Stars and Stripes and Shadows

How I Remember Vietnam

Tim Haslam

Bloomington, IN   Milton Keynes, UK

AuthorHouse™
1663 Liberty Drive, Suite 200
Bloomington, IN 47403
www.authorhouse.com
Phone: 1-800-839-8640

AuthorHouse™ UK Ltd.
500 Avebury Boulevard
Central Milton Keynes, MK9 2BE
www.authorhouse.co.uk
Phone: 08001974150

© 2008 Tim Haslam. All rights reserved.

No part of this book may be reproduced, stored in a retrieval system, or transmitted by any means without the written permission of the author.

First published by AuthorHouse 1/9/2008

ISBN: 978-1-4259-6309-5 (sc)
ISBN: 978-1-4343-6171-4 (hc)

Library of Congress Control Number: 2006910515

Printed in the United States of America
Bloomington, Indiana

This book is printed on acid-free paper.

Cover design by Terry DeGraff

*For Diana, who's made all the difference, filled all the voids
and who has always wanted to share all there is and was.*

*For Alec and Austin who someday must venture out into the
reality around them; approach it all with courage, patience and
appreciation for the better nature of the people around you.*

For Jane.

*Dedicated to the grunts of the 3rd of the 8th, to all the
grunts of the 4th, to all the grunts, to all who know!*

February 2003

"Some day I'll be home and will forget how shitty this all really is!"

I remember with crystal clarity having that thought over and over again while in Vietnam. I was right. I can't remember how shitty it was. After thirty five years those components of my character; emotions, passions, fears and the like that carry the intensity of experiences into ones consciousness are buried under years of better living experiences; mostly happy, often rewarding, many uplifting. Thus, I now look back on those days, so long ago, through the glaze of intervening remembrances of better things, better places and better results. Time allows that to happen, experience ensures it happens. I guess, maybe even some determination on my part to always move on has helped to disintegrate my experiences in 1968 from my being today.

The emotional components aside, I'm not sure now how well I can trust the intellectual residue left in my mind. There was a time when I could remember nearly every day in Vietnam, where I was, whom I was with, and what I was doing. Today, the days, the places, the people, the events, the stories and subsequent story embellishments come together in my mind to reform pictures that may or may not be true representations. The pieces of the images are all real. I'm not sure I can glue them all back together here and juxtapose them as they really were then. *It doesn't matter.*

My mom kept my letters; the ones I wrote home while in Vietnam. She gave them to me a few years ago and I have re-read them many times to help clarify my recall of things. I wasn't much of a journalist then. There are surprisingly few clues in those letters as to what was going on there for me. I always offered up some description of where I was and what I was doing. No one reading them could get any sense of why this all was so shitty. They read now more like letters home from Boy Scout camp. Right now I'm greatly irritated with my twenty-one year old self for not being better able to chronicle the most intense experiences I would likely ever have, occurring at a time and place of historical significance for our country and the world. The paper these letters are written on and the envelopes containing them all are well worn and soiled. This dirt and residue from Vietnam, imparted to them from my own warrior hands, seems to hold as much information and fascination for me now as the limited narrative content inscribed on them. *I can't explain why.*

Apologies in advance to my mom and anyone else who might find the language I will use here to be offensive. Be warned, it will go way beyond "*shitty.*" In Vietnam we spoke to one another using a language form that was spoken by all and perfectly appropriate for the circumstances we were in. Alliteration wasn't ever our objective, gentility was never our concern. We punctuated our speech with profanity and vulgarity. We referred to the Vietnamese as gooks, zips, dinks and worse. We referred to each other and even ourselves as assholes and dumb-shits and worse. Such expressions would be offensive to our families back home. They're offensive to me now. Then, it was appropriate, it fit our living and surroundings, it was all offensive…we walked the talk.

I think there's one more aspect of all this that's important to bring up before I tell the story. It has to do with the one lingering scar that never goes away. It's the almost overwhelming sense of unfinished business.

Why should I feel this? I did my job. I did what was asked of me. I did my duty.

I still, to this day, have dreams of being in Vietnam. In some I'm still there, having never left after 35 years. I'm thinking, in these dreams that I've been here a long, long time and I'll be glad to get finished and go home. In some I've returned to Vietnam and am also glad to have another chance to finish. These aren't the nightmarish dreams one might expect a combat veteran to have. They're devoid of any fear or any horror. They're not flashbacks of anything that actually happened. I guess it's not that difficult to figure out. I'm alive and others are not. I was lucky and they were not. I was also lucky relative to many other surviving Vietnam combat veterans. What I did, what I saw, what I felt, as shitty as it all was, was relatively minor compared to what others faced there. So, perhaps I didn't pass the test. Perhaps I wasn't tested enough. Perhaps every person who survives combat experiences carries with them forever the feeling that they have failed to give, "…*the last full measure of devotion.*"

The gate of mercy shall be all shut up;
And the flesht soldier—rough and hard of heart—
In liberty of bloody hand shall range
With conscience wide as hell; mowing like grass
Your fresh-fair virgins and your flowering infants.

Henry V

March 16th 1968

On this day, Lieutenant William Calley and 150 men of Charlie Company, 1st Battalion, 20th Infantry were helicoptered to the hamlet of My Lai, in Quang Ngai province, South Vietnam. They were sent there on yet another "search-and-destroy" mission, to find Viet Cong. The several hours that Charlie Company spent in My Lai that day will be remembered by nearly everyone who knows of, or hears of the Vietnam War. The men of Charlie Company walked away from My Lai leaving behind, as a result of their "search-and-destroy" efforts, the bodies of 347 civilians. Many of the inhabitants of My Lai that day were old men and children who were bayoneted or shot by Charlie Company. Many were women, clutching their babies as they were herded into ditches and machine-gunned…many having first been raped.

Charlie Company walked away from My Lai and reported back that their mission had been a success and that they had added 120 Viet Cong to the body count.

It would be nearly a year before the truth of My Lai would begin to surface back home…not a single enemy soldier had been encountered and only three weapons were found.

Charlie Company was comprised of a typical cross section of young men from the United States of America.

They were soldiers.

At the same time these soldiers were committing these acts in My Lai, an Airlift International Boeing 707, chartered to the United States Army, was in the air somewhere over the Pacific Ocean bringing more soldiers to Vietnam.

I was a soldier on that plane.

I spent most of the tedious and restless hours of that long flight thinking about what was to come in the year ahead.

What would I do in Vietnam?

What would Vietnam do to me?

I'd never heard of My Lai.

Chapter 1

The Oracle of Route 14

March 21st 1968

It's now real, no more training, no more exercises, no more practice, no more blanks; *this is really Nam.*

The Bravo Company First Sergeant comes over and joins Heald and I at the rear of the deuce-and-a-half truck parked in front of the Battalion headquarters. The sky is gray and looking like rain, but it is, even at 6:30 a.m., hot and really humid. The monsoon season is about to begin here in the Central Highlands of Vietnam. We've been warned about the rains. A few days ago while processing in at the 4th Infantry Division Reception Center one of the veterans there was describing the monsoons. I remember him saying that of all the things he had to endure; combat, mosquitoes, heat, etc., it was the constant rain of the monsoons that got to him most. I didn't believe him. I didn't understand. I knew rain to be something friendly you usually watched from inside a warm place.

The Company Clerk for Bravo Company, a Spec-4 named Asher, appears from somewhere and gives the First Sergeant some papers.

"These two are the only ones for us Top." (*First Sergeants are always called "Top." It's the shortened version for the term top-kick. You can figure out why the term applies.*)

Top tells Heald and me to get on the truck. He tells us a Sergeant Frazier will take care of us when we get to Dak To.

"Where are your weapons?" the impatient and humorless First

Tim Haslam

Sergeant asks.

Before we can answer, Asher says that Trent is bringing them.

Right on queue, someone, obviously Trent, appears with two M16's. One goes to Heald, one is handed to me. Trent has another piece of paper where he has recorded the serial numbers of the weapons. He officially assigns them to us. We are also handed a bandolier. Mine's not full, only four magazines where there are pouches for six. I don't question this or complain. I just do what I'm told. The bandolier, even with only four magazines seems heavy. I had trained with an M16 at Fort Polk and was very familiar with it. This one seemed different. It was more real. It was a veteran. It had duct tape around the butt with something written on it, too worn and faded to read. I wondered who had had this before me. *What had happened to him? What had he done with this M16? What would I do with it?*

I follow Heald up into the bed of the truck with my M16 in one hand and a canteen of water in the other. The truck bed is open with a few crates and some other loose stuff lying around. There's nothing to sit on, so we take up positions down on the bed floor with our backs up against the cab of the truck. I watch as Top, Asher and Trent head back to the Battalion headquarters area to go about their base camp duties. It was now just Heald and I. We were about to be absorbed into B Company, Third Battalion, Eighth Infantry Regiment, the "3rd of the 8th."

When I left Fort Polk, Louisiana, a few weeks ago at the conclusion of my advanced infantry training (AIT), I said goodbye to all the friends I'd made since entering the Army. From that moment to now, I was on my own. There were no familiar faces to accompany my odyssey from Fort Polk to here, with stops at home, Fort Lewis, Washington, Yakoto Air Force Base in Japan, Cam Rahn Bay on the coast of Vietnam and finally here to Pleiku in the Central Highlands. A ragged paperback copy of Leon Uris' *Exodus* and an equally ragged crossword puzzle book provided some distraction from thinking about my future plight over the long hours of my journeys. There were of course other travelers on the various airplanes and busses shuttling me onward toward the conflict in the Republic of South Vietnam. Most of these travelers were just like me, soldiers just out of training, on their way to "*Nam.*" Many were

Stars and Stripes and Shadows

willing, and in fact some anxious, to carry on conversations. Perhaps it was just my natural shyness that motivated me to keep such discussions to a minimum or, perhaps it was some other internal mechanism that selfishly wanted the time to reflect on the twenty-one years of my life so far and the life to come in the next year. It was easy to reflect while scanning the pages of *Exodus*, or trying to determine a three-letter word for "pismire." It was not so easy when someone else wanted to tell you all about their car, or their girl, or how scared they were.

I met Bob Heald last night at dinner. Now, he and I are best friends. Up to this moment in our military careers we had been told everything we needed to do. We didn't have to think for ourselves or make any independent decisions.

Now what do we do? There are decisions to make. Can we take our helmets off to get some relief from the heat? Our M16s aren't loaded. Should we take a real magazine with real 5.56mm bullets out of our real bandoliers and insert them into our real rifles? If so, do we then pull back the charging handles to insert live rounds into the chambers rendering the weapons ready and lethal? I don't know. Heald doesn't know. We're paralyzed here, as we've been trained to be. We can't resolve this dissonance, so we explore our situation with chitchat.

"Where's Dak To?"

"How far is it?"

"I hear it's bad there."

"I hope we get more ammo than this."

"I hope it doesn't rain."

"It's fucking humid!"

We're soon rescued from our independence. Two guys approach the truck from somewhere behind us. They each have M16s in their hands and two bandoliers draped across their chests. There are no patches or other indicators of rank on either of them. They each wear helmets and are carrying several canteens. One has a .45 in a pistol belt worn around his waste. The other has a transistor radio.

The one with the pistol belt plods up the drivers side of the truck and looks at us. Without an introduction, he asks authoritatively, "You guys ready?"

"Yea," is the only smart thing either of us can think of as a response. As he climbs into the truck cab he solves our first big problem.

"Get magazines in those weapons. In five minutes we'll be out the gate and on our way to the shit."

He starts the truck as the other guy climbs into the shotgun side of the cab, saying nothing to us—we're just cargo. I look into the back window of the truck cab hoping for more information. I can see only the helmets on their heads. The driver's helmet says *Cleve Browns* scrawled across the right side in fading black ink over a poor rendering of a football. Other names and messages worthy of lesser billing are scattered around the rest of the helmet. The guy in the shotgun seat's helmet has the name *Norton* more carefully inscribed in an almost perfect representation of the Norton motorcycle logo. The camouflage cover of my helmet is new and clean it says nothing. Actually, it does say something...it says "new guy."

The truck lurches forward beginning the next step on our journey out to "*the shit.*" We get only about two hundred yards and the truck stops. We're in front of the 1st of the 12th Battalion area where a single man with a weapon and much more gear than we have steps toward the cab of the truck. He says something to Cleve Browns and Norton, moves to the back of the truck, tosses up his gear and climbs in the back with us. Heald and I can tell immediately that he's not like us. Although, he's our age he looks different. He's going back out to the "*shit.*" He knows the "*shit.*" He's not happy. We later learn he's just come back from rest-and-recuperation—R&R. He had five days of living like a human being in Singapore...he's not happy.

The R&R guy who knows the "*shit*" and is not happy gets settled in between some of the crates and asks us what unit we're assigned to.

"Third of the Eighth," we reply.

"They got the shit kicked out of them up on a-thousand-and-one a few weeks ago during Tet. (*Mountain peaks are designated on military maps by their altitude measured in meters.*) I guess their still putting things back together," he tells us, putting us in our proper place in the food chain. He looks us over for a few more moments without comment then pulls out a ragged paperback book from his pant leg pocket and starts to read. We're not very interesting apparently to someone who knows the "*shit,*" who's been to Singapore on R&R and who has a book to read. None of us are too happy now.

Our truck again starts off and in just a minute exits the main gate

Stars and Stripes and Shadows

of Camp Enari, the 4th Division base camp outside the town of Pleiku. The camp sits at the base of Dragon Mountain, a stark dry looking peak in the middle of a large valley. Armed Forces Radio broadcasts from a transmitter atop Dragon Mountain because of its height and its location roughly in the middle of the country. We head eastward along with a couple of other trucks and one jeep with two MP's aboard. I feel now, for the first time like we are really exposed. We are outside the barbed wire and in open country. The landscape is mostly rice fields interspersed with pockets of heavier vegetation. There are occasional Vietnamese on bicycles or tending fields adjacent to the road. They seem to be people minding their own business, paying no attention to us.

We pass along the edge of Pleiku city. It doesn't look like a nice place through the dust kicked up by our trucks and the morning overcast. After another mile the road takes us along a plateau that overlooks Pleiku Air Force Base. I arrived there a few days ago on a C-130 cargo plane from Cam Rahn Bay where I'd been processed into the world of the United States Army Vietnam (USARV). The Air Base now is a flurry of activity as we pass by it and it's exciting to see and hear and feel the real machines of war preparing for a normal day's activities.

One plane is taking off, moving southward down the runway away from us. It's a small gray, funny looking plane. It has a small fuselage with a propeller on the nose and another propeller on the opposite end. The tail section of the plane is held on by two pieces connecting it to the wing on either side of the fuselage. I will learn later that it's a Cessna O-2 Skymaster. It's also a FAC or Forward Air Controller plane used for spotting targets and directing artillery and air strikes.

The plane hustles down the runway a few hundred meters before hopping up into the air. It struggles further up into the gray sky, banking eastward until it has come around to a northern heading. *I think that's the same direction we're going.* Two other planes now take off together side by side on the same runway. They're more serious looking in their camouflage paint. They are also propeller driven aircraft, looking like conventional WWII era fighters. I can see bombs and rocket pods under the wings. I will learn soon that they are Douglas A1E Skyraiders. The grunts call them hobos. We will soon be grunts. I will learn that the grunts love the hobos. They think of them as "pee-bringers" because of all the destruction they can bring to Charlie. They bring

Tim Haslam

"*pee*" into the "*shit*!"

We've progressed eastward enough so that the hobos pass directly over us as they follow the FAC plane northward. They're at less than 50 feet above us and I can clearly see the pilots, the bombs and the rockets. These planes seem to be very strong and stable as they race to somewhere important. *Are they going to Dak To?* I wonder. *Is the 3rd of the 8th getting the shit kicked out of them again?*

I wish I had more ammo.

It's not quite seven thirty in the morning and I have a coating of sweat over all my skin. It will remain there for as long as I'm in this country.

The road is turning slightly northward as we approach the east side of the valley and rises sufficiently to give a pretty good view back behind us. I can see the air base, Camp Enari in the distance and several other smaller military-like complexes arrayed around the southern outskirts of the town of Pleiku. From this vantage point, I can see that all these facilities are encircled by concertina barbed wire with sandbagged bunkers spaced at about thirty yard intervals forming the next internal ring. Jeeps with heavy machineguns, similarly equipped armored personnel carriers (APCs) and tanks are also in abundance within these mini-fortresses. Glancing up from this vista I can see the dullness of the sky in full panorama. Darker clouds are coming from over the mountains to the west and I notice rainsqualls here and there across the valley chasing us out of this place. All of the manmade elements of this scene seem very isolated, ending abruptly where the surrounding jungle and mountains have yet to yield to our purposes. It is a fearful place that I'm glad to be leaving. My gladness lasts only long enough to look forward up the road to where that same mountainous jungle is now only a few hundred yards away.

This feeling of isolation sinks in deeper as I consider the meager military wherewithal of our little convoy.

My spirits are almost immediately lifted however, as our truck rounds a bend in the road that leads down into another small valley. The road runs directly through the middle of this valley, which is perhaps a mile long by a few hundred yards wide. To my great relief the entire length of the road is congested with military vehicles; trucks, jeeps, APCs and tanks, all bristling with guns. We pull into the tail

Stars and Stripes and Shadows

end of the pack just as two Huey helicopters pounce over us from our rear, flying so low that their air vortex jostles us around in the back of the truck. They're gunships with rocket pods and mini-guns mounted above their landing skids. The first gunship follows the line of vehicles up about two hundred yards, slows somewhat over the clear area to the right of the convoy then seems to come to an abrupt stop in mid-air, nosing up slightly then settling down to the ground. The second Huey does the same thing landing just behind the first.

My heart is now pumping rapidly as I take in the full impact of what's going on around me. The sounds of the helicopters, the smells of road dust and diesel exhaust and the image of so much military power massing together impinge on all my senses beyond anything I've ever experienced. The sensations offered by this scene are truly awesome. Nothing I have ever experienced comes close to the scale of all this. I am no longer isolated. I am a small piece of this loud, dangerous beast that is about to invade the forest ahead. *I think we're well equipped to take on the mountains and anyone in them that might try to resist us. (It won't take long for me to be proven wrong.)*

Cleve Brown and Norton are quickly out of the cab and walking up the line of vehicles in front of us. They again offer no information to the unworthy cargo in the back of the truck. The R&R guy who knows the *"shit"* and is not happy reads on. His heart doesn't seem to be pounding. People similar to Cleve' and Norton are milling about the vehicles. Boxes and crates are being shuttled between trucks. Norton comes back and tells us to leave our weapons and come with him. Heald and I hop out and do as we're told. R&R-guy reads on. We follow Norton up the road about fifty yards to a stack of crates and boxes. He tells us to take these back to the truck. We retrieve the things in the pile as instructed and lug them back to the truck. R&R-guy actually puts his book down and offers us a hand lifting the crates onto the truck. He seems interested in the possible contents. Two of the boxes turn out to be crates of Carling Black Label beer. R&R-guy has found what he was looking for. He opens one box, removes two bottles of the warm beer and inserts them into pockets on either side of his pant legs. It's his entitlement for providing protection for this refreshment on its journey north to the grunts in the *"shit."* Heald and I are not offered a similar share. We are not yet real grunts. We'll have to earn our warm

Tim Haslam

Carling Black Label beer.

Cleve', Norton, Heald and I are all now back on the truck. The Huey gunships lift off, nose down like bulls about to charge and lunge forward, flying low on a northward heading, one on either side of the road. They are out of sight in an instant. The lead vehicle in the convoy starts forward initiating a snake like response from the chain of various, olive-drab machines following in line behind it. Cleve' grinds our deuce-and-a-half into gear and we jerk forward, requiring the human components of the cargo to re-adjust the equally valuable inorganic provender that is sliding around in the truck bed with us. We pass some of the heavily armored tanks and APC's that are pulled to the side of the road.

"Why aren't they coming along?" I wonder to myself.

The road takes us to the end of the valley where it starts a gradual climb into more mountainous terrain. There is now heavy vegetation on both sides of the road. I recognize bamboo in dense clusters and small trees with leaves looking like banana trees. The rest is just a tangle of green stuff. There is too little separation between our vehicles and the vegetation. Anyone who wanted to shoot us could do so, well hidden within this jungle. For the next six months this will be a fact of life. I will always be within the range of anyone hidden behind this green veil that wants to kill me. It's unsettling. *R&R-guy doesn't seem concerned?*

Not far beyond the valley I see a twisted old sign along the side of the road. "14" is all it says in fading black on a graying, rusty background. The old French Route 14 runs most of the length of Vietnam. Many years ago it was probably the main thoroughfare between Saigon and points north within the interior section of the country. Now, it hardly qualifies as a highway. The constant traffic of tanks, APC's and heavily laden army trucks combined with the scars from mines and bombs have etched the ancient asphalt into a ragged track nearly unsuitable for civilized vehicles. The trip from Pleiku to Dak To is about fifty miles and will take several hours due to the condition of this trail and the caution that we must exercise. We learn there are *"bad"* places along the way. Places further up the Chu Pao Pass where Charlie seems more likely to interrupt our progress. Places where Charlie brings *"pee"* back on us.

Stars and Stripes and Shadows

I again wish I had more ammo.

Cleve' wrestles the truck around one particularly tight right hand curve, shifting the cargo again. This time, some of the smaller bits that had been hidden among the general clutter of the truck bed slide into view. I'm amazed to see two loose hand grenades come rolling out in front of my feet. These are real fragmentation hand grenades.

"What the hell?" I think to myself. I have seen these only in training, where they were treated with the greatest of care and discipline because of their destructive potential. Now, they're rolling around at my feet like empty beer cans.

R&R-guy comes alive at the sight of the two grenades and I'm more startled by his reaction than by the shock of being in such close proximity to the grenades.

"Pick those fuckers up now," he barks at me.

I do, without hesitation, but then stall at the next step. *What do I do with these?*

"Here," he says, reaching toward me.

I gingerly hand him the frags, one at a time. He very carefully puts them into one of the pouches on the pack he's been sitting up against.

"I hate these fucking things," he says in a somewhat more human tone.

His demeanor continues to down shift to something more relaxed. He takes off his helmet, re-inserts his book into his pant leg pocket along side the Carling and lights a cigarette. He makes eye contact now with Heald and me almost like we were people.

From that moment until we arrive at Dak To, R&R-guy becomes our mentor on grunt life. He shares everything he knows; facts, tips, tricks, lore, legend and superstition. He imparts more seemingly useful knowledge to us in these few hours than I obtained in nine weeks of infantry training at Fort Polk. Having our attention this way at this time somehow implants the lessons of R&R-guy deeply into our psyche. Later, my own experiences and opinions to the contrary from other real grunts will have difficulty trumping the pronouncements R&R-guy shares with us this morning. I will do things for the rest of my tour, just because of R&R-guy's admonishments on the trip to Dak To this day.

As any true oracle would do, he first settles down his audience to enable our full attention. He can tell that both Heald and I are con-

Tim Haslam

stantly scanning the edge of the jungle as it passes along beside us and that we have firm grips on our M16s.

"Charlie won't fuck with us as long as those gunships are around," he affirms confidently. "If the rain starts in further up the pass we'll have to get our shit together. The gun ships can't get to us and the going is really slow. Then, we're target practice for the gooks."

With this knowledge, Heald and I both shift our scanning from the flora around us to the weather conditions above us. It's still gray overcast, but doesn't look like rain. I put my rifle down to my side and light a cigarette. Heald follows my lead and we settle in for our schooling.

Only a minute or two has past since R&R-guy secured the two grenades. This experience is fresh in all our minds and so becomes the subject for lesson one.

"I hate fuckin' frags," he reminds us.

We want to know why.

"When we get up to Dak To, you'll see why. This road we're on now, these mountains and this jungle are nothin' compared to what's up there. When you get with your company and start humpin' around in the real shit you'll learn fast. The jungle will get you! Everything in it wants your ass! Everything that grows there has thorns or razor-fucking-sharp leaves. If isn't cutting you, it's grabbing at you. It rips into the camouflage cover on your helmet. It snags your rucksack and clothes and wrestles you down to the ground. As you're going down, you'll reach out for support and grab the elephant grass blades or broken bamboo shafts or some other well defended plant, slicing the shit out of your hands and arms."

"And," he says with more emphasis, "it'll grab anything you have hanging on your gear—like frags. It'll yank those fuckers away from you; yank the safety ring and pin out and drop them into the ooze under your feet. You and the guy behind you will be shredded wheat before you know what happened."

"If you have to carry these things, put 'em in an ammo pouch or someplace where the jungle can't use them on you!"

This isn't grunt lore he's spreading out to us. Everything about his tone and body language validate the personal-ness of the advice. Later, we will learn to differentiate grunt bull-shit stories from that which is or was real for somebody. I'm beginning to hate fucking frags myself.

Stars and Stripes and Shadows

It won't be long before I learn to hate them even more.

R&R-guy pauses and makes his first scan of the sky and surroundings while re-establishing his composure. It seems a good opportunity for questions and so, I ask him about his pack. I saw lots of them back at Camp Enari, but never saw anything like it during training.

"Fuckin' AIT is a joke," is his opening to the next lesson.

"Nobody ever even sees a rucksack until you get one strapped onto your back out here in the boonies. Your ruck is your life out here. Everything you care about, everything you need goes in or on your ruck."

Heald and I study the ruck and its metal frame as the lesson progresses. R&R-guy's ruck has lots of strings and bits of rope and snap-rings hanging from various loops and cloth tabs stitched on and about the pockets of the pack. When we get to Dak To, he will attach all the things he deems necessary for his survival making it more complete for his "life out here."

"You couldn't keep toilet paper in that little-ass pack you run around with during AIT," he offers, further invalidating our training, "but you'll also learn quickly that Mr. Ruck will kick your ass every minute of every day you're out here. You'll dread the thought of having to climb into it and the effort it takes to get to your feet. After about a half-hour humpin' with Mr. Ruck on your back, his full weight will start to drive you down into the ground. If you try to stand up straight, he'll pull you over backwards, or to the side into the jungle thorns and blades and shit. As the day goes on, the straps will begin to seem more like claws and you start to think real hard about how important all that shit is you have inside Mr. Ruck."

He pauses from this rant for a moment. Then, he says, "You don't need much toilet paper out in the shit anyway," laughing at his joke.

Route 14 continues to rise gradually as it winds its way northward. Occasionally the terrain slips away on our left side affording us broad vistas looking out to the west. The mountains are high and rugged-looking in their lush green cloaks. There are no signs of civilization beyond our convoy—not that we are particularly civilized. There are periods when the sun comes out giving all we see a much more benign appearance. Actually the superficial image is quite beautiful in the full light.

Tim Haslam

Norton's radio is providing background music. Otis Redding is singing, "Sitting on the Dock of the Bay."

I light another cigarette. I take another drink of warm water from my canteen.

The day's getting hotter and the humidity keeps increasing as the forest around us gets thicker. The layer of perspiration expands sufficiently to form rivulets of sweat. My fatigues are starting to feel sticky. Still, we're all pretty relaxed now, fully attending to R&R-guys tails and not paying attention to the sky.

Suddenly its pouring rain and we're instantly soaked. Following the lead of R&R-guy, we make some effort to cover the cargo with an old poncho that is crumpled up among the other litter in the truck bed. Most of the stuff is in wooden crates and made to survive the elements. The Carling is in cardboard boxes and gets first priority under the poncho. Nobody seems to give any thought to putting us under there.

I put my helmet back on too late. My head and face are already awash. My fatigues are now glued to my skin, secured there tightly by the rainwater and sweat amalgam. For just an instant the cold shock provides a little relief from the heat. That feeling doesn't last long, as the overall effect feels terrible.

The rain lasts only a minute or two, passing into the foliage falling off to the east behind us. Mercifully a patch of intense sunshine, starting the steamy transition back from rain soaked to sweat soaked, follows the squall. This will be a constant cycle throughout the monsoons.

R&R-guy uses the rain as an object lesson for his next sermon.

"You know you'll never be dry again," he starts. As he delivers this headline, he's extending both his arms forward toward us. His sleeves, like everyone's, are rolled up above his elbows and the bare portion of his lower arms reveals a lattice-work of scabs and scars.

"Jungle rot," he declares. "Nothing ever heals out here; cuts, scratches, mosquito bites, leech wounds all end up the same way. You watch. This time next week, count the festering sores you have. Every fucking one of them will itch like crazy. You'll have to scratch at 'em, spreading it around even more. About once a month one of the medics will check everybody over for jungle rot. He'll swab Merthiolate all over you that'll sting like a motherfucker and make everything itch even more."

The lesson takes an instantaneous turn from jungle rot to medics.

Stars and Stripes and Shadows

"There are two kinds of medics out here. The first kind can do almost anything. They're better than fucking doctors. Most of the medics in the 1st of the 12th are like that. A bunch of our guys were wasted bad up on thirteen-thirty-eight a few months back and our medics got 'em all together and dusted off to the hospital alive. But, some medics are Merthiolate and Darvon assholes. If there's anything wrong with the outside of your body, you get Merthiolate. If there's anything wrong on the inside you get Darvon. They always get too much of this stuff and they don't want to hump it around, so, that becomes their remedy for everything. I had a toothache back in November, and some numb-nuts medic put Merthiolate on my gums and gave me a bunch of Darvon."

I don't know about Heald, but for me, this day keeps getting less and less inspirational and I'm not sure I want to hear much more. But, want to or not, mile after mile, R&R-guy indoctrinates us further; what the best and worst C-ration meals are, how many magazines of ammo we'd better have...at least 30; how many canteens of water we'd better have...at least 5; what brands of cigarettes to accumulate for bartering; how to burn leeches off your body or your buddies body; more and more how-tos, what-tos and when-tos each illustrated with practical examples from his experiences. At one point he asks for one of my magazines and I give it to him. He presses down into the rounds at the open end of the magazine pushing them out into his helmet until the magazine is empty.

"See, the base camp commandos loaded these magazines; there's twenty rounds in here. Twenty rounds will jamb the gun. Load eighteen rounds, maybe nineteen."

I strip two rounds out of the rest of my magazines and listen on.

It's all too believable. We know now that the whole 4th Division had a rough time of it in the mountains around Dak To during the Tet offensive. His regiment, the 1st of the 12th was engaged in one of those really ugly slugfests with NVA regulars dug in up on thirteen-thirty-eight. He was there. He earned his Carling, his bragging rights and his transformation from a guy just like me or Heald into a real grunt. Like it or not, intentional or not, independent of any specific thing he may or may not have done there, he has been initiated into the fraternity of those who know the "shit."

His comments about the Tet offensive divert my attention for a

13

Tim Haslam

few moments. The Tet offensive started when I was still in training in Louisiana. I remember it brought a greater sense of urgency and seriousness to the remainder of our training. When I was home on leave before coming here, I remember the cover of the March issue of Newsweek Magazine. It was a picture of a tank with many wounded Marines on it. "The Agony of Khe Sahn" the caption read. To the extent a static image can portray "agony," this picture did. I thought about those Marines and their agony a lot. At that same time, there was a popular song being played on the radio. It was an instrumental called, "Love is Blue," by the Paul Mauriat Orchestra. I liked it and bought the album, playing it almost continually while home on leave. I will have the picture of those Marines coupled with the "Love is Blue" melody in my mind forever.

Most of the Tet stories in the papers and on TV then were of the Marines at Khe Sahn and of the Marines fighting street by street in the city of Hue. I don't remember hearing anything about the 4th Division and what they had to do around Dak To. I'm sure those Marines will never forget what happened to them during Tet. I'm just as sure they would relate to all the other grunts fighting the day to day battles in Vietnam that go on without photo coverage or any journalistic recording of their terrible struggles.

I shake off the 'agony' image, the "Love is Blue" melody and the brief thoughts of home. Charlie was and, according to R&R-guy, still is all over these mountains. This is the first reference he's made to anything in the present. I can somehow tell that he's talking so much about what has happened to him in the past because it keeps him from thinking about what's going to happen in the future. We're all apprehensive about things to come. He has good reason to be. Despite all he tells us, Heald and I still don't get it. Our fraternity affiliation is still with our friends back on the block. We also don't yet get that we will never be able to re-join that fraternity or return to the same block.

Our convoy's slow progress up Route 14 is intercepted by rainsqualls a few more times. We just sit and take it. There's nothing else we can do. The road seems now to be more level, traveling along a high plateau. Very tall trees are being added to the jungle canopy making it dark and shadowy even when the sun is out.

Cleve' and Norton have been generally minding there own business

Stars and Stripes and Shadows

up in the cab but have occasionally chimed in with comments validating R&R-guys stories. Cleve' suddenly turns back to us and points off to his left to ensure we see something that way. I lean out to get a better look forward to see what he's pointing at. There's a dirt road running westward away from the highway along a narrow ridgeline. About sixty meters down this road is a bizarre appearing complex. The crude looking little enclave is an ARVN outpost. The South Vietnamese Army doesn't have the resources that our army does, and so their fortress is constructed largely of bamboo and tree poles. It's not a large post, maybe forty meters in diameter sitting atop an open knoll at the end of the ridgeline. The jungle has been cleared away for thirty or forty meters down the sides of the knoll sloping away from the post. The actual construction of this fort is incredible; the bamboo and poles making up the outer wall are tightly laced together, rising up twelve to fifteen feet. At a height of about three feet, protruding out from the spaces between the poles are fans of sharpened bamboo stakes. The pattern is repeated at about four foot intervals up the wall. The whole structure thus bristles porcupine-like. They don't need barbed wire to keep intruders out.

I wonder how long it took them to fashion all these spikes, as there are thousands of them. Completing the image of this medieval looking battlement is a guard tower rising above the gated entrance.

At the top of the wall a few feet down the internal side is a scaffolding-like walkway similarly constructed out of bamboo. Machineguns are spaced all around the perimeter on fixed mounts, loaded and ready to fire. I can see a few ARVN's milling around, some up on the walkway and others down on the muddy ground toward the center of the compound. They all seem to be loitering without any apparent purpose. The ARVN's are dressed in traditional fatigues; stateside fatigues to us, different from the lighter weight tropical fatigues that we wear. The fatigues they wear however, all seem to be tailored to ensure the tightest fit possible. This further emphasizes the small stature of these people. Those that wear helmets look, from this distance, like children playing soldiers. They're all smoking cigarettes; so are we. They're all looking at us; we're all looking at them. It somehow seems important to all of us that each other sees the weapons at our disposal.

At the intersection of the road going down to the compound there is an armored personnel carrier with the South Vietnamese flag painted on its side. Atop the APC, sitting behind the big fifty-caliber machinegun, is another one of those children-playing-soldier. As we pass just a few yards from him, I can see his face is serious, humorless, without a trace of admiration or humility towards his American saviors. He has the dull expression of someone without hope; someone isolated; someone whose life has been very different from mine. He knows the "*shit*" in ways none of us will ever understand. I can't tell what he's thinking as he studies us going by.

The sky seems to have darkened further as we pull past the bamboo fortress. As it shrinks into the distance behind us its apparent how isolated the place really is—it's being swallowed up by the jungle. Watching the last vestige of the bamboo tower disappear, I can't help but think how easy it would be for Charlie to wipe out the little ARVN complex. I can't help but think that Charlie's all over the mountains surrounding this place right now, studying the compound—studying us. My feeling now is not yet fear, but a deep sense of foreboding, totally unfamiliar in my prior, comfortable San Fernando Valley life.

A few miles further north the convoy enters the city of Kontum. It's difficult to see this as much of a city. Route 14 passes along the western side with the bulk of the ragged buildings and muddy streets fading off and up into the mountains to the east. The atmosphere here is foggy and there is a light drizzle keeping us well saturated. The fog gives Kontum a ghostly appearance. The people and vehicles visible down the intersecting streets look surreal to me, ethereal as they fade in and out of the hidden realms of the shrouded city. Again the foreboding feeling swells from within me and I'm glad that our time here in Kontum will be brief.

More tanks and APCs are stationed at intersections as we pass through town. More serious looking MPs scurry up and down the line of our vehicles in their jeeps, each jeep showing long belts of 7.62mm ammo hanging down from the machineguns mounted behind the front seats. Everybody seems nervous and anxious to move beyond Kontum. The feeling is clear that there's nothing here for us but trouble.

As soon as this trouble feeling really sets in the convoy comes to a stop with our truck halted along a row of aging, faded storefronts

Stars and Stripes and Shadows

adorned with signs in Vietnamese, mostly red and yellow, identifying their purposes. I don't know what they say, but many of them must offer Coca-Cola and Marlboro cigarettes, as these familiar logos are everywhere.

The value of advertising is not lost on the local residents of this isolated mountain town. The instant our truck comes to a complete stop, Vietnamese kids emerge from everywhere offering up all sorts of merchandise; many have bottles of Coke, many have simple brass bracelets that are popular with the GI's, none however have Marlboros as they know that we can usually get all the cigarettes we want for free.

Norton is approached by a kid I guess to be about ten years old. The barefoot kid, dressed in ragged shorts and dirty tee shirt, has a box containing eight or ten bottles of Coke.

Norton asks, "How much?"

The kid doesn't speak English but knows the routine well enough to reply, "Fit-ty."

"Fifty?" repeats Norton, highly insulted. "Di-di," he offers back to the kid making a hand motion accentuating the 'beat-it' translation.

"Fit-ty," repeats the kid standing his ground.

Norton holds out a 25-cent Military Payment Certificate and says, "Twenty-five."

The kid takes the MPC note, hands Norton one of the bottles of warm Coke and concludes the transaction marking Norton with, "GI numba ten!"

He moves back toward the three of us in the bed of the truck. R&R-guy and Heald each give the kid one of their 25-cent MPC notes and are handed their warm Cokes. I give the kid a 50-cent note and in return get my warm Coke and a, "GI numba one" evaluation. GI-numba-one in this context means *sucker.*

R&R-guy looks at me like I'm an asshole, then opens all three bottles using the little P38 can opener he wears on a shoelace around his neck.

I ask him about the MPCs. I thought they were for military use only.

Within the Vietnamese free enterprise, black market system, he explains, everything works; MPCs, real greenbacks and Piastres, the actual currency of Vietnam. With this explanation he admonishes me not

Tim Haslam

to influence the open market with back-on-the-block sentimentality.

Even warm, the Coke tastes good as I contemplate my reputation as numba-one-GI, sentimental, asshole.

More kids approach offering their wares; more "di-di's" and "di-di-mou's" from us; more "GI-numba-tens," are expressed from them.

Business is concluded

Quickly emptied, the Coke bottles have joined the rest of the litter rolling around the truck as Cleve' jerks us forward again. Kontum ends abruptly and we're back into the forest. The triple canopy jungle around and above us traps the hot, humid air and it feels like we've driven into a sauna. Rain now would be welcome.

The remainder of the trip to Dak To is sameness, more forest, some openings with vistas generally to the westward, a few more bamboo fortresses with vulnerable, loitering ARVNs; occasional rain, constant heat, humidity and sweat and a million hiding places for anyone who wants to kill me.

R&R-guy is pretty quiet for the rest of the trip. He checks through the stuff in his ruck; he naps, he reads, he smokes, he grows less and less happy.

It's just past noon as the convoy starts down a gradual grade leading into a fairly broad valley. Over looking the valley to the west is a very high steep ridge known to the grunts as Rocket Ridge. It runs southward as far as we can see blending into the high mountains all around. The north end of the ridge however, drops off at an acute angle down into the valley. Below this ridge, at about the point of the drop-off is the 4th Division's forward support base at Dak To. Approaching the base it looks like a mini Camp Enari. There are permanent hut like structures, many large tents and again many tanks, APCs and other vehicles of war. There is an airstrip currently occupied by two Hueys. The whole base is surrounded by rows and rows of concertina barbed wire within cleared fields of fire on the north, east and south sides. The west side, the side adjacent to Rocket Ridge is the dangerous side, the bad side. The whole compound is in easy range of rocket, mortar and even sniper fire from the forested ridge and the steep slopes dropping down to the perimeter line of the base. Thirteen-thirty-eight caps the ridge at a distance of about 3 kilometers above Dak To. This is why there's been so much

Stars and Stripes and Shadows

fighting up there. Anyone in control of Thirteen-thirty-eight controls the whole valley below and controls Route 14.

To the west of Rocket Ridge is nothing but dense mountainous jungle. The terrain is like this into Cambodia a few kilometers to the west and to Laos a few kilometers further northwest. The Ho Chi Minh trail, Charlies main supply route, runs down from North Vietnam roughly along these borders. Hundreds of trail arteries branch off from it and penetrate eastward into this rugged landscape. Soldiers of the North Vietnamese Army along with their supplies flow into South Vietnam this way almost without disruption. Vehicles cannot get into this area; there are no roads. The thick, triple canopy vegetation hides the activities of anything terrestrial from airplane or helicopter observation. It's an environment difficult to penetrate even on foot. I will learn how difficult.

The Central Highlands are vital to Charlie. They can hide here. They can stockpile everything they need here. They can patiently plot and plan here. They can observe, harass and kill us here. There are vast underground tunnel complexes buried under the duff of these ancient forested mountains. There are so many of these, that none of them are individually vital. Charlie puts thousands of men into these mountains deployed in small units, free to move about and harass us at will. None of these units are individually vital either. Sometimes these units will swarm together and attack our firebases, our hilltops, our places. They will come at us at these places, hurt us as badly as they can with little regard for any hurt we put back on them and fade back into the forest, dissipating into their little, non-vital, "gook" molecules.

This is the world of the 4th Division grunts. You hump into this miserable realm trying to root out and destroy these tunnels; trying to find and destroy these little bands of "gooks," all the time knowing that neither the tunnels nor the little bands are very vital but your own ass is. Then you find an advantageous hilltop, hack away the vegetation and make a firebase. You dig into the mud and set up housekeeping in a sandbag covered bunker. Your job here is to provide protection for the artillery battery that's been helicoptered in to provide fire support in a feeble attempt to control the real estate within range of the guns. The jungle absorbs the 105mm artillery shells as readily as it absorbs raindrops while Charlie slowly reforms around you for the next attack as the cycle repeats itself. This is what R&R-guy has been trying to tell us about. This is why R&R-guy is so unhappy. This, for the 4th is the shit.

The skies have cleared almost completely as we come down into the valley. The rays from the intense midday sun drill down into us as the reflected heat from the metal truck bed sautés us from below. The sunlight however, seems to give this place a friendlier feel than the overcast and fog that disguised Pleiku and Kontum. Maybe it's the mass of military might that's visible within the Dak To complex that feels friendlier. Whatever the reason, I know that there is food and water there. My one canteen has long been empty, I've not eaten since early this morning and cigarettes no longer satisfy any appetites.

The convoy zippers apart at the junction of Route 14 and the westward heading Route 512 and the Route 14 contingency continues northward to other shitty places further up country.

Cleve' accelerates our truck through the left hand turn on to 512 anxious to get to Dak To, ending this leg of his assignment.

As the area surrounding the Dak To base has been de-foliated there is nothing to keep the surface layers of red dirt in place. Thus, our final approach is through clouds of fine dust; dust that binds with our perspiration adding pigment to our first coat of filth; dust that absorbs any remaining moisture in our mouths and throats. We're all glad that Cleve' has his foot to the floor as we approach the gate into Dak To.

We barely slow down as we pass through the heavily guarded gate into this no-bullshit realm where the tanks, APCs and heavy guns are all tactically positioned. This is not the land of the base-camp-commando. Everyone here is under a constant real threat and never strays too far from the shelter of a bunker or trench line. "Incoming," is a common proclamation to the residents of Dak To. Craters in the ground and burned hulks of vehicles give testimony to Charlie's presence on Rocket Ridge.

We pull up abruptly and the final bow wave of dust washes over us.

We're here.

Heald and I clamber out together looking for Frazier or anyone else who can give us our next instructions. Several men approach the truck,

Stars and Stripes and Shadows

talking with Cleve' and Norton, seemingly concerned with the cargo, ignoring us. They're all helmeted and wear dirty, sweat soaked tee shirts above their dirty fatigue pants. There again is nothing to identify any rank or authority. After a moment or two, one of these men, the one with an M16 slung over his back comes over to us. It's Frazier. He knew we were coming. He seems friendly.

After almost human-like introductions, Frazier points over to an open sided tent, one of several clumped together at about the middle of the compound. He tells us that this is the mess tent and we can get hot food and something to drink there. He'll meet us in about thirty minutes.

As we grab our gear I look back to see what's happened to R&R-guy. He's no where to be seen. He's disappeared, drawn back into the stuff of his lessons and stories. I'll never see him again.

Chapter 2

First Blood

Frazier has collected us up from the mess tent and leads us over to the 3rd of the 8th billet. Inside the hut are supplies held in reserve for the units out in the boonies. There doesn't seem to be a lot there and it all has the look of used Army surplus. There are also cases of beer and soda that must have come in on our convoy. They'll be forwarded out to the grunts in the field later today after the Dak To guys take their cut.

At Frazier's direction, we pick through a pile of rucksacks looking for compassionate ones, ones less likely to "kick our ass." They all appear the same, they're all well worn, and they all have apparently done their share of ass kicking, so we grab ones that appear to be in solid condition. As we do this, Frazier has started a pile of canteens, ponchos, poncho liners, pistol belts with empty ammo pouches and other miscellaneous vital stuff. He instructs us to take what we want from this pile suggesting that we take at least two ponchos and three canteens. I remember R&R-guy recommended at least 5 canteens. I don't do the math that converts pints to pounds as I take my 5 canteens and commit to 10 pounds of water.

We've made our selections from the pile and have most of our vitals. Next, Frazier is kind enough to offer us some of the upgrades. He gives us a length of nylon line and a knife advising us to cut off small pieces to use as ties for securing things to our rucks. He then hands us the extra bonus; two "beeners" each. These mountaineering carabineers or snap rings will really come in handy for hanging things on Mr. Ruck and they are prized among the grunts that have them. As new guys we are fortunate to get them. Finally, acting almost as though he were Santa

Claus he hands us each a faded but clean green towel. These too are prized possessions. They help fight the futile war against perspiration, they can shade and protect your exposed neck, and they can provide some padding between Mr. Ruck's claws and your shoulders. Again, we're lucky. New guys generally inherit their towels from grunts leaving the shit.

"What about ammo?" I ask, as this has been on my mind all day.

"Get this stuff secured on your rucks and I'll take you over to where you can get ammo, frags and C-rations," he replies.

Frazier disappears outside as Heald and I hurry to pack up our gear. This takes only a few minutes and we are again on our own without orders. Just outside the hut we can see a water trailer with the word "Potable" painted on it. We know that potable means drinkable and so we boldly proceed out to the trailer and, without permission, fill our canteens. We hang the canteens on the rucksacks and try them on. They're not so bad.

Nearly an hour passes without any sign of Frazier. We take the initiative to move outside with our stuff, as it's even hotter inside than outside. We light cigarettes and study the details of the Dak To base. There are war machines here that neither of us has ever seen before. Near the northwest edge of the camp are two tracked vehicles with large twin guns mounted on them. They are 40mm anti-aircraft guns used for strafing the adjacent ridgelines in response to rocket or mortar attacks. They put out dozens of rounds in the same time it would take an artillery piece to fire one or two. They are referred to as "dusters." Artillery requires trajectory calculations to put shells on designated targets. The dusters are like big machine guns and when fired, the gunners simply follow the streaks of the tracer rounds while adjusting their trajectory to the desired area. Between the dusters and us is a huge tracked machine that looks like a giant armored tow truck—that's just what it is, a Vehicle-Tank-Retriever, VTR. It's a reminder that everything here, even the tanks and APCs are vulnerable.

Through the course of our labors and studying we've each drained one of our canteens. We realize how quickly water gets consumed as we refill them from the trailer.

A look down at the Timex watch demarcating the grimy wetness of my left arm from the moist filth of my left hand tells me it's a little after three o'clock when Frazier finally returns. We follow him over to the back of another deuce-and-a-half truck. On the ground behind the truck is a pile of full bandoliers and Frazier says to take what we want. I again revert back to my morning lessons ensuring I have a total of thirty magazines. Offering no options, Frazier says to take four frags each. I nervously take my four out of a wooden crate full of fresh grenades. I'm not at all sure how to secure these considering R&R-guys impassioned warnings. I find that I can get two of them in each of the two ammo pouches I took from Frazier's pile earlier and now wear on the pistol belt around my waste. The safety rings and pins seem protected from any snagging plants, but the grenades are heavy and their weight, along with that of two full canteens pulls the belt down onto my hips and is really uncomfortable.

Finally, we are instructed to pull out nine C-ration meals from other open cardboard cartons sitting up on the trucks tailgate. I wasn't paying full attention when R&R-guy ranked C-rations, so I randomly select nine of the individual, cardboard-boxed meals. Without coaching I figure out that it's better to remove the little cans and packages contained in the meal boxes and stuff them into my ruck as space allows.

That's it; we're now adequately supplied to go out into the boonies. Once there, the real grunts will peruse what we have, make recommendations for additions and deletions and set our place in the line of inheritance for the good stuff held by the more tenured members of our squads and platoons. Neither of us want to put are rucks on yet. We can estimate how much weight we've added since our first trial fitting and we want to put off confirmation of the coming relationship with Mr. Ruck as long as we can.

I see that Frazier is looking out toward the airfield about 100 yards away. There's a Huey parked just off the runway with its rotor turning. About half way between the Huey and us are two more guys with M16s and fully packed rucks heading for the helicopter.

"Saddle-up, and come on," Frazier says with urgency in his tone as he quickly moves off in the direction of the two grunts and the Huey.

Assisted perhaps by the adrenaline rush of the moment, Heald and I have hurriedly lifted our rucks up and twisted ourselves into the shoulder straps. Mine's heavy, it's out of balance and the dangling canteens and bandoleers make it difficult to walk in a straight line.

Stars and Stripes and Shadows

Frazier's moving away at a quick pace and we're almost running to keep up. The two other grunts are now at the Huey, stepping up on the skids and wrestling themselves and their rucks on board. Frazier, nearly there, beckons us to hurry up. The pilot is giving us an anxious, irritated look.

The first two guys occupy too much space on this side of the Huey for us to get on, so Heald and I follow Frazier around to the right side. The wash from the rotor is intense, pressing us down, further even than our own natural instincts to avoid the whirling blade above us. I get to the tubular skid and try to duplicate the entry maneuver the first two guys used. Mercifully, the door gunner on this side of the helicopter reaches out from the seat behind his M60 machinegun and offers a hand. I can't see his face behind the darkened goggles of his aviator's helmet. I'm sure he can see mine and can easily see that I'm new, anxious and pretty much out of control. I'm in, Heald's in, we're all in. Before we're anything like settled, the Huey starts lifting off. Frazier is out of sight, never to be seen again.

The first time I was ever in an airplane was just three months ago when I flew from L.A. to Houston on my way to Fort Polk for infantry training. Nine weeks later I flew back, then up to Seattle and Fort Lewis, then to Vietnam. I'm not a seasoned flier. Airplanes however, based on my limited experience, seem to have an easy time rising up gracefully into the air and staying there. The Huey is different; every piece of the machine, including the pilot, crew chief, door gunners and grunt cargo seems to be involved in the struggle to overcome gravity. Everything vibrates shudders and shakes as the churning rotor strains to free us from the clutches of the Dak To ground.

There are no seats or accommodations for making passengers comfortable. We are sitting on the floor; the side doors are wide open; there are no safety barriers to keep anything in. Centrifugal force is the only thing working for us in this regard. The noise is deafening. I find some part of the machines interior to grab on to.

The helicopter, just like the gunships back at the convoy rallying point, lifts up to about ten feet, noses down and charges forward. The Huey's powerful jet engine is now driving us ahead, accelerating rapidly as the rotor continues its labors in opposition to the laws of physics. The

Tim Haslam

view out the side door is of the runway passing rapidly beneath us just a few feet away. We don't seem to be gaining any altitude.

Then, perhaps necessitated by the oncoming terrain or perhaps just as a way to further initiate the rookie passengers, the pilot pulls us into a steep ascent, at the same time banking hard to starboard. The Huey is now at an angle of about 45 degrees and I'm looking directly down at the ground—not out and down—directly down. The strength of whatever I'm holding on to is being thoroughly tested. As nothing seems to be falling out, especially me, I start to appreciate the sheer thrill of the experience. Anywhere else this would be the ultimate A-ticket ride.

We're back to level flight, having risen to an altitude well above the valley floor with the lower ridges and fingers spreading down from the higher mountain peaks that are still above us on either side. We seem to be following a lush green valley northward. The view is spectacular in the long rays of the late afternoon sun and everyone on board seems to be settling in for the rest of the flight. Scanning around the inside of the Huey I can see the pilot up front. He is constantly adjusting the control stick positioned between his legs. Frequently he moves one of his hands over to some other kind of control stick making quick adjustments to that. All the while his feet are busy working pedals. The co-pilot in the left front seat is studying a map while talking into the radio microphone fastened to his helmet. The door gunners on either side are strapped into their mesh seats and have firm holds on the trigger grips of their M60s. They scan the jungles and hillsides passing below us with the intensity of hawks searching for field mice, the barrels of their machineguns stroking back and forth like oars pulling through the air.

One of the other two grunt guys is saying something to me. The pulsating air pressure, engine noise and vibrations of everything around make it difficult to hear him. We lean toward each other and he introduces himself as, "Fernandez." He is surprisingly able to manipulate his face into a friendly expression. I feel better as I tell him my name and offer my hand. He extends a closed fist, which I tap from above with the bottom of my fist. He returns the tap. Heald identifies himself with similar tapping. Fernandez introduces the other guy as Westerly. Westerly says nothing, but seems willing to participate in the tapping ritual. Further conversation takes too much effort so we all go back to

Stars and Stripes and Shadows

the silent contemplation of our plight.

I can see that the valley below is split by a river—the Dak Poko—winding its way southward. Occasionally small, primitive looking villages appear, surrounded by the dense forest. There are no roads connecting these little communities to anything or anyone. These are the homes of the Montagnards, the native people of the Annemite Mountains of Southeast Asia. Montagnard is the French word for mountaineer. The ruggedness of this habitat has failed to keep these people isolated from the politics and purposes of their North and South Vietnamese neighbors, their neighbor's friends and their collective weapons and machinery. At this time, our side seems to be winning the courtship of the "yards." Many, in fact have been conscripted into military units referred to as the Civilian Irregular Defense Group or CIDGs. It's good that their current alliance is with us. They know these mountains. They know them as home. It's been many years since their home has been the quiet, peaceful place of their ancestors. With our help, it's been evolving into the "*shit*." The "*shit*" comes to them.

Many of the gaps between the finger-ridges entering the valley are pock marked with bomb craters. Sometimes the individual craters look, from this distance, to be very large, maybe fifteen to twenty meters in diameter. Sometimes dozens of the individual craters link together for hundreds of meters up these canyons leaving the surroundings a devastated snarl of broken trees and bamboo shards all covered in the red laterite soil ripped out of the ground by the explosive force of the bombs. This is the terrestrial footprint of the B52.

The area we are flying over now must be heavily contested. There are many of these B52 scars as well as many lesser individual bomb and artillery craters in smaller concentrations. From both sides of the Huey, nearly all the ridges and gaps I can see are thusly blemished by our efforts at extermination. I have to believe that we're kicking the shit out of Charlie too.

Today has so far been unlike anything I have, or probably ever will experience. Hour by hour, sensation by sensation, mile after mile the real world of the conflict in Vietnam is opening up to me, exposing its awesome power and consequence. At the same time, the world of home that has always been my frame of reference is being pushed further and further away. It will soon be pushed out of reach. It will be beyond

Tim Haslam

my abilities to ever retrieve.

It has only been a few minutes since we left Dak To. The pilot puts the Huey into a banking turn to the right, heading us directly for the mountains to the east. We're maintaining our speed and seem to be closing with the mountains very quickly. He's not making any effort to increase our altitude. The mountainside is coming fast. The view is no longer of a diffuse green forest, it is of well-defined individual trees and plants coming at us.

Just short of contact with the trees, the pilot makes a brody-like turn to the left, stopping in mid air. We are over a clearing on the top of a small ridgeline and the opening in the vegetation is clearly manmade. The rubble of fallen trees and hacked down bamboo covers the ground just a few feet below us. The pilot is carefully trying to back down into this.

As we touch down, I see men approaching us from out of the surrounding jungle. I see others blended into the shadowy green at the edges of the clearing. The indelible impression is that these figures are not so much American soldiers but some kind of filthy, green clad creatures fully adapted to this place. I'm hesitant to jump from the helicopter and start the transformation into their kind but the door gunner, now very anxious, is yelling and gesturing for us to get out…now!

I step on the helicopters vibrating skid and jump to the ground. The weight of my rucksack follows a fraction of a second later, jerking me backwards, nearly causing me to fall into the splintered bamboo at my feet. Keeping low I move out from under the rotor, heading in the direction that the men-creatures are coming from. The Huey lifts up behind me, generating a shower of leaves and jungle debris, then banks southward and down back toward the valley floor. The sun is now just above the peaks on the west side of the valley and the Huey crew is anxious to complete the return trip to Pleiku before the night sets in. In two hours they will be putting away cold beers and watching movies at Camp Enari. It will be a long time before I can enjoy such luxury. I am now irrevocably a captive of Bravo Company. I have reached the final destination of my journey from home and the starting point for my life in the shit.

As soon as I reach the tree line at the edge of the landing zone I'm amongst an array of tent-like structures, hooches, fashioned from pon-

Stars and Stripes and Shadows

chos and bamboo poles. Several men are standing at what seems to be the center of camp. One beckons us toward the group.

"Captain Collins," he states in a relaxed and civilized manner as we approach the group. "You must be Haslam and Heald."

"Yes sir," we both reply, unsure of the military protocols or formalities appropriate to the situation; nobody salutes, nobody cares.

Captain Collins is a man of medium stature with dark hair and a moustache grown well beyond regulation length. He's bare headed, dressed in fatigue pants and the now common sweat stained tee shirt and looks much the same as every other man visible in this strange community. He has several days' growth of stubbly whiskers. His face, as are all the faces I can see, is a portrait of deep fatigue, strain and weariness, stained by dirt and perspiration naturally acquired in his attempts to co-exist with the jungle. It is clear that bathing is not part of the Bravo Company routine. After a few months in the world of the jungle grunts even soap and water will be unable to remove all of this many layered veneer. The faces once reflected back from the mirrors back home are gone forever.

Captain Collins offers no other greetings or introductions. "Five-Nine, you take Heald and Six-Two you take Haslam," he says, apparently directing these orders at two of the men standing to his left.

Bravo Company is made up of four platoons designated as Five-Nine, Six-Zero, Six-One and Six-Two plus the small company headquarters staff. The officer in charge of any of the units is the "Six," so Captain Collins is our "Six." The officers in command of the individual platoons take on the platoon number designations as their individual identities. Thus, "Six-Two," the man smoking the pipe, turns out to be Lieutenant Falck.

"Haslam?" Lieutenant Falck asks, unsure of the pronunciation.

"Yes sir," I answer as Six-Two approaches from the clutch of officers around Captain Collins.

"Terry Falck," he replies offering a real handshake, which I gladly return, attempting a smile. This Terry, Six-Two, Lieutenant Falck person is of similar stature to Collins, also with overgrown dark hair and an even bushier moustache. However, Falck, even under similar layers of filth, fatigue and strain has the look of an ivy leaguer. Where Captain Collins' appearance and mannerisms were cordial enough, they were

Tim Haslam

also basically military and belied nothing of any civilian life form underneath. With Six-Two, I can easily discern the "Terry" within. Both Captain Collins and Lieutenant Falck will earn my respect. Six-Two, back in a world where people just went by names, would be easy to befriend.

Six-Two leads me across the cleared landing zone (LZ) and back into the tree line on the south side. Again, there is a little community of hooches with several guys seemingly lounging around. My presence quickly catches their attention, as new guys always represent a change, new guys sometimes have news, and new guys give the seasoned grunts another chance to tell their stories, to vent their frustrations. Most significantly, new guys bump everyone else up a notch in the hierarchy.

One of the men rises to his feet as we enter the group's space. I'm not surprised when Six-Two introduces him as the squad leader for this group, Sergeant Stevens. Stevens, "Steve," is a black man with the mature look of someone willing and able to take responsibility but also with a genuine friendly air about him. We perform the fist tapping ritual.

"Don't get too excited Steve, Haslam's going into Taylor's squad. Take care of him tonight. Bob will get him tomorrow when they get back." Six-Two explains to me that Bob Taylor's squad, my squad, is out on a night ambush and will be back sometime tomorrow.

Six-Two spends a few more minutes with us, allowing the others to question why Taylor's squad is entitled to replacements and not them.

"Jeter's short and could get called out any minute," Six-Two explains.

Whoever "Jeter" is, his status launches the whole group into a frenzied dialogue.

"Fuckin' Jeter's gonna dee-ros?" someone questions.

The military orders that authorize someone returning home are labeled, Designated Return from Overseas Station. Every GI in Vietnam refers to the timing of these magic orders as their DROS date.

"Jeter's that short and he's gotta be out on a fuckin ambush patrol?" Someone else chimes in without thinking that Six-Two is the one who probably sent Jeter's squad on the patrol. Six-Two lets it slide.

More banter follows about how lucky Jeter is and how glad he's going to be to see me. Everyone seems glad to hear about Jeter, it's a confirmation that there can be an end to the shit, that their turns will come.

Six-Two patiently absorbs the barbs for a few minutes more. Then he leads Steve off away from the group a short distance telling him something as he points out into the jungle surrounding the camp. Steve returns to us as Six-Two heads off in the direction of the company command post.

The guys sitting around are pointed out by Sergeant Stevens and identified either by their last name, their nickname or even in some cases by their first name but nobody is introduced using a full name. I'm brought in as Haslam. More fist tapping. All of them react to me in a friendly way, perhaps too fatigued to exert themselves with any further hazing rituals, perhaps leaving that privilege to Jeter and the rest of Bob Taylor's squad.

Sergeant Stevens quickly breaks up the get acquainted session and advises us that Six-Two wants us to expand the area that has been cleared away in front of our position. The field of fire is too limited and Charlie can get too close to us, still hidden and protected by the vegetation. Grudgingly everyone pulls himself up, grabs some kind of cutting implement and heads off into the trees. One of them hands me a machete without comment and I follow their lead into the trees passing over a line of foxholes dug down about three feet, each with a short wall of sand bags on the outer edge.

Two of the guys have axes and immediately go to work on the bigger trees. The rest of us, all with machetes, start hacking away at the smaller trees, bamboo and viney stuff.

After sitting most of this long day, it feels good to be up and moving around. I've never used a machete before and lopping down the defenseless bamboo is a good stress reliever. The machete is really sharp and slices through things with surprisingly little effort.

In a few minutes I've chopped my way several meters into the jungle and realize that I'm also several meters from anyone else in the squad. I suddenly feel vulnerable out here even though I have my M16 slung over my back. I start looking more carefully into the forest growth out in front of me. I start looking to see where the other guys are. While doing all this looking, I keep on swinging the machete. One downward swipe from the machete in my right hand cuts through the narrow

Tim Haslam

trunk of a small but tall tree. The trunk offers so little residence to the machete blade that it continues on its arc until it reaches the next obstruction…my left leg.

Shit!

There isn't enough inertia left in the blade to do serious damage, but the instant pain, bleeding and slice in my pant leg scares me. I look around to see if anyone else witnessed my first attempt at a self-inflicted wound. No one seems to take notice that I have stopped cutting and am wiping at the blood dripping down my lower leg with the prized towel that I've been wearing around my neck. I'm determined that no one will know about this, so I alternate between more carefully controlled swings of the machete and swabbing my leg. I have good platelets apparently and the blood flow soon stops. I still feel like an idiot.

Sergeant Stevens has come most of the way out to where we are and says that's enough clearing. He yells out to a guy named Bennis and tells him to set trip-flares out just beyond the cleared area.

"Show Haslam how it's done," he adds to the instruction.

I make a mental note to add trip-flares to the ever increasing roster of relevant subjects omitted from my advanced infantry training, along with rucksacks, MPC and Merthiolate.

I follow Bennis a little distance into the jungle where, at about knee height, he wraps one end of the trip-flare wire around a tree, and then moves off in a line roughly paralleling the edge of the clearing feeding out the wire, hiding it within the undergrowth as best he can. He stops after about twenty feet. He now ties the trip-flare securely onto the trunk of another tree. Next, he very carefully ties the wire to the pull ring on the flare. The pull ring is fastened to a cotter pin that holds down the triggering mechanism that sets off the flare when released. With his left hand he holds the pull ring firmly and with his right hand he carefully pinches the bent-out sides of the pin together until there is just enough bend left to hold the pin in place against the strain of the taught wire pulling in the opposite direction. Any additional strain and the pin comes out, setting off the flare. Before he lets go with his left hand, he gets to his feet and looks around to ensure he has an avenue of escape in case he's pinched the pin together too much. The flare is dangerous. If it goes off, it would very likely ignite anything in close proximity. It feels right to Bennis and so he let's go, at the same time

32

Stars and Stripes and Shadows

stepping back quickly.

Nothing happens…success…my turn.

Bennis watches me nervously try to duplicate his every move. It goes OK with successful results. There are two more flares to be set, so we each take one and go about setting them so that we have trip wires running fully across the front of our position. I'm feeling glad to be done with this assignment as we return to the hooch area and I'm also much more confident than I was following my machete work.

The day's work is done for me and the rest of Steve's squad. Darkness is setting in as we dine on C-rations and warm water followed by cigarettes and small talk. No one stays up late here, we're all too worn out and too anxious to get one more night over with. Everyone here knows too that Charlie comes out at night, comes closer to watch, to listen, and sometimes to hurt. Its time for those on guard to go to work; to be left alone to concentrate on the silent blackness surrounding us.

Before anyone turns in we need to work out the guard assignments for the night. With my temporary addition to the squad and with Sergeant Stevens, there are eight of us to pull guard shifts. Our section of the perimeter is fairly large and requires guards in two of the foxholes all night. We divide ourselves into two four man teams and work out the rotation so that we each have to stand watch for two hours and fifteen minutes starting at 9:00 p.m. My team gives me, the new guy, the first choice of shifts. I know how hard it would be, once I've gone to sleep, to wake up and stand guard, so, I opt for the first shift. Nobody seems to object and as soon as the rest of the rotation is established my three partners crawl into the hooch and are quickly asleep.

I'm left alone now at the foxhole just a few feet out from the hooch and it's just a little past eight o'clock. Officially, my shift doesn't even start for nearly an hour. The extra hour was apparently understood to offset the obvious advantage of the first shift. I'm learning.

I'm unclear on exactly how to do this, should I be down in the foxhole, sitting on the edge of it, lying down, or what? Although it's quite dark already, I can just see the silhouette of someone sitting upright at the edge of the next foxhole, about twenty meters off to my left. OK, I'll sit on the edge, feet dangling down into the hole. I then arrange the two bandoliers I have at my side so that I can get at them quickly.

Tim Haslam

I double check my M16, tapping upwards on the bottom of the magazine to ensure that it's fully seated, feeling upwards with my right hand thumb to check the position of the selector switch—safety on. Then, *Shit! Shit!* I think to myself. I don't have a round in the chamber. I haven't had one in all day. No one ever told me to chamber a round. *Shit!* To chamber a round now means I have to pull back on the charging handle and then release it. This causes the bolt to spring forward pushing the top bullet in the magazine into the firing chamber. The M16 is an assault rifle. It's designed to give us fire superiority in close combat. It's not designed to be quiet in its operation.

I make a mental calculation of how long it would take me to chamber a round and switch the selector lever off the safe position in the event of a sudden attack. I decide to leave the weapon as it is. I take off my pistol belt and lay it next to the bandoliers. I open the top flaps on the pouches that contain my four frags but don't take them out. All the weaponry I have at my disposal is now as ready as I can make it. I start performing my night's work —sitting, waiting, listening.

If I bring my wrist up in front of my eye, there is just enough of a glow on the face of my Timex to make out the time. It's finally nine o'clock. It seems that I've been sitting here for hours and my shift is now just officially beginning. I'm really tired. The heat of the day is gone and the air is getting cooler, almost cold. I take a drink of water from my canteen. I look over toward the foxhole on my left. It's now too dark to make out any silhouette. I strain to see the jungle edge out in front of our position. It's now too dark to see anything. Looking upwards, I can see a patch of clear sky through a break in the trees overhead and see one star. One star, no clouds, no rain…things could be worse I think to myself.

The total blackness of the surroundings is matched by the silence. There are no animal sounds, no leaves rustling, no water coursing, no distant drone of aircraft…no nothing. There is no external stimulus to help in the struggle to resist sleep. There are only the internal processes of my mind churning through the events of the day to keep me awake.

The seconds and minutes loiter along with a stubborn disregard for

Stars and Stripes and Shadows

my fatigue and boredom.

I reach down to feel the machete wound on my leg…it hurts…it itches. R&R-guy was right. It's not scabbing. There's just a glob of gooey blood stuck there. The pain is a good stimulus. It wakes me up a little. I try to concentrate on the pain but that too is soon pushed aside by my fatigue and boredom. I need something to stimulate me. I need a cigarette.

I drop down into the foxhole and light a cigarette, careful to minimize the light flare from my Zippo lighter. I remain in the foxhole, leaning against the side-wall keeping the smoldering tip of my cigarette hidden within my cupped hand. I don't bring the cigarette up to my mouth, but drop down into the foxhole for drags of smoke.

The cigarette works at reviving my attention. Now, more relaxed but also more alert, my thoughts wander out of Vietnam and back home. I wonder what my mom and dad are doing. I wonder what my friends are doing. I wonder mostly about what Rosemary is doing. I relive our last moments together and think about the torture of being without her for a whole year.

Somehow I've managed to stay awake through the millennia of my shift. At exactly 11:15, I crawl back to the Hooch and wake up Sergeant Stevens who has the next shift. He slowly exits the hooch, pulls his boots on and staggers toward the foxhole collecting up his gear on the way, never saying anything to me.

Without removing boots or any other articles of clothing I fall into the warm place vacated by Steve in the hooch and am asleep instantly. This day has finally come to an end.

Tomorrow will be my first full day as grunt. I will be a grunt twenty-four hours a day seven days a week for a long time to come.

Chapter 3

Bonding With the Forest Creatures

The first shafts of light filtering down through the leafy jungle canopy bring the encampment to life. The air is still and cool, yet heavy with humidity. For most of the drowsy inhabitants, the first morning ritual is cigarette lighting. It occurs to me that Charlie could employ blind scouts to find us, as the distinctive clicks of Zippo lighters snapping open and shut echo around the camp and the odor of freshly ignited tobacco wafts throughout the neighborhood.

There now seems to be little attention paid to the surrounding tree line and the dangers that were assumed to be in residence there during the hours of darkness. The men of Steve's squad seem surprisingly jovial this morning as they go about there preparations for the day. Actually, no one really seems to be preparing for anything; no face washing, no shaving, no teeth brushing, no equipment readying...no urgency. There is mostly just banter without much substance while people rummage around in their rucksacks. The rummagers seem hopeful of discovering something forgotten within the reaches of their rucks. The reality of the contents takes over and C-ration cans start to emerge.

I follow this lead and examine my own supply of C-rats looking for something appropriate for breakfast. I start pulling out the bigger cans, reading the printing on the lids; Beef Steak, Turkey Loaf, Ham and Lima Beans. The smaller cans aren't much better; Crackers, Cheese Spread, Bread-White; then, a prize; a can of peaches. I'm not yet far enough removed from civilization to consider 'Ham and Limas' for breakfast, so I open the can labeled, 'Bread-White', the peaches and a couple of mystery packages where I find some cookies, a package of

Stars and Stripes and Shadows

instant coffee, a plastic spoon, some toilet paper and a small package of Salem cigarettes. The coffee introduces a new challenge; heating water.

By now the other guys are far enough along in their own breakfast preparations to start taking an interest in what the new guy might possess. Bravo Company has been out on this "hump" for many days and their supplies have dwindled down to the bare necessities.

"You got any heat tabs?" someone asks me.

"No," I reply, not knowing what a "heat tab" is. I think I can figure it out however.

Since I can offer no heat tabs, the guys revert to other means of generating heat to cook their meals. I'm surprised to see them passing around a block of stuff that looks like white Playdough. Each person pulls apart a walnut sized hunk and pinches up a little spike, lays it on the ground and lights it with a match or Zippo. The stuff ignites instantly with blowtorch intensity. By bending the partially attached C-ration can lids, they've fashioned handles and are able to hold the cans over the fast burning globs. The contents heat up quickly over the blazing Playdough.

I have to ask, "What is that stuff?" formally exposing myself as a rookie.

"C4," they all reply as though expecting my question.

"C4! Like C4 explosive?" I ask rhetorically.

"Don't worry…it won't go off unless you step on it while it's burning."

Apparently concerned for the welfare of the new guy, Bennis tosses me an empty can to use for heating my coffee. I now have my own chunk of the explosive, but really have to think twice before lighting it. Everybody in the group stays seated around me as I approach the little pinched up spike with my Zippo, so I guess it's OK. Like the others, my piece is immediately ablaze and I'm heating my first cup of GI coffee.

The peaches and cookies seem really good and whet my appetite for more. Further rummaging in my rucksack turns up a can labeled, Ham Slices. Ham would be OK for breakfast, I think and my C4 blob is still burning. I get the can opened and over the heat in time to warm up the contents before the remaining plastic explosive sputters out. Even warm, the grayish rubbery disks pretending to be ham are pretty bad.

Tim Haslam

I assume that whatever they really are, they are a source of protein and therefore finish them all.

I once again survey the group for clues as to what I should do next. Based on the survey results I settle into a comfortable position using my ruck as a seatback. I light a cigarette, casually sip my coffee and join in the morning discussions. The nourishment, tobacco and caffeine combine to make me relaxed and comfortable. There are no dishes to wash, no bunks to make up; no formations to stand. No one of higher rank has hassled us yet today and the whole experience still feels like an adventure. Everything around me is new and stimulating. It's not like that for the others. This, for them, is all part of a routine that blends together in sameness day after day, just as the flora of the surrounding forest intertwines into one giant mass with little separation of hue or purpose; where the only noticeable change comes with catastrophe...where contrast invites predators.

The naïve, comfortable, excited, new guy represents a stimulus for the grunts in Steve's squad. They start to interrogate me, not so much in an effort to find common bonds, but because the Q and A session is a diversion. Maybe a response from me will trigger a discussion that they haven't had before. Maybe I have news that hasn't come to them via Armed Forces Radio or in the occasional copies of Stars and Stripes, the military newspaper, which they sometimes get. Maybe something I say will afford one of them the opportunity to re-tell a story that they all have heard too many times. It doesn't much matter what I have to say, as long as the saying of it takes up time.

"California, the L.A. area," I reply to the obvious first inquiry, figuring nobody has ever heard of the San Fernando Valley or Van Nuys.

In return, I learn where back-on-the-block is for them; Waco, Texas, Ankenny, Iowa, Hawaii, Guam and one other Californian from, "up by Fresno." Small talk stemming from our geographical revelations follows. Each of us offers our knowledge of the various places discussed with the same sophomoric expertise that accompanies most grunt conversations. Actually, I guess the same formula; 10% fact, 30% perception and 60% bullshit forms the foundation for the expressions of most men this age, it certainly did for my fraternity brothers back on my block...myself included.

Our chat meanders around from professional sports teams to the

Stars and Stripes and Shadows

weather patterns known to predominate at any city or town discussed, to cars and girls. At some point every grunt discussion I will ever participate in will revert to cars and girls. With these transitions, the formula nearly always shifts to 100% bullshit.

We've managed to entertain ourselves through mid-morning. There's been no attempt by any officer or senior NCO to interfere with our cigarette smoking, coffee drinking knowledge exchange. They're probably up by their own hooches doing the same thing.

The conversation has just shifted to the inevitable ranting about our current situation when a guy approaching from the headquarters area behind us interrupts. He's holding the frame of his rucksack, with a radio strapped to it in one hand and the handset, connected to the radio with a spring cord, in his other hand.

"What's happening, Wee John?" someone asks as the radio guy enters our space.

"Don't go fuckin up the day for us Wee John," someone else requests, assuming he's a messenger from the upper echelons.

Wee John is Lieutenant Falck's radio operator, his RTO. Wee John is Six-Two-Charlie to everyone who is privileged enough to use the company's radios. I'll never know why or how he came to be known as "Wee John."

"Relax," he says, "Taylor's squad is coming in up through your position. They'll radio in when they're close. I told them we probably wouldn't shoot them."

"Only Jeter," Sergeant Steve, says, "I think we should put a few rounds into the trees overhead as they come up just for Jeter's sake."

Everyone laughs understanding the symbolism for Jeter, the short-timer, but no one reaches for their guns. This platoon in particular does not play games with their weapons. Bob Taylor's men will make it clear to me why later.

"Six-Two-Alpha-Charlie, this is Six-Two-Charlie. Over," Wee John says into the handset in response to a muffled voice breaking the steady squelch of the radio.

"Roger that, Ed. I'll let you know when we hear you. Tell Jeter to keep his head down when you guys get close. Over."

"Wee John, tell them we have trip flares out there and to be careful coming in. I'll send someone out to guide them through," Sergeant

Tim Haslam

Stevens says, at the same time instructing Bennis to go out and guide them in through the wires we set last night.

Wee John relays the warning and the rest of the guys in Steve's squad start paying more attention to the surroundings. They make sure their weapons are close at hand and ready. They know that Charlie can follow a small patrol on its way back home.

The morning sun is already hot on this cloudless day and the ever-present humidity further increases our discomfort as we watch Bob's squad work their way through the trip wires towards us. As they get closer, I forget about my own little miseries, as these guys really look beat. Although their night ambush position was only about a klick (one kilometer) out, it required them to navigate up and down several steep ridges. The going here is always slow as the point man must hack his way through the heavy vegetation with a machete, never able to clear enough to save those following from the snags and spikes left in the narrow corridor.

The seven men of the returning patrol say nothing as they plod into our position. They are heavily laden with weapons, ammunition and canteens. They don't have their rucks or any thing affording creature comfort. If they slept at all last night it was on the bare ground, with little more than the fabric of their fatigues separating them from the damp tangles of vines, fallen vegetation and insect life in residence at the lower levels of the jungle eco-system. As it is with all other organisms in this realm they were part of the food chain, constantly being nibbled away by tiny creatures feasting on their fresh blood, their living and dead skin and the salty brine that covers their bodies.

I study each man as they pass into our little circle, dropping their gear before dropping themselves. The first is tall, slender and looks to be my age. He has a radio similar to Wee John's, a PRC25, strapped to the ruck frame on his back. He's not actually a member of Bob Taylor's squad. Ed Arter is the platoon sergeants RTO. The platoon sergeant, Bruce Bollman, is designated Six-Two-Alpha, so Ed is known on the company net as Six-Two-Alpha-Charlie. Ed and Wee John are the only RTO's in the platoon and so they must alternate on patrols. RTO's are possessive about their radios and their responsibilities and therefore unwilling to let anyone else take a turn humping the 10-pound PRC25's on patrol to even out the workload. They will however, complain about this continuously.

The next three men file in and drop their gear and themselves into our midst. The third man in this file is lugging an M60 machinegun and wears belts of ammo over each shoulder and another around his waste. Each of the other men, except Ed also has a belt of machinegun ammo along with their own M16 bandoliers. The last three men of the squad and Bennis are lagging behind a few meters and its not difficult for me to tell which one is Jeter. Bennis, who is black, is engaged in a spirited dialogue with the only black member of Taylor's squad, Jeter. Jeter is the only one from the patrol with the energy to talk. He's the only one with enough spirit to engage in light banter with a brother, he's the only one going home anytime soon.

The last man to reach us must be Bob Taylor and I'm amazed at his appearance. He is, even through the mask of accumulated filth a ringer for the movie actor Robert Taylor. For a moment, this resemblance adds another surreal aspect to my first impressions; *maybe I'm just an extra in a movie.* Taylor too joins our group, crumples to the ground under the weight of his weaponry and like most of the others proceeds to empty any remaining water in his canteens down his throat or over his head. The last man in the squad to arrive drops his gear down next to me without comment or any acknowledgement of my presence.

As the seven weary men continue to re-hydrate and re-nicotine I study them and their gear. *So this is what real soldiers look like.* Their weary, sweat covered faces and their tattered dirty fatigues disclose a new dimension of the reality of this life. The amount of weaponry they have now heaped down on the ground in front of them attests further to what this is all about. In total there must be a thousand rounds of ammo for the machinegun, even more for the M16s. One man has an M79 grenade launcher and a large canvas pouch full of ammo for that. Ed, the RTO has a shotgun instead of an M16, as his job requires shooting only as a last resort. There are many frags, several smoke grenades and a few pouches I recognize from training as containing Claymore mines. The total destructive power of their arsenal is awesome. Humping this arsenal through the jungles just about kills them. I wonder what it was like the times they set out with all this stuff and came back with less. Then, humping it through the jungles probably saved their butts and killed somebody else.

Tim Haslam

After a few moments, Sergeant Stevens introduces me to Sergeant Taylor. Everyone's attention is now on me and all seem glad to see a new person. Jeter is especially glad and asks Steve if his DROS orders have come. He reminds everyone how short he is, "Three days and a wake up!" If he left the boonies today there is just barely enough time to get him out-processed and on his way home as scheduled. His rapture over the thought of going home has overshadowed his knowledge of the Army's ability to meet schedules of this nature.

Steve's "Nothing yet," reply, doesn't seem to upset Jeter much. He knows that the arrival of the next chopper can bring his ticket and ride out of the shit.

Jeter's eminent freedom dominates the dialogue for several minutes more before everyone's attention returns to me. Taylor formally introduces himself as, "Bob Taylor." His voice too is that of the actor Robert Taylor *(I'll have to explore this incredible coincidence at some later time)*. Bob, like Steve, comes across first as a genuine, friendly person with little need to emphasize his rank or authority. He introduces the squad in no particular order; Bob Price, Mike Beasley, Elmer Charette, James Jeter and finally the guy sitting down next to me is Mike Danko.

Danko, up to this point has been sitting quietly. He's not said anything to anyone. He's not bothered to open any of his canteens. He seems sort of sullen and serious, mostly just staring straight ahead out from under the helmet coming down well over his forehead nearly covering his eyes. Danko's dark moustache surpasses anything I've yet seen within the Bravo Company clan. It completely covers his mouth, arcing even further down at the sides. The overall image of Danko is that of a silent movie villain.

Immediately after Bob introduces him, Danko utters something without changing his posture, orientation or fixed stare.

Geesoder…is what it sounds like to me. The others seem to understand but offer no help in translation.

"What?" I reply, thinking I must have missed some of the original transmission.

"Geesoder," he repeats with more emphasis.

OK, I heard it right the first time. *What the fuck does "geesoder" mean?* Is that tribal language or some other military code word or acronym omitted from my training? As a part of speech, it was apparently

Stars and Stripes and Shadows

a declarative predicate, an instruction and it was obviously directed at me. The others now seem to be watching intently, enjoying the interaction. They know Danko. They know that I don't know Danko. They're watching a puppy twisting his head from side to side as his master tries to give him his first obedience lesson. It's great entertainment for the veterans.

"Geesoder?" I inquire back, intoned with submissiveness.

Danko remains silent, apparently bothered by my limited understand of the language. He lets another few seconds pass and then twists his head slightly over to his right looking for someone to assist with a translation.

"Give...Him...Some...Water!" Elmer finally says, emphasizing each word, providing me with the Danko-to-English translation, ending this round of stump-the-new-guy.

With that clarification, I offer Danko one of my canteens, which he takes, still without changing his posture or straight-ahead orientation. He takes a big swig from it, removes his helmet, pours some over his head, takes another big swig and hands it back. As I recover my now empty canteen, he reaches over toward me with his right hand and says, without breaking his forward gaze, "Danko."

I clasp his hand firmly, relieved to have progressed beyond this step in my indoctrination.

Jeter, still standing, comes over and offers his fist for the tapping ritual. I stand up to give and receive taps with Jeter. Then, since I'm already standing, I move to each of the men in my squad in an effort to complete the introductions in a civilized way. There's a variety of responses; firm hand clasps, firm thumb grips, some tappings, various combinations, all rendered with as much warmth and sincerity as their fatigued personalities can muster. These are all nice guys hidden within their grunt exteriors. This is a big relief to me.

The guys from the patrol have had sufficient time to recover somewhat and start stirring around. Some dig out C-rations and prepare their lunch, others begin arranging and organizing things within camp, making it home-like as well as making it more defensible. Mike Beasley is watching his can of beans and franks heat up over one of the last remaining heat tabs in the Platoon's possession when he pulls up his right pant leg revealing the sweat streaked filth of his lower leg. Just above

Tim Haslam

the top of his ragged green sock is a slimy slug looking thing. Further up the calf muscle is another one.

"Fucking leeches!" he proclaims, both as a reaction to the disgusting parasites and as an alert to the others.

The alarm triggers an immediate response from everyone on the patrol. Pant legs are lifted, shirts are removed, towels and bandanas are cast aside as each man checks as much of his flesh as he can see, and solicits assistance from others to check the places he can't see. They all prove to be hosts. Danko and Price find theirs on their lower legs too. Elmer has one on the back of his neck. Sergeant Taylor discovers one on the soft fleshy part, inside his right bicep as Elmer shows him a second one just above the waste band of his pants toward his backside. Although each discovery brings an echo of Beasley's initial sentiments, "Fucking leeches!" or "Fucking bloodsuckers!" or just an emphatic, "Fuck!" the men seem to be taking it as part of the routine.

I had just lit a cigarette at the time Beasley discovered the invaders. The search process is still underway when Danko reaches toward me and says, "Geesigrit."

I don't need any translation. Danko takes my cigarette and presses the burning tip into the bloated leech clamped onto his lower calf. Reflexively, the leech releases its hold as well as most of the blood it has transfused from Danko. The surrendered blood blends into the sweat streams flowing down into his sock. He brands the second leech on him with similar results, flicking off the sizzling remains with his fingertip and then passes my cigarette along. Price gets it next and goes after the gluttonous passengers on Elmer's neck and Bob's back before attacking his own stowaways.

The skirmish is quickly over and the body count is tallied up. Beasley has taken one of the wounded leeches prisoner and is stretching it out between his fingers, testing its elasticity. Elmer takes a drag on the remains of my cigarette, and then casts the butt down into the foxhole beside us without any acknowledgment of my contribution to the squad's effort. I'm now rather uneasy about my own status in the food chain and even though I haven't been where they've been this day I feel a need to do some checking. I'll wait for an opportunity to do so less conspicuously.

With things back under control, they tell me of the place they

Stars and Stripes and Shadows

spent the night. How it was down at the bottom of a ravine, wet and overgrown and apparently alive with leeches brought out by the first rains of the monsoon season. Although they're around during the dry season, it's during the monsoons when they're a constant menace. The men of the squad spent the long night alternating their struggles to stay awake while on guard with their attempts at sleep while trying to get comfortable within their cold, wet habitat; trying not to move or make a sound, hoping they've attracted little attention from the forest. Admittedly they had not anticipated the leech population in residence and taken no precautions. Next patrol, we'll tuck in our shirts, button our collars, roll down our sleeves and tie off the bottoms of our pant legs. We'll wrap our towels around our heads and necks and we'll douse ourselves with mosquito repellent. Mosquitoes are so much a part of the daily living here, that they haven't even mentioned them and, so far I have only had a few bites. Applying the repellant as a weapon against leeches is mostly psychological and probably just adds seasoning to the leeches grunt buffet.

The rest of the day progresses in this leisurely fashion. Whether from necessity or boredom, weapons get cleaned, equipment gets organized, another foxhole gets dug, and more sandbags get filled. On two separate occasions, Hueys show up and drop off cases of C-rations, lister-bags with fresh water and mail. The mail lifts everyone's spirits. I haven't had time to write home to give people my address, so my spirits, not yet in desperate need, go un-lifted. The mail reading festival reminds me to write home. I get quick notes written to Mom and Dad and Rosemary advising them of my current whereabouts and my new address and am able to get the letters out on the second Huey.

Neither Huey proves to be the "freedom bird" for Jeter, even though he heard the distinctive whir and pop of each helicopter's approach before any of the rest of us. He watched optimistically as each lowered itself down into the clearing, dropping off its cargo, returning to the sky and the unobstructed path to Dak To or Camp Enari without a passenger, without him. Sergeant Taylor, recognizing Jeter's anguish, goes up to company headquarters shortly after the departure of the second helicopter to see if there is any information about Jeter, to see if anything can be done.

45

Tim Haslam

Taylor's gone a long time. It's late afternoon before we see him again. He's hurried down from the company CP and burst into our squad position looking for Jeter.

"Jeter's over with Steve's squad," Beasley tells him.

Taylor moves a few meters in the direction of Sergeant Steven's squad and spots Jeter, hovering restlessly among some of his friends there. Taylor calls out to him, beckoning him with his arm to return. Jeter doesn't need any further coaxing and starts sprinting back toward us with Sergeant Stevens, Bennis and another black man, Ernie Jefferson, following along behind.

"Get your gear!" orders Taylor.

Those three words reverberate through the squad and all those within earshot, bringing everyone to their feet. Those three words that Jeter has heard a hundred terrible times before, this time enter into his awareness like the voices of the Methodist choir on Christmas Eve. Suddenly, he's totally out of control, not knowing what to do next.

There's too much to do. What gear should he take? What should he leave? He has to say his goodbyes. Is this really happening? Have his DROS orders really come? Jeter is uncharacteristically speechless.

Bob Taylor re-takes control and fills everyone in. "No DROS orders yet," he says, quickly adding that, "Captain Collins and Six-Two have decided to send you back to base camp to wait for your orders to show up. They've even managed to get a bird coming down from Dak Pek to swing by here and pick you up. It'll be here any minute, so don't screw around. Just take your personal stuff and leave everything else with us. Give Haslam the stuff you think he'll need or want."

The rest of the squad and, in fact the whole platoon is now trying to aid and abet Jeter in his escape. He quickly empties out everything contained in his ruck, starting a pile for me and one for whomever, with a few special things doled out directly to worthy individuals. My pile grows quickly; two trip flares, a Claymore mine, more machinegun ammo, a machete, an entrenching tool, a smoke grenade, a prized poncho liner, and a flashlight. I'm trying to estimate the additional weight being bestowed upon me and wondering how much of the "whomever" pile will also find its way on to my back.

After a year of relying on all this stuff for survival and comfort; after a year of humping it all over the Central Highlands; after a year of hav-

Stars and Stripes and Shadows

ing all these things conspire with Mr. Ruck to kick his ass, it seems that their disposition should take longer than these few minutes. But that's all it takes and the only things left in Jeter's possession are his personal stuff, his nearly empty ruck and his weapon. Now, there are only a few minutes more to separate himself from the men of Bravo Company, his fellow grunts…his friends. This isn't easy for Jeter, as so many things are suddenly vying for his attention. Each man around him deserves time and words and closure. Each of the black brothers now collected around deserves a special acknowledgement for their bonds and perspective. But the Huey's coming—there isn't time. Fist taps, hand grasps and a few nervous superficial sentiments will have to suffice.

Sergeant Stevens offers up the perfect queue and opportunity for Jeter to make his break toward the clearing.

"What about your ruck? How are you going to say goodbye to that, or are you going to take it home?" asks Steve, shifting the attention from the awkwardness of the moment. His question gets everyone focused on the real enemy that has nearly vanquished them all.

"If it was me, I'd shoot the motherfucker right now!" someone says.

Others chime in with recommendations of a similar nature involving frags or Claymores. Jeter though has the final solution.

"Y'all watch," he says smiling. "When me and Mr. Ruck are airborne on the slick out of here…you watch…at about a hundred feet over the jungle, Mr. Ruck gets pushed out. Mr. Ruck and Mr. Jeter part company for good. That's right…y'all watch. That's when Mr. Jeter starts in as a person again and nuthin's ever gonna ride on this back again."

The sound of the Huey coming for Jeter reaches all of us at the same time. Six-Two is coming down from the CP in a hurry. Jeter and the rest of us meet him on the way up to the clearing. Six-Two and Jeter share a few brief words and a handshake closing their relationship as officer and subordinate, as grunts who have known the shit and as an Ivy-league kid from Penn State and a blue collar kid from Huntsville, Alabama, whose paths crossed in the worst place on earth. The experiences they have shared and the individual courage and character of each man will bond them together forever.

The chopper sets down among the bamboo rubble. Captain Col-

Tim Haslam

lins, ducking in low under the rotor blade, intercepts Jeter just short of the Huey's skid and offers his hand. Jeter shakes hands with him, climbs in and takes one last look at the faces of his comrades, the faces of the grunts who haven't yet survived their ordeals. He takes one final cerebral snapshot of the shit.

Having no other purpose than chauffeuring Jeter back to life, the Huey lifts up, rises above the treetops and deliberately moves off towards Dak To as we all watch for the promised execution of Mr. Ruck. The Huey's climbed as far as it's likely to climb and nothing's been cast out. All eyes are on Jeter's side of the helicopter as it fishtails out of site over the next ridgeline and still no jettisoned passengers. Everyone is disappointed, but no one's surprised.

"Too much respect," says Sergeant Stevens, as the little band of still imprisoned grunts sadly return to their hooches and their own rucks.

N N N N

The rest of the day and the next two days pass by slowly with little variation. Hueys come and go. Six-Two makes an appearance now and then for no apparent reason, there are no orders or instructions or information. It's unclear to any of us what our contribution to the war effort is as we sit here, drinking warm water, smoking cigarettes, talking and napping. Our supplies of good cigarettes are getting pretty low, and we're now relegated to smoking the less desirable brands that come with our C-rations. The weather's remained hot, with clear skies and no rain. As relief from the boredom, people write letters or re-read special letters they've kept up in the webbing of their helmet liners. Some have tattered paperback books or old copies of Stars and Stripes that get read and passed around. Nearly everything we have now is a re-run. There's nothing new to stimulate us. Whenever Ed Arter or Wee John comes around, they're questioned about any information they may have heard over their radios. They don't know much. The Battalion is convinced that Charlie's building up all around us and they want us to confirm the belief. I don't know if it's better to confirm it by sitting here waiting for them to come to us or by going out looking for them.

Around noon on my fourth full day here, Six-Two comes down and explains our next mission to Sergeant Taylor and the squad…another ambush patrol. We're to leave later this afternoon and will be going out

Stars and Stripes and Shadows

further than the squad went before, almost three klicks. We're to travel light; ammo, water and two meals of C's. This doesn't make anyone too happy, but no one voices any complaints. Personally, I'm glad to have the chance to break the monotony and do something.

It's after 3:00 when we saddle up. I have my M16, 23 of my magazines, my share of the machinegun ammo, frags, trip flares, my meals and three of my canteens full of water. Because we need to move and react quickly on patrols like this we don't take our rucks. Without the ruck though it's difficult to attach all this stuff to me in any efficient way, there still seems to be too much stuff. The tropical fatigue pants have lots of pockets and so I stuff them with the little meal cans and packages plus one of the canteens plus two of the M16 magazines. Most of this stuff goes into the biggest pockets on the outside of the upper leg. All this is nearly pulling off my pants, causing me to cinch up my belt as tight as possible. Above this is my pistol belt with two more canteens, the ammo pouches with the four frags and the trip flares; the weight of all this rides higher up on my hips, above my pant waistband. I place two more magazines in the lower pockets of my shirt. I have a bandolier over each shoulder and another tied around my waste so the bulk of the weight is toward the back, offsetting some of the pull from the pistol belt on the front side. The 100 round belt of machinegun ammo is the only remaining piece to deal with and the only option is to drape it over my head and shoulder like my bandoliers. The problem with the machinegun belt is the orientation of the bullets. I can either have the points of the bullets sticking into my neck or into the side of my torso. I opt for the torso.

I stuff four of the little packs of Salems into the webbing of my helmet liner and I'm ready for my first patrol. Everything hanging on me feels awful. As I take steps everything shifts and jostles around flopping out and back into me. The afternoon heat and humidity have found an ally in all this gear, joining forces to extract as much moisture from my body as possible. I start to wonder if this really is better than the monotonous routine of the last few days.

Wee John has the radio duty with this patrol and has joined us along with another guy I haven't met before. He introduces himself as Dick Charlebois, the platoon medic. He's traveling lighter than the rest of us. He does have an M16, but only one bandolier and no other weaponry.

Tim Haslam

He also has a canvas pouch with his medical supplies hanging from a strap slung over his shoulder. His presence is another reminder of the reality of what this is all about. I wonder if he's a Merthiolate and Darvon guy or not. Whatever Doc Charlebois is, I hope I don't have to find out first hand.

Six-Two, Taylor and Wee John huddle around a map for a few minutes more as the rest of us stand around sweating, trying to adjust our gear into more cooperative configurations and checking again the readiness of our weapons. Then we start off with Taylor directing the order of departure; Danko on point with a machete to cut trail, followed by Beasley, Bob Taylor, Wee John, Doc, Elmer with the machinegun, me and Price bringing up the rear.

The only specific instruction I get from Sergeant Taylor is, "Keep up."

For the first few hundred meters we follow the same trail that the squad had made coming back in the other day. This takes us away from camp along a ridgeline gradually sloping downward toward the southeast. As we turn more eastward following another finger ridge, more steeply inclined, the going slows as Danko must now cut a path for us through the dense tropical growth. I can only see Elmer and Doc in front of me and can barely hear the machete slicing through the vines and branches and breaking through the bamboo up ahead. Price is following closely behind me, the only one paying any attention to the world behind us.

We've only been gone about ten minutes when all the elements impinging on me start to settle in. The heat radiates down through the trees above as the humidity presses at me from all sides. Every few minutes I need to wipe the sweat from my eyes and brow with one end of the towel I'm wearing around my neck. Gravity too must be increasing here, as the weight of each magazine; each frag and each ounce of water exert their downward force. Again, I have not balanced my load very well. My right pant leg pocket has more weight than my left. My lower right shirt pocket also has more weight than the left pocket. I have my M16 in my right hand and so with each step I have to adjust for the extra burdens on my right side. Danko's best efforts with the machete make an opening, not a trail and so the footing is through and over bent and broken bamboo, branches, vines and roots with little

50

Stars and Stripes and Shadows

actual ground visible. This requires me to watch my feet constantly to avoid tripping. The corridor width is also narrow with only the larger obstructions cut away so that we're all in constant contact with the plants surrounding us. It doesn't take long for me to discover another dilemma I'll have to face for most of my time out here. At six foot three inches tall, I'm the tallest person in the squad and the platoon. Danko, typical of the guys who usually cut point, is about five foot nine and so whacks away enough stuff for people his size to wrestle through generally in an upright posture. I have to constantly hunch forward and duck to avoid the still intact growth that is often overhead. So much attention is required just to stay on my feet and make forward progress that I can barely attend to what may be going on around me. Snipers, mines, booby traps or even large enemy forces could be within a few feet from me. The density of the forest however absorbs sounds pretty well and so Danko's chopping isn't likely to attract the attention of anyone who isn't already in our path.

We've progressed steadily downward for about thirty minutes following the same finger ridge. I hope Taylor is skilled with map and compass, because there are no landmarks visible to use to verify our position. Every step we take looks the same and the limited view of our surroundings can easily deceive us about the slope and contour of the land we're on. It's critical to any unit like ours to always know our exact position and map coordinates. Should anything happen where we need help; artillery or mortar support, an air strike or a medevac, we cannot make a mistake about our position. The jungle hides us from everything except friendly fire rounds that may have been directed on to the wrong position.

I'm wondering if anyone else is feeling as weary as I am at about the time the squad comes to an abrupt halt. Then suddenly, everyone ahead of me moves more quickly forward and forms a little group at the edge of what seems to be a clearing. As I get closer, I can see the clearing is formed by bomb craters. Sergeant Taylor choreographs the squad's movements so that we can cover each other as we move into and through this exposed area. Bob Price and I, being at the end of the file, remain in the trees until most of the squad has maneuvered across the clearing. This gives me a little time to study the intrusive effect of the bombs. They have thoroughly devastated everything within their

Tim Haslam

explosive radius. Huge trees have been sliced off at various points leaving splintered trunks protruding up from the rubble of broken branches and the shredded remains of smaller trees and lower story vegetation. There is so much annihilated plant mass laying in this tangle that the actual depth of the craters is hard to determine. Everything is covered with a coat of fine red dust from the dirt blown out of the ground. The sun now has unobstructed access down into this scene and lights it up almost like a spotlight against the contrast of the filtered light fading off into the surrounding jungle darkness.

The others have worked their way across and taken up covering positions on the far side of the clearing allowing Price and I to proceed through. This proves to be a real obstacle course requiring us to climb up, over and through the rubble. As I do this, I can also see some of the metal bomb fragments imbedded into the remains of trunks and branches. I think for a moment what it would be like for any human or other animal species to be here at the instant the bombs breech the protective jungle canopy, burrow into the ground and then, a split second later violently transform all living things into decaying shreds and pieces. I wonder if these bombs found their intended victims. I wonder if I'm climbing over shreds of Charlie.

A small stream flows down between two of the finger ridges at the far side of the clearing and provides an opportunity for us to take a break. Everyone naturally forms a small perimeter, scanning the surroundings for vulnerable points of access by intruders or projectiles. Then everyone reaches for his water, then cigarettes. As I drink, I try to gage my rate of water consumption and realize that my three canteens won't be enough. Doc Charlebois is sitting on a rock within a few feet of me and so I ask him if the water in the stream is OK to drink.

He says, "Probably" and reaches into his pouch, pulling out a vile of iodine tablets.

"Put a couple of these in your canteen, if you're going to try the stream water," he says without much confidence in the likely outcome of his suggestion. Wee John, Beasley and Danko are all soon dipping canteens into the stream, so I do too. Next, we all take the opportunity to use our towels as a way to convey the cool stream water to our heads and faces. This effort is not only refreshing but reveals patches of skin pigment that we've not seen for many days. This partial cleansing how-

Stars and Stripes and Shadows

ever leaves our faces with a mottled sort of camouflage look.

My body, aided by the water and nicotine, is starting to rejuvenate and so my mind starts to pay attention to the ground around me. I look for leeches but see only ants. They are huge ants though, maybe half an inch long, black, with oversized heads and mandibles. They are crawling all over the place. *They're crawling all over me!* No one else seems concerned about them as I watch one of them track over my shirt and on to the bare skin of my arm. The ant doesn't seem to find my flesh of any interest and so continues his searching back off of me and on to the ground. R&R-guy was wrong; everything here isn't out to get me. The mosquitoes however are, and down at the bottom of this ravine, near the stream, they're fierce. I have a little bottle of repellant under the elastic band around the camouflage cover of my helmet along with another little bottle of gun lubricant for my M16. I apply the repellant liberally to all exposed skin wondering if this method of prevention might be worse than the mosquitoes themselves. The smelly, oily repellant blends with the dirt sweat and salt, giving the thickening veneer an even more uncomfortable viscous feel to it. The sense of adventure is rapidly being overwhelmed by the myriad of little elements nibbling off the soft shell exterior of my body and my character.

Taylor concludes his work with map and compass and tells us that he thinks we have about another forty minutes of humping until we get to the ambush site. We set out again in the same order staying close to the stream and following the ravine downward on a southwest heading. The going is a little easier now as we don't have to go up and over any large ridges and, as the ravine starts to open up, the vegetation too starts to thin out. As we progress further down there are several areas where the under-story is very sparse, leaving nearly clear areas between the large trees. Taylor is cautious about moving through these areas. Although our visibility is much less obstructed, we're also easy targets for snipers who could fire at us from hidden positions far enough away to escape any reactive fire from us.

It's at the edge of one of these clear areas that Taylor halts the squad, signaling us to get down. He once more confirms our position with his map and compass, then takes the handset from Wee John's radio and calls back to Six-Charlie, advising of our whereabouts and status. We have clumped ourselves together close enough for everyone to hear

Tim Haslam

Taylor describe the situation. The belief is that Charlie has taken up residence higher up in the adjacent ravine and comes down across this clearing to get to our ravine which leads down to the Dak Poko. From the Dak Poko he has his pick of avenues to several small ARVN bases, and American Special Forces camps. Our objective is to lay an ambush at the end of the clearing nearest the stream and then, if no one comes along tonight, to search around tomorrow morning for any signs of trails or tunnels. Wee John completes Sergeant Taylor's explanation by reminding everyone that the real objective is of course body count. The whole chain of command will be thrilled if we can claim even one kill. Charlie's chain of command probably feels the same way.

As quickly and quietly as possible, the squad sets three trip flares between trees a few meters out into the clearing, across what would be the anticipated approach down to the ravine. Then we take up positions within the jungle at the northwest edge of the clearing, spreading ourselves out in a semicircle with a radius of about twenty meters. I'm in the second slot from the left end with Price to my left and Doc Charlebois to my right. It's nearly seven o'clock and darkness is coming. I can just make out where everyone else in the squad is, trying hard to imprint their positions in my mind. If the desired outcome of our ambush is achieved, I don't want to shoot any of our own guys. I hope that they all have similar concerns and have imprinted my position.

Price and Doc are close enough that we can converse quietly as we prepare dinner. This is my first opportunity to eat C-rations cold. I'm hungry enough to extract and eat the bits of ham, lima beans and coagulated globs of fatty stuff that fill up the can without thinking too much about how awful it is. Some crackers and cookies complete the meal and leave a more palatable taste in my mouth. I finish off the canteen that I had partially filled from the stream…the one with the iodine taste. For dessert I have the Chiclets gum that's in the foil pack with the toilet paper and cigarettes. An after dinner smoke is out of the question under the circumstances and so we begin to give our full attention to our responsibilities as ambushers. There will be nothing else to do or say between now and when the sun rises in about ten hours. The four men on each side of the semicircle make up a guard team with each man pulling a two and a half hour shift. We agree that we will simply work from the edge to the middle so Price will have the first

Stars and Stripes and Shadows

shift, then me, Doc and Beasley. Price has propped himself up against a tree trunk with his rifle across his lap as the rest of us try to establish a nest for sleeping.

Fortunately, the area we are in is pretty dry and so I can burrow into the ground cover a little. I can't see any leeches, ants or anything else crawling around my space but still try to cover myself up as much as possible. I have buttoned everything on my fatigues and have my towel over my head and as much of my face as I can, allowing only an opening for breathing. I have my left hand wedged down between my legs and my right hand on my M16. My mind is occupied only with my surroundings, situation and discomfort as fatigue quickly facilitates the transition into sleep.

It seems that only moments have past when I feel Price tugging at my shirt.

"It's ten thirty, you're up," he says quietly.

"Do you need my watch?" he asks as I get re-calibrated to the dark reality.

"No, I have one." I whisper back while pulling myself out of my terrycloth cocoon, watching Price prepare his for the rest of the night. No other communications, situation updates, or words are necessary; Price has done his duty and now it's my turn.

The changing of the guard takes only a minute; Price is fast asleep and I'm wide-awake. This night's guard duty takes me one more step down into the depths of danger and isolation. As bad as guard duty was back on the perimeter line at the Company's position the last few nights, this is worse. I trust that someone else on the other side of our position is also awake, but for all I know I'm the only friendly living thing awake and alert in this place of nocturnal creatures; this place where Charlie believes he can move about freely; this particular place where our leaders believe we will intercept Charlie, prevail in a violent struggle for survival and report more bodies tomorrow than they do. For the next two and a half hours the outcome of this whole scenario seems to depend on me alone. Price sleeps soundly knowing he succeeded at his turn. Doc sleeps soundly, not needing to know anything but fatigue for the next two and half hours. They all sleep soundly, secure in the belief that I will stay awake.

Tim Haslam

In the darkness, I think I can just make out the clearing a few meters in front of me. It's as much a feeling or residual image of the clearing as it is a visual confirmation of anything really there now. I try to mentally pace off the distance between the trip flares and me. *It's not far enough!* I think Charlie will be right on top of me when his foot snags the trip wire. The flare will light both of us up like a spotlight on gunfighters in a western movie. I mentally rehearse my reactions and movements all the while hoping that Charlie's taking the night off.

The stream flowing down the ravine behind me provides a steady interruption to the silence but is irregular enough to confuse my senses. There are other sounds around me too. There are sounds of the sleeping squad, rustling sounds up in the trees above me and occasionally there are little muffled surprise sounds coming from somewhere, caused by something, at some distance I can't determine. The more I try to attend to every vibration the more artifacts I collect for analysis. *This isn't working!* To do my job here, I have to get my mind out of this place but only far enough that I can quickly return when the real threats materialize. This is the real task for each of us during our guard. We are constantly trying to re-establish the correct thresholds, trying to find the lines between meaningful signals and background noise, trying to separate what we think and know and feel when our abilities to differentiate are obscured by darkness, fatigue, isolation and fear. I have to endure two and half hours of this without company, without diversion, without even a cigarette.

As the moments go by, my need and desire to sleep keeps increasing. My only countermeasure is to keep my mind active and, as my senses can offer no stimulation, my memory is the only mechanism available, so I try to remember things. I try to remember the names of all the kids in my sixth grade class. I try to remember every teacher I had in high school. I try to name every Steve McQueen movie, every player on the Dodgers, every state capital. The recall game gets me through about half of my shift when my fatigued brain refuses to offer up any new categories. My determination to stay awake now starts to negotiate with my fatigue. *Just close your eyes for a minute.* I think to myself. *Just a minute wont hurt. I'll still be able to hear things—I can't see anything anyway. Just for a minute.* There are just enough alert brain cells to override this beguiling suggestion. I know that my eyelids, once shut, would refuse to open. I know that shutting my eyes would be the all-clear signal shutting down the whole system. I know that the instant my system shuts down things will crawl out from their hiding places and add us to the body count tally.

Twelve-fifty-five, my watch says. *Five more minutes to endure…five minutes…three hundred seconds; two hundred ninety nine…two hundred ninety eight…*

"Doc, its one o'clock," I say, gently shaking the warm body laying to my right, "Doc, wake up!"

"What? OK, OK." The body mumbles with eyes still closed, belying any real commitment to the acknowledgement.

It's now 1:02 a.m. and I'm on overtime.

"Doc, it's your turn on guard," I plead, shaking him more vigorously.

I continue the pleading and shaking until the eyes are open and Doc has rejoined me in the shit, leaving whatever better place his dreams had taken him to. Doc pulls himself up trying to stretch his towel around him as some protection against the now chilled air, taking my Timex to consummate the transition of responsibility. I burrow back into my nest, unconcerned about the other things crawling over me, or Charlie, or who my tenth grade English teacher was, or how shitty this is starting to get. Sleep takes me away for the next few hours.

"Six-Two-Alpha-Charlie, this is Six-Two-Charlie, say again. Over." I hear Wee John saying into the radio as my eyes open, confirming that I really have spent the night as a forest creature in this place so far from home.

"Roger, wait one," Wee John responds to the little amplified voice coming through the handset. "Bob, Six-Two's on the horn," he says offering the handset to Sergeant Taylor, who's coming to life at about the same rate as the rest of us down among the decaying compost, on this overcast, cool morning.

"Taylor," is all the Sergeant says, too tired to think through the correct radio protocol.

"Roger," he repeats several times without any other verbiage that might elucidate the rest of us now eavesdropping on his conversation.

Tim Haslam

He continues the "rogering" as he pulls his map out of his pant leg pocket signaling to us that something has changed in our mission. Still on the radio, he gestures for us to bring in the trip flares and to get things packed up quickly.

"Maybe two and half hours that way," he replies to some Six-Two inquiry, "...if we hump our butts off."

The rest of us, hearing this, look at each other registering the same non-verbal sentiment...*shit!*

"I can't tell from the map," he responds to another option from Six-Two. "Maybe if we work down to the finger that intersects the stream at nine-four-five-two-eight-two we can come pretty much straight back up."

This description coupled with the concern on Taylor's face elicits the same reaction from us as option one.

"Roger. Out," Taylor says concluding the dialogue, handing the handset back to Wee John.

Bob keeps us in suspense while he lights a cigarette.

"Good news," he says in an unconvincing sort of way. "The Company's going back to Dak To for a few days and we have to get back up to their position ASAP. So, get something to eat quickly and get packed up."

Taylor opens up his map in front of us and explains the route that he and Six-Two have chosen. My minimal training on map reading and land navigation back at Fort Polk is enough for me to recognize how close together the contour lines are going up the selected ridge. The route is probably about half a click shorter than the way we came down, but none of us like the idea of making a climb that steep in a hurry. Still, at the end of the hump is a ticket out of the jungle for a few days; a ticket to the support base at Dak To and all the luxurious creature comforts available there. We tell ourselves that this image will sustain us through the next few hours' work.

This time, Beasley will cut point with me following and everybody else in some assigned order behind. Beasley's about the same stature as Danko and so I prepare myself to climb and duck my way up the mountain. We've hurried our way through our chosen canned nutrition and saddled up. Our first opportunity for a smoke is just as we start off and so, most of us set out with cigarettes dangling from our lips,

Stars and Stripes and Shadows

eyes squinting from the smoke, pretending to get some positive benefit from the nicotine.

Beasley moves quickly, following the stream down for about two hundred meters. A finger ridge rises up to our right on the opposite side of the stream, so Beasley waits for Taylor to catch up and confirm that this ridge is the route up. Taylor instructs Mike that it is and that he should try to work up the right side of the ridge rather than to go directly to the crest. He emphasizes the importance of keeping the upslope always to our immediate left.

The slope and density of vegetation gradually increase and in just a few minutes Beasley is busy swinging his machete. In some ways, working upwards seems easier than coming down. My forward motion swings the weight forward, closer to the ground and my head is more naturally oriented toward the obstacles approaching at foot level. The load on my back and shoulders is drawn downward through my body's center of gravity as opposed to the constant pull backward experienced when going down. I have also done a better job of balancing my load today. For a few minutes I can tell myself that this isn't going to be so bad.

I watch Beasley toiling ahead of me as we progress obliquely up the ever-steepening slope. The heat and humidity are catching up to us and my, *this isn't going to be so bad*, feeling starts to sweat away. The advantages of balance and posture moving upwards soon give way to the muscle exertion required to keep lifting my body and gear up the mountain, step by step. I can't help but reach out to the branches and vines for assistance pulling myself up some of the steeper inclines. R&R-guy was right, most of the vines have thorns and too many of the branches turn out to be the razor sharp, broken shafts of bamboo that Beasley's cut. The flesh of my uninitiated hands and forearms offers little resistance to the slicing and snagging from the permanent residents of this neighborhood. The resulting scrapes and scratches on my arms don't bother me much, but the little slices on the palms of my hands sting enough to hold my attention, exacerbating all the other little miseries. Maneuvering over and through the obstacles requires my full attention. My mind can't separate itself from the rest of my body struggling up the monotonous track. It can't drift off to somewhere else with images of friends and comfort and fun, where time moves more quickly.

Tim Haslam

It seems like hours have past before another finger ridge appears out of the jungle ahead, sloping off eastward, obstructing our path. Beasley stops and waits for Sergeant Taylor to determine a course correction. After studying his map and compass he concludes that we're drifting too far eastward and must now move as directly as we can to find the crest of the ridge leading up to Bravo Company's position. To do this, we have to zigzag back and forth up the steep slope to our left for several minutes. Its tough going and we're all greatly relieved when we reach the ridge crest and find that it's nearly clear of low vegetation. Taylor again checks his map and compass and confirms our position with more confidence now that he can identify the terrain features around us. He tells Wee John to radio up to Six-Two and to give him our position, telling him the map coordinates. The rest of us take a standing water break. We've been working up the mountain for nearly an hour and a half without a break and no one has the stamina to add a burning cigarette to our mouths, already gapping open to pull in as much oxygen as possible.

"Twenty minutes," Taylor estimates, "if things stay pretty much like this, and we should be there." He advises us to stay separated now as we move along the top of the ridge crest, as we're exposed targets from the adjacent ridges and the jungle below. We all become more alert to our surroundings. The others in the squad automatically calibrate their reflexes in anticipation of the unmistakable crack of an AK47 or the muffled pop of an enemy mortar lofting its deadly projectile in our direction. This is a situation they've all been in before. This is the way it is when Charlie gets the first shot.

Beasley, now highly motivated at the thought of ending this hump, or determined to be an impossible moving target is setting a blistering pace. It's all I can do to keep him in site in front of me and I can only hope that the group behind, particularly Sergeant Taylor can see me. We move through another two hundred meters or so of this open ground before the bamboo starts to thicken up again, slowing our progress. As the squad catches up with me and, the once again machete wielding, Beasley, Taylor yells out to hold up.

Beasley, with a big grin on his profusely sweating face asks Taylor what the problem is.

"I think I'd better call up to the Company and alert them that we're

Stars and Stripes and Shadows

coming in before they pop a cap on your buzz-saw ass!" Taylor says, laughing and panting along with the rest of the squad now caught up in Mike's frenzied drive to the goal line.

Wee John radios up the alert giving us just enough time to take a swallow of our remaining warm water. Taylor takes one more reading with his compass and points forward and slightly to the right activating the Beasley-jungle-harvester.

Our path back in to the Company's position is verified by a Huey vectoring in from our left. We break into Six-One platoons cleared field of fire just as the chopper lands in the LZ and we can see six rucksack laden grunts scramble on board. The trip flares have all been pulled in and, in fact most of the Company has already been lifted out. Our platoon is the last to go and the other squads have spread themselves out into a protective perimeter around the LZ. Six-Two is waiting for us and instructs Taylor to have us pack up the rest of our gear quickly. Four more Hueys are in route now to get the last of Bravo Company out of the shit. We don't need Bob to repeat the order and it takes just minutes for us to reclaim the rest of our households and form up around the LZ. Danko, Price, Beasley, Elmer, Doc and I are invited to take the next bird that's now approaching and none of us hesitate at the offer.

The UH1-D arrives with the familiar left hand mid-air sliding stop and backs down into the LZ. The six of us are pretty casual as we approach and, in fact heave our rucks inside instead of trying to struggle on board with them on our backs. The rucks, laden with gear and weaponry fill up most of the cargo room and so we take up positions sitting at the side openings with our feet dangling out over the skids. As the chopper vibrates upwards I reflexively reach for something to hold on to, my faith in the centrifugal force concept still incomplete. The Huey lifts nearly straight up until it's above the trees then banks leftward, accelerating down and away from the LZ. I watch the LZ and the few remaining Bravo grunts shrink away until they're just a blemish on the jungled mountainside. There's a great feeling of relief that I've been extricated from this landscape, even if it's just for a few days.

The day is bright, clear and hot and the unobstructed view from the side of the Huey is spectacular. Danko and Price are on my side of the bird and seem to be really happy. The noise of the Huey makes any conversation impossible, but their facial expressions tell the story.

Tim Haslam

Just a few moments ago we were struggling our way through the jungle and up the steep mountain ridge, exposed to hostile fire, minimally fed, thirsty, exhausted and unsure of anything. Now we're on our way to Dak To. At Dak To, there's real food, plenty of water, maybe even beer and soda. At Dak To, there are showers, there might be clean clothes, there is a little PX with candy, things to read and there are plenty of cigarettes of all brands, even the prized, unfiltered Camels that the most macho image conscious among us prefer. More than anything else, we hope there is mail at Dak To.

The pilot understands who we are and where we've been. He adjusts the collective to optimize the rotor angle for speed and throttles up the jet engine. With its nose down, the Huey seems to like to show off this way as it races over the terrain below. The vibrations have settled down, the flight is smooth and the passengers are like kids at Disneyland on a school day. The M16s clutched in our grips are the only connection to the hard truth still surrounding this momentary interlude...*this is fun!*

The fun increases as we drop down lower until we're just a few meters above the water of the Dak Poko. The gentle meanders of the river result in a series of left and right hand banking turns that keep our stomachs engaged in the thrill ride. Suddenly, a bridge appears ahead and the pilot noses up dramatically to clear the structure, banks sharply to the left and starts following the road; Route 512. We can all see ahead down the highway. We can all see the forward support base in the distance...*Dak To!*

The open air of the Dak To base is less humid than the steamy air compacted within the jungle we've just come from but the unobstructed rays of the sun are more intense as they bore directly into us while we separate ourselves and our gear from the Huey. The pilot acknowledges our appreciative gestures with a wave as we're herded over to a larger group of Six-Two grunts surrounding Sergeant Bollman at the edge of the landing field. Taylor hurries ahead to get instructions from Bollman with the rest of us moving less quickly under the full weight of our gear. Each Bravo Company platoon is being assigned to a section of the perimeter with individual squads assigned to specific bunkers. The bunkers here, spaced at about forty meter intervals, are wooden frame

Stars and Stripes and Shadows

structures with sandbagged walls and roofs. Trenches and foxholes fill in the spaces between the bunkers so that one is never too far from a place to jump into when incoming rounds start to fall.

It works out that Six-Two platoon gets four bunkers on the open side of the base, facing eastward, the side away from Rocket Ridge. The main gate into the base is on the southeast with a complex of bunkers and towers adjacent to it. The next bunkers moving northward are assigned to us. Sergeant Taylor, Elmer, Beasley, Price, Danko and I are in the third bunker with the guys from Sergeant Stevens's squad taking the two bunkers between us and the gate and the rest of the platoon and Company filling up the bunkers up the line to our left.

The inside of our bunker measures about eight foot square. The south and east sides have been dug down so that one can walk nearly upright and take up firing positions out the narrow opening on the east side. The northwest section, a square about six feet by six feet, forms a platform about four feet above the floor level, leaving just a few feet of headroom. This is where we'll sleep; at least this is where four or five of us will sleep, as at least one of us will be on guard throughout the night. Of course, the interior of the bunker is entirely dirt, but its dry dirt and there doesn't seem to be any sign of other inhabitants. Taylor offloads his gear up on the platform just inside the door, the rest of us staking our claims in available space heading toward the business end of the bunker. With personal spaces established, we collectively start decorating, carefully placing the machinegun, ammo, grenades, and star shell flares at the bunker opening, accessible and ready to deploy should Charlie interrupt our holiday here.

As we prepare the bunker, Taylor lets us know that we're pretty much free to do what ever we want the rest of the day. We can go to the mess tent at meal times. We can use the showers, perhaps even when there's hot water. The little PX will be open for two hours starting at seventeen hundred hours and there are two Vietnamese barbers available all day for us.

"You will get haircuts!" he suggests strongly. "Tonight, after chow, there will be bravo-two and three for anyone who might be interested. For Haslam's benefit, that's beer and soda," he proclaims with the enthusiasm of a waiter at a fine restaurant describing the brandy available after a six-course dinner.

Tim Haslam

"Any chance it will be cold?" inquires Elmer. "Of course," says Taylor sarcastically. "They've modified a Huey specially for delivering refrigerated beer out to the grunts. I think it'll be on tap too."

"Well, hell Bob, they do have generators and electricity here." Price offers optimistically.

"How hard would it be to get a refrigerator up here? Plus, the permanent party guys here are pretty resourceful and could make a fortune selling cold beer."

"I'll pass your suggestion on to Sergeant Sweeney, the new Company Supply Sergeant." Taylor responds, leaving us all with the expectation that warm beer will be our final reward at the end of the day. Under the circumstances, even warm beer is something to look forward to.

"Before anyone heads for the showers, see Sweeney over at the Bravo Company supply tent and get clean clothes," Taylor further orders. "I think he even has clean towels, so bring these vile rags that you've had around your necks for the last two months and trade them in."

"Any questions," Taylor asks, as anxious as everyone else to start taking a brief break from Sergeant-hood and jungle dwelling.

There are apparently no questions and so Bob sets us free saying only, "Be back here at twenty hundred hours!"

Through no intentional action on either of our parts, Price and I have paired up as we head off to find Sergeant Sweeney and his offerings. Elmer and Beasley seem also to be paired, talking in a relaxed fashion, walking a few feet ahead of us. Danko follows a few feet behind us, seemingly content to be on his own, without the need or desire to converse, but still close enough to be part of the group. Bob Taylor doesn't appear to be interested in joining us as he heads up the bunker line, perhaps seeking one of his fellow NCOs as more appropriate company. Perhaps, he feels that we would be more relaxed without his company. Perhaps he just has something else to do that has nothing to do with his rank or any concern about military protocol.

Like ants, the Bravo Company grunts form random walk trails from the bunker line into the camp interior ultimately discovering Sweeney and his supplies. He has bars of soap for us; toothpaste, toothbrushes; clean socks, clean towels, clean tee shirts, clean fatigue shirts and pants. He does not have underwear. As I head for the showers with all my clean stuff I'm troubled by the underwear situation. I have now been

64

wearing this particular pair of Army green boxers since I left Pleiku, more than a week ago. Even by fraternity house standards, this is extreme. By my mother's standards this is a felony. I have been wearing this underwear twenty-four hours a day. It's very hot in Vietnam. It's very humid in Vietnam. There are no appropriate words, even in the grunt vernacular, to describe my underwear. But, they are mine and I've been raised to believe that one should always wear underwear. I can't replace them and I can't get rid of them. There is no laundry at Dak To.

The fifty-five gallon drum of water up on the small tower above the showers at Dak To takes about three hours to heat up using the jury rigged propane system assembled beneath it. After three hours the fifty-five gallons of sort-of-hot-water takes about four minutes to drain out, allowing three or four people to have something like a hot shower. The fortunate three or four people from Bravo Company are long gone and so I and the rest of Taylor's squad are content using the eighty-five degree water that comes from the much larger water tank on the bigger tower adjacent to the water heating system. There's plenty of this water and with Sergeant Sweeney's soap we take our time excavating through the accumulated geology, ultimately revealing the skin and hair we've not seen for so long. My clean arms confirm R&R-guys predictions. The myriad of small cuts, scratches and scratched at bites are all naturally trying to mend themselves but the environment of constantly moist filth limits the repairs to incomplete scars surrounded by reddish patches. Now that it's clean, it itches more than ever. Maybe Doc has something for this…maybe Darvon or Merthiolate.

The shower water and Sweeney's soap are my only solution for the underwear problem. It's a poor solution at best and the end result is wet underwear with some of the filth replaced by soap residue that refuses to rinse out. I tell myself that it's a satisfactory improvement and that my underwear is now suitable for continued personal service into the future. Right at this moment however they're still wet and so I'm forced to violate my ancient ancestral dress code and go bareback. As our bunker is much too far away, I also have no option except to carry around my boxers and towel as I visit the other amenities here at Dak To.

The Vietnamese barbers speak four words of English, "How you

Tim Haslam

want cut?" They apparently don't understand *any* English as each of our replies results in the same mowing of our heads with their electric clippers. The entire process, opening dialogue through cutting, takes maybe twenty seconds for which we are expected to give them fifty cents. They stuff the tendered MPCs into their pockets without so much as a "GI numba one" and direct the next head into clipper range. Their efficiency and dedication to customer service suggests to me that they must, by Vietnamese standards, be very wealthy men.

Its early afternoon and we are briefly clean as the sweat and Dak To dust begin to rebuild the veneer. We've had a leisurely hot meal, washed down with warm cherry Cool-Aid and have partaken of all that Dak To has to offer. Returning to the bunker we spend the next several hours mostly in private space. There hasn't been any new mail delivered yet, so people are hesitant to write letters, waiting for news from home to respond to. Old letters get re-read again. A few new paperback books have been acquired here as well as several newer copies of Stars and Stripes.

One of the back issues of Stars and Stripes tells about the murder of Martin Luther King Jr. The impact of this news is disquieting and seems to diminish the picture of America that I want to have with me here. With Jeter gone, everyone in the squad is white, and so, I can't see or hear the reactions of any of the black men here. Perhaps, it's disturbing to them in a different way. Perhaps it's no surprise to them that a black leader can be assassinated in America. It gets clearer to me that the concept of America must be different for each of us. The concept of being a grunt in the Central Highlands of Vietnam is, however the same for us all and so, the various images of America and home exist only as abstractions, to be visited privately or together in the few brief moments that life in the shit allows.

For the rest of the day we read, we sleep, we're more comfortable than we've been in a long time, but we are, more than anything, still bored.

Five o'clock finally arrives and the anticipated opening of the small PX. Everyone in the company seems to be in line outside, sharing the same hope that the twenty-foot by twenty-foot shed somehow magically maintains an inventory of merchandize similar to Sears Roebuck. My

Stars and Stripes and Shadows

place, in about the middle of the line, gets me inside in about twenty minutes. What's left is not very exciting and so my shopping spree adds only a pad of letter writing paper, an Abba-Zabba and a Turkish Taffy to my personal possessions. A few of the lucky shoppers at the front of the line were able to purchase 16mm Minolta cameras; about the size of a pack of cigarettes, and film. Ed Arter got one of these, and so, everyone in Six-Two will have their pictures taken numerous times throughout our stay at Dak To.

Sergeant Taylor intercepts us coming out of the mess tent after dinner and suggests we swing by Sergeant Sweeney's. This can only mean one thing and our pace quickens to ensure that we get our share of any beer that Sweeney may have available.

The new supply sergeant—Sergeant Thomas Sweeney—has attained a place of reverence for himself in the eyes of the field grunts of Bravo Company. Not only does he have plenty of beer for us but, the beer is almost cold. There are two fifty-five gallon drums filled with Black Label and Miller High Life beer cans floating in water that only a few hours ago was ice. Sweeney, standing proudly between the two drums, keeps repeating that we each may take three cans. Master Sergeant Madison, the senior NCO in the field with Bravo Company stands behind Sweeney, passively ensuring that no one takes advantage of Sweeney's benevolent offer. Sergeant Madison is a career Army person who saw action in the Korean War and is a no-nonsense all-military type who has everyone in Bravo Company, including the officers, scared to death. Each of us retrieve our share from the drums offering an appreciative glance up at Sweeney and, at the same time ensuring that Madison can see that we only have three cans.

Off to the side of the vigilant Madison, the saintly Sweeney and his almost cold beer are about a dozen cardboard cartons labeled "Sundry Pack." The boxes have all been opened and the contents carefully stacked on two adjacent tables. There are several boxes of candy, ballpoint pens, letter writing tablets (*de-valueing my prior investment*) and cartons and cartons of cigarettes. Someone knowledgeable about their relative value within this macho-grunt market has organized the cigarette cartons. The unfiltered Lucky Strikes, Pall Malls and especially Camels are at one end of the table with a hand written note, limiting

Tim Haslam

access to two packs. In the middle of the table is a more massive stack of Marlboros and Winstons with the allowance bumped up to five packs each. Finally, at the other end of the table is the stack of menthol cigarettes and other brands that young American men don't want to be associated with, even though there is apparently no limit to the take within this group.

The scrum around Sweeney's gifts slowly starts to untangle and the Company begins to disperse away, back to our assigned positions along the bunker line, each of us protectively clinging to our cigarettes and almost-cold-beers.

There is still an hour or so before the nights guard watch starts on this pleasant, dry evening. The air is cooling somewhat as the last long rays of sunlight squeeze through the trees at the top of Rocket Ridge, illuminating the Dak To valley out beyond our perimeter in clean, soft light. Our bunker is now in the full shadow of the ridge providing the first relief we've had from the sun today. Danko, Beasley and Elmer fashion chair-like structures for themselves out of sandbags and rucksacks just outside the bunker entrance while Price and I jump up and sit on the edge of the bunker roof facing them. Each of us seems to be similarly motivated and directed to first get comfortable, then to slowly approach our refreshments, savoring each draw of cigarette smoke and swallow of beer. For a few minutes, no one thinks about anything except the relative pleasure of the moment. There is no need to validate the feeling verbally.

Although the shade and the evening air have cooled things off, it's still warm and humid. We've taken our fatigue shirts and tee shirts off and sit bare-chested keeping our clean towels close at hand to swat at the mosquitoes now out in force. We'd rather fight them off this way than to douse ourselves with mosquito repellant and have the foul smell interfere with the enjoyment of our smoke and drink.

Beer drinking anecdotes are offered up to start the relaxed dialogue. Each of us in turn seems to be able to contribute something to the conversation and each contribution is afforded appreciative responses; "*right-on*," "*fuckin-A*," etc. This gets us through the first can of beer and two cigarettes.

There's a lull in the conversation as the second round beer can tabs

68

Stars and Stripes and Shadows

get pulled off. Danko's effort results in a foam spray burst that washes down his chest earning him a scolding from the group for wasting good beer. The foamy trail down his front passes between two scars, each of about an inch and a half in length, one slightly higher on his torso than the other. No one in the squad has said anything to me up to now about being wounded, but these look to me to be the artifacts of something recent and so, I ask Danko how he came by them.

The whole atmosphere changes as my question penetrates into the consciousness of the squad. All the eyes are drawn first to Danko's scars, then to me, then back to Danko. No one is relaxed any more. Danko takes a long drag on his cigarette and, reverting back to his cryptic style, mumbles something in Mike Beasley's direction.

"You don't want to know," replies Beasley abruptly, looking up at me, irritated that I have spoiled the party with my inquiry.

"Tell him," says Elmer after a long uncomfortable pause, acknowledging that the cat is out of the bag now.

"You tell him," Beasley replies, acquiescing to the inevitable disclosure but looking to Danko for some sign of concurrence.

Danko continues to stare straight ahead, puffing on his cigarette and sipping at his beer, seemingly uninterested in the outcome of the exchange. Elmer and Beasley look up at Bob Price sitting next to me. Price is the most senior of the group and is also the most educated and articulate of the squad, having had some college education back in Oregon before he was drafted. He also looks studious in his thick gray-framed Army issue glasses. It seems that he's been nominated as the one who should fill me in.

"All right, I'll tell him," Price says deliberately, followed by another suspenseful pause while he retrieves the pieces of the story from somewhere deep inside him not readily accessed.

"You see that?" Price asks, pointing back at the mountainside somewhat north of us, as a way of breaking the silence but still affording him time to organize the story he's about to tell.

"That's Dog-bone ridge," he says, with his finger tracing the sharp line up the mountain.

"The peak at the top of that is a-thousand-and-one. The ridge runs from there over to that high peak, thirteen-thirty-eight," he says, his finger guiding my eyes to the top of the high ridge that runs diagonally

Tim Haslam

out to the west of us. The distance between the two peaks is maybe two thousand meters.

"Behind all that are more ridges, valleys and mountain tops," he declares, still sorting through the details of what he's really trying to say.

"A few months ago, the Company was somewhere up in there humpin' around."

He pauses briefly and looks to the others to ensure that he's getting this right. They all sit quietly, seemingly as interested in Price's rendition as I am. The mountainous jungle beyond Rocket Ridge that Price is describing is the same area that R&R-guy warned Heald and me about. Right now I'm glad that the high ridge is there, forming somewhat of a barrier between us and this storied land of danger beyond.

"At the end of one of the days, we made camp early and we were happily surprised to hear that hot food was being flown in to us. Not only hot food, but beer too. It wasn't anything approaching cold like this, but there was plenty of it. We'd been humpin' our asses off, and so the beer and food had everyone feeling pretty good that night and the squad was sitting around shootin' the shit pretty much like we are now.

There were two guys in the squad then; Freddie and Pineapple. I think they were both from Hawaii or Guam or some place like that and they were best friends. The two of them were always kiddin' around and always fuckin' with each other. They were like two brothers, always trying to get over on each other. Anytime one of them said anything, the other one would say they were full of shit. They were like that all the time, it was their way of having fun and although it always seemed like they were fighting and arguing, they were never really mad at each other." Price pauses for a moment and scans the other faces for assurance that he's providing all the necessary background.

"This is no place for fuckin' around like that," clarifies Beasley, "Pineapple especially, you'd think this was all one big playground the way he was...*asshole!*"

"Anyway," Price continues, "this night, we were all sitting around, drinking the beer and bullshittin' about stuff and we start talking about cars and Pineapple starts telling us how fast his car is. Freddie tells us that Pineapple is full of shit and that his car barely runs at all. He says this just to piss Pineapple off and it works. So, they keep drinking beer and arguing over whose more full of shit until Pineapple finally warns

Stars and Stripes and Shadows

Freddie that he's going to shut him up. Freddie tells Pineapple that he'd better get his gun if he's going to shut him up but he's laughing, so nobody takes this too seriously. Pineapple looks around like he's looking for his M16, but he's not really serious either.

They're both pretty drunk now and can't seem to break out of this stupid argument. Pineapple keeps looking for his M16, but can't find it, so he reaches down to his ruck and pulls out a frag. 'Maybe I can shut you up with this!' he says, and walks over until he's right in front of Freddie. Freddie calls his bluff and says that he probably doesn't know how to use the thing. So, Pineapple pulls the pin on the grenade and starts jumping around right in front of Freddie still taunting him, but still not serious and with a firm hold on the safety spoon. The rest of us are now all trying to get Pineapple to put the pin back in the grenade and put it down. The joke's gone too far. Pineapple then steps right in front of Freddie so that they are practically nose to nose, both of them laughing but continuing their badgering of each other. Then, before anyone can do or say anything, Pineapple sticks the hand holding the grenade down Freddie's shirtfront. Reflexively, Freddie reaches up to grab Pineapples hand and pull it out of his shirt.

It wasn't funny anymore. In an instant, the interaction of Freddie and Pineapple's hands dislodged the grenade. The rest of us sitting around barely had time to even understand what was happening as Freddie and Pineapple frantically tried to recover the live grenade being pressed and jostled within this nest of flesh and fabric. The four or five seconds it took for the grenade fuse to burn down passed too quickly for any of us to react at all.

Freddie took most of the grenade blast and it pretty much cut him in two. Pineapple's hands shielded him somewhat, but with his hands blown off and both his arms mangled and with the other fragmentation wounds he was pretty fucked up. All the company medics were down there in a minute, but he was already in shock and died before he could be dusted off. Danko was hit with two pieces of shrapnel and one piece caught Beasley in the penis, just about cutting it off. He's OK though, the surgeons at the hospital in Japan repaired it pretty well…right Mike?"

"I'm fine," is all Beasley says, uncomfortable with the shift in attention.

Tim Haslam

Price takes a long drink from his last can of beer and gazes around at his audience. His narrative is complete, the story's been told. No one else has any elaborations or modifications; no summaries, no epilogues. There is nothing else shared that connects these five men with the story just told except the two little lines of scar tissue that barely divert the perspiration rolling down Danko's chest. I will hear this story repeated several times over the next six months. Each new man to the squad will learn about Freddie and Pineapple; about frags and beer and Danko's chest and Beasley's penis. None of us hearing this story will ever know of the deeper scars left within the men of Taylor's squad.

By 9:00 p.m. the squad has all settled onto their individual two-foot sections of the bunker's dirt shelf and are fast asleep, all except me. I've drawn the first watch and am sitting up on top of the sandbagged roof, looking out across the rows of barbed wire toward the dark interior of the Dak To valley. My M16 is laid across my knees, a fresh pack of Camels and my Zippo are laid at my side next to my bandoliers and pistol belt. The air too seems to have concluded its day's work capturing the scorching rays of the sun and directing the convection currents of heat and humidity at and around everything trapped within its reach. In its resting state, the air allows an occasional intrusion of cool breeze to sneak through. In the civilized world, such a balmy evening would coerce its inhabitants into a relaxed state of wellbeing. A state to be celebrated and accompanied by iced drinks and romantic conversations conducted on beaches or candle-lit restaurant verandas or even, just backyard patios. Here, the coercion must be resisted. The weapons within my reach belie any pretense of wellbeing and, even if I were to surrender briefly to this seduction, my only accompaniments are my Camels and the residual effects of the Carling Black Label. Still, this moment, here atop the sandbagged bunker, all alone, feels like the best I've had since I left home.

I spend the hour and a half of my shift reflecting on my new life in Vietnam. I replay R&R-guy's stories and attempt to validate some of them with my own experiences over the past several days. So far, he's got it right and yet, no one's been shooting at me, there's been very little rain and the guys around me all seem to know what they're doing. There are even rumors spreading around that peace talks will soon be

Stars and Stripes and Shadows

taking place. I think that maybe this whole thing really won't be so bad and that I'll be going home sooner than I thought.

Occasionally I glance back over my shoulder at the dark outline of Rocket Ridge and wonder about the land beyond. R&R-guy feared this territory more than anything, as do Price, Elmer, Beasley and Mike Danko. The valley in front of me too has its dangers. Out there, my enemies are hidden within the villages, disguised as farmers; disguised as women; disguised as children. In the mountains and jungles behind Rocket Ridge, my enemies are uniformed NVA soldiers, disguised only by the tunnels and vegetation that hides and protects them. My only friends rest below me within the meager shelter of these sandbags.

As I light the final cigarette of my shift. I wish I hadn't given in to the macho self-image that desired these Camels. The unfiltered smoke is strong and harsh and over-rides the comfort offered by the milder brands. Next time I'll re-position myself back into the general population and take the Marlboros. Rights-of-passage opportunities are plentiful here and no one is likely to use my choice of cigarettes to validate my place in the culture.

It occurs to me as I sit here alone on top of this bunker that today is Easter Sunday. There was nothing through the course of the day that would distinguish it from any other day here; no colored eggs or choco-late bunnies, no baked ham dinner or religious services commemorated the occasion. No one said anything. No one seemed to notice. Such things have little meaning here except perhaps as a reminder of another life that continues to fade off into the past.

I start to collect my things in anticipation of the end of my shift and my opportunity to sleep. The pistol belt catches my attention and my eyes and mind are drawn to the four grenades secured to the two ammo pouches clipped on the belt. I look closely at one of them, partially il-luminated in the starlight, studying the size and shape, contemplating the effectiveness of the crimped end of the cotter pin that holds the pull ring. I think about Freddie and Pineapple. I think about R&R-guy. I think about how everything around me is somehow connected to purposeful death and how easy it is for accidental death to find its victims. I'm starting to get it.

Chapter 4

At War With the Forest

The fine red Dak To dust being sucked up by the Huey's vacuuming rotors automatically starts adding layers of camouflage to our faces. We're less sympathetic to the helicopters purposes this time as it lifts us up and away from Dak To and starts vectoring up country. We're going back out after less than three days of rest. It wasn't all rest though, as the Army doesn't tolerate idleness much. So, we spent most of our days stringing barbed wire, filling sandbags, digging holes, assisting Sergeant Sweeney moving things around for unclear purposes and firing our M16s at paper targets placed on stakes outside the perimeter. The hot meals and bathing opportunities at the end of each day still made it feel somewhat like a vacation and the arrival of mail on the second day raised the spirits of the entire company; except mine, as it's still apparently too soon to expect anything.

The evening conversations with the squad back at the bunker were more cordial than our first evening's revelations. Anything to do with the war itself was carefully avoided. I still have much to learn from my squad brethren about the realities of life out here, but I have learned to be respectful of their few relaxed moments. The time and place and circumstance will come where each member of the squad will share every experience they've had. Now it's best for me to just listen and perhaps seek opportunities to establish myself in the hierarchy of bullshitters with my own claims of conquest and accomplishment back on the block. The beer we now have to wash down our stories with however is only as cool as the shaded floor of the bunker where we've stored it throughout the day.

Stars and Stripes and Shadows

Our guard shifts each night pass without incidence, the strength of our defenses perhaps lulling us into an artificial sense of security.

Whatever the brief moments at Dak To were, we all knew they were better than what was to come.

The train of Hueys ferrying Bravo Company back out into the shit starts to slow and queues up to the southwest of a high mountain peak. The peak affords a 360-degree view of the surrounding ridges, valleys and jungled river basin spreading out further to the west. Because of its commanding position, the 4th Division has established a firebase on this hilltop.

I'm sitting with my rucksack up against the rear panel of the UH1-D and so I have a forward view of the approaching landscape. As the little base comes into view I'm once again struck with the dissonance of the image. People don't belong out here. It's a place for creatures more suited and adapted to this environment. Yet, instead of the native ants coursing in, out and over their anthill home, I see, from this distance, ant sized, dirty green humans shuffling in, out and over the holes, trenches and sandbagged bunkers dug into the mud of this scarred hilltop, stripped of all its natural vegetation.

Four nearly circular pits, surrounded by sandbagged walls, are spaced within the center portion of the hilltop. Inside each pit is a 105mm Howitzer aimed out at the country below. Two smaller pits contain mortars, one, a big 4.2" piece and the other, a smaller 81mm tube. Ammunition for all these weapons appears to be in abundant supply, stacked within the moderate protection of the pit walls. This is Firebase 30. Bravo Company is replacing Delta Company up here. Our job is to protect the guns and mortars here and patrol the surrounding mountains looking for Charlie.

Our chopper bucks up slightly and stops in mid-air, hovering while the Hueys ahead off load Six-One Platoon. The somewhat abrupt stop causes me to shift focus back inside. Bob Taylor's facial expression catches my attention for no particular reason. I study him for a moment then scan over to Elmer, then Mike Beasley, then Price and finally Danko. Each of these very distinct faces wears the same subtle expression. Their look is similar to the way Captain Collins first appeared to me. Having more time to study them however, I'm puzzled by the depth

Tim Haslam

and substance of whatever feelings draw these faces into such masks of weariness and concern. At the time I have no way of understanding all that's portrayed. I'm still too new to this to recognize their common reaction as we return to the shit; their dread of more tedious days struggling under the rucksacks and bandoliers; their useless attempts to resist the onslaught of mosquitoes, leeches, mud, and dust as the jungle environment starts once again to break them down and consume them. I don't get it yet, that each day out here, although bringing us one day closer to DROS also brings us one day closer to fulfilling our purposes—contact with the people out here who are determined to kill us, contact where some of the people engaged will surely be killed. I don't yet understand that each return trip out here erodes our individual spirit and determination a little more, further confuses the purposefulness of our mission and adds irretrievably to the expanding separation from the lives we have known before Vietnam.

A light rain starts falling just as we haul ourselves off the Huey and try to orient ourselves to the complex of sandbagged lined trenches, bunkers and weapons emplacements that blemish the hilltop sloping up gradually to the east of our landing zone. The rain is quickly congealing the surface dust into a mortar-like consistency that clings to our boots as we plod up the narrow opening in the wire that separates the LZ from the base. Each mans passing along the narrow trail compresses the accumulating surface moisture further into the dust layer so that soon it's a slippery pudding. Several men ahead of us slip and fall making the passage even more treacherous for us. Reacting as a team, our squad carefully maneuvers upwards, setting our feet firmly and pulling up the following man with our rifles, minimizing our individual down time.

Six-Two catches Sergeant Taylor's attention as we reach the interior of the base and points to a bunker near the crest of the hill. The squad follows Taylor along a trench line and into the bunker. Our bunker at Dak To by comparison was spacious and luxurious. There is barely enough room for all of us and our gear in this hole. The ceiling is so low that even the shortest man, Mike Beasley, has to duck down. For me, I have to bend over so much that I must remove my ruck for fear of toppling over forward. The interior layout is similar to the bunker at Dak To, with a shelf for sleeping rising above a deeper trench on two sides. The southern facing side has open firing positions. With all of

Stars and Stripes and Shadows

us and all our gear pressed into this space, barely illuminated by the cloud filtered light coming in through the firing ports, the feeling is pretty claustrophobic even for those of us not usually subject to such reactions.

The others are used to this. They've set up housekeeping in many such places. For me, the adjustment is disturbing. I can't see any way to be orderly about this. There simply isn't enough room for all of us, and our gear. There isn't enough room near the firing ports to organize our weapons and ammo in any effective way. Even in this light rain, several obvious leaks are beginning to liquefy patches of the shelf and floor and with the mud we all carry in on our boots, this place will soon be a sludge pit. I find myself momentarily paralyzed. Standing here, bent over uncomfortably, wet from the rain, with no evident escape or relief available, I wait for a brief instant to be rescued.

Sergeant Taylor apparently sensing my condition comes to the rescue in a nurturing sort of way.

"Haslam, get your ass with the program! Offload your ammo and gear and get up to the platoon HQ and get a D-handle shovel. We've got some home improvement work to do."

"OK," is all I can offer as an appreciative response, as I hand over my belt of machinegun ammo and two of my bandoliers to Elmer who's closest to the firing-port. The rest of my gear stays on the edge of the sleeping shelf as I scuttle off in search of a shovel.

I find Wee John and Ed Arter setting up their radios under an improvised shelter made of ponchos and ask if they know where a D-handle is.

"I think Ferlik has one," Ed replies pointing back down the hill to another bunker about twenty meters east of ours.

"Thanks," I offer back, pondering the best route down there.

Just as I start out the rain stops and the sky begins to clear, instantly restarting the heat and humidity cycle.

I get two and a half steps down toward Ferlik's when my foot hydroplanes off the corner of a poncho that's partially draped over some wooden crates. The splashdown of course draws the attention of Ed, Wee John and fifteen or twenty other Bravo Company veterans within earshot. I look back up over my shoulder toward the platoon HQ with both my hands buried into the mud behind me just as Lieutenant Falck

Tim Haslam

appears out of his bunker.

"Haslam," he acknowledges as though taking note of my agility. "Do you know how to use a prick twenty five?" he asks incongruously.

"Yes sir," I answer wondering what his question has to do with my present circumstance. My knowledge of the PRC25 radio doesn't seem very relevant right now. Six-Two continues on toward the Company HQ further up the hill without any further explanation. I pry myself up out of the mud and carefully head off on my quest for the shovel wondering all the while about the PRC25.

N N N N

The rains are coming daily now; squalls, that pass over us quickly, drenching everything enough that the intervening dry periods are no longer sufficient to harden the surfaces of the firebase or the trails leading toward and away from our compound of pits, trenches and sort-of protected holes in the ground. Our home is liquefying. Like all the creatures that live here, we must now accept the water from the sky and adapt to its influences. Dust transcends to mud and, instead of fragrant spring flowers, mildew colonies blossom in this April environ, adding another foul odor to the air. The confined space of our bunker collects and holds the mildew smell, adds it to the stench of sweat and the other body odors of our squad, mixes it with stale cigarette smoke and the noxious smoky cordite residue from the 105's firing throughout the day and night leaving a pall that only a captive grunt could endure. Even outside, the air encapsulating the firebase is pungent and acrid. Smell, mercifully, is a sense that we accommodate to pretty quickly.

From nearly every vantage point on Firebase 30, one can see for several kilometers in any direction. There are almost always clouds in view at some point around us and thus rainsqualls can usually be seen hosing over some track of jungle off in the distance. When the squalls are clearly heading for us there is little we can do in the way of preparation. Things will just get wetter. We are things.

Based on some misguided logic, the Army has established certain guidelines for how we are to dispose of bodily wastes while residing at places like FB30. The company medics are in charge of compliance with these guidelines and the actual construction of the appropriate facility...the "*shitter*." Having limited resources to work with, the medics usually construct the shitters the same way. Artillery shells come in wooden crates with approximate dimensions of 36"x18"x6." The medics remove the top of the empty crate, then, using an axe, cut a hole in the bottom with a diameter of approximately 6-8 inches (*ensuring that numerous splinters surround the ragged edge of the opening*). This 'seat' is then placed over a hole dug approximately two feet down into the mud. If a role of toilet paper is available, it's placed on a stick stuck in the ground next to the seat. However, one is generally expected to bring his own paper. In an effort to avoid contaminating the air quality of the FB, the shitter is located out on the landing zone adjacent to the firebase.

Forced, by shear necessity to avail oneself of this facility is the final right of passage that utterly strips away any residual modesty that may have escaped our military living up to this point. I can only laugh to myself as I settle in for my initiation experience here. Happily, the weather is good. It's not raining, the view is spectacular and I'm basically all alone. I am however, also sitting here with my pants down, clearly visible to everyone on FB30, clearly visible to every North Vietnamese sniper within miles around, totally unprotected from incoming fire of any caliber and vulnerable to being blown down into the basement part of the facility by any approaching Huey. No one brings the latest edition of <u>Stars and Stripes</u> down here as accompaniment to this activity; an M16, yes!

On our second morning at FB30, Sergeant Taylor rallies the squad and invites us to participate in a short patrol. We should be out and back in less than three hours he clarifies. We are to scout out the neighborhood to our southeast, have a quick look around for any signs of Charlie and then head back. We will just need weapons, ammo and water.

Taylor advises me that the platoon has been issued a third radio and I'm elected to be the RTO. I will still be in Bob's squad, but will provide some relief for Ed and Wee John. Now, each RTO only has to go on every third patrol. I'm not sure I'm coming out ahead here as being an ordinary rifleman meant I went on every fourth patrol and I now can add at least another ten pounds to my back. However, there is some bizarre prestige in being an RTO and so I accept without objection, trying to overlook the other salient reality that RTOs are the first target in any firefight. Taylor sends me up to the platoon HQ to get the radio and some additional instruction from Ed and Wee John.

Ed gives me a refresher course in the care and use of the AN-PRC-25 radio. He provides me with an additional long-stick antenna and two extra batteries. (The batteries must weigh another five pounds each.) He fills me in on the current Company, Battalion and Artillery Support frequencies, referred to as the "pushes" and calls in "commo-checks" to each to confirm that the radio is functioning. My call sign is Six-Two-Three on the company net.

Officially released by Ed, I carry my new toys back to the bunker thinking nervously about this added responsibility.

N N N N

The intermittent rains of the early monsoons have already changed the jungle from the way it was on our last patrol; nothing is dry. Everything seems to have an odor about it. More creatures are apparent; large beetles, large spiders, small lizards and snakes, frogs of various sizes and colors, tree dwelling crabs and more ants. The ants are moving from the ground up into the foliage to escape drowning and are easily brushed off the plants and onto us. Clouds of mosquitoes hover around many of the streams. Our liberal applications of repellant afford a poor deterrent to their appetites. We've yet to see the leeches that we know are stretching and pulling their way toward the places they instinctively know we will stop at. The constant passage of the clouds overhead followed by the contrast of filtered sunlight creates a kaleidoscope of changing shadow patterns. Thus, everything seems to be moving, swaying, creeping or crawling.

My senses are on overload trying to work through this territory and keep up with Sergeant Taylor in front of me. The rest of the squad has just their weapons and ammo to carry. I have my weapon, ammo and the radio strapped to my rucksack frame on my back and it gets heavier with each step. I must also pay close attention to the handset that is hooked onto the frame strap coming over my left shoulder. It emits a constant squelch sound, broken only when someone is transmitting on this push. Later, I will be able to attend to this without thinking, but

Stars and Stripes and Shadows

now its one more thing to be concerned about. I should mostly be concerned about Charlie. Charlie's out here; that's why we're doing this.

Bob Price, who's been cutting point for us, has stopped at a small clearing at the end of the ridgeline we've been following for about the last half hour. The terrain ahead of us slopes down in all three directions and is covered by heavy vegetation. Sergeant Taylor signals for us to form a small perimeter around the clearing and then tells us to take ten while he studies his map to confirm our position. We are each about ten feet apart with Taylor in the middle, also about ten feet from where we are on the perimeter. We are all spread too far apart to carry on any conversation without giving our position away so we sit quietly, smoking and taking measured sips of warm water from our canteens. I can see that the others are checking themselves for leeches and other unwanted passengers.

As I pull my pant leg up to check my lower left leg, something catches my attention down the slope in front of my position. It was too subtle a stimulus to even register whether it was a sound or some kind of movement detected out of the corner of my eye. I pause from my leech check, look carefully out and down the slope for something that would confirm my alert reaction. A few seconds pass before a repeat of the stimulus reaches me. This time, I know it to be a sound. It's clearly a rustling sound coming from some distance down the slope. Something is there, something much bigger than the usual insect or reptilian inhabitant. The confirmation that I've heard this has my heart pumping. I need to engage the rest of the squad in identifying what or who this is. Fortunately Taylor and Elmer, who is to my left, both react to my twisting around and bringing my M16 into a forward ready position. Glancing back at Sergeant Taylor, I point down the slope and back up to my ear. He seems to understand and starts to crawl slowly toward me. The rest of the squad sees Taylor's movement and knows what to do.

Just behind me now Bob Taylor hears the next rustle and gestures back to the squad to keep down and quiet. He too, is unsure how far down the slope the movement is. We both continue to listen. The next rustle confirms that it's getting closer, but we're still unable to assess how much distance is between us and whatever it is approaching. Taylor, taking no chances, whispers to me for the radio handset.

Tim Haslam

"Six-Charlie, this is Six-Two-Three. Over," he says into the handset, his voice volume calculated to be just enough to stimulate the handset membranes that will connect us to the Company.
There's no response.

"Six-Charlie, this is Six-Two-Three. We've got movement out here. Over," this time raising his voice somewhat. Still no response.

"Six-Charlie, this is Six-Two-Three, get on the goddamn horn. We've got movement out here. Over," Bob says with nervous irritation in his voice.

Another rustle sufficient for everyone in the squad to hear comes up to us just as Taylor releases the handset talk button.

"Six-Two-Three, this is Six-Charlie. What's your position? Over," says the nearly garbled voice of Roy Houston, Captain Collins' RTO.

"Six-Charlie, this is Six-Two-Three. We're at nine-five-five-two-six-four. Over," says Taylor glancing between his map and the slope in front.

"Roger, Six-Two-Three...wait one."

"Wait one?" says Taylor apparently to himself. "Shit Houston, we don't have one!"

"Six-Two-Three, this is Six," says Captain Collins before Taylor can vent his frustration further. "What's going on, Taylor?"

"We've got unidentified movement within fifty meters of our position coming up at us from the east slope. Will advise when we have positive ID, meanwhile, how about bringing around one of those 105s in this general direction, just in case. Out."

Taylor hands me back the handset and whispers for me to turn off the squelch and turn the volume all the way down. He doesn't want Captain Collins' or anyone else's voice coming through on the radio to give our position away.

The rustling is now steady...coming up pretty fast. About thirty meters down the slope I can see the tops of some of the plants move, disturbed by whatever is coming up at us. Taylor crawls up along side of me so that he too has a clear path for firing at the intruder. The rest of the squad is frozen still and silent, but ready.

At about twenty meters, we can start to see the shape and mass of whatever this is, but cannot yet determine exactly what or who it is or what their intentions are. The slightly visible shape disappears quickly into a heavier

82

cluster of brush, still moving deliberately forward toward us.

A few more seconds pass before the movement abruptly stops. Whatever is there seems to be oriented towards us and has perhaps, somehow detected us. No one moves.

Two minutes at least pass before the rustling starts again just a few meters out from where Taylor and I lay, ready to unleash the full fury of our M16s.

A moment later, I glance over at Taylor as he lifts his helmet off his head and smiles.

"Shit!"

"Shit is right!" I respond, laughing at the sight of the large grayish wild pig that snuffles out of the brush just a few feet from us.

The nonchalant pig casually acknowledges our presence with a grunt; turns around and scurries back down the slope. The six of us simultaneously slump out of our alert, scared posture, re-set the selector switches on our M16s to SAFE and reach for another cigarette.

The pig has served a useful purpose for the squad. The adrenaline charge cleared out the fatigue and monotony accumulated from the patrol so far. Each of our reactions to the potential threat and danger has sharpened our senses, pulling us away from our selfish, petty concerns over bugs and thorns and mud and soggy boots. This cigarette is our reward for reacting properly. It's our reward for being able to avoid any body counting, either as counter or countee.

ϟ ϟ ϟ ϟ

We're all cooling down outside the bunker, listening to Bob Taylor debrief Six-Two about the pig assault and the rest of the patrol when the popping rotor sound and vibration of an approaching Huey catches our attention. It's obviously a logistics helicopter, a "log-bird," bringing supplies out to us. Such arrivals always stir up interest among the mud-hole dwellers and all of Bravo Company watches to see what's being off-loaded. The starboard side door gunner starts tossing stuff out onto the muddy surface of the LZ; C-rations, Sundry Packs, a couple of crates of mortar rounds and finally, the only thing any of us really care about, several mail bags. Four guys from Six-Zero platoon hurry down to retrieve the Huey's offerings. They, of course, grab the mailbags first, in case there should be a sudden attack or rainstorm or something, and

Tim Haslam

lug them back up the hill to the Company command post. They can come back and get the rest later.

Six-Two hurries off up toward the CP, Bob Taylor close behind in his wake. The whole company is sitting around now, waiting. There's no point in starting anything that would just get interrupted by the mail being distributed. The Platoon reacts in unison to the site of Lieutenant Falck heading back down from the CP with a bag of mail, followed by Taylor trying to maintain his hold on at least ten packages of various sizes. The twenty members of the platoon jockey into position like nested baby birds anticipating the exact landing point of their worm-bearing mother.

The Lieutenant starts reading the names from the variously sized and colored envelopes he pulls out of the bag; Bollman, Fisher, Fernandez, Ferlik, Ferlik, Charette... Everybody seems to have had their name called at least once and still, Six-Two keeps retrieving handfuls of envelops from the deeper reaches of the bag, repeating names already in receipt of some vital transfusion of spirit from home. Then, in what must surely be the last handful likely to be drawn from the now slack bag I hear it; Haslam, Haslam, Haslam, Haslam, Haslam, Price, Danko, Haslam, Haslam, Haslam, Charlebois, Haslam, Haslam. The rest of the platoon reacts with envious but supportive appreciation for the bounty of pink, purple and white clad messages that Six-Two tosses out to me.

I sort the ten unopened letters by return address, easily recognizing the senders, as Bob Taylor starts to read off the names on the packages. He doesn't bother to read the name on the first package. He just tosses it out to me as though everybody would be expecting the trend to continue. The rest however find their way into the grateful hands of others in the platoon.

With the Santa Clausing finally concluded, we all retreat to some private place to study and savor our connections with home and real life. I shuffle through my ten envelopes several times before commencing the opening ritual. The three pink envelopes and two purple ones are from Rosemary, each hand addressed in her characteristic left handed cursive. Three are in business sized white envelopes with the addressing carefully typed. These are from my dad. The last two are in plain white stationary envelopes, also hand addressed, but this time in my mom's

Stars and Stripes and Shadows

impeccable penmanship. I struggle for a moment trying to determine the optimum order in which to open and read the letters. The package, from my mom will be saved for later. Maybe I should order them by postmark date so that the senders would be in some more random order. No, Rosemary's letters will be last. I want to maintain the anticipation of what she has to tell me as long as possible. So, is it Mom or Dad first? As I continue to shuffle the white envelopes, I notice my dad's each have a number hand written down in the lower right hand corner; #1, #3 and #4. My curiosity about the missing #2 forces me to put Dad's messages first.

"Dear Tim," his perfectly typed #1 letter begins. The "Dear Tim" grabs at me more than the formal structure of the letter might warrant. My father was not one to share what was dear to him in anything but the most objective ways and yet, without reading any further to find additional context for the salutation, I believe him. I believe that the whole presentation of this message is his way of saying that I am dear to him. I know from writing numerous school reports on our old typewriter that it's impossible to get through a letter this long without typing errors, even for my dad, who is much superior to me on the keyboard. This letter is flawless; no typos, no erasures, and perfectly centered. It had to have taken several tries, several pieces of paper and a long time. He wanted it perfect. He wanted it perfect for me.

He starts with sad news. My grandmother, his mother, died on March 27th, his birthday. He matter-of-factly fills me in on the details of her passing, the funeral and logistical after effects. There's nothing about how it feels, what she meant to him or perhaps failed to mean to him. I think about what she meant to me. I remember how she always pinched my cheeks, gave me soggy kisses and often, in recent years confused my name with Barney, our German Shepard. I think about how her small apartment in Beverly Hills looked and smelled. I think about the hard life she had and some of the superficial characteristics and mechanisms she used to elevate her self-image and supposed stature within the well-to-do community she lived in. Dad's success and executive role at 20th Century Fox provided most of the substantiation for her credentials. Her shortcomings aside, I will miss her and am sorry there wasn't some chance for personal closure with her. I don't yet see her passing, along with Barney's while I was at Fort Polk, to be part of

Tim Haslam

the rearranging of my world back home as the world here increases its hold on me.

The rest of his letter fills me in on things at the studio and at home. He asks questions about where I am and what I'm doing. The #3 and #4 letters are similar, each adding new information. Letter #3 makes reference to information he must have sent me in the missing #2 about the proposed peace talks. I wonder if I will ever get it. I wonder how long it will take for the peace talks to end the shit.

Mom's letter does more of the same. She too, reiterates the facts around Grandmas death and the funeral. She fills me in on things in the neighborhood. They played bridge last Saturday night with the neighborhood group that they have played with once a month for as long as I can remember. All of the group is concerned for me and sends their best wishes. I try to think back to what I was doing on that Saturday evening when they were all playing bridge over scotches and sodas in one of the comfortable living rooms I knew so well. I can see all of their faces and miss them all. My mom concludes her letters, as did my dad, with the oxymoronic admonition to be careful while I'm in Vietnam.

I order Rosemary's pink and purple envelopes by postmark date to ensure the continuity of her stories. By the time she received the first letter from me, with my address, she had written all five of these letters. She fills me in on everything. She hasn't had much contact with any of my fraternity friends but has had news that two more of them are on their way over here. One I know to be in the Marines, and the other was in the Army's helicopter maintenance school the last I knew. I doubt that I will run into either of them here. She tells me that she and her dad have been doing more things together and her job at Judy's keeps her occupied during the day. She says she's a little bored on the weekends and that leads into how much she misses me, how concerned she is for me and how awful it is thinking about how long this year will be. Her letters ping back and forth from elation at having contact with me this way to sadness at being limited to contact this way. My feelings, as I read her letters, ping along, back and forth with the same rhythm and underlying agony.

I read all the letters over and over, finally placing them carefully up under the webbing of my helmet liner. I open the package from my mom and segregate the bounty of cookies, candy and canned goods

Stars and Stripes and Shadows

into two groups. The first group is stuff that I will share with the rest of the squad now in a short feeding frenzy. The second group, are the few things that I will selfishly keep, rationing them to myself over the next few days as some kind of daily reward. The mail experience has reconnected me to home and yet, looking around now at this place I feel farther away than ever.

✘ ✘ ✘ ✘

A steady rain invades down through the darkness, washing over the poncho that covers most of me as I sit here on the top layer of wet sandbags that cover our bunker. It's 3:30 a.m. I have the last guard shift and must endure this misery until dawn. The rain hides everything from my site. The rain blocks every other sound from reaching my ears. If Charlie's working this shift too, he can easily get to within a few feet of me before I could detect his sloshing in the mud near me. I would have only a second to redirect the slippery wet metal and plastic of my M16 toward him, hoping that the saturated internal mechanism reacts appropriately when I pull the trigger. I hope that Charlie isn't dedicated enough to any cause or opportunity to want to be out and about this night. I hope that Charlie is safe and dry in his tunnels somewhere out there.

Staying awake isn't the problem now. I'm too uncomfortable to sleep. Staying sane is more the challenge. I can't work my way to any kind of solution for what I'm up against here. I'm not sure I can do my job as required; it's too dark, too noisy, too wet and too shitty. I can't quit and I can't escape. There's nowhere to go, the breadth of the surrounding shit is too vast; I can only retreat again mentally. I can only try to bring up some mental imagery as a distraction. The letters in my helmet are the only things that can save me.

There is, of course, no way to read them again in this darkness, nor could I possibly remove them without having them instantly soaked into pulp. I must re-read them from memory.

It works; remembering each paragraph from each letter takes me away from the reality of this dark, wet, dangerous place and brings me to someplace else.

The air is in transition this evening, as it should be in Southern

Tim Haslam

California in mid March, somewhere in between the crisp coolness of the winter nights and the soft balmy summer evenings to come. It's getting later and later, nearly 1:30 a.m. Time is running out for us too quickly. I must go soon. I must go home and then, tomorrow go on to Vietnam. The front door of Rosemary's apartment must be opened soon, she will have to go in, closing that door between us, starting the separation that will span such a long distance and last so long. Vietnam will reveal itself to me on my side of the door. California life in 1968 will reveal itself to her on the other side. Yet, for one more moment we need not think of such things. She's been in my arms for at least an hour now and we've run out of things to say—out of ways to say goodbye. I can only continue to absorb the soft warmth of her body clinging tightly against mine. I can only savor the salty taste of the tears falling down her cheek as I kiss them away and savor too the fading scent of the remaining Shalimar essence on her neck. Everything we've shared over the last two years melds into this moment—every laugh, smile and touch; every argument, reconciliation and discovery; every playful, carefree moment alone and with friends merges now with the disheartening knowledge that in just another minute it will all be denied to us for the next year—denied perhaps forever. All I care about for this minute is how I feel about her and how she feels about me.

I must stay here. I must stay in this moment, this place, this feeling. I can't let time or responsibility or rain or shit or Charlie dislodge me from here. I can stay here until dawn.

Something's pulling me away from Rosemary's grasp. Something is compelling me to release my grip on her and this moment. Vietnam is jealous and insists on my full attention. The outlines of the trees surrounding FB30 are just starting to separate themselves from the dark background of this long night. Dawn is coming and I must transition back fully into this place where there is intense heat but little human warmth, where close contact enervates the heart for surviving not flourishing, where tears are not bittersweet, they're just bitter

N N N N

Bravo Company has been ordered to thoroughly scour the neighborhood surrounding FB30. This means that several patrols go out each

Stars and Stripes and Shadows

day, which also means my new role as RTO has me going on patrol about every other day. I now "hump" the radio for the other squads in the platoon and this affords me the opportunity to get to know the rest of the men in Six-Two. The platoon is comprised of a good mix of American culture and it's pretty easy for me to find some reason to like each man I meet. I'm probably the only representative of the comfortable upper middle class within this mix, but still seem to be accepted into the tribe, albeit at tenderfoot rank. As grunts here, the importance of our cultural facades are being continuously washed and eroded away revealing who and what we really are at the core of our being. This is what will bond us together or separate us within the tribe.

The northwestern approaches to the firebase drop off steeply, similar to those to the south and east, but then, instead of rising back up to the higher ridgelines and mountain peaks, they slope gently down toward the verdant valley of the Dak Poko River. The landscape on this side varies from dense jungle to open fields of tall grasses to forests of tall thin trees with little undergrowth. Each of these environments contains different risks and hazards for the uninvited visitors. The edges of the elephant grass blades are razor sharp and slice any exposed surfaces of arm, neck or face that brush by. The grassy areas are also spotted with bamboo thickets that are home to the bamboo viper. The *"two-stepper,"* as the grunts call this small green snake, has earned its reputation because of the potency of its venom—a victim will die within two steps of being bitten. This is probably an exaggeration, but we all believe it and react with terror at the sight of any of the many species of green snakes that slither into our jurisdiction. Scorpions, spiders and poisonous centipedes the size of lizards reside within the decaying duff under the tall thin trees who's trunks all seem to be protected by protruding thorns. The thick jungly places are, of course, an almost uninterrupted tangle of perils.

Charlie has found ways to ally with each of these realms against the grunts. Charlie has learned how to blend in here. Charlie knows that mines and other manmade destructive devices can easily be concealed here. But, Charlie doesn't need to rely on mechanisms manufactured in some Russian, Chinese or Romanian factory. Charlie can fashion deadly spikes out of bamboo and hide them within the grass, or line the

Tim Haslam

bottoms of camouflaged pits with them. He can make his own snags and snares and traps that are designed, not so much to kill us, but to wound us sufficiently that we must be cared for, that we must be sent home with permanent disabilities that will illustrate what happens to imperial invaders.

My next turn in the patrol rotation has me and my radio assigned to Sergeant Ferlik's squad, about to depart on a short exploration down into the western surrounds. Ferlik estimates that we'll be out on this one for about an hour. We just have to trek down one of the finger ridges sloping down from the firebase about a klick, cross northward over the gap between ridges and back up the next finger. It looks pretty easy on the map. Sergeant Ferlik describes the task to us in a way that makes it sound simple enough and so we all set off relieved that we have drawn one of the easy ones. This is a one-canteen hump.

Sergeant's Mike Ferlik and Grady Talbot lead the other two squads in Six-two with skills and abilities similar to Bob Taylor and Sergeant Stevens. All four men are however unique as individuals. "Grady" is the most serious, the most Spartan in his personal tendencies and the least congenial of the four squad leaders. Grady is an Oklahoman, of Plains-Indian ancestry and therefore seems to prize the warrior image. Grady's power is in his determination and steadfastness and his men respect his leadership. Taylor and Stevens are both highly competent, responsible and always play the military game as required, when required. Their human sides however, show through in ways that tend to enhance the respect they command from the grunts around them. Mike Ferlik is the least seasoned of this cadre but knows his business and like Bob and Steve has earned respect for who he really is as well as what he does. Over time I will find that Ferlik and I have a lot in common and we will frequently divert and amuse each other with our similar senses of humor. For now, I'm the new RTO and will stick close to each of these men on patrols and do what I'm told – congenially or not.

Sergeant Ferlik, four members of his squad, Doc Davis the medic and I route step our way easily down the finger like the Seven Dwarfs skipping off to work. We break out of the heavier vegetation that surrounds the FB within a few hundred meters and have an easy time getting the rest of the way down to the bottom of the finger; so easy, in fact that we reached this milestone without stopping, without checking any map and without ever confirming our position.

The ridge finger unfolds into a swampy basin that is difficult to navigate through. The patches of standing water, heavy growth thickets and small hillocks that fill up this area require us to meander around the obstacles, all the while trying to stay generally aligned to our target position estimated to be another two hundred meters out. It's hot and humid down here and our struggle through this territory takes long enough to change our opinions about how easy this patrol will be. Sergeant Ferlik stops us a few times as we weave our way through this, checking his map and compass and scanning the landscape for any terrain feature that would confirm our position. Each scan results in a look of deepening concern on his face. We all start to wish we had brought more water.

At the western edge of the basin there is a slight rise up into a more overgrown section. The machetes come out slowing the pace even more. Our one-hour has long passed, as have any remaining optimistic attitudes. We try to follow the clearer areas that open up in the general direction we should be going, requiring us again to move circuitously instead of vectoring directly as Ferlik's compass requires. It's impossible to see anything to our northeast that would lead us up to the ridgeline we seek for our return trip. The way we're maneuvering around in this stuff also makes it nearly impossible to gage how far we're actually progressing in any direction. Sergeant Ferlik continues to direct the point man with short arm thrusts pointing variably this way and that. The determination of his thrusts seems to be diminishing and everyone's confidence is beginning to ebb.

The patrol struggles on this way in a generally northward direction for about another hundred meters when we come to a small clearing that seems to funnel off eastward into something appearing almost trail-like. There is no evidence of bordering vegetation being cut or footprints or anything else that would firmly establish this as a trail. Mike Ferlik carefully checks his map, which has known trails marked on it. There are no trails on the map anywhere around here. There should not be a trail here. Although unsure of our exact position, his

Tim Haslam

compass suggests that the clearing seems to be headed upwards toward where FB30 must be.

Normally, we avoid trails. They're too obvious a place for Charlie to set traps for us or to ambush us. But, under the circumstances this seems to be the best way to get us back on track. If this isn't a man-made trail, it's an amazing facsimile and the going is pretty easy as we follow the nearly straight path that progresses gently upwards through the triple canopy jungle. The patrol is moving pretty quickly now and everyone is feeling more confident. Sergeant Ferlik continues to scan the surrounding terrain looking for something that will match the abstract contour lines on his map. It all feels right, but nothing within our view can confirm it.

Any concerns I may have had for our situation are interrupted by a pained outburst from Gino Lombardi, the guy behind me. He's fallen to his knees as I turn in reaction to his distress.

"*Shit, shit, shit!*" he keeps screaming as he rips the bandoliers off his shoulders and reaches frantically at the back of his neck.

"*Motherfuckers, shit,*" he exhorts as he tears his shirt off, flinging it to the ground in front of him. The next guy behind him hurries in and starts slapping at his bare back turning him around so that I can now see what's happened.

Dozens of red fire ants were brushed down from their nest in the foliage at the side of the trail as Gino passed by. Their landing zone happened to be the back of his neck and their stinging response affirms their dissatisfaction with the disruption in their afternoon's activities.

The fight is a brief but fierce struggle and Gino seems to be in a lot of distress. Doc Davis is summoned and quickly takes charge. He does all the right first-aid kinds of things to determine the actual level of damage and condition of the patient; then, after certifying the grunt as damaged, but OK, he applies the appropriate remedies; Merthiolate for the bites and an offering of Darvon for the pain.

The skirmish with the ants has given Sergeant Ferlik an opportunity to sit down and really study his map and he comes to the conclusion that he can't confirm our position...we're lost!

"Get Six-Two on the horn," he directs me. "I need to fill him in."

Stars and Stripes and Shadows

The filling-in takes only a minute as Ferlik tries to describe our route and confesses that the last time he had a true confirmation of our location was when we were still at the firebase. He takes the subsequent reprimands for his carelessness pretty much in stride trying to turn the conversation into a game plan for finding us and getting us back home. Lieutenant Falck is not one to be overly dramatic or authoritarian in such situations and so, he too gets right to the issue at hand.

"Roger," Ferlik keeps repeating as a response to whatever Six-Two is saying.

"Roger. Out," he concludes and hands me the handset.

"Listen up." He instructs everyone. "One of the 105's is going to fire off a round in a minute. I want everyone to listen for it, so we can figure out the direction back."

He looks specifically at me and says that someone from the artillery battery will call me just before they shoot.

"Six-Two-Three, this is Trigger-Five. Over," says an unfamiliar voice through my handset.

"Trigger-Five, this is Six-Two-Three. Over," I reply immediately waving to the squad to pay attention.

"Six-Two-Three, this is Trigger-Five. I'm going to count down from ten and then listen for the shot. Over," he instructs, pausing for only a few seconds before starting the countdown.

I manage to get everyone's attention and use my fingers to show the final countdown from five.

"...three, two, one, fire. Shot. Over!" The battery RTO announces.

None of us hear anything.

"Trigger-Five, this is Six-Two-Three. We didn't hear a thing. Over," I tell him, looking at Ferlik for some direction on the next step.

"Shit," is all I get back from Mike. Then, after another moment, "Get Six-Two back on the horn."

Sergeant Ferlik seems to have a plan as Six-Two comes on. He's sitting on his upturned helmet with his map spread out in front of him on the ground as he engages Lieutenant Falck.

"Go to nine-six-nine-two-eight-five, sir. Do you see that short, flat

Tim Haslam

knoll coming off the ridge line there?" he respectfully directs Lieutenant Falck. "How about putting a mortar round on that knoll? If the knoll is coming off the ridge we're on now it's on the reverse sloop and we should be out of danger, but within range to hear it. If it comes off the finger to our north, there's enough separation between the ridges to keep us out of danger but close enough to hear a round go off. Whadda ya think?"

Lieutenant Falck seems to be in general agreement with the plan, but wants to clear it with Captain Collins and Lieutenant Reese, our artillery spotter. Nobody likes the idea of sending a live mortar round in our general direction. The experienced men in the squad have many times been sent out on patrols that marked artillery and mortar targets. They know that the usual method is to call back the target coordinates and adjust the firing until the rounds actually hit on the requested grid position. The six-digit grid coordinates used with the resolution of these maps narrows target areas down to about an acre, so sometimes the initial rounds are hundreds of meters off the mark.

Several minutes pass before a voice—that of Lieutenant Reese—breaks the squelch of my handset. Reese's reputation as an A-number-one-asshole has already been brought to my attention and so his surly request for Ferlik comes as no surprise.

With the radio handset tucked between his ear and shoulder, Sergeant Ferlik starts marking points on his map with a ballpoint pen, all the while "rogering," back to Reese without additional commentary.

"OK, roger. Out," Ferlik says, letting the handset spring back to me.

The plan is to put a mortar round on the spot that Ferlik suggested and then, if we still can't hear that, to put additional rounds out from that point at one-hundred meter intervals, alternating north and south until we can hear them. The theory is that we will still be able to hear the approaching rounds from a safe distance.

Again, the first round is fired and given ample time to land and explode without us hearing anything. The second round too is lofted off a hundred meters further to the south without a sound reaching us. Finally, there is a dull sound some distance to the southeast of us at about the time the third round should have struck the ground. Hearing this, Ferlik grabs the handset and calls back acknowledging the hit.

Stars and Stripes and Shadows

He suggests that they fire one more round, adjusting the target one hundred meters to the north. He tells us all to cover up with this one knowingly coming closer.

This time the *kachunk* of the exploding round is unmistakable and we can all estimate it to be about two hundred meters to our southeast. Ferlik makes one more mark on his map and calls back up asking for Six-Two.

"Roger that sir. That puts us just over the next ridge to the north and about fifty meters west," he says, relieved to know where we are.

"Hell if I know sir," he says next, obviously answering Six-Two's inquiry into how we got so far off track.

"I don't get it," he says to me eyeing the map looking for some clue that could explain what went wrong. "We had to have strayed off northward almost from the beginning, and then followed the wrong ridgeline down." Pointing to a ridge that moves down from the firebase, but in a much more northwestward direction than the one we should have been on. "Then, we must have started up this next ridge, taking us still further north. Shit!"

Ferlik carefully plots the course up the ridge we're on that will lead us back into the north side of the firebase. It's been nearly four hours since we started out on this "little" patrol and only the most frugal of us has any water left. Sergeant Ferlik estimates that we have at least an hour of uphill climbing to do to get back if we push ourselves. No one really blames Mike Ferlik for our situation as we all know how challenging and deceiving this terrain can be. Still, no one is too happy as we drag ourselves back up into the higher realms.

We've only been on the move a few minutes when my call sign comes over the radio.

"Six-Two-Three, this is Six-Two-Alpha. Over," says the now familiar voice of Platoon Sergeant Bollman.

I quickly answer back and am informed that Six-Two is sending Sergeant Stevens and his squad down to intercept us and guide us back in.

"Goddamn it! What kind of off-the-wall-shit is that?" says Ferlik when I pass the message on. He knows that the Lieutenant has either lost faith in his abilities to bring the squad in safely, or is just fucking with him. The latter being the most likely possibility and probably

Tim Haslam

instigated by the other platoon NCOs just to have something to needle Ferlik with forever.

We meet up with Steve and company in about half an hour and the taunting begins, not to end until we're back at the firebase and everyone in Bravo Company has had an opportunity to pile on their critiques of our afternoons journey. All of the commentary comes from people who know it can happen to them and, for many of them, it has.

The rest of our time at Firebase 30 is sameness; a few patrols, a few duties usually involving shovels and sandbags, tedious hours of guard duty each night. Rain, mud and boredom will be the lingering after images from our time here. We've been fortunate here to have two hot meals provided to us each day courtesy of the 6th of the 29th artillery. Artillery batteries generally have mess units attached to them with sufficient supplies to feed the infantry units that protect their guns—a fair trade. This will be the only aspect of FB30 that any of us are likely to miss.

Hueys seem to come in at least a few times each day, dropping off mail, fresh water and any other supplies that we may need; everything except underwear. We've been re-supplied with clean fatigues, socks and tee shirts but still no underwear. My jockeys and I are now approaching the one-month anniversary of our intimate relationship

Chapter 5

Who Would Fardels Bare?

Eight more pounds, I think to myself as Ed hands me two extra batteries for my radio.

I don't know where I'm going to put them?

We're moving out this morning for an extended trip into the boonies. We're going "humpin." Everything we have comes with us. The inner compartments and pouches of my ruck are stuffed with C-rations, personal gear, field bandages, ponchos and liners, cigarettes and everything else I've deemed necessary for my comfort. The gear that 's necessary for my survival; ammo, grenades, flares, mines, entrenching tool, machete and water (all six canteens), either gets clipped to the outside of the ruck somehow, strapped to my body in some way or draped over me. We have also just been issued gas masks without clarification of the necessity. *Has Charlie been using poison gas on us somewhere, or are we now using gas on them?*

My radio is strapped to the back of the metal rucksack frame so that it rests between my back and the ruck. At Ed's suggestion I've obtained another poncho to use as padding between my back and the hard corners and edges of the radio. My ruck's ready, as is all the rest of the panoply that I must attach to myself; *everything except the two batteries*.

Ed, sensing my dilemma comes to the rescue with another lesson in tribal knowledge.

"The plastic bags," Ed exclaims, pausing a moment for the lights to come on for me.

"What about them?" I respond, trying to dislodge the rest of the solution from Ed.

"The bags are valuable," Ed explains, referring to the clear plastic bags that the fresh batteries are sealed in.

"Everyone in the platoon wants them. They can use them to protect their personal gear from the moisture. You control the supply, so you make deals. They hump the batteries, they get the bags."

I test Ed's economic theory on Mike Beasley and Mike Danko and, sure enough, both jump at the opportunity to earn a plastic bag.

"Saddle up," shouts Bob Taylor, over the thumping vibration of the first Huey approaching the LZ.

Captain Collins, Lieutenant Reese and their RTO's will get on the first bird, but will stay airborne until the whole company has been dropped off at our destination up country. Six-Two is to be the first platoon on the ground and four Hueys will be required to get the whole platoon in. Our squad, drawing the short stick, wins the opportunity to be on the first one. This means that the six of us will be put on the ground somewhere out in the boonies, tasked with securing the area for the arrival of the rest of the Company.

Charlie would love to catch a point squad like this coming into their neighborhood. If they know we're coming, they can take all of us and our helicopter out with a single rocket or rocket propelled grenade or cut us to pieces with machinegun and small arms fire from the protection of the forest surrounding our landing zone. But, the forest is large and remote, how could they know? The forest is also a forest, with trees and plants that block access to the ground for helicopters filled with invaders. The usual way for us to overcome this problem is to dispatch a flight of B52s the night before. Their bombs easily clear space for helicopters and grunts. If Charlie's figured out this routine, they know where we'll be this morning.

There is a palpable adrenaline rush pumping through the whole company as we work cooperatively to get attached to all our gear. The weight of the ruck and all the things hanging from it make it extremely difficult to put on while standing up, so, we work together in an effort to gang up on the individual burdens. One man sits down with his ruck at his back, squeezes into the shoulder straps and then is assisted to his feet by someone else. The process is repeated until everyone's on their feet.

Stars and Stripes and Shadows

Having thusly, "saddled-up" I reach for Price's outstretched hand and together we pull until I'm standing. I'm immediately stunned at the weight pulling down on me. Even bolstered by the adrenaline boost of the situation, it's all I can do to steady my legs beneath this awkward load. My first reaction is fear, bordering on panic. How can I possibly move through these jungles, up and down these mountains and over and around the snags and snarls I know await us with this much weight on my back.

I can't do this, I think to myself, as I look around at my squad mates all having the same thought.

They however know from experience that they *will* do it. They also know what it will take to get it done and what doing it will do to them.

These people, this morning, wear a new mask I have never in my life seen before.

The "shit" is getting shittier.

It's an ordeal just to get from our bunker down to the LZ. The footing down the slippery, mud path is tricky enough without carrying any kind of load. With all this gear, I have to really strain to maintain balance and forward momentum. Everyone is having the same kind of experience. The veterans are clearer on what's in store though; I can only imagine what is foreshadowed by the experience of these first few steps. There is no sense of adventure now, only doubt that I will be able to pull my weight and dread at the effort it will take to try.

Taylor has ordered all of us to clear any rounds from the firing chambers of our weapons. He doesn't want any weapon discharging accidentally into a helicopter or grunt if someone stumbles or falls trying to get to and into the Huey. We all know the additional dangers associated with the exposed portions of our ammunition and frags that could snag on parts of the helicopter or one another's gear as we attempt to wrestle ourselves on board. There are far too many details to worry about in the last seconds before the downward churning Huey completes it's landing in front of us; we've run out of time for preparation and caution.

The door gunners at the sides of the Huey seem even more nervous then we are as they urge us to increase our pace toward their flying

Tim Haslam

machine. My attempt to comply and increase my gate nearly topples me over just as I reach the skid on the starboard side.

Somehow, we have, with some assistance from the anxious gunners, managed to get everyone and everything on board quickly and without complication. The bird is airborne an instant later and there is a brief moment of relief for the squad and the Huey crew. The pilot and crew-chief up front are the only one's with responsibilities to fulfill for the next several minutes, guiding the UH1-D helicopter around in expanding circles until all the other choppers have collected up the remainder of Bravo Company. The armada then queues up behind us, arraying for our airborne assault into Charlie's backyard somewhere to the northwest.

Having confirmed the readiness of the airborne force, the pilot points the Huey towards our destination and accelerates to full throttle, all the while making the necessary adjustments to trim, roll and yaw necessary to keep this vibrating hulk in the air. The orientation of the helicopter is nosed down, but moving forward in level flight. It can't take long for us to get to our destination at this rate of speed.

This time, my back is up against the forward bulkhead of the chopper, and so my view is to the rear. Once again, I look to the faces of the others in the squad for some guidance on what to do or say or think or feel. What I see validates everything that I do think and feel...it was better to be bored back at Firebase 30!

My scan gets to Sergeant Taylor, sitting opposite me, straining to look forward, just as he swallows deeply and yells out to us to, "lock and load!"

The charging handles on all the M16s and Elmer's machinegun are pulled back and released almost in unison. Our postures stiffen up, taking a strain back on the straps of our rucks and all the gear that must exit the Huey with us in just a few seconds. The collective anxiety percolating up within the squad must be brought under control to avoid a chaotic scramble to get out of the machine when it touches down. The pilot must quickly adjust for any weight shifts within the helicopter and anticipate acute changes such as a grunt's weight suddenly stepping onto the skid while still hovering. Such an external load could easily lever the Huey over far enough for the 44-foot rotor to strike the ground, resulting in disaster.

Stars and Stripes and Shadows

Sergeant Taylor is aware of the dangers and starts choreographing the exit. He points to Mike Danko sitting to his right, nearest the starboard door and holds up one finger. Danko acknowledges with a head nod. Looking then to me, he holds up two fingers. I know what he means and acknowledge in similar fashion. He works quickly through the rest of the squad assigning numbers until the order is complete.

"If we have to get out before the chopper can set all the way down," he screams, "I want everyone out this side," he says, pointing to the opening on my side. He wants to avoid any rocking reaction that the helicopter would go through if we tried to jump out alternately from each side.

With another hand motion he directs me to slide closer to the opening so that I'm clear of the door gunner who sits to my left.

Complying with Taylor's directive I can now see forward as the freshly cratered landscape races towards us. I can also see that there's a separation of only about twenty meters between our rotor blades and the tree line off to our right.

Suddenly, my view of the trees to our right is obstructed by something flying by, just beyond the rotor tips of our Huey.

It's a Cobra gunship racing to get ahead of us.

As it passes, I can see and hear the gattling gun under the nose unleashing a spray of bullets out into the cratered area just ahead. Hundreds of brass bullet casings are streaming out the sides of the gun and the foliage around the clearing ahead is being shredded by the fusillade of lead. A fraction of a second later I can see rockets pulling out from the pods under the little wing-like protuberances on each side of the Cobras narrow fuselage. The twisting contrails of the rockets lead up into the forested area just beyond the clearing, ending in light flashes and billowy clouds that slowly waft back toward the craters.

Just a few meters before meeting the trees, the Cobra noses nearly straight up, banks slightly to the right and disappears over the trees, now just a few meters away.

The Huey slows dramatically as it enters the cratered clearing. The door gunner next to me opens up with his M60, so close, that I instinctively reach up to try to protect my ears from the defining bursts. He's sweeping the barrel of the machinegun back and forth in small arcs, but I can't see what he's firing at. The foliage at the edge of the clearing is

Tim Haslam

being pulverized by his strafing and with so much stuff flying around I can't really tell if any of it is associated with fire being returned at us.

The helicopter is now hovering unsteadily about six feet above the lip of one of the bomb craters and the pilot is frantically trying to maintain trim on his Huey, knowing that he has to deliver us safely to the ground; knowing too that he's a sitting duck here. There's no way he can get any closer than this and so, his crew-chief leans back towards us gesturing with up and down finger points screaming for us to jump.

"Jump...now!" The panicked door gunner starts to scream too, all the while continuing his fire into the surrounding jungle.

Danko is at the edge of the opening trying to rehearse the movements required to get out of this moving platform as requested.

"Jump, goddamn it, jump," the gunner screams, trying to be heard over the blasts coming from his own firing.

I watch Danko step gingerly out toward the skid rocking up and down in front of him.

Nothing else about Danko's jump or my exit registers with me until I realize that I'm falling toward the ground sloping into the crater, just inside the lip. My feet dig into the loose dirt as I land. A fraction of a second later the full weight of my ruck and gear reaches shoulder level, gaining downward momentum, and jerks me over backwards. Pulled now by my ruck, I tumble down to the bottom of the crater, ending up in a jumble of gear and forest debris. I don't seem to be hurt in any way, but am concerned by all the firing that's still going on above me.

Danko has landed with the same results and is scrambling to untangle himself. The others, behind us, are jumping with greater success and are able to establish positions within the protection of the crater's raised up berm. As they stabilize themselves they too start firing into the surrounding vegetation.

It's actually only been about thirty seconds or so since the Cobra unleashed its rockets into the trees just beyond the clearing and this crater. The smoke I saw billowing up from the rocket strikes is just now reaching us. *Only it's not smoke...it's tear gas.*

The struggle to get myself upright and recover my gear is made more compelling by the burning in my eyes and throat and the continuing heavy machinegun fire coming from the Huey hovering just a few feet above me as the last man jumps out.

Stars and Stripes and Shadows

If this Huey does get hit, it comes down right on top of me, I think to myself.

If there really is someone firing back at the rest of the squad, I need to get up there and add my efforts to their suppressing fire, I think to myself.

I have the radio and need to get in touch with Six-Two and Captain Collins to fill them in on what the situation is here, I think to myself.

What the fuck is the situation here? I think to myself.

All this thinking is going on in parallel with my body's efforts to get back upright; to get my gear together and to claw my way back up the side of the bomb crater and face whatever it is that's stimulated such a response from all these trigger fingers.

"Cease fire," Sergeant Taylor yells out, just as I get to the top of the crater. "Cease fire, cease fire," he repeats as Elmer runs out the rounds remaining on the belt being churned through his M60.

I don't get to use my weapon! I'm too late to use my weapon!

I've spent my first moments in real combat trying to recover myself from the bottom of this goddamned crater.

My heart is still pounding, my eyes are watering, my throat is dry and burning and my nose is running profusely from the chlorine gas.

I've finally got myself into position to be a participant and everything's over.

"Get Six-Two on the horn and tell him to bring in Ferlik's squad," Taylor says to me, calmly but somewhat out of breath. "It looks like we're clear down here and with Ferlik's guys we can secure the LZ."

"OK," is all I can say in reply as I wipe some of the various fluids coming from all over my face onto my shirt sleeve.

There's too much to do right now for me to ask what everybody was firing at.

� ✺ ✺ ✺

Captain Collins and the other officers are anxious to get the company organized and away from the LZ. There are about eighty of us out with the Company on this hump and a group this size doesn't move quickly or quietly through this environment. If Charlie doesn't know where we are right now, it won't be long before he does. Although, the body-count objective doesn't necessitate us finding him first, our own bodies would prefer encounters on our terms.

103

Tim Haslam

Except for the officers and NCOs, no one knows for sure how far we have to go today or where we're going. Rumor has it that we must go about two klicks—two kilometers— two thousand meters.

Two thousand meters doesn't seem that far to anyone who thinks in terms of straight lines and flat, clear land. Two thousand meters doesn't seem that far to anyone who thinks in terms of hiking shoes and trails maintained by the Department of Parks and Recreation or the Forest Service. Two thousand meters without a rucksack and eighty pounds of gear can be thought of in terms of a pleasant afternoon outing. But, no such terms are available to the Bravo Company grunts about to head out into the jungles of the Central Highlands with the objective of killing people before those people can fulfill their objective of killing us.

The water-courses draining down from the highest peaks have formed the landscape of this part of the Central Highlands. The smallest capillaries wash down from firmer ground at the highest points until finger ridges are formed, radiating out in all directions from the ancient smoothed down pinnacles. The capillaries come together into larger streams between the fingers, deepening and widening the separations. The streams come together to form canyons and valleys that will eventually flow down into the wide valley of the Dak Poko. All of this is cloaked in the thick green vegetation of the forest, hiding the contours, concealing rise from fall. This is the topology that we play hide-and-seek with Charlie in, alternating in the role of predator and prey.

For most of what we do and where we go here, the finger ridges become the reference points. We go up them and down them; we go across them and the separating valleys, canyons and gullies. There is almost always land, vegetation and animal life forms above us and below us from wherever we are on the ridges. Most of the ridges are well within rifle range of the adjacent ridges. It's easy for a motivated person with a rifle to hide within the flora along any ridge crest, fire one or two shots at a target on an adjacent ridge and then retire safely down the opposite slope of their ridge. Sometimes we're the targets; sometimes Charlie's the target; we're all motivated. When there are eighty of us trying to go somewhere at one time, we get to be the targets.

The Company tries to move in such a way as to minimize the number of men exposed to rifle fire. There is a point platoon that leads,

104

Stars and Stripes and Shadows

followed by the Company Headquarters people, followed by the drag platoon. All these men, maybe forty or so are stretched out in one long file, trying to maintain separation of about two or three meters. On each side of this file are the flank platoons; twenty or so men on each side of the main file at a distance of thirty to fifty meters away, give or take, depending on the terrain, trying to keep pace with and abreast of the point platoon. The men in the flank platoons shield the sides of the main body of the company. The Company, thus deployed, tries to follow the route of the point squad; six to eight men who set off twenty to thirty minutes ahead of the main body in an effort to expose any traps, mines, ambushes or snipers that might threaten the main body. Everyone on point squad knows that their role is sacrificial. Success for them doesn't require survival.

Six-One platoon is on point today and their point squad was sent off as quickly as possible after the LZ was secured, having had barely enough time to confirm the route and destination on their map. Because of the rush to get the Company away from the vulnerable LZ, the point squad started off less than ten minutes ahead of the main body. For Six-Two platoon, our assignment this afternoon is the right flank. We'll have to cut our way through the jungle trying to keep aligned with the center file at a close enough distance to ensure that Charlie can't get between us, but far enough off to provide a sufficient warning for any attacks coming from the right as well as a barrier against any inbound projectiles launched from this side.

The going is frustratingly slow. When the front end of any file slows or stops the men behind come to a complete stop and wait for the proper separation to be re-established. The farther back in the file one is, the longer the wait and the shorter the intervening periods of movement are. When the front of the file speeds up, the trailing mass tends to speed up too much, closing on the man in front too quickly; again, they slow or stop to adjust, affecting everyone behind in a similar fashion.

Many factors determine the pace of the point units; the gradient, up or down, the density of the jungle to be hacked away and the clarity of the route ahead and its perceived dangers. For the men behind, there is an added element that increases in influence in direct proportion to their relative position in the file—the ooze factor. Each man's footsteps compress the moist ground a little, squeezing the water out, separating it

Tim Haslam

from the soil somewhat. Our boots tend to collect and carry away much of the solid bi-products of this process. The following man's path is thus a little bit muddier, a little bit more slippery. This time of year with the early monsoons contributing moisture, the ooze factor builds quickly. Eight or ten men following the same narrow path is sufficient to render the footing treacherous for everyone trailing, particularly when the path is up or down and here, the path is always up or down. From this point on back in the file, one has to plan each footstep, carefully plotting a landing spot and foot orientation to reduce the possibility of slipping. The effort required to control Mr. Ruck and his contents requires a good deal of our attention as does the ever present realization that we should be looking out for Charlie and so sometimes we pay too little attention to a particular footstep and end up on our ass. Sometimes, if the path is steep enough the grunt in front or behind us ends up on his ass too as a result of our failure to beat the ooze. Under these conditions, every grunt in Bravo Company will spend some time on his ass each day of the hump. We will make feeble attempts to overcome the ooze factor. Our M16's sometimes cease to be weapons and become walking sticks used to pole us up and over some of the short, slippery rises in the path. The jungle foliage adjacent to the path frequently seems to reach out, offering some limb or vine or branch that, if grasped would pull us up and out of the ooze. So tempting is this offering that we overlook the thorns and razor sharp edges of the leaves until they slice and sting us back into reality.

Time has little meaning for us. Time is not measured for us by the changing position of hands on a watch, but by the steady build up of pain we all experience. Mr. Ruck contributes, the thorns and blades contribute, the slips and slides and falls contribute, the salty sweat finding its way into the little open wounds contributes and the mosquitoes contribute. The contributions build hour-by-hour, step-by miserable-step.

Distance is what matters to us. We have to go two klicks. When we've gone two klicks, we can cast off Mr. Ruck. We can do a better job of protecting ourselves from the thorns, blades, slips, slides and falls. We can even fight back at the sweat and mosquitoes. We can concentrate more fully on killing Charlie and not being killed by him. Each one of us spends some portion of these monotonous hours trying

Stars and Stripes and Shadows

to calculate how many steps it takes to go two klicks. When we divide these estimations by the time it's taking us to go a few steps, the result is disheartening, there's much pain yet to be endured.

Rays of the late afternoon sun pierce through the few openings in the low clouds and wash sections of the otherwise shadowed ridgeline the Company is slowly climbing in crisp clear light. The ridge is too narrow for all three flanks and so our platoon, on the right flank, has to scramble along the right hand slope of the ridge trying to keep up as we deal with the lesser ridges that branch down from the main finger. The separation between the ridgeline the Company is on and the adjacent finger to the west is only about fifty meters and so our platoon is sometimes on it and sometimes down in the depression between the two fingers. Neither ridge rises up too steeply, but the climb is steady and the summit seems to be nowhere in sight.

The work for our platoon has the same stop and go character to it as that of the main file, but, because we must maneuver over and around different terrain features, we must cover more actual ground. It's been two and half hours since we left the LZ and everyone has reached the point where we're just plodding along, physically exhausted and even more weary mentally. The going now is a test of will, character and determination. *I don't know how much longer I can keep at this.*

Six-Two has halted the platoon at a point where he has some visibility and is studying the ridge running gradually upwards on our left. We can just make out some of our guys in the main file as they pass through some of the sunlit openings along the crest. We're falling too far behind. Our point is now adjacent to about the mid-point of the main file. We need to kick it into high gear to get back up where we should be.

None of us need Six-Two to clarify the situation as we stand there, stooped over under the burdens of our rucks, propped up by our weapons, gasping to pull oxygen out of the heavy, humid air. None of us is under any misconception that our ordeal is almost over, that we are almost there.

As I look to Six-Two to confirm what I already know, a shock blasts through the air, causing me, and everyone around me to reflexively hit the ground.

Tim Haslam

It's a loud, crisp, precise crack, followed a fraction of a second later by another crack, then another.

I know exactly what it is. I know, because I've never heard it before. In my training, I've heard the M16 hundreds of times. I've heard all the weapons that we carry and use. I know by process of elimination that this is the distinctive crack of an AK47. It's Charlie's weapon of choice. It's Charlie!

The shots came from up on the ridge to our right, maybe forty meters from us. None of us in the platoon saw the muzzle flashes or any smoke and there were no apparent bullets coming our way. But, we're all concerned about what comes next; what might be coming our way?

"Six-Charlie, this is Six-One-Charlie. Over," the voice coming through my handset declares with urgency. "We've got two men down and need more medics up here."

"Roger that, Six-One, they're on the way give me your situation. Over." The voice responding is that of Captain Collins who must have taken up the radio handset the moment the echoes from the enemy rifle shots faded off.

"Six-Two-Charlie, this is Six. Over," the Captain continues, his voice transitioning from concern to control.

"Six-Two. Over," Lieutenant Falck responds within a second, circumventing his RTO, Wee John from the dialogue stream.

"Six-Two, get some men up on that ridge crest pronto and neutralize those fucking gooks. Over."

"Roger," Falck replies into the handset while almost simultaneously instructing Sergeant Stevens, whose squad is on point and nearest to the area where the shots came from, to get up there. Steve responds with a hand wave to his squad and they, along with Ed Arter who has the nearest radio, start the treacherous climb up the side of the ridge towards the general proximity of the shots.

"Wait one," shouts Lieutenant Falck, realizing that Steve and his men are about to head directly into an open field of fire, fully exposed to the weapons up on the crest, without even being sure where the shots came from.

"Six-One, this is Six-Two. Can you put some fire on where you think those shots came from? Over," Lieutenant Falck says into the

Stars and Stripes and Shadows

radio from a semi-crouching position, all the while holding his hand up as a signal to Sergeant Stevens to continue waiting.

Without any reply over the radio, two M16s and an M60 machinegun open up from the ridge crest above us to our left. Every fifth round from the machinegun is a tracer, making it easy to follow the bullets streaming across our front, up into a clump of tall trees on the ridge top to our right, violently shredding off bark and scattering the foliage of the surrounding plants. Sergeant Stevens and his squad can see exactly where the rounds are going. Lieutenant Falck can see exactly where the rounds are going. We can all see exactly where the rounds are going. We can all see where Charlie was when he shot us. Sergeant Stevens, Bennis, Ernie Jefferson and the rest of the men of Steve's squad that I have just started to get know start moving as quickly as their burdens will allow up toward Charlie's blind, hoping that Charlie's running as fast as he can down the opposite slope and away from us. The rest of us remain pressed down into the meager protection of the plants around us hoping that this isn't just a set up. Hoping that five hundred more gooks aren't about to come charging over the ridge toward us. Our widened eyes are all on Steve's men, while our minds wonder about whom the two men reported as "down" are. Later, we will wonder why it was those two men when every one of us could just as easily have been aligned with the sights of the AKs and the eyes of the NVA soldiers squeezing the triggers.

There's much activity going on within my sensory perception. Sergeant Steven's men are nearing the ridge crest up to my right. Doc Charlebois is struggling up the slope to my left as fast as he can to offer help tending to the wounded men. Six-Two is gesturing for the other squad leaders to reposition forward to better support Steve and his men and the radio is a steady stream of communications, orders and status updates. Six-One advises everyone that we'll need a medevac helicopter, a "dust-off," for the two men shot, as quickly as possible. Five-Nine replies with orders to start cutting a clearing on a generally flat spot that his forward squad is on. Six-Zero offers to send some of his men with machetes and axes to help in the assault on the various jungle obstacles protruding upwards, forming barriers between the summoned dust-off bird and the ground where the wounded men are to be rescued from. Everyone seems to know what to do; everyone but me has done this

Tim Haslam

before.

"Six-Two-Charlie, this is Six-Two-Alpha-Charlie. Over," Ed's voice breaks into the radio chatter. "There's no sign of anything up here... nothing. Over."

"Roger Alpha-Charlie, this is Six-Two. Hold your position. Over."

"Six-Charlie, this is Six-Two. Put Six on the horn. Over."

"This is Six. Go."

"There's no sign of anything up there. What do you want us to do? Over."

"Get the rest of your platoon up on that crest and move upwards until you're back even with Six-One's point. Then stay put until we get these wounded out of here. Over." Captain Collins follows up those instructions with similar orders to deploy the whole company into a defensive perimeter around the LZ that's now being barbered out of the jungle by the men with the machetes and axes.

Every grunt in Bravo Company has earned the right to complain about everything that happens to them out here. The ever increasing misery endured over the last few hours has sufficiently weakened our bodies and our wills to the point where our primitive nature nearly refuses to accept any further opportunities for stress or strain or work or risk. That is every opportunity except the work required to help the wounded men. Without ever thinking about it, without the slightest hesitation or resistance, and readily overcoming our physical weariness, everyone rallies to the work required to save the injured men. Everyone's complete focus is on securing a landing zone for the dust-off helicopter.

It's been just under thirty minutes since Charlie's three bullets penetrated our space and our people. The dust-off Huey with the two damaged men safely aboard is rising quickly up from the LZ, the on-board medics now tending to the wounded grunts.

Captain Collins re-focuses the Company on the work yet to do. The three files are re-formed and forward motion begins again. The pace is just a little bit quicker as we start moving back up the ridges, we know we've lost time and have ground to make up. We know too that Charlie knows where we are and that we're vulnerable.

110

Stars and Stripes and Shadows

The Captain, after much map studying, has ordered our platoon to stay up on the ridge crest where the shots came from. That ridge parallels the one the Company is on for several hundred meters and he doesn't want any more sniping coming from the high ground to his right. Sniping from the ground to our right; my right, is apparently OK.

The next hour passes more quickly as the concern over Charlie and his bullets diverts much of our attention from our other woes. Our eyes and ears scan and probe the plants and trees, the rocks and ridges and the shadowy shapes of the jungle. Charlie will not get away from his next shot so easily.

Six-Charlie finally calls over to us on the radio and says that the main body has reached our objective for the night and that we should move off our ridge and re-join them. With the end just a hundred meters off, the Platoon energetically traverses the little intervening valley and climbs up the opposite slope bringing us into the Company's position where the rest of the men of Bravo Company are already at work making camp.

We trudge the last few yards to our assigned position, again on the right of the perimeter. All of the men of Six-Two Platoon acquaint themselves with our new home in nearly similar fashion. I lean up against the trunk of a large tree and just sort of slide down until I'm sitting on the ground and then wrestle myself free from the clutches of Mr. Ruck. I'm exhausted and don't want to move, but I can see that there's still work to be done. We have to clear the vegetation away from where our hooches are to be set up as well as fields of fire out and away from our position. We must dig foxholes and fill sandbags to go around them. We must string the trip flares and set the Claymore mines. We must set a guard plan for the night. Then, the work's done and we can heat up our favorite C-rations, smoke a cigarette, check for leeches and, if our turn in the guard rotation allows, crawl into the hooch and fall asleep.

The foxholes we've dug are spaced at approximately even intervals around the full Company perimeter with three men usually assigned to each hole. We're on one-third alert and so, one man is awake and on guard while the other two men can sleep within the relative comfort of their hooch. Listening posts are also set up out beyond the perimeter line maybe thirty or forty meters. LP is the worst of the worst jobs as it

Tim Haslam

involves three men sent out with nothing but their weapons and some ammo to spend the night clustered together, unprotected from the elements, tasked with alerting the Company to any intruders. LP at night performs the same sacrificial function as that of the point squad when the Company is in motion during the day. In front of the men on LP is Charlie, armed motivated and stealthy. Behind them is the rest of Bravo Company, fatigued, anxious and dedicated to the proposition that nothing out in that jungle will get close enough to inflict harm. The dedication is supported by M16s, machineguns, frags, trip flares and Claymore mines.

The Claymore is the most powerful and destructive devise in our defenses, being comprised of one and half pounds of C4 explosive behind a matrix of 700 steel ball bearings all packaged into an arc shaped plastic case. When detonated the ball bearings are blasted outward with the shattering force of the exploding C4, obliterating anything within fifty meters over a sixty degree arc. A wire runs from the Claymore back to the perimeter line and is attached to a detonator that can be activated by two quick compressions of the trigger—two required as a precaution against accidental detonations. There is usually a Claymore hidden out somewhere in front of each foxhole, the detonator close at hand to the nervous grunt on guard who knows the power of the device and what it could do to anything perceived to be a threat out in the darkness, whether it be Charlie, a wild pig or a fellow grunt on LP. The men on LP know to be quiet. They know that any noise they make can elicit a deadly reaction of fire and metal from any direction.

The Company uses their radios to communicate status throughout the night. These situation reports, or sit-reps, are called out every twenty minutes. The Company headquarters people are camped somewhere in the middle of the perimeter and initiate the sit-reps. Each platoon has one of their radios in a hooch just in back of the perimeter line and another radio out with the LP. Throughout the night, hopefully, the process is repeated exactly…

"Five-Nine-Charlie, this is Six-Charlie. Sit-rep. Over."

"Six-Charlie, this is Five-Nine-Charlie. Situation negative. Over."

The ping and return of the sit-rep dialogue is repeated for each

Stars and Stripes and Shadows

platoon; Six-Zero, Six-One and Six-Two. The LPs are pinged the same way. However, because of their vulnerability, they respond simply by keying the handset button which breaks the steady static squelch sound on the network; one or three breaks for negative, two or four breaks for movement or alert or oh-shit!

I have the first guard in the rotation tonight, the nine to midnight watch; which is always my preference even if the duty really starts about eight o'clock. For the pre-nine o'clock segment, the work seems a little less lonely. Some of the other men are still milling about quietly in the dark spaces between the foxholes and the hooches, illuminated only by the red tips of their cigarettes. Others are attending to personal business within their hooches; reading letters or books, or writing letters, using a flashlight, all the while making sure they have a towel or poncho liner over them, blacking out their space, concealing them and their activities from Charlie and his gun sights.

By nine o'clock the camp is still and silent, the man made contours and silhouettes now fully absorbed into the overarching darkness. Once again my struggle to stay awake, to stay alert, to stay sane begins. The uniqueness of this day in my life makes the struggle somewhat easier as there is much to relive and sort out, to ponder and clarify. I remember so long ago when this day began in the relative comfort of our mud hole at Firebase 30 and how it progressed, under the persistent burden of my ruck and gear, via helicopter into this cratered, tear gas shrouded jungle realm with only the occasional brief break to eat or drink or smoke or react to people shooting at us.

Doc Charlebois returned to the platoon area just as we were settling in for C-rations and cigarettes this evening and filled us in on what had happened up on the ridges above us today. Everyone assumed and Doc's story confirmed that there were most likely only two snipers firing at us. Their first shot was aimed at a rifleman named Adamson in Six-One platoon. He was lucky; the 7.62 millimeter Warsaw-Pact round impacted with the metal frame of his ruck at a velocity of just under 700 meters per second, deflecting its trajectory slightly to the right, tearing through the soiled fabric of Adamson's fatigue shirt, ripping a furrow of flesh straight across his back. The metal-jacketed bullet left a clean wound damaging only flesh and the muscle tissue just below the surface, exiting out through the opposite side of his shirt. The rent to

Tim Haslam

his back was nearly eight inches in length and spread open slightly wider than the width of the searing bullet, damaging thousands of nerves, leaving Adamson in excruciating pain. He was lucky because he was easily tough enough to outlast the agony of his body's initial reaction to the shock and trauma. He was lucky because no bone or organ or limb blocked the invading missile. He was lucky because a-half-dozen medics in Bravo Company were more than Merthiolate and Darvon assholes who knew what to do. He was lucky because tonight he is in a hospital, out of the shit.

The next shot, probably fired by the second sniper was aimed at Staff Sergeant Johnson, the platoon sergeant for Six-One, who was two men in front of Adamson in the column. He was lucky too. Reflexively his body reacted to the first shot by pulling itself instantly downwards into a crouch. The velocity of his jerking motion downward was just sufficient to remove his head from the line of the second bullet as it bore through the air just above his helmet, marked by the whooshing sound of the air molecules colliding back together, filling the vacuum left by the bullet. His luck wasn't sufficient to get him out of the shit however. Charlie will have other opportunities to change Sergeant Johnson's luck.

Between Adamson and Johnson in the column was Brent Grieve another Six-One rifleman. Grieve wasn't so lucky. The NVA sniper who shot at Adamson—who was knocked away the instant the bullet struck his ruck frame—quickly re-oriented the barrel of his AK47 up slightly and to the right until the next target came into his sights—Grieve. The snipers own internal system was excitedly pumping adrenaline now, limiting his ability to stabilize his rifle barrel, limiting his ability to sta-bilize his focus and his willingness to wait another fraction of a second to lock the sites onto a vital part of Grieves anatomy. So, as soon as his senses suggested there was an American grunt in his sights he pulled the trigger. His second shot, fired in actuality just a second or two after his first, and traveling at the same velocity struck Grieve squarely in the right shoulder. The bullet entered into Grieve and directly encountered a nearly solid sequence of bone. The bullet tip, almost unimpeded by fabric, skin, muscle and connective tissue reached the top outer bulge of Grieve's right humerus bone. The compact tissue of that knobby protuberance and the other bones connecting to it at the shoulder joint impeded the progress of the bullet. Seeking the path of least resistance

Stars and Stripes and Shadows

the bullet started to bend and flatten as it continued inward, splitting, breaking and crushing the stiff but fragile bones forming the ball and socket joint that just a fraction of a second ago allowed Grieve to move his arm. As it flattened out, the bullet started to slow until the additional resistance of the clavicle and scapula were sufficient to stop its forward motion. Then the reaction caromed the remaining energy back, erupting outward, expanding the entrance wound. The force of the blow knocked Grieve sideways and literally pushed him out of the right shoulder strap of his ruck. The weight of the ruck now swinging off his back and the remaining energy from the bullet impact yanked him to the ground, writhing in agony.

Grieve wasn't so lucky. Although he would most likely survive and he would be in the same hospital with Adamson tonight and out of the shit forever, it's unlikely that his arm would ever again function fully.

Doc described how two of the Company medics attended to Adamson while all the rest, including himself, tended to Grieve. His injury would require more than a field dressing and a syrette of morphine for the pain. The bullet had done considerable damage to several of the skeletal structures that held his right arm on as well as the blood vessels and nerves that enervate and control his lower arm and hand. Any further movement could easily extend the damage beyond the remedial abilities of the Army's most skilled surgeons. This was the main concern of these young men, whom we all referred to as "Doc," but who, in actuality, had only a few months of extensive first aid training. They were trained well enough to know that they could only do the minimum to aid Grieve now, but that they could cause severe damage by trying to go further. Their training and teamwork was sufficient for them to carefully arrange Grieve and his arm onto a litter fashioned out of a poncho and to move him gently to the LZ. There, they sheltered him from the jostling effects of the spinning helicopter rotor and the associated debris flying about until he was handed off, along with Adamson to the on-board medics. The future of Grieve and his arm was now dependent on how quickly the dust-off pilot could urge his Huey back to Pleiku and the 71st Evacuation Hospital, and how quickly and effectively the doctors and nurses there could evaluate, prioritize and attend to him. As was typical of such events, none of us in Bravo Company would ever know the outcome.

Tim Haslam

Such were the thoughts that accompanied the first two hours of my guard duty, alternating with thoughts about the perpetrators, the violators, the NVA, gook, sniper, bastards who had so easily accomplished their mission. *Who were they?* I wondered. *What did they look like? How old were they? What did they say to each other as they scrambled away from our feeble counter attack? What did they say to their fellows when they returned to their tunnel complex homes somewhere out here? What are they talking about doing tomorrow? What will Captain Collins and the other officers do differently tomorrow?*

The hours seem to have gone by more quickly with these things churning around in my head, but I don't like to be in this mental place and I don't want the churning to continue when it's finally time to surrender to my fatigue.

Go home, I think. Go home for a few minutes. Go back to Mom and Dad, my backyard and my car and my friends. Go back to Rosemary.

So, I try to go back to all of them for a little while. But the images have changed slightly. The slide show of remembrances seems to be fading in some subtle fashion and something is prohibiting me from refining the focus and clarity of the associations and feelings. They seem so far away now as though they are transitioning out of reality and into a dream.

ᚾ ᚾ ᚾ ᚾ

"Let's go, let's go!" Taylor says, lightly kicking the boot heels on the feet extending out of the hooches, trying to roust the sleeping bodies attached. "We're moving in thirty minutes."

Thirty minutes is barely enough time to take down the hooches, pull in the flares and mines, empty the sand bags and prepare Mr. Ruck for another day of ass kicking. Breakfast will have to be consumed in parallel with these other efforts, coffee is out and morning cigarettes will have to be smoked down, dangling from our lips, instead of being savored slowly over casual morning conversations.

It's not yet six o'clock as we scurry to break camp in the cool morning mist while the officers huddle around Captain Collins, each with an open map, following the tracings of the Captain's finger over the abstract images of our desired route today. There seems to be an unusual amount of attention paid to the officers and the perceived conviction

Stars and Stripes and Shadows

of their discussions. They've been told where we need to go today by higher headquarters and probably what route to take, but the strategy and tactics that the Bravo Company grunts must employ is up to these six men. The desired outcome for our work is not simply to get to some designated place by the end of the day. Our job is to find North Vietnamese and kill them. These officers, because they are human beings too, will also endeavor to achieve the secondary objective of reducing injury and death within our ranks.

By ten o'clock the sun has burned away the overcast above the trees that blanketed us during the night and early morning and enough rays penetrate through the layers of foliage to keep the ground level water molecules active and the humidity oppressive. The Company has, by direction of Captain Collins, spread itself out more than on yesterdays hump. A greater percentage of the men are deployed on the flanks, which are also moved out to about a hundred meters from the center file and the prescribed individual spacing has been expanded to about ten meters. The idea is that Charlie's snipers are less likely to get off more than one shot before the Company can react and with the elements spread so far apart, a substantial detachment could be peeled away and deployed out to block avenues of escape. The concept seems pretty good. *Except for one of us!*

The whole company will have to cover much more territory today as the officers want our movements to be less direct and predictable and the point squad, from Five-Nine really has their work cut out for them with this strategy. The officers fear the point squad may be tipping off the route of the rest of the Company to Charlie and so they've been ordered to sweep back and forth to adjacent ridges on both sides of the Company's track and to occasionally circle back in hopes of catching snipers laying an ambush. The incentive for the point squad enduring the fact that they will have to hump three or four times as far as the rest of the Company is a night free from any guard duty. For grunts with very little available in the way of creature comfort, this is actually a pretty strong motivator.

Around eleven o'clock there is a simultaneous change in the terrain and the weather. Mercifully, the ground has leveled out and we seem to be moving along a large flat plateau. The forest here however is still thick, the upper canopy even denser than that of the rising fingers

Tim Haslam

we've spent the morning climbing. The Company, still spread well apart, is moving more quickly, following the lead elements hacking out the pathways with their machetes. There is no longer any evidence of any sunlight shafts penetrating down to the ground as we plod along through this darkening world where we seem to be getting smaller in relationship to the things growing above us. Because of the relative flatness and the lack of any apparent ground above our flanks, this area also feels less dangerous.

The malaise-like concentration on my footsteps is suddenly disturbed by a steady, pervasive sound interrupting the familiar, rhythmic compressions of my steps, building steadily, overcoming all the noises that I've grown used to as accompaniment to my struggles. It's coming from above me, high up in the trees, increasing in volume, rapidly spreading completely over the whole plateau. All of our eyes are drawn upwards to identify the source; rain.

The monsoon squall passing over us pours its contents down into the upper canopy trees above us where the drops splash apart over the branches and leaves. The spray and trickling water works its way down into the middle canopy where broader leaves catch and route the water down still further to the next level; the level of the ground vegetation, the level of the terrestrial animals, the level of the uninvited grunts. Several minutes pass between our reaction to the first sounds coming from above and the arrival of the first drops splashing lightly into our zone. It doesn't seem like much at first, just a few scattered drops sliding in among us. But those are soon followed by others and others and others until everything above us seems to have lost the ability to resist the water, becoming part of a gigantic hydraulic conspiracy trying to wash us away from a place we don't belong.

Six-Charlie's voice comes over the radio accompanying a halt in our forward progress and announces a lunch break. I pass the word forward and back to the men around me and to Mr. Ruck.

In an instant Ruck is off and on the ground, the little cans are out, opened and cooking over the heat-tab I've ignited in a little nest I've made under the protection of a gnarly root buttress anchoring a huge tree to the forest floor. Neither the root nor the tree affords much protection for me from the rain however. It doesn't seem to matter much though, the water striking me now just roles or bounces off the well-

Stars and Stripes and Shadows

saturated fabric of my clothes.

I have set four goals for myself on this break; check thoroughly for leeches, eat, keep a cigarette dry long enough to light and smoke and, finally to sleep. Sleep will come the moment I stop trying to accomplish the other three goals. It's the same for everyone. Sleep is one of our appetites that never gets satisfied fully and so always beckons. We've learned to sleep in short increments. We've learned to sleep soaking wet. We've learned to sleep in uncomfortable positions. We've learned to sleep in the shit.

Pulling up my left pant leg to check for leeches, I'm startled to actually find one. Reflexively I swipe at it with my hand as though it were a mosquito or fly. This only flips the bloated tail end of the slimy thing over the head end that has firmly clamped itself into my flesh and, for the first time I can actually feel the connected parasite. Goal number three quickly jumps up the priority list and I scramble for a cigarette. The first one hastily retrieved from the Marlboro pack is fumbled onto the wet ground, lost forever, never to provide me any reward or comfort. *Damn!* Number two is withdrawn more carefully but still with panicked urgency. My flaming Zippo ignites the tip of the cigarette adjacent to the half inch of dry paper and tobacco toward the end; the rest of the shaft already soaked from my wet hands. The instant the red hot Marlboro touches the leech it releases its grasp, expelling out some of the blood it has stolen.

"*Shit!*" I say out loud, but to myself, my face pursed up in a disgusted reaction.

The soggy cigarette goes back into my mouth for safe keeping while I carefully explore the rest of my leg, up to my knee and back down under my wet filthy sock and as far into my boot as I can see and feel with my finger; *all clear.*

Raising the right pant leg reveals two more of the disgusting creatures, eliciting an equal or greater startle response from me. These two must have had a later seating time for lunch as they both seem to be anemically thin and appear to be writhing themselves into a more comfortable position for their repast.

"*Die you bastards!*" I think to myself as I reach for the execution device hanging from my lips.

"*Goddamn it!*" I exclaim loudly as a reaction to the now saturated

Tim Haslam

tobacco tube breaking in two at my touch, the business end splashing down next to the waterlogged remains of its former roommate from the red and white box.

I throw the filter end into the forest and retrieve another one from my dwindling arsenal. The party-for-two on my right leg is quickly sizzled off and subsequent, thorough inspections fail to find any others.

Three leeches at the cost of three cigarettes is not a sustainable ratio. I'll need a better strategy. I'll need to be more efficient and skilled. I'll get lots of practice.

The rain continued through the whole break, limiting any rejuvenation afforded by the barely warm C-ration pork-pucks, the next two soggy cigarettes or the brief involuntary drifts off into semi-sleep. Mr. Ruck however was fully refreshed and ready for the afternoon rounds, having gone up a level or two in weight class with the added rainwater collected within its fabric and folds.

Somehow Elmer and Mike Beasley, the men to my front and rear have managed to get their rucks on and up on to their feet on their own and so, apparently must I. With Mr. Ruck staring belligerently up at me, I set my feet as firmly as I can in front of Ruck's frame, approaching it like a skinny, drenched Sumo wrestler. I take charge of the situation with the next move, grabbing the shoulder straps with the intensity of Humphrey Bogart taking hold of some bad-guy's shirt front and then with all my might, I thrust the ruck up to shoulder height, slam it against the massive trunk of the tree, twisting myself into position so that I'm holding the weight of the pack up against the tree with my back. Then, with ballet-like finesse I force my two arms through the straps and, just like that, Ruck is captured; *round one to me.*

Elmer and Mike have taken in the whole confrontation.

"Nice move," says Elmer, obviously impressed.

"Fuckin-A," confirms Mike, obviously speechless.

Within an hour all the fond memories of the lunch break have been left far behind, as has the level plateau. Mr. Ruck has reclaimed his dominant position jockeying me up the next series of steep, slippery ridgelines. As a mental diversion I've gone to the music category of stored remembrances. Words and melodies come into my consciousness, overshadowing the pain and discomfort signals constantly vying for my attention.

> *We gotta get out-a this place*
> *If it's the last thing we ever do*
> *We gotta get out-a this place*
> *If it's the last thing we ever do*

Somehow, these lyrics have been subconsciously selected first from my cerebral jukebox. They seem appropriate, and are repeated over and over again while I simultaneously try to remember the group behind the words. Is it the Rolling Stones; the Kinks; the Animals? I don't know. It doesn't matter. The words do take me *outta this place* for a little while.

"We're old enough to go to Vietnam and fight and die," Jack advises the Ranger. "We oughta be old enough to drink a beer!"

"Yea, that's right!" Davis, Mahoney, Wirt and I chime in as the supporting chorus.

The Park Ranger has heard it before and he's sympathetic with the philosophical disconnect. However, the law is the law and his job is enforcement.

"I want you gentlemen to pack up your gear and leave the park now," he says sternly, emptying out the remaining contents of the Coors bottles he's confiscated from us.

A second Ranger joins him and they both watch us carefully, illuminated by their flashlights as we pack up our things, all the while reminding them of Vietnam and death and injustice. They're not paying any attention to the substance of our limited arguments, but are paying close attention to our abilities to articulate the feeble mantra. Any slurring of speech or stumbling about as we collect up our things would likely result in some kind of detainment. It would be irresponsible of them to send five inebriated young men off onto the narrow roads exiting Yosemite Park this late at night.

Apparently we pass the visual sobriety test and the Ranger's allow us to climb into the two Volkswagens and leave the scene of the crime.

It's pretty late, we don't know where we're going to go, and we're

Tim Haslam

a little bit pissed off that our camping party has been spoiled, but we are also five middle class young men from good families who have just driven away from our first encounter with *the law*. In some way, the episode has validated our liberation as young men and our escape into the night, unconstrained even by a destination has left our free spirits pretty high. Life is good and can only get better.

Jack turns on the radio as I steer my VW out of the campground and on to the dark road leading westward out of Yosemite, the second VW following closely behind.

> *We gotta get out-a this place*
> *If it's the last thing we ever do*
> *We gotta get out-a this place*
> *If it's the last thing we ever do*

...the voices declare through the crackly little speaker on the Volkswagen's dash. Jack cranks up the volume, mostly increasing the crackle, initiating enthusiastic participation from Mike Mahoney in the back seat and me, behind the wheel.

> *We gotta get out-a this place*
> *If it's the last thing we ever do*
> *We gotta get out-a this place*
> *If it's the last thing we ever do*

...we shout out as loudly as we can, rocking the little white beetle along its escape route, just glad to be free young men out in the world, late on a summer's night.

> *We gotta get out-a this place*
> *If it's the last thing we ever do*
> *We gotta get out-a this place*
> *If it's the last thing...."*

The crack is less loud and crisp this time.

We are on the left flank and towards the back of the pack. The shot has once again come from the right and slightly ahead of the

Stars and Stripes and Shadows

main body of the Company but it has the same effect, bringing all of us instantly to the ground, orienting our weapons out toward the surrounding jungle.

Nothing comes over the radio for several minutes to clarify the situation or to confirm the success of the sniper. This time the officers were prepared and free to react without any additional approvals. Six-One Platoon is on the right flank today and Lieutenant Nelson dispatched his two trailing squads an instant after the shot was fired without even knowing if anyone was hit. The thirteen men in this detachment nearly sprint up and over the ridge where the shot came from, staying thirty to forty meters down slope from where the AK47 was fired. They take up positions on the next finger out to the west, which rises gently up nearly parallel to the sniper's ridge. The other two squads of Six-One also deploy westward forming a line between the Company's position and the top of the sniper's ridge and soon all of Six-One starts the upward sweep. Charlie must go up to avoid the grunts spread out below him, blocking any downward escape route.

Meanwhile, Lieutenant Elliott has wheeled Five-Nine Platoon, which is on point around to the right in an effort to cut off the uphill avenues. All the men of Five-Nine are pressing hard, driven by adrenaline, fear and rage to trap the NVA soldier...all the men but three. Doc Hayes and Sergeant Fesi are attending to Warren Boothe. Boothe, who is Five-Nine-Alpha-Charlie, turns out to be the one man sacrificed in the successful strategy of limiting the sniping to one shot. It may have just been random bad luck that put Boothe in the enemy gun-sights this afternoon, or, it may have been the whip antennae trailing downward from the radio strapped to his back that gave him away as an RTO, a communication link within the grunt Company, a preferred target. Whatever the sniper's reasons were, his bullet has critically wounded Boothe. Like the attack yesterday, the shot came in from the right and at a downward angle. As Boothe and all the men in the file would have presented themselves in profile to the snipers sights, this shot probably hit exactly where the shooter intended. At this range, the bullet was traveling at nearly full muzzle velocity when it slammed into Boothe's ribcage. The collision shattered the sixth rib, which, fortunately for Boothe, redirected the path downward and toward the back, away from the main mass of his lungs and his heart, which were right in line

Tim Haslam

with the initial vector of the projectile. Still, the hot steel and lead slug continued to drill downward through Boothe, nicking both the middle and inferior lobes of his right lung, finally coming to rest against the interior wall of his right hipbone.

Sergeant Fesi, better known as Five-Nine-Alpha, assists Doc Hayes as much as he can. Together, they carefully separate Boothe from his ruck and radio. Fesi, then grabs the handset and sends out the call for more medics to help, announcing to all ears on the net that the man down is Boothe and that he is pretty fucked up.

Captain Collins again has much to do. All of his right side elements are actively attempting to trap and destroy the sniper. The rest of the Company is spread thinly over a one hundred meter section of jungle out to his left, vulnerable to any kind of attack. Even without his map, he can see that there is no place anywhere around suitable for cutting an LZ to dust-off his wounded man, the terrain is too steep and irregular. Boothe will have to be lifted out somehow.

Ten minutes, at least have past since the shot transformed Boothe and the Company.

The voice of Six-One-Charlie finally breaks the unnerving squelch of the net.

"Six-Charlie, this is Six-One-Charlie. Over."

"Six-Charlie. Go."

"We've met up with Five-Nine on the ridge at about the place the shot came from and there's no sign of any fuckin' gooks anywhere and there's no fuckin' way anybody got by us!" Six-One-Charlie's voice clearly portrays the frustration and anger all of us feel, punctuated dramatically by his almost trembling, breathless delivery. His expressed anger seems to be the only weapon he has to hurl back at the situation, the sniper and the shit to counter the diminishing confidence he, and we all, feel. Like Agatha Christie's Ten Little Indians, we're being picked off one by one. Unlike those "Indians" though, there's no mystery about who's doing it. The only mystery is where he is.

While the rest of us anxiously reflect on the situation, Boothe continues to suffer the primary tangible consequence of the sniper's success. Nothing within his central nervous system has been damaged and so his mind is actively connected to what has and is happening to his body. There is pain at the site of the entrance wound and at the splintered rib

Stars and Stripes and Shadows

and a less acute burning sensation running downward somewhere inside him. He can understand most of this pain. He has felt pain before and can use it as a gage for assessing the damage. But there are other signals coming from within him that he doesn't understand, that he's never felt before, that confuse his ability to discern the outcome. His body is reacting to the intrusion of the scorching slug. The severed capillaries at the nicks in his lungs are dripping just enough blood into the alveolar sacs to make him want to cough. The muscle and connective tissues ripped and burned by the auguring metal are releasing small amounts of blood and fluids, dropping the pressure of these normally closed systems just slightly. He struggles to gain control of his senses so that he can fight back somehow. But his mechanisms aren't working very well. His awareness is acute and yet his ability to control is clouded, diffuse and disintegrated. He cannot rally himself enough to overcome the effects of the little bullet that now lies still, cooling down at the end of its destructive foray through his body. He cannot intellectually clarify the circumstances, the consequences or the fear.

Doc Hayes knows what's happening and what he must do. Boothe's body is reacting to the trauma as anyone's would. His pulse is rapid, he's taking deep and rapid breaths, sometimes coughing, and the pallor of his face is cool and growing pale. These first signs of mild hypovolemic shock are apparent to Hayes. With Sergeant Fesi's help he places Boothe's ruck under his legs, being careful not to turn his torso completely onto his back, using his own knees to prop up the injured right side. Then, Doc Hayes, who is a very large black man, starts applying his more naturally acquired skills. Hayes is a gentle giant, an affable, good-humored human being, naturally calm, honest and trustworthy. He begins his easy, confident dialogue with Boothe as readily as any surgeon might begin an operation they have performed a hundred times. He steadily and reassuringly draws Boothe's attention away from the internal distress and uncertainty that is compounding the shock reaction. Hayes' on going, unpretended questions and comments gently retrieve Boothe from that fuzzy, sfumato state that he was slipping into. Boothe is, at least for the moment, under the control of Hayes more than he is under the influences of his body's responses.

Doc Hayes still has real work to do to tend to the physical attributes of the damage; work that will require his full attention. He needs

Tim Haslam

Boothe to participate actively in the fight against the deadly shock reaction and so, he intentionally offers Boothe an unlikely distraction—his own pain.

"Where does it hurt most?" he inquires with characteristic sensitivity, but without really caring what the answer is. Doc's strategy is to draw Boothe's attention onto something he can focus on for a little while. Something he can work on. Doc knows this is a risky strategy as there is a fine line between the modest level of pain that one man can endure and moderate through his own personal strengths and capacities and the more severe level that is unendurable, that demands a disconnect from the sensations overburdening the consciousness, hastening the shock. Weeks later, Doc Hayes will share all of this with me and clarify the basis for his belief in pain. He will tell me how he's seen severely wounded men whose angered response against the pain seems to have kept them out of the clutches of shock and how he's seen others who slipped quickly into the deadly shock syndrome as soon as their internal mechanisms disconnected their consciousness from the pain. I don't know if this is sound medical practice or not. Hayes believes it and right now it seems to be working for Boothe.

"Six-Two-Charlie, this is Six-Charlie. Over," Houston impatiently beckons.

"Six-Charlie, this is Six-Two-Charlie. Over," responds an equally impatient Wee John.

"Six-Two-Charlie, what's the situation down there? The dust-off is inbound, ETA in about three minutes. Over."

Wee John surveys the work going on by the rest of us in the platoon in front of him before he responds to Houston. The only terrain accessible from the air turns out to be near our position. There's way too much vegetation to clear and the ridges are too narrow and steep to make a real LZ. We are just trying to clear enough of the canopy away to allow the medevac Huey to lower down a litter.

"There's one more tree to bring down, then there should be enough of an opening to drop down the basket. Over."

"Rog. You'll need to pop smoke when they get close. Over."

"Roger that. As soon as we hear him close enough, we'll pop blue smoke. Over."

126

Stars and Stripes and Shadows

The Huey arrives just as the last tall thin tree comes down. Wee John pulls the pin on the smoke grenade and tosses it out into the little clearing. The blue smoke is drawn up quickly into the newly opened shaft ventilating the jungle.

"Six-Charlie, this is Six-Two-Charlie. I don't have the push for the chopper, so you'll have to be middleman in this. Over," says Wee John, meaning that he can't talk directly to the Huey pilot now hovering directly above the opening.

"Negative Six-Two-Charlie, you'll have to be in direct contact with him to pull this off," says Captain Collins taking charge of one more aspect of the situation. "Wait one."

"Wee John, drop off this push and go to six-six-point-fiver. Over," Houston comes back on advising the Hueys radio frequency.

"Rog. Six-six-point-fiver. Out."

Four of the Company medics along with a string of other helpers, all under the stewardship of Doc Hayes have brought Boothe down the ridge in a poncho litter. Hayes and Boothe have done everything they can to stabilize his condition, but time is now working against them. He needs to get up into the hands of the medics on the dust-off bird and then to the 71st Evac as quickly as possible. The challenge is now for the Huey crew to drop the litter down nearly eighty feet through the narrow chasm in the swaying trees while countering the updraft effects on the rotors. Medevac pilots and crews are usually the best of the best when it comes to Huey drivers, as this kind of rescue is typical of what their job requires. At least this time no one is firing at them—so far.

It takes three minutes for the basket to reach the level of our out-stretched hands and another two minutes to get Boothe strapped in and lifted up by us until the slack can be taken out of the line by the Huey crew without jerking Boothe out. The Huey is oriented at such an angle that the pilot can't possibly see all the way down the shaft to the litter and Boothe. Even if he could his full attention has to be on maintaining position, altitude, yaw and trim. The slightest shift in the Huey's position up above the trees could amplify down the steel cable resulting in a spin, sway, rock or bounce of the basket with disastrous results for the passenger. Right now, this dust-off pilot is like a pianist trying to play Beethoven's Fifth Piano Concerto in a hailstorm. Every

Tim Haslam

fiber of his concentration, reflex, sensitivity and skill is engaged in the effort. He cannot miss a note or beat or intonation of this opus. The pilot isn't alone however in the effort. The whole crew is engaged in the process; watching, communicating and preparing for the next move, all the while extremely careful not to add to the pilot's problems by suddenly shifting the internal load.

Slowly, steadily, Boothe is drawn up out of the shit. The rest of us below, our feet still firmly affixed *in the shit*, watch the basket shrink upwards until it's pulled safely aboard the helicopter.

Our numbers have now been reduced by three. Two fuel guzzling helicopters have flown hundreds of miles. Surgeons, medical staffs and equipment have been deployed and our progress in the last two days has been delayed by several hours at a cost to Charlie of four 7.62 millimeter bullets. Adamson, Grieve and Boothe are worth more than this.

N N N N

Bob Price swings his machete deliberately through the vines and branches that block our way and yet he's being careful to minimize the sounds he's making. He knows that he's the man out in front. He thinks that Charlie knows where we are and that today it could be his turn. Six-Two is the point platoon today and our squad, now about thirty minutes ahead of the Company, is the point squad. I'm next in line after Price, back a few meters and using my own machete to clear away the higher vines and things that he misses. I don't want to spend another day hunched forward trying to avoid the overhanging stuff. I'm also aware that if and when the vegetation opens up, Price and I will pop out like clay pigeons and that I'm the pigeon with the radio antennae differentiating my value as a piece on the board.

For most of the morning we've been working our way through lower ground, a narrow valley carved out by the meanderings of one of the larger streams. The valley is a catch basin for all the water draining off the surrounding ridges and varies in character from marsh to swamp to ultra-dense jungle. Some of the marshy areas seem to be solid fields of sharp edged elephant grass, rising up seven or eight feet, limiting our vision to just a few inches. In this realm we're like claustrophobic blind men struggling through a field of razor blades.

We stop to roll down our sleeves and to wrap our faces in our towels as a way to shield our flesh from the grasses defensive efforts. It feels to me like we've entered into some giant Venus Fly Trap and are about to be digested.

"*We gotta get out-a this place*," plays continually in my mind, a true reflection of how each of us feels. We're all thinking the same things. We're all starting to believe that the slicing grass may only serve as a diversion within this conspiracy, distracting our attention away from the leeches and vipers that slither and squirm after us, herding us all the while toward Charlie's hidden booby traps, or into target areas already dialed into his mortar tubes. I want Price to move more quickly. I want to be cautious somewhere else. I want to *see* the dangers that surround me. *I want air.*

Price's abrupt stop interrupts my paranoia and gets me re-focused just in time to avoid a collision with his rucksack. Together, we take a couple of cautious steps out of the grass maze and into a small clearing, sparsely populated with tall slender trees. The landscape gently rises up to our right, leading back up to the familiar fingers and ridges. Beyond the little clearing, the valley, clad in its triple-canopy forest raiment's continues its gradual ascent up away from us to the north. Bob and I turn and watch the rest of the squad break out of the elephant grass, each man gasping the fresher air, as though they had just surfaced from the depths of the ocean.

Sergeant Taylor leads the way to a thicker cluster of trees on the opposite side of the clearing where, without any communication to us, he drops his ruck, plops down onto the wet ground and opens his map.

"Haslam, get Six-Two on the horn," he instructs me without shifting his gaze from the map.

"Rog," I reply, moving close enough for Taylor to reach the handset as all the others drop out of their rucks and reach for water and cigarettes.

Taylor starts his comments into the Prick-25 handset with a long description of the grassy marsh we just passed through; carefully identifying its grid location on the map and advising Lieutenant Falck to have the Company steer clear of it. Then he just listens for a long time, occasionally placing his finger on his map, rogering dispassionately back through the radio. As he continues to listen, the look on his face gradually transitions from simple fatigue to concerned fatigue. The look on

Tim Haslam

the rest of our faces unconsciously mimics Taylor's expressions, all of us suspecting that the mysterious dialogue isn't about rest or relief or hot meals and cold beer on the way out to us.

"Roger. Wait one...I'll put Haslam on. Give it to him."

"You'll need a pencil and paper," he says to me, handing me the handset, shifting himself around so that he can fill the whole squad in.

"You ready, Six-Two-Three?" Ed Arter's voice asks, inquiring as to my readiness to write something down.

At my acknowledgment Ed tersely declares, "Six-two-six-zero...you got that? Over."

"Roger. Six-two-six-zero. Is that it? Over."

"That's affirm. Out."

"All right, listen up." Taylor instructs, naturally wielding every NCO's most frequently used expression. "Here's the deal. Six is pretty sure that our gook friends will try to ruin our afternoon again and so he's planned a little surprise."

Taylor shifts around again, pointing to the finger ridge rising up to our right. "This ridge runs for almost two klicks before it intersects with another ridge crossing eastward." He shifts back and points down to the map spread out on the ground in front of him.

"This is that ridge and, this other ridge here, as you can see, parallels our ridge the whole way up. It offers Charlie just the kind of conditions he's had the last two days. In other words, it's sniper paradise."

"I can't wait to see where we come in," says an uncharacteristically bold Elmer.

"*Guess* where we come in," challenges Mike Beasley sarcastically.

"What's this other push for?" I ask Taylor, referring to the channel frequency that Ed gave me, thinking there is more to come in the plan.

"That's the surprise," Sergeant Taylor begins his clarification. "At least that's supposed to be the surprise. That's the push for Robin-One-Eight, a Loach that's gonna join us further up the ridge. The Captain's pretty sure that Charlie's watching us and as soon as he sees the point squad—us—start up this ridge he's going to know where the Company's going. As soon as he thinks he knows where we're going, he jumps up ahead on this other ridge and waits for another easy target."

Stars and Stripes and Shadows

"So, we're gonna be the easy target and then the Loach flies in and blows the shit out of Charlie. Is that it?" Elmer offers, confident he's figured out the strategy.

"Negative. Our job is just to convince Charlie that we're leading the way and that the Company will be following along. The Captain and the rest of the brain trust have figured out that there is a stretch of ridge running for about two hundred meters up about a half a klick from here that is both ideal for sniping and has good escape routes. They figure that's where Charlie will be."

"So Bob, what if Charlie's smart enough to think he'd better change his pattern and decides to pop a cap on the first guy he sees in the point squad?" asks Price, reminding everyone that he's the first guy in the point squad.

"It won't matter," Taylor answers, drawing everyone's attention back to the map.

"See, this is the prime real estate for the sniper, right here, up on this ridge and this is the only route for anyone coming up the ridge we're on. But, right here, about twenty or thirty meters below the primo target area, we stop. That's where the Loach comes in." Taylor pauses for a minute and points to another spot on his map.

"When we get to this point, we'll radio back to Six-Charlie who'll be in contact with the Loach. Then, Haslam, you switch over to the push you got from Arter and get in direct contact yourself. The Loach will sneak in low and search for Charlie, as we start moving up this ridge again. The belief is that there's no way Charlie'll fire at us with the Loach hovering around. Belief number two is that Charlie may find the Loach to be irresistible and fire at it."

"Suppose Charlie finds the Loach *and* us to be irresistible. Did anybody think of that?" Price adds to the discourse, still shaky about his likely role relative to Charlie's reactions. "A Loach doesn't really have all that much fire power and would likely di-di pretty quick if somebody starts shooting at it."

"Oh, yea, I guess I forgot something important," Taylor responds to an opportunity he was obviously waiting for. "You're right, the Loach will di-di the instant he thinks bullets are headed his way but the Loach won't be alone. Somewhere, hidden off behind one of the ridges will be the Loach's partner, a Cobra gunship. The whole idea is for Charlie to

Tim Haslam

actually take a shot at the Loach. If he does, within about three seconds, the Cobra jambs in and defoliates the whole goddamn neighborhood including any NVA campers."

"It seems like there's an awful lot of beliefs involved in all this," I say, looking at Taylor to gage his level of confidence in the plan.

"Well, that's the plan," he says, authoritatively. "At least, if Charlie really is up there and if he really does something, he'll pay. If he really is up there and doesn't do anything, we'll be above him and the rest of the Company will be spread out coming up all the nearby ridges. The Loach and the Cobra will be watching over everything from the air. Charlie'll be fucked."

"Robin-One-Eight, this is Six-Two-Three. Over." I nervously say into the handset, becoming acutely aware that I've never in my life had the responsibility of anything like coordinating the activities of two airborne helicopters trying to find and kill human beings, trying to avoid killing friendly human beings —us — and trying not to get shot out of the sky.

"Six-Two-Three, this is Robin-One-Eight. Over."

The strength of the signal carrying the pilot's voice surprises me. The chopper has power much greater than that of the batteries that drive the signals around our net. The character of his voice and the cadence of his delivery are also more deliberate and military-like than I've grown accustomed to, although, everything he says carries with it all the background noises of the little helicopter.

"Robin-One-Eight, this is Six-Two-Three. How do you hear me? Over." I ask, trying to conform to the more serious style of the Loach pilot, still surprised and intimidated by the fact that I'm actually in contact with the operators of these powerful and expensive war machines.

"Lima-Charlie," the voice in the Loach responds instantly, confirming that he can hear me loud-and-clear.

"Robin-One-Eight, this is Six-Two-Three. We're at point alpha. Over," I say, confirming that we have reached the designated hold point on the map.

"Roger, Six-Two-Three. I'll be over you in a minute to confirm your position. Over."

Point alpha was agreed to because it appeared on the map to be just

Stars and Stripes and Shadows

below the crest of the ridge on the slope opposite Charlie's supposed position and likely to be clear enough for the Loach to be able to see us. The area turns out to be just as predicted and although there is some vegetation around us, we can easily be seen from the air.

I let the squad know that the Loach will be flying over and they all straighten up, looking and listening for the little chopper.

The Loach surprises all of us, actually popping up from our northeast, seemingly rising out of the trees, passing over us quickly just above the treetops.

"Six-Two-Three, this is Robin-One-Eight. I've got you confirmed at alpha. I'm proceeding up into the search area. Go ahead and start up again. Over."

"Rog, Robin-One-Eight. We're on our way. Out."

I look over to Sergeant Taylor and with my index finger pointed up make a circling motion suggesting that we move out.

Everything we do now is predicated on the belief that Charlie is up here watching us and, if the beliefs are right, he will take a shot at something or someone. Charlie by now knows that the Loach is searching around for him and he can probably figure out that the American helicopter must be in contact with the grunts on the ground. He can figure out that this contact is over a radio...a radio just like the one I have strapped to my back. *Why would he shoot at Price when I have the radio?*

The nickname Loach comes from the letters LOH, which stand for light-observation-helicopter, more formally known as the Hughes OH6-A Cayuse. The Cayuse is a bumblebee like aircraft that can dart in and out of all kinds of terrain, spot enemy targets and dart back out of range usually before drawing fire. Sometimes, up here, the Loach's just have a single occupant, the pilot and sometimes an observer rides along in the shotgun seat. Loach jockeys are at about the same level of esteem as medevac pilots in the hierarchy of Vietnam helicopter pilots but are as different from their Huey driving brethren as James Dean is from Laurence Olivier. The Loach pilots have to be true adrenaline junkies who like nothing better than to sneak up on Charlie, drawing fire and then backing off to a safer distance, hovering like a hunting dog pointing out a covey of quail. They don't really pilot the little choppers; they wear them, like tight fitting ski boots that react immediately in

Tim Haslam

unison with every twitch of their feet or hands. The OH6-A is made for this kind of work and these pilots are born for it.

The James Dean at the stick of this Loach is no exception. After passing over point-alpha, he dipped down into the separation between our ridge and the supposed sniper's ridge, hustled up the gap about two hundred meters and then made a mid-air stop, kicking around the tail of his Loach so that he was facing directly toward the crest of the ridge. He is now positioned so as to be face to face with anyone along the ridge top. From this orientation he somehow maneuvers the chopper slowly up-slope sideways, all the while maintaining his front toward the ridge. After proceeding this way for about another hundred meters the Loach jerks up like a hummingbird and crosses over the ridge top out of our sight.

J. Dean has a sidekick today, an observer...another adrenaline junky. One who must participate however, without having the ability to maneuver or withdraw the helicopter from harms way. The observer is simply a thrill rider, a rollercoaster passenger with complete faith in the machine and its operator. The observer's overt focus isn't on the ride however; it's on the search. He scans down into the jungle below with the intensity of a hungry winged raptor, hyper-sensitized to any incongruous movement or oscillation, shape, form or shadow. J. Dean, like his partner, also scans the terrain below with similar determination, but part of his attention is always working out future escape solutions. He is constantly re-appraising his position relative to his surroundings, determining the openings available to him and his machine should he need to react. He knows that his well-honed reflexes will move the Loach the instant a threat materializes. He wants his reflexes to be coupled with a planned escape route.

In actuality, my radio contact with Robin-One-Eight has been with the observer riding along and not the pilot. J. Dean is on another frequency in constant contact with the Cobra.

For the next several minutes, as we continue our climb up into the target area, the Loach searches up and down the ridge, occasionally coming into our view or earshot. When we get to the area that was determined to be the likely attack zone I call back to them, advising that we're at point-bravo. *As I make this call with the handset up to my mouth and ear I can't help but think how excited Charlie probably is right now to have an RTO in his sights.*

"Roger, Six-Two-Three. Confirmed at point bravo. Keep moving. Over," the observer responds quickly, something in his voice suggesting his attention is not entirely on our conversation.

"He says to keep going," I advise Sergeant Taylor, at the same time feeling really sympathetic to the idea of getting us *out of this place* as quickly as possible and glad to have the handset hooked back onto my ruck strap on the left side, the side away from any sniper's view.

Before Sergeant Taylor can respond, the quiet is shattered by bursts of machinegun fire coming from somewhere off to our right.

"Six-Two-Three, thiz Robin. We think we've got gooks up on the ridge slope," the excited observer advises over the sound of the continuing bursts reverberating through the open air and over the radio. "Get to point-charlie, ASAP!"

"What's happening?" asks an anxious Taylor, representing the sentiments of the rest of the squad.

"All he said is that he thinks there's gooks up on the ridge and that we should get to point-charlie ASAP."

"How many fuckin' gooks? Are they moving? Where?"

"I don't know, he just said gooks," I respond knowing that Taylor really just instructed me to get more information.

"Robin-One-Eight, this is…"

Before I can get any further, the Cobra barges up from the terrain just behind us, racing up over us so close we can clearly see the pilot and feel the rotor wash. Another fifty meters up, the shark-like gunship banks hard right and crosses over the opposite ridge, following the scent of its likely victims, dipping out of our sight, leaving us behind as he sniffs out the men who would shoot us. The only thing that Taylor and the squad and I can do now is to listen.

The bursts of firing that had been coming from the two M60's mounted to the skids of the Loach abruptly halts. Then two short AK47 bursts. Then an eruption of fire and explosion obviously discharged from the Cobra. Then, there are only the fluttering vibrations of the helicopter rotors off in the distance.

J. Dean and his observer had apparently spotted something suspicious down in the vegetation and started firing in an effort to flush it out. They kept firing until they knew the Cobra was about to strike

Tim Haslam

and then started to back off to get out of the way. At that point, an NVA soldier several meters off to the right of where the Loach had been firing made the fatal mistake of shooting at the withdrawing Loach. His timing was poor. The Cobra breeched the tree line just in time to see the muzzle flashes of the AK47. Charlie's full attention was on his excited efforts to bring down the little American helicopter that was pulling away from him, off slightly to his left. Before he could react to the sudden appearance of the whirling dragon coming down from the sky just over the trees to his right, the Cobra crew had him locked into the sights of their mini-gun and their rocket launchers. In an instant, the person in the NVA uniform with the Chinese made assault rifle, who ever or what ever he had been in life, was mutilated savagely along with everything around him by the hundreds of rounds slamming down from the mini-gun and the shrapnel from the two rockets unleashed at him. The first rounds spewing forth from the mini-gun were dead on target, tearing into him with such force that his life was ended instantly; no pain, no suffering, no recognition that his role as soldier and human being was ending. Whatever his last thoughts were, they would dissipate away quickly, unlike the physical remains of his body that would be consumed slowly by the surviving creature's resident in this dark, lonely place.

"Six-Two-Three, this is Robin-One-Eight. We have one confirmed kill and maybe one or two others down in the bush. We're gonna prune some more of the shrubbery around here to see if we can flush out any more zips. Hold your position when you get to point-charlie. My guess is that if anybody gets away from us, they're headin' right for you. Over."

"Roger, Robin-One-Eight. Understood. We should be at point-charlie in about five. Over," I respond, looking at Taylor who is standing right next to me.

"So?" Taylor says with somewhat of a shrug, inviting me to fill in the details of what has just happened.

"All right," I begin, buying a moment to organize my summation. "They wasted one gook for sure and maybe one or two more. I guess they think there's still more around and so they're about to strafe the area some more. He says we should get to point-charlie ASAP because any gooks that might get away from them will be heading that way." As

Stars and Stripes and Shadows

I'm saying this, something inside of me is evaluating the euphemisms coming out of my own mouth. *Wasted* and *gooks* are no longer grunt jargon terms, they've just been validated by real fire and real death for real human beings. *I wish I'd used other words.*

The better part of an hour has past since the little OH6-A dropped in as our bodyguard. No one has approached the ambush position our squad has set up at point-charlie and the Loach and Cobra team have just withdrawn quietly off to other opportunities, having completed their additional "pruning" work. Six-One platoon has worked its way up to the pruned area and is carefully scouring the territory for evidence that might confirm the results of the skirmish. The rest of the Company is cautiously working its way up towards us trying to flush out anyone fleeing or hiding from the eyes and venom of the two helicopters. My role as point of contact with the men in the flying machines has come to an end, concluded with a final, "thanks; out," before switching my radio back to the Company push.

The familiar voice of Six-One-Charlie breaks the squelch on my radio and begins describing the results of their search. Sergeant Taylor is sitting next to me, both of us leaning against the base of another huge tree with the rest of the squad spread out down slope from us, forming a barrier to anyone trying to get up this ridge. We both straighten up in reaction to the muted voice calling back to Six-Charlie. As Mr. Ruck is propped up next to me with the radio control knobs just inches from my hand, I reach over and turn the volume full up and hold the handset up so that both Bob Taylor and I can hear.

"...we've got three gook bodies down here," advises Six-One-Charlie with slow deliberation, a tinge of nervousness detectable in his voice. "There's also a blood trail heading up the ridge toward the southwest. Over."

"Six-One-Charlie, this is Six. How do you know the blood isn't from one of the dead gooks? Over," asks Captain Collins, obviously a little frustrated that he can't assess the situation and the damage with his own eyes.

"Well sir, I guarantee that these three gooks never moved from where they were hit," clarifies Six-One-Charlie. "All three of 'em are totally fucked up...pretty much obliterated! We followed the blood trail for about twenty or thirty meters until we lost it in some really

Tim Haslam

thick shit. What blood we could see was all on the ground at pretty regular intervals, like it was probably a leg wound. With the choppers gone, about all we can do now is toss some frags out into this shit and see what happens. Over."

"Roger, Six-One-Charlie. Go ahead with the frags. Then I want y'all to work your way southwest another half klick. Then call back. Over."

Taylor pulls off his helmet and lights a cigarette, a little more relaxed knowing that no one is known to be heading our way except friendlies. I do the same just as four muffled *ka-chunks* from Six-one's grenades break through the forest silence. We both listen intently for a few moments for some follow up sound, but there's nothing

"You have a leech on your neck," Taylor says to me matter-of-factly, his unconcerned intonation indicating the situation on my neck is of a pretty low level of concern. With a surprisingly similar attitude, I reach up and feel for the blood-lusting slug. It surrenders immediately to my initial grasp, apparently not yet fully committed to the A-positive entrée just a stab away. Without really giving it much thought, I just roll it around a few times between my thumb and forefinger and then toss it down into the mud. Leeches are moving further down the list of things to be concerned about here in the shit.

N N N N

The Company wearily plods on in similar fashion for another three days, although happily without any live interaction with Charlie. Our wanderings take us another eight or nine klicks further out into this wilderness, further away from everything familiar until the wilderness itself starts becoming too familiar. The vegetation blocks our way at nearly every step. The saturated ground slides from under our feet at every rise and fall along our path. The intermittent rains ensure that we never dry out completely, but they also seem to chase the mosquitoes away. The leeches are now familiar passengers, burned off dispassionately at each rest break for those who have the energy to bother with them. Occasionally, I'm startled out of the sameness of the surroundings at the sighting of some large, multi-colored spider or insect species that I've never seen before, and hope never to see again. We never see any larger animals though, as they must know that our coming can

Stars and Stripes and Shadows

bring a swath of death across the land. The scavengers within the realm would do well to follow us.

Where are the birds in this country? There don't seem to be any birds.

Each step, up and down each ridge, over each long klick is a little more difficult than the one before it. Each of the dozen times a day that I have to pull myself back up onto my feet after slipping down into the ooze requires strength and effort that I don't think I have. Most of the time we help each other getting back up after the slips and falls; sometimes however, because we are so weary we just stand and wait, while the grunt obstacle in front of us struggles back up; nobody says anything, nobody thinks anything; it's just his turn, not mine.

Rest breaks are always yearned for and welcomed, but are also the source of some dissonance. Our bodies are in need of so many things; nourishment, water, sleep and nicotine. The pain and itching from our cuts and scrapes and bites also suggest that repairs are required. *How can I rest when there are so many things to attend to?*

The nicotine desire, as always takes priority. A cigarette seems to fill more than just a need, it still serves as the only little reward we have to offer ourselves that is discretionary, that isn't Army issue. Watering is easy and eating is reduced to whatever food can be obtained and consumed quickly and easily—taste doesn't matter. Screw the rest. There's nothing I can do about all the little wounds anyway, accept to scratch and make them worse. Then, until someone yells out to "saddle up," I can sleep, holding a burning cigarette in my hand, partially satisfying two requirements.

Except for the three encounters with Charlie this is the way it's been for the six days we've been out here. Each night too, has been the same; long hours as lonely sentinels, battling every second against the need to sleep. A battle where the darkness and the jungle silence ally with our fatigue to draw down our eyelids, to close off our senses entirely, to encourage surrender. We're in a place now where only the strong and adaptable survive. None of us feel very strong and none of us want to adapt very much. The truth is that we *are* getting stronger and more

Tim Haslam

adaptable. We have conquered fifteen to twenty klicks of everything the forest has offered up against us. We have prevailed over at least three enemy soldiers and we have adapted to the leeches and mosquitoes to the point where we don't much care about them anymore. We are much stronger than we were six days ago. *The question is, are we strong enough for tomorrow?*

✎ ✎ ✎ ✎

This is the worst. I think to myself. *It can't get any worse than this.*

Danko, Beasley and I have drawn the listening post duty tonight. Just before dark and through a light rain, we worked our way down about twenty meters into the jungle as quietly as possible. As soon as we were out of sight, the trip flares were set behind us as a way of locking the gate, and the Claymores, now pointing out in our direction were wired up. It's our turn in the in-between-zone. All we have with us is our weapons and a little ammo. The rules say we can't even bring a poncho to shelter us from the rain. The fabric can make too much noise rustling around.

The light rain that accompanied us coming down here has been steadily reinforced over the last few hours. It's not rain any more, it's just a flood of water, cascading off all the foliage, pooling on the ground around us, treating us as though we're just more decaying debris on the forest floor. Without the rays of the sun or the radiant heat gathered within the plants during the day the water stays cool as it splashes and courses around through the blackness of the night. Our body heat transfers enough energy to warm the water molecules in contact with our skin pretty quickly, as long as we stay perfectly still. Any slight movement however unleashes a cold shockwave, slapping us rudely out of any pretended comfort.

I can't stand this. I tell myself. *I can't stand this and I can't do a damn thing about it either.*

It must be about eleven or twelve o'clock. It's not even my shift on guard and I'm still awake. I'm just lying here on the wet ground, drawn up like a soaked stray dog, trying to avoid any movement that might result in another cold sting. I can think only of the water draining through my matted hair, dripping over my eyelids, down the edges of my mouth, and of my saturated fatigues clinging uncomfortably to

Stars and Stripes and Shadows

my shivering flesh. I can do my job and listen for Charlie, but unless bagpipes and drums accompany his approach I'll not hear him. I can't even go somewhere else mentally. The elements bombarding my senses supersede all access to my consciousness.

"You're up," Beasley says to me, confirming that my midnight estimate was pretty close. He passes over my ruck frame with the attached radio and hands me the handset.

"The next sit-rep should be coming anytime. Have fun." Beasley's punctuating comment is just enough to bring me back to life a little. *There are still human beings out here who can turn the misery into sarcasm.*

N N N N

We all stand around Sergeant Taylor looking like olive drab penguins, our arms hanging obliquely down at an angle away from our slouching bodies so that the rain water runs down off our hands instead of down the inside of our shirts. The three of us on LP have re-joined the platoon, having just endured, what for me was the longest night of my life. Somewhere, between the end of my guard shift and the first hint of daylight, shear fatigue overcame everything else, ushering me gently into a shallow sleep. It may have latest a couple of hours or just a couple of minutes. It was long enough to take me to a warm place that I used to know. A friend was there, a black furry friend, my dog Barney. He was licking my face, leaving a wet residue as he tried to get my attention.

I don't know if it's Barney's image, or the little bit of sleep or just the realization that the night's over, but I feel surprisingly renewed as Taylor starts to fill us in. The rain has stopped and lighter skies appear through the canopy off to the south and west also elevating my spirits a little. A dry cigarette may be possible before too long.

"It looks like we'll be staying here a couple of days," the Sergeant says, scanning our faces for some response. The reaction from each of us is mixed. There's great relief that we'll be free from Mr. Ruck for a few days but there's also great disappointment that we're not being pulled out of here anytime soon. The veterans in the Company know that these humps usually last four, sometimes five days. This is day seven.

"How much longer we gonna be out here?" the usually muted

Tim Haslam

Danko asks, surprising all of us with his firm voice and understandable diction. The circumstances are severe enough to have worn away some of his quirky, disengaged facade.

"I don't know," answers Taylor honestly, without any command pretense. "I don't think the Captain knows either. The Division wants body count bad and, I guess our contribution the other day makes them think we can contribute more. Anyway, we'll be running daily patrols out from here for a while. After breakfast, I want you all to dig out these foxholes and expand the fields of fire. This is going to be home for awhile, let's get it squared away."

The veterans of Bravo Company have been on many missions like this, humping up and down the mountains of the Highlands, but few have lasted this long and most of their prior humping experiences were during the dry season when the going was a little easier. This one's different. The days and nights in the rain and the frustrating skirmishes with Charlie are starting to take a toll. The weariness has now spread through the entire Company, as has the discontented grumbling about the whole situation; the hump, the ruck, the Nam, the Army, the war...the shit. Our circumstance has even taken on a name—*misery hump*. For me, I derive some satisfaction from this. I'm a participant in something that will be remembered and relived; that will be spoken of in front of new replacements that are yet to be initiated. I'll be able to speak from experience now as a veteran. I was there on *misery-hump*! I experienced the misery! There's still however much more misery to come for all to share, to endure and to survive before anyone of us can tell or brag about it.

Although I have earned some bragging rights within the tribe, I'm still a long way from being able to understand much of what my comrades here think and feel. The others in my squad arrived in Vietnam at various times in the fall of 1967 and so they have six or seven months of experiences behind them. They are about half way through their one-year tours. They've learned what it's like out here and they've learned what it does to them. They've learned what it takes to get through each day and each night and they've learned how lucky they've been in this world where survival is as much a factor of luck as it is of cunning or training or skill. They all think about their remaining time and look

Stars and Stripes and Shadows

toward the fall of 1968 as though it were a far distant land across a vast sea of shit.

И И И И

"What the hell are you doin'?" Ernie Jefferson asks Elmer, interrupting the casual chit-chat session we're all having as we lounge around our campsite, enjoying having nothing to do on this so-far-dry afternoon. Elmer's been fiddling around with his mouth for the last several minutes until everyone in our little group has become distracted from the topic under discussion.

"Shee-it, it's my goddamn teeth. They never did fit right and they just keep get'n' worse," Elmer explains in his usual unperturbed way, referring to the nearly full set of dentures that he wears.

Elmer reminds me a little of Ray Bolger's scarecrow character in the Wizard of Oz movie. He's tall, thin, almost gangly and it's difficult to estimate his age. He's probably in his mid-twenties. However, with the natural narrowness of his face and the constant, subtle pursing of his lips adjusting to his dentures, coupled with the influences of the filth and fatigue, he could easily pass for forty. He seems to take everything pretty much in stride, never complaining as an individual but always willing to join the chorus railing against all the conspiracies and conspirators that are out to get us.

"Where'd you get those teeth?" Doc Charlebois inquires of Elmer, pulling himself into a more upright posture as though some scheme has just entered his mind.

"Fort Rucker, Alabama. They're genuine Army issue. I got 'em when I was still in boot camp."

"So you've had them for over a year now?" asks Doc, looking for confirmation from Elmer.

"Yea, that's about right, just over a year now."

"You know you can get new ones," Doc tells Elmer, still apparently holding back the real point of his inquiries.

"Even if I could, I doubt they'd be any better'n these. This is Nam. Things like false teeth probably come over like everything else, pallet loads of 'em, one size fits all." Elmer presses his thumb firmly up against his upper plate and laughs at the image he's just created for all of us.

"He's right," says a laughing Mike Beasley. "They'd be just like

143

Tim Haslam

fuckin fatigues. If the Army finds out that a Bravo Company grunt needs replacement false teeth, next thing you know we'll get a Huey load of 'em dropped on us out here instead of something we really need."

"Like underwear," I break in, reminded that I'm approaching the two-month anniversary of my relationship with this particular pair of skivvies.

"We'll all have to hump 'em around with us to keep Charlie from get'n 'em," resumes Mike.

"Bullshit, man," interjects Steve Fernandez from Sergeant Steven's squad, who's been part of our focus group, "a rucksack full of dentures would be worth a fortune here. You ever see the teeth on the gooks? Those that still have any, have teeth that are all black from chewing betel nut. They'd love to get their gums around some good solid American made teeth. If we had 'em, we'd make a fortune."

"*That's* what makes their teeth all black?" I ask, having seen a few such mouthfuls on some of the Vietnamese working at Camp Enari and on the road through Kontum.

"That's it," confirms Doc. "It's an ancient tradition…supposed to prevent cavities."

Doc should know. He seems to be the medic in charge of dental care for Bravo Company. The day before we left FB30 we were all required to brush our teeth in front of him using some fluoride solution that he gave us. The whole platoon was standing in a line brushing and brushing until we were frothing like a pack of rabid hounds, cursing at Doc for the brackish taste filling up our mouths.

"It doesn't matter whether they're any good or not, or even if they fit or not," Doc exclaims, capturing our full attention. "They can't fit you for false teeth out here in the boonies. You'd have to go back to base camp for at least a few days. It'd be a way to get out of the shit for awhile."

"Can you make something like that happen, Doc?" asks Elmer perking up at this surprise possibility.

"Yea, I think so. I have to send a report back to the Battalion medical officer whenever anybody reports some condition that I can't fix. I'll just say that your Army issue dentures are worn out and that you're unable to fully enjoy your C-rations like the rest of us."

Stars and Stripes and Shadows

"Shit Doc, I can't enjoy mine either," Bob Price says, beating the rest of us to this opportunity, "I seem to have this condition where I apparently still have working taste buds in my mouth. Maybe I'd better go along with Elmer and have that condition looked at."

"No fuckin' way! I can fix that with a swab of Merthiolate," Doc responds.

Everyone listening in on this dialogue chimes in with a description of their own unique condition, volunteering to accompany Elmer on his possible journey down the Yellow-brick-road, to the Dentist of Oz...out of the shit. Doc Charlebois parry's away each of these imaginative rationalizations with the skill and ease of Zorro disarming Sergeant Garcia. Whether by design or not, Doc Charlebois has also just rallied us all out of the weary doldrums of our plight. There is work to be done and a goal to focus on that doesn't involve Charlie or Mr. Ruck. *Elmer can get out of the shit to get new teeth.*

Ɲ Ɲ Ɲ Ɲ

"Watch out for the bullet that has your name on it," one of my fraternity brothers cautioned me sarcastically on my last day at home, stealing a phrase we'd all heard many times on TV and at the movies.

The bullet with my name on it, I think to myself, as I fidget with the handful of AK47 rounds in my hand. Although I'm not one prone to superstition, I can divert and amuse myself a little with the possibility here.

On the morning of day ten of misery-hump we discovered an entrance to one of Charlie's tunnel complexes as well as some gear and ammunition scattered around above ground, near one of the tunnel entrances. Someone must have been surprised by the sounds of Bravo Company approaching and di-di'd away in one big hurry, carelessly leaving behind souvenirs for their pursuers. It was my good fortune to find the half-dozen copper clad bullets lying in a little cluster a few feet from the hole that connected to the rest of the underground complex. This entrance hole was only about two feet in diameter, barely wide enough for an average sized American body to squeeze down into. It appeared to drop straight down about four feet and then connect to another shaft of similar diameter coming in from the northwest.

As I contemplate the value of my find, our leadership, all gathered

Tim Haslam

around the entrance to Charlie's lair, are trying to determine the best way to motivate a grunt of lesser rank to crawl down into this subterranean nightmare and have a look around. This is one of those times in my military career when I want everyone to take note of the fact that I'm nearly six-foot-three inches tall and definitely not a good match for this kind of work. There must be someone in Bravo Company of more compact construction who could, enthusiastically, be lowered down head first into this hole; someone who would particularly appreciate the adrenaline enhancing opportunity of crawling into this narrow, dark realm with just a flashlight and a .45 pistol; someone who would appreciate the opportunity to explore Charlie's architecture and workmanship, perhaps even his hospitality and, most of all, appreciate the opportunity to forever claim to be an experienced *tunnel-rat* telling everyone forevermore what it was like down there, in Charlie's warren, alone. Whoever steps up to it, will earn the bragging rights.

It turns out there are several men in Bravo Company of appropriate dimension and character. Three step forward, even before the call for volunteers from the officers goes out and one, Dale Rimmer from Five-Nine Platoon is quickly elected based on some apparent prior experience. One of the other volunteers, as a consolation prize will get to be dropped down behind Rimmer, to serve as a communication link.

Rimmer's orders are not to attempt to explore the full extent of the complex, but to try to determine which direction the main arteries appear to head and to see if there are any signs that might confirm how recently this place was occupied. He's given a compass to bolster his sense of direction as he worms his way through the claustrophobic ant-farm.

As Rimmer performs his terrier duties, the rest of the Bravo grunts search around the surrounding forest for other points of access into the complex while the officers continue to plot the best strategic reaction to our find. Captain Collins and Lieutenant Reese both seem to be spending a lot of time on their radios and, as none of their conversations are coming over the Company net to my handset, I know they must be conspiring with external entities. Whatever is being discussed and planned, we all know that it will involve a change in the afternoon's plans for the rest of us.

The solution apparently involves putting as much distance as pos-

Stars and Stripes and Shadows

sible between Charlie's tunnels and us before night sets in. We're now being driven hard toward some objective off to the southeast of the tunnel complex. This way is a ninety-degree shift from the northeasterly vector we were on this morning when we discovered Charlie's lair and involves climbing up and over several of the finger ridges that fan down across our path. The going is particularly brutal, alternating between up and down, with the weather too alternating between hot and humid, and rainy hot and humid. Everyone in Bravo Company is now worn down by *misery-hump* to where the fabric of our physical capability is so threadbare that each of us must draw upon some inner reserve of character or stubbornness or sense of duty to keep going. Each small step is a struggle under the oppressive weight of the rucksacks; over the slippery ground; through the clouds of mosquitoes queuing up to invade our filthy, sweaty flesh. Everyone's attitude is a reflection of the surroundings and circumstances. *Everyone's attitude is shit!*

It's finally over for the day. We can go no further in the fading twilight. We must dig in and set up camp quickly.

Sergeant Taylor along with all the NCOs is summoned to a pow-wow as soon as we drop our rucks. The rest of us start the nightly ritual of chopping and digging with little zeal for the thoroughness of our work or even for the consequences of our minimalist efforts should Charlie feel obliged to reciprocate our house call tonight.

"Listen up," comes Taylor's familiar preamble, bringing a halt to the halfhearted flailings of machetes and shovels.

"Listen up. Here's the deal for tonight. Ranger's agreed to arc-light the complex we found today. We'll be on full alert until after the attack, which should be about midnight. So, dig these holes deep, we're less than a klick and a half from ground zero. Any questions?"

I've learned by now that *Ranger* is the code name for the Battalion Commander and that *arc-light* is the term used to describe a B52 air strike. Full alert means that nobody sleeps until after the bombs have been dropped. If the pilots or bombardiers make a miscalculation it's apparently better for us to be awake to experience the side effects.

Dinner conversation is all about B-52's and thousand pound bombs and what they do and what a safe distance from them is. There are varying opinions as to how many planes comprise an "arc-light" and how many bombs each plane carries and what altitude they drop the

Tim Haslam

bombs from. There is debate over how deep the bombs burrow into the ground before exploding and what diameter tree trunks can be severed and how much such an attack costs in dollars. The whole process and consequence is explored on and on before the conversation turns to the fact that no one will be allowed to sleep until after midnight. The good news is that the guard shifts for the rest of the night will be shorter. The bad news is that no one can expect to get more than two or three hours of sleep this night. Two or three hours of sleep will do little to rejuvenate our spent bodies and even less at mending our ragged spirits.

Each of us struggles through the long hours leading up to midnight in similar fashion. Mental fatigue brings conversations to an end around nine o'clock. Feeble attempts to administer to our various wounds, pains and itches occupies some time, as does minimal efforts at gear and weapons maintenance. Anything and everything we attempt to do seems to require effort and energy we don't have and so, mostly we just sit silently in the pitch-blackness, chain-smoking our way through the tedious vigil, waiting for the bombs to rain down from the sky on to our neighbors.

We can't hear the Stratofortresses approach; they fly too high. The crews of the great death birds are probably miles away by the time their cargo trumpets its entrance into our space. The first sounds from the invading half-ton bombs is a terrifying roar as they bore down at ever increasing velocity through the humid air above the highlands. So many of the massive bombs are falling so closely together that they combine to disrupt the atmosphere they penetrate, reverberating the air pressure for miles around, awakening or alerting every living thing with their horrific sound. The weary grunts of Bravo Company are the only creatures in this forest that understand the implications of the awful noise; the only creature's confidant that the noise is not after them. We are the creatures who can summon the noise and the monster that will momentarily follow. The noise and the monster serve us.

Our attentions have been drawn to the sounds of the falling bombs for just a few seconds before the ground starts shuddering as the rapid sequence of explosions tears into the mud, soil and rock that had been protecting and hiding Charlie. For several more seconds the rumbling blasts continue as Charlie's complex is clawed out of the ground and hurled viciously into the surrounding jungle by the indiscriminate

Stars and Stripes and Shadows

bombs. The light flashes preceding the blast sounds seem farther off than the rapport would suggest. The thunder and feel of the bomb's collisions and explosions seem very near to the stunned grunts being shaken out of their weariness. For a brief moment I think of Charlie as a human being. I think for another moment how glad I am that Charlie doesn't have B52s.

⚡ ⚡ ⚡ ⚡

By 7:00 a.m. on the twelfth day of *misery-hump* we've all had breakfast, coffee and cigarettes and are nodding off as a reaction to our sleep deprivation coupled with our boredom. Six-Two and Bob Taylor intrude on our convalescing after just a few minutes with orders to start packing up again. We need to go back and check out the bombed area to assess the damage. No one moves in reaction to the announcement. *We should give Lieutenant Falck and Sergeant Taylor a moment to come to their senses, or to fess up to their joke. They can't be serious.*

"I don't like it any better than you," Lieutenant Falck acknowledges, his posture and facial expression fully consistent with his words and with the way we all truly feel.

"Let's go," is all Taylor can add, also too weary to elaborate on the situation.

Our worn out but resigned expressions and silent reactions serve as acknowledgement to our superiors that we're coming, but before any of us can actually drag ourselves to our feet the crack of a gunshot shocks us into alertness and action.

"What the fuck?" Beasley blurts out, as we all scramble for our weapons, "that was an M16 and close too."

We all recognize the sound of the M16 and we all can tell that the shot came from somewhere inside our perimeter. Excited voices can be heard from across the camp and several people seem to be converging around something not clearly visible to us through the vegetation. No one however seems to be reacting as though there was any threat or danger. My radio offers no information as to the source or target or purpose of the shot.

"Everybody stay put. I'll go check it out," says Lieutenant Falck heading off in the direction of the excitement, boosted by the same kind of adrenaline jolt we all feel.

Tim Haslam

"Porter! A guy named Porter in Six-Zero shot himself in the foot," Falck tells us upon his return a few minutes later.

"Porter? Ray Porter?" asks Ernie Jefferson, obviously familiar with the name, his face tightening into an expression of deeper concern than the rest of us probably register. Although, we all know who he is, Ray Porter turns out to be a friend of Jefferson's. "What happened? How bad is he hurt? What the fuck happened? What..."

"He says it was an accident. That's all he's saying. Nobody else seemed to be near him when it happened. Nobody else knows anything for sure. The right side of his right foot has a pretty good-sized chunk taken out of it. Doc Hayes seems to think the damage can all be repaired though. It looks like..."

"Whadda ya mean nobody knows *for sure*? Does somebody think he shot himself on purpose?" Ernie's questions betray a transition in his thinking. A transition from simple concern over the well being of a fellow grunt who's been injured to a more complex concern for a black brother who may now be under suspicion from elements within the establishment. The rest of us listening to the exchange are feeling the building tension in Ernie's reaction. The effects of *misery-hump* and all its allied shit are now exposing sensitivities and vulnerabilities that we can normally repress or moderate.

"Nobody's saying anything, Ernie," replies the obviously exhausted Lieutenant.

"Nobody's say'n anything, nobody's think'n anything," interrupts Sergeant Stevens. "Except that maybe we're all pretty tired and nobody's think'n too right about what they're doin' or what somebody else might be doin'. *It don't mean nothin'!*"

Sergeant Stevens' language has also undertaken a subtle shift in character. Up to this moment, every word I've heard from Steve, the respected black squad leader, would have passed muster in any English grammar class. He's not one prone to colloquialisms, vernacular or street jive. Now, however his message rides to us on the easy shortcuts of language evolved back on the block. It's not because he's too tired to uphold the rigors of subject, predicate and pronunciation. It's because he has the energy and natural inclination to care about connecting with his audience on a more human wavelength, the wavelength of the regu-

Stars and Stripes and Shadows

lar guy grunt, and perhaps, specifically of the regular guy black grunt.

It don't mean nothin' is a phrase used constantly by the grunts. It's a common form of punctuation in the patois of the Nam. It's a common response to someone's expressions of irritation, frustration or attitude. Few grunts, in country more than a week or two are able to resist the ready flow of this expression from their adapting tongues, along with the equally popular, *off-the-wall-shit.* These clichéd utterances are heard throughout the grunt community, but the *it-don't-mean-nothin'* idiom has special meaning for the black soldiers out here. For them, it's an acknowledgment of a deeper recognition, a declaration of liberation and independence, an affirmation that they are who they are and that's enough no matter what they're up against. The black grunts are more intimately familiar with barriers and obstacles, with bigotry and discrimination, with consolations and condescension than most of their white comrades here, and so they have, between them, a shared mantle of words, clichéd phrases and gestures that the rest of us pick up on and mimic, albeit at a more shallow level.

✍ ✍ ✍ ✍

The hump back to Charlie's former subterranean camp is arduous and yet, as we plod back over the difficult ground, each of us seems to be more contemplative than usual, distracted from the normal miseries by introspective self-assessments of our character. Every one of us suspects that Porter's wound was self-inflicted. The most compelling evidence in the indictment is our own feeling, our own sense that we must be approaching the threshold of our individual rational control. Did Porter unwittingly or subconsciously work out a solution or, did he knowingly calculate the consequences of a well-aimed gunshot against the consequences of taking one more step back into the shit under the bullying burdens ravishing the Bravo Company grunts? Right now he's on his way to a clean bed at the 71st Evac Hospital. Right now we're on our way to a place where unseen planeloads of thousand pound bombs have just obliterated a thousand life forms. Right now we're all way into the shit.

There's nothing familiar about the shattered landscape we've returned to and are now probing around in. The devastation seems utterly thorough. The bombs have slammed into this section of forest like a

Tim Haslam

tornado through a Kansas trailer park. Only a few of the very largest trees still stand within the cratered swath that extends for hundreds of meters. Direct sunlight washes down onto ground denied its luminescence for the last thousand years and the red soil that now covers everything, having been returned violently to the top layer, once again starts settling into its stratification cycle. The vegetation from all levels of the canopy lies compressed into the splintered rubble that surrounds the great craters.

The monstrous force that transformed this section of forest did so quickly and completely. There are no residual fires or smoking embers or anguished cries from wounded creatures; or people; or gooks. There is in fact a pervasive stillness and silence. The rattling, rustling sounds of gear and the unusually muted tones of our voices fill this newly opened auditorium with surprising clarity and volume. The feeling is somewhat surreal as we search about for bits or scraps of evidence that would confirm the success of this action; this investment; this show of strength. The ants seem to be the only survivors, searching along with us for bits and scraps meaningful to them and necessary for their crude survival.

Our platoon is scouring our way up to the farthest end of the bomb's path. The devastation starts, or ends (*there's no way for us to tell*) on a slope rising to the northeast of the line of craters. The end forms somewhat of an amphitheater with the huge surviving trees towering over and surrounding the wounded section of forest. As we enter the bowl, the sunlight is at such an angle as to bathe the ancient trees at the very far end in crisp clear rays of morning sun, making them appear like venerable wards watching over the amphitheater below them that is rapidly filling up with little foreign invaders. I'm struck for a moment by the dissonance of this scene. There is a subtle beauty to this dramatic rendering of such a terrible event. Were it not for the contrary reality of this scene, there is an impression of some natural old cathedral; damaged, defaced, but still standing; a scene reminiscent of Dresden or London during the Second World War.

"There's still an entrance intact over here!" Doc Charlebois yells out, redirecting everyone in the platoon to his position. He's standing over a nearly round hole in a patch of unbroken ground between two of the craters. The hole goes straight down into darkness.

Stars and Stripes and Shadows

"That's no tunnel or entrance," advises Sergeant Stevens with a measure of excitement in his voice. "That's a dud. There's a thousand pound bomb down there that didn't go off. I'd stay back away from there if I were you."

Each of us steps back quickly fully aware of how far we'd really have to go to survive if the dud came to life.

The Captain, paying little attention to what the rest of us are doing, is carefully surveying the area, trying to match any surrounding terrain features that seem familiar from our prior visit and perspective with those indicated on his map. This is the place he concludes. The bombs were dead on target but the force of the bombs was also so violent as to have shredded or buried or simply disintegrated every trace of Charlie, his complex and his supplies. We find nothing.

N N N N

After less than an hour of combing through the rubble, we reform and once again return to the routine of *misery-hump*. Our feelings are mixed as we plod off, away from the bombed area. There is recognition that if Charlie was anywhere around here last night he probably never saw the light of this day, but there is also the familiar sense of frustration that we can't confirm the effectiveness of our tactics and our strength. Charlie's snipers can see us go down as they pick us off with their little rifles, confirming their tactics and validating their strategy. We can only assume that we're wearing him and his cause down with our planeloads of well-directed ordinance.

Another grinding hour passes as we settle back in under the ruck when a surprise announcement comes over the radio from Five-Nine-Charlie, working with today's point squad.

"Six-Charlie this is Five-Nine-Charlie," begins the seemingly routine communication. "Two gooks just walked out of the jungle in front of us and surrendered. Over."

The word spreads quickly, initiating an excited response from everyone and a series of directives over the radio from Captain Collins.

"Form up a perimeter and keep a sharp eye out. Bring 'em back down here to us. Don't hurt 'em."

Six-Two platoon is in the center file right behind the Company Headquarters people and so we all get a clear view of the two prisoners

Tim Haslam

being delivered to the Captain. They're both dressed alike, in seemingly fresh uniforms, with black sneakers on their feet, their heads covered by pith helmets with red stars on the front. Both have their hands raised high above their heads and one has a small piece of orange paper in his left hand. Their escorts from Five-Nine Platoon are in possession of two AK47's obviously confiscated from them.

The two men are of similar stature; small, maybe five feet four or five inches tall and each seems to be pretty young, maybe eighteen or nineteen. The one in the lead, the one waving the orange paper, keeps repeating, "Chieu-Hoi, Chieu-Hoi," at the same time trying to force his terrified face into a smile. The other echoes the *Chieu-Hois* with much less vigor, unable to even attempt any facial expression that might disguise his fear. Each Bravo Company grunt they pass fixates on them, studying them, sizing them up. Each grunt wears a similar mask of curiosity carried upon an exaggerated confident posture. These two don't look very threatening on the surface. A look at their AK47s however modifies that impression. In some ways, they look just like us. They wear the same veneer of sweat and dust over a facial expression confirming their daily struggles with the jungles. They don't want to be here either.

Captain Collins is on the radio with higher headquarters when the two prisoners are delivered. They've already been thoroughly searched by the men of Five-Nine and, without their weapons, they seem pretty harmless. Sergeant Madison directs them with hand motions to sit down as the Captain places his hand over the radio handset and suggests to no one in particular that the prisoners should be given water. Doc Davis offers a canteen to them. Someone else hands them each a bar of Hershey's Tropical Chocolate. Cigarettes followed by an active Zippo, come from still another host. They're being treated pretty well. Perhaps they're even being overwhelmed by the hospitality. They're not sure what to do with the chocolate and neither of them seems to want to join the two dozen grunts gathered around smoking feverishly. Each however takes the canteen without hesitation but limits their intake to just a few swallows.

The little orange piece of paper has fallen to the ground in front of them for all of us to see. We've seen them before. Occasionally, along the route of our humps we've come across such papers littering the jun-

Stars and Stripes and Shadows

gle. They're propaganda messages air dropped by the Army's Psy-Ops teams. This particular one has a picture of a B52 raining down bombs, surrounded by some narrative description in Vietnamese describing a better alternative, surrender—*Chieu-Hoi*. Actually, Chieu-Hoi means *open-arms*. It means throw down your weapons and come over to our side. You will be welcomed with open-arms.

So far, the grunts of Bravo Company are fulfilling the promise of Chieu-Hoi. The two frightened visitors are being treated with cordial hospitality under the watchful eye of Captain Collins and Sergeant Madison. Within half an hour they've relaxed enough to start making eye contact with some of the American grunts surrounding them. They're studying us now with the same sort of curiosity that we have about them. Those of us not involved in the studying are busy clearing an LZ or watching the surrounding jungle for possible rescuers or potential assassins of our prisoners. Another half hour of quiet study passes before everyone's concentration is interrupted by the sound of an approaching helicopter. For them, the sound of the Huey resurrects the full measure of fear and uncertainty associated with their plight.

The Captain, Lieutenant Reese and Lieutenant Falck all head off in the direction of the LZ as the chopper settles in. Four men in clean fatigues jump out of the Huey and crouch their way toward the three officers approaching from out of the jungle. The two groups collect together and spend several minutes in discussion before the Captain leads them back towards the prisoners. Two of the men are U.S. Army officers, First Lieutenants, armed only with holstered pistols, followed closely by a man of obvious lesser rank clutching an M16 by its carrying handle. The forth man is Vietnamese, dressed in an ARVN uniform adorned with patches and insignia that mean nothing to me, but seem to be the trappings of an officer. His uniform is also conspicuously clean, starched and tightly pegged, accentuating his small, wiry frame. He too is armed only with a pistol.

Captain Collins and his entourage fan out in an almost choreographed sort of way as they approach the group gathered around the prisoners. The Captain tells Sergeant Madison to clear away most of the closer-in gawkers. Madison immediately fulfills his responsibilities like a beat cop shoo-ing away onlookers from a crime scene, unveiling the two captives for inspection by the visitors in the clean, starched

155

Tim Haslam

uniforms. One of the Lieutenants walks confidently forward until he's standing right in front of the two men, whose posture and expressions have returned to terrified. The Lieutenant, obviously aware of the prisoner's reaction, squats down in front of them, removing his helmet, carefully arranging his own expression into a friendly smile as he rakes his fingers back through his hair.

"Tell 'em they'll be OK. Tell 'em they'll not be harmed and ask them if there is anything they need," he says to the Vietnamese translator in the well-tailored uniform, all the while maintaining his compassionate expression and eye contact while stooped down at the level of the vanquished men.

The ARVN officer remains standing a few feet off to the left of the squatting American officer, his posture and expression more a reflection of someone asserting dominance than soliciting trust. There is no attempt to bring a smile to this chiseled, businesslike face. Everything about the ARVN in fact suggests that smiles rarely serve his purposes or are appropriate within his world. He's been assigned to help the Americans, but it's pretty clear from his demeanor that we should all be there to help him and his cause on his terms. He will however, do his duty, whether it comes naturally or not and so he offers up the Lieutenant's sentiments using the closest approximations he can retrieve from the Vietnamese lexicon.

To my ear, the spoken Vietnamese language sounds clipped and impatient, characterized by runs of short regressive syllables requiring more work by the tongue against the roof of the mouth than English. Although I don't understand a word of what the translator says, it's hard for me to connect the abrasive, high-pitched utterances emanating from this steely-eyed man with the pacifying suggestions tendered by the American officer. The captives however attend to each phoneme with proper respect and interest. At the conclusion of the translation, the two young NVA soldiers glance briefly at one another, each then answering tersely, seeming to accept the explanation. Their only needs are apparently implied in the Chieu-Hoi promise; safety, good treatment, and a new place within the southern capitalist society, far away from these mountains and the *whispering death from the sky*. The starched ARVN relays this back to the stooped down Lieutenant and everyone else within earshot in perfect, Americanized, Army variety English.

Stars and Stripes and Shadows

Having established this level of rapport the Lieutenant presses forth diplomatically with his interrogation and requests the translator to, "ask them how long they've been here." The Lieutenant can see, as we all can that they're in good physical shape and dressed in new uniforms. He has the same suspicion as the rest of us—they're new recruits.

This time there is considerably more dialogue back and forth between the translator and the two men. Their answers must have gone beyond the minimum expectation and the ARVN officer apparently seized the initiative on his own to further the exploration. The American officers wait patiently, aware that whatever is being exchanged here is important, also acknowledging that the ARVN has aptitudes for more than just interpreting. Several minutes of this uninterrupted exchange go by. Periodically, I can hear one party or another refer to Chieu-Hoi and on more than one occasion the bolder of the two prisoners' points to the B52 illustration while shaking his head followed by glances up toward his grunt captors. *"No! No!"*

Both of the prisoners seem to respond to the ARVN without hesitation. As the dialogue continues to develop, the one previously in possession of the leaflet takes on the role of primary spokesman. His narrative is so lengthy that the South Vietnamese officer finally has to hold up his hand to stop the flow of information and relay it to the English speaking audience intently awaiting a translation.

As we all suspected the two men have not been down here long. They came down from the North just over a week ago to reinforce the 66th NVA Regiment that operates within these parts. This regiment is believed to have suffered considerable loss during the Tet Offensive. Apparently, they, like many other young men were hurried through their military training, receiving only limited political indoctrination, mostly proffered during their weeks spent in route down the Ho-Chi-Minh trail. The hardened, more dedicated members of the veteran 66th are scattered all around in small units and so these two have only had minimal contact with their more committed comrades.

It turns out that their first real assignment was to hump supplies back to the tunnel complex that Bravo Company stumbled upon yesterday. They had nearly returned to the complex last night when the bombs fell. A few minutes more and they would have been annihilated along with everything else within the arc-light zone. As it was, they

Tim Haslam

were just far enough away to survive, but close enough so as to be emotionally pummeled by the thunderous explosions and violent reactions of the rupturing ground. Nothing in their young lives up to that point, including the most impassioned and patriotic appeals could prepare them for the utter terror of last nights encounter with the power of the Americans. They want no part of any effort that might place them in such a circumstance again. Taking the fight to American grunts with rifles is one thing. Being vaporized by an unseen monster from the sky is something else entirely.

All of the officers listening to the steady relay of information from the interpreter react in similar fashion. They're all stunned over our good fortune. We've hit the jackpot with these two. Once back at Division Intelligence, these two simple, frightened, young soldiers are likely to provide a wealth of information. Right now, there's only one more piece of information required by Captain Collins and the tired grunts within his command.

"Ask them how many men were in that complex," Collins instructs the translator.

The ARVN checks first with a glance down to his American partner and then, upon receiving a simple nod in return poses the question. The Vietnamese translation seems to be even more direct then the Captain's English version. The few syllables jabbed out by the ARVN are followed by an uncomfortable pause, then a short, quiet exchange between the two captives and finally a summary by the spokesman.

They were only there a few days and were kept busy. They were never shown much beyond the place they ate and slept and some of the areas where they put new supplies coming in. Men were coming and going all the time in small groups, mostly at night. It was hard to know how many men were there at one time; maybe twenty or thirty.

"What about the other men they were with last night?" adds the Captain. "What happened to them? Where are they?"

The ARVN passes on the questions without seeking any approval while shifting his posture into a slightly less rigid form, inadvertently resting his right hand on the butt of his holstered pistol. The prisoners each react with similar concern, attending more to their interrogator's hand than to his question. Their uncertain eyes climb back up into contact with the ARVNs downward gaze and then slowly scan around to the other faces of their captors, then to one another. They each must think there's a right answer to this question.

As I take all this in, I begin to feel sorry for these two people. They're no longer soldiers. Perhaps they never really were, or perhaps they've shamefully disqualified themselves as NVA soldiers. Their whole identity and purpose in life is now determined and regulated by us. They can decide nothing. They can control nothing. They can only answer our questions and await the consequences. Their South Vietnamese cousin may shoot them regardless of their answer, either of his own volition or at the insistence of the Americans now in control of their destiny. It is disturbing to me to realize that right now, these two men are probably thinking that my friends and I are about to kill them. Even if they're more trusting than that, they must realize that their future has been relegated to the whims of this war. They must realize that they will never go home again. The whole interaction with these two people, these two sad, vanquished enemies, taking place in this hostile, damp, dark place weighs heavily on me. Home seems further away than ever now. *Perhaps what they must realize is true for us all.*

Once again, a helicopter full of people noisily shrinks off into the open sky away from me. As it was with Jeter and his freedom bird and Adamson and Grieve, and once again with Boothe and their dust-off rescues, I watch helplessly as two more pieces are removed from the board. The sky seems to be the only thing that connects me to the rest of the world. Everything below the sky is part of this other primitive, dangerous world, where we, the remaining pieces, must go back to the work of repositioning ourselves on the board. The weary pawns and knights of Bravo Company once again reset for the next gambit.

"We'll dig in here for tonight," the Captain directs the other officers still collected around the site of the recent interrogation. There is apparently much digesting to do of the information recently handed over to us by the two NVA visitors. The officers here and back at higher headquarters need to re-think the situation and the next best move and so the rest of us will get a break from humpin' for the rest of the day.

We're rousted early again on the thirteenth day of *misery-hump*,

Tim Haslam

hurried out of our hooches and into our rucks. We're going back once again to the bombed out area. This time each platoon is going to take a separate route back. The orders are to move quickly and quietly along a broadened front in hopes of surprising any remnants of the 66th that might be surveying sites for a new home. The other possibility is that we'll sneak up on them attempting to salvage something from the wreckage of their old complex. Whatever the hopes are, they're under the sole proprietorship of the officers. For the rest of us, our hope is to be surprised with the word that we're getting out of here. A slender hope even exists that the whole thing may be over soon, that the rumored peace talks may succeed. For me, my hope is that this is as bad as it's going to get. Yet, at the same time I cling to this hope, something else is beginning to happen to me. There is a subtle urge building within me, an urge to raise up my M16, to look down the sights at a *gook*…to pull the trigger.

> *What a day for a daydream*
> *What a day for a daydream'n boy*
> *Now I'm lost in a daydream*
> *Dream-n 'bout my bundle-of-joy*
>
> *And even if time ain't really on my side*
> *It's one of those days for take'n a walk outside*
> *I'm blowin' the day to take a walk in the sun*
> *And fall on my face on somebody's new mowed lawn*

I re-read the latest letters from Rosemary and Mom and Dad at each rest break. The images stay with me long enough to divert my attention for the first few hundred meters after the breaks. I guess I've been overly influenced by the movies growing up, as the images of home are always accompanied by the background lyrics of some song. I can daydream about all the times I had with my *bundle-of-joy*. I can daydream of all the Saturday mornings reluctantly pushing the lawn mower around our yard. *I wish it were one of those days!*

The hump back over this now familiar ground yields nothing. Our fights are limited to the usual skirmishes with mosquitoes, leeches, mud and thorn, all fought under the whips and scorns of heat and humidity and, of course Mr. Ruck. Our supplies are once again low. The most frugal of us have C-rations enough for one more day and we are nearly out of water. We've been filling our canteens with the rain water draining down from the forest vegetation, but there's been no rain for the last few days. Worst of all, we're down to the unpopular cigarette brands in the little four packs that come with our C-rations. We do have plenty of ammo though, and frags and Claymores. We have pounds and pounds of these.

> *All the leaves are brown*
> *And the sky is grey*
> *I've been for a walk*
> *On a winter's day*
> *I'd be safe and warm*
> *If I was in L.A.*
>
> *California dreaming*
> *On such a winter's day*

I hope this doesn't explode! I think to myself as I twist the tip of my knife into the copper and steal amalgam of the bullet casing.

We've set up camp by noon, at one end of the cratered zone and are free to do whatever we want for the rest of the day, whatever we want within the constraints of this patch of jungle, whatever ever we want within the limits of our resources, whatever we want within the residue of our energy. There's not much *whatever* available and so each of us sits quietly cleaning something, re-reading something, fidgeting with something, occasionally raising up something as a topic for discussion. For me, the *whatever* is the bullet with my name on it, or the bullet about to have my name on it.

It takes me the better part of half an hour to twist my way through the metal on one side of the casing. The hole allows me to pour out the black powder inside, reducing my anxiety over a friction-generated explosion. Another twenty minutes of more rigorous twisting opens another hole on the opposite side of the cylinder. I'm stalled for a minute at the next step, unclear on the correct protocol for applying

Tim Haslam

my name; Tim Haslam or Haslam, Tim? Or does it need to be my full name; Timothy Lee Haslam? I solicit opinions from the rest of the squad, receiving back a range of responses from, "Any of those is OK," to, "Just use your Army serial number," to, "It don't mean nothin.'" I conclude that Tim Haslam will suffice and so, carefully carve that into the casing. The hole is just big enough for me to thread a shoestring through, which I also run through the hole in my P38 can opener and then tie it around my neck. I'm now in possession of the bullet with my name on it. I've rendered it harmless. Now, if I can, in similar fashion, find the pieces of grenade, rocket and mortar shrapnel with my name on them, or the bayonet tip, or the shard from an anti-personnel mine reserved for me I will be invincible. There may however be pieces of a stray thousand pound bomb or 105mm howitzer round or a Cobra rocket with my name on them too. There are too many perils; too many charms to be collected. The AK47 round will have to do. It'll be lucky. I'll be protected.

⚡ ⚡ ⚡ ⚡

The morning of the fourteenth day of misery-hump finds the creatures of the forest going about their usual business. The living vegetation is busy photosynthesizing the water and nutrients drawn up from their intertwined root systems at a furious pace, turbocharged by the intense heat and energy provided by the searing tropical sun. As new plant mass is generated, the less vigorous segments are sloughed off and fall to the ground, joining a thousand years of their ancestors in an afterlife where there is no longer any differentiation between family or species or phyla. The new bits arrive and immediately begin composting. It will not take long for the first scouting representatives of the thousand species of insects and micro-organisms that dwell down here to discover the additions to the menu. Sooner or later, part or all of each bit will match the appetites of something struggling for its own survival down here. The bits will satisfy the appetites of some small life form, sustaining it until some other, larger life form, with appetites for different kinds of proteins consumes it. The process is continuous up the hierarchy of the forest. Things that crawl get consumed by things that slither or walk, they in turn get consumed by things that run and grab and tear, who ultimately get consumed by things that think.

Stars and Stripes and Shadows

The grunts of Bravo Company are thinking about how bored we are this morning, about all our little pains and discomforts, about our adversaries here at the top of the food chain; Charlie, leeches and mosquitoes.

I'm thinking how shitty this all is.

At least I'm thinking about the shit and boredom while sitting quietly in the shade, on a day when the heat is particularly intense and the oppressive humidity punishes every movement. At least I'm thinking about the shit separated from the clawing strains of a rucksack and the determined thorns of the jungle. At least I have warm water to drink and a dry cigarette to smoke. At least I have friends to share the experience with.

It's mid-morning when Six-two and Sergeant Taylor quietly appear at the edge of our little grunt group, raising the suspicions of everyone as they move in among us, plopping down without any seeming purpose other than to join in on the fidgeting and banter. Their presence has to be more directed than that. It always is, and so we all perk up, focusing our attention on them. *Now what are we going to have to do? What bad news do they have for us that would require penetration of our ranks in such a benign way?*

"The prisoners have proven to be pretty useful," Lieutenant Falck offers up to the group, as casually as any topic being thrown out for furtherance. A long pause follows during which, each of us considers advancing the topic in some way but don't because we suspect there's more to come from our leader.

"It seems the Division's been able to use the prisoner's estimates of gook numbers in the complex," he says slowly, then pauses, removes his helmet, swabs at the sweat on his forehead with his shirtsleeve and then looks nonchalantly around to confirm that each of us is growing more anxious about where this is all going. The confirmation comes easily via our expressions, posture and the number of cigarettes being lit.

"It seems the Division can estimate the effectiveness of the arclight the other night based on the number of gooks thought to be in the complex and our input that the destruction appears to be pretty complete." Another pause…another swab…another glance around, this time he gets a bite.

"Sir, with all due respect, is there a point to this?" asks Bennis impatiently.

163

Tim Haslam

"The point, Specialist Bennis, is this...body count! Those B52s dropped their bombs where *we* told them, *where Bravo Company told them*? The body count therefore belongs to us, just as if we'd pulled the triggers of our own rifles on them. We were sent out here for body count and now, along with the three gooks that the helicopters got the other day, also at our direction, we have tallied up thirty kills."

The Lieutenant once again pauses, swabs, glances and pauses again.

"So sir, does this mean that we should all carve thirty notches into the stocks of our M16s or what?" Bennis pushes back, just as Falck had hoped.

"Well no, but you're certainly entitled to do that," the Lieutenant responds, apparently in no hurry to get to the real point.

"Sergeant Taylor, perhaps you'd like to explain to these men what happens next."

"Yes sir. We're getting the hell out of here...today!"

"No shit?"

"No shit!"

"Right on!"

"Fuckin-A!"

"About goddamn time!"

"Where?"

"We're going to guard a bridge over the Dak Poko for awhile," says Falck, gradually slipping back into officer-ness but still savoring the change in attitude brought about by the announcement and his preceding dramatic tease. "There's a battery of big guns there to be protected, which also means that there'll be three hots a day at their mess tents."

It's not Dak To or Pleiku, but it means an end to misery-hump, it means real food, maybe even cold drinks, maybe even a chance to bathe. The announcement is therefore cause for much excitement and celebration as we prepare ourselves to move away from misery-hump and on to the next phase of our lives in the shit.

N N N N

There's a different feeling this time as the Huey pulls me up out of the shadowy green mass. On my prior rides in and out of the forest, I was a visitor, a stranger intruding where I didn't belong, where I was

Stars and Stripes and Shadows

unequipped to participate fully with the creatures that live here. I look at my arms and hands for a brief moment as the helicopter churns upward. I look at the open sores, bites and cuts and then back down into the darkening shapes and shadows shrinking away from me. I try to understand how a body count of thirty can be claimed without seeing the bodies. That doesn't really matter though. I can think about that later. It's the jungle spreading out around me as far as I can see from the rising Huey that has wrested my focus and attention away from all other thoughts. I think about the things I now know to be down there, the things that did this to my flesh and the things that would have done more if the timing were different; shoot me, kill me or be killed by me. I think about the people who were alive when we landed out here fourteen days ago who's dead bodies now lie decaying somewhere below in this vast, rain soaked wilderness, forever entombed within the suffocating isolation of these mountains. These last two weeks have completed my initiation. I'm a reluctant journeyman in this world now. I can say I know the shit. I know I will come back into it. I know I will be a part of it again.

Chapter 6

Where's the beef?

The Dak Poko collects much of the water from the western watershed of this part of the Anemites. It meanders southward from its source somewhere around 15° north latitude, 108° east longitude, until it crosses under a bridge a few miles northeast of Dak To, along Route 512. From that point it flows south and westward until it passes into Cambodia and merges into the San River. The San continues on southwestwards until the much larger Mekong swallows it up. The water that began its journey high up on the peaks and ridges of the Central Highlands is blended there with water that has come all the way down through most of Southeast Asia from somewhere up in the Himalayas. The mighty Mekong pours down through central and southern Cambodia, through its capital city Phnom Penh where it turns abruptly to the east and enters South Vietnam. The southern end of South Vietnam, from Saigon southward is the delta, a land defined by the Mekong. The many mouths of the Mekong drain into the South China Sea exiting past the Vietnamese towns of Can Tho and My Tho. From the Route 512 Bridge the water must journey some 500 miles to reach the open sea. Ocean currents and tides will carry the water eastward another thousand miles into the Philippine Sea and on into the Pacific Ocean. Pacific currents and trade winds push the water another 9000 miles to the east until it eventually finds its way to the west coast of the United States. Along the Southern California coast, waves carry the water up and onto the sandy beaches. Beaches like Playa Del Rey where I spent most summer days in high school with my friends, riding our banged up old surfboards, or beaches like Santa Monica where the water caresses the pilings of the Pacific Ocean Park pier where I first learned the thrill of speed on the park's old wooden roller coaster.

The water and the air are the only things that connect me directly to the beaches and amusement parks and remembrances of home. But the air is by nature ethereal and capricious. It goes everywhere and nowhere. I can't count on the air in its hot humid guise to leave here and go home, but the water is purposeful and determined. The water wants to connect things, to find things, to carry things. I've always felt connected to water, and now I can feel connected through it. I can imagine the path all the way home along the route of the water.

The Dak Poko has been rising steadily since the beginning of the Monsoons, gradually climbing up its banks as more and more water seeks the path of least resistance on its way to Playa Del Rey. Just upstream from the bridge the southern flowing water encounters stiff opposition from a rocky section of ground and is caromed westward. The abrupt turn also slows the silty river flow considerably, forming a large pool that funnels out just under the Route 512 Bridge. On the southern edge of the pool, the rocky land rises up quickly to a plateau twenty or thirty feet above the water level. Up on this plateau the 4th Division has placed two of its largest pieces of artillery. A long barreled 175mm self-propelled howitzer along with one of it's stubbier but more powerful cousins, an 8-inch self-propelled gun. As these two giants are of significant value in controlling the surrounding terrain, they are well protected. Several rows of stacked concertina barbed wire, liberally populated with trip flares, encircle the outer perimeter of the plateau. A few yards in from the wire is a trench line, protected by a low sandbag wall. Within these protective circles, are a collection of sandbagged bunkers, tents and pits, each fulfilling some role in support of the fire-breathing masters they serve. The pits contain mortars that will react in kind to Charlie's mortars and rockets that can easily lob shells into the compound and onto the big guns and the big gun crews and onto the grunt pawns protecting these valuable pieces. The whole compound is vulnerable to rocket and mortar attack from the jungles sloping up into the mountains on the east side of the river. Our mortarmen have preset targets onto their weapons, so that anything Charlie hurls at us can be responded to quickly. One or two rounds are all Charlie can expect to send our way without swift retribution from us. But Charlie is patient.

Tim Haslam

One or two rounds are enough for now; one or two bursts of the slicing shrapnel among the Americans will serve a purpose.

Across the river from the big guns is a similar encampment, with three 155mm howitzers providing the muscle on the north side. So, the 4th has laid claim to the high ground overlooking both the north and south banks of the Dak Poko with Route 512 serving as the line of demarcation to the west. Charlie has jurisdiction over everything to the west, to the north and across the river up into the mountains to the east. We have the bridge, the plateaus on either bank and we have five really big guns. The road, running southeast down towards Dak To, is usually occupied by heavily armed American vehicles under cover of watchful Hueys and impatient Cobras, allowing us to feel like we control that part of Route 512.

About two hundred meters up the road from the bridge is the village of Dak Mot Kram. This long, slender shaped village has it's northeastern edge on the banks of the Dak Poko and gradually fades off southward toward the Dak Kal, a smaller tributary feeding into the Dak Poko about 600 meters below the bridge. Route 512 bisects Dak Mot Kram on its way westward to Laos about 15 miles away. The village is populated with Vietnamese, not Montagnards and the loyalty of the Dak Mot Kram residents is suspect. Trails running eastward from Laos and Cambodia course through and around the village and ultimately connect with the river and the road south. It's not hard to find Charlie's footprints along these trails and there are at least a dozen known NVA strong-points within a three mile radius of Dak Mot Kram. If the villagers here aren't supportive of the NVA out of philosophical conviction, they probably are supportive out of fear or intimidation. Their attitudes towards Americans are, at best, neutral, more likely passive-aggressive and possibly hostile. Most of the people that reside in these mountains however would probably just like to be left alone, without politics, without manifestos, without economic theories and without weapons. They probably don't want to have to take sides. They probably just want to carry on their daily routines, tending to their rice and banana crops and their cattle and pigs. The river provides them with fish and the forest provides them with betel nut. The road provides them with tobacco and Coca Cola. The spirits of the forest and of their ancestors provide the answers to their questions and their concerns. They need and want little else.

Stars and Stripes and Shadows

On the afternoon of our arrival here, the grunts of Bravo Company know nothing of the territory. We know nothing about the trails and the known NVA strongholds or the allegiances of the local villagers. We don't yet even know that there is a village just up the road. We know only that misery-hump is over. We know only that whatever is in store for us here should be an improvement. We can see that the complex is well established. We can see that the wire is already in place, as are the trip flares and Claymores; that the holes are already dug and that the sandbags are already filled. We can see the mess tents that provide hot meals for the "redlegs" (*the artillerymen*); the mess tents that will do the same for us in exchange for our services as sentinels, and defenders of the giant, tracked cannons that lord over the realm of their effective range. We can see that the "shitters" have walls made of ponchos to re-establish our modesty and we can see the water of the Dak Poko.

Six-One and Six-Two platoons have been deployed around the smaller 155mm guns on the north side of the river, and Five-Nine, Six-Zero and the Company Headquarters staff are placed up on the higher plateau on the opposite side. Each side has a mess tent and so there seems to be little advantage to one location over the other. The impact of the guns also balances out. The rapport of the smaller 155s is somewhat less of a shock than that of the two bigger guns, but they fire more often. All of these guns however make the sounds of the 105's and mortars back at FB30 seem like bashful children gently pawing through their first piano recitals. When the 175 or the 8-inch howitzer go off, the effect is literally stunning to everyone in the camp. The 155s make their best efforts to mimic the violent thunder of the bigger guns and lift the tracked under carriages abruptly with each firing. We don't yet know that all these beasts are predominantly nocturnal.

We're barely out of our rucks when a few members of Six-One find their way down to the river's edge, strip down completely and dive into the muddy water. Without any further encouragement or authorization, most of the rest of the north side contingent stampedes down into the water like a family of lemmings. Within moments, the south-siders take notice of what's happening and assault the river from the other side. Soon there are sixty or so naked grunts splashing about in the chest deep water of the big pool. An empty canteen is thrown into the group from somewhere and a spontaneous variation of water polo breaks out.

Tim Haslam

For the first time since any of us arrived in this country, we're doing something nearly forgotten; we're playing. Playing like the boys we so recently were back home. The water has reconnected us with who we once were. The water has cleansed off most of misery-hump's residue, separating us even from the uniforms that blend us into the shit around us. The water wants to carry away the facades of war and release the boys beneath.

Everyone participates equally in the game. The canteen is tossed about to and from the jumping and diving bodies; bodies of PFCs, Spec-4s, Buck Sergeants and Staff Sergeants; even a Lieutenant or two; everyone is equal here. The stripes and bars and affiliations with rank remain on the bank of the river conjoined with the sweat and blood stained fatigues cast off by the boys drawn into the comfort of the water. There are a few Vietnamese in dugout canoes just up river and more up on the bridge watching the spectacle of the grunt game as it unfolds without any apparent purpose or point. *GIs are beaucoup dinky dau they must surely be thinking.*

N N N N

Although mail found its way out to us a few times while on misery-hump, providing some brief measure of distraction and mental escape, the bags full of letters and packages awaiting us at the bridge can be savored slowly on our own terms. Here, we can take possession of the prized links back to the world, steal away to some private shady spot and immerse ourselves in the images and feelings abstracted from the ball point cursive or the carefully typed script. We can linger over the warm feeling brought on by each brief salutation and the casual references to names and places that were once so familiar and are now so distant. References to names and places and things that once were so comfortably taken for granted as natural extensions of a safe and happy life. These few private moments with the letters from home restore some of the luster of life and, along with the waters of the Dak Poko, help to scour away some of the wars influences, slowing, for the time being our transition away from safe and happy.

"Haslam, Haslam, Haslam…" Taylor repeats, once again tossing out to me several of Rosemary's orange envelopes along with others from Mom and Dad along with a package from my sister. There's enough here for me to read and re-read for at least an hour longer if the Army will leave me alone.

Rosemary starts each letter describing how much she misses me, how hard it is for her without me, how she can't wait for me to get home. She fills me in on everything she's been doing, which sounds pretty much the same in each letter; she goes to work, on the weekends she and her dad take in a movie or visit family friends. She seems to be seeing our friends less and less. There's something subtle underlying her narratives that suggest she's in transition too.

The main news from both Mom and Dad is that they've sold our house and bought a new, smaller home out in Woodland Hills. They've enclosed a few Polaroids of the new place. It has a nice view back over the San Fernando Valley from the small backyard. There's nothing there like the swimming pool that my friends and I spent our summer nights in, playing Marco Polo. There are none of the big walnut trees to climb around in that populated our yard, nor any walnuts to throw at each other across the street and no big front lawns to play football on. The inside is nice and new and modern. They will have an easier time maintaining this place. It will be a nice home for them.

✴ ✴ ✴ ✴

The three 155s on our side of the river take turns each night firing def-cons. About every twenty minutes, a shot is fired out at a pre-registered target just outside the perimeter of some grunt unit that's taking their turn humpin' around out in the boonies. The def-cons are supposed to catch Charlie off guard as he tries to sneak up on the grunts. The shells exploding out there may or may not keep Charlie off guard but they certainly keep many of the grunts out there awake and anxious as to the continuing accuracy of the calculated trajectories. They certainly will keep me awake this night. The gun that has the duty tonight is about twenty feet away from the hooch that Price, Elmer and I have set up and are now attempting to sleep in. For the three of us, the cycle starts with a brief episode of shallow sleep, interrupted by the booming shock of the outbound projectile and the jolting quake of the big machine's recoil. As the dust and cordite residue settle over us, we try to re-start the cycle. Our fatigued central nervous systems have become a battlefield of their own. The forces of serotonin and the

Tim Haslam

chemistry of sleep struggle to overcome the invasions of adrenaline and the chemistry of alertness that are allied with the concussions of the big guns. The sleep chemistry fulfills its settling-down function more slowly than the sharp jolts of adrenaline. The sleep chemistry just starts to win when the next round is fired.

Once again we're trapped. We're prisoners, not of our adversaries here, but of our own tactical imperatives. There's no place else for Bob and Elmer and I to go to find peace and quiet. There's no chance a friendly request to our neighbors will coax them into quieter pursuits the rest of the evening. We can't call the police and complain—the big guns are the police. We turn, as always when we're trapped, to cigarettes. Not however in surrender, to sit passively and smoke our way through the night's ordeal. This time we'll apply the full force of our ingenuity and resourcefulness, cleverly using cigarettes as the solution. Actually it's just the cigarette butts that are required in our defense. The cigarette filters just fit into our ears as plugs to block the shattering vibrations. *Now we can get some sleep. Let the guns fire.*

The guns continue to fire every twenty minutes through most of the night. The shock wave of each blast reaches our ears, passing through the fiber barrier of the cigarette butts without any diminishment. We've wasted two perfectly good cigarettes each and now we *will* surrender and sit passively smoking our way through the rest of the night. Sometime around four o'clock, the gun crew ends their shift and the three of us collapse into real sleep, the filter ends of our Marlboros still lodged within our ears.

The next three days here pass uneventfully in typical Army style. The mess units of the 15th of the 16th Artillery provide us with pancakes and ham and toast for breakfast, and coffee, real coffee, not the instant coffee that comes with our C-rations, but wonderful, thick, black, oily, sludgy stuff, choked with grounds and supercharged with enough caffeine to keep our morning bullshit sessions lively and impassioned. These mornings, under the cool overcast skies are a great relief and afford all of us an opportunity to get-our-shit-together; our military shit, our personal shit, even our emotional shit gets restored to a more serviceable level. By late morning however we can expect our first dose of *off-the-wall-shit*. The officers always seem to feel obliged to put us to

Stars and Stripes and Shadows

work, and so foxholes and trenches get dug deeper, more sandbags get filled and more barbed wire gets strung. The Huey's ferrying supplies out to us always seem to have spools of barbed wire or coils of concertina wire included in their manifest and since we have it, we must use it. I wish that some of the quartermaster's investments in barbed wire would be diverted to investments in underwear. There's still no sign of a replacement for the shorts I've had on since Pleiku.

There are usually some similar work assignments for the afternoon or some sort of training session that occupies a couple of hours of our time. Late in the afternoon each day however, we return to the river, to play a little and to get refreshed before dinner. The hot meals provided for lunch and dinner are a great improvement over the C-rations even though most of it still comes out of cans. The cooks in the mess unit really are pretty good at transforming the contents of the number 10 cans into decent meals.

So far, each evening's meal has been accompanied by milk. Enough milk is flown out each afternoon for anyone who wants it to have their very own quart carton. Because of the heat and anticipated time away from refrigeration the milk has been cut with coconut milk to keep it from spoiling on its way out to us. The only thing that's spoiled is the taste. For some of the lucky grunts at the front of the chow line there are even a few cartons of chocolate milk. The chocolate masks the coconut milk taste and these cartons can command a high return for anyone willing to part with theirs for a price.

N   N   N   N

On the morning of day three at the bridge camp, Sergeant Taylor sends Danko and me off to stand guard up on the bridge, the specifics of our duties left unclear. We should just take our weapons and get instructions from whomever it is we relieve up there. So, we grab our M16s, a bandolier of ammo and fresh packs of cigarettes and head up onto the cantilevered span. Two guys from Five-Nine are leaning up against the bridge railing at the southern end as we approach. They're glad to see us, and start to head back to camp before we have any chance to clarify our responsibilities.

"Hey, wait up," I yell out. "What are we supposed to do up here?"

"Don't do anything! If any of the gooks crossing the bridge pulls

Tim Haslam

out a weapon, shoot 'em," one of the men says, slowing his pace away from us somewhat as he passes on the vital aspects of the assignment.

"Are we supposed to stop anybody, or search anything, or what?" I ask, still in need of a little more guidance.

"If you want," is all that comes back as a reply from our mentors as they turn up the dusty track heading back toward the plateau, each puffing out a trail of cigarette smoke.

"Well shit, I don't know what we're supposed to do," I say to Danko, anxious to get his take on the situation.

"Nothin'," he elaborates in his typical cryptic style while placing a cigarette between his front teeth, taking up his position leaning back against the bridge rail.

"Nothin'," he repeats to ensure that I'm clear on the concept, now pointing at the tip of his cigarette.

"Right...don't do nothin'," I say with a resigned smile as I light his cigarette with my Zippo.

Where are these people going? I think to myself. *Who are these people and where the hell are they going?*

There is a fairly steady stream of foot traffic crossing the bridge. Most of the travelers are crossing south to north, but the north to south volume is pretty constant as well. There are a great variety of people in the parade passing before me. Mostly there are women pushing carts or carrying large bundles, usually accompanied by children. The bigger children carry smaller children, the smaller children carry babies. A few older men in ragged clothing sometimes riding bicycles, more often pushing them, pass by with their own variously sized bundles. The biggest mystery to me however is the number of men in ARVN uniforms walking past, some south bound and some north bound. Many plod along slowly all by themselves. Some are in pairs or groups of three or four. Some have weapons and other military gear. Some appear to have nothing at all.

Yesterday, because of my RTO responsibilities I was given a map of this section of Vietnam. With nothing else to do, I pull the map out of my pant leg pocket and study it. Dak Mot Lop is the name on the top of the topo-map. It takes a lot of searching over the busy contour lines of the green map to find a small village with the same name, Dak

Stars and Stripes and Shadows

Mot Lop, up in the top right hand corner. It's easy to find the Dak Poko however, and I trace it down the right side of the map until I find the bridge and Route 512 just in from the right hand margin. From the bridge, I follow the little line designated as 512 as it winds its way northwestward until it ends abruptly at the Laotian border. I survey the route carefully and the surrounding territory. There's nothing there but mountains and forest; no towns, no real villages above Dak Mot Kram and no military outposts or camps. *Where are these people coming from and going to?*

"Look at this." I say to Danko, showing him the road on the map and sharing my concern as to what these people are up to.

"It don't mean nothin'," he mumbles, confident that his assignment here is limited to the protection of the bridge only.

I study each person passing by me more carefully, torn between a natural curiosity about who these people are and a developing paranoia about what they're up to and their possible roles in support of the NVA and Vietcong and their efforts to kill me. The bundles they carry could be full of weapons or explosives just as easily as clothing or food or household goods.

Few of the adults passing by make eye contact with me. Nearly all of the children do, their expressions varying from child to child and mood to mood; frowns, smiles, curiosity, concern, fear. I'm not afraid of the dirty faces of the children. Occasionally, an adult will look my way, some apparently just studying me out of their own curiosity or boredom, some attempt to offer a weak smile or friendly expression, usually exposing a mouthful of black teeth. I want to return the expressions to some of them, but don't. Some, I react to with greater misgivings and simply stare at until they shift their attentions back to the road. Some, I just look away from as though they didn't exist at all.

Sometime around my third cigarette a group of Vietnamese approaches, coming up the road from the south catching my attention. There are three adult men, two pushing carts, followed by four animated children. The group stops about ten yards short of the bridge and gathers around the two carts. The children, ranging in age from about ten to twelve are handed boxes pulled off the carts by the serious looking men. Danko and I both assume a more upright position as we study the group, their carts and their boxes more carefully. Our M16s

Tim Haslam

are raised up slightly and brought around in the general direction of the group that's stopped within our jurisdiction for unclear purposes. For a brief moment we each have the same terrible thought. *Are we going to have to use these weapons on these people…these children?*

A boy about ten years old turns away from the cart and starts heading up towards us as quickly as he can under the burden of the box he carries but slows quickly in response to the reaction of the two GIs raising up their guns, orienting the barrels right at him. He stops completely—the expressions on the faces of the two Americans and the direction of their guns indicating some dangerous confusion. He carefully puts the box down on the ground in front of him, tilting it towards us, exposing the contents; bottles of Coke!

"Coca-Cola…you wan Coca-Cola?"

Danko and I say nothing as we return to the bridge railing, happy to have avoided an armed confrontation with the band of soda peddling gypsies. The boy, once again carrying his box, follows us repeating his inquiry.

"How much?" I ask, remembering the going price of Coke down in Kontum.

"One dollah," he declares assertively, smiling at the realization that negotiations are open.

One dollar, I think to myself. *You little prick. You just about got your ass shot off, scaring the shit out of us and now you want us to give you a dollar for a bottle of warm, probably poisoned, Coke?*

"Di di. One dollar number ten. Beat it," I tell him, still more disturbed over whether or not I would have shot him a minute ago than by his opening price.

"OK, OK, fit-ty," he says, taking a quick look back towards the three men at the carts.

His glance over at the little band of skinny Vietnamese in the soiled, torn garments changes my thought process. These people have nothing I think to myself and then I wonder what the three men do to the kids who don't make quota or command the necessary price. I wonder too where they get the soda and what they pay for it. I wonder what the consequences are of me giving him fifty cents for a bottle of warm soda that I don't even want, and I wonder what Danko will think about whatever I do. I wonder if a grunt on guard duty is supposed to conduct

Stars and Stripes and Shadows

business with a raggedy little peddler of warm soda.

I'm still wondering as I pull a rumpled fifty-cent MPC note out of my pocket and hand it to him. *He's a kid! He has nothing! What can it hurt? Screw Danko if he doesn't like it and screw the Army if they don't like it. Next time give me clearer orders?*

"Fit-ty," the kid says, crossing over the bridge to where Danko stands, quietly staring at us, out from under the helmet that nearly covers his eyes.

Without saying a word, Danko hands the kid a fifty-cent MPC note that he's had in his hand, takes his Coke bottle, pry's off the cap with his P38 and leans back out over the bridge rail, staring down into the Dak Poko, probably not wondering about anything. Mike Danko seems to find all of this much less complicated than I do.

The hours up on the bridge, like everywhere else in this country, pass slowly. All there is to do is watch the almost uninterrupted parade of people; people heading northwestward following Route 512 further into the wilderness, where, according to my map, nothing awaits them and, more people trudging along in the opposite direction along the same route coming back from the same nowhere. My imagination starts to conspire with my boredom to explain what these people are doing.

They're fucking with us. They're taking their bundles and their carts and their kids up the road a mile or so where they must swap around everything and return back across the bridge in front of Danko and me as some form of entertainment or as a diversion. They've choreographed it so that only kids heading northwestward will try to sell us sodas and trinkets, as several do.

A few individuals catch my eye for one reason or another. Perhaps it's the unusual blackness of someone's teeth, or some limp or scar or other physical deformity, of which there are many, or maybe it's the high pitched sound of someone's voice as they squeal off an instruction to one of the kids following along behind them. Whatever it is, I know I've seen this person earlier, going the other way across my bridge. I can't remember for sure if they had a bundle or a cart last time or not.

It's getting hotter up here. The sweat pours down off my face as I look longingly down through the heat waves shimmering off the old steel struts of the bridge into the cool water of the river below. The caffeine lift from this morning's gritty coffee has been fully metabolized

Tim Haslam

and there's no longer much of a nicotine boost from the steady chain of cigarettes I've been smoking. The last swallows of hot Coke do nothing to quench my thirst, leaving instead a furry residue around the inside of my teeth and along the sides of my tongue. I'd give every cent I have right now for about five minutes with a toothbrush and a cool glass of water. I'd give more than that for some clean underwear. I'd give almost anything I have right now for almost anything I don't have.

Just as my level of personal discomfort reaches this crescendo, I notice two ARVNs heading up the road toward me from the south. They stay close to the side of the bridge that I'm leaning against, heading nearly straight for me. They each have rifles, old M1 carbines slung over their backs. The one closest to me also has a holstered .45 pistol attached to a belt he wears over his shoulder. As they approach, their conversation stops, each of them making eye contact with me at about the same time. They continue to stroke up towards me like two street punks, trying to establish dominance with their stern stares and their testing smirks, until they pass within a few inches of me, all the while maintaining their fixed, hateful gaze into my eyes. Six feet past me they return to eyes-front and re-join their conversation.

What's with these two assholes? I say to myself, now more irritated with them than anything else. As I'm having this thought, I find myself giving in to a compulsion to stand upright, face the backs of these two little shit-heads and pull back the charging handle of my weapon and release it so that the recoil spring loudly snaps the bolt back into place. The ARVNs jerk around quickly in reaction to the sound of the M16 waking up. *This reaction from them is all I need.* With my weapon still pointed at the ground I return to the rail and lean back, smiling just slightly at my two rude allies in the war against communist aggression. *I get the last smirk. I win!*

Danko looks over at me lifting the front of his helmet exposing more than the usual amount of his face.

"Don't mean nothin'," he says.

"Don't mean nothin'," I say.

N N N N

Six-Two has summoned the whole platoon for a meeting late one cloudy afternoon. He and Sergeant Bollman are sitting next to one

Stars and Stripes and Shadows

another on a stack of crates full of artillery shells as the rest of us slosh up towards them through the fresh sticky mud created by the most recent squall to spray over us. The Platoon Sergeant and First Lieutenant seem pretty relaxed as we all gather around just in front of the two men, dwarfed by the big gun carriage in place just behind them. They gesture for us to sit down, before either of them wakes up to the fact that the only seating available is down in the sludge at their feet. As none of us go anywhere around here without our helmets, they can serve as our chairs. Because of the muddy ground, it's best to orient the helmet so that the top outer part is down in the mud, leaving the inside, bucket to sit in.

"Alright, listen up. I've got a few changes I want you all to be aware of," Falck says, looking out over the little clutch of curious grunts rocking around in their upturned steel pots. "First, some changes in the line-up. Captain Collins is up for rotation and will be leaving the Company. Actually, he's already left. He was called back to base-camp yesterday, thinking that he'd be coming back out with his replacement. I guess the Division has other plans and so he won't be back. I know he wanted to say his farewells to the Company in person but it looks like that's not going to happen. His replacement, a Captain Hilton, should be joining us within a few days.

"What do you know about this guy, sir?" Sergeant Stevens interrupts.

"Only his name and rank and that he's a West Pointer. Oh, and that this is his second tour here.

Next change, you may notice that Wee John is not among us this afternoon. Doc says that he's got an ear infection and so he's on his way back to Pleiku to get that fixed up. Haslam, you're going to take over as Six-Two-Charlie. Congratulations, you're now my personal RTO, starting immediately. Chuck Bragg, one of the headquarters RTOs is also up for DROS and so when Wee John gets back, he'll probably be taking his place. He'll then be Six-Charlie or Six-Alpha-Charlie, depending on how the new CO wants to arrange things.

Next, there's some good news, at least for some of you. Ed Arter, Bob Taylor, Bob Price, Raul Fernandez and Ernie Jefferson, you're R&R requests have all come through. You leave this afternoon."

"Yes," shouts out Fernandez, followed closely by similar expressions

Tim Haslam

from Bob Price and Ernie Jefferson.

Once again, Lieutenant Falck's timing and method of relaying information serves to rejuvenate all of us just a little. Certainly the guys who will depart for R&R today are ecstatic, but the rest of us benefit indirectly from the surprise element too. We're all always so anxious about the next surprise that Charlie, or the Division, or the Army, or the jungle has in store for us, that we have buried any anticipation of being the beneficiary of a positive surprise of such magnitude and consequence. Each of us now thinks for a brief moment that someday we too will hear, "*You leave this afternoon.*"

"This must be a mistake," Six-two exclaims as he scans one of the pieces of paper he's been shuffling through. "Where's Charette?"

"Here, sir," Elmer says, rising up out of his steel-pot rocking chair.

"There's something here from the Battalion medical officer that says you're supposed to go back to base-camp too; something about your teeth? It also refers to some report by Doc Charlebois. One of you two wanna fill me in?"

"It's Elmer's dentures, sir," Doc clarifies. "They're pretty worn out and don't fit so well anymore. I'm obligated to report such things to the medical officer. I guess he needs to go back to Camp Enari to get a new set."

"Are these worn out dentures somehow limiting Charette's abilities to carry out his duties out here?" the Lieutenant inquires, in what seems to be a playful manner.

"I'm not really sure about that, sir. I only know from my observations that they're not up to Army standards and that Specialist Charette is constantly fiddling with them."

"How about it Elmer, how bad are these things? Are they interfering with your duties?"

"Not really, sir. They're just kind of a bother some times," Elmer says, not really sure if Six-Two is just playing around or not. He's torn between his natural inclination for total honesty and respect for authority, and his rapidly increasing desire to get out of the shit for a little while. Six-Two, with Docs unwitting assistance is providing all of us with some entertainment at Elmer's expense.

"They whistle, sir," someone declares softly from within the audience.

Stars and Stripes and Shadows

"What was that? They whistle?" the Lieutenant asks, searching out for the source of this new information.

"Yes, sir, that's right," Bob Price says. "The last time we were on LP Elmer was whistling away in his sleep. I'm surprised you guys didn't hear it and pop a Claymore on us. I think his teeth in their current state represent a risk to the whole platoon."

"Is that right? Anybody else in this platoon think that Elmer's teeth might represent a risk to us?"

After about two seconds, heads start turning around looking for the group response, then, almost simultaneously everyone raises his hand.

"So, I guess everyone thinks that Elmer should be sent back to get better teeth?"

"Yes, sir," responds the chorus.

"OK," the Lieutenant pauses for a minute. "Anybody else in this platoon wear dentures?"

No reply.

"OK then, this is the last time the denture story gets anybody out of here. Elmer, you go out this afternoon with the rest-and-recuperation crew."

All right, last item. We need to send a patrol out tomorrow. Because of all the vacations, we're going to pick a few lucky volunteers from various squads to go. Sergeant Bollman will lead, Haslam will be RTO.

Shit! I thought being the Platoon Leaders RTO would have some benefits to be enjoyed before my next patrol!

✗ ✗ ✗ ✗

Staff Sergeant Bollman, Six-Two-Alpha, the Platoon Sergeant for Six-Two Platoon, is of average stature and looks much younger than he really is. Under his helmet and the accumulated filth is a boyish face, framed by reddish, blond hair. Cleaned up and dressed in appropriate civilian attire he would pass un-noticed among the surfers of the world. In a relaxed moment, his behavior, demeanor and the substance of his communication would also fit into the surfer image. He's not a surfer however; never has been. His Yankee upbringing in, Brockton, Massachusetts compels him more naturally into his role as senior NCO for the platoon. He, like the rest of us, is fulfilling a temporary

Tim Haslam

role however. None of us here are professional soldiers. Like the men at Valley Forge, Gettysburg, or Belleau Wood, at Bastogne, Iwo Jima or Pork Chop Hill, we've put on the uniforms and been sent off to do the work of the citizen soldier. When the work is done some of us can go home and back to our pursuits of happiness. This process requires a lot of citizen sorting so that stars and bars and stripes are allocated, hopefully to the worthy and capable. Sometimes these allocations miss the mark. Sergeant Bollman works hard to be worthy and capable of his allocated responsibilities and does a good job fulfilling a role he is probably not naturally suited for. Staff Sergeant Bollman, like most of the rest of us is really a kid. Bruce Bollman however, can play the role of a rifle company platoon sergeant well.

I watch the back of the dingy cloth covered steel pot bob and twist around a few feet in front of me as Six-Two-Alpha leads the patrol up the road away from the bridge. Sergeant Bollman's helmet seems oversized for his smallish head and provides me with a momentary distraction as I consider my relationship with this new boss. Ed Arter is Bollman's regular RTO, Six-Two-Alpha-Charlie. Ed is on R&R and so, for the duration of this patrol, anticipated to be a couple of days, I will take on that call sign. When we get back, I can officially start my Platoon Leader's RTO role as Six-Two-Charlie.

Bollman churns along up the road at a pretty rapid pace, his short legs dislodging a cloud of fine red dust for the rest of us to suck in. This is a full ruck patrol and all of us trailing Sergeant Bruce wonder if he'll be able to maintain such a pace. Behind me in the file is a collection of unhappy "volunteers" from various squads within the platoon; Jerome Bennis, Scotty Morris, Toby Lamberti and Mike Beasley. Doc Davis is the volunteer medic. Once again, we don't know much about our mission, except that we're only supposed to be going out about a klick.

As we approach the edge of Dak Mot Kram, Sergeant Bollman slows up, looking westward away from the road, into the vegetation that surrounds the village. There is a clear, well-traveled trail heading off that way, which Bollman turns on to, shifting gears back into full speed. The trail parallels the length of the village along its southern side so that we get an unobstructed view into the hamlet. The villagers in sight seem busy this morning, many wielding farming implements within sectioned plots of ground. *I can't tell what the plots contain.*

182

Stars and Stripes and Shadows

Many children are around, some appear to be working, some appear to be following adults around and some appear just to be doing children things. Few adult males seem to be around, except for elderly men. Several of these slight, wrinkled forms loiter about this side of the village with little apparent purpose, observing the six Americans passing by, all the while smoking their pipes and chewing their betel nut.

The trail starts to arc northward around the west end of the village where the forest growth starts to thicken up. Just at the beginning of the arc, Bollman startles everyone as he slams on his breaks in reaction to something only he can see around a sharp jog in the trail.

"Jesus H. Christ! The goddamn thing scared the shit out of me!" he exclaims, as the rest of us come around far enough to see up the trail and the huge water buffalo obstructing our way. The large black beast stands obliquely across the trail; the horned end aligned a few degrees off perpendicular to our course. The buffalo seems aware of our presence, but hasn't changed its demeanor or behavior as a result of our intrusion into his space. He just stands there, head upright and oriented straight along the plane of his body so that he appears to be looking off to our right. Occasionally though, his eyes shift towards us as he chews away on something. The intensity of his shifted gaze is enough to communicate a clear determination not to be disturbed. The animal and his reputation for fierceness, has the six of us literally buffaloed.

After a moment or two of the standoff, we look to our leader for a solution.

"Well Sarg; what's it gonna be, shoot the son-of-a-bitch, or what?" Beasley inquires, observing along with the rest of us that the vegetation is too thick around the back side of the animal for us to get through easily and, although the ground in front of it is clearer, all of us have ceded this territory to the bull's control.

"Maybe if we just throw something at it, it'll go away," Morris suggests, scanning around for a suitable projectile.

"Maybe if we throw something at it, we'll just piss the shit out of it and the motherfucker'll eat us," Bennis replies, apparently mis-categorizing the obstacle as a carnivore.

"All right, all right," Bollman asserts, taking command of the situation. "Here's what we're gonna do. Bennis, Toby and Morris, you guys start around slowly in front of him. The rest of us will stay here and if

Tim Haslam

it looks like he's gonna do anything, we'll distract him somehow until you all can get passed and out of the way. Once you're far enough away, we'll follow. OK?"

"Right on!" Bennis says, shoving Toby Lamberti into position to lead the right flanking maneuver.

"That thing moves at all, you shoot it Sarg...OK?" Morris says, sort of laughing but sort of serious too, sort of unsure if this thing is really dangerous or just some villager's property.

As we complete the planning phase of the operation, an old man and two small children, all dressed alike, in what seems like raggedy diapers appear at the edge of the village, about twenty meters away from the contested zone. If they're in fact VC, or loyal to the communist cause, they're about to learn a valuable lessen in American military tactics. If they're in fact just three diaper-clad villagers without political affiliations, this is probably just entertaining. Whatever their perspective, it's the most interesting diversion available to them today and they quietly jockey for optimum viewing positions.

"Don't look it in the eye!" Toby admonishes the first wave unit just as they set out. Lamberti is an Iowa farm boy and apparently has experience with bovine sensitivities. The advice however creates an obvious dissonance for Bennis and Morris, who are each of more urban backgrounds and who have been starring at the beast almost continuously since we got here. They are reluctant to trust the buffalo blindly as they pass through the danger zone. However, if Toby has some first-hand knowledge of water buffalo psychology they will do as instructed. And thus, the trio sets off nervously.

They made it. They're out of harms way, well up the trail beyond the buffalo's killing zone. The two younger spectators from the village have moved up closer too, perhaps out of concern for the animal or, perhaps just to get a better view of the anticipated struggle between the remaining three Americans and the stubborn animal blocking their way.

Don't look it in the eye. Don't look it in the eye. Bollman, Beasley and I remind ourselves as we take our turn moving gingerly through the exposed terrain until we reach the safety of the rest of the squad far up the trail. None of us can be sure about what the animal was thinking as it chewed its way through the whole episode, having never moved anything but it's lower jaw accompanied by a few flicks of it's tail at the

Stars and Stripes and Shadows

flies collecting around it's hind quarters. All parties seem to be pretty satisfied with the outcome.

While the six of us debrief ourselves over cigarettes, the smallest of the trio of spectator's marches up boldly toward the water buffalo, until he's adjacent to the great beast, just inches from the horns curving back from the huge head. Then, after the boy applies a few light taps with a small stick to the back of his neck, the fearsome creature obediently follows the boy's lead back into the interior of the village.

Another hundred meters up the trail we're back into territory with real dangers, the village and all its perceived perils having disappeared from our sight. The ground is relatively open and exposed, sloping up very gently toward the west. The Dak Kal River has carved a little gorge blocking our access to the west and the steeper mountains beyond. The gorge drops down about twenty feet from the flat ground we're on and measures about twenty meters across. The river itself is nothing like the Dak Poko in water volume, but is substantial enough to represent great risk to anyone attempting to wade across it under the unsteady burdens of ruck and gear, and so, Bollman continues to head northward along the eastern rim of the gorge scouting for a place with easier access down to the river and with a suitable place to ford. Our mission is to take up an ambush and observation position somewhere up on one of the forested ridges that climb out of this valley about a half klick to the west of where we are now. From this position up on the ridge, we should be able to observe much of the open territory that fans down from the mountains, across the Dak Kal and the approaches to the village. Several trails pass through this area that connect ultimately with the supply route trails a few miles to the west in Laos. This is known to be a popular route for Charlie.

It looks like something from a Tarzan movie; a tangle of vines, ropes, sticks and bamboo shafts, intertwined together and tethered to large trees on either side of the gorge. The hanging bridge in front of us was obviously constructed by the most primitive of civil engineers and does not appear to be very well traveled. It would however afford the most expedient way across the gorge and the river below for anyone willing to attempt the crossing. None of us immediately express such

Tim Haslam

willingness, offering instead a litany of legitimate concerns, such as; "It's a trap," "It's probably booby-trapped," "I'll bet no one's used this in years," "NO FUCKING WAY!"

As the latter sentiment is the expression of Sergeant Bollman himself, it seems like little additional analysis will be required before we continue our exploration for an alternate route.

"I'll try it," Toby says, basically setting the dare for the rest of us.

"You heard the man. NO FUCKIN' WAY!" Morris reminds him, drawing on his unfailing respect for authority as his justification for nixing Lamberti's suggestion.

"Come on Sarg, we can get across in just a minute and we're on our way. Who knows how far up stream we'll have to hump to find a better place to get across." Toby's now getting pretty hyped about the idea and is enjoying his role as team daredevil. "Come on guys we can do this…how about it, who's coming?"

A dare is a dare and cannot go unanswered just because the authority figure thinks it's a bad idea. I spent a lot of time as a kid climbing around in the walnut trees that populated our neighborhood as well as a lot of time walking along the narrow top of the interconnecting slump-stone wall that separated the homes on our block. I've never been afraid of heights. In high school, I would get a lot of satisfaction showing up some of my less adventurous friends when out exploring or hiking, by scampering up some rock or ridge they were unwilling to challenge. During summer vacations from college, my more adventurous friends and I climbed many of the rocks and domes around Yosemite—*at least until the Park Rangers ejected us from their jurisdiction, objecting to our evening refreshment choices.*

"I'll do it," I respond to the challenge, irritating the four remaining contestants.

"Man, you're fuckin' crazy!" says Bennis, characterizing both Lamberti and I.

"NO FUCKIN' WAY," Morris confirms. "Sarg said, NO FUCK-IN' WAY!"

"Go one at a time. The rest of us will see how it goes," a cautious but curious Bollmann directs, disappointing the others greatly with his lack of commitment to his initial, very sound evaluation.

So, the challenge has been accepted and Lamberti and I must deliver. Toby approaches the bridge threshold, stops, and more closely surveys the engineering and construction of the mostly organic span. He quickly realizes that he'll probably need to engage the full capacity of both hands and so he slings his M16 over his back with the muzzle pointed down and away from his right side. He thrusts his left foot forward slightly, probing around among the sticks and bamboo shafts that must support him over the first few steps away from solid ground, carefully shifting some of his weight onto his left leg. Then both arms reach out and grasp at the main ropes that seem to support the whole structure. With his right foot still anchored to the ground, he tests the stability of the system, gently but firmly shaking the two ropes. There is barely a ripple down along the span away from him.

Good news, it seems pretty solid, solid enough to justify commitment of his right foot, bringing his full weight and that of his ruck and gear completely onto the span. Once his right foot comes up even with his left, he restarts the process; step, probe, grasp, shake, shift, step. He repeats this cycle six or eight times, eliminating the shake part after the third repetition. This gets him almost ten feet out onto the bridge where he glances back confidently. The movement of his head is just enough to upset the geometry slightly initiating a subtle chain reaction. His head twist has shifted the weight just a bit to the left, off center-line, and the bridge structure at his feet compensates with a somewhat greater shift off to the right. Toby reacts quickly to the swing and sway, realigning his head to the front, steadying himself with his hands on the ropes, applying enough force to counteract the reaction. He's learned a valuable lesson and continues on.

After reaching the one-third milestone, each additional step results in a visible increase in the sag of the bridge. This adds another dimension to Lamberti's concerns. Every step through this sag zone sends a wave forward and back along the now creaking span reverberating off the supporting trees and back toward Toby. He now has to control each movement and countermovement flexing the bridge fore and aft and the twisting response resulting from any side-to-side shifts. At mid-span, he must stop completely to settle down the springing, swaying and twisting. He makes no attempt to look back at us, but each of us is pretty sure what he's thinking…*Me and my big fucking mouth!* What's left of his work is now all uphill, changing the mechanics once

Tim Haslam

again. His center of gravity, determined largely by the mass of his ruck, has shifted out and back from his body. The rucksack, already thought to have a mind of its own, reacts to each step with a little fishtail like motion. Where careful plotting, probing and balance characterized his approach to the first half of the transit, the second leg is more a test of arm and upper body strength as he pulls himself forward adjusting to each countermotion with the strength remaining in his arms. With his eyes focused on the solid ground to his front he pulls and tugs at the ropes, bringing his feet up quickly to share the load, until the final step takes him back up onto steady ground at the gorge rim.

"OK, come on, it's not so bad," he says, a moment after he reaches the other side…lying through his teeth. We (*especially me*) can see the sweat pouring out from under his helmet and the shaky hand attempting to light the cigarette jammed into his mouth. "Come on. I'll cover from here."

I wish I would have paid more attention in my 11th grade physics class when Mr. Fife explained the principals associated with pendulums, fulcrums, harmonics and wave dynamics. In fact, I wish I were in Mr. Fife's class right now. But I'm not. I'm on Sergeant Bollman's patrol and it's my turn to show off.

A quick glance around at my friends on this side of the gorge fails to elicit any helpful suggestions or expressions of enthusiastic support. In fact, the silent expressions seem to be unanimous…*You got yourself (and probably us) into this. You're on your own now!* Bollman can't even offer a reprieve at this point. Lamberti can't be left alone on the other side and he's not about to ask him to come back. *I have to go!*

Toby Lamberti, like everyone else on this patrol, is of average height, five-nine, five-ten, something like that. At my height, if I do everything exactly as Toby did, each little mistake will be exaggerated. Each movement of my head off center-line will result in a significantly greater compensating shift in the opposite direction down at my feet. I know this. Mr. Ruck knows this. I'm very aware of my height and my center of gravity as I set out. I want to crouch down as much as I can, but the weight on my back puts such a strain on my thigh muscles that I'm forced to stay pretty erect as I pull myself along. At the mid-point of this tightrope walk, just as I'm starting to feel some confidence in the ultimate outcome, another thought crosses my mind. *I'm totally*

188

Stars and Stripes and Shadows

exposed out here! I'm easy prey for a sniper who could shoot me, or the ropes holding me up. Looking down at the sticks and poles beneath my feet I wonder too if Toby was just lucky to have missed the mines that could be hidden here. The little bit of excitement that accompanied me along the first half of the crossing has completely abated. The dangers associated with falling from the bridge were measurable and tolerable. Now, I associate the dangers with the predators thought to be around here. I can't run, nor hide. It would be nearly impossible to bring any of my weapons into action here against the snipers firing away at the tall American with the radio struggling slowly across the bridge. My avenues of escape are limited.

If Charlie's anywhere around, I'm fucked!

Get to the other side as quickly as possible! Forget about being careful. Just pull or push or leap along, up the remainder of this obstacle course. Don't think about it—just do it!

This self generated guidance launches me onward, reaching, grasping and pulling at a rapid clip, until Toby's outstretched hand hauls me up onto terra firma, leaving the entire span of the bridge behind me bouncing and twisting wildly.

"Damn," is all I have to say to Lamberti as I un-sling my M16, simultaneously probing for my cigarette pack.

"OK, come on across," he exhorts to the others with a beckoning gesture as I settle myself down.

There's no immediate reply and no obvious forward motion from any of the others. Toby and I know exactly what's going on and what's about to happen. We can read their lips from here.

NO FUCKING WAY!

Our heroics have earned nothing for Lamberti and I except isolation on this side of the river. The others, with Sergeant Bollman's unhesitating approval, have started off, continuing along the opposite edge of the gorge looking for some simpler way across. Toby and I keep pace with them along our rim, keeping in visual contact while nervously scanning our side for any signs of Charlie. One thing in our favor is my radio. Bollman knows that he can't be separated from it for too long. He also doesn't like having his little band divided this way.

Fifty meters further up, the river turns slightly westward at a point where the gorge walls have broken down, providing easy access to the

Tim Haslam

water as well as a stepping stone path across. Lamberti and I are rejoined with the squad, trying to exact some recognition for our pioneering spirit. Bollman's rapid pace however, away from the river, out across the open grassy slopes leading westward toward the mountains, eliminates any opportunity for discussion or valuation of our experiences crossing the bridge.

The sun bears down hard on us as we cross this open exposed territory, all of us anxious to get up into the shade and protection of the forest. The gradient is steadily increasing and the humping takes on the familiar feel of agony setting in. The village behind us, the water buffalo and the vine bridge are soon dropped from our consciousness, replaced by the realization that there are only seven of us, heading into Charlie's yard. The edge of the approaching jungle offers the allure of shade—a false promise we all know—as the shade is always accompanied by the compacted humidity, the mosquitoes and a thousand places for Charlie to hide, to ambush, to mine and to booby trap. The jungle just ahead is a vast hungry monster with appetites for everything that enters and stays too long. Our brief, leisurely respite guarding the big guns at the bridge is now just another memory. The shit is once again our reality.

⚔ ⚔ ⚔ ⚔

"Six-Two-Alpha-Charlie, this is Six-Charlie. Over."

"Six-Charlie, this is Six-Two-Alpha-Charlie. Over."

"Put Six-Two-Alpha on. Over."

"Rog. Wait one."

I have to pull myself up, walk over ten feet to where Sergeant Bollman is curled up in a leafy nest, sweating his way through a light mid-afternoon nap.

"Bruce," I say, too tired and hot to form the extra syllables denoting rank or surname.

"Six-Charlie's on," I say, tapping his shoulder with the radio handset, until his eyes open, reconnecting him with Vietnam.

"This is Six-Two-Alpha. Go," he says, taking the handset, allowing me to return to my own nesting place, my own sweat; my own boredom.

Six-Charlie's muffled voice squeezing through the crackly handset and my subsequent movement has provided a break in the tedium for

Stars and Stripes and Shadows

the sorry little band of grunts encamped here, just at the edge of the forest. Six or Six-Charlie must be advising Bollman that we've done our job and it's time to return to the bridge camp, the hot meals and the cool water of the Dak Poko. We've been sitting here in this same hot, humid spot for three days now, diligently observing the open ground down below us, watching for Charlie. Watching all day and trying to watch all night. Bollman has brought along a Starlight scope, a telescope-like instrument that uses starlight or moonlight to enhance night images. We've worked in two man teams throughout each night, taking turns scanning over the landscape with the scope, trying to make some sense out of the fuzzy yellow-green shapes that appear through the scopes eye piece. The vague outlines of things start to become familiar, but it's almost like studying the echoes on a radar screen. It's a limited abstraction of reality.

Movement is what we're looking for. If it moves, it's Charlie. If it moves, we get on the radio and call in a fire mission. If it moves, we tell the fire direction center back at the bridge where the movement is, using predetermined map locations as a starting point. The fire direction center works out a firing solution and sends it on to the crew of one of the 155mm Howitzers. The turret of the big gun will traverse slightly to the precise azimuth prescribed along the horizontal axis. The gun barrel will be elevated to the precise angle up the vertical axis and the exact powder charge required to loft the explosive projectile will be determined and loaded into the breach of the gun. One of the redlegs will pull the lanyard, the primer will fire, the powder will explode, the conical shell will be launched, the grunts at the bridge will be jarred out of their sleep and the fire direction center will declare over their radio, *"Shot out!"* The ninety-seven pound high-explosive projectile will spiral its way through the Central Highlands air until gravity pulls it down into contact with the ground. If the round lands where everyone hoped it would, we'll provide the necessary information to adjust subsequent rounds more precisely onto the spot where the movement was observed. *"Drop one hundred, right fifty. Fire for effect. Over."* If all of this works according to plan, we'll add bodies to the count the next morning. If anybody in this communication chain made an error, or heard a number incorrectly the deadly rounds could fall anywhere and our bodies could be added to the count. It would be better if nothing moves.

Tim Haslam

"You've gotta be shit'n us Sarg," is Morris' reaction to Bollman's summary of his discussion with Six-Charlie. *You've gotta be shit'n us,* is the reaction we all have.

We're to stay here another two days. The Division is getting lots of reports of heavy movement between the bridge and the border. They have to be moving our way. They have to come right by us. We have to see them. We have to stay until we do. We have to direct someone with a Howitzer or someone flying an airplane full of bombs or someone jockeying a Cobra gunship full of rockets to unleash their weapons onto the movement we see. We have to estimate how many gooks were on the ground at the time and place of our directed attack. We have to add bodies to the count.

"We don't have food and water to last another two days," Beasley adds. "I'm down to my last canteen now!"

"He's right Sarg. I've got two meals left and just over a canteen of water," adds Lamberti. We're all in the same fix. Water is the particular concern.

"We'll have to conserve. We'll have to make it last," says Bollman, knowing that we can survive the two days, knowing too that we have no choice.

"I'm on my last battery," I say, bringing up a problem with greater significance and consequence than our remaining food and water. "I put it in last night. I don't think it'll last through two more days."

Bollman knows, we all know, that without our radio, without our communication, we're useless out here to the Company and the Battalion and the Brigade and the Division and to General Abrams. We all know that without our radio we're just seven grunts a long way out in the boonies, the same section of boonies where heavy enemy movement has been reported. Without the radio we're disconnected from the big weapons that can protect us from superior numbers of gooks with rifles and machineguns and rocket propelled grenades that are reported to be heading our way. Without the radio we're fucked!

Bollman only needs a second to think through a countermeasure to our latest problem and then tells me what I need to do.

"Six-Charlie, this is Six-Two-Alpha-Charlie. Over."

"Six-Two-Alpha-Charlie, this is Six-Charlie. Go."

"Six-Charlie, I'm on my last battery and it's not going to make it for two more days. I'm going to shut off the radio. I'll come back up every hour and call in a sit-rep. Over."

"Roger, Six-Two-Alpha-Charlie. I guess you know to turn off squelch to save power too. Over."

"Rog, I've had it off all day, it still won't make it. Over."

"Roger that. Call in your sit-reps on the hour. Out."

I turn the power switch to OFF, disconnecting us from the rest of the world. We all have the same thought. What if something happens five minutes from now? What if an 02-Skymaster flying around a klick to our west spots a thousand gooks flowing over the ridge behind us, heading right for us like army ants devouring everything in their path? What if the peace talks are successful and the war ends five minutes from now? What if…?

"Ensilage," Lamberti responds without hesitation to my inquiry; "What's an eight letter word that ends in a-g-e that means…*Ferments within a silo?*"

He's from Iowa, he should know.

The crossword puzzle in the now ragged copy of <u>Star and Stripes</u> that I've dragged along is the only diversion I have. We've all read every story and article in the paper by now, passing around the rumpled sections, occasionally initiating a brief dialogue usually preceded by some expository condemnation. "Fuckin' peace talks are never gonna happen!" "Goddamn hippies don't know shit about shit!" "Numbnuts Johnson just wants out of office!" "Fuckin' Abrams and MACV don't know their asses from their elbows." "Fuckin' gooks!" "Fuckin' Army."

Morris, Bennis and Doc Davis, the three black members of our patrol are lounging along a line to my right with Bollman, Lamberti and Beasley forming a semi-circle off to my left. We're all close enough together to be involved in every conversation and the boredom ensures that everyone's attention is drawn to each and every comment uttered. Morris and Doc start a conversation about home in which Morris mentions something about L.A.

"I didn't know you were from L.A.," I interrupt. "What part? I'm from the San Fernando Valley."

Tim Haslam

"South Central," he says, denying me much of an opportunity to explore common ground. The white, middle class suburbs of the Valley and the ethnic neighborhoods of South Central Los Angeles are worlds apart, connected only occasionally by political rhetoric or cross-cultural transgressions. And, so it is that our conversation this humid afternoon, two klicks west of Route 512, on the Dak Mot Lop map, turns to issues of race and strife and our unique perspectives on such things.

"I worked for awhile in the summer of '65 down on Western Avenue, just south of Robertson. Are you anywhere near there?" I ask Scotty in an effort to narrow the gap and maintain the momentum of our discussion.

"No, I'm pretty far south of there, down toward Compton. The only time I was really up that way was during the Riots."

His response, and particularly the word *riots*, signals everyone that this little chat is about to get more interesting. Several of the limp bodies sit up and a few of the remaining cigarettes in our possession are ignited. This is a lot better than revisiting the stories of someone's '57 Chevy. This is something new to explore and reflexively several of us take a quick scan around out to our front, checking for Charlie's presence before we dedicate our total attention to the matter now at hand.

"You mean the Watts Riots?" asks Doc.

"Yea, what else?" responds Morris, knowing that he now has the burden of rounding out the story for the rest of us. It seems however that he's not yet ready to take up the narration by himself and so he invites me back into the limelight.

"What were you doing down there on Western Avenue?"

"I worked my summer vacations at 20th Century Fox Studios and they have a small lot down there where they film TV shows. I was there during the riots. It was pretty uncomfortable for awhile." The rest of the audience takes note of my claim to have worked at a motion picture studio, filing that away temporarily, to be further explored after we wrap up the "riot" stories.

"Yea, it was bad man, but it had to happen, man, it had to happen." Morris seems to recognize that he's heading into sensitive territory. There's one way to continue on explaining all this to the brothers; Doc and Bennis, but it's not so clear to him how Mike Beasley and Toby Lamberti from Iowa and Sergeant Bruce Bollman from Brockton, Mas-

Stars and Stripes and Shadows

sachusetts will react.

The Nam and the shit are where the seven of us find ourselves now. The Nam and the shit make everything else seem different, less serious…less real. Even an event like the Watts riot takes on a different meaning. Different even for Morris, who was there when 32 people lost their lives, who was a participant, who felt the frustration of the little injustices that people in such communities endure each day. Watts and South Central Los Angeles were his places, for better or worse, they were his places. Now this little patch of jungle overlooking the grassy slopes is his place. It's our place. We're all in this together, black and white, Iowa and Watts and the San Fernando Valley. It doesn't change where we've been or who we are, but adds another layer of experience to be considered when we look at the world and each other. We each still have our own perspectives and bias and propensities for prejudice. But here, we're all just grunts and feel the same daily frustrations with the little injustices that our grunt community must endure. This allows all but the most extremely bigoted within our ranks to find ways to get along, to overcome the alignments and requisite dispositions that divide our culture back home. It sometimes allows us to see more deeply within the people around us.

Everyone has a perspective and an opinion to share in the discussion about the riot, about life in big cities and small towns, about police and pigs. When the subject matter becomes too tedious or too tense or too opinionated, humor seems to come to the rescue. Young grunts tend to be sort of bi-polar in this way. When we've exceeded our quota of railing against the fuckin' this or the fuckin' that, someone usually comes to the rescue by pointing out some aspect of the fuckin' situation that strikes everyone as funny. It brings it all back into perspective. *It don't mean nothin'!*

Bennis contributes an anecdote to the discussion, recalling an experience he had in boot camp at Fort Ord. Someone in his training company was in the National Guard at the time of the riots and was deployed along with his unit to Watts. Bennis tells how the guardsman was actually showing off a campaign ribbon on his khaki uniform that his unit was awarded for their role in the Watts Riot.

"How the fuck can someone get a medal for something like that?" Doc asks, rhetorically.

Tim Haslam

"That's complete bullshit man," adds an agitated Scotty Morris, "I was in the Watts riots too, I didn't get no motherfuckin' medal!"

Everyone has a good laugh at Scotty's unique observation, never really considering that maybe he wasn't kidding.

Mother Bollman hands out bars of Hershey's Tropical Chocolate for breakfast on the morning of the last day of the patrol. All of our other food is gone and the good sergeant had secreted these away in reserve. The hard, chalky candy bars are made so that they won't melt in the tropical heat. No one is sure what ingredients go into them that preclude the melting. Among the grunts they're known as Yard-bars because the Montagnard CIDGs are usually willing to trade something they have for them. The Montagnards actually like them. The "Yards" are the only ones who like them. For us, Yard-bars are a last resort. They'll provide some energy and a little bit of a needed sugar boost, but they'll also require a swallow or two of our remaining water to wash away the taste and no one has more than a half a canteen of water for the return trip.

Staff Sergeant Bollman has been on the radio this morning with Lieutenant Falck and has received the OK to bring the patrol back in. Charlie has failed to cooperate with the plans objectives. Charlie has failed to participate with the seven of us in the body counting game. We'll come home with all of our ammunition and all of our bodies. Maybe next time we'll do better.

N N N N

No one objects to the pace that Bruce Bollman sets on the way back. No one is tempted to use the vine bridge to prove anything and, happily, no water buffalo obstruct the trail. In an hour and a half we're back, surrounding the water trailer, filling our canteens and ourselves with water, ready for the break we've earned. *What to do first? Head for the river, or the mess tent, or the mailbag, or the shitter, or just some shade?* This is why the Army has a chain of command. This is why the Army has officers. Six-Two comes over to the water trailer and organizes our agenda for us.

"There's clean fatigues over by my bunker. Why don't you get those, then take a swim, then chow," he says to the magnificent seven.

Stars and Stripes and Shadows

"Then, at eleven o'clock, an hour from now, I want to have a platoon meeting."

No further discussion is required and we all head for the bunker with the clean clothes. There's a big bag full of the one-size-fits-all shirts and pants and another bag full of tee shirts and socks.

"Where's clean underwear?" I ask Doc Charlebois, who's sitting up on the edge of the bunker overlooking the menswear department.

"Look in that bag," he says pointing to a smaller duffle bag lying off to the side.

All right! I think to myself as I lift up the duffle and reach down for the long anticipated clean underwear.

"It's empty. Come on Doc, you've gotta be shittin' me. Where's the underwear?"

"If it's empty it's empty. That's all there was…sorry!"

I can't even comprehend the implications of this. It's been over two months since I put these on. It's been over two months since any clean underwear was delivered out to us. What if it's another two months before the next re-supply? What if I'm on another damn patrol then?

Doc hands each of us a bar of soap that he pulls out of one of the Sundry-Packs next to him as we head down to the river. At the river's edge, we each make a little neat pile of our new, clean stuff and start a community pile of the filthy garments. Everyone wades into the water with similar expressions of relief. The bars of soap are quickly put to use in vigorous attempts to scrub off the mud and dust and sweat, to expose the bare skin and open sores. The bars of Ivory Soap are all we have to cleanse our bodies and our hair and, for me, my underwear. All the rubbing and scrubbing I can do just seems to blend the Ivory residue along with the filth accumulated over the last two months into the worn fabric. Repeated wringing out and shaking improves the condition only slightly, but enough, I tell myself to allow our relationship to continue into the foreseeable future.

A few minutes up on the flat rocks at the river's edge is all that's required to dry us (and my underwear) and it's off we go as instructed by Six-Two.

Doc Charlebois' little transistor radio provides the background music for the discussions he and I have undertaken since I got back

Tim Haslam

from the Fifteenth-of-the-Sixteenth mess tent. I have had sufficient time to settle into the platoon's command bunker now that I'm officially Six-Two-Charlie. Lieutenant Falck, Sergeant Bollman, Charlebois, Ed Arter, when he returns from R&R, and I now make up the platoon headquarters and will live together in this bunker. Right now Six-Two and Sergeant Bollman are off at some meeting and so Doc and I are left alone to relax.

Scotty Morris finds his way over to us, drawn mostly by Aretha Franklin's voice coming through the little radio's speaker. He climbs up on the top of the bunker with us and is soon followed by Ernie Jefferson and another black man that I've not met before. James Littlejohn, a sergeant from Six-One Platoon introduces himself with a friendly smile, offering a fist for tapping. Littlejohn seems older than the others. Older in fact than anyone I've seen in the Company accept maybe Sergeant Madison. He could be in his early thirties but is as easy going and as relaxed as the younger brothers being persuaded out of the shit by Aretha's familiar seduction.

I pass around my fresh Marlboro pack and settle in as a new student to this aspect of American culture. It turns out that AFVN radio is playing Aretha exclusively for the next hour this morning. My three black grunt friends are in heaven, sharing their remembrances of home against the soulful backdrop of the music, but also courteously including Doc and I in the dialogue as opportunities arise.

"Hey Sterling, listen to this, come over here and listen to this," Littlejohn shouts out to Sergeant Johnson, Six-One's Platoon Sergeant, who's walking by.

"Aretha," is all Johnson says as he joins the group. Johnson, who also appears to be in his early thirties, is more quiet and reserved than the others. He, like Littlejohn, has been in the Army for a long time, it's his career and he takes his work seriously. Right now however, Aretha and the relaxed clutch of brothers are sufficient enough motivation for him to revert back out of his military role for a moment. He seems to be pretty shy and less apt to contribute or validate opinions expressed. He smiles easily however and reflects a gentle friendliness when invited into any specific topic. Johnson is a good person, respected NCO and his presence within this little group seems to add great value to the pleasant interlude.

Beyond the obvious black and white distinctions within this little group of grunts, the six individuals here are all really very different. Sergeant James Littlejohn Jr. from rural Georgia has been in the Army since he was seventeen. It's been his life. It's taken him from place to place, home to home; he has no other meaningful roots. He's not always been as dedicated to his profession as he could have been, and so his progression up through the enlisted ranks has been slow with occasional retrograde adjustments due to minor breeches. Today, after nearly fifteen years in the Army he's a buck sergeant, an E5, the lowest NCO rank. But, for him it's OK. He knows the choices and decisions he's made that have brought him to where he is; he's not a victim. Morris, the kid with the inner city smarts and perspectives is as different from Littlejohn as I am. Scotty is a draftee who can't wait to get out of the Army. His south central Los Angeles is, in most ways, completely different from the poor Negro realm of rural Georgia and the Deep South, or the dusty plains of west Texas where Ernie Jefferson grew up. But, their color, their race and the history of their people in America bonds them all together and precludes any equivalent bonds with Doc and me. All that doesn't really matter though; right now, we're all just grunts on a break from the reality of this place that bonds and binds us together.

Dinner at the 5/16th mess tent today was an extra treat—real roast beef and mashed potatoes. Of course the portions were pretty small and left everyone yearning for more. Fortunately a fresh supply of beer has arrived and there is enough for us to fill up on. Bob Price and Bob Taylor have returned from R&R and so, after dinner, I join them, Mike Beasley and Doc Charlebois back at the squad's bunker to hear the stories Price and Taylor have for us. Mike Danko actually volunteered for KP duty up at the mess tent as a way of avoiding some less desirable assignment involving the shitters and is absent from this relaxed discussion, and Elmer is still somewhere, out of the shit, having his dentures tended to.

Bob Taylor had been in Singapore and Bob Price in Hong Kong. Their experiences were similar; lot's to eat, lots to drink and never a moment without a female companion. There's some debate about

Tim Haslam

which R&R site has the most beautiful women, the friendliest women, the sexiest women, the most experienced women, the least expensive women. None of us in the audience care much about the food or the drink descriptions or the site seeing, but hang attentively on every detail that can be gleaned regarding the women. Where do you find them? What do they say to you? What do you say to them? What do they do? How often? How long? How much?

The sections of each city where the bars are, the standard routine with the mama-sans and the introductions to the bar girls, the get acquainted drinks at the bar with different girls until the perfect match is made, the negotiations with the mama-san and finally the "date" are all described with the appropriate flourishes and enthusiasm. Each adjective and adverb used to describe the girls and the activities with the girls refreshes distant images for us. For some of us the images are only fantasies as our real experience is much more limited. For Taylor and Price, reliving the experience for us keeps it alive for them for a few more treasured moments. For the rest of us it carries the promise of things yet to come. If we can survive, some day there will be R&R for us too. It will be our turn. Right now we all want this conversation, accompanied by the warm beer to linger through the evening until guard duty and radio-watch must start. We all want it to distract us from the shit around us for as long as possible.

Sergeant Taylor interrupts one of his narratives, observing Mike Danko shuffling down the trail from the mess tent towards us. Danko, his long dark moustache pointing down and out from under the shadowy face hidden beneath his helmet, seems to be in no hurry to join us and yet he seems to be aware that we are all watching him. His slow pace is now intentional, ensuring that the spotlight and everyone's attention is fully on him. *What's he up to?*

Finally, Danko, guided along by our curious stares, arrives at the edge of our little gathering outside the squad's bunker. He stops—says nothing—only his eyes move, shifting left and right verifying that everyone's full attention is on him. *It is!* Still nothing is said. The drama is prolonged. We glance around at one another to see if anyone has a clue as to what's going on. *We don't!* Apparently the tension is not yet sufficient for him to disclose whatever it is—if it's anything at all—that's behind his subterfuge.

Stars and Stripes and Shadows

"So, Danko, what's happening?" Taylor asks, hoping that his rank will be sufficient to pry open Danko and reveal his secrets.

Danko continues the pause for a moment longer, then very slowly, with each hand, reaches into the large pockets at the sides of his dusty, oily fatigue pants. There's something there we can all tell. We hadn't noticed the bulges in his pockets before now. The bulges are what this is all about. Very slowly, with as much drama as he can maintain, his eyes continuing their scans across our impatient faces, he exposes the bulge objects.

"All right Danko!" the audience responds to the objects now presented in front of us within the filthy hands of the man with the subtle smirk on his face.

Danko has, within each of his grimy, greasy hands an entire beef roast. No one considers for a moment the environment of Danko's pockets where these roasts have been or the sanitary implications of his hands as we scurry about for mess kits or other suitable vessels for distributing the bounty in front of us. We set upon the beef with our own eager, filthy hands, clawing and pulling it into parcels, handing them around, consuming them like a pride of starving lions. Danko's gift and his method of presentation have turned our pleasant evening discussion into a night to remember. Beef, beer and images of willing young women will accompany us into our lonely duties this night, into our attempts at sleep and hopefully into our dreams.

At 11:30 p.m. I finish my shift on radio watch and attempt sleep. This usually easy transition is somehow more difficult this night. There is a restlessness attached to my thoughts. Thoughts brought about by Taylor and Price's shared experiences. Thoughts and images of young women; of soft, smooth skin, of shape and contour, of fragrance and warmth and touch all remind me of how far away I am from such things. The imagery of the bar girls transitions into images of Rosemary and every intimate moment I've had with her and every intimacy I only imagined having with her is brought back as I toss and turn within the black, claustrophobic confines of the bunker. The pleasantness of the images enhances the anxiety of my reality and the frustration of our separation, of our ever-fading connection. Sleep will not come any time soon.

Sleep does come. Perhaps only for a few minutes when it's in-

Tim Haslam

terrupted by something, disturbed rudely by something angry and insistent shaking me back toward the shit. The boom and shock and reverberation of the 155s bring everyone at or near the bridge camp out of their sleep. These aren't the planned periodic def-con firings. This is a sustained series of salvos. This isn't harassment and interdiction fire. This is a desperate defense. These rounds are aimed at movement. Charlie has come!

Six-Two pulls himself up and reaches for the radio. He calls up to Six-Charlie for some clarification.

Charlie Company is being hit up on Firebase 25!

"Switch Ed's radio over to the battalion push!" he orders me.

I change the frequency and turn the volume up all the way.

Lieutenant Falck, Sergeant Bollman, Doc and I listen intently to the chatter coming over the radio, trying to piece together what's happened, what is happening, all under the accompaniment of the pounding guns just outside our bunker.

"Six-Two-Charlie, this is Six-Charlie. Get all your people up and out to the perimeter line…full alert. Over," instructs the voice on my radio that's still tuned to the Company push. The order is repeated to each Platoon in Bravo Company. The Tet offensive taught everyone in the U.S. military a lesson about the scope and magnitude of Charlie's capabilities for surprise attacks. In the last few weeks Charlie has been more active, seemingly recovered from his Tet wounds. Battalion and regimental sized units of NVA have hit several camps and bases recently. Firebase 25 is in our neighborhood. Charlie is close.

The angry Howitzers seem much larger to me now as they boom and recoil and settle and boom again. The four of us in this bunker are small and fragile and uncertain about life's purposes and consequences and duration, but the Howitzers have come fully alive, heaving their deadly wrath out into the darkness, chasing it away with flame and thunder. All the little men supporting the awakened machines need do is continue to feed them the explosive fodder. The little men and the great machines seem to know what to do.

It seems odd to me for a moment that my job is to stay here in the command bunker, not to go out to the line with the other squads in the Platoon. My job is now to be an extension of Six-Two. Wherever he goes, I go. Right now, he's going nowhere. His job is to understand

Stars and Stripes and Shadows

the situation and deploy his Platoon accordingly. My job is to listen and to relay commands and status and requests. My job is to communicate clearly and concisely and accurately as this night continues to erupt around me.

Bob Price has the Six-Two-Three radio with Taylor's squad and calls back to me to let me know that the whole Platoon is now in place out on the line. Six-Two Platoon is positioned along a section of the perimeter facing out towards Route 512 looking westward. Star shell flares are popping off above the camp illuminating everything and the muzzle flashes of the 155s add to the kaleidoscopic shifts in brightness and contrast dancing over the nervous activities of the camp. Within the bunker, our attentions are divided between the activities surrounding us, the instructions coming over the Company net radio and the reports and requests pinging back and forth over the Battalion net about what's happening to Charlie Company up on the firebase.

Dust off birds! They need medevac choppers up to FB25 ASAP!

"They're on the way!"

"Is it safe for them?"

"Will they come under fire?"

"Everything's under fire here! We need to get the wounded out!"

"Charlie's right at the wire at the northeast sector!"

"We're taking heavy fire from RPGs, B40s, machineguns and mortars! At least ten men down!"

"Put up more flares over us!"

"Adjust rounds twenty meters right!"

Charlie Company is being hit hard.

Bravo Company waits within the trenches, and bunkers to be hit hard. It no longer matters that its night or dark or a time we should be getting our much needed sleep. Bravo Company will remain awake and alert; waiting through the rest of this night.

Chapter 7

FB25

Three dead at the firebase, seven more wounded, at least 20 dead NVA littering the perimeter of Firebase 25, where Charlie Company welcomes the dawn filtering through the clouds and rain, still on full alert. The shooting has stopped, the rain of artillery shells exploding out in the jungle just beyond where Charlie was has ceased and now the rain and the whir and pop of rotor blades are the only sounds for the Charlie Company grunts to attend to. Within the muddy trenches and bunkers they have only their cigarettes and each other to offset the lingering terror of the nights struggle. The squads and platoons on the northeast sector took the brunt of the assault. Their machineguns, their M16s, their grenades and Claymores, the wire, the mud and the steep approaches to the perimeter combined to stop Charlie's siege.

For the grunts of Bravo Company, a few klicks away, we lost only sleep and perhaps some of the cilia within our inner ears. We are active this morning however, pulling our shit together; packing it all up. We're moving out today. We're going to relieve Charlie Company at FB25.

Like most of the firebases around here, 25 resides atop a high peak. It has a commanding view out toward the south and a somewhat obstructed view to the west. To the east the landscape drops off sharply and then rises again steadily up into the surrounding mountains. The north side is the dangerous side. The firebase actually is dug into the top of a ridge that runs generally west to east. At the far eastern end the ridge is connected via a saddle to another ridge running parallel back towards the west. The gap between the two ridges is steep and deep

Stars and Stripes and Shadows

and heavily forested but the gap is also narrow. These two ridges are within easy rifle range of each other. The firebase has been carved out of the jungle canopy that once shielded this high ridge. With the big trees cut down and the lower story vegetation hacked away, the ridge is open and exposed as are the inhabitants who stray from the protection of their holes and burrows—their trenches and bunkers.

Once again an anxious Huey crew urges us out of their machine, not wanting to spend a second longer than necessary sitting here on the exposed LZ at FB25. We exit quickly into a light rain and into the grip of heavy mud. The choppers bringing us in are also ferrying Charlie Company out of this place and back to the bridge where we just came from. Just beyond the down wash of the rotor blades we pass each other. I've grown accustomed to the mottled masks of filth and fatigue that we all wear but the faces of the Charlie Company grunts have something overlaid that I've never seen before. They're glad to be alive this morning and yet they're not sure how or why they've reached this dawn and these helicopters. The shock of the prior night's battle is still reflected in the eyes of the exhausted men as they dispassionately study us going by. A few have the energy and the need to say something to us.

"Charlie's all over this place!"

"Stay close to your bunkers!"

"This place is the worst, man! This place is the worst."

None of us say anything in return as we contemplate the implications of the places we're trading.

Six-Two leads us off the LZ and up into the interior of the base. It's not FB30. FB30 had the appearance of order and control. FB30 was a secure place that we used to launch our attacks and to harass our enemies that might stray into the surrounding forests. FB25 has the look of a defensive enclave. The network of capillary trenches that meander all over the place is deeper than the trenches at FB30 and shows signs of heavy use. The bunkers carry more layers of sandbags, each layer seemingly added as a reaction to another mortar attack. There is clear evidence of Charlie's efforts here; small craters, rubble of splintered ammo crates and C-ration cases, twisted shards of green metal and other bits, pieces and damaged fragments of things litter the muddy ground between the pits and bunkers. There's a battery of 105s well dug in here, as well as several mortar pits, each with an ac-

Tim Haslam

cumulation of packaging debris discarded haphazardly as the mortar men launched their flares and high explosive rounds as quickly as they could throughout last night. There is no one lounging around casually outside anywhere at FB25.

At the center of the base is a complex of bunkers distinct from the rest because of the array of radio antennae sprouting out of and around them. This is TOC, the Battalion Tactical Operations Center. The Battalion has placed its most important command and control facility up here on FB25, out at the edge where our zone meets their zone. FB25 is an important place. Charlie knows this. Charlie can see the 105s, the mortars, the antennae and the volume of helicopter traffic coming and going to this place. This is just the kind of place they can hurt the Americans. This is just the kind of place they can tear away at us to test our will and wear down our determination. Perhaps they can even take it all away from us for a few hours before the B52s are summoned to exact retribution...to rip FB25 away from everyone.

Charlie has an ally in the terrain here. The adjacent ridge paralleling the base on the north side affords the perfect approach. The opposite slope of that ridge falls away to the north. All of our artillery support lies to the south; the big guns back at the bridge, the 105s in range at FB30 and the guns at Dak To are all to the south. Their shells can reach only the forward slope of the ridge, they cannot elevate to a trajectory steep enough to bring the rounds down onto the reverse slope. The reverse slope is also protected from most air strikes. F4 Phantoms approaching from the north could easily overshoot their designated targets and fling their 500-pound high explosive bombs, their cluster bombs and their napalm canisters right onto the grunts at FB25. Only the slow flying A1Es and the Cobras can attack the reverse slope from the air, attacking in short west to east arcs. Only the mortars from FB25 can reach Charlie on the reverse slope. Charlie can build up his forces and his strength hidden within the jungles of the reserve slope. He can lob his mortar rounds at us from there. His snipers can retreat there after fulfilling their daily assignments. But, Charlie can only really get at us from the saddle that connects the two ridges.

We follow Lieutenant Falck up over and around the maze of obstacles, unsure of where we're to be assigned within this complex. It doesn't take long to confirm what we all expected. Six-Two starts down

Stars and Stripes and Shadows

the north sloping face of the hill, heading for the bunkers out on the perimeter line facing the other ridge. Two Cobras prowl back and forth over the opposite ridge to discourage Charlie from disrupting our changeover. As we work our way down we see the saddle down and to our right. The saddle is a jumble of fallen vegetation interspersed with cleared openings. Where the firebase perimeter connects with the saddle there is an abundance of interwoven concertina wire. The open ground coming back up toward the bunker line is crosshatched with regular barbed wire and tangle foot razor wire. Within this wire zone it's easy to see the trip flares and the Claymores with their detonator wires streaming back up into the firing ports of the bunkers. Two bunkers have clear fields of fire out over the wire onto the saddle and the gentle rise up to the base, one at the eastern limit of the firebase and the other about thirty meters back along the north side. Thirty meters further up the north side is the next bunker…our bunker.

Our bunker is similar to the one we had at FB30 only somewhat larger. As the prior residents had to spend so much time in this hole they've made some useful improvements. They've dug out the sleeping shelf so that one can crawl back there and actually sit up. They have also dug out an additional little shelf at the head end of the sleeping shelf that is ideal for storing personal gear. The firing port too has been well tailored to facilitate the business at hand. There is ample room to lay out ammo along a ledge just below the bunker opening. Above the ledge, at the lip of the opening are nine Claymore detonators each connected to a mine emplaced somewhere in the tangle of barbed wire at various distances down the slope to our front. We can put out a lot of fire from here, out into the cleared zone to our front and across onto the other ridge, the ridge where Charlie can see us and can shoot back at us. This morning our bunker has four layers of sandbags over the log roof. The new residents will find it necessary to make additions to this part of the architecture.

There is an entrance on the west, front side of the bunker. The entrance way is through a trench that snakes along to the west connecting us with the next bunker, another twenty meters away. Half way between the two bunkers an intersecting trench leads back up toward the center of the firebase where it connects with the other trench highways leading to all points within the complex. Another trench runs behind

Tim Haslam

our bunker heading eastward, connecting us with the two bunkers that sentinel over the saddle. Fifteen meters along that trench and about five meters up above it, is a remnant of twisted metal and debris with the recognizable parts of 50-caliber machineguns. Six-Two has learned the story of what happened last night and what happened to these guns.

Somehow, the Brigade had in its possession a quad-fifty machine-gun mount. This is a weapon system comprised of four, heavy 50-caliber machineguns mounted together on a turret base. The quad-fifty is really an anti-aircraft weapon but someone thought it would be just the thing to protect the one vulnerable approach to FB25. The 50-caliber rounds can penetrate armor, trees and anything else that Charlie could possibly use to conceal him in this territory. The fabric and flesh and bone would barely diminish the velocity of the 50-caliber rounds should Charlie's path intersect the bullets path. The idea is sound. Charlie is detected moving on the saddle. The quad-fifty responds and shreds Charlie and everything else. Apparently, no one thought that Charlie might figure this out' that Charlie might recognize the potential of the quad-fifty, sitting right out in the open up on the hillside, that Charlie might consider a countermeasure.

The countermeasure last night was a rocket-propelled-grenade. Just as planned, the quad-fifty opened up as soon as movement was reported out on the saddle last night. Twenty-six rounds blasted out of the barrels, slamming viciously into the things and occupants of the saddle. It took the three man crew from Charlie Company about three seconds to direct the twenty-six rounds out into the invaders before the RPG round, fired from the opposite ridge, exploded the quad-fifty, all its ammo and transformed three American grunts into three KIAs.

Each of us in Six-Two Platoon will pass along in the trench below the quad-fifty mount many times during our stay at FB25. Each time we pass it we'll study the demolished skeleton of the guns, the turret mount, the ammo and the bloody remains of the three men. The remnants that weren't substantial enough to be placed into the three body bags used to convey these men home.

As we settle into our new home, studying the view to the front, scanning the neighborhood for any signs of life, the sounds and smells of this hilltop community follow our steps, rounding out our sensory familiarization with the place. Most of the smells and odors are famil-

Stars and Stripes and Shadows

iar to us; mud, wet sandbags and canvas, decaying vegetation, cordite residue and C-rations heating up over heat tabs and C4. But there is something else in the air here; something subtle. Only occasionally, when the air and breeze are just right can I detect it. It's so faint that at first I'm not sure it's even real. It's new to me. Each time it registers within my consciousness I try to figure it out. There is something of a sweetness to it, but there is nothing pleasant about it. Once in awhile I'll get a dose of it sufficient enough to find an overpowering sour stench blended with the sweet smell. With each breath, the pungent, vaporous residue builds up within me until I understand what the vile, disgusting odor is…death!

The bodies of the NVA invaders—thought to be about twenty—remain down on the saddle, just at the edge of the wire. Early this morning a detail from Charlie Company went out there to count. They took shovels and made an attempt to bury the bodies. They didn't have the time or the inclination to dig proper graves. Their efforts, in fact amounted to little more than covering the bodies in a few shovels full of dirt and mud. The rain and humidity and increasing heat of the morning are steadily breaking down the tissues and fluids and metabolic bi-products, releasing the smallest of the putrefying molecules up into the air, spreading them over the surrounding terrain, bringing them to the attention of all things still living here. The cycles of sun, rain, heat and humidity rapidly transform such things. For the next several days it will be impossible for us to avoid or ignore the ever-increasing potency of the death odors wafting over us from the decaying bodies out on the saddle.

Hueys are coming in at a regular clip this morning, re-supplying FB25 with the commodities consumed last night. They stay only long enough for the nervous flight crews to throw off the crates and boxes. Occasionally, one will come in with a sling load of crates hanging from ropes below it. These birds are particularly vulnerable hovering above the LZ with their dangling cargoes, the anxious pilots looking down at a wind blasted grunt volunteer giving hand signals in an attempt to place the sling safely on the ground. At mid-morning a huge double rotor Chinook helicopter comes in with a water trailer slung beneath it. It gets the trailer just close enough to the ground to cut it loose, drop-

Tim Haslam

ping it rudely onto the edge of the LZ as its rotor wash blows away every loose thing on this side of the firebase. With each arrival, more grunt volunteers are dispatched to the LZ to retrieve the cargo and hump it back to appropriate places within the bunkers and pits.

"Ed, you and Tim go up to the LZ and bring down some C-rations that are for us." Sergeant Bollman orders. "Some of Grady's and Steve's guys are already up there sorting it out; bring back whatever they have for us."

"Should we take our guns?" I ask.

"No, you won't be there long and you'll need both hands to hump the stuff back here. Just stay near the trench lines."

Grunts from all around the base are moving to and from the LZ shuttling the mortar rounds, the artillery flares the light weapons ammo and the C-rations back to their required places. Few seem concerned enough to stay within the trenches, preferring instead to take the quicker, more direct overland routes. Ed and I merge into the traffic and make our way down to the LZ where we find our guys sorting out our stuff. Grady is overseeing the process and he's started to build a little cache for each platoon and one for platoon headquarters. Ed and I study the pile for us, both happy to see a good supply of batteries for our radios but bothered a little by the amount of stuff to be humped back. This will take several trips.

Ed and I are pretty casual as we head back to the LZ for our third load, more casual than the recent history of FB25 warrants. As we reach the Six-Two Platoon guys on the LZ we light up cigarettes feeling like we're entitled to a little break, not yet understanding that open air breaks here are dangerous. There are two more trips worth of stuff to bring back and no one seems to be in too much of a hurry to finish the chore.

After only a moment or two our casual conversation, out here on the open edge of the LZ, is interrupted by a muffled sound coming from some distance off to the north. Each of us reacts at the same time. Even I know what this is and know what I'm about to hear.

"Incoming!"

Everyone on the firebase heads for cover. Those of us on the exposed LZ must seek cover, but we must also get to our weapons, we don't know what the incoming rounds portend. We don't know what else is com-

Stars and Stripes and Shadows

ing our way. Ed sprints back up toward the center of the base with me in close pursuit. Just as we get to the first bunkers the mortar round explodes behind us on the LZ with a loud *kachunk*. A second after the explosion there is another muffled *thwump* sound, then another. We continue making our way in the general direction of our bunker and our weapons, crouching as low as we can with each hurried step, some of the steps within the relative safety of trenches and some crisscrossing between the bunkers along the way. The second round lands fifteen meters to my left, with an even louder *kachunk*, on top of a stack of C-ration cases piled next to a bunker. The contents of the C-rations join the jagged shrapnel pieces spraying over everything adjacent to the explosion.

I'm OK. Keep going. Get to the bunker. Keep down. Where will the third thwump hit?

The adrenaline rush and the attention required for maneuvering over and around the obstacles in between the supposed safety of the bunker and I have superseded my fear. But there's something else coming up into my consciousness that isn't fear or a concentrated effort to find safety. There is a bizarre sense of excitement about all this. Clearly, the incoming rounds have disturbed the boredom of grunt life but they also provide some validation for it all. My months in the Army, my training, the weapons and gear I've been humping around, all of these things are symbiotically connected to the mortar rounds falling my way, launched by the men I'm supposed to encounter out here, encounter in just this way. The third round explodes loudly well off to my right, down toward one of the bunkers overlooking the saddle just as I jump down into the last trench, following a breathless Ed into our bunker. No one's been hurt and little damage has been done. Charlie's attack has gone unanswered and I have a nervous smile on my face as I get calibrated to the activities within the relative safety of our bunker.

"Shit!" is all I can say as I try to digest a feeling never felt before in my life; a sense of excitement coupled with real fear.

◢ ◢ ◢ ◢

Each day here is about the same. We stay close to the bunkers. No patrols go out. When we do go out, it's to shore up the defenses somehow; more wire, more sandbags, more Claymores. We always have

Tim Haslam

men with weapons, M16s and machineguns, watching out across the ravine at the opposite ridge, watching and listening for the cracks and thwumps of Charlie's weapons. Our weapons will respond quickly to anything seen or heard.

Two men are always stationed in a small foxhole down at the edge of the saddle keeping a close eye on the tangle of debris that Charlie could easily crawl through, concealed from the eyes of the grunts back up in the bunkers. The two men are well stocked with grenades to lob out into the snarl of trunks and branches that cloak the best approach to our base. The two men know that they perform one of those sacrificial roles. Charlie would have to get by them to invade our base. Charlie would have to make noise getting by them. The job of the two men is to ensure noise is made.

Twenty meters up the hill from the trench separating our bunker from the bunker to our west is a mortar pit. The 81mm mortar there is the first line of defense against anything coming at us from the reverse slope of the other ridge. Our mortarmen have preset trajectories and determined the appropriate charges and fusing for several targets at various points along the top of the other ridge and down the far slope. They just need a vector and a distance estimate and they're ready to drop rounds into their tube. Our guys can have their rounds *thwump-ing* into the air before Charlie's rounds can *kachunk* into the ground on our side. No one has much of an advantage. We each have the ability to slice and shred one another with our mortars.

Cobras and Huey gunships regularly prowl around the firebase as an added deterrent to Charlie's efforts at harassment. Nothing is more comforting to the grunts at FB25 than the sounds of the heavily armed choppers daring Charlie to show himself and nothing is more isolating than the same sounds fading off into the southern sky as the helicopters return to Pleiku as night approaches.

When it's not our turn to watch or listen or hump supplies from the LZ we're free to lounge around our bunkers, to read the latest copies of <u>Stars and Stripes</u> or the latest paperback books being passed around, to read and re-read the latest letters we have from home and to write our own letters in response. No one can do too much of any of this before the necessity for sleep takes over, and so napping tends to be the predominant activity. It's also OK for us to move back and forth

Stars and Stripes and Shadows

between bunkers to visit the guys beyond our squads or platoons, to get acquainted with the broader array of grunts sharing this experience, to exchange new stories and perspectives, to appreciate life in each FB25 neighborhood.

At nearly anytime of day, for anyone so inclined, there is usually a poker game to be found. Five or six grunts squeezed into a smoke filled bunker, passing their accumulations of Military Payment Certificates back and forth as their luck and skills dictate. The actual winning and losing and the wealth associated with either outcome are relatively unimportant. Having two or three hours go by this way is the real reward. Familiar songs coming over someone's transistor radio are always in the background and the images of home exchanged through our superficial dialogue make the games the most pleasant diversion available for many of us. My fraternity house experience with this game seems to have given me an advantage and I usually come away with more MPC than I entered with. So much in fact, that I will be able to send some of it back to Camp Enari for safekeeping until it's my turn to go on R&R.

Nighttime here, like everywhere in the grunt world, is dramatically worse than the daylight world. Here at FB25 we are always on two-thirds alert, two men awake and on guard for every man that gets to sleep. This makes for long nights and little sleep. Here too there are listening posts set each night. Three-man teams that sneak out to the edge of the wire, where they'll spend the night, frequently in the rain, listening for Charlie slithering up to kill us. The LP on our side is down somewhere in front of our bunker, just beyond our nine Claymores, hidden within the branches and trunks of the fallen trees. The concertina wire has been laid in a convoluted maze so that there is a route through it, out to the ground beyond, a route hopefully known only to the grunts on our side. At dawn each morning the cold, wet, weary men of the LP can be seen carefully weaving their way back up the hill, trudging miserably through the maze, patiently disarming the trip flares strung across their path, glad to be alive and thrilled that they won't have to do this again for a few days; hopeful also that there isn't some off-the-wall detail awaiting them, that will interfere with their plans to find a dry place for some sleep. Whatever torments there were for those of us pulling our guard shifts within the protective shelter of the bunkers, they were nothing like the slow motion miseries encountered second by

Tim Haslam

agonizing second out on LP...the worst of the worst.

One of the rewards of my new job as Six-Two-Charlie is dispensation from LP duty. *If being the number one target for Charlie's snipers is the price of this benefit, it's worth it.* My nightly job now is radio watch, responding to the sit-rep calls every twenty minutes, with the understanding that should our LP or the Six-Two-Three radio fail to respond to any sit-rep call, it's my problem to resolve. There's no guidance offered as to how I should go about resolving such a situation and so, each sit-rep call carries with it a measure of anxiety. It's a big relief to hear whoever has the Six-Two-Three radio answer back with *"Situation negative. Over"* and even more of a relief to hear the *"phhtt, phhtt, phhtt"* sound coming over the net as the poor LP guy squeezes the talk button on the handset indicating the same negative situation. For him the situation is about as negative as it can get without Charlie adding to his woes.

The five of us in Platoon Headquarters, Doc, Ed, Bruce, Lieutenant Falck and myself work out the nightly rotation so that two of us sleep while the other three stay awake, sharing the radio duty. Every hour one of the sleepers gets exchanged so that we sleep for two hours then stay awake for three hours. This is as close to the two-thirds doctrine as we're willing to go.

There is a great advantage to having others awake along with you. The main advantage is that we keep each other awake. The bunker provides enough sound insulation for us to carry on quiet sporadic conversation, albeit limited to the energy we have left for such work within the musty blackness. On the dry nights, the nights when the clouds are separated enough to allow views up into the stars, we climb up onto the top of the bunker with the radio and take in the panorama of little lights arrayed above us as we perform our alert duties, careful not to offer a human silhouette to Charlie's nocturnal snipers. These moments are easier to endure than those within the claustrophobic confines below. The balmy night air and the clear skies are more able facilitators for our remembered, anticipated, perhaps pretended trips home. A cigarette carefully lit and puffed, so as to block Charlie's view of the meager illumination, adds another little pleasure counteracting for a moment the great pall of shit that surrounds and hangs over us.

Our first night at FB25 passes slowly, quietly, without visitors, leav-

Stars and Stripes and Shadows

ing only added weariness and fatigue to mark its passing.

⚡ ⚡ ⚡ ⚡

Four-point-two inches in diameter; it's an amazing feat to hurl a conical shaped hunk of iron, four-point-two inches in diameter, four or five or ten thousand meters onto a precise target. So many things impinge on the path of the projectile; the elevation and direction of the launching device, the amount of powder in the explosive charge used to push the round out of the barrel, the wind and humidity and air pressure, the steadfastness of the ground resisting the recoil all must be accounted for and counted on. Maps have been used to determine the desired target. What if the map is off a little? What if the supposed declination angle off of true north has shifted slightly? What if the finger ridge indicated on the map is in actuality a fraction of a degree off its relative position to the Howitzer or mortar? What if the Forward Observer, the FO, overestimates the distance between the Bravo Company grunts and the desired targets? *What if...?*

Each day the officers at FB25 get together to plan the days strategy, the improvements necessary to shore up any perceived weakness in our defenses and to prepare for the next night to come. Lieutenant Reese and the other artillery officers at TOC reconsider the value of the targets they've already established around our perimeter. The targets that the guns over on FB30 and down at Dak To will be asked to shoot at should something happen up here. They evaluate the efficacy of these targets against what they learned two nights ago when Charlie attacked. The targets are too far out they determine. They must bring them in closer they decide. They carefully plot another firing plan, marking reference targets at several points all around the firebase. On our side some of these targets are as close as eighty meters out. The rules say such targets must be a minimum of seventy meters away from friendlies. The 105mm high explosive rounds have a killing radius of 25-meters. There isn't much margin of error.

Just as the last long rays of sun slip over the mountain tops to our west on day two, my radio advises that everyone should seek the shelter of their bunkers. The 105s over on FB30 are going to fire a few defensive targeting rounds — Delta Tangos — DTs. The DTs are the final check in the process. Live rounds are fired at the plotted reference targets.

Tim Haslam

If they actually hit these targets, all the variables are logged for future reference. If the rounds miss, adjustments are made until subsequent rounds find the mark. Just in case the initial error approaches us, we are advised to stay in the bunkers. All aircraft heading home from points north are also advised of the site lines for the DT firings to avoid possible collisions. Everyone's ready!

"Shot. Over!" Lieutenant Reese relays over the Company net, echoing the advisory from the Battery down at FB30.

Everyone waits. Everyone listens.

In a few seconds there's a great explosion off to our left, much closer than anyone expected.

Another moment passes before we figure out where the first round landed.

The water trailer brought in yesterday by the big Chinook wasn't the planned reference target. The water trailer was brought in to provide drinking water to the thirsty inhabitants of this hot, humid place. The remnants of the trailer and its contents litter the LZ, having, apparently offered little resistance to the high explosive round that detonated right next to it, leaving a small crater. That wasn't supposed to happen. The American taxpayers are out one perfectly good water trailer and we are back to conserving the water remaining in our canteens. Reese and company pow-wow for a few minutes before coming to the same conclusion all the grunts have already arrived at...*left one hundred!*

The adjustment made to bring the second round properly onto its reference target seems to have fixed things in general and the rest of the DTs explode out and around just as planned. All of our guys now know where the rounds will land if summoned. Charlie too probably knows where the rounds will land. Charlie too knows about the seventy-meter rule and his officers will try to carry the fighting into this zone.

The board is set for the night. Our defenses are all in place and prepared. Charlie determines what happens next.

At 2:20 a.m. Five-Nine-Charlie breaks the squelch on the radio, sending a subtle shock through everyone within earshot of the radios.

"Six-Charlie this is Five-Nine-Charlie. We've got movement down to our front. Over."

Five-Nine Platoon has the section of perimeter to the north of us,

Stars and Stripes and Shadows

partly facing the opposite ridge and arcing around toward the LZ on the western end of the firebase.

"Five-Nine-Charlie, this is Six. Fill me in on the movement. Over."

"This is Five-Nine. The men in our second bunker up from Six-Two believe they heard something out past the wire down in the gully."

"What about your LP?" asks Captain Hilton. "Where are they relative to all this?"

"Our LP is further around to the west, down from the LZ. They haven't reported anything and replied negative at the last sit-rep about ten minutes ago."

"What's their call sign?"

"Five-Nine-Three. Over."

"Five-Nine-Three, this is Six. How about it? Give me a sit-rep. Over."

"*Phhtt, phhtt, phhtt.*" The radio says in response to the Captains request, indicating situation negative; they've heard nothing.

"Six-Two-Charlie this is Six. Give me a sit-rep. Over."

I look at Lieutenant Falck before responding to confirm my negative situation assessment. He reaches out, in response to my look, requesting the handset.

"This is Six-two. Wait one. I want to check with the next bunker up the line toward Five-Nine. They're closer that way. Over," he tells the Captain and then instructs me to go over there and see if they've heard anything.

It takes me only a few seconds to transit through the trench separating our bunkers and another few seconds to fill in the awake guys there on what's going on.

Nothing, they've heard nothing. Another few seconds gets me back home where Six-Two relays the confirmation that the situation is negative from our perspective.

"Six-Zero-Charlie, this is Six-Charlie. Sit-rep. Over."

The Captain has decided to call out to all stations for a sit-rep. They all come back negative and so he's faced with a command decision. Should he do something or just assume that the Five-Nine guys have heard something benign or perhaps, in their weary states, heard nothing real at all. The nervous men in Five-Nine's second bunker up from

217

Tim Haslam

us could have heard any of a million things; another wild pig rooting around or one of the many other carnivores or scavengers who prefer working the night shift, a falling seed pod, a dead tree limb dislodged by a gust of breeze or the shifting nighttime temperature, or a careless man trying to crawl up silently to the American's night defensive position to learn something about how the inhabitants spend their nights. Or possibly they only think they heard something. Sometimes our blind listening out here in the lonely blackness reacts to sounds we have manufactured within our own minds.

If the Captain decides to do something, Charlie will learn something; something about our defenses, something about the way we react, something about our nighttime resources. If the Captain does nothing and Charlie really is crawling up to us, crawling up to turn our Claymores around 180 degrees, to aim his RPGs at our bunkers, we're fucked.

"All stations, this is Six. I want everybody up. In five minutes, on my signal we're going to conduct a mad-minute. Bring in your LPs and radio back when they're in. Over."

At 2:42 a.m. everyone at FB25 is awake awaiting the Captains command.

At 2:43 a.m. every M16, M60 machinegun and M79 grenade launcher starts firing out into the darkness surrounding the firebase. The *kachunks* of exploding grenades provide the rhythm for the steady cacophony of small arms blazing away from the trenches and bunkers. Tracers sweep back and forth from the machineguns, adding visual effects to the show of force and a few trip flares pop off, as the flood of fire coming from all around the firebase hits the wire suspending them. The intense light from the flares, filtered through the building layer of smoke, illuminates everything out to our front. No one however sees any signs of Charlie within the diffuse contrasts exposed before us. If Charlie is anywhere around he's just learned that the Americans can pour thousands of rounds of ammunition out into the night at any time for any reason. *Madness!*

И И И И

I'm just about to open the little cans that represent my breakfast, sitting comfortably with Ed on the back of our bunker on this bright

Stars and Stripes and Shadows

clear morning when the *thwumps* come. Two in quick succession, followed after a short pause by a third and fourth.

"Incoming!" Ed and I yell out simultaneously, along with a dozen other voices as we scramble down into the trench that leads back into our bunker, leaving the unopened little cans sitting out, exposed to the mortar rounds now plummeting downward towards us. We're barely into our bunker when the 81mm mortar in the pit up behind us starts *thwumping* back in response. There's little difference between what we're doing this morning and what our ancestors did a thousand years ago. Our slings and catapults and trebuchets hurl stones back and forth over the battlements as we curse each other, preparing ourselves for the likely struggle to come where we must stab and slice, rip and rent each other until the less vigorous and determined withdraw or surrender. In another ten minutes however we can commence twentieth century warfare. In another ten minutes the Cobras returning northward from their nocturnal nests at Camp Enari will swoop in to assist the warriors on the inside of the citadel. Industry will be added to the equation.

Before the Cobras can churn their way up the valley to us a pair of A1Es appear, arcing across the northern ski, banking leftward back around towards us. The lead plane vectors its camouflaged fuselage onto a path paralleling the firebase, steadily dropping in altitude. Its gently rocking wing tips are still tilted into the left-hand bank as it approaches the reverse slope of the opposite ridge from the west. The right hand wing of the Hobo seems to jerk slightly to the right, bringing the growling machine into level flight just as two objects separate from the underside of the wings. The objects disappear from our site over the crest of the forested ridge. A second later, a long series of popcorn explosions zippers back to us from along the target line. The individual bomb-lets expelled from the cluster bomb canisters are exploding within this section of jungle like a thousand hand grenades. The Hobo pulls up hard to the left to the cheers of the firebase residents.

The second A1E follows the same path in, unleashing two cylinders at about the same point. These however, turn out to be napalm, exploding in a deafening blast, followed quickly by a wall of flame jumping up over the ridge top, so intense that we can feel the heat sweep over us. The two planes circle out again into a longer arc until the trailing Hobo overtakes the lead plane. With Hobo number two now in the

Tim Haslam

lead they return for another run. The A1Es in turn pass through the residual napalm smoke, flying another hundred meters along the ridge before releasing their weapons in the same sequence; cluster bombs followed by napalm.

Again they bank off to the left but circle around more abruptly until they are heading directly towards us from the north. They rip through the dark smoke and roar right over us, less than a hundred feet up and waggle their wings left and right, again to the cheers of all the appreciative grunts, awestruck by the breakfast performance.

With the show over and the belief that Charlie's mortar positions are now smoldering ruins, Ed and I return to our little cans and the doldrums of the day to come. Everything is as we left it. The incoming rounds fell further up into the interior of the firebase, damaging only sandbags.

OK…now a cigarette, then coffee, then breakfast.

Wrong!

"Haslam," Sergeant Bollman interrupts in a tone reminiscent of my mother's orders to get out of bed on a Saturday morning. "Go down and relieve Morris down at the observation post. Take your breakfast with you." Bollman's directive is in reference to the trench overlooking the saddle where apparently Scotty Morris has finished his shift guarding the vulnerable approach. As this post is manned throughout the day, every grunt in the Company below the rank of sergeant gets a turn.

With my M16 and lots of ammo I head down toward the observation post, a cigarette dangling from my lip, my still unopened breakfast stuffed into the pocket on the side of my fatigue pants. Thirty meters down I climb out of the trench that forms the outer perimeter and start working my way carefully down through the tangle foot wire, fully aware that I'm now totally exposed to anyone with a rifle on the other ridge; anyone with a rifle and the inclination to shoot me. Each breath I take working my way step by well-planned step down through the slippery mud draws in an increasing measure of the sickening stench wafting up from the dead bodies rapidly decomposing out on the saddle. Morris and his partner in the foxhole, Rich Green, turn in unison toward me as I make my final approach, each with a bandana tied across their face in an attempt to limit the number of noxious molecules entering into their nose and lungs. Both look as though their

Stars and Stripes and Shadows

bandanas are pretty ineffective.

Scotty is quickly up and out of the foxhole, nearly sprinting his way upwards toward fresher air. I look at Green, through eyes watering in response to the airborne residues of rotting flesh as I pull my towel around from the back of my neck, plugging it over my nose and mouth. It doesn't, even with its own accumulation of odors help much.

"Cigarettes help a little," he says, lighting two of his Winstons, handing me one as a replacement for the butt I just flicked off into the sludge at our feet.

"They didn't do a very good job at burial detail," says Green, pointing out to the ground just beyond the concertina wire in front of us. There, maybe ten meters away, I can see the stiffened arms and legs of several bodies pressed into a trench. The recognizable contours of human anatomy have by now conjoined with the mud and other decaying vegetation to form a tar-pit like scene. The image in front of me is such a macabre mosaic that it barely registers with me that these are the first dead human beings I've ever seen. The stench overpowers everything. I can't even rally a measure of sympathy for these former men. It's their fault they attacked. It's their fault they put themselves in front of our machineguns and Claymores. It's their fault that they object to our points of view and it's their fault that even in death they continue to assault me and the other grunts here with their stinking transition. It's their fault that I have lost my appetite for breakfast this morning.

Throughout the long two hours of my turn down here I long for a breeze to come along and chase the odors back down the saddle, back towards Charlie's side, but the steamy air remains still, wrapping me up completely in the morbid vapors. Two hours is not enough time for my senses to accommodate to this smell, it's too strong, too stinging, too clear in its message. Observation is the assignment down here and we completely understand what the consequence of failure to observe can be. Our searching heads, scanning out across the saddle and into the hiding places out beyond are exposed targets. We have to spot Charlie's snipers before they can get off enough shots to eliminate us as searchers and scanners. I've never been more anxious with an assignment here in the Nam; here in the shit.

N   N   N   N

221

Tim Haslam

Just before dusk two Hueys ferry in a group of visitors to the firebase along with a good deal of gear that seems out of place here. The four uniformed men, armed only with holstered pistols start to drag what looks like an electric generator, and several large loudspeakers up toward the center of the base, assisted by a couple of volunteers from Five-Nine Platoon. One of the men is Vietnamese, the other three look like typical clean, base-camp type American GIs. Lieutenant Falck breaks away from our after-dinner conversation and heads up toward the men assembling their gear to find out what this is all about.

"We can forget about much sleep tonight," he says, rejoining us on the top of our bunker.

"They're an Army Psy-Ops team and they're going to be broadcasting propaganda messages over their speakers all night. They think they can encourage more of the dinks to Chieu-Hoi."

The officers have decided to change our regular nighttime strategy. Everyone seemed to like the Captain's "mad minute" exercise last night and have choreographed one in for tonight as well, to be launched at some point after the Psy-Ops team finishes telling Charlie about all the benefits of surrendering to us. The good news for some of the men is that we will not bother to send out any LPs tonight. The bad news for all of us is that this will be a long noisy night.

I don't remember the transition from dusk to darkness. I must have fallen asleep lying up on the top of the bunker and when the first loud pronouncements blare out from the loudspeakers somewhere up above me I'm totally disoriented. It takes a few seconds to get recalibrated to the what and where and when of my reality. The usual corrosive strains of the Vietnamese language are amplified into an unbearable harangue of clipped syllables being forced through the hissy, slurring, overdriven speakers. Fingernails scraping on a chalkboard being broadcast over the poorest quality, but loudest possible PA system come to mind. I can't imagine how anyone hearing the rhetoric echoing around the jungle would be able to separate the ideas expressed in this libretto from the cacophonous grating tones of the orchestration. The little Vietnamese man at the microphone, impassioned either through conviction or sense of duty, has plenty of stamina; on and on he bleats, without pause, without any modification to rhythm or tenor or tone, hour after deafening hour. If I were Charlie, I'd surrender if the Americans would just promise never to subject me to this kind of torture again. Sergeant Bollman and I observe cynically that Charlie's probably running as fast as he can away from FB25 right now. These amplified words are mightier than the sword, mightier than the M16 the mortar and the Howitzer.

Sometime around 1:00 a.m. the auditory assault ceases and the black night starts to return to its normal silent status. Sometime around 1:10 a.m. Six-Charlie starts the five-minute countdown to tonight's mad-minute. Sometime around 1:15 a.m. we all open up with our weapons on full automatic, spraying as much lead as we can out into the jungle and the shit surrounding us. Sometime around 1:16 a.m. the creatures resident in the neighboring forest cautiously return to their sleeping, their scavenging and their predatory schemes. The raucous party at FB25 is finally over.

N N N N

The first Huey of the day scuttles in around eight o'clock, sent to retrieve the men and gear of the Psy-Ops team waiting on the LZ. Perhaps the atmospherics are just right for the Huey's noise to obstruct all other sounds. Perhaps our ears are still ringing from the pounding, blasting jolts they were subjected to through most of last night, or perhaps we're just too weary to be alert. Whatever the reason, no one apparently heard the first of the three *thwumps*. The first indication we have of incoming fire is the shell exploding between the helicopter and the bunkers up at the edge of the firebase. We all hear the following *thwumps* and the subsequent explosions stepping across the top of the hill and we all hear what we hoped not to hear.

"Medic!"

Our mortars are just starting to respond as Doc, his medical bag in hand, hurries down toward the LZ where the plea came from.

"Medic! Medic!"

This isn't a repeat of the prior request. This time the call comes from down to our right, somewhere around the lower of the two bunkers guarding the saddle access. Something doesn't add up here. None of the incoming rounds landed anywhere near there. I've had the radio handset pressed to my ear since the first explosion, listening for any status updates or deployment orders. The ongoing radio chatter is steadily clarifying the situation over near the LZ. Two men from Five-Nine

Tim Haslam

have been hit; one peppered by small shrapnel fragments to his upper leg and buttocks, the other more seriously wounded by a large piece lodging in his back, his neck nicked by another. Still, nothing comes back from Six-One to explain the need for medics down there.

"Six-One, this is Six. What's going on down there? Over," our new Captain asks.

"Six-One, Six-One, this is Six...give me you your situation. Over," the Captain repeats more forcefully after a short pause.

"This is Six-One. I've got a man down in my number two bunker. I'm on my way down there now. Give me a minute. Over," Lieutenant Nelson answers.

Several long minutes go by before the Lieutenant's voice breaks squelch to fill in all the listening ears anxiously awaiting news.

"Sergeant Johnson's dead," the somber voice of the Lieutenant begins. "It looks like he...wait one."

How can this be? I think to myself as I pass along the message to Bruce and Lieutenant Falck. He was inside his bunker and there weren't any rounds close to there? *How can this be*?

"This is Six-One again. Johnson was shot...right through the heart. It looks like a sniper must have been able to shoot right into the firing port from somewhere over on the ridge to the right of the saddle. Over."

There's another long pause while everyone tries to digest and process what we've just heard. Captain Hilton, the new Bravo Company CO must digest and process this more quickly than the rest of us. He must realign the Company and react.

"Six-One, this is Six. Put as much fire as you can on wherever you think the sniper was. I'll bring the mortars around there too. Over." The Captain knows that the sniper is long gone. The Captain knows that the men of Six-One and of Bravo Company need to respond somehow, to let some of their emotional shock ride with their bullets slamming into the jungled plant life that concealed the killer. We have plenty of bullets. We will have plenty of tears. We no longer have Sterling Johnson.

Six-Two, Bruce and I are all stunned at what we've just heard. The reserved and respected Sterling Johnson, Six-One's Platoon Sergeant, alive just a moment ago, is dead, killed by a sniper shot that no one heard. Shot and killed within the supposed protection of his own bunker. Shot and killed doing the same thing that all the rest of us were doing. *Why him? Why not us? Why not me? When?*

Two Huey gunships accompany the medevac bird coming for our wounded men. They prowl slowly over the opposite ridge as the injured men are carefully handed over to the crew of the helicopter with the red cross painted on it. The gunships add a few bursts from their mini-guns into the foliage where the sniper was thought to be as the two Bravo Company grunts are lifted up out of this place, fluttering their way to the 71st Evacuation Hospital within the care of the onboard medics. The heavily armed Hueys with the shark-tooth painted muzzles continue to circle and search for nearly an hour, until another Huey sticks itself down into the mud of the LZ, where the crew hands off a couple of crates of something in exchange for the poncho wrapped body of Sterling Johnson.

It don't mean nothin', we try to tell ourselves, when, in fact it means everything.

With Doc back at the bunker we replay the events of the morning trying to piece together what happened; trying to understand what Charlie did; trying to understand what we did right and what Johnson did wrong.

The first Huey came in. The incoming rounds exploded. Two men are wounded. Johnson is dead. Somehow a sniper fired his AK47 at the exact same time one of the mortar rounds exploded masking the rapport of his rifle shot. Was this just an incredible coincidence? Did the sniper somehow watch the plummeting mortar round with one eye, the other aligning his sites with Johnson's heart, squeezing the trigger just as the round hit the ground? However Charlie did it, the truth for Bravo Company remains the same; we're being picked off one at a time by the patient men with their little rifles hiding out there in the shit.

Rain today…a lot of rain, making it a good day for staying in the bunker, for reading, for napping, all the while considering how much of a target we might be presenting to someone over on the opposite ridge. Late morning brings a let up in the downpour and the sky clears out

Tim Haslam

enough for Hueys to find their way out to us. The first ones coming in bring something new for us, something of value. Each of us is issued a brand new air mattress. The kind you inflate with your breath, just like the ones we used to play on at the beach, except that they're olive drab. Our bunker quickly fills up with the air cushions and our napping takes on a level of comfort nearly forgotten.

The third chopper churning in doesn't quite touch down when an AK burst from the other side chases it away. Bollman, Doc and I, lounging at various points within the bunker all heard the gunfire and each of us detected the smoke burst and muzzle flash at the same time. A machinegun from Five-Nine opens up in response but we can see that they're firing too far left. They have wrongly assumed the snipers position. The tracers streaming across the ravine attract others to fire. Several M16s join in the reaction, all firing in the wrong place. I call over to Five-Nine-Charlie and advise them of their mistake.

"Six-Two-Charlie, this is Five-Nine. Put some fire on where you think he is. Over."

"Roger," I say, as Bruce and I grab for our rifles, scrambling out toward the trench out on our left side.

"Elmer!" Bollman yells out, up toward the next bunker. "Put some M60 rounds out where we're firing! He and I both start firing into the vegetation up on the opposite ridge top where we saw the gun smoke. Tracers from Elmer's machinegun follow along quickly, marking the target for everyone. Doc and Six-Two have joined Bollman and me in the trench, increasing the volume of lead tearing into the opposite ridge. Up behind us, the 81mm mortar crew is frantically setting their tube angles and charges to add their contribution to the stuff being hurled back at Charlie. For some reason, the first *thwump* from the mortar behind us doesn't sound right. The four of us react in unison to the wrongness of the sound, jerking around in an effort to find an explanation for the dissonance. In an instant we all can see what's happened.

"Short round!" the mortar guy's yell out, validating what we have already determined.

The projectile puffs out of the tube, rises up lazily twenty or so meters before losing interest in its purpose and destination and starts collapsing back down toward the earth.

Shit! It's falling right down towards us.

Stars and Stripes and Shadows

There's barely enough time to wake up and react to the reality and consequence of what we're seeing. All we can do is hurl ourselves downward as deeply as we can into the muddy bottom of the trench, trying to pull our helmets down over as much of our bodies as possible. The round *splushes* into the same mud in the same trench just outside the entrance to the next bunker up the line just a few feet from us and the slicing, ripping pieces of shrapnel surrounding the explosive charge contained within the round, all meant for Charlie, remain within the structure of the shell. The round happily didn't reach an altitude sufficient to fuse the charge. The impotent missile just lies there quietly in the mud having scared the shit out of all of us.

The mortar guys more carefully prepare the next round before dropping it into the tube as we watch from below. Their careful preparation wasn't enough. This round too takes life with the same disingenuous *thwump*, the same apathetic puff, the same wiffleball ascent and the same *"oh shits!"* from all of us down range from the tube. It lands just above the trench, maintaining its inert form, nearly as successful as its predecessor in its affects on us.

Enough is enough!

"What the fuck are you trying to do?" We inquire of our friends in the pit up above us as we retract ourselves again from the muddy recesses of the trench.

"Get your fuckin' shit together! What are you trying to do, get somebody killed?"

Get somebody killed...that's what we're all trying to do!

ℳ ℳ ℳ ℳ

There's an hour or two left before dawn, when I crawl up onto my air mattress, taking my last turn in the sleep rotation, careful not to climb over Sergeant Bollman who's asleep somewhere nearby in the black den. I'm exhausted, but still need something other than the day's events to accompany me into sleep. I want to read the latest letters from Rosemary one more time tonight. I remember leaving them up on the little shelf dug into the ground just above my head. My flashlight is up there somewhere too. I probe around with my hand for a moment in the pitch-blackness of the bunker until I feel the flashlight. Then, with my towel over my head forming a barrier between the little ray of light

Tim Haslam

and the outside world, I look for the letters. Instead of the longed for orange stationary, the ray of light reflects off the red eyes of a huge rat. One more time, something startles me out of my readiness for sleep. One more unwanted tenant is sharing this dark, mud-pit with us.

"Goddamn it!" I blurt out as I jerk backward away from the over-sized rodent. The volume of my proclamation along with the suddenness of my body's retreat jars Sergeant Bollman out of his peaceful sleep.

"What's going on?" He asks into the darkness as he attempts the transition back from wherever his sleep state may have taken him.

"There's a fucking rat in here!" I explain, naturally trying to engage someone of higher rank in the problem. The rat, still bathed under the flashlight beam, hasn't moved in reaction to anything that's transpired since its discovery, apparently determined to hold its ground up on the ledge.

"Jesus! It's a big sucker! We gotta get that thing outta here!" says Bollman, his adrenaline and level of alertness now equal to mine, as he fumbles around for some implement to use against the intruder. He knows right where his rifle is and grabs for that, at the same time I reach over for my machete that's been stabbed into the side of the bunker, just barely visible in the reflected light.

Now that we're both armed, what are we going to do? Obviously Bruce can't shoot it in here and there's no room for me to wield the machete after it within the confines of the little shelf that the rat controls. Also, if I'm going to have to move at all as part of our strategy, I'll be unable to follow the scurrying beast with my light. Before either of us can formulate a plan the rat bolts out of the light beam, disappearing within the darker reaches of the shelf off to the right. I track it down quickly with my light causing it to race over to the far left side of the shelf. Sorry rat, no good. I've still got it in my light beam. Off again; this time like a broken field runner it sprints back to the right about two feet staying just ahead of the pursuing spotlight. Then, it slants hard right and leaps down off the shelf onto one of the air mattresses. We can hear it skittering around over the plastic surface of the mattress but I can't get a bead on it with my light, it's too quick. It's close combat now; the little sucker is right down here with Bruce and I, ready with fang and claw, pumped up for a fight. Bruce and I are not ready, I don't

Stars and Stripes and Shadows

want him shooting me and he doesn't want me decapitating him. We both reflexively jerk back toward the walls of the bunker just as Lieutenant Falck ducks through the entrance.

"What the hell is going on down here?" he asks, just before the rat trampolines off the air mattress onto the startled officer's knee and then off into the darkness somewhere.

"What the fuck...!" Six-Two cries out in reaction to the unidentified assailant, jerking himself back out of the bunker.

"It was a rat, sir."

It'll be awhile before I can get any more sleep tonight.

⚡ ⚡ ⚡ ⚡

The last time I had at least four hours of uninterrupted sleep was before our last patrol back at the bridge. The fatigue is setting in, my spirit is pretty low, energy is nil. I can't rally enough enthusiasm to work my way around the trench network in search of a poker game. I'm not sure I want to spend much time out there anyway, where everybody's mortar rounds keep falling from the sky. Six-Two doesn't fraternize with the enlisted men where money is changing hands, although he can occasionally be enticed into a game of Hearts with Doc, Bruce and I. Ed and Doc are almost always good for an hour or two of Gin Rummy and so we spend most of our awake time playing rainy-day games within our dank smoky hovel. Ed's transistor radio plays continuously in the background, its muted delivery serving as our only umbilical back to something recognizable from our past lives. It feeds and nurtures our spirits somewhat when a particular song draws us back to a better time and place, suggesting that such a place still exists. Ed is the most musical among us, claiming to be a drummer of considerable skill, proving this with his continual rhythmic slapping of anything around, keeping time to the beat of whatever song is playing. He and Bruce also seem to be about equal in their knowledge of popular lyrics and never hesitate to conjoin their voices with those of the real artists transducing out of the little speaker. This adolescent energy is contagious enough to keep all of us talkative, laughing and distracted from all that resides just outside. The adolescent energy gets us through the mornings.

It all seems to catch up with us after our lunchtime C-rations. The weariness, the boredom, the claustrophobic confines of the bunker and

Tim Haslam

the pervasive dampness of everything; air, skin and clothes all become too much to ignore. Sleep is the only escape and we are all so deprived, it comes easily. Our bodies seem to be able to find the sleep stage that's received the least attention so that sometimes I'm into a dream the instant I dose off, other times I fall immediately into a deeper realm of nothingness where everything within me just shuts down and rests. No matter how it transpires, it's never enough, always interrupted too soon by something or someone.

I don't know what's brought me out of my light slumber this afternoon. Someone else's fidgeting, a disruption in the PRC25s constant squelch sound or perhaps it's Judy Collins trying to reach out to us through Ed's little transistor radio.

> *Bows and flows of angel hair*
> *Ice cream castles in the air*
> *And feathered canyons everywhere,*
> *I've looked at clouds that way*
>
> *But now they only block the sun*
> *They rain and snow on everyone*
> *So many things I would have done,*
> *But clouds got in my way*
>
> *I've looked at clouds from both sides now*
> *From up and down and still somehow*
> *Its clouds illusions I recall*
> *I really don't know clouds at all*

The bunkers firing port frames a gray-green landscape out in front of me, the view diffused by a light mist. The little ribbon of sky visible above the opposite ridgeline is just gray and ponderous, no ice cream castles, no feathered canyons, no illusions.

It's not unusual to see grunts out in front of the bunkers, adjusting Claymores, or stringing more wire. If I don't have to be involved, I don't pay them much attention. So the first glimpse I get of someone moving down at the edge of the wire doesn't really get my full attention. Then, something about the figure just entering my peripheral vision sends a

Stars and Stripes and Shadows

shiver down my spine. The helmet appearing up out of the lower right hand corner of the bunker opening is different; it's a pith helmet with a red star on the front.

Shit!

"There's a gook in the wire!" I yell out, jumping up off my air mattress, scrambling for my rifle. Six-Two and Sergeant Bollmann are away somewhere up the hill with the other officers and senior NCOs of the Company and Doc is off socializing at someone else's hole. Ed jerks up a fraction of a second behind me, lunging for his shotgun. We each ready our weapons, take aim, and then start to more fully evaluate the situation.

"Chieu Hoi, Chieu Hoi, Chieu Hoi!" the man in the ragged uniform with the red-starred helmet yells out, flinging both his arms skyward. By now at least twenty weapons are zeroed in on him and he knows it.

"Chieu Hoi, Chieu Hoi!" he keeps repeating as several men from Six-One Platoon materialize and start heading down cautiously toward him, each with an M16 aligned with some vital component of his anatomy. The man freezes just at the edge of the outer wire, his arms outstretched upward as far as he can reach. This time the person surrendering has the look of a more seasoned veteran. His threadbare uniform is as filthy as ours, ragged at the sleeves and pant legs, his black tennis shoes caked with mud. His AK47 is slung over his back and he wears a pouched vest full of magazines for his weapon. Despite the fear and uncertainty tremoring over his face, everything else about this man suggests that he's been here a long time, that he's an experienced soldier; that he's encountered the Americans before. His weapons too have the look of experience.

The whole north side of the firebase has by now reacted to the red-starred visitor and no one is yet convinced of the sincerity of his plea. No one yet believes that he could be alone out there. We all shift our attention back and forth between the gook at the wire and the forested gully and ridge behind him where people have been shooting at us, where, perhaps even he's been shooting at us.

"Keep your hands up!"

"Don't fuckin' move!"

Each of the Six-One men maneuvering down through the wire cor-

Tim Haslam

ridor maze seems to have some instruction for the NVA soldier awaiting them at the front door, even though he's unable to understand a single word being barked out at him. He does understand what will happen when the triggers are pulled. His best response is no response, just stay frozen, just keep repeating Chieu Hoi, keep looking for the open arms promised the other night by the voice echoing around through the dark jungle shit surrounding him. *Where are the open arms, he must be thinking.*

As quickly as they can, the Six-One guys take possession of the AK, the 7.62mm ammo and everything else that Red-star has on him. With a couple of men in front of him and a couple more behind, the neutralized soldier is escorted back up through the access route that weaves and zigzags around the concertina wire barriers. The Bravo Company officers, accompanied by a whole cadre of others from TOC, advance down toward the edge of the bunker, hurrying to take command of the situation. They reach the trench line just as the prisoner and his escorts break out of the concertina swirls and start their way carefully up through the tangle foot razor wire and Claymore covered slope in front of us. A few of the unfamiliar TOC types continue out until they meet the group coming up, taking custody of the still Chieu-Hoi-ing man. His new captors seem more hospitable. One apparently speaks Vietnamese and is offering the promised assurances previously withheld by the M16 toting grunts. The ensuing conversation seems pretty lively as the whole party meanders quickly up toward the TOC bunkers out of our sight.

Sergeant Bollman has rejoined Ed and me in the bunker, all of us with weapons in hand, still nervously scanning the land to our front. My Zippo arcs around and ignites the three cigarettes that will bring us back to our more relaxed, bored state.

"I can't believe that guy could get all the way over here without his own guys seeing him," I observe.

"Maybe they've all pulled out and he saw his chance to break away," Ed offers hopefully.

"I don't know," says a more pensive Bollman. "I don't know. Something doesn't feel right about that guy."

N N N N

Stars and Stripes and Shadows

The Army Corp of Engineers has been trained to do all sorts of wonderful things; build roads and bridges and military structures, clear away major obstacles from the path of strategic progress and solve any number of problems that involve rearranging nature for the betterment of our side. Up here in the Central Highlands of Vietnam, way out in the boonies, there aren't that many opportunities for the Engineers to apply their trade. Nature up here is too vast, too well dug in, to quick to counterattack; our strategy and deployment too ethereal to be bounded by roads and bridges. The bombs from the B52s do most of the engineering work. There are Engineers assigned to the 3rd of the 8th however, and like everyone else they search for things to do. Good Army Engineers are resourceful. They can make useful things out of whatever materials are available to them. Good Army Engineers have a strong intrinsic need to contribute to the war effort.

This afternoon, up on the isolated hilltop designated Fire Support Base 25; the Engineers have finally broken out of their boredom and come up with a project. They believe, and have convinced the other officers, that their project will add significantly to the defenses of the firebase. They have, in fact, been able to generate a great deal of enthusiasm among the senior staff present here. They will need just a few things to construct their prototype:

1	55 gallon drum
1	2.5 lb. block of C4 explosive
1	Blasting cap
1	30' length of detonator wire
1	Hand detonator
30	Gallons of gasoline
25	Gallons of napalm

The bill-of-material for this project alone should have been sufficient to bring any sane person to their senses—any high school chemistry teacher —any responsible grown-up. But this is war. Resourcefulness and ingenuity win wars. Boldness in the face of danger wins wars. Things that explode and burn with great force, unleashed and directed by well trained, confidant practitioners win wars. Insanity wins wars. This isn't a good place for responsible grown-ups anyway.

Tim Haslam

All of the solid materials described on the BOM are available right here on FB25. All that we need to bring in is the gasoline and napalm. There must be plenty of both down at Dak To where the thirsty trucks re-fuel and where the flame-throwing tanks and APCs re-load. Major Geiger, the Battalion Executive Officer who resides up at the TOC bunker has the clout to requisition the required fluids. He may have some negotiating to do to convince a Huey pilot to fly in such a cargo to a place where sniper's bullets frequently greet incoming helicopters. Major Geiger has the clout and the enthusiasm for the project to overcome any such reason-based objections. We'll get the gas. We'll get the jellied explosive.

A few grunt volunteers with shovels are all that's required in the way of labor.

By mid-afternoon, all the required materials are at FB25 and the perfect place for the prototype has been determined. Right in front of our bunker! The idea is to fill up the drum with the gas/napalm mixture, affix the C4 with an attached blasting cap to the bottom of the barrel, attach the detonator wire and string it back to our bunker. Then, bury the drum in the big hole dug by the volunteer grunts, carefully angling it out toward the barbed wire-covered approaches to our position. When Charlie comes up this way, we'll compress the detonator, just like we would if it we're a Claymore, the C4 will explode and the 55 gallons of manmade lava will erupt out and over everything to our front.

The Engineers supervising the work take careful measurements of the hole dug by the volunteers, ensuring that the precise angle has been achieved. The empty drum is then carefully placed down into the pit, with the C4 attached. Finally, a crew of non-smoking grunts relays the cans of gasoline and napalm down to the non-smoking Engineer in charge of filling up the drum. At this point they figure out the angled barrel precludes the full charge of 55 gallons and so the leftovers are returned to the LZ. The drum is tightly sealed and covered over with a layer of dirt. All that's needed now is Charlie.

First Lieutenant Terry Falck, Staff Sergeant Bruce Bollman, Specialists Ed Arter and Dick Charlebois and PFC Tim Haslam carefully study the new mound that is a short thirty feet out in front of our home. The Engineers have constructed a volcano in our front yard and are anxious to see it erupt; to see it erupt from somewhere way up on top of the hill behind us.

234

Stars and Stripes and Shadows

"This better fuckin' work!" is the unanimous sentiment of the personnel who'll have to ignite the experiment from a mere 30 feet.

⚡ ⚡ ⚡ ⚡

Another long nearly sleepless night and tedious day pass without incident. We add another layer of sandbags to the bunker. We clean our weapons again. We watch another water trailer find its way down out of the gray sky onto the LZ. We get re-supplied with clean fatigues. *No underwear.* Hearts, Gin Rummy, Ed's rhythmic slapping, Ed and Bruce's renditions of the hits of the sixties, cigarette after cigarette, moment after moment hobbles by.

At 2:21 p.m. another Huey vibrates up from the south, bumps down onto the LZ, casts off several bags, allows two TOC officers to board, strains itself back up into the heavy air and pulls away back toward the southern world, abandoning us with the contents of the bags...mail bags.

Life is good again. Six-Two and Sergeant Bollman dole out the letters and packages to the appreciative men of the Platoon. There's something for everyone. There seem to be many things for everyone. For me, there are multiple letters from Mom and Dad, five from Rosemary, one from my sister, one from one of my fraternity brothers, a package from my sister and another mystery package. The weather is clear and dry and so Doc, Ed and I each take our bounty to a different corner of the bunker, hop up on top, arrange everything according to our individual systems, light cigarettes, get comfortable and slowly expose the contents of the messages and gifts. Bruce and the Lieutenant prefer the interior of the bunker, allowing each of us to have our own space for the few minutes we will have re-connecting to home. Charlie and the rain just need to mind their own business for a few minutes.

The large package, wrapped in brown paper, has had the return address obscured with some kind of postal stamps. Without knowing the sender, I don't know how to prioritize it within my mail opening and reading system. By default, it has to go first. The contents prove to be a wealth of goodies; packages of candy, cookies and canned goods of all types, a new deck of cards, some stationary and a sealed envelope. Within the envelope is a type written letter from the Young Republicans, thanking me for my service and sacrifice, wishing me a safe return,

Tim Haslam

reminding me to vote in the election next November. This will be the first election since my twenty-first birthday and my political susceptibilities are still up for grabs. I know which of our neighbors back home are staunch Republicans and likely to be behind the good wishes of the YRs. I know which of our neighbors are staunch Democrats and now look forward to their retaliation.

My sister's package is next. It's nearly as large as the one from the YRs, similarly wrapped in brown paper. The contents of her package represent the same basic food groups and so I co-mingle them with the others for further disposition later. Within the recesses of the box I also find a button about two inches in diameter with a pin on the back that simply reads; *I Like Asphalt!* My sister, the UCLA art school graduate, has a subtle appreciation for my situation and thought I might appreciate the contrast of the buttons declaration with the organic world of the Nam that I have described to everyone back home. I pin it onto the camouflage cover of my helmet.

Once I've organized the contents of the packages and planned out their consumption over the next few days, some to be shared, some to be selfishly hoarded, I shift into the stack of letters. With these, I really don't want to be disturbed. I want to disengage completely from everyone and everything around as I savor each sentence, each sentiment, and each portrayal of once familiar things and places and people.

The letter from Rick Wright, my fraternity brother updates me on all the superficial, frivolous activities still going on within my circle of friends back at Phi Delta Psi. The circle continues to shrink however as more and more of the brethren are drafted or seek less risky alternatives in the reserve units of the various military branches and the National Guard. Nearly everyone is either in the service someway or has a permanent medical deferment, usually the result of some football injury. The images of the beer and the parties and the carefree life portrayed in Rick's narrative, entering back into my consciousness as I read his letter here within the hot, humid confines of the shit, seems to simultaneously elevate and sadden me. I somehow want to tell them all to grow up. At the same time I want desperately to be there with them. I want desperately to be anywhere but here. I look at the button on my helmet. *I Like Asphalt!*

The thrust of my sister's letter is mostly political. She is enamored

Stars and Stripes and Shadows

with a Senator named Eugene McCarthy who is running for President. She says, that he says, he will end the war. *I like him already.* She doesn't think he has much of a chance though, as Bobby Kennedy seems to be the favorite among the Democrats and likely to win the nomination. She likes him also and says that he too seems to be growing in his opposition to the war. *So, who's in favor of the war? How long will it take for somebody to end it?*

Mom and Dad each fill me in on the new house. Dad tells me that he found a buyer for my 1957 Porsche. He got $1700 for it that he put in the bank for me. I'll miss the car but that's a pretty good price and by the time I get out of the Army I should have saved enough money for something better.

All the letters tell me about the things that are changing back home. They're not really described that way though by the writers, they're just the normal little evolutionary things that happen as life goes on within the familiar context of their daily lives. For me, a million miles and a world away from that context, it seems that things are unraveling, that things are being gradually but steadily erased from the life I remember. My house, my car, my dog, my grandmother are all gone. Each departure has been independently related to me. Each described with journalistic accuracy; who, what, where, when, why and how. Each annotated with the appropriate impact and sentiment. I don't yet understand what the sum of this all really means to me. I understand only that I'm glad to hear from them.

Finally, there is nothing left but the orange envelops. I have lingered through all the preliminaries as long as I can, knowing that the five orange envelops were still to come. The five orange envelopes will bring to me what I need and want. I order them chronologically by postmark and carefully slice open the top of the first one.

The annual cycle of the May/June gloom has set in around Rosemary and all of Southern California. The marine layer keeps the mornings gray and cool when everyone wants it to be warm and clear and summer-like. It's a depressing time of year. Rosemary seems depressed; she misses me. She doesn't like her job much anymore; she hasn't been spending any time with our friends and her dad is drinking more and more. Just one scotch and soda at the end of each long workday shouldn't be much concern, even for a former alcoholic who has suc-

Tim Haslam

cessfully abstained for the last fifteen years. He always made one for Rosemary's mom Raylene before she died. Administering to her nightly habit seemed to be enough to satisfy his own obsessive alcohol connection. Just one, or two, each night isn't a problem for anyone. Just one, or two, in combination with the other drugs she took to help smooth out life's ripples killed her a year ago on another May/June gloom day. Now he has only himself to administer to; he can enable only himself.

The four following letters are variations on the same theme. She has written them more out of boredom than anything else. Each is short and empty of her usual warmth and exuberance. Each is a plea that I don't recognize, too veiled and distant for me to resolve. She makes no inquiries about the latest events in my life over here, no comments about anything I have described in my latest letters to her. I can't see her face as I read these; her smile. I can't feel her hand in mind. *What else is being erased?*

> *Hello darkness my old friend*
> *I've come to talk with you again*
> *Because a vision softly creeping*
> *Left its seeds while I was sleeping*
> *And the vision that was planted in my*
> *Brain*
> *Still remains*
> *Within the sound of silence*
>
> *"Fools," said I, "You do not know*
> *Silence like a cancer grows*
> *Hear my words that I might teach you*
> *Take my arms that I might reach you"*
> *But my words, like silent raindrops fell*
> *And echoed*
> *In the wells of silence*

◢ ◢ ◢ ◢

"Sit-rep negative. Over," I report back to Houston and the others listening to the 1:40 a.m. situation check. I, in turn listen to the others repeat my message around the perimeter. Happily, they're all negative.

Stars and Stripes and Shadows

There are no LPs out this night as we're likely to have another mad-minute sometime before dawn, and so there are no *pffit pffitts* to count as the outposts are polled. Bruce, Doc and I are all awake, each sitting here in the bunker, wrapped up in our poncho liners, trying to stay alert, watching out into the darkness, listening for something other than the steady brushing, dripping sounds of the rain coming down.

Maybe it's just a diversion, or perhaps he has suddenly developed a real concern. Sergeant Bollman stands up and moves closer to the firing port. He feels for the Claymore detonators he knows are resting up on the edge of the opening.

"Which ones are these?" he asks, leaving us to assume he's referring to the three detonators nearest the center of the port.

"You mean which Claymores?" I whisper back to confirm my understanding.

"Yea…which Claymores?"

"Those three, the ones in the center are for the center row of Claymores. They're in three groups of three. The group over here to the right is for the three mines furthest down the hill. The group farthest over to the left is for the highest row."

"What about the gas? Where's the detonator for the gas?" I know now that these are just quiz questions from the Platoon Sergeant. It was his idea to hang the detonator for the canned volcano on a stick jammed into the side of the opening.

"It's hanging over at the far left side," I remind him, passing the final question on his what-do-you-do-when-your-disoriented-in-the-nighttime-pitch-blackness test.

"Good. Remember, set off the lower ones first."

He doesn't need to re-educate us on this either. We all understand that if we set off any of the mines in the top row, they'll obliterate everything out to the front including trip flares, men on LP, Charlie and all the other Claymores down below. With the top row, we also have to remember to duck, as the back-blast would be of sufficient force to rip us to pieces.

"What about the gas?" Doc asks. "If we set that off, it will incinerate everything down below. Do we have to set off the lower mines first?"

"Yea, I guess so," says Bruce, making a solid command decision.

239

Tim Haslam

Each of the nine Claymore mines has the wherewithal to kill everything within fifty meters out to the front. All of them, placed within such close proximity to one another have the wherewithal to kill everything many times. The real reason for placing the mines this way is based on the belief that Charlie may be able to infiltrate unseen and unheard up through all the other obstacles and turn the mines in the first row around. Then, if he makes any noise, the Americans up in the bunker, about thirty meters away, will detonate the mines. The Americans up in the bunker will obliterate themselves. Having three rows of mines at our disposal gives us the upper hand as obliterators even if Charlie gets to the first two rows.

At 3:00 a.m. it's my turn to sleep. I shake Ed out of his comfort, remind him where he is and watch him slide down reluctantly off his air mattress as I slide up enthusiastically on to mine. A few wriggles and adjustments to my poncho liner and I'm ready for my two hours of sleep. Almost ready; my boots have my attention; my boots are heavy and uncomfortable. Should I take the time to take off my boots? Should I take the risk of taking off my boots? *Goddamn boots!* Now I have to make a decision before I can allow myself to sleep. Boots? No boots? Comfortable sleep? Fight Charlie in my socks?

Boots!

Now, having resolved the internal conflict, I'm really ready for sleep. Just get my imagination calibrated with my fatigue and ride away someplace else, someplace better.

I picture Rosemary and her dad. I picture the disappointing grayness of the May/June Southern California sky. I picture Rosemary struggling to push my old blue Porsche through the parking lot at the mall, trying to get up enough speed for me to pop the clutch and start the engine. I picture Rosemary climbing into the passenger seat, gently encouraging me to invest in a new battery. I remember a time when a dead car battery was a big deal. In another second I remember nothing, I picture nothing. My fatigue is too great to sustain even a dream.

✶ ✶ ✶ ✶

Even in the darkness, still shrouded in my own sleepiness, I know right where I am as the Lieutenant shakes my leg. The bunker...Firebase 25...the shit, but I don't know the what or the why of it for a moment or

Stars and Stripes and Shadows

two. *Didn't I just go to sleep a few minutes ago? Isn't it still my turn?*

"Everybody up," Six-Two says to me and the other slumbering body—Doc's body—in a nervous voice, his volume set just above a whisper.

"Another mad-minute?" I ask, at the same time trying to understand why the helmet I've just put on feels odd. *I know it's mine. It was right where I left it before I curled up under the poncho liner.* Further investigation with my right hand determines that it's on backwards.

"No, we've got movement," the Lieutenant says quietly, as I correct the orientation of my steel pot.

Someone else is in the bunker with us. My eyes have adjusted enough to detect the outline of an extra person over near the doorway. *I think its Beasley.* Sergeant Bollman is very close to the extra person. *It is Beasley.* I can hear a few whispered words between the two of them and recognize the voice.

"Right about where our LPs have been going," I hear Beasley say, "Down at the edge of the wire, just about where the opening is.

"Six-Two, this is Six. What about it, anything more? Over," the Captain's voice enters the conversation via the PRC25 handset.

"This is Six-Two. Two of my men in the next bunker up from mine confirm they saw something down at the edge of the wire. One of them is with me now. Over."

"Saw something, or heard something? Over."

"One of them thought they saw something, alerted one of the other guys who saw it too. There's just enough starlight to make out outlines of things down there. Over."

"Don't you all have a Starlight Scope? Over."

"That's a rog. My Alpha's taking a look now. Over."

I can see enough now to confirm that Sergeant Bollman is, in fact, scanning the ground out in front of us with his scope.

"Here, take this and stay close," Falck says to me, handing me the handset. I strap on the radio and grab my M16, ready to follow the Lieutenant. Ed's doing the same thing with his radio and will be glued to Bollman. Doc knows his job and has his tools at hand.

"I don't see anything," Bruce says continuing his search via the amplified images of fuzzy green shapes coming through the optics of the scope.

Tim Haslam

The pop of the trip flare reaches our ears a fraction of a second after the blinding flash of light. The initial burst of the flare is so intense that we're all blinded for a second, unable to see anything. Reflexively we all crouch down as far as we can, bumping into one another in the crowded pit at the front of the bunker. There isn't room for six people, radios and weapons in here. There isn't room to get re-set and study the now fully illuminated ground out in front of us.

Without saying anything, Six-Two pushes his way out of the bunker and into the trench outside, stopping after a few steps, his RTO, Six-Two-Charlie, following close behind.

It's really bright out here. I can see the Lieutenant's helmet and face clearly, peering out over the sandbags at the front edge of the trench, lit up by the flares burning phosphorous. I can tell that my head and my radio are similarly visible to everyone around.

The bright green light is starting to fade as we try to find what set off the warning device. The light from the waning flare starts pulsing out, creating the impression that everything is moving. The shifting shapes and shadows of the scene in front of me look like some ancient silent movie; streaked, jerky and artificial, revealing just enough to suggest what's going on, what might be there. Abruptly the stage returns to total darkness, leaving a momentary after-impression within my minds eye.

There was someone there. There was a gook there. I know there was someone there. I think there was a gook there. I think there was something.

"Did you see that?" I ask the Lieutenant, hoping he will fill me in on what it was I may have seen.

"I think so. I'm not sure. I'm not sure what I saw. Get Six-Charlie on the horn and tell him we need more flares."

"Six-Charlie, this is Six-Two Charlie. We still think there's movement down here. Something set off one of our trip flares but we couldn't really see anything for sure. We need more flares. Over."

"Roger that, Six-Two Charlie. We'll get some up over you. Over."

Within just a few seconds, the mortar behind us *thwumps* a sequence of three star shell flares up into the sky above us. As they ignite and start drifting back downward, tethered to their little parachutes, we are again

Stars and Stripes and Shadows

challenged to find Charlie or whatever may be moving around down there within the dancing array of light and shadow out to our front. But there *is* something down there within the shifting contours and shapes that catches my attention. I can't really see it or tell exactly what it is. It was more a movement that seemed out of step with everything else, a left when everything else was a right, an ebb when everything else was a flow. I start to point down to help focus my impression.

"I saw it," Six-Two says before I can say anything. "Give me the handset."

"Six-Charlie, this is Six-Two. Put Six on. Over."

"This is Six. Over."

"I've got positive movement down in front of my position, just at the edge of the wire. I want your OK to pop the closest Claymore. Over."

"Wait for the next star shell...then do it. Out."

"Bruce...Bruce...when the next flare goes off, set off the Claymore that's furthest down and on the right," the Lieutenant instructs an unseen Sergeant Bollman, trusting that Bruce is paying attention within the dark interior of the bunker."

"Right," a nervous voice responds from within. "Just a second, I need to find the right detonator."

"OK...OK, I've got it."

"Wait, wait," Six-Two shouts just as the next flare pops to life up over the trees. "Let us know before you set it off."

The Lieutenant doesn't want any of the curious onlookers up here taking the brunt of the back-blast.

"Fire in the hole! Fire in the hole!" Bollman yells out, sucking everyone down into his respective trench.

The blast hammers onto my steel-pot and into my eardrums with a deafening shock; too loud, too crisp and too short-lived to be compared to a thunderclap. Within an instant, the 750 steel ball bearings hurled away from the two and half pounds of exploding C4 have pulverized, shredded or vivisected everything in the kill zone. The ringing silence that follows is quickly interrupted by the pops and spraying sounds of the trip flares going off all along the perimeter. The blast shock has whip-lashed along the concertina wire with sufficient force to yank out all the trip wires.

Tim Haslam

Things seem to be happening all along the northern side of the base; loud things, bright things; anxious grunts trying to find—trying not to be found; but still no firm validation that Charlie's out there.

What the fuck is going on? Is anything really going on?

The scene curtains back into silence and darkness as the last flare fizzles out, all of our weapons are still pointed out toward the wire, all of our senses set on acute alert, all of our hearts pounding.

"I can't confirm anything, sir," the Lieutenant advises Captain Hilton over the radio. "Whatever we saw out there must have been hit by the Claymore; but, until we get people down there in the morning there's no way to tell for sure what was there. We'll have some repair work to do on the wire down there too. I think there's probably some gaps blown through. Over."

"Keep a sharp eye on that area. I've seen this before. Charlie makes enough noise to get our attention, hoping we'll pop a Claymore, knowing what that will do to the wire. The front door's open. Be careful. Out."

By now Bob Taylor, Grady, Mike Ferlik and Sergeant Stevens have worked their way over here to our bunker to confer with the Lieutenant about the plans for the rest of the night. We're all clutched together as close as we can get within the narrow trench connecting the two bunkers. The red tips of cigarettes, carefully cupped within our dirty hands, trace up and down, hip to mouth, as we listen to the Lieutenant choreograph the rest of the night. No one at Firebase 25 is asleep now. No one at Firebase 25 is likely to sleep anymore tonight and so, it's no surprise and it's not too disturbing to hear Six-Two order full alert for the rest of the night.

"What about another mad-minute, sir? It seems like that might be a good idea under the circumstances," asks Grady.

"Yea, you're probably right. I didn't even think about that. I guess the Captain didn't either considering all the ruckus we just created with the Claymore. Let me find out about that. Get Six-Charlie on the horn."

"Six-Charlie this is…"

Apparently one trip-flare survived the Claymore blast. The pop and sudden bright light coming from the wire, thirty meters down to the left, initiates a collective jerk downward from all of us in the trench.

244

Stars and Stripes and Shadows

"What the hell?"

"Wait one Six-Charlie. Over."

"Six-Two-Charlie, this is Six. What's going on? Over."

We all quickly spread out along the trench line, looking out toward the burning flare. Again, it's so bright against the sheer blackness and such a blinding shock that the illuminated images are difficult for us to process. But, within a second our eyes have adjusted sufficiently to see something; to see the same something. There's no confusion about the image this time. The prone man bathed in the greenish glow, with the AK47 cradled in his arms, has nowhere to go to conceal himself. He knows he's visible to the Americans now. A half a dozen grunts within the bunkers and trenches up to our left know the same thing and do what they've been trained to do; do what their fear and adrenaline compels them to do. M16's, some set on semi-automatic and some on full-automatic, crack and sputter out their deadly responses to the exposed intruder.

The Six-Two squad leaders, the Lieutenant and I watch together as the lives of the NVA soldier and the Judas flare come simultaneously to an end. This, now dead man is not the focus of our concern however. The shadowy shapes worming and crawling around thirty meters to the right, directly down the hill in front of our position have stolen our full attention, denying any further reflection or sympathy for the body of the careless dead man.

"We've got gooks in the wire for sure!" I relay into the radio handset, not bothering to preface the alert with any formal radio protocol. "One's dead down in front of our number three bunker and there are others right in front of us. Over."

If Six or Six-Charlie, or anybody else is trying to respond to me over the radio I'm unable to hear it over the bursts of gunfire coming from everyone around me. I can just hear Six-Two scream out to the squad leaders to get back to their positions before he ducks into the bunker. With Bruce and Doc's weapons blasting away steadily out into the darkness, the noise inside the bunker is even more deafening. I press the handset up as tightly as I can to my left ear, as some protection against the shattering reverberations, trying to separate out any voice commands coming through the radios meager amplifier. My right ear is taking the full brunt of the sound blasts as my right hand and arm

Tim Haslam

are wrestling my own M16 up onto the firing port ledge.

"Pop the other two Claymores on the lower row," the Lieutenant yells out.

"Pop the Claymores!" he repeats, reaching over and shoving Sergeant Bollman further over toward the detonators.

Bollman reacts to the shove without comment, grabbing the first detonator, squeezing it immediately; once, twice. *No time for any preparatory warnings. Fuck the back-blast.* The sloping terrain in front of us absorbs most of the repercussion from the first exploding Claymore as Sergeant Bollman sets off the remaining mine in the lowest row. A second or two pass before a layer of smoke roles up the hill out of the darkness towards us, like some great silent specter, curling into the bunker and our lungs, eliciting an undeclared cease-fire. The other rifles and machineguns along the northern perimeter also come to rest, echoing the transition back into smoky silence. Everything that was there, everything we think we saw maneuvering down there, must surely have been destroyed by the devastating blasts. But the protective wire too must now be blown completely away. The ground between the opposite slope and us is now wide open, unobstructed except for the debris of formally living things.

Another series of aerial flares are launched. Popping a moment later at their apogee they start drifting downward to help clarify the situation. Nothing is clear however. The gyrating images illuminated through the haze of dust and smoke fail to disclose any living threats to us; fail to confirm the effectiveness of our Claymores and fail to foreshadow anything to come.

I follow the Lieutenant back outside into the trench where we both scan the vulnerable approaches to our position, careful not to offer anymore than our helmets and eyes as targets above the sandbag wall at the forward edge. I'm glad to be out of the bunker, the accumulation of smoke and smell and sound was overwhelming within the close confines of the protective crypt. The air is only slightly less polluted out here, but there is a feeling of space and room to maneuver, a feeling that there are more options available.

"Give me the radio," Six-Two says, shifting another step to his left, peeking up just a little bit more. He fills in Captain Hilton and everyone else listening over the Company net on what's happened. The

Stars and Stripes and Shadows

Captain responds with a few questions, a few requests for elaboration. "How many...Exactly where...Are we...Have we...Did you...?"

"Several."

"Not sure exactly how many."

"Five or six...maybe more."

"Right in front of my position. One confirmed down to my left."

"Roger."

"Roger."

"Negative."

"Roger."

"I gotta believe there's more to come," he says at the apparent conclusion of the Captain's interrogation. *A statement I wish he hadn't made.*

"I think we'd better get our mortars ready for firing close in support, H-E and willy-peter," Falck suggests to the Captain, raising my level of anxiety another notch with his belief that high-explosive and white-phosphorous mortar rounds may soon be falling, "close in."

The Captain validates the belief and advises that flares for the rest of the night will be provided by the 6th of the 29th Artillery over at FB30 and confirms that all the mortars here are being readied to fire close-in def-cons.

Six-Two is still on the horn when he's proven right. A *thwump* from out to our left breaks the silence, followed by one just over the ridge directly across from us, and a third from down across the saddle somewhere.

"Incoming! Incoming!"

Suddenly my appreciation for the space and room and options available to me out here in the open trench is relegated to a secondary concern. Explosive missiles are falling from the sky. The bunker is a much better place to be.

A new sound chases the Lieutenant and I into the bunker, a short, quick *whoosh* through the air followed by a muffled thud up in the muddy berm above the trench. Another *whoosh* slams into one of the sandbags at the front of the trench followed by others, *whooshing* and slamming into various surfaces around us.

The whooshing bullets and the kachunks of exploding mortar rounds tearing into our earthen battlements changes the perceived

Tim Haslam

momentum of the game, elevates our emotions and confuses our priorities. The incoming lead and steel declare unequivocally Charlie's fealty to his manifesto and his passionate desire for retribution. These people are no longer sniping at us from concealed positions within the jungle. They're here in force. They're calling us out to fight. They want something we have and they're determined to take it. They want our firebase, our guns, our ammo…our lives. They want everything we have or ever will have.

A few greenish tracers streak obliquely across our front, heading more toward the bunkers down to our right than directly toward us. Most of the incoming fire seems to be shifting down that way. No flares have yet to arrive from the 6th of the 29th and thus only the mortar bursts and gun flashes break the darkness and these are too short lived and localized to disclose any real targets for us. It's now like just another mad-minute. Everyone is firing out into the night, occasionally shifting the direction of our shots back along the line of an incoming tracer, hoping to find the shooter over on the opposite ridge. Our mortars too are now pumping out rounds as fast as they can. Concentrations of explosions and muffled flashes mark the crest of the opposite ridge and the ground just beyond the saddle. Ten, twelve, fifteen high-explosive rounds *kachunk* into the darkness of Charlie's side before a white-phosphorous round bursts just beyond the saddle, spraying out streamers of burning phosphorous in all directions, illuminating the fallen trees and other debris littering the land bridge connecting our two ridges.

The sticky white-hot phosphorous blobs continue to burn, on and through anything they come in contact with; tree limbs, bamboo shafts and human flesh. Small fires start to flare up within the heaps of dead vegetation, glowing just enough to confirm that Charlie is down there. Most of the perceived movement seems to be on the saddle, crawling along toward our side, but spidery shapes can also be detected at the limits of the fires glow, down below our position where the wire used to be. The intense gunfire from our side becomes focused on these areas and unidentified grunts in the trenches on either side of our bunker start lobbing hand grenades down at the vague shapes feeling their way up toward us. Charlie's offensive tactics have met stiff resistance from the sleep deprived Americans. *So many weapons, Charlie has to be thinking. Too many weapons! Too much exposed ground to get passed! Too many obstacles! Too many bunkers and trenches and fortifications! Too much determination to survive!*

The first flares lofted up above us from the 105's over at FB30 are too far to the west. They light up the LZ and the quiet expanse of jungle arcing along that end of the firebase. They provide just enough light in the night sky however to silhouette everything and everyone on the firebase against the lighter contrasted sky. Charlie's riflemen over on the other ridge take notice and fire a few more rounds. As the wayward flares drown out into the forest to the west the shooting slows to an arrhythmic series of sporadic pops and bursts and then into silence.

Lieutenant Reese has apparently advised the supporting artillery battery on how to adjust their trajectories and the next salvo of flares comes to life right above our position. Air currents up above the trees however, are drawing the parachute flares off to the north too quickly, leaving us with only a short, sweeping, spotlighted view of the slope in front of us. Again, nothing is clear enough in the brief swath of illumination to identify with certainty; to aim at, to neutralize. There is apparently just enough disclosed or suggested to some of the grunts to draw a few bursts of M16 fire. No return fire. The mortars on both sides remain silent. Six-Two shuttles once more out into the trench, with me close behind.

The Lieutenant is on the radio with Captain Hilton when the next flares paint over the dark slope and ridge, strobe-lighting the various pieces of the dangerous puzzle stretching and shrinking eerily in front of us. My attention shifts away from the officer's conversation and the searching for a moment, distracted by a sudden concern for the number of rounds remaining in the magazine in my rifle. *How much did I fire? Two bursts...three...more? How many rounds is that? How many left?*

Fuck it...put a new magazine in.

Just as I slap up the bottom of the new magazine, making sure it's fully locked in, Six-Two turns to me and says, "Get Bruce!"

As the Lieutenant still has the handset pressed up to his ear, the cord, tethering us together stretches just far enough to get me to the bunkers entrance.

"Bruce, Bruce...get out here," I say in as loud a whisper as I can, assuming the Platoon Sergeant will disregard the insubordination of my directive.

Tim Haslam

"The gas," the Lieutenant says, as Sergeant Bollman's helmeted head pokes out of the bunkers entrance. "Six wants us to set off the phugas."

"Oh shit! I hope this thing works without blowing us all up! How do you want us to do this? Where do you want everyone?" Bollman replies, trying to think through what's about to happen.

"Send Doc up to Taylor's bunker and have him tell 'em what's going on. Tell them to make sure everyone is in the bunker and to keep down.

Tim, you'll let everyone on the radio know just before we blow it. OK? Everybody got it?"

"OK."

"OK."

Doc brushes past us on his way up to alert Bob Taylor as Lieutenant Falck and I return to the still hazy interior of the bunker.

"I've got the detonator. You tell me when," Bollman says.

"All right, let 'em know on the radio that we'll count down from ten."

I pass on the alert and pause, looking at the Lieutenant for the final go ahead. He's just close enough and visible enough for me to see his head nod as he starts crouching down. By the time my count gets down to seven, I'm also snuggled down as far as I can into the muddy bottom of the firing trench.

"…three…two…one."

The C4 blast sounds for the first instant just like a Claymore, but doesn't echo and rebound into silence like the previous ones. Instead, there is a steadily building roar, monstrous in its intensity, storming in through the firing port over us.

It's daylight now. The sun has suddenly risen and planted itself in the ground just outside our bunker, its light and searing heat quickly floods through the interior of the bunker.

"*Oh shits,*" are forced out and repeated from us all as we reflexively lurch toward the bunker entrance. Most of the oxygen in the bunker has been either burned off or sucked out by the mushrooming ball of flame roiling upwards just outside. We have to get out of this broiler fast.

Streamers of the burning contents of the drum are falling everywhere; over the bunkers, down within the connecting trenches and onto

Stars and Stripes and Shadows

the ground rising up behind us. Everything to our front seems to be aflame. The carefully engineered volcano has erupted. Not at the prescribed angle out toward Charlie, but straight up, cascading its napalm and gasoline lava directly down onto our bunkers and trenches.

The four of us meld into a clog at the bunker door trying to escape the heat building up, anxious to get out and away from the convection oven behind us, but equally fearful of the fiery rain falling to our front. No one is yet panicked but the shared level of anxiety and uncertainty is nearly overwhelming. Within a second or two all the flaming airborne slush has splashed back to earth leaving a thousand little fiery blobs and puddles each contributing to a rising pall of black smoke. The brilliant light of the initial fireball has dissipated away, leaving us in a candle-lit realm of choking, gasoline scented smoke. We all crouch our way further into the trench, following Lieutenant Falck who's surveying the damage.

The bottom of the trench between our bunkers is so saturated with monsoon rain that it oozes back over any burning particles cratering into it, quickly suffocating them. The canvas and plastic fabric of the sandbags covering our bunker fizzles back or melts away, retreating from the searing napalm globs scattered over the top of our home, but the wet mud contained within the bags patiently resists any fire-induced transformations. Fortunately for us the volatile concoction fails to ignite any significant secondary fires. Fortunately for us our bunker and Taylor's bunker were oriented at just the right angles to preclude any of the initial fiery blast from entering into the firing ports and onto the people huddled down below. Miraculously we have all escaped the phugas experiment with little more than ringing ears and a sunburned like feeling under the layer of smoke residue added to the mantle of filth coating our exposed flesh.

Lieutenant Elliott saw what happened when the drum exploded and immediately figured out the other obvious danger. The Six-Two positions were now lit up and fully exposed to Charlie. He ordered all of Five-Nine Platoon to concentrate their firepower down to our front and across the ridge in an effort to keep Charlie's head down while the grunts over to the right recover from the consequences of the blast. Then, over the radio, Five-Nine requested another mad-minute for all the elements on the north side, to be focused in front of our positions.

Tim Haslam

The automatic rifles and machineguns on either side of us slice across our front, out over the smoke shrouded glow and into the darkness beyond. The steady fire sweeping down the slope and over onto the opposite ridge must have worked. There's no answering fire from Charlie. Charlie's had enough for tonight.

The Captain comes back on the radio and polls each platoon for a casualty report. Doc Charlebois has been up to all of our four bunkers and confirms that no one in our platoon is hurt. It turns out that the only real injury to anyone at FB25 this night is a sprained ankle suffered by one of the mortarmen hurrying ammo back to his pit. Everyone on our side of the perimeter however will have some small physical reminder of what has just happened. Each of us can find cuts or scrapes or contusions that weren't there an hour ago. Bob Taylor and Ed Arter have each shown Doc small burns on their hands. Neither Bob, nor Ed nor Doc can determine the source with any certainty; napalm, gasoline, cigarette, gun-barrel?

No one seriously injured. No one killed. How could that be?

No one killed on our side.

The commanding officer of the NVA unit that attacked us must be getting a different kind of casualty report. *How could they even determine the status of the men sent forward into the American's wire and mines and bullets? How could they account for any of the individuals caught in front of the American's Claymores and machineguns? How many have crawled back? How many have returned whole? How will he justify the losses? How much damage do they think they did? How will he explain this? What have they learned? What have they gained?*

The last of the napalm candles have burned out and the thick black smoke has disintegrated into a remnant of odorous haze hanging close to the ground as the first subtle glow in the eastern sky suggests the approach of dawn. All of us become more animated as the increasing light climbing over the higher mountain peaks starts chasing away the blackness; chasing away anything still concealed out there, evicting anything left alive. The senior officers from TOC are coming down toward the bunker line to get a first hand look, anxious to tally up the bodies, excited about the reports they will send up to higher headquarters. The grunts who've been searching the darkness all night are anxious to assess the damage we've done, to confirm what we did to whatever we saw and

Stars and Stripes and Shadows

thought we saw, excited to be alive for another morning. Everyone is anxious to determine what happens next. Hopeful that nothing happens next; we know how lucky we are.

The first rays of the sun squeezing through the higher reaches of the forest foliage start to reveal the evidence. Sections of concertina wire that were interlaced tightly across our front yesterday are now scattered down into the jungle below, leaving a gap in our defensive line of about twenty meters. Three small craters clearly mark where the first row of Claymores was. The second row of mines up towards us seems to be intact, each one surrounded by the blackened residue of the burning napalm and gasoline. The site of the three passive Claymores sitting out there, undisturbed, serves as another reminder of our good fortune. What would have happened if any of the lava-like napalm had splashed down over the plastic casing of the mines? Could it melt its way through, re-orienting the device before it came into contact with the C4 inside? Would the C4 just ignite and burn like it does when we use it to heat C-rations or, would the heat simply be intense enough to set off the explosive chain reaction? Which way would the ball bearings fly?

The early morning light is sufficient enough now to see clearly down the slope to our front, out over the gully and onto the opposite ridge. The senior officers searching down the slope with their binoculars fail to find what they're looking for, as do the grunts scanning the same landscape with their tired eyes.

The bodies? Where are the bodies? Where are the dead gook bodies that should be littering the muddy ground out there?

"I can't see a single body out there," Ed says, apparently directing his observation over toward Six-Two, who now has his Army issue binoculars pressed up against his eyes.

"There…over on the saddle," he answers, after pivoting slowly to his right. "There are a few new bodies over there. They must have dragged all the others off."

"How the fuck could they have done that, sir? With all the shit we were sending down there. How the fuck could they have pulled all those bodies out of there?"

"All those bodies? How many do you think were there? I know of one for sure that we wasted over there," he replies, pointing at the spot where we all saw the surprised prone man gunned down under the glow of the trip flare. "I only know that I *saw* more of them over this way, down there where the wire used to be. I can't say that I actually *saw* more of them go down. I gotta believe the Claymores had to have taken some of them out and I gotta believe that all the firing we did had to hit some of them, but, if any of them were left alive, they must have managed to pull the bodies out of there. My guess is they pulled 'em down as far as they could, down into the gully out that way; down far enough to be hidden in the vegetation where others probably helped get them up and over the ridge."

"Maybe the bodies are still down there in the gully," Bruce suggests.

"Maybe."

Maybe there really weren't any bodies. Maybe this whole, unreal night, never really happened. Maybe I'll open my eyes slowly, crawl down off my air-mattress, light a cigarette and casually study the same old shit that surrounds me. Maybe I'll open my eyes and be home.

И И И И

By late morning the wire has been repaired, new Claymores and trip wires have been set and Six-Zero Platoon has returned from a short sweeping patrol out over the saddle and along the opposite ridge. The nervous men on the short patrol radioed back their discoveries as they were made; seven "fresh" bodies added to the decaying population of corpses in amongst the rubble littering the saddle, blood trails up along the ridge crest, an AK47, ammo pouches, another AK47, a tattered wallet with a family photograph taken back in Hanoi and two dead bodies, nearly unrecognizable as human, splayed out down in the gully. Teams of Loaches and Cobras have been combing the land to our north and west, flying back and forth stripes out to the Laotian border and back. Charlie's gone. At least for now, Charlie's gone.

The inhabitants of Firebase 25 have collected into small groups around the various bunkers along the north side. There's no need to seek out the company of those sharing the usual cultural or rank or seniority affiliations this morning. Everyone is bonded together with the same experience, the same after effects and the same need to talk it through someway and to hear other voices. We each get as comfort-

Stars and Stripes and Shadows

able as we can, slouched up against some part of the bunker, having predetermined the best routes to greater safety should something else happen. Each of us seems to have the same array of assets placed close at hand; our loaded weapons, our ammo, canteen cups full of coffee, Zippos and cigarettes.

Bruce, Doc, Lieutenant Falck, Ed and I have been joined by Lieutenant Elliott and are re-living last night, minute-by-minute, event-by-event, perspective-by-perspective. Each of our comments helps to fill in some gap in everyone else's understanding, but, at the same time, many of the comments confuse our personal images. *How could what I remember be true if what he says is right? The flare didn't pop before the incoming mortar rounds went off. Did it? We weren't inside when that happened. We were outside. Weren't we? I thought they were over that way...not that way?*

Some of the disputed points are resolved by polling—the majority view is truth. Some are dispassionately discarded as irrelevant and some are simply left as confusing. Most of the salient facts are unanimously stipulated. Charlie was out there. Charlie was firing at us with rifles and mortars. We were firing back with everything we had. The Claymores must have killed some of them. The phugas was a total fuck-up on somebody's part and we're lucky to have survived it. We are all lucky to have survived any of it. No body was killed or seriously hurt. We're goddamned lucky. *Fuckin-A!*

"Here comes Six," I advise the others in our group, spotting the Captain working his way down one of the vertical trenches that connects our position with the upper reaches of the firebase. I haven't met our new CO before, never even really had a close look at him. He's a big, burly sort, looking less soldierly however, than his predecessor Captain Collins. His helmet is shifted off center giving him a sort of un-squared-away look. He has his M16 in his right hand, but I don't see any additional ammo. He's not quite as filthy as we are, but, from here, he sure doesn't look like a West Pointer either.

"Everybody OK?" is all he says as he sits down on the sandbag wall next to me.

"Yes, sir," Ed, Bruce, Doc and I chorus back representing the NCOs and enlisted men within the little group.

"Pretty damn lucky, I'd say, sir," Six-Two says, more confidant in

Tim Haslam

his status with the Captain than the rest of us.

"That was a long night," is all Lieutenant Elliott wants to add.

"Well, you all did a great job. Everyone in the Company did a great job last night," the Captain adds in a quiet, believable way. Lieutenant Falck uses the Captain's comments as an opportunity to introduce Ed, Doc and I. He's already become well acquainted with Platoon Sergeant Bollman and Lieutenant Elliot. Captain Hilton shakes our hands and repeats the "great job" comment.

"You want some coffee, sir?" Doc asks as the Captain lifts off his helmet, indicating he's interested in settling in with us for a while.

"Yea, if you've got it."

Doc and I had built a little wood fire earlier and have kept a helmet full of water warming over the embers.

"Sorry sir, it's not real hot," Doc says, passing the can full of instant coffee he's just mixed over to me.

"If it's warm at all, it'll be great. Thanks," the Captain replies, taking the dirty can from me. The character of the Captain's voice and his relaxed posture put everyone at ease. Within another few minutes it becomes clear that he's come down just to be with his men; to learn what the night was like for us and to share in surprisingly honest terms what the night was like for him.

"I thought we were really in for it for awhile there. Large North Vietnamese units have hit Special Forces camps in the II Corps area over the last week or so and we all thought they might start to come after some of the firebases, or hit everything all at once, like they did at Tet."

"So, do you think that was some sort of a diversion last night, or what?" Bollman asks.

"I guess I do, but I can't really be sure. There's something screwy about it that I can't figure out for sure."

"Do you think it was maybe just some kind of a probe…you think more of them will be coming back now that they know what we've got up here?" I ask.

"I don't think so. I've been mulling that over all morning with Major Geiger and Ranger. We've all come to the same conclusion about that."

"So, you think they had enough last night, sir? You think they've

Stars and Stripes and Shadows

di-di'd back to Laos?" Ed asks, optimistic about the answer.

"What I really think is that somebody on their side screwed up. They've known what we have up here for a long time. They confirmed that when they hit Charlie Company and they've been patiently building up their knowledge ever since."

"How do you mean that, sir? You mean they've been watching everything we've been doing?" Six-Two asks knowing that they've been watching us. We all know that.

"I've been thinking about that this morning too. They've been doing more than just watching us. Think about what's happened since we got here. Think about the incoming mortar rounds splashing down all over the place. There was never any concentrated fire. They never really hit anything vital. Nothing seemed to be really targeted. They were just mapping the firebase with rounds, fixing locations and setting targets for later. Think about the snipers. They could have picked off a dozen men by now but they shot only at incoming choppers."

"And Johnson…they picked off Sergeant Johnson down in his bunker, don't forget!" Doc reminds us all.

"Yea, that one stumped me for awhile too but I think they needed to know that they could shoot into those two bunkers down there. If they can shoot in there with rifles from over on the other ridge, they can put RPGs in too. If they could take out those two bunkers, they'd have a real opportunity to get up inside the wire and into the perimeter.

The other thing I think we all need to learn from is that guy that walked up here the other day; the Chieu Hoi. Think about what we did with him. We walked right down there in broad daylight and escorted the guy right back up into the firebase, showing anybody watching the best way up through the wire."

"You don't think that guy really wanted to give himself up?" Doc asks, unintentionally diverting the Captain's expressed concern away from what we did and onto the motives of our captive.

"My guess is he was carefully picked and sent over to us while his pals watched and sketched the route in. I'd also guess that he didn't object too much. Right now the son-of-a-bitch is getting three square meals a day and sleeping on clean sheets courtesy of Uncle Sam and the Republic of Vietnam while his still living buddies are hiding out in a tunnel somewhere."

Tim Haslam

"You said you thought they screwed up. How?" asks Elliott.

"I've been in a few fights like that before and Charlie usually had his stuff together pretty well. We always came out on top, but after it was over you could figure out what they were trying to do; why they did what they did. What happened last night, the way it happened, makes no sense. That's why I think something got really screwed up for them. I think you were right a minute ago Sergeant, when you ask about it being a diversion. It would make sense for them to do what they did if there had also been another attack down on the Green Beret camp at Ben Het, or even at Dak To. There job would have been to keep us busy and particularly to keep the 105s up here and over at Firebase 30 engaged in the action away from their main attack. But, nothing happened last night at Ben Het or Dak To or anyplace else around that we can tell. So, I don't know. Maybe something got called off at the last minute and these guys never got the word. Whatever it was, it just doesn't make a lot of sense to me. But I'll bet some NVA officer has some explaining to do."

"Six-Two-Charlie, this is Six-Charlie. Over," Houston's voice breaks over the radio that's sitting next to me.

"Six-Charlie, this is Six-Two-Charlie. Over," I reply ensuring I use the proper protocol with the CO sitting next to me.

"Put Six on. Over," the Captain's RTO says.

"Here, sir. It's Six-Charlie." I hand him the handset and at the same time glance up the hill and see Houston looking down at us waving.

"OK, OK….I'll take it up there. I'll be right up," the Captain says into the handset gathering up his rifle and helmet as he rises to his feet.

"I gotta go talk to the Colonel again. Thanks for the coffee…great job last night."

"The Captain seems to be a pretty good guy," Ed says watching the large West Pointer hurry back up the trench.

"Right…we're lucky. When Collins left I wasn't sure what we'd end up with," a smiling Lieutenant Falck says. "He seems to know his stuff."

"So what do you think happens now, sir?" Doc asks. "Are we gonna stay here much longer?"

"I don't think so. I think the Captain was going to tell us that. I

Stars and Stripes and Shadows

think we'll be out of here in a day or two."

"I hope its back to the bridge. I could get used to that," I say. "I'm ready for some more of Danko's roast beef."

"We gotta be due for a break back at Dak To," Ed says pointedly, looking at the two officers for some clue.

"I think we're overdue for a real stand-down back at Pleiku," Lieutenant Elliott says giving away the true depth of his weariness. It's been many months now since any of these men have seen base camp and I can tell by there expressed attitudes that any other next destination will be a bitter disappointment.

Chapter 8

Hey! Mr. Tambourine Man

His name is Maebon—Jay I think he said—Jay Maebon.
I watch him standing there hunched over like the rest of us under the unfamiliar weight of his ruck, although his doesn't seem quite as well stocked as most of ours. His face is what captures my attention though, not his ruck. His freckled face is that of a teenager. He may not actually be that much younger than most of the rest of us, but he sure looks like he is. He's cleaner than we are too, hasn't built up the layers of dirt and smoke and weariness that hide the younger men the rest of us still might be deeper down. I'm gratified to see his wide-eyed expression, his alertness, his anxiety, his uncertainty, his isolation and his fear. *I'm no longer the new guy.*
Maebon arrived yesterday, flown out to FB25 along with two other new additions to the Company. Six-Zero Platoon got one, Six-One Platoon got one and we got Jay Maebon and Jay Maebon got us. His reception was less cordial than mine a few months ago, not because of him or anything about him. A new guy is always a welcome addition. Maebon also came to us armed with an M79 grenade launcher and a big pouch full of ammo. Another grenadier in the Platoon will be really useful. We need Jay Maebon and his weapon, but Jay Maebon was introduced to us just after we were all informed of our next destination; our next mission. Not a stand-down at Pleiku or a break at Dak To or a hot meal and a swim back at the bridge over the Dak Poko. No; another hump, *another goddamned hump; another off-the-wall, bullshit, somebodies-gotta-have-their-head-way-up-their-ass hump.* And so, Jay Maebon entered the world of the 4th Division grunts at a time when

Stars and Stripes and Shadows

all his new found brothers are at their lowest. Jay Maebon hasn't done anything wrong but he also hasn't earned the right to echo the shared expressions being uttered all about him; F-T-A, fuck-the-Army! It-don't-mean-nothin'!

We're to be flown out seven or eight klicks to the west, about half-way between FB25 and the Laotian border. From there we'll zigzag our way back eastward and find Charlie, find out what he's up to, find out how many are out there, kill some and add bodies to the count. Ranger — the Colonel — the Battalion CO— the guy who's head is probably way up his ass is sending Bravo Company out to the west and Delta Company out to the southwest. Alpha Company will replace us up here at FB25 and Charlie Company stays at the bridge. We don't have all the facts to verify that Bravo Company is getting screwed, but that's the general feeling. Maybe it's because Captain Hilton is new and didn't raise an objection with Ranger. Maybe Captain Hilton wants a chance to prove his worth at body counting. Maybe it's our reward for such a good job the other night.

Each of us in the Platoon, except Jay Maebon, can count on our two hands the total number of hours of sleep we've had in the last week. The last time I can remember having more than four hours of sleep at night was back at the bridge, before the water buffalo patrol. We all know how tired our bodies are. We don't yet realize how far we've stretched and thinned the sinews of our spirit. The grunts struggling onto the vibrating Hueys are not sorry to be departing FB25, but the dark, rainy, jungled world ahead is approached with dread and anxious irritation. None of us give a fuck what Charlie's doing out here. Let him have this shit-hole. Let the smarmy, smirking ARVNs come out here and deal with their cousins from the north. Let the B52's remove the communist threat from these useless forests. Let the Bravo Company grunts fight for something tangible. The threatened values of our flag, our country and our cause are hard to find looking out the side of the noisy helicopter at the shadowy dismal realm below. We're soldiers though; everything around us reminds us of that and we're soldiers together. We still think we'll do what we're being told to do. We still believe that there's a reason for us to be out here.

N N N N

Tim Haslam

The first day's trek was thankfully short; less than two hours from the LZ, over ground that was mostly low, brushy hills. The steady rain that accompanied us would have made climbing the expected higher mountains a torturous effort, leaving us feeling like we got a break today. The rain clouds continue on eastward in their pursuits, not ready to stop and rest as are the grunts of Bravo Company and so we dig into our night defensive position under a clear, bright sky. There's enough of the afternoon left for us to dig our foxholes, fill our sandbags, lay our trip flares, set our Claymores, dry out our fatigue shirts and still have a little time to do nothing.

The Company is spread out along a narrow, low hilltop surrounded by heavy vegetation, interspersed with tall thin trees. The trees make perfect poles for supporting our hooches and can usually be felled with one or two vigorous swings of a machete. Ed, Doc and I have pre-planned our hooch architecture, each contributing ponchos and pieces of rope to the structure. Two poles pounded into the wet ground with our entrenching tools provide the vertical support, with a longer pole laid horizontally into the Y-shaped tops of the four-foot high stakes. One poncho is spread out below the horizontal pole for the floor, two ponchos tied together and draped over the center pole make the roof, another gets tied across the back. One more is fashioned awning-like protecting the front door and still another is laid out on the ground in front that allows us to get in and out of our boots without having to sit in the mud outside. There's just enough room inside for the three of us to lie down on our air-matresses. Lieutenant Falck and Sergeant Bollman are hooch mates and are set up next to us. Because we make up the Platoon Headquarters, we get to be back off the line. All the other squads build their hooches behind the foxholes they've dug around the perimeter. They will all have to pull guard duty rotations out in the foxholes all night. Doc, Ed and I will just have to pull radio watch from the comfort of our hooch. Maybe Six-Two and Bruce will feel benevolent and share in the duty, cutting down the awake time considerably.

With the daylight work done but lots of sunlight left, both Ed and Doc have taken up positions within the Hooch. Ed is busy writing letters and Doc is fully absorbed in the latest Louis Lamour paperback to be passed around. I'm too antsy for some reason to settle in this way and so I wander down the line of hooches in search of some more ac-

Stars and Stripes and Shadows

tive diversion. A short ways down I find Bob Price, Mike Beasley and Mike Danko indoctrinating Jay Maebon. This is exactly the kind of diversion I need.

Price and Beasley are re-living the events at Firebase 25 when I join them. I light a cigarette just after sitting down and am a little surprised to see Maebon pull out his own pack of Marlboros and light up too. A real, burning cigarette doesn't belong in that freckled boyish face. *I hadn't ever given any real thought to how a cigarette dangling from my own sophomoric lips might look.* Maebon seems familiar with the appropriate affectations of the habit and smokes along without raising any other concerns from the senior grunts gathered around. He also seems to be getting comfortable with the group and asks lots of questions about things being described to him. After a time the conversation turns away from grunt war talk and on to grunt home life BS. Maebon's background and credentials, his pedigree and experience all need to be explored. I'm not surprised to learn he's from the mid-west, Muncie, Indiana, and that he was drafted within a year of graduating from high school. Everything about him seems to be pretty regular, almost Norman Rockwell regular, too regular to be of any real interest to the rest of us. The whole background check turns out to be pretty boring, but Maebon comes across as a friendly, good natured sort, taking his first lessons out in the shit pretty much in stride. He's OK.

Just after lighting his next cigarette Maebon makes his first real rookie mistake.

"So, where are you guys from?" he asks to no one in particular and no one responds very quickly.

"Where are you from Danko?" he re-aims the question at the body to his right.

Why he specifically directs the question at Mike Danko, the silent grunt nearly hidden within the shadows of his oversized helmet is a mystery to us all. Why he would start with the least cordial, least talkative, least seemingly attentive member of the group present will never be known to any of us; but, he did, and we all know that we're about to be entertained. We all know that one more fly has just flown into the spider's web. Another new guy is about to meet Danko.

Three, just barely audible syllables filter out through the long dark moustache bristles that curtain over the unseen mouth.

Tim Haslam

"Newk-eyeoh."

"What?" Maebon says, as we all knew he would. None of us really knew what the exact bait would be for the first round of pawing and we all have to think hard to come up with the correct translation. We have to review our knowledge of Mike Danko to decipher the short burst of para-words that Maebon believes he has misunderstood. I can tell by the subtle grins that the others seem to have it. I need one more try.

"Sorry, what?" Maebon repeats after a short pause.

"Newk-eyeoh."

The utterance is exactly the same in volume, tone, pitch and emphasis.

OK, I got it. I remember something Danko once told us. I know what it is.

"New something, Iowa?" is that what you said?"

There's no change in posture or orientation from Danko—the Rodin sculpture—the hungry leopard.

"Newk-eyeoh." The volume is raised just a notch this time.

"OK, I give up. I have no idea what he's saying," Maebon declares, sitting up straighter, scanning the rest of our faces for some clue as to the answer or what he should do next."

"Newark, Ohio," Bob Price says in a calm condescending tone. "Danko's from Newark, Ohio."

"No shit! I know where that is. It's over by Columbus. My cousin lives there."

"Geesigrit." Danko looks over at Maebon.

Without hesitation or comment, Jay Maebon hands Mike Danko the red and white box. *The kid learns fast.*

Maebon starts telling us about his cousin, who lives in Newk-eyeoh, when he's interrupted by Bob Price reaching for the Six-Two-Three radio. Price now humps this radio and is reacting to the voice breaking through the squelch. After a couple of "Rogers" Price tells us that they're going to be firing DTs around us in a few minutes.

"Make sure you have your helmets on," he advises, looking at Mike Beasley and I, the only ones without head cover. Beasley and I return our steel pots to our heads and we all resume our casual conversation. In another minute or two Price announces the first shot heading our way. The alert doesn't even disturb the flow of our conversation and

Stars and Stripes and Shadows

the resulting muffled explosion, well away from us to the south, barely gets a reaction, even from Maebon. Lieutenant Reese is calling in the coordinates and setting the adjustments for rounds to be fired closer in should they be needed later tonight. Reese and the redlegs at the other end seem to be getting it right as the next two rounds also fall well away from us working their way up the west side of our position.

The fourth round fired is the closest one yet to where we are, but still explodes far out into the expanse of brush beyond our perimeter and elicits little concern from any of us. A few seconds pass, the rapport and echo of the round have faded off when Bob Price, sitting next to me tumbles backward suddenly. We all see Price jerk backward before the dull thud sound registers with us.

"What the fuck?"

"You all right, man. You OK? What the fuck was that?"

"Yea...I'm OK...I'm fine," Price says, pulling himself back up. As he returns to full upright he pulls off his helmet and examines it carefully. A piece of spent shrapnel from the artillery round glanced off the top of his helmet with sufficient force to bowl him over.

"Here it is. Look," I tell the others, spotting the jagged edged, egg-sized piece of steel resting on the ground between Bob and me.

"Shit! It's fucking hot!" I blurt out after attempting to pick up the piece to get a better look.

"Man, that's a big hunk of shit. You're lucky that hit you in the helmet!" Beasley tells Price. Maebon is taking all this in with concerned curiosity, trying to figure out if this kind of thing happens all the time.

Price pours some water from his canteen over the ragged chunk, cooling it enough to be handled. He looks it over carefully and then passes it around for each of us to inspect. All of us perform the same hypothetical analysis as we gauge the mass and weight and run our fingers along the sharp edges, imagining what would have happened had it hit any of us somewhere other than the helmet. *Bob Price was lucky. We were all lucky.*

"What are you gonna do with it? You gonna keep it?" I ask him as the hunk is returned to Price.

"I dunno...I guess so."

"You should keep it and you should put your name it," I tell him.

Tim Haslam

Price, Beasley and Danko know what I mean. They each wear AK rounds around their necks like I do, their souvenir charms, their indemnification fetishes.

"You'll have the piece of shrapnel with your name on it. It'll be lucky."

"Yea…I guess that's right," he says and starts trying to scratch his name into the surface of the hard metal with his pocket knife. Jay Maebon looks at all of us like we're a little crazy.

"Is that an AK47 round?" Maebon asks me, pointing to the bullet dangling from the shoelace around my neck, next to my P38 can-opener. "Can I see it?"

He studies the bullet for a minute or two, noting the differences between it and our M16 rounds.

"How can I get one of these?" he asks, "I gotta get one of these and get my name on it."

"You gotta find yours. It won't work if somebody gives you one. You gotta find yours out in the shit somewhere. Too bad you didn't show up at Firebase 25 a day sooner, they were all over the place out there."

"You think we'll find more out here soon?"

"Yea…we probably will. I think we will."

и и и и

The short easy hump of the first day, Price's encounter with the flying metal and Jay Maebon's first lessons in grunt superstition have all been left far behind, distant memories, irrelevant to anything we try to do now. It's only been two days since we humped away from that comfortable, dry position and entered again into the higher mountains. It feels like we're still on misery-hump. It feels like we never ended misery-hump. The rain's been off and on, day and night. We've been slipping and sliding our way up and down ridges and fingers, higher even than those we struggled through on our last hump. The going is treacherously slow and people are already starting to discard bits and pieces of gear, deemed to be relatively un-necessary given their potential value and their weight. Government-issue litter marks the muddy trails we etch through the jungle. Ponchos, empty ammo cans, full C-ration cans and an array of personal items is left behind for Charlie or any

Stars and Stripes and Shadows

other scavengers likely to be following us.

No one says much. Even on breaks there's a selfish silence. No one has the energy to converse. No one has anything to share verbally. We all know how shitty this is and we all share every aspect of it as though we were conjoined into one miserable creature, enslaved by this jungle. Spirits are low. Morale is low.

A little after midnight on the third night out, the first sit-rep of my watch comes over the radio. Five-Nine, Six-Zero, Six-One and their LPs all report or signal back negative. I report back negative for Six-Two from the relative comfort of my air-mattress and poncho liner and wait in the quiet darkness for the last signal from our LP.

"Six-Two-Three, sit-rep. Over," Six-Charlie calls out with the casual assurance that a negative reply is automatic.

The silent pause slaps everyone listening on the net out of his supposed sense of relative well-being.

"Six-Two-Three, Six-Two-Three. Gimme a sit-rep. Over," he repeats, getting irritated with the delay.

Six-Charlie waits again. We all wait again…a good long while.

Come on guys, wake up and answer the sit-rep. Everyone listening thinks the same thing; somebody's fallen asleep out there. One of the three guys out on our LP is supposed to be awake out there, listening to the jungle surrounding him and listening for sit-reps; trying to listen through the silence, curled up into a wet ball under some thorny jungle plant, fighting with ever-diminishing capacity against his own exhaustion. We all feel the same exhaustion. We all want and need to be sleeping right now. We all know how hard it is to stay awake through the long, dark, isolated hours of our shifts. But the guys on LP have to endure it all out there pressed as deeply as they can get into the shit. If they close their eyes for anything longer than a blink, they may not be able to re-open them again.

"Six-Two-Charlie, this is Six-Charlie. Your LP isn't responding. Over."

I know, I know. What am I supposed to do about it? Go down there and wake them up?

"Roger that Six-Charlie. Let me try. Over," I acknowledge.

"Six-Two-Three, Six-Two-Three, this is Six-Two-Charlie. Give me

Tim Haslam

a sit-rep. Over."

I look over to see if Ed or Doc is awake; to see if they can share in the anxiety and maybe offer a solution; but Ed and Doc are a long way from the shit right now, comatose, their bodies trying to hyper-rejuvenate during the short hiatus.

"Six-Two-Three, Six-Two-Three. Get on the goddamn horn and give me a sit-rep. Over."

"Six-Two-Charlie, this is Six-Charlie. You've gotta do something. Over."

"Roger."

I pull my boots on, strap on the radio and probe my way cautiously over to the neighboring hooch and wake up the Lieutenant and Sergeant Bollman.

"Who's on the LP?" Six-Two asks as soon as he's clear on who I am and what I've just told him.

"I dunno, guys from Steve's squad."

"Well, go down there and tell Sergeant Stevens what's going on. See if he's got any ideas."

As I pull out of the hooch and start my reluctant trek down toward the foxholes I hear the Lieutenant say, "Bruce, go with him."

Bollman is right behind me when I reach the closest hole. The two of us surprise Ernie Guitierrez who's got the duty at this hole.

"Where's Steve?" I ask.

"Second hooch down that way," Ernie whispers back, pointing to his left. "What's going on?"

"Your LP's not answering."

"Shit, I'll bet they're asleep."

"Man, I hope that's all it is."

Sergeant Bollman takes the lead as we pick our way carefully along past the next hooch and up to the next foxhole.

"Is Steve in the hooch?" Bollman asks the dark outline of a person standing up in the next hole, too dark for me to identify.

I can't here the muted answer but Bollman takes a few steps toward the hooch and squats down at the entrance.

"Steve, Steve, get up. It's me, Bruce Bollman. Get up."

"What's happening?" Sergeant Stevens says, poking his head out into the open air where Bruce and I have collected.

Stars and Stripes and Shadows

"Your LP's not answering sit-reps. We need your help to get down there to them without getting somebody's ass shot off. Where are they?"

The rest of Sergeant Stevens' snails out of the hooch and rises up to his feet.

"They should be down there...about thirty meters down, a little over to the right. You're not really going down there are you?"

"Your fuckin-A right I'm not going down there," Bollman responds, emphasizing the *I'm*.

"Well I'm sure as hell not going out there."

Stevens follows the same *I'm not* philosophy, but neither of the Sergeants has categorically ruled out some less-than-sergeant rank person going down there.

I'm starting to get more nervous about the direction of this conversation, readying my objection. Whoever goes, by rights should be from Steve's squad.

"Hold on a second," Steve says, looking around for something. "I've got an idea."

Sergeant Stevens turns back towards his hooch and squats down next to an open cardboard box sitting off to the left of the entrance. I recognize the box as a Sundry-Pack. Each platoon got one today, helicoptered in along with our fresh water re-supply. The Sundry-Packs contain a collection of miscellaneous stuff; toothpaste, candy, cartons of cigarettes, writing paper and large useless bars of Ivory Soap. The North Vietnamese Army units that scavenge around after us are probably well stocked with Ivory Soap. There's no way for the grunts out here to bathe and there's sure as hell no way anyone's going to hump around a big heavy hunk of soap. There must be a dozen bars in each pack and if the Company gets five Sundry Packs, that means sixty Ivory Soap bars to be left behind. *Maybe Charlie makes candles for his tunnels out of sloughed off bars of Ivory Soap.*

I can't imagine what Steve could be thinking of as he rummages around through the box. He can't be going through all this to get a cigarette or candy right now and what good would writing paper do? He comes up with both his hands full of soap bars.

"Here, hold these," he says, handing two bars to Bruce and two to me. "Come on."

Tim Haslam

"Bruce and I, armed with our rifles and our Ivory Soap follow Sergeant Stevens, who is now similarly armed, down in front of his foxhole a few feet. Steve shuffles around a few steps looking upwards. By now, Bruce and I have figured out Steve's plan.

"Le' me call back first and let everyone know what we're going to do, so nobody starts shooting."

"Six-Charlie, this is Six-Two-Charlie. We're going to make a little noise out to our front to try and wake up the LP. So don't be alarmed if you hear anything out this way. Over."

"Roger, Six-Two-Charlie. Understood. Out."

Steve lobs the first bar of soap high up through a clearing in the trees above us having calculated the trajectory necessary to bring it down close to his LP. We can hear the outgoing Ivory missile rustle down through the trees and brush, thirty meters out.

Steve can't have all the fun.

Bruce launches the next tallow-based bomblet, arcing it into the same neighborhood with a similar noisy result. I add a third shot to the attack and then go to the radio.

"Six-Two-Three, this is Six-Two-Charlie. Give me a sit-rep. Over."

Pfftt, pfftt, pfftt.

"Six-Two-Three, this is Six-Charlie. Stay awake...goddamn-it. Over."

Pfft, pfftt, pfft!

"You better have a little talk with your guys in the morning Steve," Sergeant Bollman says as he and I toss our unused ammo back into the cardboard box and head back up to the headquarters hooches.

"What's going on?" a half-asleep Ed says as I crawl over him getting back to my station.

"Nothin'...go back to sleep."

N N N N

The early mornings up here, wherever we are, seem cooler than we're used to. The agony starts early, as we have to crawl out from under our poncho liners into the cold, damp mist. There isn't time to build fires to get warmed by, there's barely enough time to heat up a can of C's and water for coffee. Take down the wet ponchos that sheltered us

Stars and Stripes and Shadows

through the night, empty out the wet, muddy sandbags that surrounded our foxhole, pack all the other damp things into Mr. Ruck. This has been the morning routine each day. Everything stays wet. I've had no trouble getting helpers to hump my extra radio batteries; the plastic bags are in high demand in this environment. I need more of them myself and have selfishly humped one of the five-pound batteries, feeling the extra weight every step of the way, but dry letters from home and dry writing paper is worth it.

Six-Two, Sergeant Bollman, Ed and I get together before we start out each day. We all have maps and the Lieutenant shows us the plan for the day, tracing the chosen route with his finger. We look for the separation between the contour lines as clues for what we're in for. When the lines are close together we know the going will be extra tough, up or down steep terrain…steep, slippery terrain.

The Division has determined that Charlie is getting better at monitoring our radio communications and that he probably has the same maps. As a countermeasure, we're no longer allowed to give our position over the radio using map coordinates. Instead, someone has designated four points on our map at major grid intersections three kilometers apart, so that the area we're working in fits into this big square. Each of the four points is given a category, like; states, cars, baseball-teams or girls names. So, if we're closest to the point designated "states" and I want to call in our position I would say something like; "from Iowa right point-four up one-point-two." The next time I might say, "From Nevada right point-six up one-point three." The idea is that Charlie wouldn't be able to figure this out and would think that Iowa and Nevada are two different reference points on the map. Then, to make it even harder for Charlie, we also now have words of the day. These are simple alpha for numeric substitution codes…

Day 1 Z E B R A F U N D S
6 3 1 0 9 5 2 8 4 7

Day 2 F I R S T W O M A N
4 1 8 7 2 3 9 5 0 6

Tim Haslam

With these, we can call in our map coordinates substituting the letters on the words-of-the-day code for the grid numbers. We're supposed to randomly use the category method and the word-code method to ensure that Charlie stays confused. All of this means that Ed and I have more to do. We must make sure that our maps are marked properly with the reference points and proper categories and that we have the right words for each day and the corresponding numeric equivalents. We have to make sure that we don't lose our marked up maps or our slips of paper with the codes scribbled on them. We have to make sure that we don't get killed now that we are in possession of vital military secrets.

Once we've all calibrated our maps and codes and starting position we're off, Ed following close behind Bruce, me right behind the Lieutenant. The Platoon Leader and the Platoon Sergeant are superiors in rank to the rest of us in the Platoon. As such, they are expected to conduct themselves through this shit without complaints, without gripes, without showing any overt signs of their own fatigue, their own frustration or their own discomfort. As military leaders they should not be compelled to verbalize their reactions to everything around them with crude obscenities, as those of us in the lower echelons do. Terry Falck and Bruce Bollman are pretty good at conducting themselves appropriately, at least through the mornings.

The regular chatter that comes over the radio provides somewhat of a diversion from the monotony of humping. The point squads call in their position and describe the route and the terrain ahead, giving me a heads-up on what's to come. It's often disheartening to hear them call back to us, describing the steep, thickly-jungled ridge they're fighting their way up or the swampy, bamboo thickets their chopping their way through. *Maybe the Captain will opt for an alternate way; I sometimes think to myself. Maybe we won't have to mule our way up one more brambled, slippery incline today; I sometimes think to myself. Maybe we've seen the worst of it for today;* I always think to myself and I'm always wrong in my thinking. Sometimes it's better not think too much. Sometimes it's better to concentrate on other worlds far away.

> *Hey! Mr. Tambourine man, play a song for me,*
> *I'm not sleepy and there is no place I'm going to.*
> *Hey! Mr. Tambourine man, play a song for me,*

In the jingle jangle morning, I'll come followin' you.

Take me on a trip upon your magic swirlin' ship.
My senses have been stripped, my hands can't feel to grip,
My toes to numb to step, wait only for my boot heels to be
wanderin'
I'm ready to go anywhere, I'm ready for to fade
Into my own parade, cast you're dancin' spell my way,
I promise to go under it.

Hey! Mr. Tambourine man, play a song for me,
I'm not sleepy and there is no place I'm going to.
Hey! Mr. Tambourine man, play a song for me,
In the jingle jangle morning, I'll come followin' you.

Six-Two has switched positions with me for a while this morning, following behind me. We've been moving for the last hour at a stop and go, bumper to bumper, asshole to elbow pace along a narrow trail winding its way up along the side of a high ridge. The rain's been light but steady all morning and I'm thankful that the incline we're on isn't any steeper. My consciousness has drifted off, away from the slow plodding file of grunts, away from the pain of the sodden mass of gear anchoring me downward, away from all things. I'm in a foggy nether world, without thought, without dreams, without feeling, without awareness. When the body in front of me moves I move. When it stops I stop. My eyes continue to take in the muted light reflected off the dank green mass that surrounds me, my ears continue to hear the steady static rush of the radio squelch and the boot steps splashing and squishing somewhere below me, but all deeper mental processes have been shut down. Something around me will have to change to break the spell and bring me back into a state of mental alertness.

A tiny, unobtrusive object entering onto my mental radar screen breaks the spell. I'm not sure why it's even a sufficient stimulus to catch my attention. I hone in on it though, visually refocusing out of my disengaged malaise and back into the reality of the Nam. I watch it move slowly, purposely along its course, seeking its objective. I watch the leech work its way up the filthy green sleeve of the grunt in front of

Tim Haslam

me. It stretches itself out, the full one-inch length of its body and then grips onto the fabric with its front end and pulls up its hind end forming a U-shape. It slowly repeats these moves several times. Then it stops after one of the pulls and instead of forming the U-shape, it rises up its narrower front end, so that it appears to be standing upright, held fast by its anchored-in hind end. It waves around...searching. It's looking, or sniffing, or using whatever sensory apparatus it has to find the nutrients it seeks. It seems to know its getting warm. It's on the right track.

"La Bamba," it says on the side of the helmet next to where it says *Ernie G.* I remember now that it's Ernie Gutierrez in front of me. I can see that he too has the glazed over look of the sleepwalking grunt. Ernie has no idea that the leech is climbing up the back of his arm. Ernie has no idea that the grunt behind him, Six-Two-Charlie, is carefully studying the slimy parasite stretching its starved body up towards his shoulder and the exposed flesh of his neck just beyond. Ernie doesn't know of the mental diversion his leech offers to Six-Two-Charlie. Right now, for Ernie, *it-don't-mean-nothin.'*

The leech moves more quickly over the coarser material of the ruck strap that pulls down over Ernie's shoulder. Three quick pull-ups and it's across the strap and back onto the shirt fabric, just below the wrinkled collar. There, it rises up again for another waive around, confirming that the warmth detected is increasing. The sensors within its mouth and over its skin acknowledge that it's getting close. Its appetites will soon be satisfied. Its protein deficiencies will soon be overcome. Its life will soon be revived and sustained for a while longer, perhaps for as long as a month if it can steal enough blood to fill itself.

For a second I think about saying something to Ernie. For a brief second I think about telling him, saving him. It would take too much energy though; too much energy for both of us right now. I want to see what happens anyway. I want to be distracted from all else around me for a while longer. I want to see if Ernie will react to the actual strike, the penetration of the little teeth, the injection of the anti-clotting enzymes or the pumping transfer of blood out of his neck into the segmented body of the leech. *Ernie will probably reach back and pull it off as soon as it comes in contact with the bare flesh of his neck anyway.*

A mosquito hovering around my left ear elicits a feeble swat from my left hand just as the leech stretches over the upper folds of Ernie's

Stars and Stripes and Shadows

collar, stepping gingerly onto the warm, pulsing tissue of its human host. There's no reaction from Ernie, his mental separation from the shit around him is uninterrupted by the first subtle probes of the hungry invader. Both ends of the leech are now establishing holds, wading through the film of sweat and filth that will season the reservoir of protein plasma just a few layers of epithelial tissue away. The first penetration attempt isn't quite right for some reason. The narrow end rises up again, waives around vigorously and then cranes down off to the left a little, settling in quietly. *Still no reaction from Ernie.* Still no alert or rescue attempt from Six-Two-Charlie. There's still more to be observed; still more to learn.

Nothing seems to happen for several minutes and I'm becoming bored with the lack of activity. My consciousness is starting to pay attention again to the weight of my ruck, to the sweat in my eyes and the feel of my wet socks sponging between the heels of my feet and the inside of my boots. I look away from the inanimate leech for a while, up into the green mass of leaves and vines all filtered into sameness by the heavy damp air. I listen more attentively for a moment or two to the hissing squelch of my radio, anxious to hear Six-Charlie's voice break through declaring a rest break. I realize how thirsty I am, but don't have the energy to reach around and unfasten one of my canteens. I want a cigarette, but that would be way too much trouble. *I want to be out from under all this shit and out of this place* but that's too distant a dream.

I don't know how long it's really been since I took my eyes off of Ernie's leech. It's been long enough for it to have grown though. Its slender body has doubled in size and its color is darkening. I reach up with my left hand and scour my own neck. No response yet from Ernie.

Another few minutes and the leech has tripled in size, engorged itself into a hideous black blob. *Ernie has to sense the mass of this thing hanging from his neck. He has to feel its weight pulling on the teeth still embedded in his skin.*

"All Eight-Two stations, this is Six-Charlie. We're taking ten. Over," Houston's voice comes through, rescuing all of us.

"Ernie, we're taking ten. Pass it up the line," I say to Gutierrez, without any other notifications.

"We're taking ten, sir," I repeat back to Six-Two coming up a few

Tim Haslam

meters behind me.

I throw off my ruck, retrieve one of my canteens and nearly empty it. I light a cigarette and take two long drags.

"Ernie...hold still a second, there's a leech on your neck," I advise him as though I had just made the discovery. I walk up next to Ernie, who's still standing and take a close look.

"Hold still, I'll get the sucker off."

I press the burning end of my cigarette into the fat purplish blob clinging to Ernie's neck. It releases its grip immediately, as well as a flood of blood and falls down under Ernie's collar somewhere. Gutierrez reaches back, fumbles around for a second or two and comes up with the vile blood-ball.

"Thanks, man," he says to me as he throws the rubbery carcass as far as he can off into the jungle.

"Sure...no problem."

N N N N

Each day out here seems a little longer than the one before it. We go a little slower, a little further, a little deeper into the mountains and a little deeper into our own individual silent suffering. There's been no sign of Charlie so far this hump, no external interruption to our meandering progress, nobody seems to know or care that we're here. Today we did have to stop and cut an LZ though. One of the guys in Six-Zero has malaria pretty bad and had to be dusted off, sent back to the clean sheets of the 71st Evac.

Dusted off for malaria?

Everyone has the same thought. Everyone thinks hard about skipping our daily Dapsone pill or spitting out the Chloroquine/Primequine pill that Doc hands out each Monday morning as dictated by USARV Regulation 40-4. We all re-consider how much of a nuisance the mosquitoes really are...*Do the ones that carry malaria look any different?*

> *Tonight I'll sing my songs again*
> *I'll play the game and pretend.*
> *But all my words come back to me in shades of*
> *Mediocrity*
> *Like emptiness in harmony I need someone to comfort*

Me.
Homeward bound,
I wish I was,
Home where my thought's escaping,
Home where my music's playing,
Home where my love lies waiting
Silently for me.

Lieutenant Falck wrestles his way up a steep slippery stretch ahead of me, grabbing onto vines to maintain his forward progress up through the wet mud that's been trampled into slush, insufficient for traction on such a gradient. My own similar struggle takes all of my energy and my full attention. I don't see the vine that's been supporting the Lieutenant give away. I don't even really see the Lieutenant and all his gear tumble down into me. I just become part of the avalanche. Reflexively, I try to break the fall. Bowled over to my left, it's my left arm that automatically juts out as the brake. In my left hand is my M16 and so my fingers can't help to cushion the contact with whatever I'm about to land on. The exposed knuckles of my hand take the full brunt of the impact and there seems to be more than the usual jolt of pain as I slam down into the hacked away stumps of bamboo. It takes a second or two to figure out the best way to get myself and my splayed-out gear separated from the Lieutenant, back in order and under control. Sergeant Bollman has climbed up to help Six-Two and I get back up to our feet and without comment we all return to our positions in line and start once again to make our way up the treacherous slope.

Once the whole Company has reached the top of the ridge we take a break, affording me the first opportunity to fully investigate the damage to my stinging hand. Several more small cuts have been added to the array of little wounds attempting to scab over within the wet filth. My index finger is the source of the greatest pain and I can see several splinters of bamboo protruding out of the second knuckle. It's easy enough to pull most of them out but one has buried itself pretty far up under the skin. Bolstered by a cigarette I try to reach the tip of the shard with the tip of my knife but my unsteady probing only serves to push the splinter further down into the flesh. *Oh well.*

Maybe I should have Doc take care of this?

Tim Haslam

I can see Doc resting comfortably up against a tree, three men down the file from me. *He looks awfully relaxed.* I don't think I want to call out to him and ask him to pull a splinter out of my finger. Doc is a combat medic. He deals with metal that's penetrated into people...not splinters! I don't think Darvon would help anyway and it doesn't hurt that much anymore. I don't think I want him pouring Merthiolate into the latest vents in my flesh as that would sting like hell. Maybe tonight, after we make camp, I'll have him take a look at it. Right now it takes too much energy to fret about. I'm thirsty and hungry and we've only got a few minutes for reparations and mending. *Fuck the bamboo in my finger. It-don't-mean-nothin.'*

The ridges here prove to be too steep for us to maintain anything like the pace required and so the Captain has chosen to work down through a narrow stream-cut canyon snaking its way generally eastward. At the canyons narrowest points the stream itself becomes the only avenue for our passage and we have to criss-cross it several times. A few places we find it easiest just to wade down stream, sometimes hip deep in the rain-swollen watercourse. With all the weight on our backs and the unsure footing beneath the surface of the gently flowing water the going is slow and difficult. Several men lose their footing or their balance and end up fully submerged in the murky water, cursing furiously along with their rescuers as they struggle to regain their upright position and their place in the file. Each of us suspects that the stream is alive with leeches. Each of us is sure that we're being set upon from under the surface of the water by a whole new array of parasites. We all understand that should Charlie find us here, nearly immobilized by the water, below the heavily forested higher ground on either side of us, we're dead.

Six-Two Platoon is walking drag in the formation today, bringing up the rear. This means that the going for us is extra slow as the long file ahead of us constantly re-adjusts to the movements and shifting pace of the individuals picking their way over and around the obstacles ahead. We do a lot of waiting, just standing, hunched forward trying to shift some of the weight of our rucks onto our backs and off of our shoulders. We try to keep a close eye on the land behind us as Bravo Company has left a trail that's easy to follow.

Stars and Stripes and Shadows

I smoke too much on days like this. It's the only diversion there is but with the wetness of my hands, the cigarette paper gets quickly saturated, usually rendering the last inch and half of tobacco un-smoke-able, so I keep lighting them, taking a few hits and throwing away the soggy last half.

At one point the stream is compressed through a narrow rocky cleft, cascading down steeply ten to twelve feet. The water has an easy time adjusting to the abrupt drop off but the grunts of Bravo Company are less able to flow gracefully down and over the mossy rocks. For us, the way down is via a flight of natural rocky steps dropping down on the south side of the stream. The rocks here are of a flaky construction and extremely slippery with the mist fed moss and lichen. Between the rocks are steep sections of mud, and thickets of bamboo spears, shafts and shards bound the whole route down. Various techniques are employed by the grunts trying to descend down through this trap. Some men don't trust their feet at all and simply take most of the route down on their ass, using both hands and both feet as moving braces. Others try to team up on the slope with mixed results. Some back down as though climbing down a ladder and some, too weary to strategize, just slip, and stumble their way down taking the bumps and bruises as inevitable.

Whatever Dennis Jernigan had in mind as his turn came; it didn't work out very well. Only a few feet down, his right foot twisted suddenly off the front edge of a rock plate. The full weight of his ruck reacted to the short lurch forward and to the right, swinging out over into the bamboo, pulling Jernigan backwards down into the nest of leaves and spikes. Jernigan, who I played poker with back at Firebase 25, landed hip first, his full weight centered right over one of the bamboo shafts, splintered by someone's earlier machete stroke. For him it was like sitting on a knife blade. The whole Company could hear his screams as he twisted himself off of the impaling shaft.

The men around Jernigan had a tough time trying to get him down the rest of the drop and into the hands of the medics down below. Once there, the medics could size up the extent of his wound and begin tending to it. They find a two-inch slice at the surface, penetrating down nearly to the bone just below his buttocks. There's no way for them to tell what's been left inside the wound. They apply everything they have

Tim Haslam

that might counteract foreign organic matter infecting the interior tissues. They liberally disinfect the wound with sulpha and albumin powder that will help coagulate the blood, slowing its flow out of his body. Then they wrap up the wound as tightly as they can in a field dressing. That's all they can do to mend the wound. Surgeons will have to get in there later to complete the disinfecting, the cleaning and the mending of the torn tissues. Now the medics must try to minister to Jernigan's panicked reaction to the pain and sense of damage to his hip.

"You gotta be shit'n me!" Sergeant Bollman says handing the handset of Ed's radio back to Ed.

"You heard him. Let's get going."

The weary Lieutenant has just been given orders to take our squad back nearly a klick to a place where we can cut an LZ for the dust-off bird needed to get Jernigan out. He knows that it's the only way. He knows that it's our turn and, he knows too, how hard it will be to go back over the same ground that we've struggled through all morning, hack away the LZ and then make it all the way to the Company's night defensive position, wherever that might be. The Company can't wait for us. It will be for us to make up the expanding distance between us. He knows what it will be like when he tells the rest of the Platoon.

"Six-Two-Charlie, this is Six-Charlie. Six wants you to go ahead and get started. A squad from Six-Zero will bring the dust-off guy to you. Over."

"Roger."

I tell Six-Two of the Captain's instruction; my news breaking the agitated silent pause that followed the Lieutenant's disclosure to the squad leaders.

"This is so fucked up," Sergeant Taylor says rhetorically, expressing the shared sentiment for the other NCOs.

"What else can we do?" Lieutenant Falck says, hunching his ruck further up his back. He doesn't have time to negotiate and nothing to negotiate with. He knows that Taylor and Steve and Grady and Mike Ferlik understand. He knows that all the men in the Platoon will realize that a man's life is at stake. He may not know the effect this work will have on the spirits of his men over the long run. He may not know what's happening to his own spirit.

Stars and Stripes and Shadows

"Let's just get it done. Steve, you take point," he says, closing the discussion.

The squad leaders spread the word to the others who already suspect that things are about to get worse. The reactions are predictable, divided into two camps of expression.

"This is so fucked up!"

"It-don't-mean-nothin'! It-don't-mean-nothin'!"

� ✶ ✶ ✶ ✶

"Hey Ed, bring your radio over here," I shout across the freshly cut hole in the jungle over the fading pops of the medevac bird trailing off to the south.

"The signal's not very good, sir. Six is on, but keeps breaking up. Maybe Ed's getting it better," I advise the Lieutenant as Ed arrives.

His radio is no better, the distance and terrain and clouded weather have all teamed up to suck the energy out of the Captain's radio transmission.

"How about a fresh battery' maybe the batteries going?" the Lieutenant suggests.

"I put a new one in this morning," I tell him.

"Me too," says Ed, eliminating one possible remedy.

"I'll put on the long-stick antennae and get in the middle of the LZ."

Six-Two and Ed follow me into the center of the cleared circle.

"Roger," the Lieutenant keeps saying. "Say again. Over," he requests about every third roger.

"Roger. Out."

"OK, listen up," he says to the group gathered around him; the squad leaders, Ed, Bruce, Doc and I.

"We've gotta hump our asses off to get back to the Company before it gets dark. The Captain says they're getting lots of reports of activity up in this section," the Lieutenant says, squatting down over his map, pointing to a train of high ridges three klicks to the north.

"He also doesn't want us to follow the same trail back to them; too many opportunities for snipers and ambushes. We're gonna have to move as quickly as we can along the top of this ridge here and then down this finger, crossing over the stream about here and up to the

Tim Haslam

Company's position, here."

My Timex says its five after four. The distance and terrain indicated on the map make it clear that the rest of the afternoon will require an effort like nothing I've yet experienced in the land of the shit. We must drive ourselves through two and half klicks of uncut jungle before nightfall, with Charlie thought to be gathering along our left flank.

This is so fucked up.

An hour out from the LZ we take our first short break, stopping at the crest of a high ridge with unobstructed views off to the north. The panorama exposed to us holds little attraction though. It's just more of the same. All we care about right now is water and the chance to be off our feet and out from under Mr. Ruck for a few moments. The sweat-streaked faces around me mirror the same level of fatigue and anguish that I feel and betray the same understanding of what's yet to come. We still have a long way to go and time is running out. We'll have to push harder.

"Saddle up!" the Lieutenant says much too soon. No one really wants to sit here any longer though. We just want this to be over.

Just as I help pull Doc up onto his feet, a jarring blast of sound shakes down through the trees over us. An F4 Phantom jet just above the treetops screams out into the clear sky, heading northward. A second Phantom follows an instant later a little further to the east. The whole Platoon watches as the two camouflaged planes tighten up their formation, bank sharply to the left and head for a high ridge that cuts diagonally away from our position, up to the northeast. The first plane swoops down, seeming to head right at the mountainside, maybe a mile away from where we all stand transfixed by the spectacle of the loud, fast aircraft about to attack something unseen off in the distance.

The released bombs wobble downward only a short distance before exploding into the forested hillside as the first Phantom banks hard left, climbing back around toward us. The second F4 duplicates the attack, circling around and re-joining the lead plane back where they rallied for the first assault. Again they bank left and again the first plane swoops down. This time the tumbling object jettisoned from the plane erupts into a huge wall of fire climbing up the mountainside. The flaming napalm clearly marks the target area for the grunt spectators and the second Phantom waggling its wings into alignment with the flight

Stars and Stripes and Shadows

path of its predecessor. We all watch with nervous anticipation, glad the F4s are pounding Charlie's position, but concerned that Charlie is that close.

"Jesus Christ!" Doc shouts out in reaction to what he's just seen, hoping that his eyes have played some trick on him.

I too can't believe I've really witnessed what just happened. I study the gray sky over the distant ridge, searching through the napalm smoke to find the evidence that my eyes have deceived me. There's nothing in the air except Phantom number one, which is roaring right over us, locked into an extreme left banking turn heading back toward the burning patch of forest.

It just can't be. That just can't be.

But we all saw it. The second F4 pilot adjusted his Phantom onto its final vector, trim and angle of attack, heading right for the same target area. Then, suddenly it was just swallowed up by the shadowy green hillside. It just flew straight into the mountain. I don't know if it released its bombs or not. It happened too fast. After a second or two, a muffled explosion reaches us and a smoky fireball roils up out of the forest right above where the American Phantom jet disappeared.

It just can't be.

"What the fuck happened?" I hear familiar sounding voices ask.

"Did it get shot down?"

"Shouldn't we do something?"

"What are we gonna do? It's at least three klicks away and whoever was in that plane is for-sure dead," Sergeant Bollman says, trying to be matter of fact.

"Call it in. Let Six-Charlie know what just happened," Six-Two tells me, feeling as helpless and as much in shock as the rest of us.

Six-Charlie acknowledges the information and asks for a map coordinate. The location is off my grid of categorized reference points, so I transpose the location using the word-of-the-day and give it to Houston along with our own current location.

"You better get your asses in gear," Houston advises. "We're at the night location and you guys have a long way to go."

No further mention of the F4 or the two men that just road it to their deaths in front of us.

"Let's go," the Lieutenant says, starting off. He too has nothing

Tim Haslam

else to say about the surreal event that we all just watched. It was just another don't-mean-nothin' little piece of this whole shitty mess. We'll never know what happened to the American airplane and the two men who just a minute ago buzzed over us, doing their job in this war. *We have to go now. We have to get our asses in gear.*

I re-adjust the ruck straps digging into my shoulders and set off, trailing close behind the hunched over Lieutenant, both of us lost within our own confused world.

Hey! Mr. Tambourine man, play a song for me,
I'm not sleepy and there is no place I'm going to.
Hey! Mr. Tambourine man, play a song for me,
In the jingle jangle morning I'll come following you.

Then take me disappearin' through the smoke rings of my mind,
Down the foggy ruins of time, far past the frozen leaves,
The haunted, frightened trees, out to the windy beach,
Far from the twisted reach of crazy sorrow.
Yes, to dance beneath the diamond sky with one hand waving free,
Silhouetted by the sea, circled by the circus sands,
With all memory and fate driven deep beneath the waves,
Let me forget about today until tomorrow.

Hey! Mr. Tambourine man, play a song for me,
I'm not sleepy and there is no place I'm going to.
Hey! Mr. Tambourine man, play a song for me,
In the jingle jangle morning I'll come following you.

※ ※ ※ ※

The seventh day of this hump opens the same as all the others. We crawl out from under our damp poncho liners into the mist shrouded encampment and start the daily cycle over again; light a cigarette, heat up enough water for a can of luke warm coffee, heat up the most palatable of the remaining C-rations, perform another careful check for leeches, scratch at all the itching open sores and get the gear together. Ed and Bruce and I gather around Six-Two to go over the maps and codes and to discuss the day's movements. Another long day, two klicks

284

Stars and Stripes and Shadows

as the crow flies, close together grid lines and higher mountain peaks, most over a thousand meters and the weather forecast calls for rain.

Doc Charlebois has skipped the planning session this morning. He's been over with Mike Ferlik checking on Tom Novotsky who last night was feeling feverish, complaining of chills. Aspirin was all that Doc could offer to help him through the night and Sergeant Ferlik gave him a night off from guard duty.

"How's he doing?" asks Sergeant Bollman as Doc hurries back up toward us.

"He says he feels better this morning…a little headache and a little weak. We'll see how he does. I think it might be malaria. It's too early to tell for sure."

"I've gotta go over and talk to the Captain. I'll let him know about Novotsky and see what he thinks we should do," says the Lieutenant heading off bareheaded and empty handed.

A few minutes later Lieutenant Falck returns and starts getting into his gear without saying anything, signaling the rest of us to do the same. Tom Novotsky and the rest of us must pick it up where we left off yesterday, regardless of our attitude or physical condition.

"We'll be walking center file. Grady in front, then Steve then us, Taylor and Ferlik bring up the rear behind the CO and headquarters. Let's go. The point squad's long gone," Six-Two says to the pack being herded together around him.

Each man's tired face sags with dread, anticipating another long familiar day in the boonies. I can see Tom Novotsky coming up behind the rest of the men. His face reflects more than physical fatigue and knowing anticipation of the tedious work ahead. Fear shows through the dullness of his eyes. He's afraid that today won't be like all the others. He's afraid that he won't be able to do it today, that he won't be able to keep up, that the weakness spreading over him and the subtle ache overtaking his whole body from somewhere deep within will make his ruck and gear un-endurable; the next step impossible. Something in his mind tells him he can't survive out here in the jungle with the rest of Bravo Company today.

"Hold up," I can hear Wee John say, somewhere behind me.

Its a few minutes after ten; we've been crawling our away up and

Tim Haslam

down the ridges for three hours. The rain accompanying us has varied from light to moderate to heavy but always present. Much of the filth has washed off our hands and faces, only to be replaced by newer layers of fresher residues. No one has been able to avoid slipping and falling this morning adding layers of mud to our boots and our fatigues. Pant legs and shirt backs are being torn and shredded. Flesh is being similarly violated by the jungles defenses.

We can't possibly do this all day, I think to myself as I turn to see what Wee John wants.

I can't possibly do this all day, I've been thinking to myself for the last half hour as the misery steadily overtakes me.

"What's going on? Are we taking a break?" Six-Two asks up toward Wee John.

"One of your men's down back behind us."

"Novotsky," the Lieutenant says, wrestling out of his ruck. Doc Charlebois has stayed back with Ferlik's squad all morning just to keep an eye on Novotsky. This morning's hump has just about killed all of us. *Maybe it has killed Novotsky.*

Bob Price calls up to me on the radio just as Six-Two starts back along the line of men behind us.

"Novotsky's in pretty bad shape. He can't go any farther. Doc says he can't go any farther. Over."

"Roger. Six-Two's on his way back to you. Over."

I want to say more and to know more about what's happened to Tom, but don't have the energy. The Captain will be coming on the radio any time now anyway to start orchestrating another LZ cutting effort. I hope some other platoon gets the assignment. We had to do it yesterday for Jernigan. *Or was it the day before yesterday?* It's got to be somebody else's turn. I have just enough strength to search the terrain around us to see if there is any ground suitable for clearing. There isn't.

"Six-Charlie, this is Five-Nine-Alpha-Charlie...we're about three hundred meters up from your position. The ridge flattens out here and there's mostly bamboo covering the area. We can cut an LZ here pretty easily. Over."

The men on the point squad have been asked to head back toward the Company, to find ground that could be used to bring in the dust-off bird for Novotsky.

Stars and Stripes and Shadows

"Roger, Five-Nine-Alpha-Charlie. Start clearing. The rest of Five-Nine will head up that way now to help secure the area. Six-Charlie. Out."

Without his ruck, Tom Novotsky is led along the freshly carved pathway toward the place where the medevac helicopter will soon arrive to take him out of the shit. His gear has been doled out to the others in Ferlik's squad who must wrestle the extra burdens all the way to the LZ. People they pass along the way offer help, until the gear is spread amongst a half a dozen men. Once again the grunts find enough strength to help in the effort to get a damaged man out of here. Each of us studies the pale, fever-glazed face of Novotsky as he passes, Doc Charlebois at his side. There's no doubt that he's really sick. There's little doubt that it's malaria. Still, as he passes slowly along, heading for the air-ambulance ahead, everyone is in some measure envious of Tom Novotsky.

◢ ◢ ◢ ◢

Roy Houston is Six-Charlie. He's humped the Bravo Company CO's radio for a long time now. He's on his third CO. Roy's been in the Nam since October of last year. He's endured eight months and must endure four more. He's seen just about everything that the shit has to throw at a grunt. He was there last November when Bravo Company ran into Charlie up behind Rocket Ridge and lost 20 men in vicious fighting. He survived the Tet offensive. He's been in other firefights, other mortar attacks and other sniper assaults. He's seen a lot of men, a lot of his friends leave the shit, dusted off to cleaner places where they could mend their bodies and rejuvenate their spirits. He's never been seriously wounded himself, just the same thousand little wounds that the jungle inflicts on all of us, not official wounds "received in combat," no Purple Hearts. Roy Houston has humped a million klicks, through a million mosquitoes. His R&R is a long faded memory. He just has to endure four more months and then he can go home. He can quit being Six-Charlie.

The rain's been falling pretty hard most of this afternoon. At the last break Six-Two and I studied our maps carefully and estimated at least two more hours to reach our destination for tonight. The good news is that the map shows the way along a finger ridge, gradually slop-

Tim Haslam

ing downward on a southwestward arc. If it weren't for the rain this would be pretty easy going; *if it weren't for the rain.* As it is, the track turns out to be a series of twisting mud chutes waiting in ambush for the heavily laden grunts. Each slip and fall takes its toll. Each time, the effort to get back up is greater, until my mind starts pleading for surrender. *Don't get up. Don't try. Just stay here. Fuck this!* The quiet curses from the others around me, dragging themselves up off the jungle canvas, tells me I'm not alone in my tired, angry, nearly beaten state.

I follow Lieutenant Falck carefully down one of the short chutes, zigzagging sideways, until we reach a patch of flatter ground. The Lieutenant and I stop there for a minute, celebrating our victory over the one, ten-foot section of jungle trail that has failed to ensnare us. The celebration is brief however, as the view to the front shows another hundred meters or more of treacherous ground, littered with grunts struggling to regain their footing or their upright posture.

Shit! Shit!

Our slow, sideways, zigzagging approach will take forever down this. Mr. Ruck will kick my ass every unsteady step of the way and who knows what's down there, beyond the stretch that we can see. *What if it's like this for the whole rest of the way.*

Wee John, Houston and Captain Hilton are coming down the section right behind us. Wee John makes it all the way to us on his feet and takes in the view ahead, verbalizing the same reaction we've had with a disheartened, "Oh, fuck!"

Roy Houston is only about two more steps away from the bottom of the slippery slope when his feet hydroplane out from under him. He goes down hard, square on his ass. The weight of his ruck continues to curl over down the remaining section of the slide, pulling the helpless Houston another few feet until the whole mud coated mass comes to rest a few feet behind us.

We all look back for some reaction. Wee John takes a few steps back and offers his hand to help Roy up, but Houston just lies there.

"Here, take my hand Roy. The grounds pretty solid here," says a sympathetic Wee John.

Still, Houston remains still, saying nothing. After several seconds, he roles himself into a more upright seated posture and yanks his arms out of the straps connecting him to his ruck and gear. He looks up

Stars and Stripes and Shadows

briefly, scanning for just an instant the three faces in front of him his eyes welled up with tears.

"Fuck this!" he says in a choked quiet voice, throwing his M16 down into the brush beside him. "Fuck this!"

"Are you OK, man?" Wee John asks, just as the Captain takes his last careful steps down the chute, joining the rest of us on the flat patch of ground.

"What's the matter?" the Captain asks.

None of us have an answer. None of us know how to describe what we know is the matter. None of us can speak for Houston right now. The Captain can tell by our silent orientation that Roy is the focus of attention.

"What's the matter Roy…you OK?" Captain Hilton's voice reflects a natural, honest concern. The big man with the two black bars on the front of his helmet must now take command of a new circumstance. He must add whatever has happened to his RTO to his responsibilities to the Company, to Ranger and higher headquarters, to his mission and to his own personal misery, all of which demand his full attention right now. No one would be surprised to see an Army officer in such a situation attempt to curse and berate Houston back into line. He has bigger things to worry about than the insubordinate sniveling of one man, but Captain Hilton is something else before he is an Army officer.

"What is it Roy? Are you hurt in some way?" asks the Captain crouching down at Houston's side.

"Fuck this shit! I've had it. I'm not going any further. I'm not takin' another fuckin' step!" Roy responds, not so much to the Captain, but to the whole shitty world around him.

"Wee John, call a ten minute break," the Captain says, pulling off his ruck.

The rest of us move off a little toward the far end of the flat ground, giving both the Captain and his RTO a little more space to work through a solution; a reconciliation; a reconstruction. None of us say anything as we detach ourselves from our gear. None of us say anything as we settle down into the soaked ground. Everyone has the same thought as we each work to retrieve and light a dry cigarette. Everyone understands that Houston may have taken the last-straw fall for all of us. There isn't anyone who doesn't understand exactly what

Tim Haslam

Roy Houston feels right now and yet there is a strange sense of selfish relief that it was Roy Houston and not any of us. *It was somebody else first, not me. What if I had come down that little slope on my ass instead of my feet? What would I have done?* For some odd reason, just seeing and hearing Roy Houston's pain has helped each of us. If it has come to this for him, someone as strong and respected as him, the measure of our own mettle and endurance has been raised. Most of what we felt a few minutes ago has changed, re-evaluated, partially cleansed of the fear of failing. Whatever else happens today, we'll get through it.

"Listen son, just take some time. Tell me what you want to do," says the Captain, now sitting next to Houston, as he pulls off his helmet. He's not in Houston's face or space. There's no preaching or condescension in the Captain's voice or posture. Even his orientation is casual and relaxed, patient and respectful. His demeanor suggests that he too is taking a much-needed break, swabbing his face with his towel, swigging water from his canteen. Only his use of the term "son" suggests his nurturing motive. The Captain may be thirty years old himself, too close in age to the rest of us to be believably viewed as fatherly. But something about the term adds a subtle measure of personal warmth that finds its mark with each of us.

The Captain shifts around facing Houston, saying something in a voice too muted for the rest of us to hear. He speaks for quite a while in this quiet tone, directly to Roy. His message is for Houston only. None of us will ever know what Captain Hilton said to Roy Houston this day, sitting here in the rain and mud. We know more about what this Officer didn't do and didn't say. We know that we're glad this man leads our Company.

Six-Charlie continues to sit quietly, staring down into the mud that welds him into this vast valueless cesspool. For a few more moments he needs to not care. For those same moments the thoughts of the rest of us shift back and forth from concern for Houston and concern for ourselves. *This is all pretty fucked up.*

"This is all so fucked up, sir," Roy Houston finally says, turning slightly toward the man seated to his right. "Sorry."

"Forget it. We'll have to go in about five."

"Wee John, give me a smoke," Houston says in a stronger voice, taking off his helmet but avoiding eye contact with any of us. Wee

Stars and Stripes and Shadows

John tosses over the plastic case that holds his Lucky Strikes without comment.

Some day I'll be home and will forget how shitty this all really is!"

After a couple of minutes we follow the Captain's lead and climb back into our gear, help each other to our feet and ready ourselves to move on.

"Saddle up," Wee John orders over the radio.

"Sorry, man," Six-Charlie says, seemingly to Wee John.

"Don't mean nothin.'"

N N N N

"Save that one for last. Don't put the floor down yet, it'll just get soaked," Ed points out to me as I start to spread out one of my ponchos. He's right. In this rain, it'll just collect water while we set up the rest of the hooch. I crumple it up. Jam it under my ruck and help Doc tie down the two ponchos that make our roof. The three of us work steadily through our now familiar process of hooch raising and have it up in a few minutes. With the hooch up, the three of us collect at the front door, under our awning poncho, hesitant to go inside as muddy as we are. For the next few minutes we attempt to clean ourselves, shaving the mud off our fatigue pants with knives and machetes. We take off our shirts and try to shake most of the crud away from the soaked fabric. Our boots also come off and get several layers of the heavy clay-like gunk sliced off. The only housekeeping task remaining is to inflate our air-mattresses.

"Goddamn-it! I always do that," I blurt out jokingly. The moustache I've been growing since I left Pleiku, the first facial hair of my life, is now of sufficient length to cover my upper lip and curl down into my mouth. Once my air-mattress is fully inflated I try to close the plastic valve cap as quickly as I can after my last blow into the little tube. I can't seem to remember to get my moustache hairs out of the way in time and always end up pinching some of them into the cap.

"I'm not sure that moustache is Army regulation," says an unsympathetic Doc. "You're air-mattress, which is Army issue, is probably just trying to trim it up for you."

"Doc's right," adds Ed. "Everything that's olive-drab out here is out to get us."

291

Tim Haslam

"I think everything's out to get us, no matter what color it is," I add.

With the mattresses inflated, we lay out our wet shirts underneath, knowing from experience that the warmth from the ground below and our body heat from above will dry them out. Then we wrap up in our dry ponchos, light cigarettes and enjoy a moment of relative peace and comfort. The experiences of this whole shitty day start to fade back into the world surrounding our green, plastic home.

Lieutenant Falck, knowing how tired everyone is after this day has volunteered Ed, Doc and I to pull our radio watches out in the perimeter foxholes, giving the other Platoon guys shorter shifts. The Lieutenant's charitable gesture is met with enthusiastic support from the three of us. *You gotta be fuckin' shittin' us!*

I get to help out Mike Ferlik's squad and they kindly give me my choice of guard shifts. Given the choice, I will always take the first shift and so at eight o'clock I'm alone in the foxhole out in front of Ferlik's position on the perimeter. I spend the first few minutes trying to arrange a place within the hole where I can be relatively comfortable until ten-thirty when my shift ends. My weapon's ready. My ammo's ready. My frags are ready. My canteen's ready. My cigarettes are ready and, should I become totally desperate, I have two Yard-bars ready in my pocket. Thankfully the rain has stopped.

After about an hour the dark clouds start to drift apart above the cleared field-of-fire out in front of me. The clearing sky reveals the Milky-way band surrounded by millions of sharp bright dots. The sky is the one beautiful thing to behold from my foxhole. It's pushed itself away from all the shit that resides down here. It remains clean and free and bright and it shares some of its distant hope through its twinkling illumination. It gives me a few pleasant moments. It remains connected to home.

My thoughts try to find their way home, using some of the familiar star configurations to navigate back out of this world. But there are too many other things to think about, too many things of *great pith and moment* to think about. There's too much that's happened here in the shit that needs to be sorted out, to be understood, to be reconciled. I think about the darkness of the jungle out beyond the clearing in front of me. I wonder if Charlie's there right now. I wonder if he can see any

Stars and Stripes and Shadows

of the glow from my cigarette as I take drags on it burrowed down in the foxhole. I wonder if it's good that we've not encountered any signs of him on this hump. Then, I think that it really doesn't matter much to Charlie. We're losing men to malaria and bamboo shafts as fast as we lost them to snipers on misery-hump.

Nothing disturbs me more or dwells on my mind more than the residual image of the F4 Phantom jet disappearing into the forested mountainside. I still can't accept fully that I witnessed such a thing—that it was real—that there really were two men in that plane, alive one second and obliterated along with their machine an instant later. *Will their bodies ever be found? How will they be accounted for? I wonder if their families know what I know.*

It's only nine-fifteen.

Hey! Mr. tambourine man, play a song for me,
I'm not sleepy and there is no place I'm going to.
Hey! Mr. tambourine man, play a song for me,
In the jingle jangle morning I'll come followin' you.

Though I know that evenin's empire has returned into sand
Vanished from my hand,
Left me blindly here to stand but still not sleeping
My weariness amazes me, I'm branded on my feet,
I have no one to meet
And the ancient empty street's too dead for dreaming.

Hey! Mr. tambourine man, play a song for me,
I'm not sleepy and there is no place I'm going to.
Hey! Mr. tambourine man, play a song for me,
In the jingle jangle morning I'll come followin' you.

Chapter 9

The Troll on Twelve-Forty-Seven

Our Huey circles down out of a bright clear sky and settles down onto the apron of the little airstrip. Six-Two jumps off and hurries over toward a larger group of officers gathered together behind the line of dust-raising helicopters. The RTOs attached to these men bunch together in a pack adjacent to the huddle of officers. I find a place in the circle of Prick25 antennas, hike the bulk of my ruck further up onto my hunched over back and plant my M16 in front of me, cane-like, butt end down onto the ground.

"Now what?" I ask of no one in particular.

"We're going further north we're flying way up north on those," I'm told by one of the RTOs, pointing off to a line of four dark colored Air Force planes down at the far end of the strip. The planes are identical. From here they appear to have a narrow boxcar shape with the tail section extending up at an acute angle away from the fuselage. Two propeller engines jut out in front of the wing that extends across the top of the machine, one on each side, and set close to the fuselage. The planes aren't very big. It seems to me that it will be a chore to stuff all of Bravo Company into these four if we're to make it in one trip.

"Caribous...C7 Caribous," clarifies another one of my more experienced colleagues, "where we're going is out of range of these choppers."

"Where are we now? What's this place?" I ask, looking back at the little complex of shacks and huts up on top of the low rise behind us, encircled by concertina wire.

"This is Ben Het. It's a Special Forces camp. A Green Beret team

294

Stars and Stripes and Shadows

works with the Yards up here."

The camp seems pretty isolated, settled in the middle of a small oval valley surrounded by higher mountains. The thick forest comes up nearly to the edge of the airstrip. A neck of the valley continues on southeastward narrowing between lower hills and ridges. A road follows the valley out that way. The edge of a village is visible off to the northwest, just beyond the end of the airstrip. I can see a few people milling about around the camp and along the paths that connect with the village. Only a few of the people I see appear to be American military. The whole place seems to be too casual—in denial about the dangers all around. The place doesn't seem to be that strongly defended either. *What's to keep Charlie from walking out of the woods, crossing over the airstrip and assaulting the camp through the thin web of barbed wire? What's the matter with the Green Berets here? Don't they get it?*

"Come on," Six-Two says to me as the group breaks up. The Lieutenant and I collect up the rest of the Platoon and head down toward the planes at the south end of the runway.

"Where are we going, sir?" I ask along the way.

"Dak Pek. Its north of here, close to the Laotian border, there's another Special Forces camp up there. When we get there we'll find out more about where we're going."

"Are we humpin' out of there?"

"No...I don't think so. There are a couple of mortar bases up in the mountains above the camp at Dak Pek. I think that's where we're headed."

"Do you know anything about that area, sir?"

"I know that the mountains there are really high. I know that it's close to Laos and that the Division thinks we need to have more men up there."

"Doesn't sound like much of a rest break."

"No shit!"

The ride in the C7 is another new adventure. We're herded up the loading ramp at the rear of the plane by two anxious Air Force men of unknown rank and directed onto the long row of flip-down webbed seats running along both sides of the length of the cargo compartment. There isn't room for us to take off our rucks, making it almost impos-

Tim Haslam

sible to sit down on the narrow seats. Most of us sort of half sit and half lean, resting the weight of our gear on the ledge of seats. There are a couple of round porthole windows along either side providing a little light into the compartment, but affording no view outside.

We're not anything like settled in when the ramp closes and the pitch of the engine noise shifts up loudly. The plane shudders and vibrates heavily as the engines continue to increase revolutions. Finally, at what must be full-throttle the Caribou lurches forward and starts churning quickly down the short runway.

The C7 Caribou is a class of airplane known as STOL, short-take-off-and-landing. The grunts of Six-Two Platoon learn why in just a moment as the attitude of the plane shifts instantly from its horizontal plane following the runway to an angle of about sixty degrees, causing all the grunts within to reflexively flail out for anything to grab onto that will keep them from tumbling back toward the tail. *I'm sure the crew is having another good laugh at the expense of the Army ground-pounders on board.*

All we have to look at is each other as we ride along northward in the Canadian manufactured aircraft. I can tell that we've climbed pretty high and that the air up here over the high peaks is unsettled, buffeting the Caribou up and down through the bumps in the sky. There is a general claustrophobic feeling shared by all of us crammed into the noisy little cargo plane. No one is sure if we're allowed to smoke in here or not, so no one does. Sleep is the only thing that we can try to do—that we need and want to do. Our fatigue is great enough to overcome everything else happening around us. The sudden rises and drops through the bumpy air, the waggles and twists and shudders of the flying box and the shifting tones of turboprops and air currents may be of sufficient concern to keep normal people alert and awake. I sleep.

It seems that only a few minutes have passed before the plane shifts its orientation downward, disturbing me back to awareness. The angle down seems to be steep, confirmed by the increase in whooshing air sounds flowing around the C7 and the higher pitch of the engines. For a long time the Caribou continues on this vector—down and down. *How long can this take? How far have we dropped? How far are we from the ground? Is the pilot awake up there in the cockpit?*

Finally there is a subtle adjustment in the descent angle slowing

Stars and Stripes and Shadows

the fall somewhat, but we're still coming down fast. Everyone in the Platoon has made the same mental calculations—the ground has to be coming up soon. Everyone's trying as best they can to brace themselves for the impact as the plane just keeps on dropping. Our complete concentration on the descent is broken for a moment by a short series of alternating little dips of the wings along with a similar series of left and right wags of the planes tail section. The plane seems to be slightly out of alignment—the tail doesn't seem to be following the same line as the nose. The Caribou at last bounces onto the ground, jarring the nervous grunts. The engine noise shifts dramatically, straining to overcome the ground speed. Now, we have to hold on to keep from tumbling forward.

Assisted by the engines, the brakes and the stubby design of the Caribou, the pilot is able to slow the plane quickly. Just before it comes to a complete stop, the engines rev up again and the tail section kicks around 180 degrees, confirming for all of us that the crew of this aircraft doesn't want to be here on this ground any longer than they have to. The Air Force guy who's been strapped into a more substantial seat at the back end of the hold presses a button and the ramp starts to drop down.

"Let's go. Everybody out, everybody out...now...now...let's go!"

The engines still seem to be turning at near full throttle as we file down the ramp, out onto the few feet of runway left behind the anxious C7. Bruce Bollman's the last one off the plane and his feet are barely on solid ground before the door starts to close behind him. The whole Platoon scurries off to the side as quickly as we can to escape the prop wash sandblasting everything to the rear of the straining machine. A second later the pilot releases the brakes and the Caribou lurches forward, accelerates rapidly over the perforated steel plate runway and then pulls up into the gray sky at a sharp angle. From where we stand it appears to be a struggle for the pilot and his STOL airplane to gain enough altitude to clear the high ridge he's heading for to the south. The dullness of the overcast sky must have confused our depth perception as the plane clears the ridge top easily a moment later and disappears off into the southern sky, heading back to safer territory.

The rest of the Company has collected along the side of the landing strip about fifty meters down from us, just past a mass of charred

Tim Haslam

wreckage. As we skirt the burned out hulk we can all tell what it once was...a C7 Caribou.

The complex at Dak Pek appears to be even more casual than Ben Het with native looking people milling about. The camp itself sits up on a plateau about a hundred meters to the northwest of the landing strip and is a hodge-podge of shacks, thatch-roofed huts and tents arrayed around a network of trenches and tunnels. The camp seems to be part of a larger village and here too the visible population is mostly Yards. Much of the land surrounding the complex and the airstrip shows evidence of agriculture. Rice fields, sections of banana trees and corn crops quilt this portion of the valley. High peaks and ridges surround the valley itself. Higher than anything I've yet seen in the Highlands. The little green valley, walled in by the high, forested mountains is really a beautiful place; a Shangri-la in this distant wilderness. The Montagnards who live here might have a simple paradise if weren't for the squabbles of their neighbors; if it weren't for the war that's come to their land; if it weren't for the machines and weapons and reluctant men dragging their quarrels across their peaceful homeland.

Apparently we're not done with our travels for the day. Chinook helicopters that will take us up into the mountains to the southwest are inbound to Dak Pek from somewhere. As we wait I can get a better look around at the surrounding territory. There are several other small villages visible from here. Each is perched on the top of a low hilltop and many of the closer ones are protected by the same kind of bamboo walls with sharpened spikes that I saw on the little ARVN complexes along Route 14. It turns out that there are nearly eight thousand of the Jeh people living in and around Dak Pek and that there are two companies of CIDG "strikers" stationed here along with the twelve American Green Berets. VC and NVA units harass the population of the little villages with mortar and rocket fire, steal their crops and occasionally mount full-scale attacks against one or more of the villages. The Yards that make up the CIDG units here are local Jeh men and are known to be fierce fighters. They have no use for Charlie right now, although the Jeh have shifted allegiances before. The Strikers spend most of their time out humping around the surrounding mountains scouting for NVA strongholds under the protection of the American four-deuce mortars that reside up on the mortar bases that cap some of the highest peaks to the south and west. The closer I look the more I can tell that this is, in fact, no Shangri-La. This is the front line in one of the most distant and isolated parts of this country. Laos is just a few miles to the west. Laos is safe haven for the NVA. This is still the shit.

Two of the big CH47 Chinooks approach us from the west, looking like giant grasshoppers plowing through the overcast sky, their twin rotors lifting the hulking bodies along over the ground. The two cargo helicopters circle around to the east of the landing strip and settle down gently onto the steel plated surface. The two Chinooks will have to make two trips to ferry all of Bravo Company to wherever it is we're going.

As our Platoon queues up behind the loading ramp of one of the big choppers, a crewmember hustles down out of the belly, seeking someone in charge. It's probably my radio antenna that has marked Six-Two as an officer, attracting the Chinook man in the aviator's helmet. He approaches the Lieutenant and shouts out a few instructions. Everyone is to unload their weapons, remove the magazines and make sure that all frags are secure. He looks at me specifically and tells me to be sure that my antenna is pointing down when I enter the cargo hold. He tells me I should turn off my radio anyway, something about the static electricity generated by the huge spinning rotors. He tells us to hurry. The twisted remains of the Caribou are a reminder to the crews of airplanes and helicopters that the landing strip at Dak Pek is in easy range of Charlie's mortars and rockets. We need to get in the machines and out of here quickly.

The Chinook seems to take off in two moves. The tail section lifts up first, tilting the big bird forward and then the front strains up until the whole thing is airborne. Our chopper sets out in front followed by the other one carrying Six-One Platoon. The arcing course straightens out somewhere off to the north of Dak Pek putting us on a southwest heading at an altitude of a few hundred feet. The powerful Chinook pulls quickly through the sky, steady in its orientation but vibrating heavily as it ferries us further out into this new wilderness.

A muffled *tink, tink, tink* sound, loud enough to be heard over the mechanical sounds of engines and downdraft gets the attention of all of us on board. A second later the pilot jerks the CH47 to the left and

Tim Haslam

throttles up into a steeper climb. The crewmember back in the hold with us seems to be examining the interior section of the fuselage about where the *tinks* came from while talking into the microphone built into his helmet.

"Relax," he announces to the grunts anxiously watching his every move. "A little ground fire, but no damage," he says, as though this happens all the time. As though *it-don't-mean-nothin'*.

A little ground fire?

I think about the wreckage of the Caribou back along the side of the runway at Dak Pek. *Maybe that was "a little ground fire" too.*

After another few minutes, without further disruption, we're hurried out of the landed Chinook and onto an open grassy knoll, unsure of where we are or what we're about to do. *Are we humping out from here? If so, this will be really bad.* High peaks and steep ridges, all heavily forested surround us. The only good news is that the sky is clearing and clean sunlight is washing over the green, grass-covered knoll.

"All right, I guess we're staying right here for a while," says the relieved Lieutenant returning from a short pow-wow with the other officers. "We'll dig in on the south side of the knoll, foxholes and bunkers. We may be here for a while."

Relieved at the knowledge that we won't be humping out into these mountains — at least for a while — we set to work transforming this serene little hilltop into an armed camp. Accompanied by the clear mid-afternoon sunlight we start chopping and digging. The hill and the forest surrounding it cooperate with our efforts and yield to our crude tools without much resistance. The ground proves to be soft and easy to dig in and the tall thin trees further down the slopes are perfect for fashioning the roof supports we will need for our bunkers. They come down with a few machete swipes and the branches are easily hacked off. In less than two hours we're dug in and our perimeter secured with mines and flares. There's still time to relax and dry out under the light balmy breeze sliding down from the higher mountains.

One of the Chinooks returns and offloads additional stores of sandbags, containers of fresh water and several mail bags. The day gets better still.

There is a wealth of mail for us all. It's been almost two weeks since

Stars and Stripes and Shadows

anything has found its way out to us. For me, there are two letters each from Mom and Dad, one from my sister and three from Rosemary. I'm glad to have the eight letters to linger over but somewhat disappointed that there are only three letters from Rosemary after a two week void.

My sister's letter gives me the first information I've had that Robert Kennedy was assassinated. It was nearly a month ago in Los Angeles, at the Ambassador Hotel. *I know where the Ambassador Hotel is. I think I've been to the Ambassador Hotel.*

I think back to the day that John Kennedy was shot in Dallas. I remember coming out of my third period physiology class and hearing that the President had been shot. I remember the long silent hours spent in each classroom the rest of that Friday afternoon. I remember going to the movies that night with my best friend Bob Storey. Perhaps it was wrong for us to go. Perhaps it was disrespectful of us to sit and watch Lawrence of Arabia with our President so recently murdered.

Why would somebody shoot Robert Kennedy?

I don't know much about Robert Kennedy except that my sister wanted him to be President and that he apparently wanted the war here to be brought to an end.

Why do people shoot people like the Kennedy's and Martin Luther King?

Why am I sitting here in this place thinking about this with an M16 by my side?

My dad too makes mention of the killing of Kennedy, less passionate in his description than my sister, focusing more on the deterioration of discipline in our society. My father likes things to be orderly and predictable. He likes to stay inside the lines where he's most comfortable. He's a good man there. He's earned his comfortable place there, struggling through the Depression era as a youth and young man, taking care of his mother and step brother; fatherless, without a role model to help him venture into unknown territory. He's worked hard his whole life. He's worked through in his own mind an understanding and appreciation for what freedom and liberty mean. He respects the rights of all people but, at the same time, wants to maintain his distance from anyone too dissimilar to himself.

Mom keeps her reports closer to home, well inside the lines. Her routines are unaffected by the politics and protests going on around her.

Tim Haslam

She too has built up her inner defenses against much of the complexities of life. For her though, it comes from growing up as a perpetual guest, passed around to aunts and uncles and cousins and family friends, her own father too busy for her, her mother too consumed by her own needs and weaknesses to be there for her. My mom never had a place that she felt was truly her home, her place, until she started sharing a life with my father. She could never express her own feelings or react with too much joy or anger to any situation. Such luxuries belonged to the legitimate residents of the Iowa farms and Chicago flats that she spent her childhood moving between. Sharing a home with my father was difficult for her too. Maybe it was for them both. Marriage was for her an opportunity for real security, a chance to partake of the American dream at least partially on her terms. My parents never shared their feelings about what the world had done to them during their youth. They never shared their feelings about each other. They somehow convinced me that my home was safe and secure and that my family was as normal as they come—*Father Knows Best*—*Leave It To Beaver*—*Ozzie and Harriett.*

Having her son away in Vietnam is the only disturbance in her life. I'm not sure how this really affects her. I'm not sure how this really affects either of them. I miss them both. I want to tell them how much I miss them and how much I appreciate what they do and what they've done for me. I don't care about their shortcomings.

The three letters from Rosemary are the same. Brief updates expressing little more than her boredom. The letters seem to be from someone else, someone unfamiliar. I can't form an image of her face as I read and re-read the short notes. I retrieve a photograph I've kept up in the webbing of my helmet liner and stare at it, studying the two young people frozen in a happier moment. I look a little stiff in the tuxedo, but I remember actually being pretty loose. I'd managed to put away several glasses of Champagne right under my parent's noses, right there in our own backyard. My sister was married a week before I went into the Army last October and her wedding reception was the last party of my civilian life. It was the last time Rosemary and I could play dress-up…play grown-up. The Rosemary that I knew, that I was in love with, was captured perfectly within the little picture. The light green, mini-skirted suit was made for her slender, just-beyond-adolescent figure.

Stars and Stripes and Shadows

The flash from the camera enhanced the shine of the short blond hair framing her soft, half-smiling face, her expression a combination of coy bashfulness and incomplete confidence in how beautiful she really is. *Will there ever be such a moment again? Will I ever see this girl again?*

The wind from the Chinook nearly blows the photo out of my hand and sends my helmet tumbling down off the top of the bunker I'm sitting on. The sun has disappeared into the land beyond the high ridges to the west and I'm surprised that the big helicopter would venture out this far with so little daylight left. Whatever brings it out to us in the fading light must be important. Several guys from Five-Nine crouch their way toward the ramp-end of the CH47 and assist in off-loading the cargo; coming away with several green metal containers as well as baskets full of milk cartons. They also come away with beer...lots of beer.

The metal containers are made for transporting hot food. Within these are steaks, grilled back at Dak To or maybe at the bridge camp, fried potatoes, and green beans. There are also containers of lettuce salad. There's bread and butter. There's milk and there's beer. None of the hot food is really hot and neither the milk nor the beer is cold. It is however, magnificent and there's plenty of it. The Bravo Company grunts file quickly through the spontaneously formed line, fill up the paper plates provided and happily return to comfortable places back near our bunkers.

I sit down with Six-Two and Mike Ferlik on the top of Ferlik's sandbag covered bunker and start feasting. There's just enough afterglow in the evening sky to illuminate the bounty on my plate as well as the myriad of mosquitoes and other little bugs that are flitting and crawling over everything that I'm trying to eat. It's annoying having to pick off the moving things before taking a bite of anything.

Sergeant Ferlik and the Lieutenant are both relaxed and comfortable shoveling bites into their mouths between their plate preening and their intermittent swatting at the flying bugs hovering around them. We talk about home and summer nights and barbecues. The Lieutenant remembers how good the steaks were at some little place just off campus at Penn State where he was going to school before he enlisted. He tells us a lot about Penn State and his life there. Mike Ferlik knows western

Tim Haslam

Pennsylvania and the area around Pittsburgh. None of it's too far from his home outside of Akron, Ohio but he's never been to the center of the state where the big University resides. Ferlik, like me, has attended a junior college and thinks of places like Penn State as otherworldly institutions beyond our intellectual and financial reach. Good places to educate officers though.

The conversation remains lighthearted and continues along with our meal as the darkness settles in. We're still talking and eating when Mike Ferlik asks, "What happened to the bugs?"

None of us can see what's on our plates any longer. We're just shoveling whatever's there into our mouths. Mike's question has aroused my curiosity enough to light my Zippo over my plate.

"They're still there," I advise the others.

"I guess they're mostly protein," Ferlik responds with a shrug followed by another spoonful.

"If I can't see 'em, I'm not worrying about 'em," says the Lieutenant.

"Fuck 'em! This is still good."

И И И И

For the next couple of days we seem to have been forgotten by the Army. We don't have to send out any patrols. We don't seem to be preparing for anything. We're getting away with being lazy. Even the weather's been pretty good. I'm able to add $76 to my capital assets during one long afternoon huddled within one of the Six-Zero bunkers. No one person seems to lose too much and the outcome of the poker game seems to be of little consequence to anyone. The banter and bullshit that accompanies the card playing is the real recreation that helps us get through a few hours of one more day out in the shit.

Six-Two calls Ed and Bruce and I together early in the afternoon of our third day on the grassy knoll. He has new maps to pass out to us all. D. GO KRAM it says at the top of the one he hands to me. For the next few minutes the Lieutenant gets us oriented to the map, where we are and what's around us. It's easy to find Dak Pek over on the right side of the map at 950680. Our current position is about five klicks west and three klicks north, 902705. To the southeast of us is a high ridgeline, running nearly north-south that connects two peaks,

Stars and Stripes and Shadows

Ten-seventy-nine and Eleven-eighteen. No one in Bravo Company could help but noticed these two high peaks off to the east of us that tower over the lower reaches around Dak Pek to the north. Everyone in Bravo Company could see that the peaks were occupied. The one closer to us, Ten-seventy-nine, looks from here to be a mortar base and the more distant one, Eleven-eighteen has the look of a full firebase. Six-Two refers to the two mountaintops as Crow's Nest and Ranger's Roost—the "Roost" being the higher and more distant of the two. There is another high ridgeline to the west capped by peak Twelve-forty-seven. The two adjacent ridgelines drop off steeply into the narrow valley that separates them. From here the two ridges look ominous, more rugged than any terrain we've been on, isolated up against the overcast sky. The two bases seem remote and disconnected from the rest of the Army, abandoned twins left to survive on their own in the wilderness. I'm getting the feeling that whatever comes next is going to be bad. Tomorrow we'll move up to Crow's Nest and experience whatever comes next from there.

⚔ ⚔ ⚔ ⚔

The mortar base at Crow's Nest is much smaller than FB25. It's dug into the ridge top covering a length of maybe seventy-five meters. At the widest point it's only about thirty meters. The east facing slope falls off gradually down toward the valley overlooking the complex of villages around Dak Pek. The first fifty meters down on this side the slope is covered in the same knee-high grass as the knoll we just left. The west side drops off more steeply into a forested ravine. The western approach is pretty rugged and naturally protected by dense jungle. Across the ravine the opposite ridge rises up in a mirror image of our ridge. The same steeply angled slope. The same canopied jungle. The opposite ridge continues to rise even higher though as it climbs away to the south. Twelve-forty-seven sits atop this ridge looking down upon Ranger's Roost and us. Crow's Nest is in range of mortars, rockets and small arms from across the ravine, just like FB25. There's no saddle connecting the ridges however. It's a long arduous and circuitous hump to get from one ridge to the other. The four-point-two-inch mortars up on Ranger's Roost cover us. The mortars here cover them. Together, all the mortars cover Dak Pek. Charlie's mortars cover all of us. As it

Tim Haslam

was at Firebase-30 the view from the shitter that sits out on the side of the little landing zone is spectacular. Anyone there can see everything around. Everyone around can see anyone on the shitter.

Our job for the foreseeable future is to guard the mortars here and patrol around the neighborhood to keep Charlie from getting too comfortable. The patrols from here will always involve at least two squads and will stay on our side of the ravine to the south and west. We don't need to send patrols to the north and east, the CIDGs working out of Dak Pek have that territory covered.

Crow's Nest and Ranger's Roost are more difficult to re-supply than the firebases closer to Dak To. It's a stretch for Hueys to get up here and there aren't that many Chinooks to come up here all the time. The Chinooks also make easy targets trying to settle onto the little LZ here. We're encouraged to be frugal with our food and water.

Ed, Doc and I move in to one of the recently vacated bunkers with a northern exposure at the west end of the camp. We add another layer of sandbags to the roof and make a few improvements to the cramped interior. The forest is too far down the slopes for us to go and get more trees for making additional improvements. This will have to do. Lieutenant Falck and Sergeant Bollman share the adjacent hole and the rest of the Platoon has burrowed in around the western quadrant. Everyone is now free to do nothing.

Less than an hour has passed since our arrival when the first, "Incoming!" alert scrambles everyone into the bunkers. Two rounds hit squarely in the middle of the camp damaging nothing, injuring no one. The rounds came from somewhere to the west. Charlie wants the new residents of hill Ten-seventy-nine to know that they're marked.

Although we all carried several days C-rations with us up here, we were less concerned about our water. All there is for us here is in our canteens. Fresh water is due in later today we're told. The welcome clear skies bring with them the heat, and up here on the top of this exposed peak the sun really drills down into us. Knowing that more water is coming, it's hard for us not to drink what we have. It's hard to just sit and do nothing when you're hot and thirsty.

From our bunker we can see the Chinook turning back towards us off in the northern sky at about eye level, a water trailer dangling from

Stars and Stripes and Shadows

lines beneath it. It increases its altitude slightly as it continues inbound with the welcome cargo. The pilot is being directed to the center of the camp, not the LZ. They want the water inside the protected perimeter. The big helicopter approaches slowly from the western side, its crew watching a grunt below giving directions via hand signals.

The big turbines and spinning rotors make too much noise for anyone here to hear the *thwumps* emanating from across the ravine. No one knows of the incoming rounds until they start exploding. The guy giving the hand signals reflexively hits the ground and starts crawling for the nearest protection as quickly as he can. The pilot banks his machine hard left pumping as much acceleration as he can into the escape attempt, reacting either to the sudden movements of the man below, or the two eruptions of smoke and debris in front of him or someone on the radio advising him of the dangers. The desperate machine pulls away just far enough to miss the next round exploding on the ground within its shadow. The helicopter continues away from the base out to the northwest, heading for Dak Pek, unwilling to attempt another passage until he has assurances that Charlie's been neutralized. We'll have to wait awhile longer for water.

A series of booms coming from the bigger mortar tubes up on Ranger's Roost echoes over us. The booms are followed by a string of louder explosions over on the ridge across the ravine. Our catapults answer the inbound insults. I don't know if the rounds have been directed on to a target or are just being fired into the general area where the enemy mortars might be. Ten, fifteen, twenty rounds pound into an area of about 600 square meters, each one characterized by a sharp *kachunk*. Each *kachunk* followed by a gray cloud of smoke filtering up through the vegetation. If Charlie was in that area, we probably won't hear from him again.

The next water bearer turns out to be a Huey, sent up from Dak To the next afternoon, full of fuel and empty of cargo. At Dak Pek it was loaded up with containers of water and sent along toward Crow's Nest. The Huey buzzed along, staying low over the valley fields, gaining altitude only as the northern slope of hill Ten-seventy-nine impeded its progress at level flight. The chopper quickly reaches the crest of the ridge, slowing as it peeks over the mountaintop until it hovers over the LZ. If the pilot can bring the Huey down just a few more feet the water

307

Tim Haslam

containers can be shoved out onto the LZ and the bird can retreat back behind the protection of the ridge.

Charlie's too quick. Short bursts of machinegun fire spread over the LZ, coming from up near the top of the higher ridge. The distance between the shooter and the LZ is about at the maximum effective range for an AK47, but the machinegun can deliver its lead pellets at high velocity into our space and through the thin skin of the helicopter should they hit the mark. The machinegun is more frightening than the mortars. Someone behind the machinegun is picking out the specific target, aiming the weapon and redirecting the fire until the selected target is hit, whether it's man or machine, grunt or Huey, me or something else.

The pilot reflexively kicks the tail of the vulnerable helicopter around, simultaneously adjusting throttle and rotor pitch to push and pull the machine out of harms way back over the ridge.

This time we can give the four-point-twos a firm target. Two, maybe three minutes go by before the first salvo booms away from Ranger's Roost. The rounds seem to be right on target, bursting all through the jungled ground hiding the gooks and their machinegun. If we haven't killed them, we certainly must have sent them scurrying away. It should be safe enough now for the Huey to return and give us our water.

Through the firing port of our little bunker Doc and Ed and I can see the dull green shape of the UH1-D fluttering its way back across the valley toward Dak Pek like a frightened puppy that knows it's strayed too far. We know there's no way it's coming back today.

✕ ✕ ✕ ✕

"OK, we've got nine full canteens between the five of us," Six-Two says after confiscating the green plastic bottles from us. The whole Company is going through the same process of rationing the remaining water. The more frugal individuals have gained nothing through their sacrifice and thrift. The economy has turned to socialism in this moment of vital scarcity. Everyone on Crow's Nest will be given the same amount of water and must conserve it until more can be delivered.

Where's the rain now? We've cursed every drop of rain that's fallen on us for the last several weeks and now the gods of the monsoons are reacting to our vulgar offenses. As punishment the rain-laden clouds

Stars and Stripes and Shadows

skirt these high mountain peaks, choosing instead to favor the respectful Jeh down in the valley below us, bestowing the water upon them in return for the pigs and chickens that have been sacrificed to their ancestors who speak to the gods on their behalf. *I wonder how the gods feel about ham and limas.*

Two cans of peaches!

I still have in my possession, two prized cans of peaches that I've been saving. The peaches are the best of the C-rations and I've hoarded these two cans in hopes of getting my hands on an equally scarce can of pound cake. The combination, peaches and pound cake, is actually good, especially for breakfast. The thought of peaches and pound cake for breakfast can help motivate me through a guard shift or out from under my poncho liner on a cold, misty morning. My hope has been to trade one of my cans of peaches for a can of pound cake but now the two cans are of greater value. The juices surrounding the peaches, although sugary, are liquid. It's been two days since we arrived here at Crow's Nest and no other attempts have been made to get water to us. I'm down to a half canteen of water and I'm thirsty; very thirsty; we're all very thirsty. A cup of coffee on this gray morning would be awfully good too. One of the cans of peaches will have to do to satisfy all of my cravings, except for nicotine, and the wet fruit squishing around in my mouth helps at least for a few moments to slack my thirst.

"Get Grady and Steve over here," the Lieutenant, returning from a meeting he's just attended tells Ed and me.

With Grady and Steve present, Six-Two tells them that they've volunteered to take a patrol down to the Dak Ja River that flows eastward through the valley below us. They are to take all the canteens they think they can carry back, full of water. Doc Charlebois and Doc Hayes will come along to oversee the collection of water and to ensure that iodine tablets are placed in each of the canteens. Tim Haslam will come along with the radio. I'm actually happy to have been volunteered for this one. It means I'll get water that much sooner. It should take us about an hour to work our way down to the river and probably twice that long to hump back up the mountain under the weight of the full canteens.

I stay behind Grady, whose squad is in the lead starting the trek

Tim Haslam

down off the LZ, following a little dirt trail that runs diagonally across the grassy slope. We move quickly, our own thirst pulling us toward the river. It looks like easy terrain, at least until we get to the thicker forest that's down about two hundred meters. Our dry mouths will soon taste cool water; iodine flavored, cool water. The mood of the volunteers is pretty good.

Our reverie is quickly broken however when shouts of "incoming" come from up above us where the rest of the parched Company watches our departure. The series of *thwumps* is coming from somewhere down below us off to the west. The first round to hit lands and explodes in the grass a few meters to the east of where our patrol is and several meters down toward the tree line. The next round bursts closer to us.

They're firing at us, not the base. We're wide open where we are right now. There are no trees or rocks or holes to hide behind or within.

"Get back up the hill!" Grady shouts out as he turns and starts plowing through the grass. I make my turn in unison with Grady and start to run as fast as the thick grass and the weight of my radio and other gear will allow. Another round explodes down below us, just beyond the trail that we've abandoned. All the men of the patrol are scrambling up through the grass toward the shelter of the bunkers and trenches that are thirty meters above us. Charlie must be trying to get his fire realigned to our movement toward the base as the next two rounds hit up at the edge of the perimeter, one right in front of Grady and I and the other fifteen meters over to our right...no one's hurt.

Three more steps up into the knee-high grass my right ankle makes contact with something hidden down within the thick blades. At first there is a dull sensation right at the front of my ankle where my leg and foot come together. Some internal mechanism, beyond my conscious control, refuses to take another step with that leg. I fall straightforward, face first into the grass. The instant I hit the ground I role over onto my back pulling my knee up toward my chest. There's a bamboo spike protruding through the heavy canvas fabric at the front of my boot, between the laces. The pain has now changed from dull to sharp. The straight shiv of bamboo is imbedded in the little fleshy depression at the front of my ankle. There isn't time for any further examination of the extent of the damage. I pull the spike out and for some reason keep hold of it as I try to regain my footing. It's OK, I can stand. I can run.

Stars and Stripes and Shadows

Taking my next few panicked steps, trying to build up momentum, I can see that there are lots more of these stakes lying about down within the grass, each one, just like the one in my hand, about a foot long, sharpened at each end. The exploding mortar rounds however represent the greater danger and I keep running as fast as I can.

The closest bunker turns out to be ours. I get there first, followed an instant later by an equally out of breath Grady. Doc Charlebois dives in a moment later as three more rounds *kachunk* somewhere outside our bunker, all inside the perimeter. Our mortars over on Ranger's Roost come alive just as the last gook mortar round explodes; all of the big tubes are slamming out rounds as fast as they can into the area where the little puffs of smoke from the mortars were seen to be accumulating. Grady and Doc watch the concentration of exploding mortar rounds tearing into a thicket of light vegetation that separates two swaths of open ground down in the valley below us. Grady and Doc are happy to have escaped the incoming mortar rounds and are excited to see the answering American fire shredding through everything in and near Charlie's position. I too am happy to have escaped the mortars, but don't care too much about what's happening anywhere outside. I unlace my boot as quickly as I can, yank it and the filthy sock beneath it off and study the hole in my flesh.

"What happened? Did you get hit?" Doc asks, taking notice of my activities.

"No…I kicked this piece of bamboo. It went right through my boot and into my ankle."

"A punji-stake," says Grady. "I saw them too. The whole hillside is covered with them. Charlie had control of this hilltop for a longtime before we got here. Charlie put those there for us."

"Let's see," Doc says, grabbing my foot, taking over the analysis.

There's not a lot of blood coming out of, or around the puncture, but Doc's swabbing and poking sends a shock of pain back up my leg.

"I need to clean this out. The gooks dip the ends of these things in their own shit as a way to poison anybody that might get stuck with one. This could get infected pretty easily."

Go for the Merthiolate Doc. Lot's of Merthiolate, I'm thinking to myself as I look more closely at the sharpened ends of the spike. I can't see any shit on either end. *Maybe they didn't do that to this one. Maybe*

311

Tim Haslam

it's been out there in the grass and the rain for so long that it's been washed clean.

"Jeez, Doc...what are you doing?"

"I've gotta try and get this stuff as far into the wound as possible."

"Jesus Christ, Doc! I think that's far enough! Fuck!"

"OK, OK, that's about all I can do with this," Doc says, over my sighs of relief that he's finished pressing the burning Merthiolate into the opening in my ankle. "I'm going to give you some antibiotics to take too...some sulpha pills. I'll check this every few hours for signs of infection.

"You want anything for the pain; some Darvon or anything like that?"

It took all but the last few remaining swallows of my water to get the little yellowish sulpha pills down. I don't want to commit the rest of my supply to float Darvon down my throat.

"No...it doesn't hurt much now that you've stopped fucking around with it. So, I guess this isn't the million dollar wound, huh Doc?" I say, half hoping that he's going to tell me I'll need some hospital time.

"Are you kidding?" the stoic, humorless Grady responds. "You still have a foot...you stay!"

He's not kidding.

I'm sorry I said anything in front of Grady who must now think of me as some kind of slacker.

N N N N

"Doc, Doc, wake up," I whisper at the sound asleep body curled up under the poncho liner next to me.

"What's going on? What's the matter?" asks Doc, rolling back toward me.

"I'm not feeling so good," I tell him. "I'm really hot, fevery hot. A minute ago I was shivering cold and I just feel like shit all over. I don't know if it's the punji stake or what."

"Let me see your ankle," he says to me as he pushes away his poncho liner.

"Yea...it's a little bit red around the wound. Not too bad though," declares Doc, poking around at the opening in my ankle under the beam of his flashlight.

312

Stars and Stripes and Shadows

Doc searches around in his bag for a minute and comes up with a little bottle of something other than Merthiolate and swabs it on and around the hole. It might as well be Merthiolate. It stings just as much. He replaces the bandage and starts digging around in his bag again.

"Here, take these and try to get some sleep."

I take the two pills and quickly wash them down with water from the canteen he's also handed me. The pills are down before I realize that Doc has given me his canteen and that I've just swallowed half of his remaining supply.

"That was your water, Doc. Why'd you give me your water? Thanks."

"Don't worry about it. I'm sure we'll get more tomorrow."

Whatever the pills were, they take effect quickly and I'm asleep, no longer aware of any pain or fever or chill or thirst. I've floated away from the shit for a few hours, gliding off on Doc Charlebois' medicine into some other ethereal world where nothing makes sense but I recognize all the characters. I'm flying above high mountains, soaring like Superman, in and out of clouds. Mom and Dad come from somewhere telling me I'm going to be late for school. Rosemary's there with her dad and they seem to playing poker. President Kennedy and my friend Bob Storey are standing together down below me in a dry sandy desert looking for something. Barney's jumping up at me. A huge dark gray storm cloud comes up over me and an unseen voice from the cloud keeps repeating, *"Too bad...too bad."*

"Wake up...Tim, wake up. Let's have a look at your ankle."

Doc shakes me out of my strange sleep and back into the sunlit world of hill Ten-seventy-nine. Rays of early morning sun slant into the bunker's firing port, dispersed by Ed's cigarette smoke.

"You don't feel like you have any fever. How do you feel?" asks Doc with his hand up on my forehead.

"I feel fine," I tell him, almost disappointed that I do, truly feel fine. No fever, no chill, no pain, only a little itch down around my ankle and the same thirst that we all have. I guess I was just fighting off infection last night, fighting off Charlie's shit attacking me from the inside. I guess it wasn't Malaria. I guess that I won't be seeing any clean sheets anytime soon.

Tim Haslam

I don't care how dry my mouth is. I want a cigarette.

ℵ ℵ ℵ ℵ

The O-2 Skymaster shows up first, flying tight circles, initially around us and then over and around Twelve-forty-seven and the ridge-line to the west of the high peak. After several turns around the ridge it banks over us and heads off to the north out over the valley. A half-mile out it turns back toward us and starts gaining altitude. A boom from Ranger's Roost draws our attention away from the little gray plane and the following explosion over on the opposite ridge clarifies what's going on. Purple smoke billows up from out of the forest where the mortar round exploded. They've established a reference point for the Air Force pilot in the spotter plane. A second round booms off and explodes five hundred meters closer to the high peak, this time red smoke marks the reference point. The Skymaster makes one more long sweeping turn out over the valley passing in front of a Huey churning its way up toward us from Dak Pek.

The helicopter continues on its way westward at low altitude until it's about a kilometer out to the north. The spotter plane then arcs towards us from the west, throttles hard down through the gap between the two ridges and banks out again toward the north, heading toward the complex of villages. As it swings over Dak Pek a pair of Hobos pop out from behind the mountains to the east of the valley and fall in behind the Skymaster. The trio of Air Force planes flies close together for only a moment before the spotter plane breaks away back toward us, climbing quickly. The two A1E's continue on their northwestward heading.

The Huey's changed course toward us, still flying low and slow. The lead Skyraider makes a sharp left turn putting it on the same heading as the Huey about a half a kilometer behind it. A moment later the second A1E waggles into the same line. The two camouflaged planes quickly pass over the Huey, climbing toward the crest of Ten-seventy-nine, climbing right straight at us. They seem close enough to touch as they rumble over us with their full array of weapons clinging to the underside of the stubby wings. The lead plane banks slightly to the right heading toward the last wisps of purple smoke hanging within the treetops over on the other ridge, as Hobo number two goes left toward the fading red plume. Each plane unleashes three or four rockets into the vegetation before veering away from the approaching mountain. Number one goes to the west. Number two goes east. The rockets are swallowed up by the trees a fraction of a second before they explode. White clouds, denser than the colored smoke, waft up a moment later, partially occluding the hillside above.

The Hobo pilots each accelerate their machines through hard turns that bring them back around for another pass at the high ridge. This is the Huey's chance. The UH1D hops up over the crest of Ten-seventy-nine, noses forward toward the center of the base. With clear space below him the warrant officer at the stick of the helicopter kicks the tail around and eases down toward the ground. Hovering at about eight feet, the door gunners start throwing off the bags of precious water. The first bags ejected hit the ground at the same time that the Skyraiders snarl over us, daring anything to their front to show itself. Another spread of rockets stays the course into the mountain as the A1Es turn again west and east. The hovering Huey is vulnerable for the moments that the Skyraiders are vectoring out and away from us. The last of the water is hurriedly kicked out over the skids and the Huey scampers back down over the north side of our hilltop, eager to get to Dak Pek and the hell out of this territory altogether.

A spray of machinegun bullets chases the Army helicopter off of Ten-seventy-nine. Charlie's still there, accepting the challenge of the American's airplanes and mortars. His bold burst of fire toward us brings a quick response from the Hobos and the four-deuces. Bombs and napalm from the A1Es on their next sortie are followed by at least twenty high explosive mortar rounds *kachunking* all around the forested area hiding the gooks. *How stupid can they be?*

One more cry of *"Incoming,"* disrupts attempts at retrieving the water bags scattered about the open ground at the center of the hilltop. The mortar is somewhere higher up the ridge than the machinegun, closer to Twelve-forty-seven. All three rounds fired explode within the perimeter near the center of the base but none hit the water and, again no one is hurt.

With the Skyraiders circling well out over the valley, the spotter plane swoops in out of the eastern sky and knifes toward the ridge crest coming down off of Twelve-forty-seven. Two rockets curl away from the

Tim Haslam

under-wing pods on the O2 just before the little gray plane tilts away from the jungled wall to its front. Billowy white smoke mushrooms up out of the vegetation that absorbed the rockets. The Hobos already have the scent and are aligned for the kill. They've used up their bombs and napalm, but still have high explosive rockets and ample stocks of 20mm ammo for their wing guns. The Hobos take their time, flying slowly, deliberately toward the white marker. At this speed they can unleash hundreds of 20mm rounds along with their remaining rockets. They have space and time enough to maneuver their machines as they fire. Everything beneath the white smoke is being shaken and shredded by the Hobos streaking wrath. The mortars up on Ranger's Roost add a few rounds for good measure. *How stupid can Charlie be?*

I now have two full canteens of water. I wonder what it cost the American taxpayers for these two quarts of water. I wonder if my next two quarts will require a similar effort. With the help of three Army helicopters and crews, plus fuel, three aviation-gas guzzling Air Force planes, and barrages from the 6th of the 29th artillery, each of us up here on Ten-seventy-nine has two full canteens of water. *How stupid can Charlie be?*

Every couple of hours for the rest of the day another mortar round arcs across the gorge that separates Twelve-forty-seven from Ten-seventy-nine. Mortar and artillery rounds arc back across the gorge in response. Rocks hurled by catapults and trebuchets into the battlements, angry knights taunting their foes. *How stupid can this be?*

So far no one here has been hurt by anything sent flying our way. Maybe we shouldn't be that surprised that Charlie too seems to be unhurt. Charlie's supply lines however, remain intact, unimpeded by our rocks. Up on Ten-seventy-nine things are getting scarce. Two quarts of water won't last long and food supplies are dwindling. *What if someone does get hurt? What if someone is struck by the hot metal shards that burst away from the inbound rocks? How would we get the wounded out? How would we get them to the 71st Evac? What if it's me?*

It's time to get serious. It's time to change tactics. It's time to take the offensive. It's time for Ranger to say, "That's enough. That's *a—fucking—nough!*"

"This should be interesting," Sergeant Bollman says, watching the

316

Stars and Stripes and Shadows

approaching pair of F4 Phantom jets angling down from the northeast.

"Bring it on," adds Ed.

Their first pass plants two parallel walls of flaming napalm about where the last incoming mortar rounds came from. The second pass does the same thing over where the enemy machinegun fired the last time. The lead Phantom streaks by again and unloads canisters of cluster bombs along the top of the ridge, starting a chain reaction of a hundred little explosions. His partner follows up with bombs a little further down the finger. These bombs are much bigger than anything unleashed by the Skyraiders; five-hundred pounders. The explosions and shock waves are massive. There's no way to hide from these. Charlie has to be paying a price for his harassment.

Each of us in Six-Two watches the Phantoms closely as they circle and strike, studying each movement, each motion; each adjustment. Breathing a sigh of relief each time the slender triangular shapes pull up and away from the mountain sides they are attacking. They belong in the air. They're beautiful things in the air around us. The pilots are fully alive and free when the F4s are in the air.

Down on the dusty ground we feel a little more secure venturing out from the bunkers after the Phantoms have gone, after they've delivered their flame and iron onto Charlie's nests. Six-Two and Sergeant Bollman are hailed up to a meeting with the Captain. Ed, Doc and I add another layer of sandbags to the roof of our bunker, all shirtless, catching the rays of the hot afternoon sun, thinking we can relax out here for a while.

"Son of a bitch!" Ed yells out as he stumbles into the bunker grasping his wrist. We were all lounging up on top of the bunker when the next three mortar rounds *thwumped* up off the high ridge toward us. Doc and I jumped off the west side and clamored into the bunker from there. Ed went the other way, stumbling as he hurried for the entrance, spraining his wrist slightly as he fell down through the entrance. Doc has the wrist wrapped tightly in a bandage almost before Ed can explain what happened.

"I don't think I really need that, Doc. It just sort of surprised me. I can't believe those assholes are still up there."

"I'll take this bandage off in a little while. I don't want it to swell up. The gooks must really be dug in deep up there. I think..."

Tim Haslam

Doc's commentary is interrupted by Six-Zero-Charlie's voice breaking over the radio advising that one of their men is hit; shrapnel wounds to his legs and back. We've got to get him dusted off...soon!

There isn't time to get a medevac chopper all the way up here. The nearest log-bird will have to do it. The closest logistics helicopter turns out be the Huey that brought us the water. He's just departed from Dak Pek on his way back to Dak To when the medical priority call came. Without hesitation the Huey crew turns westward at full power heading back toward Ten-seventy-nine and the ground so obviously marked by Charlie's mortar crews. There isn't time to work out an elaborate strategy for diverting the gooks attention. Fire superiority is the only option available to us. Our mortars start to lob high explosive and white phosphorous rounds over at the opposite ridge top and all of the Bravo Company machineguns start hosing across the ravine hoping to keep the enemy's heads down. The 105s up on the Roost can't yet engage. The Huey's flying right through their trajectory zone.

Captain Hilton has instructed the inbound Huey to pick up the wounded man over near the eastern end of the base and to stay away from the LZ and the clear ground near the camps center. It may take Charlie a few seconds more to adjust their mortar traverse and elevation settings over to this new target area. Men from Six-Zero already have the wounded man, suspended face down in a poncho litter up on top of the bunker nearest the designated pick up point. Doc Davis is doing everything he can to slow the bleeding from all the punctures and slices while Doc Hayes does everything he can to convince the frightened grunt that the damage is minor. The man's body is reacting too quickly and too completely for Hayes' words to prevail. He's slipping into shock.

The Huey overshoots the bunker slightly as the pilot try's to make the mid-air stop. He backs the resistant machine down over the clutch of men straining to lift the litter against the wind pounding down from the big rotor blades above them. Both door gunners, un-strapped from their safety harnesses, lean out over the skid of the rocking helicopter trying to grasp enough of the plastic fabric to pull it aboard. There's a lot of weight over on the port side of the helicopter now and the pilot's struggling with all the controls to counter balance the off-center load.

An unheard mortar round hits fifteen meters behind the chopper,

Stars and Stripes and Shadows

half way up toward the center of the camp. One more quick adjustment to the angle of the mortar tube and ten seconds of flight time and the next round should be right on target. The grunts from Six-Zero struggling to lift the wounded man on board are unaware of the incoming fire. The Huey pilot saw the round hit and knows how much time he has left. He forces the big vibrating UH1D Bell Helicopter down another two feet and the damaged man is pulled and pushed inside. Doc Davis climbs quickly up over the rocking skid and into the forward moving helicopter. Hayes hurls his medical bag into the opening at the side of the helicopter just in time. The 105s are clear to fire now and are doing everything they can to keep Charlie from getting off that one-more-round. The Huey crew, Doc Davis and the critically wounded man disappear down over the northern slope riding within the churning machine. Davis will have a lot to do to stabilize his patient until better-trained and equipped people can be reached. The 71st Evac is a long way away.

N N N N

Six-Two has summoned all the squad leaders for a briefing early on this overcast morning. Our water supplies are again nearly gone, so is our food, so are our cigarettes. Something has to be done. The Lieutenant assures us that something will be done today. Ranger has definitely had enough of Charlie up on Twelve-forty-seven and down that ridge. Ranger is an Army Lieutenant Colonel in command of a full Battalion. Ranger has convinced Saladin that enough is enough. Saladin is a full-bird Colonel in command of an entire infantry brigade. Saladin has clout. Saladin can get Major General Stone, the Fourth Infantry Division commander and Lieutenant General Peers, the II Corps commander, to authorize what he wants, and what he wants is an arc-light.

"It'll be today…later this morning. We'll have plenty of warning. In the meantime I'd recommend putting another layer or two of sandbags over your bunkers," Lieutenant Falck advises, after explaining how the combined United States military plans to dislodge Charlie from the higher ground to the south.

The announced, broad daylight, B52 strike is met with mixed reac-

Tim Haslam

tions. Everyone believes that this will do it. We've seen and heard what an arc-light can do. The big bombs will dig into the ground up there, sniffing out Charlie's subterranean lair like an army of monstrous terriers. The thousand pound bombs will explode away everything around them, reducing it all to shreds and splinters and dust and blood. *The gooks'll be fucked. Fucking gooks!*

"Isn't that pretty close, sir," Mike Ferlik asks. "I thought there were rules about how close an arc-light could be to friendlies…that ridgeline's less than a klick away."

"You're right about that, Ferlik. That's one of the reasons they're doing it during the day, to reduce the probability of error," says Falck, as familiar with how well enforced the "rules" are out here. Rules in a combat zone are more like guidelines…elastic guidelines.

"Even if those things are dead on target, sir, it seems that we could still get shrap over here," says Ferlik, seeking further assurances that this has been thought through.

"Everybody stays in the bunkers. That's your job, make sure everybody's in and down. This won't be for our entertainment."

"All Eight-Two stations this is Six-Charlie…get everybody in the bunkers. The bomb release is in sixty-seconds. Five-Nine-Charlie, do you copy? Over," Houston polls each Platoon until he has a "rog" from everyone. Every man in Bravo Company searches the eastern sky for a moment before climbing down under the little timbers and sandbags that will hopefully shelter us from what's about to fall from up there. We could all see the three little arrow shapes heading our way at thirty-eight-thousand feet.

How could these little specs bring so much destruction?

The grinding roar of the bombs accelerating down through the air is nearly as frightening in daylight as it was in darkness. It's more frightening for us this time, we're too close to be able to discern from the sound where the bombs are headed. They're coming into our neighborhood. They're coming close. *We should have put another layer of bags on! We should have dug this hole deeper!*

We've all covered our ears in anticipation of the approaching blasts. The thunder seems to begin over near Twelve-forty-seven, growling louder and louder, uninterrupted as it claws along the ridge top to-

Stars and Stripes and Shadows

ward the end nearest to us. The shockwaves vibrate around us as the excavations proceed westward, keeping our attention focused on the robustness of our bunkers construction. The beginnings of a desperate, claustrophobic urge starts rising up within me. *Get out of here! I'm about to be buried in this little hole! I'll be buried on Ten-seventy-nine!*

No one has to say anything. No one needs to hear an all-clear. The instant the trailing edge of the shockwave passes over us we head for open air. Nothing seems to be flying our way. Nothing is falling from the sky here, except dust. It's OK. We can get out. We can look to the south. Great gray-brown plumes, clouds of smoke and dust and vaporized debris, hang over the violated strip of mountain. Subtle echoes ring off into the sky conjoined with a few muffled groans from the dieing forest before complete silence shrouds everything. The grunts stare in awe at the airborne evidence of our destructive power. I'm once again glad that Charlie doesn't have B52s and I'm glad that more water can get to us now.

With the smoke still rising along the ridge top and a company of American soldiers watching intently from across the ravine, a short burst of AK47 fire spits out of the foliage just below the line of bomb craters, shattering the silence. The North Vietnamese man who pulled the trigger had no intention of hitting anyone. He probably didn't even aim at anything but the hazy sky. He just wanted to say something to us. He wanted us to know that he was still there. He wanted us to know that our machineguns, artillery, napalm and B52s couldn't get him. He wanted us to hear what he had to say, translated by the crisp loud voice of his assault rifle. *"Fuck you, American GIs!"*

The shooter may be the only one to have survived. He may have pulled the trigger with his last gasp of life. Whatever his true story, he is now the stuff of legend among the men of Bravo Company. The rapport of his short burst will linger with us long after the deafening explosions of the bombs have faded from our memories. With shoulder shrugs, head shakes and subtle smiles we all voice a response indicating some level of respect for the man and his taunting gesture. *Fuckin' gook's got balls, man.* At the same time we all wish the big planes could turn around and make another pass and finish the job.

Are we going to get water today?

Chapter 10

The World From the Roost

The architecture and civil engineering that went into the design and construction of Ranger's Roost carry the familiar trademark of the grunt and shovel; sandbag covered bunkers arrayed around the irregular contours of the high mountain peak, connecting capillaries of trench and footpath, mortar pits, ammo pits and an adjacent LZ... with open-air shitter. On the LZ are also two large black rubberized things—blivets, giant containers of water. There's plenty of water at Ranger's Roost. From up here, the grunts and their weapons sentinel over Dak Pek and the fertile valley down to the north. The finger ridge that slopes downward to the west, connected to Ten-seventy-nine forms a barrier limiting Charlie's access to the villages and food and un-indoctrinated Montagnards around Dak Pek. On the east side, another ridge curls away from the peak, bending back to the south as it falls into the deep ravine separating the Roost from it's higher neighbors. This ridge is the staircase to Ranger's Roost. It's the best way for grunt patrols to get away and it's the best way for Charlie to get in. It's the best place for trouble.

We were ferried up from Crows Nest a squad at a time on three Huey's shuttling us the short distance between the two peaks. A Loach and two Cobras prowled along the high ridge to the south covering our escape, preventing any more surviving NVA from shooting at the helicopters transporting us up to the higher base. Ten-seventy-nine was to be abandoned. We took everything we could with us, destroyed what we couldn't take and left only a bald scar. The dry little hilltop apparently isn't worth the cost of fuel, shells and bombs it's taking to defend

Stars and Stripes and Shadows

it. *It don't mean nothin.'* Charlie can have it if he wants it. Maybe it's our turn to take pot shots at anyone likely to have an interest in this real estate.

Since we're not receiving regular incoming fire up here, it's only right that we should work. Little details of men spread over the hilltop each morning; digging, clearing, stringing wire, filling sandbags, killing time, looking busy. It's been several days since we've had any rain. The red soil at the surface of the ground has dried into fine dirt and red dust coats everything and everyone. It's also hot up here. We quickly sweat out our water. We sweat out a lot as we work. The sweat attracts the red dust kicked up by the helicopters and the shuffling feet and the chopping, shoveling tools. For those of us who choose to work shirtless, it's hard to tell if our red flesh is due to the clinging dust or the searing sun. Mud or dust...which is preferable...rain or heat? Either way, there's no dry.

"A lot of guys overplay their snare drum," Ed tells Bruce and me as I add shovels full of dirt into the bag he's holding open. Ed's a drummer in a band back home and has strong opinions regarding proper technique. "I tend to use the cocktail drum more."

Bruce, whose job is apparently to supervise Ed and me, agrees with the snare drum assessment. He too has some experience with drummery. Ed and Bruce are usually of like mind when it comes to their views about things back home. I have no idea what a cocktail drum is. My experience playing the clarinet in the California School of Music Junior Orchestra left me somewhat incomplete apparently when it comes to knowledge of rock and roll musicianship.

"Which one's the cocktail drum?" I ask topping off the next bag vital to our defenses, exposing the depths of my cultural ignorance.

"It's the sort of middle sized one," Ed starts to explain, working right to left through his drum set, pattering imaginary drumsticks through the air as he describes each of the components. "Bass, snare, cymbals, cocktail..."

A real blast of sound interrupts Ed's lesson. A loud pop from down in the wire that protects the north flank of the perimeter catches everyone's attention. Such sounds always catch our attention. Such sounds always elicit a noxious jolt of adrenaline, readying us to fight or

Tim Haslam

run. Such it will be…forever.

Trip flares pop off all the time for one reason or another. Almost anything coming in contact with the trip wires will exert sufficient force to pull out the safety pin, setting off the flares. Huey's take the biggest toll on our inventory of flares, blowing debris into the concertina wire or just vibrating the air around the wire as they come and go. The grunts never ignore such pops though. We never take for granted that we know why the flare went off. We always think that it might be Charlie and so, we always investigate.

"Oh shit!" I say in reaction to what I see. Bruce and Ed jump to their feet and follow me over toward the object of our attention.

I recognize the guy as one of the new men who came out with Maebon. I don't know his name. He must have been trying to secure the flare when it went off. The screams and hollers aren't coming from him though. It's the two other men around him that are making all the noise. The two men are unsure of what to do. The new guy's shirt's on fire. The new guy doesn't know what to do. The new guy only knows that something is terribly wrong. The intense pain that now climbs over his arms and chest and face is all that he knows, all that he feels. He's consumed by the pain. He's being consumed by the flames.

Without further hesitation, the other two men throw him to the ground and role him over, successfully smothering the fire. The new guy immediately pulls himself back up to his feet, his buddies again unsure of what to do. For a moment the injured man just stands there. Then, he starts to walk back toward the bunker line, right toward me. He's just a few feet from me when I hear Doc Charlebois' voice yell out behind me.

"Don't touch him!"

Ed, Bruce and I join the two other men surrounding him, all of us unsure what we need to do. He keeps walking, zombie-like away from where the still burning flare lies on the ground. His face is a mosaic of scorched flesh and sweat and filth, a horrible portrait of pain and terror and shock. His arms are angled out away from his body in an unconscious effort to prevent damaged flesh from coming in contact with anything. He has second degree burns over thirty percent of his body. Plasma is squeezing out of the hundreds of damaged capillaries, reducing the normal blood viscosity slightly, dropping his blood pres-

Stars and Stripes and Shadows

sure. Shock and infection are the greatest threats now. His whole focus and purpose is just to get away. There is no thought, only primitive instinct.

Charlebois and Doc Hayes close in quickly and take over. They each take hold of the man, grasping him under the armpits carefully avoiding contact with any of the singed flesh that they can see. As long as he can walk they steer him toward the LZ. It's better to have him get there this way than to try and carry him. His open flesh has already been invaded by a thousand specs of dirt, debris and oily fabric, all containing resident microbes. He's an open invitation for infection. He needs the best doctors fast.

Our medics have some training in first aid for burn victims. They know of the peculiar risks associated with this kind of damage. They want to take no chances. They get on the radio with the Battalion Medical Officer who finds a trauma surgeon at the 71st who specializes in burns. Over the radio they all work out a course of treatment for the man while in route to the hospital. Both Hayes and Charlebois will accompany the man on the dust-off bird. The medevac chopper will have supplies of plasma and apparatus for intravenously restoring fluids and blood chemistry. Charlebois and Hayes will attend to the open wounds as directed by the surgeon. The Docs and the real doctors and the medevac crew will once again do what needs to be done. The man will survive. We will never know more than that. We will never see the new guy again. Our Docs will be back tomorrow, here in the shit with the rest of us.

✿ ✿ ✿ ✿

The news comes as a complete surprise. Not a pleasant surprise. I've been in the Army long enough now to know what this kind of thing probably means to me. It's inevitable though. It was just a matter of time.

"I've been summoned back to Battalion in Pleiku," Lieutenant Falck tells the gathering of dust-covered grunts collected around our bunker. "I'm not yet sure what my next assignment's going to be but I have to be back at Camp Enari tonight."

Six-Two is leaving us.

Six-Two has been the Platoon leader the whole time I've been out

Tim Haslam

here. I know him. I trust him. I like him…we all do. The Platoon has been a good team and a good family with him in charge. We don't want this to change and yet, every one of us wants more than anything to get out ourselves, to get away from all of this shit, to abandon those whose turn hasn't yet come and now it's his turn. Not to go home but to play some different role within the world of the Nam.

Terry Falck takes the time to say his farewells to everyone in the Platoon. There's too much shared and experienced to do a proper job of separating in the little time that the Lieutenant has. Falck knows and the men who have served with him know what the feelings are. We all are glad that our Lieutenant is being recognized by the higher-ups in the Army and that he's getting out of the shit…at least for awhile. It will be hard for him to drag his ruck onto the helicopter this time, leaving his men behind on this hilltop so far out in the wilderness. At the same time, he knows that he needs a break and there's gladness and relief within him as he climbs into the Huey about to take him away. His job is done out here. He's done his job out here.

"Six says that a replacement for Six-Two will be out here some time tomorrow." Bollman tells Ed and me. "The Captain doesn't know anything about him."

"I hope this isn't some fresh-out-of-OCS guy who thinks they know everything," says Ed.

"Well, the good news with some of those guys right out of OCS is that they know that they don't know shit and will pay attention to us for awhile," adds the more optimistic Sergeant Bollman.

"This is good," I say. "Either way they don't know anything."

RILEY, the patch sewn over the right-hand shirt pocket says. Over the left-hand pocket are a Combat Infantrymen's Badge and a paratrooper's jump badge. There is a Ranger patch on his shoulder along with a Fifth Special Forces Group patch.

This guy's been around. He's a Green Beret and a Ranger with combat experience. This guy probably knows something.

"John Riley," he says, extending his hand to me after Sergeant Bollman's introduction. He repeats his name again and again as he meets Ed and Doc. "It's good to meet you guys. I'm going to need a lot of help from you all. I was in Cam Rahn Bay yesterday, without an

Stars and Stripes and Shadows

assignment, wondering what I was going to be doing. Everything since then is kind of a blur."

"It looks like you could use some gear, sir," observes Bollman, taking note of the apparently empty ruck the Lieutenant carries along with his little CAR-15 rifle. "I'll take care of getting you everything you're going to need."

"I won't need much, Bruce. I prefer to travel light." First Lieutenant John Riley is a slender man, his wiry strength apparent in the way he carries himself. His face is friendly and youthful, somewhat out of character for the experienced, qualified warrior that his patches and badges attest to. He's easy to talk to, confident in his role and his qualifications and seemingly comfortable with whom he is under the uniform. He's also ready to go to work.

"I need maps first thing," he says and is immediately handed a fresh copy of D. GO KRAM. "Thanks. I'd like to get one of your plastic bags to protect this," he says to me, apparently knowing about the bags that the radio batteries come in.

"Right, sir...I should change out batteries anyway. I'll get one for you right now," I reply quickly, knowing full well that I just gave away the bag that I was saving for myself; the bag around the five-pound battery that I've been humping around myself.

Riley spreads the map out on the top of our bunker and studies it for a few moments.

"OK, I'd say we must be here right now. Is that right?" he says, placing his finger right on the irregular concentric circles that surround the number *1118*.

"Yes, sir...that's it...Ranger's Roost."

We tell him what we know about the surrounding area pointing to places on the map. We tell him about the grassy hill, about Ten-seventy-nine, about the gooks across the ravine and where their machineguns and mortars were. We tell him about how we tried to get down to the Dak Ja for water and how we were turned back by mortar fire. We tell him about the artillery fire, the Hobos, the F4s and the B52s. We tell him of the short burst of AK fire from the guy who survived it all. We tell him everything we know about the two high ridges that rise up parallel to one another to the southwest of the Dak Pek valley and then we tell him about us.

327

Tim Haslam

Riley takes it all in. He listens. He asks appropriate questions. He furthers the dialogue. He doesn't take over. He doesn't need to dominate. He doesn't yet seem to need or want to be the alpha dog. When it's his turn he tells us about himself. He's from Kansas, an Army brat, his dad a Korean War veteran Army officer. He was with a Special Forces A-team down south on his last tour. He needs real infantry and command experience to make progress up through the ranks. He carries a little Barretta pistol and a flask of Jack Daniels. He smokes Camels.

I think I'm going to like this guy.

We're fortunate, Lieutenant Riley, like Lieutenant Falck has strength and character underneath his silver bars. He knows his job. He knows his role. He knows himself. He's done all the macho things that the Army can challenge young men with. Not however to obtain the associated bragging rights and look-at-me arrogance that such accomplishments often engender. Whatever he's done, whatever he's accomplished has been motivated and maintained by more intrinsic needs and he doesn't flaunt any of it. In many ways, what shines through this man is the kid inside, friendly, good-humored, competitive and a bit of a maverick,

I think I'm going to like this guy.

"Six-Two-Charlie, this is Six-Alpha-Charlie. Over," Wee John's voice interrupts the comfortable chat session with our new leader.

"Six-Alpha-Charlie, this is Six-Two-Charlie. Over."

"Six wants to see Six-Two...send him up here. Over."

It's hard for me to think about this new officer as Six-Two. The designation has become permanently affixed to Falck. The transition of Six's from Captain Collins to Captain Hilton was easy. I never had a personal conversation with either of them. I never used the designation with them directly. A thousand times Terry Falck was referred to and talked to as Six-Two...*this will take some getting used to.*

"Rog. Out."

"Captain Hilton wants to see you, sir."

"Well guys, sorry, you may be getting screwed already because of me," the new-Six-Two says upon his return. "The Captain wants a Platoon sized patrol to go out for a few days. He wants me to lead it, to get familiar with the lay of the land. We go out late this afternoon.

Stars and Stripes and Shadows

Get the squad leaders together and we'll go over the plan."

Taylor, Grady, Sergeant Stevens and Mike Ferlik get only a limited introduction to the new Lieutenant. The announced patrol is a distraction from anything more cordial anyway. Riley explains the mission in a pretty business-like fashion. Tonight, we're to head out just before dark and follow the finger that arcs down to the east. A klick and a half down is a flat plateau that interrupts the steady drop of the ridge. We'll set up an ambush there. If nothing comes along, tomorrow we'll complete the trip down the finger, cross over the Dak Not River at the bottom of the ravine and start up toward the opposite ridge; the ridge where Charlie was, the ridge where Charlie probably still is. Our mission is to patrol over the line of bomb craters left from the arc-light, survey the damage and look for any evidence of Charlie's presence; tunnels, bunkers or bullets flying our way. Our real purpose is to let Charlie know that *we will* come over there.

Previous patrols have come down this way enough to have hacked and stomped a narrow trail for us. We must be cautious on this trail, particularly the point squad. A trail like this is an invitation for Charlie's mines and booby traps. It's easy going though and we move fast, keeping a sharp eye down to the ground in front of each step and into the brush at our sides. In less than forty minutes we're down.

The ambush site is terrible. It turns out to be a rocky knoll void of much vegetation with the trail weaving around the bigger boulders and outcroppings. A firefight here would be a free-for-all of bullets ricocheting around everyone on both sides. There's no way to deploy a whole Platoon in this place effectively. If Charlie does come up the trail the terrain features would always hide most of the men in the file. It would be a brawl not an ambush.

Lieutenant Riley surveys the site and calls the squad leaders together. He tells Ferlik and Taylor to take their squads down about twenty meters where the forest thickens up around the trail and has them set up an ambush line along the west side of the trail. If anybody comes by they're to wait and attack the trailing elements. Grady and Steve will take their squads back up the trail about the same distance and deploy in a somewhat diagonal line across the trail. When Ferlik and Taylor start shooting, it would be natural for Charlie to scramble up the trail toward the protection of the higher forest where Grady and Steve wait.

329

Tim Haslam

If any of the unsuspecting gooks choose to seek closer shelter in the rocks, Riley, Bollman, Doc and I will be there waiting for them.

The new Lieutenant seems to be excited at the possibilities. His RTO is hoping for a quiet night.

The night does go the way of my hopes and is quiet…long and quiet. There's no place to get comfortable on the hard rocks and the light of the bright full moon illuminates and adds shadows to everything on the open knoll as though it were all alive, keeping my nervous attention focused on the things around me. I don't get much sleep.

By mid-morning we've crossed the Dak Not and have climbed a few hundred meters up the other ridge, working diagonally up and to the southwest trying to skirt the areas of denser jungle. Steve and his men are on point, moving cautiously, prohibited from using their machetes here, where stealth is probably vital to our survival. Riley leads the rest of the pack following the point squad. He does travel light. He's also agile and sure-footed. He seems to be having fun.

The six men ahead of us in the point squad stop suddenly and drop in unison down to their knees. Reflexively, all the men in the Platoon filing along behind the point squad ripple down in similar fashion. Sergeant Stevens hurries down toward us, sliding the last few meters in an effort to keep low.

"There's gooks up there, sir," Steve says, pointing further up ahead and a little off to the west. "I could see four or five of them up in the bigger trees about fifty meters down from the top of the ridge."

"Did they see you?" asks Riley.

"Negative. We were lucky. Ernie was out front and on his toes and saw them just as he started into an open area. Another couple of steps and he'd of been wide open."

"Alright, let's make sure we know where we are and we'll bring in a little pee on them," Riley says opening up his map.

"I make us right here," he says to Steve and I who are crouched at either side of him looking at the map. "Where'd you see the gooks, Sergeant?"

"Right there," says Steve without hesitation, pointing to another spot on the map.

"OK, we'll ask for the first round here, a hundred meters further

330

Stars and Stripes and Shadows

west along the ridge. Then we'll adjust fire right onto them. Call it in," he says to me.

That's it? Just like that? Just, call it in? This is all up to me now?

With my pencil I mark the spot on my own map where we want the first round and find the nearest reference point. The target is in the upper left hand sector of a grid square that's two klicks up and one klick to the left of a reference point designated "cars."

"Six-Charlie, this is Six-Two Charlie requesting a fire mission. Over."

"Six-Two-Charlie this is One-Six-Alpha. What's your mission? Over." The voice and call sign is that of Lieutenant Reese our artillery spotter.

"We've got visual contact with at least five or six gooks up on the ridge in front of us. Over."

"Roger that. Give me a target. Over."

"Request one round of hotel echo on this target; from Chevrolet up two point seven, left point eight. Over."

"Roger. One round H E; from Chevrolet up two point seven, left point eight. Over."

"That's a rog."

"Wait one, Six-Two-Charlie."

Lieutenant Riley has remained crouched down, studying his map. I can tell that he's checked and verified the coordinates I've just passed on.

"Six-Two-Charlie this is One-Six-Alpha. I've got the battery commander on this push. He'll let you know when the shots on the way. After that, give him the adjustments. Over."

"Roger. Out."

"Six-Two-Charlie, this is Brandy-Three-Five. How do you hear me? Over."

"Brandy-Three-Five this is Six-Two-Charlie. I hear you lima-charlie. How me? Over."

"Lima-charlie. We're ready to shoot. Over."

"They're ready, sir," I tell the new-Six-Two.

"Let's get up to the front of the line where we can see, then tell 'em to fire," Riley says lurching quickly up along the line of Steve's men, me following in as low a crouch as I can get myself into.

Tim Haslam

"Tell 'em to fire."

"Brandy-Three-Five this is Six-Two Charlie. Fire. Over."

"Six-Two-Charlie, shot on the way. Over."

"Roger, shot on the way. Over."

I don't need to tell the others, the Howitzer is close enough for all of us to hear. As the high explosive round spirals it's way across the ravine I remember what I learned back at the bridge about how precise the six-digit grid coordinates are... *"within about an acre."* I try to remember how big an acre is and overlay it around the spot I just called in. *Shit! This better be right!*

The round hits almost exactly where we'd wanted it.

"Drop fifty, left one-hundred?" I ask, looking at Riley.

"Right on. Five rounds," he says holding up the fingers of his left hand.

"Brandy-Three-Five this is Six-Two-Charlie. Drop fifty...left one hundred...fire for effect...five rounds...Hotel Echo. Over."

"Roger, Six-Two-Charlie. Drop five-zero, left one-zero-zero, five rounds H E. Over."

"Roger that. Out."

Ever since Lieutenant Riley and I scampered up here to the front, I've kept my eyes on the area where Steve and Ernie saw the gooks. I haven't seen anyone. Then, an instant before the salvo of 105mm high explosive rounds starts to explode I see the vague outline of a man moving up toward the ridge top. Before I can really solidify the image of the man the terrain around him is clouded by the jarring bursts of gray-brown smoke. The rounds are right on target, spread just far enough apart to shred everything within a fifty-meter circle.

"Man, that was dead on," Steve says, his eyes still glued to the smoky area up ahead.

"Good job," the new-Six-Two says to me.

"Alright, we've gotta get up there and see what's left," the Lieutenant says, opening his map again. "Sergeant Stevens and Sergeant Ferlik, you two keep your squads together and stay on this route up to where the gooks were. The rest of us are going to circle back a little and come up this little finger here. We'll move along the ridge top until we're right up there," he says, pointing to the top of the ridge just above the place where I saw the NVA man. "I don't want anybody on the high

332

Stars and Stripes and Shadows

ground above us. Once we're at the top, we'll secure a line there and come down and join you. Bruce, you and Ed stay with Steve and Ferlik. You guys stay put here until we get up on the ridge top. We'll give you a call and close in together."

"There's blood over here Lieutenant and footprints heading off this way," Grady yells over toward Riley and I, who are now right in the middle of the ground pocked by the artillery craters. There are no bodies to be found but there's ample evidence that what we saw really was Charlie. There's an AK47 and a Russian SKS carbine, two ammo pouches full of AK magazines, a helmet severely damaged by shrapnel, some rice bags and one black tennis shoe.

"Hey, Maebon…here's your chance to find the bullet with your name on it," I say, holding up one of the ammo pouches. "Take your pick."

"What do you think they were doing here, sir?" I ask Riley.

"I'm not sure. Maybe they were setting up a machinegun pit. It looks like there's been some digging. The trees would make it pretty hard to use a mortar here. I don't know though; the shoe and the rice bags make me think maybe they were just taking a break; like they were on the move somewhere."

"Over toward Ranger's Roost?"

"Maybe…or maybe they saw us coming down the other side and were on their way to ambush us. They might have lost sight of us after we crossed the river. Remember, when we started up this side we started cutting diagonally over this way. If they thought we were going to keep working up that other finger they could have picked us off right through there." Riley points off to the east and an open clearing running along the top of the little finger ridge adjacent to us, a hundred meters away.

"Shit. I'm glad we saw them first," I say, thinking about how lucky we are.

"Yea…me too…only they're still around."

The top of the ridge has been totally devastated by the string of bombs from the B52s. The giant craters are littered with the debris of trees uprooted or sliced off by the explosive shock and flying metal. With so much of the natural vegetation blown away, the view in all

Tim Haslam

directions is spectacular. I can see the Roost across the ravine to the north, sitting alone, a somber filthy tumor scarring the otherwise lush green mountain. I can see Bravo Company grunts performing their duties within the red dirt, over and around the faded green sandbag walls and structures...*home sweet home.* I can see down to Ten-seventy-nine, another remnant of the fickle values of our strategy. To the south and west are more mountains, lines of higher ridges capped by protruding high peaks that twist and wind as far as I can see. A quick check of my map confirms that I'm looking into Laos. From here, it doesn't look that far away. I can see the Dak Pek River flowing along through the next ravine to the south of our ridge. It's bigger than the Dak Ja and the Dak Not, collecting monsoon runoff from most of the mountains that I can see; water from Laos, water from the sky, water on its way to the Dak Poko and Playa Del Rey.

I can see the whole length of this ridge top running off to the west. I see nothing but craters clogged with dead rubble. I can see that the going will be very slow as we search through this.

Lieutenant Riley has spread the Platoon out to comb over the bomb line. The various obstacles make it difficult to keep the twenty-six men together and on a consistent pace. There are a million places for Charlie to hide up here; a million places to snipe from and a million places to watch and call in mortars from. We're looking for him but, if he finds us first, we're fucked. *Where are the men we saw this morning? Where are the men whose blood trailed away from our explosions?*

The Lieutenant and I have been following Grady and his men, meandering along the right edge of the bomb line, skirting most of the craters. Pat Sanderson, one of the new guys who came out with Jay Maebon is out in front on this side.

Sanderson stops suddenly, holding up his right hand, turning back toward Grady who's a few meters behind.

"Hey...what's all this? Look at this Grady!" Sanderson says, pointing down toward the ground at his feet.

Grady climbs over a tree trunk and joins Sanderson.

"Shit man! Don't move," says Grady as he turns back, raising both his arms. "Hold up...everybody, hold up," he says as loudly as he can without alerting everything to our presence.

"What's the matter, Grady?" the new-Six-Two asks.

334

Stars and Stripes and Shadows

"You better come have a look at this, sir. Come up the same way that I just came, over that tree."

Riley and I duplicate Grady's approach to Sanderson until we're all collected into a tight little group.

"I think it's a dud cluster bomb," Grady says, pointing out a number of little metallic cylinders that are spread out in front of us.

"That's exactly what it is," Riley acknowledges. "Look over there." The Lieutenant's pointing to the broken remains of a large plastic container wedged under one of the fallen tree trunks off to our right. "That thing's supposed to open before it hits the ground and the bomblets are then supposed to go off as they make contact. "Something must have gone wrong. It didn't open and, I guess, the bomblets were never fused."

"Damn, they're all over the place." Grady points out dozens more of the grenade sized devices scattered out to our front.

"Don't touch 'em and be careful not to step on 'em," the Lieutenant says to everyone in earshot. "Pass the word to watch out for these."

Within a few meters we find another of the big plastic canisters, broken open, its contents also spread out all around the surrounding ground.

"Watch your step. There's more over here," Ernie Jefferson advises upon discovering the second cluster-bomb package. They must have come from the F4s that have been hitting Twelve-forty-seven and this ridge over the last few days. They couldn't have been here since before the arc-light.

Watch my step! Watch the jungle off to my side! Watch the craters up ahead! Watch the treetops! Watch the guys on point! Watch the Lieutenant! Listen for incoming mortars! Listen to the radio! Feel Mr. Ruck! There's no room for any songs in my head now, no room for images of Rosemary or beaches or Barney. Wily predator and anxious prey at the same time...it's a lot to do.

We've covered the full length of the arc-light and found nothing but the corpses of fallen trees and shattered plants. I radio back our position at the west end of the bomb-line as we take a short water break. Then, we start humping again, down a finger that falls off to the south, down toward the Dak Pek River, down into unknown land. Each step down

I can feel the high ridge behind me growing taller, forming a barrier between Ranger's Roost and us; between the Special Forces camp at Dak Pek and us; between us and our artillery and our friends. This time, more than ever before, it feels like we're going into someplace that we don't belong; someplace that is about to swallow us up.

We spend another long but uneventful night intermingled on the wet ground with the other inhabitants who feed off one another down here. We start again early, continuing on southward toward the river and the mountains beyond. A rainsquall passes over us around mid-morning, providing momentary relief from the heat but adding more moisture to the already thick air trapped within the canopy.

ϟ ϟ ϟ ϟ

"Bob, wait up," Riley says, hurrying to catch up with Sergeant Taylor, whose squad is on point today. "Hold up."

Taylor signals up to Beasley and Danko to stop. They've just started up a gradual slope that's covered with thick, chest high brush.

"Let's stay out of this open strip," the Lieutenant advises, looking up the fifty-meter swath of ground that is covered only by the low bushes, "swing around that way and head up into the woods, there, and then cut back up."

Taylor, Riley and I are down at the very end of the open section with the rest of Bob's squad up along the right side of the clearing in front of us. Steve's squad is in a line down behind us. Sergeant Bollman, Ed and Doc are about twenty meters over to our left, up in the bushes with Grady and Ferlik's squads trailing back behind them. Everyone is alert to the dangers of our position.

"Call in our position and then we'll get going," Riley tells me.

Wee John has just acknowledged the location I gave him when a short burst of AK fire cracks down from the brush covered slope and whooshes over my head into the trees behind me. With the handset up to my ear and my rifle down at my side I can't react very quickly to the bullets that spray over the three of us. The shots weren't aimed at us though; Bollman and Ed were the targets. Bollman and Ed are the furthest up the rise. They're the ones closest to whomever it is that's shooting at us. Neither Bruce nor Ed is hit and both of them have readied themselves for the next try.

Stars and Stripes and Shadows

"Hang on, Wee John, we're taking fire," I say, looking up the hill toward Ed and Bruce, and beyond up into the brush. Forty meters up a man pops up and fires wildly down toward us, again hitting nothing, but dropping us all down as far as we can get. As he ducks back down behind the bushes another pith-helmeted man, much closer to us and a little off to our left, shows himself, taking a second to swing his AK up over the foliage in front of him. The second was too long. Ed had peeked up just as the first man was dropping back under cover. Reflexively Ed raised his twelve-gauge shotgun up into firing position. Reflexively Ed swung the barrel over to the left as his peripheral vision detected the moving shape of the second man. The shotgun blast shreds through the top of the bushes and drops the man down out of our sight. Bollman now can add fire up toward the other man, keeping him down. Bob Taylor gets his squad up into the trees off to the right where they add more fire. Elmer's machinegun is enough to prevent anybody else from showing themselves. We have fire superiority now and unless there are a lot of gooks up there we've probably got whoever is there on the run.

Lieutenant Riley cautiously directs the Platoon up through the brush with Taylor's men covering the whole open strip from up in the trees to our right. Ed and Bruce hurry to the spot where we saw the closer man jerk down as the shotgun pellets hit him.

"Is he there?" Doc shouts up to Ed, staying back behind Riley and me.

"No...goddamn-it...there's nothing here. He must have crawled out this way," Ed says, starting to push away the bushes to his left.

"Be careful. Wait 'til the rest of us get up there," Riley instructs. "Mike, take your squad up through the trees over there and meet Ed coming through that way."

Ferlik and his men make it up through the bigger trees on the left of the clearing quickly spreading out with all their weapons at the ready.

"Here, look, there's a lot of blood here," Ed says. "I knew I hit him!"

For the next fifteen or twenty minutes we probe through the brush and neighboring trees searching for the bleeding man or his hidden comrades and again, we find nothing. We have only the splotches of darkening red blood to show for our counterattack. Once again we have

Tim Haslam

exchanged fire with Charlie and there are no dead bodies. Maybe it's just as well...the bodies of the grunts in Six-Two Platoon are of value to me. I don't care much about the bodies of the gooks, one way or the other. Still, there is this feeling that I want to fire my M16. Fire it at someone and see the bullet strike the target. We haven't punished Charlie for his ambushes or his sniping or his unwillingness to back away from this shit-hole. We just keep getting drawn into it further and further. *How much longer will I be this lucky?*

Ⲛ Ⲛ Ⲛ Ⲛ

Captain Hilton's been on the horn for a long time this morning with Riley. The Lieutenant's been pencil marking his map as the Captain explains the next objectives for our outing. I was hoping that we might be called back in today. It's been three days since we left the Roost. I have C-rations enough for today and tomorrow. Rainwater has kept my canteens full and I still have two full packs of Marlboros. My supplies are OK for a while longer...my spirit isn't. I'm so sick of these mountains and all that lives here. Right at this moment, with the new Lieutenant energetically plotting out the next leg of our hump, I can feel my attitude sliding out from under me. Like Houston, so long ago, I just don't want to get up. I don't want to take another fucking step into this crap. I don't give a shit about anything that's out here. *It don't mean nothin'! What does mean something out here? What does mean something anywhere?*

"Alright, here's the plan," the Lieutenant says, looking over to where Bruce, Ed and I sit quietly, bonded together in silent loathing for the world of shit that surrounds us.

"Get out your maps and I can show you where we're going."

"I guess it's not back to the Roost," I question rhetorically as I pull D. GO KRAM out of my pant leg pocket.

"How much longer are we going to be out, sir?" adds Ed. "We don't have much food left."

The tone of the questions and the exaggerated efforts to retrieve maps and drag us closer registers with Riley.

"OK, I hear you," the new-Six-Two says, straightening himself up and away from his map, orienting himself more fully towards us. He's now talking to us, not at us. He seems to recognize the real point of

Stars and Stripes and Shadows

our questions. His enthusiasm for the task ahead has been tempered by our phlegmatic response. He has some work to do to get his resources aligned with his orders and his own zeal for the mission. Straightforward honesty is the best way.

"We'll be going back in tomorrow," he begins, scanning back and forth over our faces. "We have a lot to do before then though. They want us to go to this Yard village, here," he says, drawing our attention to three little dots on the map, Dak Duat Lal, two klicks to the south of where we are now, on the other side of the Dak Pek River. "We'll meet up with two platoons of CIDGs there. While we're there at the village we need to register some targets along a trail that comes down past the village from the west. Tomorrow, we'll sweep back up this way along with the Yards, all the way back up this side of the mountain and into Ranger's Roost."

"That's gotta be at least six klicks, almost all uphill, that we'll have to hump to get all the way back up to there in one day," Bollman says, counting the number of thousand-meter grid squares between Dak Duat Lal and Hill Eleven-eighteen.

"The CIDGs are coming with us, all the way back to the Roost?" Ed asks, before the Lieutenant can comment on Bollman's assessment of the task before us tomorrow.

"Right...I guess there are about thirty of them along with two of their Green Beret advisers. They've been out for over a month and are headed back home to Dak Pek. The Battalion thinks it will be safer for all of us to come back together. Personally, I don't mind having the company. I know these guys are pretty useful in a fight."

OK, one more night; two more days of humping and one more night. I can do it!

The morning's work is typical; up and down terrain, thick and thin patches, rain and sun; hot, humid, sweat, itch, bite, scrape, slice and sting and of course *ruck! Fucking ruck!*

By mid-afternoon the skies have cleared and the sun blazes down on us. We've reached the flat plane of the little river valley where the elephant grass is thick and high, over our heads as we approach the river. The going slows to a snails pace as machetes don't really cut through this stuff very well. We've got to try and cover up all our exposed skin again

Tim Haslam

to protect ourselves. The blades of grass grab and slice at everything that comes into contact with them. We can't see anything but the grass. We can't see the ground, the snakes, the leeches or the punji-pits. We can't see anyone but the grunt in front of us. We have to stay close together. We can't tell how much more of this there is ahead of us. We can't tell how far off the river is.

The point man is suddenly at the bank of the river. The whole Platoon shoves through the grass until we're all overlooking the silty flow of water. The river is about twelve meters wide at this spot, flowing slowly eastward. Both banks are overgrown with the high grass. All we have to look forward to when we get across is more elephant grass to struggle through. *How much more? How far?*

It's impossible to tell with any certainty where we are on the map. There are no terrain features visible from down here. The only guidance we can derive from the map is the flow of the river itself. The river meanders generally eastward until it encounters a gentle ridge on the south side that bends the flow more northward. The ridge and the river bend could be a hundred meters down stream or five hundred.

Riley, Bollman and the squad leaders get together to consider our options. There are only two possibilities.

"I don't think it's too deep," the new-Six-Two says as he eases himself down into the murky water. His feet, lower legs, thighs and waist disappear down below the surface before he steadies himself, standing on the bottom with the surface of the water rolling by just below his rucksack. "OK...it's waist deep here." He takes a few cautious steps out toward the center of the flow keeping his rifle raised up over his head. "OK...the bottom seems to be pretty flat...let's go."

Being at least five inches taller than the Lieutenant, the water comes up just a little above my crotch. The current is slow, but the volume of water presses hard against me. Trying to walk along the soft unseen bottom, pushed by the dirty water is a new challenge. Mr. Ruck wants to climb further up my back to keep out of the river. I want to keep my M16 up, out of the water too. My radio is made to be weather proof, but I'm not sure how well it would survive full immersion. *I need to keep my feet. I hope there are no holes in the bed of this little river.*

I can only imagine what's swimming around in here with me; what kind of parasites and bacterium; what forms of waste and poison are

Stars and Stripes and Shadows

penetrating through the porous fabric of my fatigues. Maybe my own boxer shorts have become toxic enough to stave off some of the weaker invaders. *Maybe my boxer shorts are being cleansed somewhat as I shuffle along half submerged.* What I'm most concerned with though is how exposed we all are out here in the middle of this river. I think about how hard it would be to get out of my ruck if I were to have to duck under water with someone shooting at me. *Could I get to the protection of the bank? Should I hold on to my rifle?*

After the first right-hand jog, the river straightens out for about thirty meters. The thick high grass has filled-in every inch of bank on both sides. *It seems so well manicured.* It's almost like a canal through a park somewhere. I think about the Jungle Boat Ride at Disney-land. I look up ahead and see a dozen replications of the same thing; camouflaged helmets, faded dirty towels covering the backs of necks, ruck-sacks laced-over with belts of machinegun ammo and rifles held up overhead or spread yoke-like across shoulders. *Where am I going? Will I ever be out of this?*

Down the road I look and there's Rosemary
Hair of gold and lips like cherries
It's good to touch the green, green grass of home

Yes, they'll all be there to meet me,
All the creatures smiling sweetly
It's good to touch the green, green grass of home

Two more short twists of the river and the little finger appears on the right hand bank. It rises gently up away from the edge of the water, its bank clear of the high grass. Just bare dirt sprinkled with a few patches of scrubby vegetation and weeds. A well warn trail splits the open ground coming down from a tree covered plateau about a hundred meters up. As I climb up out of the river I can see some of the village huts within the trees. It's a great relief to be out of the water and at our destination. It's a great relief to be someplace where there are people who are just living their lives. I can see a few Yards standing at the edge of the village watching us. I can hear excited voices echoing short exclamations, apparently announcing our presence. As the last of the

341

Tim Haslam

Platoon pulls up onto the dryer ground, Lieutenant Riley starts up the trail.

"Bruce, Tim, Ed, you guys come with me. The rest of you stay here."

With each step we take toward Dak Duat Lal more villagers appear in the open spaces between the huts to get a look at us. There are lots of kids. Some eager and excited about getting close to the tall men coming up out of the water, others shy and weary, clinging to the familiar legs of bigger people near them. No one has any weapons. Many have smoking pipes in their mouths, both men and women. Many have ivory adornments plugged through the large holes in their earlobes. Most have the same bowl shaped hair-cuts. New smells…odors and fragrances blend together within the wisps of smoke that drift our way from the interior of Duat Lal. Some must be food cooking. Others must be human waste. Some must be the tobacco or whatever it is they're smoking and others are unidentifiable.

Two men work their way to the front of the pack of villagers, distinctive from the others in their dirty uniforms. They each have weapons, one an M1 carbine and the other an AK47. Their sudden appearance, coupled with the silhouette of the Chinese assault rifle slung over the second man's shoulder slows our pace for a moment. It's OK, their demeanor and the rest of their gear confirming that they're CIDGs. They're uniformed Yards. They're on our side. The small men are nearly identical in their attire; old military fatigues, open shirts over green tee shirts, black bandanas tied around their necks and narrow-brimmed bush hats.

"Hi," Riley says, apparently to the whole group collected in front of us as we approach to within a few feet. The greeting seems to me to be a little out of place, a little anti-climactic, a little too American. I expected the Lieutenant would know some Montagnard greeting or some French phrase, or at least some pidgin-Vietnamese-English comment.

"Hi," the two CIDGs respond together adding smiles to their faces, one exposing black teeth, the other a mouthful of gold.

"Hi." "Hi." "Hi," several of the other villagers add to the dialogue. Smiles all around…black teeth…gold teeth…no teeth.

"Hi," I say in return, happy that we're connecting so well, wondering how my own fur-coated teeth are being evaluated.

342

Stars and Stripes and Shadows

"Hey," a dissonant voice says from behind the pack of villagers. "You must be the third-of-the-eighth guys. I'm sure glad to see you guys." The man behind the more complete English language salutation isn't much bigger than the Yards as he pokes through the group.

"Ken Franks," the wiry little man says as he reaches us, extending his hand.

Riley does the introductions and asks where the rest of the CIDGs are.

"We've set up on the other side of the village. We thought you all might be more comfortable over here on this open side," Franks says. He has his rank chevron pinned to his collar. He's Sergeant First Class Franks. He too wears a bush hat. There's nothing apparent that would mark him as a Green Beret. His short stature and the Army issue eye glasses, laid over his drawn, creased face give him the look of a plumber or auto mechanic more than that of the fabled *"fighting soldier from the sky."* Sergeant Franks however, exudes a relaxed confidence that suggests underlying strengths, abilities and experience. Sergeant Franks has made this world his world.

"OK, let me get my men set up and then we can talk some more," says Riley.

"Right…best let me come and find you though. One of the village elders died yesterday and they're a little sensitive about where strangers go within the village. Their ancestor's spirits are apparently busy with the new addition and might be nervous about unfamiliar faces milling about. The old guy is in that big hut there," Franks says, pointing to a long thatched roof hut, open at the ends, with several people visible inside.

"What happened to him?" I ask as Riley starts off back down the trail.

"Don't really know. It was some natural cause; tuberculosis, cancer. I don't know. I hope it wasn't meningitis. They've had outbreaks of that before. It kills a lot of 'em. Our medical team is due out here in a few days, they'll find out. He wasn't killed if that's what you're worried about. The VC don't have much reason to bother these people, they can barely provide for themselves, there's not much left for visitors or thieves."

343

Tim Haslam

We set up camp in the soft soil of the open ground between the river and the village. There's no point in trying to hide here, so we go ahead and put up our hooches, dig our holes, fill a few sandbags and spend a comfortable afternoon. Small groups of CIDGs stop by to visit. They seem to be interested in commerce. *What do the wealthy Americans have to trade...cigarettes, candy, something completely new?* I'm not about to part with any of my remaining Marlboros but I do have something they might want. In my last Care-package from home, my dad sent me a corncob pipe and two pouches of Cherry Blend tobacco. At the rate I've been smoking the pipe the Cherry Blend will last a long time.

I pour half of one of the pouches into an empty C-ration can and offer it to two of the shopping CIDGs. With the appropriate body language, they ask to inspect the offering. They take a few sniffs each. The smiles and short dialogue between the two suggests a high level of interest. One of the men pulls two brass bracelets off his wrist and offers them as payment.

"OK. Thanks. Thank you," I say, taking the two brass rings. It's a tight squeeze to get them over my right hand and my new Yard friends seem relieved that the effort is successful and that the transaction has been finalized.

"You know you're now engaged to his sister," Doc, who's sitting next to me, says, joking about the possible underlying meaning of the bracelets.

"Yea...well, I've still got more Cherry Blend. For ten dollars I'll get you a wife too."

Doc and I laugh. The two Yards laugh.

All Doc can come up with to offer is two bars of the hard chalky Hershey's chocolate. These particular Montagnards don't seem to be too excited about the Yard bars, but take them as a hospitable gesture. In return one of them hands Doc four strips of dried meat retrieved from his shirt pocket and they wait politely for Doc to examine the goods and accept the consideration.

"Better try it Doc, or you're gonna hurt their feelings."

"OK, how bad can it be?" he says and gnaws off a small chunk.

"Hey, this isn't bad at all. It's like beef jerky, a little spicier and really salty."

Doc offers me one of the strips.

344

Stars and Stripes and Shadows

"This *is* really pretty good," I confirm, looking up at the two men watching us, who seem pleased at our response. One of them points up toward the top of the trees back near the village trying to tell us something about the source.

"Monkey...I think its monkey. That's what he's trying to tell us," I tell Doc. "So, what do you think that means? We've now shared monkey and Yard bars with these guys. Are we like adopted brothers or something?"

"I don't think so. I think it's gonna take cigarettes or more tobacco to get us further into the family."

The two men share a couple of brief comments between them. Probably agreeing that they've gotten all they're likely to get from the two of us. Holding up the C-ration can full of tobacco, they take their leave, smiling.

"Thanks...thanks," Doc and I say as we work to soften up the dried monkey strips in our mouths. *I'm glad I have plenty of water!*

Some of the adventurous kids come down to see us too. They're a welcome diversion for us, as we are for them. Any kind of game we can think of they want to play; tag, chase, fetch-the-canteen. We have little to give them or share with them. The CIDGs got the last of our candy. It becomes clear that they too want cigarettes. I won't give them any though. *Is it because they're little kids or, because I'm selfish?*

Sergeant Franks rejoins us after dinner along with Sergeant Robbie Mora, his Special Forces partner and one of the CIDGs who's introduced as Baul. Franks and Mora have spent a long time up here among the Jeh and know them well. The language however, is so isolated that few non-natives speak it confidently. Franks and Mora know enough to get by. Baul speaks English reasonably well and serves as the primary translator for the team whenever there is confusion.

This turns out to be a good night for them to tell us about some of the Jeh customs and superstitions. The villagers here are celebrating tonight. The good ancestral spirits are busy distracting the bad ancestral spirits to ensure that the dead man joins the proper spirit group. Rice beer helps the villagers help the spirits. The Jeh by nature are friendly people. They do whatever they can for visitors. Franks insures us that if we should wish to partake, the villagers would be glad to share the

Tim Haslam

rice beer.

"I've had that stuff before," Riley responds to the offer. "It was pretty bad. I wonder if the recipe up here is any better."

"I say we give it a try and pay our respects," says Doc.

"Yea…it seems like the right thing to do," I say, realizing I'll probably never get a chance like this ever again.

"Is there anything we should do or bring or say?" asks Sergeant Bollman.

"No," says Franks. "Just smile a lot. That will align you with the good spirits and let the villagers be hospitable."

About a dozen of us from the Platoon along with Franks, Mora and Baul traipse back up to the village, canteen cups in hand, eager to do our part at keeping the bad spirits distracted. As we penetrate the inner workings of the village the people seem glad to see us, glad to have our help. We're graciously gestured towards what seems to be a gathering point. Once there, I can see the large pots of beer sitting out in the open, just outside the longhouse where the body is. Several men are gathered around the pots. Occasionally stirring around the mucous looking brew, dipping in for re-fills, sipping along with their animated dialogue. Franks offers a brief greeting and asks Baul to do a more complete introduction. We all bring good wishes for the dead man, his family, the good spirits, all the villagers, everyone and everything—*except the VC and the NVA and the bad spirits.* All through Baul's speech, I study the contents of the pot closest to me. On the surface is a light froth, variously colored yellow, gray, and brown interspersed with clumps of floating rice husks. I can only hope that the subsurface contents are less vile. Then I scan around at the smiling, sipping faces of our hosts, carefully noting the various consequences of dental hygiene depravation. I watch several of the wooden cups travel from these mouths full of blackened teeth back down into the pots, where they're swished around, exchanging the residual cup slime for fresher measures of the fermented concoction.

If the gathered around Yards can't see through my forced superficial smile as I dip my canteen cup into the brew, I'm pretty sure that the bad spirits can. The bad spirits must surely be able to sense my concern for the biologically enriched soup I'm about to ingest. I bring the cup up slowly to my lips but hesitate for a moment, taking in the bouquet

Stars and Stripes and Shadows

before committing fully to the offering. The first close-up whiff isn't too bad. It's a little like sort-of-sour wine. *There are an awful lot of unidentifiable floaties in here. What was it that Franks said earlier today about meningitis?*

OK, OK…just hold your nose and take a slug of it…and smile!

I remember back to one of our fraternity parties when I had a sip of sake; rice wine. It's a little like that. It leaves the same impression…rice flavored gasoline.

I'm no longer concerned about bacteria or micro-organisms resident in this stuff. The alcohol is strong enough for this stuff to be used as a surgical disinfectant. The alcohol is strong enough for me to wonder how any of my hosts are still standing. Another sip and my smile re-adjusts into a more genuine reflection of appreciation for my hosts and their method of spirit distraction.

Baul, Franks and Mora return with us to our camp after a few minutes of pleasant socializing with the villagers. They tell us about the last month they've spent out harassing Charlie. They knew about what was happening to us up on Ten-seventy-nine and Ranger's Roost. They had to move quickly one night to get farther away from the arc-light planned for the next morning; the one just across from us. They've covered a lot of territory and found lots of evidence that Charlie's building up again. Sergeant Franks seems to think the signs point to objectives further to the south though. Charlie's just passing through this area.

Doc Charlebois pulls out the last strip of dried meat that he traded for earlier and asks Baul what it is. It really is monkey and Baul's further description increases the value of Doc's end of the trade significantly. The Yards really prize monkey meat but are hesitant to go out and shoot them as they used to be able to do. Gunfire attracts Charlie. Meat of any kind is prized and rare for these people. They can catch rats and bats and have a few pigs and cows for special occasions but nothing is plentiful for them. The CIDGs that work with us are given ample rations by the American and South Vietnamese Armies adding to the incentive for continued loyalty.

The Montagnards think of the Vietnamese as the lowlanders, as neighbors they would just as soon keep at a distance. The Vietnamese have nothing they want or need. The VC and the NVA have nothing for them either, except their hatred for the Americans and their ad-

Tim Haslam

monitions of how we will rape their wives and daughters and murder their children and rule over their land. The Americans tell them not to believe the VC. We give them a little food and a little medicine and a little tobacco to prove our good faith. We give them more smiles than the VC do. We play with their kids. Americans like to smile and play. The good spirits like the Americans. All the spirits would probably prefer that we all go home.

"We want to register three targets." The new-Six-Two advises us, once more pointing to the map spread on the ground in front of us. "One up here on the trail, fifty meters up from the end of the village. Another one here, right about where we are now, halfway between the river and the village and the last one further down this trail, just above where it crosses the river. There's a little bridge right here, we'll be able to use to get back across latter."

I mark all the targets on my own map and the Lieutenant and I work out where we actually want to direct the DT fire. We'll bring in rounds a hundred and fifty meters to the southwest of the village until we're on target then shift over to a point two hundred meters to the west and a hundred meters north of the village. These two points can be registered and used to adjust fire all around the village and the likely approaches.

We spend the next hour and a half, assisted by Franks and Baul, communicating to the villagers what we're about to do. We want to make sure that everyone's collected up within the confines of the village and that no one is out in the fire zones.

By noon on this hot, clear day the work is done. It took three rounds to find the first target reference and two more for the last one. The battery up on the Roost now has precise settings logged in should they ever need to surround Dak Duat Lal with protective fire. They also have precise settings logged in should they ever need to obliterate Dak Duat Lal.

We get together with Franks one more time and go over the planned route back to Ranger's Roost. We'll follow him and his team for the first two or three klicks, generally single file over the lower land along the river. When we start up the steeper ridge that bends up to the Eleven-eighteen peak we'll split into two groups, combing the whole

Stars and Stripes and Shadows

finger as we work our way up. Sergeant Mora has their radio, running on a fresh battery that I've contributed. We'll be in constant contact. Mora is Striker-Two-Five.

At a little after one-thirty we're ready to go. The heavily burdened grunts of Six-Two Platoon, the twenty-six equally burdened CIDGs, some wearing black splotched tiger suits and the two Green Beret advisers all understand that what we must do this afternoon will be an ass-kicker like nothing we've had to do before. We have to cover more than five klicks, all-uphill, through heavy forest. We have to stay together in our movements. We have to watch out for Charlie. We have to get there before dark. Darker clouds are bunching up out beyond Twelve-forty-seven. The meager comforts of Ranger's Roost are a whole world away...a whole world of shit away.

"We're never gonna make it, sir," Bollman says to Riley as we catch our breath within a small patch of open ground, surrounded by heavier jungle, "it's nearly dark now and we've got almost two klicks to go. It'll be pretty tough finding our way up the rest of the way in the dark."

"Call up there and give them our position," Riley says to me, without further comment on our situation. Even the enthusiastic, energetic Lieutenant Riley looks to be beaten down by the six hours of humping we've endured since we left Dak Duat Lal. I barely have the energy left to reach over for the handset and to form audible words. I just want to stop, to throw off this fucking ruck sack and sit until my mind can provide a better reason for going on.

"Six wants to talk to you, sir," I tell the Lieutenant, handing him the radio handset, a moment after giving Six-Charlie our position.

"Not in the dark. Two hours, at least. What about flares?" Riley's responses to the Captain are all terse and impatient. Riley just wants to get on with it. To get it over with but the darkening forest rising up ahead of us calls for different tactics. The Captain can't offer much in the way of help or advice. Riley has to make the decisions. Riley has to keep the men moving and together, to keep them alive. The new-Six-Two has to draw down a little deeper to find the leader that's needed right now.

"OK...Roger...good...let me get my map out." The Lieutenant's demeanor perks up some as he retrieves his map and flashlight, still

Tim Haslam

listening to the Captain. "Hold this for me," he says to me, handing me his flashlight.

"Right, right, OK," he says into the handset as his finger traces down one of the fingers dropping away from the Roost.

"Roger. Out."

"What are we gonna do?" I ask.

"The Captain's going to send down a patrol from Five-Nine; two squads. The first squad's going to come down to this point, about three hundred meters down from the base, and wait, the other squad's coming down all the way to this point," he says, pointing to a spot about one klick above where we are now. "They'll meet us there. If we can find them they should be able to get back up to the other squad and then we should all be able to get back in. We'll be close enough then for the Captain to send up some flares."

Riley fills in the squad leaders and Franks about the Captains relay plan. Franks has to ensure that all the CIDGs understand that there will be American grunts waiting for us somewhere up ahead. We all have to be able to distinguish between armed Americans and armed NVA hiding within the black jungle ahead.

The plan gives us an intermediate goal. It's psychologically reduced the work yet to do. We just have to go one more klick and we'll be connected with the Roost. The last klick, shepherded by the Five-Nine guys will be easy. We'll make it. We'll sleep at Ranger's Roost tonight. Let's go.

The deepening blackness obstructs our progress more than the tangles of vegetation or the steep slopes we must climb. If we lose sight of the man in front of us we're screwed. Within the denser thickets my eyes scan and search desperately up and down trying to find a contour, an outline or a movement that will identify something or someone. In the more open areas I can make out the shapes of two or three of the men in front of me. I can search a little side to side to see if Charlie is around.

I'd guess we've gone three hundred meters since Riley and the Captain worked out the plan. I don't know how long it's taken. *Thirty minutes? Two hours? Maybe the Five-Nine guys will come down further. Maybe they're just up ahead.*

After another few minutes; another few meters, a crisp burst of rifle

Stars and Stripes and Shadows

fire shatters the silence of the mountain darkness. Another burst closely follows, the first cracks still reverberating over us. *AK fire!* Other bursts follow, more rapid, more sputtering. *M16s!* It doesn't seem far ahead, yet it's too far off for us to see any muzzle flashes. The sporadic, short bursts, alternating AK and M16, suggest a hide and seek exchange.

"Six-Charlie, this is Six-Two-Charlie. What's happening? Over," I call in, crouched down behind a clump of small trees along with two other unidentified grunts.

"Six-Charlie, this is Five-Nine-Alpha-Charlie. We've got gooks down below us and off to our left...one man down. Over," I hear over the radio, before Six-Charlie has a chance to answer my call.

"Five-Nine-Alpha-Charlie, can you give me your position? Over."

"We're about fifty meters down from where we left the first squad and about two hundred meters up from where we're supposed to meet Six-Two. Over." Two more short bursts of M16 fire come through the open air and through the radio just slightly out of phase.

"Five-Nine has contact about two hundred meters up from us," I tell Riley and Sergeant Bollman who have now found their way up to me. Another short exchange of fire helps confirm the distance from us.

"Five-Nine-Alpha-Charlie, this is Six. What have you got? Over."

"This is Five-Nine-Alpha-Charlie. We're taking fire from at least three places, maybe thirty meters out. We've got one man hit in the leg. Over."

"Where's the wounded man? Can you get to him?"

"Roger. Doc's with him now. They pulled him back into some cover. He's OK. Over."

"Six-Two, this is Six. Over."

"Here, sir...it's the Captain."

The Lieutenant gives Captain Hilton his best estimate of our position based on the proximity of the gunfire sounds and Hilton instructs Riley to stay put while he sorts out the situation.

"Five-Nine-Alpha-Charlie, is there a radio with your first squad? Over.

"Roger, Five-Nine-Three. Over.

"Five-Nine-Three, this is Six. What's your situation? Over.

"This is Five-Nine-Three. Nothing happening here, sir. We can see

Tim Haslam

the firing down below us. Over."

"What's the terrain like around you? Over."

"Pretty open right where we are now; a few big rocks for cover, thicker vegetation below us and off to our right. Over."

"Alright...everybody listen up. Here's what we're gonna do. I'm going to start putting up flares out over you. Five-Nine-Alpha-Charlie, as soon as the first flare pops I want you to start firing out to where the AK fire's been coming from. Keep firing until the second flare lights up...then cease fire. Six-Two, when you see the second flare, start bringing your men up toward Five-Nine-Alpha. Just your men though. Have the CIDs stay put. There might still be gooks between you and Five-Nine and there will probably be gooks on your right flank. When Six-Two gets connected with Five-Nine, bring the wounded man back up to where Five-Nine's first squad is and then back up here. I'll keep flares coming unless you tell me to stop. Once you're connected keep everybody moving up this way, protecting your right flank. If you take any fire, answer with everything you have. When the last of Six-Two's men have reached Five-Nine-Alpha's current position, everybody stop and give me a sit-rep. If nothing's going on, we'll bring up the CIDs. Everybody got that. Over."

Everybody involved rogers their acknowledgement.

"One more thing," the Captain adds. "I'm going to start dropping mortar rounds out to the west, down on the next ridge over and into the draw on this side. Out."

As quickly as we can we pick our way up through the forested slope above us under the shifting light and shadow of the burning parachute flares. The mortar rounds bursting off to our right add a measure of rhythmic percussion to our hurried march up the hill. There are a lot of us clamoring up toward the firebase, all illuminated in the greenish glow of the flares, all of us exposed as targets from a hundred points of concealment along the route in. Charlie doesn't know how many of us are coming up this hill though. Charlie doesn't know how spread out we are. Charlie's trying to escape what might be coming his way.

Charlie's rifles provided a boost of adrenaline sufficient to drive us the last six-hundred meters up to the Roost. The wear and tear of the prior seven hours struggle were jolted back down into the confines of our aching muscles and joints by the night shattering bursts of AK fire.

Stars and Stripes and Shadows

The instant the shock wave of exploding gunpowder reached our ears everything in our central nervous system disengaged from the pain and itch, the fatigue and the dread accompanying each labored step. The last six-hundred, fear-focused meters were easy. *We're in! We're back! We're done with another one.*

⚡ ⚡ ⚡ ⚡

It's otherworldly to see them standing here; three real women, only a few feet away; three real, young American women, all in blue dresses standing between the 4.2-inch mortar and us. None of them would qualify as cover girls or movie stars. They're not adorned or made up to be elegant or alluring or sexy. But they're young American women. They smile. They speak real English. They're beautiful. We're all in love with them.

The Red Cross girls—the Donut Dollies—have been helicoptered all the way out here to Ranger's Roost as a way to distract the grunts from the shit surrounding us for a few minutes; as a way to remind us that we're not really that far away, that we're not forgotten. For half an hour or so they'll entertain us; two platoons at a time. Cookies (not donuts) and warm Cool-Aid are given to us as an added bonus. Whatever they have to say, whatever they're going to do, will be the best thing that's happened to us in months and we're on our best behavior. We're trying to remember how to act and how to talk, or, more appropriately, how not to talk.

This afternoon, they're going to test our knowledge of fashion models. They have lots of photographs of the world's most famous models. They'll ask us questions about the women behind the beautiful faces and the slender bodies. The dirty faces and the itchy bodies of the grunts can't wait. Pictures of women, even fully clothed women, warrant our full attention. The real live women holding up the pictures, asking the questions, who will be impressed by our knowledge adds some motivation to the exercise as well as a stimulus for competing in earnest. We haven't had a chance to show-off for anyone relevant for a long time.

"Twiggy," nearly everyone shouts out as the first picture is held up.

"Right, Twiggy, but the question is…what's Twiggy's real name?"

Everyone seems to be stumped…everyone except me. I raise my

Tim Haslam

hand, aware that I am apparently the only one with an answer. The three young American women in the blue-dresses all look at me. Thirty-eight grunts, including former Green Beret Lieutenant John Riley and West Point graduate Captain Roger T. Hilton all look at me. Professional soldier First Sergeant Madison looks at me. Doc, Ed, Bruce, Bob Taylor, Grady, Ferlik, Sergeant Stevens, Price, Elmer, Beasley, Danko and Maebon all look at me. The new guys look at me. Everyone's eyes are on me.

"Leslie Hornby," I say, confidently. I know all about Twiggy. Not because I'm an avid fan but because Rosemary is. Rosemary has the same lean figure, the same short blonde hair and the same young-woman-almost-too-cute-for-her-own-good look. Rosemary can also, aided by varying amounts of eyeliner and mascara, transform herself into a nearly perfect replication of Twiggy, Hailey Mills or Joey Heatherton. It was sometimes fun for me to have the opportunity to date such an array of celebrities. Sometimes though I think she took the alter egos a little too seriously.

"That's right...very good," says the moderating Donut Dolly. The audience reaction is mixed; some appreciation for my apparent knowledge, some sour grapes. Everyone's anxious for the next question.

"OK, here's an American born model that's made a name for herself in England. Who knows who this is?" Dolly number two holds up the picture of an even more slender young woman, eyes deeply shaded, long dark hair.

Thirty-eight frustrated grunts once again stymied. One hand goes up.

"Penelope Tree," I say, when called upon by Dolly number one.

Again the audience reaction is mixed. A few *"Right-on, man"* comments from the impressed faction and a *"Whoever heard of Penelope Tree?"* downgrade from the sour-grapes contingent

"Man, don't you have any pictures of women who aren't starving to death?" Sergeant Littlejohn inquires, expressing his own appreciation for the more Rubenesque female form.

The Dolly's aren't deterred by any of the commentary and in fact, may take some satisfaction in the several voiced preferences for fuller figured girls.

"Alright, this girl is a model, but is best known for something else."

Stars and Stripes and Shadows

The picture in the hands of Dolly number two is that of another dark eyed, sultry looking girl with short black hair. It's her outfit that should be the tip off though.

"Anybody know who this is, or what she might be famous for?

This is almost too easy! I'll let the suspense build for a minute on this one. I'll wait until even the sour-grapes are all looking to me. I'll wait politely and diplomatically for the others to have a turn…for the officers to have a turn.

Stumped! Baffled! Not much high fashion exposure in the background of this bunch apparently. Everybody else has had his chance. The Dollies look to me, thinking they've got me on this one.

"Mary Quant…she invented the mini-skirt."

All thirty-eight heads snap back to the Dollies for confirmation.

"Shit man, how do you know all this?" a familiar brother's voice inquires.

"Man, where are the sisters in this? There's gotta be black models." Ernie Jefferson rouses the emotions of all the black grunts in attendance. No one is really complaining however. Everyone here, regardless of his race, could spend the rest of the day ogling over pictures of skinny white girls, but some broader variety would be appreciated by the other ethnicities represented. *Haslam probably won't recognize any sister-models, is what they're all really hoping for.*

Each subsequent picture and question elicits the same response; shrugs, looks around at everyone but Haslam, followed by looks at Haslam, some in awe, others wanting to frag me. *He can't know this. Nobody could know this! Does he know this? How could he know this?*

It's my finest moment in the Nam. It's my finest moment in the Army. Six-Two-Charlie, the tall skinny guy from L.A. knows famous, celebrity, photographic, high fashion women better than anyone. All the grunts must know it, all the officers, all the Dollies. On and on I go. The game now is between the Dollies and Haslam. Everyone else is just a spectator.

"Jean Shrimpton."

"Peggy Moffitt."

"Pattie Boyd, George Harrison's wife…George Harrison of the Beatles."

The last picture, the grand finale…it would be a tough one for any

Tim Haslam

expert. She's not really a fashion model. The photograph is actually of a record album cover. The picture has the whole audience craning forward to get a better look. It's of a beautiful, smiling, longhaired brunette, the tanned flesh of her bare shoulders offsetting the pure white of the whip cream that covers her breasts and torso.

Hmmm? I raise the index finger of my left hand up and tap the side of my nose a couple of times, my chin resting upon my thumb.

Hmmm? The master repeats, as though unsure, perhaps stalling in the face of certain defeat.

Hmmm? I add one final time, savoring the last opportunity as though it were the final mouthful of Chateau Lafitte, 1939 on the planet.

"Well, the record album is Whipped Cream by Herb Alpert and the Tijuana Brass... and the girl in the picture is...Dolores Erickson."

"You seem to know your models pretty well," Dolly number one acknowledges. "How do you know so much?"

"I'm pretty good with faces," is all I have to offer, unwilling to bestow further fruits to the unworthy.

"Come on, man, no bullshit, how'd you do that? I'll bet the Biscuit Bitches gave you the answers, didn't they?" Jefferson confronts me as we head back to our bunkers.

"How could they have given me the answers? My girlfriend back home is really into the modeling scene. She has all these magazines with the same pictures. I just know who they are," I tell him honestly, still basking in the afterglow of my performance.

"No shit, man? I never heard of any of 'em."

Ernie and I reach our bunker and join Ed, Doc, Bruce, Wee John, Maebon and another of the newer guys, Mark Sturgis. They've already made themselves comfortable and are engaged in further explorations of major American babes. My advanced knowledge receives a few more accolades before the less esoteric field of movie stars replaces the category of fashion models in the discussion.

"Didn't you say something about working in Hollywood?" Sergeant Bollman says to me, re-establishing me as someone of unusual importance.

Stars and Stripes and Shadows

"Yea…I worked my summer vacations at 20th Century Fox Studios."

"No shit, man, what did you do?"

I tell them all about my dad and my jobs. I tell them how I picked up cigarette butts out of the virgin Arabian Desert sands while filming Flight of the Phoenix. Actually on Stage Nine at the studio. I tell them how I almost got to drive Steve McQueen's Ferrari, when it was parked in the way of a trailer full of sets we were moving and how "Steve" came out and talked to me about his car before I could move it. I tell them how sometimes on western films my job was to clean up after the horses that occasionally added unwanted realism to the scenes.

"What about the women movie stars? Did you ever see any real ones?"

"Sure," I reply, still relishing my role as resident expert on important females, "Ann Margaret, Raquel Welsh, Yvette Mimieaux, Candace Bergen, Leigh Taylor Young…"

"What about Debra Wally? Did you ever see her?" Ed asks. "She's too much. If I could have any woman in the world it'd be Debra Wally."

"You gotta' be shit'n me, Ed. If you could have any woman in the world, you'd pick Debra Wally?" I ask, obviously questioning his sanity and his taste in women.

"Yea, me too," adds Bollman. "Debra Wally's really fine."

"Who's Debra Wally?" ask Maebon, irritating Ed and Bruce with his ignorance of such important stuff.

"Gidget…you know, Gidget. Didn't you ever see Gidget Goes Hawaiian?" replies an impatient Ed.

"She's not even the real Gidget," I'm forced to inject, knowing that this will further irritate Ed. "Sandra Dee is the only *real* Gidget. Now, Sandra Dee *is* pretty fine. I could get behind the Sandra Dee choice for number one."

For several more minutes the whole group argues over who has the rightful claim to be known as Gidget and which one is more worthy of sharing our company should any of us ever be granted our fantasy wish.

"Natalie Wood. I'd take Natalie Wood," Wee John says, ending the Gidget debate and elevating the discussion to a more adult level.

Tim Haslam

"Diahann Carroll's for me," Jefferson adds, expanding the realm of racial and cultural possibilities.

"Yea, she's pretty fine too," Bollman acknowledges.

"I'm changing my vote," I say, anxious to re-establish my taste and level of sophistication. "Katherine Ross. I'd kill for Katherine Ross."

Apparently sensing the need to participate with a unique offering and perspective, the new guy, Sturgis breaks in with, "Man, I'd take Claudine Longet. I'd eat a mile of her shit just to smell her asshole!"

He looks around at his stunned audience as his sophomoric smile quickly fades in response to the returned grimaces of disgust.

The reaction to Sturgis' poetic description of his feelings is unanimous.

"That's really gross, man."

"Man, your one sick motherfucker! How can you even think of something like that?"

"How the fuck can you have that image in the same thought with a woman like that?"

Sturgis, who has been out here long enough to know that vulgar language is as much a part of the environment as cigarettes and C-rations is confused by the moralistic response.

"I'm just kidding, man. It's just an expression…you know, like motherfucker. You just said motherfucker. That's pretty gross too, if you think about." Sturgis raises a meager defense for his faux pas.

"Motherfucker don't mean nothin'!" Jefferson quickly meets the challenge, clarifying the long eroded away imagery associated with the MF word. "Motherfucker ain't associated with disrespect. You can't disrespect the women!"

"OK, sorry…I still think Claudine Longet is pretty foxy. Is that alright?"

"Who's Claudine Longet?" Maebon asks.

The list of women to be considered worthy of our company grows over the next half hour, their movie roles remembered, their personal attributes detailed appreciatively. It's a happy and relaxed group huddled around the exterior of our bunker thinking only of things back home. The Donut Dollies have done their job well.

И И И И

Stars and Stripes and Shadows

"Bruce, come up here," the new-Six-Two yells down toward our group from up near the CP bunker.

Bollman rises up without comment or verbal response and heads up towards the Lieutenant. Two minutes later Bollman hails Ed and me to come up there too.

"We have to get rid of these," Bollman says, pointing down to the wooden crate at his feet. "We have way too many of them and they're dangerous sitting around."

"Why don't we just put them on the next chopper out and send 'em back to Dak To?" I ask, wondering why the Army couldn't find an appropriate place for these.

"Man, don't complain, this'll be fun. You and Ed grab the crate and take it down to the edge of the perimeter, just above that clearing down there." Bollman points down toward an opening on one of the little fingers that runs away from the base on the east side. Ed and I each grab onto one of the rope handles and lift up the crate. The forty fragmentation grenades contained within are heavy.

"You mean we're just going to throw forty perfectly good hand grenades out into the jungle?" I ask just to make sure I haven't missed something in the assignment.

"That's it. I make it thirteen for each of you two and fourteen for me."

Everything I know about hand grenades suggests that this is really a pretty weird thing to be doing. In training, these things were treated as though they were fragile, high-explosive eggs. R&R-guy spoke of them as though they had lives of their own and could turn on you without provocation. Price's story of Freddie and Pineapple brings up images of what these things can do. Still, the opportunity to throw thirteen real live grenades out into the forest at specific targets of my own choosing is an exciting proposition.

"OK, we're going to take turns. I'll take one out of the crate, take it down there, behind that stump and throw it. You guys stay down back here. Then, Ed you do one, then Tim."

Bollman carefully pulls out the first frag from the crate, carries it down to the stump, looks back at us, yells "fire-in-the-hole," pulls the pin and throws the grenade. Bruce opted for the high-arc approach on his first toss, lofting the grenade high up above the trees, letting it crash

Tim Haslam

down through the foliage. The loud *kachunk* seems close but well into the vegetation and all we can see is a little smoke. Ed follows suit with the same high-arc and the same result.

As I pull my first grenade out of the crate, it seems heavier than the frags that I've been humping around for the last few months. It's exactly the same but my mind is getting calibrated to the effort required to throw this thing a safe distance out into the jungle. *It's much heavier than a baseball.* I have a firm grip on the frag as I reach the stump, my hand wrapped completely around the core, my fingers pressed tightly against the safety spoon. I look back at Ed and Bruce, shift the grenade around so that my thumb has control of the safety spoon and bring it up to chest height. It takes considerable effort to pull out the pin restraining the safety spoon. *There's no way anybody could do this with his teeth.* I look at it just long enough for it to register that this thing is live. There's no turning back. I try to follow the same arc, aiming for the same general target area out in the trees. *Kachunk*!

We follow the same routine for several cycles, Bruce…*kachunk*, Ed…*kachunk*, me… *kachunk!* Sergeant Bollman decides the appropriate trajectory for each volley. Ed and I replicate the throw. *Kachunk! Kachunk! Kachunk!* It's getting less exciting. With grenade number nine, Bollman tries a new, bolder technique and hurls the explosive device on a straight path toward the base of the trees as though he were Sandy Koufax pitching to Willie Mays. The thick vegetation swallows up the pitch, reacting a moment later with a shock of smoke and spray of shredded plant matter, clearly visible to the three of us.

"All right…cool!"

Ed comes to the mound and hurls a strike of his own, aiming off to the right of where Bruce's grenade exploded and once again, the blast is visible.

These guys got nothin' when it comes to fastballs! I think to myself as I wind up and unleash my smoker into the trees over to the left. *Kachunk*! Strike!

Bollman pitches another one in with even greater velocity, impressing Ed and I with his form. Ed, intent on taking over the fastball lead, lets fly with all he's got. The grenade slams squarely into the trunk of one of the big trees at the edge of the clearing and caroms up slightly and back out into the open space between the trees and us.

Stars and Stripes and Shadows

"Oh, shit!"

The view of this *kachunk* is unobstructed by anything. The flying bits of shrapnel are unobstructed by anything, as they spray out in all directions. Fortunately, the three of us are too far away, outside the kill zone, to be damaged by the few pieces that find their way up to us. There isn't even enough velocity left to penetrate the fabric of our fatigues. We're glad though that the fabric of our flesh wasn't similarly tested.

We complete our assignment using the less exciting, high-arc, well-out-into-the-jungle method. Bollman was right. That was fun. I'll never figure out why that was determined to be the best method for dealing with the excess hand grenades. *It don't-mean-nothin', I guess.*

N N N N

Patrols have been sent out each day to scour around the terrain surrounding the Roost and each night, ambush patrols are sent out to various spots most likely to be used as nighttime approaches to our mountaintop. There are two main avenues in and out of Ranger's Roost. One is on the north side. It's where we came up the other night, encountering Charlie along the way. The other is on the southeast corner, down below the LZ. By now, everyone at Ranger's Roost has passed along both these routes several times. We've learned where the slippery parts are, where the thorny patches are, where the steep climbs are. We always leave these familiar trails further down and head out into unknown sections of the forest, hacking our way around; sweeping, searching for any signs of Charlie. Our return path ultimately connects up with one of the two narrow trails that lead back into the front or back door to our fortress.

I've been out with Mike Ferlik and his squad today on one of those patrols. We didn't find anything but ants, leeches and a swarm of bees that hurried us onto a detour from our preferred route. Two men in the squad were stung. No damage, just another irritation, something else to hurt for awhile…to itch for awhile longer. It was my turn today to experience the fire ants dropping out of the foliage and down the back of my neck. It was my turn to feel the bite or sting or whatever it is they do when they're really pissed at American grunts disrupting their communities. Whatever it is they do, the little bastards do it with a lot

Tim Haslam

of determination, biting or stinging with all they've got until my frantic counterattack, assisted by my towel and Ferlik's hands can dislodge them. The residual stinging and itching from their assault will simply have to be endured. I can't reach back there to scrape my fingernails over the poisoned surface layers of skin. When I can't stand it any longer, I discover that I can use the radio handset to extend my reach far enough to get at the irritated tissues. It helps a little.

The patrol and all its discoveries have been put out of my mind as I sit up here on top of our bunker enjoying the quiet pre-twilight atmosphere. The irritation from the ant bites has faded sufficiently to be indistinguishable from the more general discomforts arrayed over my body. My attention now is on a new patch of red down on my ankle, just above my left foot. I don't remember it being there yesterday and it itches like crazy. Scraping away at it with my filthy fingernail provides a brief moment of ecstasy. *Maybe I should have Doc take a look at this?*

The radio interrupts my medical evaluation. An ambush patrol is heading out, two squads from Six-One Platoon on their way down through the LZ. I'm glad it's not me. I'm glad I can sit here, my boots off, smoking a cigarette, deriving pleasure scratching at the little raised, red circle on my ankle.

"Hey, Doc, take a look at this," I say to Doc after several more minutes of studying and scratching, after the pleasure of the effort has diminished.

"It might be ringworm," Doc says, reaching for his medical bag.

As Doc starts fishing around inside the bag, another call over the radio gets our attention.

"Six-Charlie, this is Six-Zero-Charlie...one of our men's pretty sick. He's throwing up. Sergeant Wells is going to help him back up to your position. Over."

"Roger that, Six-Zero-Charlie. How far out are you? Over."

"We're maybe two-hundred meters down. Over."

"Roger. Out."

The alert goes out that the two men are heading back up toward us. Everyone that heard the call over the radio wonders what the source of the man's sickness is; food, water, Malaria? For some reason I want to get my boots back on.

362

Stars and Stripes and Shadows

"Let's deal with this later, Doc."

The two men should be getting close now and we're all curious to find out who it is that's sick…how sick…why?

Doc and I have walked over closer to the LZ to see what's happened. I lug the radio along to keep up with the communications that may clarify things. There's just enough daylight left to see out over the LZ, to see the edge of the tree line where we know the trailhead to be. We're still walking when an explosion down to the southeast drops us reflexively down into the closest foxhole.

"Six-Zero-Charlie, this is Six-Charlie…what was that? Give me a sitrep. Over."

"This is Six-Zero-Charlie…I don't know. It was something back up the trail. It must be Wells and Harrison. We're going back up there. Over."

Most of the Bravo Company grunts have gathered over on this side of the Roost with weapons at the ready. We all know from the sound of the explosion that it was not a mortar round but we're not really sure what it was or exactly how far away it was.

"Six-Charlie, this is Six-Zero-Charlie…we've reached Wells and Harrison. Wells must have stepped on a mine and they're both in pretty bad shape. Wells' foot is pretty much blown off and Harrison took a lot of shrap in his chest. We're gonna get them back up there as fast as we can. You need to get a dust-off bird up there. Over."

"Roger that. Do you want any more medics down there? Over."

"Negative, Doc's doing everything that can be done. We just need to get them back up there fast. We've got ponchos for litters. Wells seems to be doing OK but Doc says that Harrison's going into shock."

Fortunately, a medical team had been up at Dak Pek all day inoculating the Yards against something. Their chopper was just about to head back when our call came in. They can be up here in six minutes. That's about how long it will take the Six-Zero guys to get back up to the LZ.

The rest of the guys in Six-Zero hurry down across the clearing and down onto the trail to meet their men coming up. Doc Charlebois, several others and I make our way down to the edge of the clearing to see if we can help in any way. Others are spread around the LZ, some with flashlights to help guide the helicopter onto the darkening landing area.

Tim Haslam

"Get a bunch of trip flares ready," the Captain yells out. "Spread them around the LZ and set them off as the chopper gets close!"

Lieutenant Reese hurries down toward the LZ, his hands full of star shell flares. As soon as he reaches the center he drops all but one that he has a firm grasp on. He slams up the palm of his hand against the lower end of the flare shaft and the skyrocket whooshes out, twisting up above the trees, bursting at its apogee, lighting up the anxious scene.

Our bunker and trench covered anthill has been transformed by the exploding mine and its aftershocks. Every one of the inhabitants is somehow engaged. There are no passive spectators. More and more men head down toward the trailhead, not to watch but to help. Others stand by with flares. Others watch for the inbound chopper, ready to help guide it onto the ground. The headquarters RTOs are all on their radios coordinating the traffic, alerting people miles to the south of us that wounded men are coming.

The men with the first litter break out of the trees, obviously exhausted but unwilling to relinquish their hold on the corners of the poncho. The slippery, narrow trail made it impossible for more than four men to bare the burdens up this far. As they break out into the clearing others quickly jump in to help. Men grab at each side. Two others take hold of the front aiding in the climb up the steep, slippery slope. The going is still slow and arduous. There's no room left for others to assist with the litters, so we assist the men carrying the load.

Doc and I each reach out to the men on the front corners. They grasp our hands with their free hands and we add our strength to their effort. Others quickly come down and grasp our hands. More and more men come down, reaching out, coupling with the growing chain of determined grunts hauling the wounded men up toward the LZ. Burning trip flares on the ground and parachute flares falling from above illuminate the human train pulling the men upward. The spotlight of the hovering Huey adds to the light and shadow array that accompanies the desperate struggle.

The Huey's down on the LZ. The poncho litters are handed off quickly and just as quickly the medevac chopper lifts up and away from the company of frustrated grunts shrinking away below it, fading under the final sputters of the dieing flares, fading back into the blackness of this Ranger's Roost place; this useless, piece-of-shit place that has just

Stars and Stripes and Shadows

brought out the best in all of us.

"Harrison's dead," Doc Hayes says to us, his eyes tearing up, as we make our way back toward the bunkers. "He was dead before we reached the clearing. He didn't seem to be wounded that bad. I just couldn't keep him out of shock. He was out of it by the time I got to him. We had to get him back up. It was too dark. I didn't have a chance to do anything for him."

Big Doc, as Hayes is known within the Company, needs somehow to feel responsible. We know and he knows that there was nothing else, nothing more he could have done. He's not a doctor, and even if he was he couldn't counteract the effects of an antipersonnel mine, hidden on a jungle trail, exploding its contents into the fragile tissues of a human body only a few feet away. He didn't have the right tools and equipment and chemicals within his little bag to stabilize the damaged man out there in the dark wet jungle. He never had a chance to ask Harrison where it hurt.

"What about Wells?" I ask him.

"That guy's somethin' else, man. When we got up to them, he was sitting up against a tree, smoking a cigarette. His foot was pretty much gone. He'd already fashioned a tourniquet out of a bandolier strap and was talking to Harrison, trying to calm him down. He didn't even want any morphine until we were almost back up here. The pain was getting pretty bad then. I gave him a syrette. He'll be all right. He's one tough mother fucker."

"Was it a mine? What happened?" Doc Charlebois asks.

"Don't really know. Wells didn't know. He stepped on something that exploded, lifting him up and forward with most of the blast and shrapnel going back behind him into Harrison. It could have been a mine...probably was. It could have been a dud mortar round too. I don't know."

"You did a good job," Charlebois says to his brother medic. "There's nothing anybody could have done out there."

"I know man...I know. Still, that guy shouldn't have died. He wasn't hurt that bad."

"Maybe there was more to the damage than you could see," Charlebois suggests. "Maybe a little piece had penetrated an organ or an artery inside or something. There's nothing anybody could have done."

365

Tim Haslam

"I don't know man. I don't know…maybe."

It will be our last night at the Roost. We'll leave tomorrow, to be replaced by grunts from the First of the Eighth. Our last night here is long, each of us sitting somewhere in the dark solitude of this isolated mountaintop contemplating what happened. A lot of tears tonight; for Harrison, for Wells, for whoever's next, for whoever's imprisoned out here in this hostile land. Each of us is remembering the times our own feet stepped along that same trail. *How close did I come? How come it wasn't me?* Each of us replays the residual images of flares and spotlights; of the Huey burrowing bravely down out of the night sky; of poncho litters jostled along by exhausted men struggling up through the mud; of anxious eyes watching the medevac helicopter probing it's way back up through the trees, hopeful ears following the hum and rotor pop fading away to the south toward the 71st Evac. I will forever carry these pictures in my mind. It will be one of the worst and best things I have ever experienced. *Another day in the Nam!*

Chapter 11

"A Little Rain"

This time it's a C-123 Provider that re-locates Bravo Company. The squatty, twin-engined cargo plane picks us up at Dak Pek, bound for Ben Het. It's a flying whale. The inside is broad and roomy...no seats, no amenities. Pack the grunts onto the floor. Hold on to something as the big, loud machine angles acutely up over the high ridges. The C-123 is fast, faster than the Caribou. The big turboprops grab and push massive amounts of air to the rear. The snub-nosed fuselage shoves the rest of the air out of our way like an Olympic swimmer slicing through the water. The ride in the Provider is a good transition out of the shit. One minute we're confined within the clutches of the jungled mountains. The next minute we're being ferried through the air at ten-thousand feet, one-hundred and fifty knots. A minute from now we'll be at Ben Het...maybe it'll be better.

Ben Het isn't a break. It isn't even an interlude. It's just a shuttle stop. There's just enough time to fill up on water, C-rations and ammo. We're going back out. Ben Het and the surrounding villages have been taking a lot of mortar and rocket fire. It looks like Charlie is building up for something around her. The Division wants Bravo Company and Delta Company to go out together and find Charlie. Don't come back without adding to the count!

The pack of Hueys is waiting for us. Waiting to take us up and away from the landing strip at Ben Het; to take us up over the high peaks to the west toward Laos, take us somewhere out in the mountains behind Rocket Ridge, take us to a place that no one wants to go.

There are already a large number of men on the ground when our

Tim Haslam

chopper settles down in the clearing and lets us off. All of Delta Company is here and about half of our Company, the rest queued up on the line of UH1s behind us.

This place is different. The forest here is not like the jungled tropical rain forest I've become used to out here. There are tall pine trees, spread well apart, towering over large rock boulders and occasional patches of underbrush. This environment seems more familiar to me. This could be the San Bernardino Mountains near my parents place up at Big Bear Lake. It could be a hundred places I've been in the Sierras. It feels a little like this should be a campout or a picnic. It doesn't feel like our guns belong here.

◢ ◢ ◢ ◢

"How far are we going tomorrow?" Ed asks Bruce who's just stuck his head into our hooch before the Sergeant even has a chance to declare his reason for visiting us.

"I don't know yet. What I do know is that we're going to be scouring around these mountains. We're not just going to be humpin' from place to place. We'll be spread out, combing these woods. I'm sure we'll be at it all day."

"Shit man, that's even worse. Humpin' around without an objective…sounds like a great day."

"Well, this should make you even happier then. I guess we're in for a little rain," Bollman declares, getting to the point of his visit.

"You mean a little *more* rain," I reply, offering my perspective.

"No, I mean a lot more rain. There's a typhoon rolling up the South China Sea just off the coast. We should start getting in on it later tonight. It may last two or three days. Don't plan on being dry and comfortable for awhile and don't count on your radios working."

The typhoon stampedes into our realm at 2:10 a.m., heralded by a steady assault of thunder and lighting like nothing I've ever experienced. Sheets of rain and hail, driven diagonally by the combined forces of wind and gravity and air pressure jackhammer onto the twined together ponchos that shelter us, keeping the three of us busy trying to prevent the total structural failure of our home.

"There's no fucking way this is going to hold together," Ed exclaims,

Stars and Stripes and Shadows

trying to ready himself for the inevitable failure of our hooch.

Doc and I follow Ed's lead, floundering around in the darkness, hurrying into our boots and shirts all the while trying to hold onto the flapping fabric of our poncho tent. We gather everything up as quickly as we can and shove it into our rucks, unconcerned with individual ownership. The six ponchos are separating from one another, giving way under the forceful push and pull of the wind and rain. Collectively, they have become useless as protection from the onslaught. The only defense now is for each of us to put on one of the ponchos and huddle closely together—make ourselves small—become a rock, just let the rain wash over us, let the wind batter our green plastic exterior. In five hours it will be daylight. It'll be better then.

At 7:30 a.m. it's just light enough to see the continuing torrents of rain and the many similar clusters of grunts, all paralyzed by the pounding force of the storm. Ed fails at an attempt to light a cigarette. I have the same result. My hands are too wet to get the shaft of tobacco up to my lips, past the curtain of water running down off my helmet.

"Let's go, we're moving out in thirty minutes," a voice yells out from somewhere over to our right. It's Bollman, standing penguin-like next to a soaked Lieutenant Riley.

"Let's go, pass it on. Try to get something to eat and then saddle up."

We have to move? We have to go about our business in this? We have to overcome the water?

All morning the rain slams down through the big trees, the heavy drops volleyed at shifting angles by the buffeting winds. We can't wear the ponchos over all this gear and stay ready for an encounter with Charlie so we're unprotected from the deluge as we slip and splash our way up through the trees and rocks. With the thinner vegetation down at ground level here, we can spread out through the forest, able to see the men around us, ghostly gray-green shapes through the rain-filtered atmosphere.

The water falling over us has come up from the south, pulled up out of the warm waters of the Indian Ocean and the South China Sea. The drops themselves are relatively warm. The wind works like a giant refrigeration system though. The wind finds its way up under the

Tim Haslam

saturated fabric of my fatigues drawing away the body heat and then sucking the cold, wet shirt cloth back up against my skin, each flutter an icy stab. New miseries to help Mr. Ruck and the Nam wear me down. *I need to get out of here!*

Kachunk. It's a perfect shot...dead on target. From this distance that was a hell of a shot. Rosemary reacts with a start to the snowball bursting against the window of the Volkswagen. She sticks her tongue out at me, safe within the warm confines of the car. She refuses to come out and join me in the snow. It's Thursday afternoon, we cut our afternoon classes at Valley College and drove up here into the mountains for no purpose or reason other than we could. No one could stop us. No responsibility could stand in our way. We were free to do whatever we wanted. All we had to do was decide what we wanted. She didn't care. I liked to drive. Let's go to the mountains. Why not?

"C'mon...let's go. Let's go get some coffee. I'm getting cold," she pleads, rolling down the window just a crack.

"Not until you come out here."

"No...it's too cold. I don't even have any gloves. I'm not coming out there."

"It's real snow! We came all the way up here and you're staying in the car? C'mon, just for a minute or two."

"No...it's cold. Let's go some place warm."

She's going to win this one. My bare hands are already getting numb. My wool Pendleton shirt is insufficient insulation against the brisk mountain air. Coffee and someplace warmer is starting to sound pretty good.

"Here," I say to her after climbing back into the driver's seat as I press the palm of my right hand up against her cheek.

"God...you jerk! That's freezing," she declares, punching me in the side.

"My face is freezing too," I tell her.

"Let's see," she replies, leaning over toward me. She presses her warm hand against my cold cheek.

"Aw, poor boy," she observes, pulling her body into contact with mine. She looks for a moment into my eyes, her own green eyes glistening with mischief. She kisses me; a short, soft tease of a kiss. She gently

Stars and Stripes and Shadows

rubs her cheek across mine. I kiss her back…a real kiss.

It's raining pretty hard by the time we get back down below the snow line. It's all the little windshield wipers can do to sweep the cascades of water away. It's all I can do to see the road unfolding ahead of us. There's a lot to concentrate on; the slippery road, the songs on the radio, everything about Rosemary, everything about being free, and I still have an hour and a half before I have to be home.

The word comes over the radio to take a break. A standing break, the puddled ground precludes any sitting. The trunk of a large tree helps me hold up the weight of my ruck for the next few moments and I'm determined to have a cigarette. I can use my wet hands to get at the plastic case in my shirt pocket. I can use my wet hands to get it close to my mouth. I can open the plastic case and the flip-top of the Marlboro pack with my mouth. I think for a moment that I can pull one of the cigarettes out with my lips or my teeth but there's too much water running down my face. If I try I'll just funnel all the water right into the box. I have to use my hands. I adjust my head until I find an angle where most of the water drips off the little bill of my helmet, over to the side, away from me. With just the tips of my forefinger and my thumb I tweeze out one of the Marlboros, grasping only the more robustly constructed filter. Careful to keep everything at just the right angles, I quickly put the case back in my pocket, pull out my Zippo and light up. *Ahhh! Life is good again.*

Like everything else that visits this country, the typhoon ultimately has its energy and determination sucked out of it by the hostile ground. As the day progresses the weakening storm swirls along northward up the east coast leaving the grunts of Bravo and Delta Companies to complete their days work within the foggy steam of its aftermath.

We find some bunkers and mortar pits. We find some ammo and supplies. We don't find Charlie. Charlie doesn't find us.

It's been several hours since the rain stopped but I'm still soaked. We've excavated our foxholes out of the heavy mud, filled our mud-bags, savored our C-rations and are ready for sleep. Doc, Ed and I have re-engineered our hooch…an extra stake here, a brace there, a few more ties

Tim Haslam

along the seams. No one thinks there will be another typhoon tonight. It's just an opportunity to solve a problem...even if it's too late.

We've been careful to lay it all out and organize everything inside the hooch so that it's all dry. My air mattress and my dry poncho liner await. I remain the only wet component, still wrapped up in my damp clothes. I have no choice about my pants. I'll just have to endure the clingy cold and itch until my body heat can dry them out. I do have options with my shirts however. I don't have to wear my tee shirt or my fatigue shirt. I can take them off. I'll be dry in moments. I can curl up under the poncho liner and be comfortable from the waist up. I don't even have to get up to pull my shift on radio watch. I can lay right here, dry and warm, with the handset pressed up to my ear.

I know only that I'm glad this day is finally over. I'm too tired to know anything else.

"...Two-Charl...Charlie..."
What is that?
Your cheek is so soft. Your breath is warm. The sun's come out. I...
"Six-Two-Charlie, this is Six-Charlie. Wake up goddamn-it and give me a sit-rep. Over."
Oh Shit! Shit! I fell asleep. I thought the sit-rep call would wake me up. Shit!
"Uh, Six-Charlie, this is Six-Two-Charlie. Sit-rep negative. Over."
"Stay...the fuck... awake!"
I pull myself more upright. Reset myself into a less comfortable position and check my watch...two-thirty. Another half hour and I can wake up Doc. Then I can relax again. Then I can go back and find Rosemary.

"Let's go in there! Ed, Tim...let's go. Six-Two wants you both... now!" Sergeant Bollman kicks at our feet, rousting us from our warm, dry nest. My body heat has worked to dry out everything during the night. It feels good. I don't want to move.

"Where's my shirt?" I ask, as I shuffle around through the gear in the hooch.

"It's out here," Ed says, standing just outside. "You must have left

Stars and Stripes and Shadows

it out here. It's soaking wet."

"Oh fuck!" I blurt out as I climb out toward Ed and see the soggy rags. *I have to put those on?* The tee shirt is too saturated to even consider wearing. My fatigue shirt is just as wet, but I don't have a choice. I'll have to put it on.

I stall as long as I can, holding the shirt, anticipating what it's going to feel like when it first comes into contact with my dry warm flesh. It's like standing at the edge of an icy pond, knowing you have to dive in. *I can't do it. I have to do it.*

"Tim, C'mon, I need you over here. Now," Riley beckons.

Oh Shit! Shit! Shit! My whole body reacts to the shock. I pull the loose fabric as close as I can around me as I head over toward the Lieutenant in an effort to accelerate the process of body-heating.

"You look like shit, man…you OK?" Riley inquires as I join the group huddled around the Lieutenant's map.

"No, I'd like to take a sick day and go back to bed if nobody minds. In fact, I think we should all take a sick day today."

"You'd miss out on big fun today, if you wasted it in your nice warm hooch. Plus, your talents are needed this morning," the much-too-cheery officer responds just as the other squad leaders splash up and join the group.

I look like shit! If I look worse than the rest of this sorry gathering I must be pretty bad.

"We're going out to the west this morning, about two and half klicks. We're on point. Ferlik, you'll have the point squad. Haslam will be your RTO. Get your Dak Mot Lop maps out and I'll go over the route."

Riley shows us the selected way down a steep finger from our current position, across a stream, back up another steep finger that angles a little southward up toward a wide, flat peak.

That's it? That doesn't look too bad.

"We've got reason to believe that the NVA are coming down through here on their way to Ben Het or Dak To. Delta Company will be working along this ridge on our left flank but will meet up with us on this peak at the end of the day."

Riley shifts his finger a few inches over to the right on his map. "You can see how close we are to Cambodia. The main branch of the

373

Tim Haslam

Ho Chi Minh trail is right there. Ed and Tim; see Houston before we go. He'll give you the new fire-push and words-of-the-day. Without any problems we should make camp by mid-afternoon. Mike, you guys need to get going in about thirty minutes."

With my ruck full, a new battery in my radio and under sunny skies, I set out, trailing Mike Ferlik, the rest of his squad falling in line behind me. The rest of the Company will follow us in a half hour or so. A few hundred meters down, the terrain shifts back into the more familiar tropical rain forest; bamboo, vines, thorns. It takes us just over an hour to reach the first stream. It flows through a narrow gully but is easy to cross. The slope on the opposite side is steep and thick with vegetation.

"We need to find this little finger here," Ferlik says to me, pointing at the little twists of contour lines.

"Man, that's going to be hard with all the vegetation up there."

"Well, since we know we came down this finger here, that means we must be right about here," I say, looking at my own map. "So the finger we're looking for should be…maybe a hundred meters over to the west…right?"

"Gotta be…OK…we'll go up a little bit into this stuff and work our way diagonally to the right until we pick up the finger."

Ferlik checks his compass. "The ridge line we want should be running across to the southeast, about 200 degrees."

"Toby, head in here. Go up fifteen or twenty meters and then start working up to the right. Look for a finger ridge that runs back up to the left," Ferlik instructs Lamberti, who has the primary machete duty out in front. Lamberti starts up as directed, slicing away the first viney impediments blocking his access to the steep slope. Ferlik follows a few meters behind, still clutching his map, his rifle slung over his shoulder. I know Lamberti to be the typical average height point man and so I have my own machete in my right hand, ready to trim the higher up branches that he will miss.

Ten or fifteen minutes along, Lamberti stops suddenly, drops down to a knee and looks back at us, gesturing for us to be quiet. We hear it too. There's movement coming from a bamboo thicket thirty meters up ahead of us. We can't see what it is. It seems to moving up the hill

Stars and Stripes and Shadows

away from us…in a hurry.

"You think we should call it in?" I ask Mike as we both strain to see something more.

"No…that could be anything. Whatever it was is probably long gone anyway."

"We should have reached that finger by now, shouldn't we?" I ask.

"Yea…definitely," Ferlik answers, redirecting his attention back to his map. "Maybe we actually came down off that first ridge here, a little further down stream than we thought before. If so, that would put us about here now and the finger we're after should be within about fifty meters."

"OK, that makes sense. You wanna keep working up this way then?"

"Toby, stay down to the right of that bamboo. Just in case, let's circle down around that area. Start back up over by those big trees. You should be able to see the ridge heading up to the left from there."

Sure enough, when we reach the big trees there is a discernable rise in the heavily forested ground running diagonally back to the southeast, just as we thought, just as it showed on the map.

"This has to be it," says a relieved Ferlik, aligning his map with his compass one more time. "From right here though, it seems to be running a little too much southward. I guess it will start turning more to the east further up. I'll check as we go."

I study my own map, carefully tracing the route we've followed so far this morning. It all fits. This has to be right. I call back to the Company and give them our position. They got a late start and are probably forty-five minutes behind us. We should keep going though, as quickly as we can. The Captain wants us to get to our objective and secure it.

Ferlik's periodic compass checks confirm that our ridge is bending around to the east as the map indicates. Everything seems to be right. The forest is heavy though, too thick to be able to see much of the terrain around. We're unable to see any of the neighboring ridges or peaks that we could use to validate our position. All through the morning we continue the steady gradual climb under the hot sun and pressing humidity.

Tim Haslam

"See that peak over there," Sergeant Ferlik says to me as I cast away the now empty can of pork slices that was my lunch. "I think that's this peak here...Nine-ten." Again, he has his compass laid down on his map as he strains to see through the little clearing that frames the mountain top off to the west.

"Yea...could be," I answer, crunching through the candy coating of the Chiclets gum included in my Accessory Pack while studying my own map. "I guess it has to be. It seems a little too far off though. By the map it should only be about a klick and a half away from where we are. Doesn't it look like that's farther off than that?"

"Maybe...it's hard to tell, but look, the compass angle is just right. It has to be it. Everything's fallen into place just like it should. We've followed this ridge along for two hours now, which should put us right about here. From here, Nine-ten would be right there and there it is."

"I guess your right. That means we should reach our objective in about another hour, right?"

"Yea...let's go."

It's not quite four o'clock when we reach what seems to be the high point on the ridge we've been climbing all afternoon. The area is heavy with brush making it hard to survey the contour to confirm the shape against the rendering on the map. It clearly slopes away in all directions though. It is a hilltop. It has to be the hilltop we're looking for.

"Six-Charlie, this is Six-Two-Charlie. We've reached the NDP. All's quiet up here. No sign of anything or anybody. Over."

"Roger, Six-Two-Charlie. We're probably an hour behind you. We'll call in when were about a hundred meters out. Delta won't be up for a couple of hours yet. Out."

The squad forms up in a twenty meter radius circle and settles in awaiting the rest of Bravo Company coming up the same route we took and Delta Company coming up from somewhere down to the north. Mike and I continue studying our maps, comparing anything we can actually see of the terrain around us with what the little lines on the map represent.

"This isn't much of a night position," I say to Ferlik. "There's higher ground on two sides and easy approaches up from the other two sides and, with two companies we're gonna be pretty cramped up here."

Stars and Stripes and Shadows

"Yea, but the ground's pretty soft, easy digging and this brush will be easy to clear. We'll be gone tomorrow anyway."

Sergeant Ferlik and I make small talk over cigarettes and Yard bars until Houston's next call, forty minutes later.

"Six-Two-Charlie, this is Six-Charlie. We're probably fifteen minutes from your position, let us know when you can hear us. Over."

"Roger, Six-Charlie. Out." I check my watch as I lay the handset back over on my ruck.

"The Company's almost up. Keep your ears open and let me know when you hear anything," I tell the others in the squad.

Ten minutes have gone by and there's no hint of a sound from anything approaching.

"Six-Two-Charlie, this is Six-Charlie. You should hear us by now, we're almost to the top. Over."

"Negative Six-Charlie. We don't hear anything yet. Over."

"We can see the top of the hill from here. Have your men stand up in the clear, you should be able to see us down the finger. Over." Houston's voice now has a hint of irritation about it.

I pass on the instruction. Ferlik and I both stand and move a little further back toward the approach we came up. There's nothing coming up from down there.

"Six-Charlie, we still don't see you. Can you see us? Over."

"Six-Two-Charlie, this is Six. We're up here on top. Where the hell are you? Over."

Oh, Shit! "Hey, Mike, Six is on the horn. He says they're on top."

"Fuck! Here...gimme it."

"This is Ferlik, sir. We're right up on top of this brushy peak. Over," the now worried Sergeant says, returning his helmet to his head as some subconscious protective response for what's about to come. I can only imagine what the Captain has to say as I listen to Mike's responses.

"Roger...roger...negative, sir...roger. Yes, sir we came all the way up that ridge. Yes, sir...roger...negative...negative...no, sir."

Mike looks over at me; his facial expression gives me the general tone of the dialogue.

"We can only see a little to the west, sir. There's a high ridge running diagonally out there, southeast to northwest, maybe two, two-and-half

Tim Haslam

klicks away. I can see more out to the east. A bunch of finger ridges run down from here to the east to a little valley. On the other side is another high ridge that runs directly north and south another two klicks away. Over."

"Roger. Over." Ferlik looks again at his map, shaking his head in disbelief. "Well, obviously this ain't it," Mike says to me, waiting for Captain Hilton to come back on the radio.

"Roger...yes, sir. Out."

"Here, switch over to the Battalion push," Sergeant Ferlik says, handing me the handset. "Saladin's flying around near here in his chopper. He's coming over this way to try and find us...call Bronco-One-Zero."

"Are you shittin' me? I gotta call the Brigade Commander? I gotta tell the Colonel where we are and how we got here?"

"Yea!" Ferlik replies with a sort of helpless shrug.

"Bronco-One-Zero, this is Eight-Two-Six-Two-Charlie. Over."

"Six-Two-Charlie, this is Bronco-One-Zero...wait one. Over," an unfamiliar voice instructs. The voice is authoritative and yet seems calm and business-like.

"Six-Two-Charlie, this is Bronco-One-Zero. My chopper's coming into your area from the north. Can you see me? Over."

I can see a Huey way off to my northeast but I search all of the sky in that general direction for any others before answering.

"This is Six-Two-Charlie...yes, sir. I can see a Huey off to my northeast. Over."

"Roger, Six-Two-Charlie. Keep an eye on me. I'm going to tell you when I'm right over your Company's position. Over."

"Mike, keep an eye on that slick way out there. The Colonel's going to let us know when he's right over the rest of the Company."

"Six-Two-Charlie, this is Bronco-One-Zero. Can you still see me? I'm right over the Company now. Over."

"Oh shit, man...he's right over them now," I say to an equally stunned Ferlik. "How the fuck could we be that far off."

"Bronco-One-Zero, this is Six-Two-Charlie...yes, sir...I've got your position. Over."

"OK, Six-Two-Charlie. Now, lead me to where you are, son. Over."

Stars and Stripes and Shadows

"OK, Roger. From the way your headed now come southwest. Over," I tell the Full Bird Colonel, Brigade Commander wondering what he's going to say when he finds out how far away we actually are.

"Turn a little more to the west, sir. Over."

"OK, sir, you're heading right for us now. Over."

"He wants us to pop smoke, Mike."

Ferlik instructs one of his men to throw a smoke grenade out in front of us.

"All right, sir...we've popped blue smoke. Over."

The Huey pulls up short of our position and hovers out about five hundred meters to the east of us.

"OK, son, I've got you...damn! I can't even tell you where you are over the radio. Get a compass reading to the Company's position...you know where that is on the map. Now follow it back two klicks. That's where you are now. Have you got that? Over."

Without saying anything I point down to my map, confirming to Ferlik where we are.

"Oh fuck! We're in Cambodia, man. How the fuck could we have gotten here?"

"Bronco-One-Zero, this is Six-Two-Charlie. We've got our position now. Over."

"Six-Two-Charlie, you'd better get moving. You've got a lot of ground to cover before nightfall. Over."

"Roger that, sir." I'm not sure what else I should say to the Colonel. *Thanks? Sorry? It'll never happen again? We wanted to be the first Bravo Company grunts into Cambodia? Sergeant Ferlik and I had our heads up our asses for most of the day, sir, but we're OK now?*

We start down the finger ridge moving as quickly as we can. There's a lot of difficult ground to cover between where we are and the NDP. It will be dark in less than two hours. We push hard down the ridges, across the valley and the little river that runs through it. Sergeant Ferlik rotates the guys cutting point every half hour. He wants the machetes swinging full tilt, burrowing a path for the rest of us following behind. At every clearing we come to, Ferlik and I make sure that we can see up to the peak where the Company is encamped. Delta Company is there now too. It's just the seven of us that yet remain out here in the

Tim Haslam

jungle as nightfall spreads over these mountains.

Bob Taylor's squad comes down and guides us back up the final four hundred meters into the dark, quiet camp. Our arrival brings out the expected commentary about our land navigation skills.

"Nice job guys. When you look at the map, DAK MOT LOT should be at the top."

"If you think this gets you out of cutting point ever again…think again!"

"How'd you like Cambodia?"

The taunts follow us over to our section of the perimeter where Lieutenant Riley greets us. We're too exhausted to offer any come-backs, too exhausted to care much.

"You guys OK?"

"Yes sir," Ferlik replies. "I don't know what happened, sir. Everything seemed right the whole way. We took a little detour early this morning around some kind of movement ahead of us. It was pretty thick stuff there and we must have started up the wrong ridge. Everything looked right though. The whole way…everything looked right."

"He's right, sir," I add, for what it's worth. "Everything looked right to me too."

"Forget it…it happens. Get your guys settled in, set guards and get some sleep. We're moving out early in the morning."

$$\textit{N} \quad \textit{N} \quad \textit{N} \quad \textit{N}$$

I have the last shift on radio watch, so, at 3:00 a.m. my sleeping is done for this night. It takes a long time for me to get fully awake and the first sit-rep call, requiring a response from me, completes the transition. I make it through the first hour re-tracing our route, trying to remember all the contour lines on the map, trying to determine exactly where we went astray. I wonder what the Colonel did after he left us. I wonder what the Colonel had to say to Captain Hilton. I wonder what the Captain will have to say to Sergeant Ferlik.

All of my wondering is so intense that it takes a minute for me to acknowledge the subtle noise coming up out of the jungle blackness. *What is that? Is that real?* It's not steady or strong. It comes and goes…faint …a little louder…again faint. I know that sound, but refuse to accept that it's real. *It can't be. Not out here. Not out here in the black*

Stars and Stripes and Shadows

isolation of these mountains. It has to be something else; something with a similar sound; an animal of some kind, maybe a monkey.

There it goes again!

"Ed, Doc, wake up!" I say softly as I shake the two warm bodies curled up under the poncho liners.

"Doc, wake up, listen...listen to this."

"What...listen to what?" Doc asks, trying to complete the separation from his dreams and his reality.

"What's goin' on?" Ed jerks up more reflexively in response to my shaking.

"Listen...do you guy's here that?" The three of us, sitting upright side by side stare out into the blackness and wait.

"Shit, that can't be," Ed says in response to the next faint replication of the sound. I'm relieved that he's heard it too, but still uncomfortable that Ed thinks it's the same thing.

"It is," Doc says, bending further forward. "It's a baby crying."

"Six-Charlie, this is Five-Nine-Alpha-Charlie. We've got some kind of noise out here. It's coming from somewhere down the hill off to our left. Over."

"This is Six-Charlie. What kind of noise? Over."

"Six-Charlie, this is Six-Two-Charlie. We hear it too. You're not going to believe this, but it sounds like a baby crying. Over."

"This is Five-Nine-Alpha-Charlie. That's it...that's what we're hearing too, a baby. Over." Within another minute, everyone awake on this side of the perimeter has heard it. Everyone with a radio calls in and confirms what they're hearing.

"What do we do? Over."

"...wait one. Over."

The image of a baby out here adds a new dimension to the horror that surrounds us. The thought of a baby, out here in this wilderness, perhaps alone, is unsettling to all of us. *How did it get here? Why is it here? Why is it crying? Who else is out there?*

"This is Six. There's nothing we can do now. Just stay alert. Over."

After another few minutes the sounds stop coming. *Why did it stop? What happened to it?*

381

Tim Haslam

Sergeant Bollman and Lieutenant Riley missed the excitement last night. They slept soundly through it all.

"No shit? There was a baby crying out there? What the hell was a baby doing out there?" Bollman replies when Ed fills him in on what happened.

"How the fuck should I know what it was doing out there. It was crying. That's all I know. It was a baby and it was crying. That's all I know," Ed answers.

"It sounded like a pretty new baby too," Doc adds.

"It probably was," Lieutenant Riley adds. "The Yards give birth that way. The women go out into the forest when it's time and de-liver...alone."

"Sir, the nearest Yard village is miles from here. Do you really think a pregnant woman would come all the way out here to do that?" Boll-man says, challenging the Lieutenant's theory.

"No, I don't think that they'd come all the way out here just to do that. But, maybe she was on her way from somewhere, or to somewhere, traveling along the river and the time came. She's probably not alone. At least there are probably other Yards somewhere around that know she's out here. That's the way they do things."

"That was just weird to hear that last night," I say. "It's still pretty weird to think that a new born baby is out here in this shit."

"Well, that baby's not all that's out here. We've gotta get going. We're walking drag today." The new-Six-Two goes over the proposed route for today with a few joking reminders about how to read a map. Delta Company pulled out earlier, working a line parallel to where we will be, off to our right. They will again rejoin us tonight. The lead platoons of Bravo Company are already on their way and we have to hurry to pack our gear up and fall in at the end of the file of unhappy grunts trudging off into the forest.

"Six-Charlie, this is Six-One-Charlie. Over."

"Six-One-Charlie, Six-Charlie. Go."

"We've got a man down. Doc says it's a leech that he can't get off. Doc says the guys gotta be dusted-off. Over."

"Dusted off for a leech? You gotta be shit'n me. Over."

"Yea...well, I guess a leech somehow got up into the end of his

382

Stars and Stripes and Shadows

penis. Doc says it's pretty far up inside and there's no way he can get it out. Doc doesn't really know what to do and this guy's getting pretty nervous about the whole thing. Over."

Everyone listening over the net cringes at the described image; *how could a leech get all the way up there? How could he not know it was there?*

"Six-One Charlie, this is Six. Send a squad back with the man to our position last night. You'll have an easy time cutting an LZ. We've got the medevac on the way. Over."

A few moments later, Sergeant Rimmer passes by us leading his squad and the leech victim back toward last night's camp. As we're at the end of the file, we're only a hundred meters or so out from there. We all study the man as he goes by, Doc Hayes following close behind. We all know him; Marty Rosenthal. He looks OK as he hurries by but doesn't seem to want to make eye contact with any of us. We each perform our own mental cost/benefit analysis of Rosenthal's plight. He's on his way to the land of nurses and clean sheets. He's on his way out of the shit. He has a leech crawling up his urethra. *We'll take the shit!*

Houston comes back over the radio and kick starts the Company into action again. Rimmer and his squad can catch up after Rosenthal is dusted off. We haven't even had enough of a break to perform a thorough leech check of our own bodies. We start out thinking that we're more vulnerable to attack than we were ten minutes ago. Rosenthal's invader has elevated the leech species up into the top position of grunt concerns. Each of us will need to formulate a better defense.

The leech species maintains its place in our consciousness for only a minute or so. The sputter of M16's behind us, answered by cracking AK fire instantly erases the leech-in-the-penis image. Six-One-Alpha-Charlie is on the horn quickly advising us that they're taking fire. Rimmer's squad has surprised some number of NVA soldiers rummaging around our vacated camp. They're unsure how many there are—about a half a dozen they estimate. Captain Hilton responds to the advisory from Rimmer's RTO and orders Lieutenant Riley to lead our Platoon back to assist. We drop our rucks, taking only weapons and ammo and hurry back toward the source of the intermittent firing. I stay in contact with Six-One-Alpha-Charlie as we approach to ensure our movements are coordinated.

383

Tim Haslam

"They're spread out in the trees over there," Rimmer says to Riley as we pull up behind the cover of a large tree trunk. "There's at least four of them...maybe more. I think there's one back in the brush over there. The rest are further back in the trees off to the right."

"Any of your guys hit?" Riley asks.

"No, they're spread out down along my left, over there."

"OK...try to work your squad around to the left. We'll swing our platoon around to the right."

Without saying anything, Rimmer jumps up and starts moving off toward his left. He gets only about two steps when a man pops up out of the brush, near the spot Rimmer had pointed out. The exposed man takes an instant to orient himself to the moving American. It's too long. Rimmer, still moving to his left, unleashes a burst at the panicked man with the AK47. The helmetless man jerks backward, as though he had been punched hard in the face and falls back behind the brush. There's no doubt that he was hit by one of the 5.56mm rounds spraying out of Rimmer's M16.

Two short bursts of AK fire come from the trees out behind the down man, a little off to our right. Grady's squad, to our far right, answers with their M16s and an M60 machinegun. The gooks know that they're outnumbered and outgunned. We can see them, retreating as fast as they can out into the forest behind them. Riley directs Grady and Sergeant Stevens to sweep carefully out through that way to ensure that they're gone and that they keep going. The rest of us cautiously approach the down man hidden behind the waist high clump of brush.

"Shit man...look at this," John James, Rimmer's RTO says, looking down at the body. Rimmer stands next to him, saying nothing as he studies the man lying on his back on the ground. The man's dead. His lower jaw is shifted a little out of alignment with the rest of his face and there is a dime sized wound an inch to the left of his chin. The wound looks more like an open sore than a bullet hole. The man looks as though he'd been knocked out; as though he were unconscious; as though he would come out of it in a minute. He's not breathing though and his empty eyes are open. He's dead.

Rimmer kneels down for a closer look. He gently twists the man's face around enough to expose the back of his head. The opening at the back of the man's head must be close to two inches in diameter; an

Stars and Stripes and Shadows

eruption of various tissues; skull fragments, blood soaked hair and soft tissues. The instant the spiraling little bullet, traveling at 700 meters per second, came in contact with the lower jaw it started to spin. Tumbling, churning, and grinding its way through everything in its path, building up a shock wave of pressure ahead of it until it all exploded out into the open air again. The mental processes associated with consciousness, which reside within these same cerebral structures, were mercifully disconnected before they could react to the trauma. Death, for this man, was an unfelt experience.

He's not very old! About my age! I wonder what he was thinking of fifteen minutes ago. I wonder what will happen fifteen minutes from now.

◢ ◢ ◢ ◢

"A squad from Delta's going to stay back here this morning," Riley tells us as we go over the maps preparing for today's hump. "If the gooks yesterday were really scavenging around after us, maybe they'll come back today. If they do, our guys will ambush 'em. The rest of us are going to spread out and work our way back up to the northwest along these ridges. Delta Company will work the right flank and we'll come up this way, Five-Nine and Six-Zero on the right, Six-One and Six-Two on the left. So, we'll be in the rear on the left flank."

The Lieutenant gives me Delta Company's radio frequency. Their call signs are similar to ours only their Platoons are designated Three-Nine to Four-Two. We've been around Delta Company on several occasions in the past and I'm getting to know many of them. Last night, we made camp early and had time to mingle with the Delta guys, exchanging stories about life back in the world and life here in the shit. Their stories aren't much different than ours. They tell them the same way. They speak the same language. There's the same "fuck'n this" and "off-the-wall-shit that" and all of it "don't-mean-nothin." Grunts are grunts.

We're about an hour out when Wee John comes over the radio and informs us that the squad from Delta is about to pull out of their ambush position and start heading up our way. The way the two Companies are deployed, it makes more sense for the ambush squad to follow the Bravo Company route and join up with us for the rest of the trek

Tim Haslam

into tonight's camp. They'll switch over to our push somewhere along the way and stay in contact until they join up with us. We're heading into steeper, heavy forest and our going will be slow for a while. The squad should be able to catch up to us quickly.

The varying contours of the sodden ground, the great trees and the heavy jungle all naturally absorb noise. But certain sounds; crisp, sharp sounds seem able to wind their way through this natural insulation, alerting all the hearing creatures that something has disturbed the steady state. Gunfire is such a sound. Even at several hundred meters the sound is unmistakable. The differentiation between AK47 and M16 is less clear at such distances. The forest obstacles change the character of the sound waves, absorbing and attenuating portions of the rippling air. Still, the surviving character of the sound is clearly identifiable. It's source unique…men with rifles.

The short bursts must be coming from the ambush squad and whomever they are engaged with. We all stop, turning back toward the shots, as we draw ourselves closer to the protection of the ground. I'm not sure what to do with my radio. Stay on the Bravo Company push or switch over to the Delta frequency to get a reading on what's going on.

"Six-Charlie, this is Six-Two-Charlie. Any idea what's going on? Over."

"The ambush squad started taking fire just as they headed out. They've got two men down. That's all I know. Over."

"Should I stay on this push or switch over to theirs? Over."

"Negative, stay on this push. Over."

There's nothing after the initial bursts. No escalation. No sporadic follow on. Just the normal sounds of the jungle now, seeming to be louder, more noticeable than a few minutes ago. *What about the two men down? What's happening with them?*

"Six-Two-Charlie, this is Six. Put Six-Two on. Over."

Riley takes the handset, listens for a moment, pulls his map out and listens for several more minutes, rogering occasionally and marking points on his map with the stub of a pencil he keeps up under the elastic band on his helmet.

"Yes sir, we're on our way. Out," he says and gives me back the handset. "Get the squad leaders over here."

Stars and Stripes and Shadows

Once everybody's gathered around, Riley fills us in. Delta Company's squad has one man dead and another wounded in the foot. The wounded man's not in too bad shape. They're bringing him and the body of the dead man up toward us. Captain Hilton is at the top of the next ridge over to our right. They can clear an LZ there to dust off the wounded man and hand off the KIA. Our Platoon is the closest and so we're being sent back down to meet them coming up and help in any way we can.

The way down seems steeper than it was when we came up and it's getting slippery, as a light rain has started falling. The RTO with the squad coming up has changed frequencies on his radio and has been in contact with me, keeping me informed as to their position. They've gotten off our track, strayed too far south and are coming up the wrong ridge. The one they're on will bend back around to the south, taking them away from the LZ being cut. They have to correct their course, climb down the steep sides of the finger their on, cross the gap and climb back up the even steeper side of the finger that we're coming down. They have to do this carrying a dead body and helping a man with a foot wound. They're going to need our help soon.

Lieutenant Riley has stayed in the lead all the way down, setting a fast pace for the rest of us following behind.

"There they are," he shouts outs, pointing diagonally over to our right as he turns down off the crest into the heavy vegetation of the slope. I can see the men coming up through the trees, thirty meters down. In another minute we reach a little clear spot and wait for them to struggle up the last few steps between us.

A man with a machete reaches us first, sweat pouring down his beleaguered face. Behind him are four men carrying the poncho litter with the dead man. Their fatigue appears to be much greater than that of their point man. If they've been carrying this litter all this way they must be nearly spent themselves. The first man up on my side, clutching the right front corner of the poncho can't go much farther. His face shows the strain of the effort required just to continue holding on to the overwhelming load.

"Here," I say to him, handing him my rifle. "I'll take it."

Without saying anything, he reaches for my M16, waits a second while I get a grip on the fabric of the poncho and then falls to his knees,

Tim Haslam

exhausted.

The litter's heavy. The body is that of a large man, lying on his back, his head at the front end, next to my hand. *I know this guy. I've seen him around. I saw him this morning. He's one of their Platoon Sergeants, I think.*

Other's from our Platoon come down and relieve the rest of the weary men who've brought their friend up this far. As we take over the work, I can see that the man's face has taken on a yellow-gray color, his open eyes staring blankly up into the treetops above us, the flesh of his limp hands gray under the accumulated filth. His fatigue shirt is open and his tee-shirt has a dark-red stain, almost black, right in the center of his chest. In the center of the stain is a small hole.

There doesn't seem to be that much blood for a man who was shot through the heart. I guess it was quick.

What was this guy's name? I remember him because of his size and that he was a Staff Sergeant.

I remember seeing him this morning as we passed by on our way out. He said something to Taylor or Grady or someone.

What's his name?

The rest of the way up to the LZ is a step-by-step struggle. I need to hold on to the poncho with both my hands to support the weight of the lifeless body. I have only my legs to pull my ruck, my share of the burden and myself up through the mud and over the obstacles. The strain on my legs and my twisted around body are secondary though. It's the vacant unchanging stare on the Sergeant's face as it jostles along next to me that wears most on the frayed remnants of my spirit. This Sergeant, this big man, this young man, not so different from myself, died out here in this nowhere place. Alive, thinking and hopeful one minute. Strong, able to endure, willing to persevere until an unseen, unheard little bullet penetrated the most vital of his physiological structures. Everything stopped. Everything came to an end.

I wonder if there's more to it. I wonder if it really is that final. I remember something. I remember Frank Rivetti.

N N N N

My fraternity brother, Rick Wright introduced me to Father Thom a week after Frank died. Steve Pickel, John Cort and I went along with

Stars and Stripes and Shadows

Rick to the Episcopal Church that Rick attended. Rick told us that Father Thom was a good guy and would be willing to perform a memorial service for all of Frank's friends. He wanted to meet some of us and get to know more about Frank first. The four of us were probably Frank's best friends in January of 1967 when he drowned. Frank, Steve, John and several others, along with their girlfriends drove up to a beach house that Steve's parents owned in Ventura on that unusually warm Sunday. I couldn't go for some reason and didn't find out about Frank until seven o'clock that night, just before the beginning of our weekly fraternity meeting, which I was to preside over as President. Rick called me and told me that Frank had gone out too far, got caught in the rip tide and disappeared into the rough surf. They tried to get out to him. They got a lifeguard boat out there as quickly as they could to search for him. He was gone.

Frank was Catholic. His parents, who we all knew, were traditional Italian Catholics who would naturally look to the church for comfort, for reason, for purpose. The Church could offer an explanation for why their nineteen-year-old son was taken from them. We all went to the funeral Mass for Frank. It was an orthodox Mass; Latin liturgy, ritual prayers. Those of us uninitiated in the religion didn't understand anything but the tears, his family's grief and the shared sense of loss. Rick was more spiritual than the rest of us and needed something more to explain and reduce the loss. He needed his own religion; his own church and he wanted his friends with him.

We met Father Richard Thom in his office at the church three days after Frank's funeral. He was a young man, maybe thirty, married and a father of a baby girl. He was casual, relaxed and friendly. He wanted to know about Frank, about us and he wanted us to know about him.

Father Thom referred to himself as a "retread." He was born and raised into the Catholic Religion. He valued it. He took it seriously, but he also found some of it to be too impersonal. He found the Episcopal Church to be the best of both worlds for him. He felt that it offered the traditions and rituals that afforded easy connections with the realm of the spiritual, the realm of higher existence, the realm of God. He found also, that it allowed a greater measure of freedom to him to doubt and explore and to minister more on a personal level. He was not yet an official Priest of the Church. His ordination ceremony was coming

Tim Haslam

up in March.

We talked for a couple of hours that afternoon, over coffee and occasional cigarettes in the relaxed atmosphere of this man's office. He didn't preach or proselytize. He had little interest in or motivation to convert anyone's beliefs or shepherd anyone into the fold. He listened. He shared. He made us feel better. He told us candidly that he wasn't sure himself about much of the doctrine of the Church, about many of the absolutes of the Faith. He was sure that it worked for many of the people he came in contact with. For them, the beliefs were something he could use to connect with them, to help them. That was his mission, to help his fellow human beings as they search for meaning in the events of their lives, nothing more. There was nothing contradictory or fraudulent for him in using the structure of his chosen religion as the vehicle for his contribution. He didn't have an explanation for why Frank drowned that day. He couldn't promise with any certainty what happened to Frank or Frank's soul. He felt in his own mind, his own heart, his own soul that whatever happened was a natural thing and that Frank and all of us were forever connected to something bigger than ourselves.

Father Thom's memorial service later that week for all of Frank's friends gave us a chance to reflect on Frank and what he was and what he meant to all of us in a way that we all could understand. The tears were still there and the grief and the sense of loss. Whatever our own personal beliefs were, we were all bonded together a little more closely that day. Many of us had known Frank since High School where he was a star football player and a popular kid.

It was good to be with friends that pleasant sunny afternoon, dressed up and clean. Celebrating our remembrances and experiences with the friend we would never see again. For many of us this was our first experience with death.

I don't know that I can get this guy all the way up to the LZ. He's getting heavier. The fabric of the poncho is getting slippery in the rain. The others are feeling the same. We have to get him back though. We can't leave his death out here. I wish I could think of his name.

Chapter 12

Once More Into the Breach, Dear Friends, Once More

HASLAM, TIMOTHY L
US56713762
A+
EPISCOPAL

I study my dog tags as I lounge up on top of the bunker. The intermittent clouds have kept the afternoon pleasant here at Dak To. We've been brought back to reinforce the forward support base as the Division thinks Charlie is likely to attack here soon, in force. We're deployed back along the same section of perimeter that we were at several months ago when we were last here. The place is the same. The same amenities; hot showers for the first ten men in line, hot meals, clean clothes, no underwear, haircuts, cool beer, candy from the PX and mail.

We've had little to do since we arrived yesterday. We've been able to clean up, clean our gear, rest, read and write. I found two extra shoe strings and have tied them tightly around the outside of my fatigue pants, just below my knees as a way to prevent leeches from getting any further up my anatomy. I'll wear these this way for the rest of the time I'm in Vietnam.

A lot of new guys joined us today and there's lots of time to indoctrinate them with our stories. Mike Ferlik, Pat Sanderson, John Batson, one of the guys in Ferlik's squad and I are sitting around reliving things for the benefit of two of the new guys assigned to Six-Two Platoon; Marion Valentine and Robert Miller. I'm not paying too much attention though. I'm still thinking about the last few days, about what leeches are capable of doing, about the crying baby and the man with the hole in the back of his head and about Sergeant-what's-his-name. I still think about Frank Rivetti's dying and about Father Thom's ordination.

Rick and John and I went down to a big cathedral in downtown Los Angeles on a Saturday morning to attend the ceremony that officially recognized our friend Richard Thom as a representative of the church. It was an impressive affair with throngs of dressed up people, robed Bishops and Priests, wine, wafers, prayers, rituals and words of hope and encouragement. I felt good being there. I felt good that someone like Father Thom was being accepted into this organization. I still didn't understand a lot of the liturgy but felt as though I could make of it what I wanted. It was a celebration. It was faith and humanity joined together.

✴ ✴ ✴ ✴

"You have to put something on there," the PFC behind the stamping machine insists. "Just pick a religion or pick "No Preference" but you have to have something there."

I'd like more time to evaluate my options before I have my faith permanently identified on my dog tags. I'd like to understand the ramifications and the consequences of such a declaration. I've been in the Army only a few days, herded from place to place, line to line, hurried along by impatient people ordering me to stand, move and answer. This seems like its pretty important…more so than my shoe or hat size. But, it's probably not the time or place where most young men make the final decision about their religious preference. "No Preference" seems pretty risky considering what I'm doing and where I'm most likely going.

"C'mon, c'mon…what's it gonna' be?"

"Um…OK…Episcopal. I remember that Richard Thom was an Episcopal Priest. I guess that's what I'll be.

✴ ✴ ✴ ✴

"We lost a guy three days ago. We were out humpin with Delta Company and a sniper got him right through the heart," Sanderson tells the new guys, slamming home the reality of what this place is all about for these people who were back home in the USA last week. They're think-

Stars and Stripes and Shadows

ing about where they were three days ago. They're thinking that death is close. They're wondering where they will be three days from now. They don't yet know the shit but know that they're heading into it.

"What happened?" Miller asks.

"The sniper fired a short burst at a group of guys from Delta Company that were coming up to join us. One of the Delta guys was the luckiest guy on the planet. The first bullet hit him right in the helmet, didn't touch his head though, but hit him with enough force to flip him up in the air. One of the next rounds hit him in the back of his heel as his leg was flying around. It's the million-dollar wound. He's out of the shit for a long time and he's got a souvenir helmet with a bullet hole in it. The other guy wasn't so lucky. The bullet hit him square in the heart…never knew what hit him."

"Shit man, one guys that lucky and the other guys dead," Miller says. "I guess there's nothing you can do."

"It's God's will," Batson says.

John Batson is a good guy, a straight arrow, a friendly, well-mannered sort. One of the few out here who has enough engrained discipline to avoid the profane language and the vulgar responses to everything. Batson is devout in his own religious beliefs. He's a Christian Soldier and has all things clearly separated into the good and bad, the right and wrong, the black and white, the us and them. He does God's work and what ever happens is God's will. He knows that many of the rest of us don't see things quite the same way as he does. He thinks we will all see the light some day. He keeps his proselytizing to a minimum though.

God's will? I think to myself. Can it really be that simple? I don't think I can blame God so easily for all of this. I don't think we can absolve ourselves and our leaders and the human race of any responsibility, any complicity and just pretend that God is behind it all. I think people brought this on. I think people made decisions, exercised judgments, chose the alternatives they thought would be best. I think that there is such a thing as free will. I think that we make mistakes sometimes when we interact within this complex world. My faith says that we learn from our mistakes and that we try not to repeat them. I don't know if I'm right or if my thinking is better than Batson's. We're both out here in the shit. Either of us could be next. God's will or man's free will.

Tim Haslam

It's the same shit for both of us

N N N N

For Six-Two Platoon, the few days we spend at Dak To result in a transformation of the unit. Four new guys join us but, more significantly, four guys leave us. Sergeant Taylor and Steve Stevens are close enough to their DROS dates to be pulled back to Pleiku. They've made it. They've survived. There leadership will be missed. They will leave a big hole in the Platoon. Bob Price has somehow managed to get himself accepted as the next Bravo Company clerk, largely because he knows how to type. He put in the application when he was coming back from his R&R and solicited help from Lieutenant Falck to pull some strings and make it happen. Price is on his way back to base camp too, to spend the rest of his tour at Camp Enari, not fully out of the shit but out of the boonies at least.

"Well, I guess the Battalion wants me to lead the Recon-Platoon," Lieutenant Riley tells us. "It's the kind of assignment I've really wanted and a good opportunity for me. I'll miss you guys. You all do a great job and know your shit. If any of you are interested in joining Recon, I'd love to have you."

"When are you leaving, sir?" I ask him, wondering about the timing and the next officer that will replace him.

"Today...now...the Recon Platoon is out west of here someplace. I'll be flying out to join them in about an hour. Not much time for goodbyes."

Packages from home, one from Nancy and one from Rosemary take my mind off the changes taking place within the Platoon. There are lots of good things within the rumpled cardboard boxes. There's only a short note though within the package from Rosemary. She hopes I'm OK. She hopes I like the stuff in the package. There's nothing about her, nothing about us. There's nothing to refresh the images or the feelings. There's nothing to take me back somewhere and little to beckon me into the future, to pull me out of this lonely empty place. I've reached the lowest point in my life as I sit here within this musty bunker doing the only things available for me to do...think, wonder...yearn. Home is so far away...changing, evolving without me. Things here are

Stars and Stripes and Shadows

changing, evolving with me. My friends and family here are separating from me. The people I learned from, the people who taught me how to endure and cope, to persevere and adapt are moving on, moving away, moving out. Other people's faces linger in my mind. Sad, vacant faces without color, without life. Faces locked into a final blank stare, looking perhaps for something beyond the wilderness that has absorbed their last breath. I can't tell myself that *it-don't-mean-nothin'*.

И И И И

"Shit Doc, who's side are you on?" I hear Elmer ask. He's two men up in front of me in line. All the Bravo Company medics have divided up the Company on this clear hot afternoon and are performing one of their periodic check ups of the grunt resources. They look over all the exposed areas of flesh, looking carefully at the open cuts and scrapes, the festering sores and the accumulated jungle rot patches. They dispense gallons of Merthiolate as the primary weapon against all of these conditions. Each application met with the same general unappreciative response from the victims of the stinging treatment.

"What's going on here?" Doc Hayes asks me as he examines the various forms of tissue damage embroidered along my left arm. He's focused on my hand though, particularly the puffy dark section just below the second knuckle on my index finger.

"I think it's a bamboo splinter," I tell him, hoping that the explanation will be consistent with the usual Merthiolate remedy.

"How long has that been there?" Big Doc asks, pressing his large fingers in and around the knuckle.

"A few weeks I guess."

"Why didn't you say something about this, can't you see that it's infected?"

"I thought it would heal itself. I think it's been getting better."

"Yea, right…when we have to cut your finger off it'll be better. OK, we're gonna have to get that out of there."

Hayes begins the reparations by pouring a pint or so of hydrogen peroxide over my hand, preceded by a lie about how it won't hurt. Then, he makes several attempts to grasp some part of the buried bamboo splinter with a pair of tweezers. His large hands are particularly adept with these, but still he seems able to grasp only bits of still connected

Tim Haslam

flesh, each tug sending another little shock of pain back up my arm.

"This ain't get'n it," he declares after a few more probes, "I'm gonna have to cut that out."

The sun seems to have dropped down out of the sky to a position much closer to me. Its heat and brightness have increased greatly as Hayes makes the first little slice down through the darkened flesh. I keep a close eye on Doc's work until I have to deal with the sweat pouring off my forehead.

"Jeez, Doc...how long is this going to take," I ask as the world around me starts to take on a sort of fuzzy look. I don't really want to look too closely anymore at the excavation going on within my finger.

"This thing's way down in there. Sorry. I've almost got it now."

"Damn!" is all I can say as the rinse off with Merthiolate jolts me back into full consciousness.

"Let that air out a little bit and then I'll bandage it up. Next time don't let anything like that stay in there that long."

"Yea, OK...next time.

N N N N

"Here they come," Bollman says, pointing out beyond the barbed wire to three Honda motor bikes churning through the dust.

"Who are they?" I ask, watching as the three bikes come to a stop at the edge of the wire across the cleared expanse of the protective zone. It's actually pretty obvious who they are and what they want.

"Boom-boom girls...local whores and their pimps," Bollman says, maintaining his aloof, non-commissioned-officer perspective about the approaching females seeking to rent their bodies to the American grunts.

"Hey, G.I....you wan boom boom?" The female voice yells over to Grady's guys in the bunker to our right. "Numba one boom boom!"

"How much?" someone over there asks.

"Fi dollah."

"I don't think we can get out to where you are...sorry."

"Is OK, we come there," the spokesperson for the group responds. The three girls, two dressed in traditional long white ao dai's and conical hats, the other in jeans and a silk shirt are now standing in front of their chauffeurs. From this distance it's impossible to evaluate the offered

Stars and Stripes and Shadows

goods much beyond their gender. They're small, skinny females, the one doing the talking is enthusiastic and assertive, the other two remain quiet, uninvolved in the marketing and negotiations.

Grady's guys huddle up to consider the possibilities, the logistics and the pricing...why not?

"OK," is all that's said to close the deal. From my observation point on top of our bunker next door I'm wondering how these three little women are going to maneuver through the wire, flares and mines that are woven all through the ground separating them from their customers. Bruce and I watch in almost stunned disbelief as the three girls sprint forward; jumping, ducking, dodging like broken field runners as they romp through our defenses as though it were some giant hopscotch game.

"Did you see that?" I ask Bruce, knowing that he did. "How the fuck did they do that? It's like they knew the way through."

"Yea...it kind of makes you wonder who else knows the way through. It makes me wonder if the three assholes back on the Honda's are really VC, using the girls to scout the route in here."

"Shit, man. I can't believe they could do that so easily. Is it OK for them to be in here?"

"Fuck, no! Here comes Grady," Bruce says diverting my attention to the always-stern squad leader, heading back toward the bunkers from the center of the complex.

"This should be entertaining," Bollman advises as we anticipate Grady's upcoming interaction with his squad and their guests.

Grady didn't see the three women slip into his bunker. He doesn't yet know that the men of his squad think that they're about to be entertained in ways long denied to them. Inside the bunker just ahead of him, the introductions are taking place, the goods are being sized up, the numbers on the tendered Military Payment Certificates are being tallied up, and the order of activities to come is being worked out.

By my watch it was about twenty seconds between the time that Grady entered the bunker and the time the three girls made their exit and sprinted back through the impenetrable array of our defenses.

"G.I.'s numba ten," shouts out one of the Honda assholes, gesturing energetically with the middle fingers of both his hands. The girls climb onto the backs of the motorbikes, take hold of their disappointed

397

Tim Haslam

male chaperones and the whole irritated little troop scuttles off on the gargling Hondas back toward the village.

"I don't think I've been out here that long," I tell Bollman.

"No shit, that stuff's pretty bad. If Grady hadn't come along when he did, you can bet that Doc would be doing a brisk business in tetracyclene next week. Save it for R&R, you get a lot more for your money and the girls are clean." Again, Staff Sergeant Bollman has sound advice to offer a subordinate.

N N N N

It's been just over a month since we were introduced to Lieutenant Riley back up on Ranger's Roost. No one was too happy to have a replacement for Lieutenant Falck then. Riley, however had credentials; Green Beret, Ranger, experience in the Nam. It didn't take Riley long to confirm his abilities and to earn our respect. He was a good guy too. He had a good sense of humor. He was easy to be with. He knew his shit.

This guy doesn't know shit is my first reaction.

First Lieutenant Grossman is tall, looking more studious than athletic. He's clean shaven. He's too clean, his hair is too short. He wears Army issue glasses. This is his first day in the boonies of Vietnam; in a combat zone. His only command experience came at Fort Benning where he served as a training officer for six months. He earned most of his officer qualifications at ROTC at the University of Missouri. He's no Riley. He's no Falck. My reaction to the newest-Six-Two has less to do with who or what he is than who and what I've become. I'm too weary to be tolerant or charitable and too worn down to be optimistic. It's all I can do to try and be friendly. My feelings are no different than the other veterans of this Platoon as Bollman introduces our new officer. Grossman has his work cut out for him.

There seems to be some standing rule that new Platoon Leaders get the next assignment. Grossman's first opportunity to lead his men in combat comes three days after joining us at Dak To. The Company was brought back up to Firebase 30 yesterday, to patrol around this area again. The good news for us is that it's familiar territory. The bad news is the rain is pretty constant. This morning, the Lieutenant is to

Stars and Stripes and Shadows

personally lead a squad-sized patrol out to the northeast. Our job is to follow one of the old trails eastward until we come to an intersection with a newer trail that is thought to branch off to the south about two klicks out from the firebase. Once we find the trail junction, we're to bring in artillery fire to register the trail junction as a target.

The newest-Six-Two fills us in on the mission as it was explained to him by Captain Hilton, goes over the route on the map and listens intently to our remembrances of the area from our prior visits four months ago. There's no outward manifestations of excitement showing on Grossman, as were obvious with Riley when he was about to launch out into action. For this young man the test is about to begin. He's wanted this for one reason or another. He's been trained at the University for this. He's passed muster as a leader during his tenure at Fort Benning, overseeing the exercises of sleepy, clueless recruits. But, Gerald Grossman knows, more than anything else, that he's the only man here who has never taken a step out into the jungles of Vietnam, into the range of snipers with AK47s, into the traps and ambushes that our adversaries prepare for us. And, Lieutenant Gerald Grossman knows too, that he is the only man here who is officially in charge.

The Lieutenant's nearly as tall as I am and I can see, as I follow along behind him down through the first few hundred meters of our patrol that he too is being snagged by the higher vines and branches that the shorter point man can't reach with his machete.

"Why don't you let me go first, sir? I've got my own machete for clearing things higher up. Until you came along, nobody else seemed to notice that there were things growing up here."

"OK, thanks. Maybe I should get one of those for myself," he says, seeming to appreciate that I'm reacting to something we have in common.

"Just let me go first. I kind of like hacking away at this stuff. It helps take my mind off the ground. If you want a turn, just let me know."

"OK, lead the way. I'll keep an eye on your technique. If it looks like you're really having fun, I may give it a try."

Another hundred meters along, Grossman takes his first fall into the shit, his feet sliding out from under him stepping too quickly down

Tim Haslam

over a knot of roots.

"You won't be the last one to do that today," I say to him, extending out the butt of my rifle for him to grab onto. I don't want him to feel bad for going down and yet I'm glad for some reason that it happened to him first this morning, before me; that I'm helping him up before he has the chance to help me.

In about an hour we come to the old trail. It's a wide, well warn track, that's been around for a long time. At this particular point the trail seems to be weaving along the side of one of the finger ridges. The ground rises up quickly to the right and drops quickly off to the left, both sides thick with vegetation.

"I guess we're going to have to follow the trail for awhile. It seems to be too thick on either side for us," Grossman says, knowing of the dangers that trails pose.

"Right, sir, I don't see that we have a choice. Maybe I should call in our position."

"Good idea. Let's get a reading on where we are."

The Lieutenant's pretty methodical with this work. He checks his watch, determines how long we've been gone, estimates our rate of travel, orients his map to his compass and traces with his finger what he thinks has been our route down.

"I make us right about here," he says with surprising confidence.

"Yes, sir, I agree," I say, marking my own map with my pencil, noting the time. Since my detour into Cambodia I've learned to temper my intuition with compass measurements and time plots. Here, there is little doubt that we're close to where we think we are. There are no trails anything like this anywhere else around. The finger we came down on is also the only one that crosses the trail within this grid square. I've no doubt about our position.

The three men on the trail in front of me have stopped and are gathered around studying something down on the ground.

"Take a look at this, sir." Bennis says to us as we reach the little group. At his feet is an incongruous looking tangle of branches and vines, woven together, partially covered with dirt and leaves. The whole mass sags downward about four inches below the surface level of the surrounding trail. This little dent in the natural contour is enough to

Stars and Stripes and Shadows

alert the grunts.

"What do you wanna do, sir? It's either a punji-pit or a spider hole," Bennis declares.

"I don't think they'd put a spider hole in the middle of a trail," Lamberti responds. "Whatever it is, I'd be pretty careful about opening it up."

"Why don't we just drop a frag on it and clear it out?"

"I don't think I want to let everybody around know that we're here just yet," Grossman says.

"Cut a couple of long bamboo poles and let's see if we can get the cover off that way."

Bennis and Lamberti quickly comply and within a minute each has a thick pole about ten feet long. Working together, as far from the hole as they can get they prod and nudge at the edge of the cover closest to them until the plug yields a little and slides away from them leaving a gap at the front edge. Then it's easy for them to pry up the cover and flip it out of the way on the far side.

"Wait a second," I say as the others start forward to get a peak down into the pit. I pick up two golf-ball sized rocks and lob them down into the hole in front of us hoping they'll trigger anything that might be set down there. Nothing hidden down in the hole reacts to the rocks and so we all cautiously inch up to the edge and peer down in. About four feet down is a matrix of bamboo spikes held fast into the ground at the bottom, the sharpened ends pointing upwards.

"Stepping into that would ruin your whole day, wouldn't it?" says Lamberti, imagining, along with the rest of us, what this trap would do to the flesh of our legs as we broke through the disguised covering. I think about the one little stake that got me in the foot and about the gook shit that the points are probably dipped in.

Ruin your day is right!

"I'm a little surprised that they would have let this deteriorate like this," observes Grossman. "It wasn't going to fool anybody the way it was."

"It looks like maybe they've split this area, sir. Didi'd off to somewhere else. There's no sign that anything's been on this trail for a while either," I offer hopefully, "but, it's probably not too good of an idea for us to stand here and gawk at this too much longer. We're easy marks

Tim Haslam

right here."

"Right," the Lieutenant acknowledges, scanning around at the surrounding vegetation, realizing that a hundred unseen snipers could be within a few meters of where we are, "let's go."

A few bends of the trail further down, the ground on the lower slope opens up enough for us to get off the trail, allowing us to take a parallel path through the safer virgin forest ground. In another forty minutes we find the other trailhead, leading off somewhere to the south. The newest-Six-Two and I carefully go over our maps and confirm our position.

"It looks like it might be clear enough back up on that little finger for us to set up and call in the mission," I say to the Lieutenant, pointing to a spot back about thirty meters from where the trails join. From there, we can set up a little defensive perimeter and walk the artillery rounds in from a safe distance out to the southeast.

"OK, we'll set up there. I'll figure out the coordinates for the first round."

"Trigger-Six, this is Eight-Two-Six-Two-Charlie. Over."

"Eight-Two-Si....oo...Char.... you're bre...ng up.. ver."

"Roger, Trigger-Six...wait one. I'm gonna put up my long stick. Over."

"I don't know about this, sir," I tell Grossman. "My signal's not very good. Way down here, in this weather, they may not be able to get us."

"How strong is your battery? Do you have a fresh one?"

"This one was new this morning. I have another new one, but I don't think it's the battery. Maybe, it's the frequency. Maybe another channel will work better...I'll try."

"Six-Charlie, this is Six-Two-Charlie. Commo check. Over."

"Six-Two-Charlie, this is Six-Alpha-Charlie. I hear you...weak but OK. How me? Over."

"Roger, same, same. We're having trouble picking up the signal on fire-push. How about relaying for us? Over."

"OK, Six-Two-Charlie...give me the info. I'll send it over to the redlegs. Over."

The Lieutenant wants to bring the first round down three hundred

Stars and Stripes and Shadows

meters off to the southeast and adjust subsequent rounds in at fifty-meter intervals until they're hitting fifty meters beyond the trail intersection. Then we'll give them a final "drop fifty and mark as target," then we can pack up and go home. I give Wee John the first coordinates along with a request for one round of high explosive.

"Wait one, Six-Two-Charlie. I'll let you know when they shoot. Over."

"Shot out. Over," Wee John declares after a pause of about three minutes.

"Rog. Shot out. Over."

"It's on the way. Listen up," I tell the men circled around me, all anxious to get this over with and to get back to the comforts of the firebase.

"Hey, Reynoso...how about it...did you hear anything?" I yell out toward Raphael Reynoso, one of the new guys whose come along with us and is positioned furthest out toward the target zone. There's been ample time for the 105mm projectile to arc its way through the dreary mountain air and explode into the ground. I didn't hear anything.

"I don't know, man. I think I heard something but it was, like way off...way out that way...just sort of a muffled kind of a sound."

"Tell 'em to drop a hundred," Grossman says.

I pass on the adjustment request and wait again.

This time we all hear it. It's just as Reynoso described it, a muffled sort of sound, hardly characteristic of an explosion. But with the ground this saturated and the heavy air...maybe. If it is, it's still way too far off.

"Drop another hundred."

"Six-Alpha-Charlie, this is Six-Two-Charlie. They're still way over. Drop one hundred. Over."

"Ro..er, dro...undred. Ov.."

"..ot out! O.r."

"Alright, it's on the way and I'm losing the signal from up there. I hope this one's a lot closer."

There's a sudden rustling in the treetops just out in front of where Reynoso sits listening intently. The rustling was preceded by a conjoined whoosh of air and followed instantly by a dull thud into the

403

Tim Haslam

ground.

"What the fuck, man!" yells out a startled Reynoso, reflexively pulling himself back toward us and away from the source of the thud. "That thing landed right out there in front of me."

"It's a dud," I offer back, reflecting both my surprise and irritation. "They've all been duds. They're not exploding."

"Six-Alpha-Charlie, this is Six-Two-Charlie. None of the rounds fired so far have gone off. They're all duds. That last one practically landed on top of us. What the hell's going on with those guys? Over."

"Roger ..at Six-.oo-Charl... Anybo.. .urt? Over."

"Negative, but something's wrong with these rounds. Somebody better figure it out. Over."

Wee John doesn't bother with a reply before he passes on the information to the battery guys. I'm sure by now the Captain's probably on his way over to investigate and have a chat with whoever is in charge of the battery firing out at his men. I try to move my radio and antennae around to see if that might somehow improve the reception.

"Six-Two-Charlie, this is Six-Alpha-Charlie. I guess they forgot to set the fuses or didn't set them right or something. They've got things squared away now. Over."

"They screwed up setting the fuses, sir. They're sorry...won't happen again," I relay to the newest-Six-Two, making almost no effort to disguise my attitude about the whole sorry mess. We've got to start over. We've got to sit out here in the fucking rain for at least another half hour and do it again before we can slog our way back up to the firebase. Days like this are taking their toll on my sagging spirits and everyday seems to be a day like this, and I don't give a shit if this new Lieutenant knows it.

The first two rounds from the re-run effort explode out at about where we anticipated they would. We can hear them clearly, even through the heavy rain that's now falling. We just need to step in one more time, verify the impact area and register the target.

"Six-Alpha-Charlie, this is Six-Two-Charlie. Drop five-zero. Over."

I wait several seconds for a reply from Wee John.

"Six-Alpha-Charlie, this is Six-Two-Charlie. Over."

Stars and Stripes and Shadows

Still no reply.

"Any Eight-Two station this is Six-Two-Charlie. Come in. Over."

"Any Eight-Two station this is Six-Two-Charlie. Get on the horn. Over."

"I'm not getting anything, sir," I tell Grossman. "I don't know if they can hear me or not but I'm not getting anything now. What do you wanna do?"

"Let's go back out to the trail. Maybe it's open enough out there to pick up the signal. Try a couple of the channels from out there."

"OK." I knew the Lieutenant would suggest that. It's the right thing to do, the obvious thing, but it forces me to drag my soaked body up onto my feet, exposing myself to another wave of cold shocks as the fabric of my drenched fatigues redirects much of the pooled water down my collar and sleeves. *Let's just get out of here. Let's just go. Haven't we screwed around with this long enough?*

I try again from the middle of the trail, fifty meters up from the junction, hoping that nobody at the firebase has decided to fire the next round without any confirmation from us...*nothing*. I go ten meters further down and try again, then fifteen, twenty and back up. No reply reaches my ANPRC25. I try the fire-push again and even take a chance with the Battalion frequency, thinking that Ranger or even Saladin, the Brigade Commander will answer. I wonder if he'll remember me as the same guy that strayed into Cambodia. Nobody answers. We're out of range. The atmospherics and the terrain are too much for the best efforts of the little transmitters. There are too many extreme undulations in the landscape, too many clusters of dense plants, too many shifts in pressure gradient and too much water in the air for the radio waves to cover the distance in a cohesive way.

"Nothing, sir."

I can tell that Grossman is in the throes of his first command dilemma out here. He hasn't completed his mission. He's one artillery round and fifty meters away from finishing the job as the book requires. He doesn't want to have to go back and explain to Captain Hilton, even if our alibi is pretty compelling. He's unsure about the impact of his next decision on the men with him. Is it OK to quit and go home under the circumstances, or should he persevere and find another way to achieve the goal. Maybe we should just try and wait it out. If the rain

Tim Haslam

lets up maybe we can re-establish contact and get it done right. What if the rain doesn't let up?

I know what Lieutenant Falck and Lieutenant Riley would do... they'd say; "fuck this, let's pack it up and get out of here." They'd say that, because of their experience out here in the shit and because they know that they have the trust of their men and their commanding officer. They know, from their own experience how to deal with the consequences of their decisions. Maybe, on their first patrols they were different. Maybe they didn't know so much then.

"Let's stay a while longer and see if the rain let's up. Keep trying the radio."

Goddamn it! I think to myself in reaction to what I was sure he would say.

"Sir, I think we'd better head back. They don't know what's happened to us. They don't know if they should send out the cavalry or what. Can't you plot the trail junction position from that last round?" I suggest to him, the rest of the men around us nodding in agreement with my assessment. We all think we've done enough on this stupid assignment.

"We'll give it fifteen more minutes," Grossman says coming to an internal compromise with the logic of my argument and the intrinsic desire on his part to ensure that he's made every effort to fulfill his assigned task.

"OK, sir. I'll keep trying." *I can last fifteen more minutes.*

Nothing changes in the next fifteen minutes. The rain continues to penetrate down through the jungle onto us and the radio waves sent searching for us from up on Firebase-30, pushed along at fifty-eight-point-nine-five kilocycles, fail to reach my radio antennae with sufficient strength to overcome the steady state squelch. I have no way of knowing if my own transmissions are reaching anyone. We've done everything we can do. If the redlegs hadn't screwed up with the fuses on the first three rounds fired we'd be done—mission accomplished. If it weren't for the rain and the jungle we could confirm our situation and our decisions. If it weren't for the inadequacy of the ANPRC25 radio transmitters we'd be connected with our leadership. If it weren't for...

We'd better not get lost now! I think to myself. Without the radio

406

Stars and Stripes and Shadows

we're cut off from everything. If we run into Charlie now, we're on our own. If anybody gets hurt, it'll be up to us to keep them alive and get them out. I don't know if I should trust this new Lieutenant with the land navigation work, even though he seems careful and diligent or rely more on my own sense of direction. I'm not sure that he's too comfortable anyway with his RTO second-guessing his interpretations even if I have more experience out here—even if I've been to Cambodia.

"I make us right about here, sir," I tell Grossman as he surveys the surrounding landscape from an opening on the ridge crest that we're climbing. "Does that seem right to you?" *Let's see how he reacts to my observations.*

"Yea, it sure does. I'm just not sure of the best route up from here. It looks like it would be about a half a kilometer shorter if we went up this way," he says, pointing up toward our left, "but it also looks steeper than if we stayed along the side of this slope until we reach this finger here. What do you think?"

OK, good...the newest-Six-Two wants my opinion.

"I'd keep to the right, sir, stay on the side of this slope. If we start up that way, within a few meters, everything's going to look exactly the same. We won't be able to see shit. If we start to stray off course we won't know it until we reach the top of the ridge and we could end up anywhere from here to here," I tell him, pointing out the possibilities on his map.

"I think it'll be faster this way too."

I notice the sweat on the Lieutenant's face washing through the first layers of filth building up. His glasses must be difficult to see through, as they too seem to be magnets for moisture and airborne particles. Maybe it's because we're heading back instead of out, but my misgivings and my resentment about this guy are lessening. Perhaps I still have enough energy and strength to look a little below the surface. *Maybe he's not so bad. He's trying. He wants to do the right thing. What do I want?*

∦ ∦ ∦ ∦

This one will be called Firebase-18. It's a round-top, grass-covered peak with only a few trees to cut down and no bamboo. The grass and the gentle slope of the hilltop have facilitated quick drainage of the rain-

Tim Haslam

water and the soil down below the surface layer is easy to dig through and easy to fill up our sandbags with. The sun's been with us for most of the two days that we've been here and our work fashioning bunkers, pits and trenches has been at a relaxed pace, performed shirtless under the clear sky. It's almost pleasant here. I get to know some of the new guys better as we work together digging and laying out the concertina wire. By late afternoon of the second day we've completed our own bunkers and the perimeter defenses and are working on the pits and walls for the 105s that are to be brought in tomorrow. Along with the battery of artillery will come their mess-unit. This means hot food for us...something to live for.

The break in the rainy weather has given us a chance to dry out everything as much as the humid air will allow. The nights too have been clear and dry, balmy and pleasant. Doc, Ed and I have chosen to sleep outside, setting up our air-mattress and poncho-liner beds up on top of our bunker. Even our shifts on radio watch are relatively pleasant with the great expanse of star-studded sky to study. I hope we stay here for a long time. I hope the monsoons take a long break.

"The water's hot. If you guys are ready for coffee, get your lazy asses down off of there," I tell my two bunkmates who are in no hurry to start another day in the shit.

Ed makes enough of an effort to pull himself upright and light a cigarette. Doc just roles over onto his back and rests his head on the interlaced fingers of his hands, taking in the unobstructed view of blue sky above him.

"I'll have mine in bed this morning, I think," Doc says. "My canteen cups over by my ruck...cream and a lot of sugar, please."

"What do I look like, your day-man?" I offer back, hoping my inflection will put a quick end to his fantasy. "I've been watching you two snore away the last three hours. Get your ass up before the omelets and croissants get cold...the Nam awaits."

"Sorry, I don't think I really want an omelet again this morning," Ed says, "I think I'll have pork slices and canned bread for a change and maybe some Chiclets."

"Yuck. I think I may just chew on my socks this morning," Doc responds, pulling himself fully upright. "That'd taste better."

Stars and Stripes and Shadows

In another few minutes Ed and Doc have joined me down at the side of the bunker, smoking and drinking coffee, contemplating what today's activities will entail. The drone of a helicopter approaching from the south catches our attention. It's a big Chinook with a 105 howitzer slung beneath it. Good, the battery will be put in place today, including their mess unit. We should get a hot meal tonight. Of course there will be more work for the grunts to do to earn a share of the prepared food. It will be our job to finish up any digging required to set the guns and to provide filled sandbags to encircle each of the five emplacements. Today will be a day of shoveling.

The CH47 veers slightly to the westward just before it reaches the hilltop we're on. It skirts the west side of the perimeter and then starts to head in toward the center bringing it right over our bunker. The rotor wash blows away everything that isn't firmly fastened down.

We should have seen this coming. We should have been able to figure out what was about to happen. But, we were so comfortable and relaxed watching the spectacle of the approaching chopper with its cargo and so intent on the promise of a hot meal later today that our guard was down. We were relaxed and comfortable right up to the point where our air mattresses and poncho liners took flight, joining all the other debris being swept off the surface of the firebase. The floppy substance of the poncho liners seems to keep them down near the ground as they flutter away off the bunker and tumble down toward the perimeter line. The air mattresses however follow more convoluted paths through the air turbulence. The first downward wash of air squirts the mattresses out and away from the bunker. A few meters out the air vortex catches the escaping green plastic balloons and lifts them straight up…five, ten, fifteen meters. Our twisting, curling beds are being buffeted through the air out toward the perimeter. By now Ed, Doc and I are giving chase, stumbling through the muddy ground, still being sandblasted by the air pressing down from the Chinook that's hovering up near the top of the hill, lowering down the dangling howitzer. The air mattresses seem to recognize that this may be their best chance to escape the shit and the smelly grunts that've enslaved them. They rise, fall, twist and jump away from the three of us until they've strayed too far. Until their fate is sealed, until the three grunts can only stand and watch their final seconds of life.

Tim Haslam

The concertina wire snags the three army issue mattresses in quick succession; Haslam's, Arter's, Charlebois'...rip...tear...pop. The wire may not always be a sufficient barrier against invading North Vietnamese Army regulars or local whores but it has proven to be a 100% effective means for preventing the escape of one of our few afforded comforts.

"Shit," is all I can say as I stare at the remains of my bed, hanging there limply, caught within the thorny barbs. I think of the scene in The Great Escape where Steve McQueen crashes his stolen motorcycle into the barbed wire and is hopelessly ensnared as his Nazi pursuers close in. "Shit," is probably what Steve's character was really thinking. He's going back to the prison camp. I'm going back to sleeping on the hard ground. *Shit! Goddamned Nazi helicopter!*

The second Chinook and Howitzer arrives a short while later, blowing in from the east this time. The fate of our bedding, witnessed apparently by much of Bravo Company, has provided a valuable lessen to everyone else. Extra efforts have been made throughout the base to secure all such valuable things before the next chopper tornados in. The rest of the Company will sleep comfortably tonight because of our sacrifice. No one however, thanks us.

Just like its predecessors, the fifth and last 105 dangles beneath the approaching Chinook. Apparently there are some last minute adjustments to be made to the destination emplacement and so the big bird pulls up and hovers just at the edge of the perimeter on the southwest side. The wily grunts over there are prepared and have secured everything of value within the confines of their bunkers. There's only one little glitch...engineers.

A detachment of U.S. Army Engineers has been up here with us, helping to design the firebase. We haven't been paying a lot of attention to them, thinking that they were really there to help. They may be the same Engineers who were with us back at FB25. The one's behind the phugas experiment. The required design work here apparently wasn't a full time job and the dedicated Engineers needed to busy themselves with useful endeavors. Once again their extra efforts involved a form of experimental weaponry. They didn't concoct this one however. The Army provided it. The Army catalog description for the object of their curiosity is E-8, 35mm Tear Gas Launcher. Our Engineers have taken

410

Stars and Stripes and Shadows

one of these units and carefully mounted it within the branches of a large tree rooted within the tangle of barbed wire on the southwest quadrant of our perimeter. To this, they have also carefully attached a trip wire. If Charlie were to attempt an infiltration from this side, they would encounter not only the usual array of trip flares and Claymore mines, but also the surprise release of sixteen small missiles containing the anti-riot gas. Charlie would be engulfed in the choking, stinging, vomit inducing gas. Their vision impaired by the watering response of their eyes, they'd be totally disoriented and easy targets for us. We would of course have our gas masks on.

The two spinning rotors on the top of the big "shit-hook" suck great volumes of mountain air from above and accelerate it all down onto the grunt domain below. Everything that's loose blows away and everything that's attached to something vibrates violently. Trip wires begin to oscillate in response to the vibrations. The oscillations transcend into harmonic motion. The harmonic motion evolves into ever expanding waves until the whiplash effect yanks the attached retaining cotter pins out of their receptacles setting off the triggering device for the flare or mine or E-8, 35mm Tear Gas Launcher.

"Gas...its gas!" Doc yells out as the cloud reaches us, following the series of little explosions spreading over the southern approach to the base. "Its tear gas," he manages to clarify through his coughing fits. Doc can barely keep his eyes open as he stumbles into the bunker in search of his protective mask.

"Where the fuck is my gas mask?" Ed inquires of no one in particular as he and I join Doc in a panicked effort to find our masks, the leading wisps of gas following us into the bunker. Already our throats are on fire and our eyes are watering profusely. Somehow I find the canvas pouch that contains my mask, attached to the side of my ruck. I pull it out and struggle to get it on. I haven't had this on since the day it was issued to me, months ago. My hair is much longer now. The black rubber straps grab at my hair as I try to pull the mask over my head. I can feel chunks of hair being pinched and rolled up into the rubber straps until they're being yanked out in clumps. Once the mask covers my face I realize that it's much too tight, pulling the flesh away from eyes and nose, adding to the discomfort. By now my mouth, throat, eyes and lungs are full of the cholorine-sulphur mixture. I can't stop coughing. I can't stop my eyes

Tim Haslam

from watering or my nose from running like an open faucet and I can't get my hands at anything trapped behind the suctioning mask. *I'm going to die in here! I'm going to suffocate in here!*

Barely able to breathe at all, I struggle back out of the bunker. Desperate for some relief, I try to see if I can determine the direction the plume of gas is moving. The clear plastic eye-pieces of the mask are now obscured with moisture from my perspiration as well as heavier remnants of the other fluids that are building up within the hot rubber muzzle. *I can't see anything through this. I can't breathe. Fuck this!*

I jerk up the mask, lifting it off my head without regard for the additional clumps of hair that are uprooted in the process. The air outside can't be any worse than the air trapped within the mask. *I need to be able to see. I need to find an avenue of escape.* By now the Chinook has churned its way up toward the last gun emplacement position and is waiting for people on the ground to direct the positioning of the gun. The air over on our side of the firebase is settling down and the remaining gas cloud seems to be following the shadow of the big helicopter up toward the center of the hill. With my mask now in my hand I run as fast as I can in my semi-blinded state down toward the perimeter wire to my left; Ed, Doc and several others following, pulling their masks off as they go. The first row of concertina wire defines the limits of our separation from the gas fumes. It's just enough. The air down here is clear and clean. An ever-increasing mass of grunts huddle together, most bent over, coughing, spitting or throwing up.

"What the hell was that?" someone in the group manages to ask between coughs.

"Another addition to our defenses, contributed by the Corps of Engineers."

"Damn, man…whose side are they on? Isn't there a bridge or something for those guys to be building somewhere? How about leaving the defenses to us! Damn!"

"That is some mother-fuckin bad shit, man!"

"These gas masks aren't worth a shit either, man! We've been humpin' these things for all this time and they don't do shit!"

"That thing would have been pretty effective against Charlie though…you'd have to admit," one of the optimists in the group observes.

Stars and Stripes and Shadows

"Fuck, man, I'll bet Charlie's sittin' out there right now watchin' us, laughin' his ass off."

Our analytic, debriefing dialogue continues for the next few minutes, until we've run out of ways to condemn the Engineers, until the flow of fluids has been slowed and our snail-tracked sleeves are heavy with collected mucus. We plod back up the hill, glad to be breathing the normal dank, humid air...anxious for a cigarette.

◢ ◢ ◢ ◢

"Seconds," a short man in a greasy tee shirt covered in an even greasier apron shouts out in the general direction of the grunts spread around outside the mess tent. Spaghetti, bread, butter, salad and chocolate milk comprise the menu for our first prepared meal in a month. It's great. Greater, because the evening is clear and balmy and there's been no indication that Charlie might be around to lob mortar rounds at us. The men of Bravo Company react quickly to the call for "seconds" and within a few moments a long line of grunts, still working through their ration of "firsts" has queued up. Doc and I are in no hurry, what we've already had is ample but as the line starts to shorten we find the temptation too great and take up our places at the end.

Captain Hilton and another officer, a Lieutenant from the artillery battery, come out of the mess tent together engaged in a relaxed conversation. The Captain takes notice of the line of men heading back toward the chow line and detours away from the Lieutenant who's on his way back up toward the FDC tent further up the hill. With his own mess kit in hand, Captain Hilton falls in line behind me.

"Did I hear the call for seconds?" he asks, a smile on his face.

"Yes sir, you did. We all did. I hope there'll be enough."

"Yea, this was pretty good tonight...the salad especially. I've really come to miss fresh vegetables."

For the next several minutes, as the line progresses slowly toward the open side of the tent the Captain, Doc and I chat casually. Prompted by some question from Doc, Hilton starts in telling us about some of his experiences at West Point. The Captain is a friendly good-humored man by nature and his anecdotes are entertaining. He's telling us about the time he and three of his fellow underclassmen were invited to join General Westmoreland, who was the commandant then, and his wife

413

Tim Haslam

for dinner at their residence, as was the tradition. He's telling us how one of his freshmen colleagues always ended his statements during the dinner conversation with a "no shit" closing validation. He remembers how uncomfortable he and his better-mannered fellows were each time the "no shit" declaration was expressed in front of the patient General and his gracious wife. What he remembers most however occurred late in the evening, during dessert when the loose-tongued plebe completed another short narrative without the usual vulgar ending punctuation. Mrs. Westmoreland, sensitive to the prior reactions of the General and the other three nervous neophytes, leans forward slightly and responds to the young man, in a casual, interested tone, "No shit?"

We're all laughing at the Captain's tale when Roy Houston, hurrying down from the inner-reaches of the firebase calls out to the Captain. "Sir, sir…Ranger's on the horn, sir…he needs to talk to you right now. You need to come back up."

"No shit," the Captain declares, still clinging to the white linen image of the Westmoreland dining room, hesitant to give up his place in the chow line.

"Did he say what he wanted me for?"

"I think he wants an update on the readiness here. I'm not sure though. I just talked with one of his RTOs."

The Captain shakes out the remnant food scraps from his mess kit, looks for a moment at Doc and me and then fixes his gaze on the now short line that remains between us and more fresh salad.

"Roy, tell the Colonel you couldn't find me," the Captain says to his messenger with a determined little smirk on his face. "I can get my ass chewed anytime…seconds are hard to come by."

"Right on, sir," I tell the Captain, appreciating the spirit of his appraisal.

Houston is completely unprepared for the Captains response. *How the hell is he going to tell a Lieutenant Colonel that he can't find his Captain within the confines of the little firebase.* Roy turns and starts back up the path contemplating the possible consequences of what's about to happen. *Maybe he should just get in line too. Maybe, he too should just take an ass chewing…on a full stomach.*

"Goddamn it," the Captain says after another few seconds of reflection. "All right, all right, I'm coming." With one last resigned shrug

Stars and Stripes and Shadows

the Captain abandons his place in line and his initial commitment to rebellion and follows a relieved Houston back up toward the expected "ass-chewing."

None of us at the end of the "seconds" line feel betrayed by our leader's failure to follow through with his declared insubordination. He had no choice. He had to go. But each of us appreciates for this one brief moment that Captain Hilton was just like us down at the core. The discomfort and depravation are taking their toll on the West Pointers just as surely as they are on the draftees. *Seconds **are** hard to come by!*

ℳ ℳ ℳ ℳ

"Hey, Riley's Recon Platoon's here," Mike Ferlik says as he joins me in the breakfast chow line. "They're up in one of those big bunkers up on top. I guess they're going to use this place for their home base for a while."

"Let's go see him after breakfast," I respond, hopeful that a reunion like this will break the monotony for a little while.

We find the old-new-Six-Two comfortably lounging within his bunker, boots off, cigarette dangling from his lip, cleaning the little Berretta pistol that he's always carried with him.

"Hey guys...what's happening?" the very relaxed Lieutenant says to us as we enter the bunker. He introduces us to three of his guys that are in the bunker with him. They're a pretty casual bunch. Riley fills us in on life in the Recon Platoon, clearly happy with his new role. He loves the independence. He loves being in charge of a little unit that moves around a lot and moves fast when they're out humping. It's kind of like his very own little army. I can tell that he's having about as much fun as anyone can out here in the shit. We fill him in on the same-old-shit experiences we've had since he left. None of us have any idea where we go next.

"You know I could use a good RTO," he says to me as he reaches over with his Zippo to light my next Marlboro. "If you're interested I'll bet I can get you transferred over here. The Recon Platoon gets first priority when it comes to personnel."

"Wow...that might be pretty good, sir," I say, surprised at the offer and unprepared for the possibility of a change like this. "That'd be great.

Tim Haslam

I guess I should talk to Lieutenant Grossman."

"Why don't you talk to Captain Hilton too, he'll have to approve the transfer. I'll talk to him too the next time I see him."

The newest-Six-Two doesn't seem too happy at my news. His reaction seems to reflect a sense of personal betrayal instead of any recognition that this might be an opportunity for me. He doesn't seem concerned so much with losing an RTO as with the possibility that I'm just the first of the veterans to tender a no-confidence vote in his leadership. Perhaps I was a little insensitive as I described the opportunity to work for my old boss again with such enthusiasm.

"You'll need to get the Captain's approval," is all he says in response. "I guess I'll have to think about how to re-arrange things here."

"You know I really need experienced people here in the Company," the Captain tells me after I explain Riley's offer. "Between now and the end of November I'm going to loose over thirty men to DROS. Both Falck and Riley spoke pretty highly of you and thought that you'd make a good squad leader some day. I've already got promotion orders signed for you to make Spec-4. They should be coming in any day. In November I can make you an E5, a buck-sergeant, if you stay here with the Company. But, if you really want this deal with Riley, I won't stand in your way. Think it over and let me know what you want to do."

The kudos from the Captain and his almost-promised promotion into the ranks of the non-commissioned officer realm add a new dimension of complexity to the issue. Being an NCO for the rest of my days in the Army carries with it a lot of benefits. Those three stripes on my sleeve would afford me a lot of privileges and a lot of respect—justified or not. Sergeants are treated way differently than enlisted men. *I'd better go back and tell Riley that I can't take him up on his offer.*

"Shit, if that's all that's standing in the way, I'm sure I can get you stripes too in November. There's nothing that says my RTO can't be an E-5," says Riley, pinging things back into confusion. "Think it over tonight and let me know tomorrow what you want to do."

"Recon's the way to go, man," one of Riley's guys adds as I head out of the cramped bunker. "This is so much better than being with a regular dog company."

Stars and Stripes and Shadows

Now what am I going to do. Two promises of promotion, each from men, superior Army officers, whom I like and respect. The Recon Platoon might just be the change I need to slow the cycle of deterioration that my body and spirit are undergoing. Being a squad leader though would be the first real opportunity I've had in my life to test my own leadership abilities. It seemed so simple and straight-forward when Riley first made the suggestion. Now I have a lot to think about. It's been a long time since I've had to make a decision about anything.

"We're moving out in the morning," says Lieutenant Grossman, interrupting my private mulling-over session outside our bunker. "We'll need to be ready at first light."

"We're not going out humpin' again, are we, sir?" Ed asks.

"No, they want us to build another firebase, somewhere north of here, up in the mountains above the Special Forces Camp at Dak Seang."

"We just finished this one. Can't Delta or Charlie Company dig out the next one? This place is pretty comfortable and nobodies taken a shot at us since we got here," I say, my tone an accurate reflection of my attitude. Everything we do seems like its temporary with no lasting value or purpose. We take some ground away from Charlie's control for a few days and then abandon it back to him a few days later. Bravo Company digs the holes and Delta Company comes along and occupies them. Alpha Company digs the holes and we come along and occupy them. We hump from mountain to mountain; up and down, never intending to stay anywhere, never finding value in any of the places we go. What difference is any of this making? What good is any of this doing?

"Haslam, since I guess you're going to be leaving us, I'm going to send you back to Grady's squad. Fernandez's going on R&R. You can take over his machinegun for the rest of the time you're with us," Grossman says to me, having apparently worked out the worst kind of punishment he could think of for my perceived disloyalty.

You've got to be shit'n me. Hump a machinegun?

A minute ago I was contemplating which offer of promotion was the most appealing; which would afford me the best opportunity; which of the men who seem to value my work I would most like to accommodate.

417

Tim Haslam

Now, suddenly I'm being demoted back down into the role of squad machinegunner. Kicked out of Platoon Headquarters; relegated back into the realm of nighttime LPs and perimeter guard. Just like a new guy, I'm being placed into a rifle squad and given the worst job. The newest-Six-Two is still the closest officer to me up the chain of command. He's the one who still has the power to make life even more miserable for me. He's choosing, for some reason, to do just that.

Ed and Doc are almost as shocked as I am at the Lieutenant's declaration, seeing clearly that the new Lieutenant's motivation is nothing more than retribution for my voiced appreciation for his predecessor. They see too that the new Lieutenant will wield his official power for his own purposes, to satisfy his own needs. He's no Falck or Riley or Collins or Hilton. He's not the kind of leader that anyone's going to risk their life for.

"Sir, I haven't made up my mind yet about leaving," I offer as my opening maneuver to avoid the machinegunner sentence. "The Captain wants me to stay with the Company. I told him I'd let him know tomorrow what I wanted to do."

"We'll be out of here tomorrow...building a new firebase somewhere. I've gotta get my Platoon ready. I need an RTO that I can count on for a while."

"Can I go and talk to the Captain now? Can you wait until I have a chance to talk with him before you do this?" I plead with him.

"OK, talk to him now. Let's get this straightened out now," he says, knowing that Captain Hilton's already taken an interest in the outcome. Perhaps he's becoming a little concerned that his own actions are going to become part of the issue to be discussed with the Company Commander.

"Sorry, sir," I say to the Captain after first apologizing for interrupting his moving preparations, "I really didn't think this thing with Lieutenant Riley was going to become a negotiation. He says that he can get me a promotion too in November. When this first came up this morning, I just thought it might be an opportunity to do something different. Now it's getting sort of out of hand. I'm not sure what I should do."

The Captain stops his ruck packing and looks at me. "So, you really

Stars and Stripes and Shadows

don't have strong feelings about going over to Riley's unit?"

"I don't know, sir...I guess not, although there are some things about it that sound pretty good."

"Alright, I'll make it easy for you...you can't go. I need you here. I'll let Riley know." The Captain's command decision has instantly solved the problem, although I'm left with a little sense of disappointment.

"Is there anything else?" he asks, returning his attention to the C-ration cans he's stuffing into his ruck.

"Well, sir, Lieutenant Grossman wants to send me back to Grady's squad as a machinegunner. I guess he wants to get another RTO."

"Bull shit," the Captain says making another command decision.

Chapter 13

Like Pigs in Shit

August 16th 1968

It's been a nearly five months since I climbed onto the back of the deuce-and-a-half truck back at Camp Enari and entered the shit world of the 4th Infantry Division grunts. *Seven months to go! How will I endure through seven more months of this? When will I ever get another full night's sleep? When will I be clean again? When will the little wounds and open sores ever heal? When will Charlie pick me?*

This morning it's my left leg that has my attention. It's that little red patch on the outside of my ankle, below the top of my sock, just above that little knob of bone that sticks out. It itches like crazy. The little circle of red that Doc thought might be ringworm the last time he took a look at it has expanded in diameter. It's now the size of a quarter. It feels good scratching it—maybe too good. I'm sure I'm not doing myself any good by digging my filthy fingernails into the flakey flesh at the surface. "Don't scratch it. You'll just make it worse." My mother would always admonish me when I reacted to mosquito bites the same way. Scratching at it is the only pleasurable thing I have too do though as I sit out here in the rain on the LZ, waiting for the men ahead of us to disembark on the string of Huey's that's shuttling us somewhere further north this morning. There isn't time for me to take my boot off and really examine the red blotch more carefully. *If I think about it later, maybe I'll have Doc take a look at it again.*

The monsoons are about at their peak here in August and today is typical…steady rain. High, dark clouds hang over the mountain peaks, darkening everything within the forested ridges and valleys. Lower puffs of clouds, connected to the ground with dark lines of falling water provide a slalom course for the pilot directing our UH1D helicopter up the valley of the Dak Poko. Our destination is in the mountains above the Dak Seang Special Forces Camp, about twenty-nine kilometers north of Dak To and ten kilometers east of the Laotian border. This camp, sitting in a little valley surrounded by high mountains may be the most isolated camp in Vietnam. On the west side of the valley is the Dak Poko and on the east is what's left of Route 14. Too much has happened to the road over the years of war for it to be of much use up here and the mountains and jungles that surround it make it too dangerous to risk valuable military vehicles on. Dak Seang has a little airstrip as it has to be supplied and supported from the air. Charlie's building up his forces around here again. Prisoners have been taken in the last week from the 101st NVA Regiment, a fresh unit in these parts. There's only one reason they would build up here —Dak Seang.

Firebase 31 was first dug into the top of Hill 925, about two and a half klicks north of the Special Forces Camp last May. A month later it was abandoned. Now, it seems to be of value again. Our job is to go back up there and resurrect the pits, trenches and bunkers, ready it for a battery of 105s and run reconnaissance and interdiction patrols around the mountain ridges that run from the valley of the Dak Poko up into the higher mountains to the west. A Company of CIDGs will join us once the base is secure and hospitable.

From the open side of our approaching Huey Hill 925 looks like a disaster scene. The old trenches, pits and bunkers are now just muddy depressions, filling up with the steady invasion of rain. Hundreds of tree poles, used to support the original bunkers are scattered over the entire surface, intermixed with an array of other army issue debris; old crates, twisted up sections of barbed wire, engineering stakes, bent sections of Marston-mat and a thousand shredded, decaying sandbags. No one seeing this can feel anything but dread and despair at the work that lies ahead. *We have to reconstruct a fire support base out of this?* We have to turn this exploded septic tank of a hilltop into a place suitable for civilized artillerymen and their cannons and for visiting Montagnard Strikers. We have to make a home for ourselves out of this garbage

Tim Haslam

dump. We have to do it today.

It's like trying to dig a hole in a lake. The ground is so saturated that our little shovels barely excavate out anything but water, and the falling rain washes off most of what does come up on the blade of the shovel. *This is never going to work!*

"We'll never get anywhere like this!" I declare, refusing to pour one more shovelful of muddy water into the sandbag that Doc is holding open for me. "We've gotta try something else!"

"He's right," Lieutenant Grossman, who seems to be letting by-gones be bygones this morning, acknowledges. "Let's see if we can't build up the sides with logs and then put a roof on it. Then we'll have to dig out the mud from inside." It's a fucking idiotic idea, but better than anything else that anyone can think of and there are plenty of large logs imbedded within the sludge all around us. We all struggle together, Ed, Bruce, Doc, the newest-Six-Two and I. Everything from our wastes down covered in the heavy mud and everything from the waste up awash in the fresher water falling dispassionately from the colorless sky.

At some point the effort becomes too much to bear along with the built up frustration and irritation. It becomes too much of a burden pushing the mud around with any serious hope of overcoming the elements to achieve our goal. The only way to get through this now is to revert back to the all-saving, all-encompassing philosophy of the Nam grunt...*it-don't-mean-nothin'*.

"Hey, I think you've got something on your boot," Doc says to me, starting the dialogue that will bring us all out of our mental despair. Everyone's attention is drawn down to my boots. We all have to laugh in response to Doc's understated observation. Actually, my boots are nowhere to be seen. My legs look like little tree trunks, upheld by burls of mud glued to the ground. The other's are all the same. We all look like we're growing out of the sludge of Hill 925.

"Thanks Doc. I think your shoe's untied," I respond as I attempt to lift my right leg up, resulting in a loud sucking sound.

"I understand we're going to have to stand inspection this after-noon. Who's got the Shinola?" Ed adds to our efforts at fighting back with the only weapons we have left; sarcasm, cynicism and adolescent

Stars and Stripes and Shadows

humor. "How about it sir, any truth to the rumor that the Donut Dollies will be coming out here today and that only those with clean uniforms, haircuts and shined boots can attend?"

"Sorry guys, actually the Donut Dollies were on that last Huey," says the Lieutenant, seemingly willing to participate in the juvenile banter. "They refused to get off here. They wouldn't accept the idea that the creatures slogging around down here were American soldiers. They didn't want to get their blue dresses dirty trying to entertain a band of primitive Neanderthals."

"Man, I thought the Red Cross was supposed to provide disaster relief," Bollman adds, watching his discarded cigarette butt disappear below the surface of the viscous ground. "If this isn't a disaster I don't know what is."

"How long has it been since you guys were back at base camp? When was the last time you had a real break?" Grossman asks, a measure of earnest concern detectable in his question.

"Five months for me, longer for the others," I answer first.

"No, I was on R&R a couple of months ago," Ed says, correcting me.

"I was there for one night about a month ago," adds Doc, further revising my statement. "I had to go back with one of our wounded men."

"Six and a half months for me but I'm going on R&R in two weeks," Bollman says, his face alternately reflecting the accumulated weariness of his first observation with the childlike hopefulness of his second.

"That long?" Grossman seems surprised. "Man, a month ago I was home."

The Lieutenant's perspective jars us out of our humorous mode and caroms our thoughts back to other images; distant reflections of things clean, dry, warm and safe. We can go on now with our shovels, pushing around the mud and water, disengaged from the here and now. Each of us wanders off mentally to the residual faded images of someplace better. Somehow we get our bunker constructed without much more thought. We scrape out enough of the surface layers of mud to allow us to spread out a layer of ponchos on the sleeping shelf. We've found places for our sodden gear and our wet, dirty weapons. We have a home.

Tim Haslam

For the rest of the day and all of the next, the grunts of Bravo Company struggle through the unrelenting rain to return Fire Support Base 31 to its state of readiness, returning Hill 925, once again, into a valuable possession of the United States Army. The wire goes up, the flares and mines are set and the artillery pieces are lowered down out of the gray sky. The first outgoing rounds, fired off at the likely approaches to Dak Seang, confirm the effectiveness of our efforts. One-hundred-and-five millimeter Howitzers can now bring pee down on Charlie if they decide to fuck with the camp at Dak Seang. The dirty rifles and machineguns of the Bravo Company grunts will have to bring pee on Charlie if he decides to fuck with FB31. Everything's ready to bring pee. There's no let up in the rain.

N N N N

The company of Yard soldiers files into the firebase around noon on the third day having humped their way up here from someplace further to the north. They're a serious looking band of men, their uniforms a mixture of old fatigues and tiger suits, their weapons a collection of various vintages. They seem to be less concerned with the rain than we are. They set up camp out in front of our positions along the north side, out between our bunkers and the rows of concertina wire. They don't bother with bunkers. They quickly set up their hooches and dig foxholes, covering them with ponchos. This camp for them is just a place to spend the nights. They expect to spend the daylight hours out searching and destroying.

"OK, here's a news bulletin from the Division," Sergeant Bollman says to the group of us ferreted away within the dank bunker as the afternoon drizzle adds to the swamp outside. "Anybody that wastes a gook gets three days at the in-country R&R center down at Vung Tau."

"You mean there's now a bounty on bodies out here?" I ask.

"Right…if you can prove you killed one, you get to go."

"The way things go in fire fights, how can anybody be sure who really got one of the dead bodies?" Ed inquires with eager interest.

"Don't worry about shit like that. If it gets to that point we'll sort it out somehow. We'll draw straws or something. I'm not sure that three

Stars and Stripes and Shadows

days in Vung Tau is that great anyway."

"Man, three days anywhere but here is worth it," I respond. "When's our next patrol?"

My comment is more than just an evaluation of the R&R alternative. There is still, building within me, a strange desire to unleash bullets from my M16 into the body of an enemy soldier. It's not that I don't think of them as human beings. It's not that I can't comprehend the transient nature of our conflict. It's not that I'm becoming a cold-blooded killer. It's because, at some deep unconscious level there has to be a purpose for all that I've done since I entered the army. There has to be a tangible result for all that I've endured. There has to be a countermeasure against the man in the other uniform who's AK47 will be unleashing bullets at me.

"I think we go out tomorrow, probably two squads on separate patrols. You and Ed will probably both be going out," Bruce answers, describing our next chance to earn three days away from the shit. "Five-Nine has patrols out now. Maybe they'll get lucky."

One of the squads from Five-Nine does get lucky it turns out. Not lucky enough to add a body to the count and earn someone a reward vacation, but lucky because they spotted Charlie before being spotted. The squad surprised a trail-watcher; a single man, sent out to sit and watch one of the well traveled trails that skirts across the ridges to the west of Nine-twenty-five. No one is sure if he was asleep or just daydreaming his way through the tedium of his assignment. Rumor has it that he was actually taking a shit. Whatever he was doing, the Americans saw him, hidden within a cluster of bamboo off to the side of the trail. A machinegun and five M16s pointed his way, less than fifteen meters away, convinced him that his work was done, that he had failed in his assignment. He surrendered without a struggle—without so much as a last-second tactical utterance of "chieu hoi."

Nearly everyone at FB31 crawls out of their bunkers and sloshes over toward the west side of the hill where the Five-Nine squad is coming back in with their captive. There is great debate among the spectators as to weather or not the live NVA body counts toward the bounty.

"It's not dead or alive," Mike Beasley offers his interpretation of the deal. "It's just dead. I don't think it counts."

"Bullshit, man…that guys worth a whole lot more walkin' and

Tim Haslam

talkin' than he'd be if he was wasted," Ed responds. "He ought to be worth five or six days. How about it Bruce, what's the deal on prisoners?"

"I don't know. They just said confirmed bodies. I guess a live body counts."

"So who's gonna get the R&R?" I ask. "Does the whole squad get to go?"

"I don't know," says Bollman, growing irritated with all the requests for details on the growing array of possibilities commensurate with the original offer. "That's Five-Nine's problem."

"The whole thing's bullshit, man," says Bennis as he pulls away from the group, heading back toward the protection of his bunker. "Nobody's going anywhere. I'll bet the gook gets some vacation time at Vung Tau before anybody in Bravo Company does."

⋈ ⋈ ⋈ ⋈

"Somebody didn't ante up...again...Lewis? Johnnie?"

"OK, OK, what's the game again?"

"Seven card stud, high-low split...the same as it was the first three times I said it," Pat Sanderson reminds the five of us squeezed into the candle-lit, smoke filled bunker.

"How about it Tim, you gonna open?"

"I'll check."

"Check to you Rusty."

Before anybody can bring this lousy hand to life, two of the regular residents of the bunker crowd in, having just returned from a long patrol. We all knew that they encountered Charlie on this one, that a firefight ensued and that they added bodies to the count. What they have to tell us about their experience is more important than the dollar fifty in MPC piled in the middle of the poncho liner we're sitting on.

"Reese man...fuckin' Reese...what a shithead," Barry Ells starts off, clearly agitated.

"What now?" I ask, registering the unanimous sentiment that Reese is known to all of us as an A-number-one shithead.

"I can't believe that asshole is an officer...that he's even on our side."

"We had two dead gooks and another one that was pretty fucked

Stars and Stripes and Shadows

up; a bullet wound in the abdomen and another bullet in his right arm."

"What does that have to do with Reese? Did he put a bullet in his head or something like that?"

"No fuckin' way…that would have been the humane thing to do. The gook somehow managed to pull himself up until he was sitting upright, kinda slumping forward. Out of it though, really out of it…he was dieing and he knew it. So Reese just walks up behind him and says something like, 'I always wanted to do this,' and tries to cut the guys head off with his fuckin' machete. The fuckin' asshole doesn't really swing hard enough though and just sort of leaves a big gash in the guys shoulder but he keeps swinging, never really cutting all the way through the guy's neck, just sort of beating the guy to death, making a bloody mess of the whole thing."

"Nobody tried to stop him?"

"It all happened too fast. He'd probably bashed the guy about three times before any of us really knew what was happening…by then the guy was dead. Anyway, Reese is an officer, man. What are we supposed to do when a psycho officer starts swinging his machete at an already wasted gook? Sergeant Margolis finally went over and checked out the gook to make sure he was for-sure dead and he said something to Reese like, 'You shouldn't have done that, sir, I think we're supposed to try to bring in as many prisoners as we can.' Reese just shined the whole thing on saying that the guy was dead anyway… that the guy was useless."

"How can Reese get away with shit like that? Couldn't the Captain do something? Shouldn't we tell the Captain?"

"The Captain probably knows. Fuckin' Reese probably told him. He probably thought that would get him his weekend at Vung Tau. Nobody said anything about how we're supposed to kill these people or how we're not supposed to kill 'em…it don't mean nothin' man, it just don't mean nothin.'"

The story adds a new set of images for all of us to wrestle with, a new dimension of depravity to consider. There's something wrong with all of this. There's something wrong with Reese. He didn't do this because he's been traumatized by constant combat or out of revenge for the personal friends he's lost or because he's been emotionally teed up to commit acts of violence. He did it because he thought it would be

Tim Haslam

fun. He did it because he's grown bored with the lack of recreational alternatives available. He did it because he's an asshole; an officer, on our side and an asshole. There's one more thing wrong with this whole shitty mess.

"What's the game again?" Someone asks.

⚡ ⚡ ⚡ ⚡

Lieutenant Grossman has volunteered to take a shift on radio watch along with the rest of us tonight. That cut the shifts down to two hours each, although he pulled rank and insisted on the first shift. I drew the last one, the four to six watch and so, at 4:30 I'm sitting up on my end of the sleeping ledge within the bunker, my poncho liner pulled over me, tent like, so that I can use my flashlight. I want to re-read all the latest letters from home. Heavy rain's again falling. I pity the poor guys out on LP. The first sit-reps of my watch pass without incident, everyone on the net responds with the desired "negative" or phfft, phfft, phfft. Twenty minutes later the process is repeated…everything's still negative…everybody's awake. I need a cigarette but can't manage to do that within the poncho liner tent, so I give up the letters for a few minutes, shut off the flashlight and hop down into the muddy trench between the ledge and the firing port. A few close-in raindrops breaking the plane of blackness is all I can see outside.

"Six-Two-Three, this is Six-Charlie. Sit-rep. Over."

I'm paying more attention to the second cigarette I'm trying to light off the butt of the first, crouched down low in the trench, than I am to the sit-rep responses.

"Six-Two-Three, this is Six-Charlie. Give me a sit-rep. Over," Roy Houston repeats.

Damn it! Not again! Not tonight! Not on my watch!

"Six-Two-Three, Six-Two-Three, come in Six-Two-Three. Sit-rep. Over."

C'mon you guys…wake up…answer the damn horn!

"Six-Two-Charlie, this is Six-Charlie…you're LPs not responding. You've got a problem. Over."

"Roger Six-Charlie. Wait one. Over."

Now what do I do? I don't want to wake the others up and I sure as

Stars and Stripes and Shadows

hell don't want to go outside and deal with this. I'm not sure where our LP even is and I don't think we have any supplies of Ivory Soap.

"Six-Two-Charlie, this is Six-Charlie. What are you gonna do? We need to know what's happening with your LP...now. Over."

I try to call them again. Perhaps a really irritated voice, punctuating the call with lots of profanity will roust them. *It doesn't. There's still no reply.*

"Six-Two-Charlie, you've gotta go down there and see what's going on." The voice suggesting my next move isn't Houston's this time, it's Lieutenant Reese.

"You need to go down there right now. We need to know what's happened out there. Over."

He's gotta be out of his fuckin' mind! He really wants me to go out there. Find my way down to the perimeter line in the dark; try to explain to the heavily armed Yards who don't speak English why I'm heading out through the wire in front of them; find my way through the flares and mines and search around out in the black jungle until I happen upon three men huddled together with their M16s ready to blow away anything that makes a noise. If I should find them, I would have to spend the rest of the night out there with them. There's no way I could get back in without the Yards shooting me. What if Charlie really is out there and has overcome our LP? I'm dead for sure!

"This is Six-Two-Charlie. I don't think I could get out through the CIDGs, sir. I don't think going down there is such a good idea."

"I don't give a shit what you think Six-Two-Charlie. Somebody from Six-Two needs to find out what's happened to that LP. Put Six-Two on the horn. Over."

I shake the Lieutenant and Sergeant Bollman out of their sleep and give them a quick briefing. I clarify my concerns about me, or anyone else interested in living through the night, trying to go down there to find the LP.

"This is Six-Two. Over," the newest-Six-Two says into the handset, trying to figure out his possible next moves.

"Negative...I'm not sending anyone down there under the circumstances. How about sending up a flare? Let's see if that'll get their attention. Over."

Way to go, Grossman! My opinion of our new leader has just jumped

Tim Haslam

up several pegs. *Now, will he stand his ground against the narrow-minded but powerful asshole Lieutenant Reese?*

"Negative…negative…that's insane. If we think there's any chance that something's going on, let's put the base on full alert. It's almost five a.m. anyway. Over."

"Whose squad has the LP out there?" Grossman asks Sergeant Bollman during a pause in his dialogue with Reese. Before Bruce can answer, the unmistakable pops of gunfire can be heard off in the distance. The continuing bursts are coming from the valley to the south, too far off to have anything to do with our LP. Something's happening down at the Dak Seang camp. The firing is increasing. Steady sprays of machineguns, grenades and something more ominous, the heavy explosions of artillery rounds can all be heard breaking through the wet night air. But the howitzers up here at FB31 haven't started firing yet. Dak Seang is taking incoming artillery fire. They're under a full-scale assault.

"Six-Two-Three, this is Six-Two, give me a sit-rep. Over." Grossman says into the handset before anyone else on the net can react to the firing coming from the valley.

"This is Six-Two-Three. What the fuck's going on? Over."

Everyone's awake now…everyone within the bunkers at FB31. All the Yards and all the trios of soaked men on LP have been jolted out of their fatigued complacency by the sounds of battle reverberating up from the valley down below us.

"Full alert! Everyone on full alert," Captain Hilton's voice comes over the radio just as the first outgoing rounds explode out of the 105s up behind us. Everyone scrambles for their weapons and ammo and heads out toward the bunkers and trenches furthest out toward the perimeter. *Fuck the rain and the mud!*

There's no let up in the pops and cracks of small arms exchanging lead pellets off in the distance. The explosions of artillery rounds, grenades and Claymore mines are also continuous. Occasionally something explodes with pyrotechnic flares sufficient to penetrate the two and half kilometers of low clouds that separate Dak Seang from FB31. We can see the flashes, we can hear every shot. We can feel the fear.

"Incoming! Incoming!" The alerts go out after the first two mortar rounds have exploded behind the first row of bunkers on the west side

Stars and Stripes and Shadows

of our base.

It's difficult for us to differentiate the muzzle flashes of the 105s from the exploding mortar rounds from where we are. It takes a minute or two to calibrate which blasts are coming from the fixed positions of our guns and which one's are the moving bursts of exploding shells falling amongst us. *Keep down! That's all I can do, keep down!"*

The incoming mortar rounds are finding their way over the whole surface of the firebase. With the battle sounds coming from Dak Seang and the uninterrupted salvos pounding out from the 105s we can't tell where the mortars are. The rounds just keep coming. Charlie's mortarmen are doing their job up here, trying to distract the Americans up on the mountain, trying to disable the big guns that are shelling their comrades assaulting the other American camp down in the valley. The heavy rain clouds that blanket the valley will prevent the Americans from bringing in their Phantom jet bombers and their strafing, rocketfiring Skyraiders. If it looks like they have any chance of breeching the defenses of the Dak Seang camp, they can continue the siege into the approaching daylight. Only the American helicopters can stop them and the weather and distance will keep them out of the fight for several more hours.

Men here are being hit. One of the incoming rounds has found its mark within the western most gun emplacement, killing one of the artillerymen instantly, wounding two others, and halting temporarily the output from their howitzer. Another round finds its way into one of the forward trenches along the southern perimeter. An instant before, two of the Montagnard CIDGs had jumped down into the same trench seeking shelter from the incoming fire. The indiscriminant missile has enjoined the two men with their ancestor spirits. The shock and shrapnel exploding through their bodies, trapped within the confines of the muddy pit has ended their lives without ceremony or celebration.

By now everyone in Bravo Company who had initially sought shelter in the closest trench has scrambled his way into the nearest bunker. Many of the Yards are still exposed though, as are the redlegs, still courageously feeding high explosive and white phosphorous rounds into the breeches of their guns...standing their ground against the stones being catapulted back over our battlements.

The only way we can put an end to the onslaught of incoming fire

Tim Haslam

is to stop our own outbound fire long enough to find the NVA mortars. If we can hear the pops from the tubes launching the projectiles our way we can estimate their locations. Our own mortars can start fighting back. We can do what they're doing. We can start raining down death in their proximity, round after round, until one comes close enough to tear through their flesh. We have plenty of mortar rounds up here.

It takes only a few seconds after our 105s quiet down for us to hear the pops. Three enemy mortars are steadily firing, all coming from the southern slope of the hill, maybe a hundred meters apart, maybe two hundred meters down. That's a precise enough guess. Our own 81mm tubes start lobbing rounds back out into the darkness. The *kachunks* seem to be close enough to the *thwumps* to continue the bombardment without further adjustment. If we can send more stones their way than they send our way, we'll prevail.

The rate of incoming rounds slows, and then stops all together. There's no let up in our own firing however. Our mortars continue the barrage for several more minutes. The welcome *kachunks* echo back up the hill from various points along the southern slope. *Keep it up!*

There's finally some suggestion that the sky is getting lighter. It's nearly six o'clock. The gunfire, more sporadic now, continues from down in the valley below us and our outbound artillery fire has slowed too. People are now directing our 105s from down at the Dak Seang camp. Precise targets are being identified to guide the next explosive rounds down onto the nests of remaining invaders. The shift in the firing rhythms suggests that we're winning, that Charlie is being pushed back away from the gates of Dak Seang.

The attack on Dak Seang must have been just what the Army needed. The inhabitants of the Special Forces camp are claiming two hundred and ten enemy dead and 27 captured at a cost of one dead and twenty wounded. Up here at the firebase where our job was to support the camp down below we have three killed and several wounded. There are no enemy bodies for us to count. Although some portion of the 200 claimed bodies littering the approaches to Dak Seang had to have been victims of the artillery rounds hurled out of the guns up here, there's no reason for any of us to celebrate. By 8:00 a.m. we've all returned to our respective mud holes busying ourselves doing nothing, reflecting on the

432

Stars and Stripes and Shadows

events of the night, wondering why mortar rounds landed in somebody else's position and not ours. Wondering too where the Huey took the two dead Yards. Wondering…mostly just wondering.

✗ ✗ ✗ ✗

The patrols going out over the next few days are anything but boring. Two more prisoners are taken; both "chieu-hois," giving themselves up to us without any resistance. They tell us that there are many others who want to surrender also. If we keep sending out patrols into this area they will find us, we're told. *If we keep sending out patrols into this area they'll find us all right—in the sights of their AK47s.* The possibility of bringing in more prisoners increases the number of patrols we're to send out. Every other day Ed and I are assigned the RTO duty for one of the squad sized searches. We find lots of evidence that Charlie's around; more fresh bunkers and tunnel complexes, new trails tracking through the wet ground and another encounter with a sniper. One of the new guys is hit in the arm…another million-dollar wound. He'll be out of the shit for several weeks. He'll miss the rest of the monsoons. Maybe the war will come to an end while he's still in the hospital. *Why can't I get shot in the arm?*

We also have scout dogs being sent along on some of our patrols now. A big German Shepard and his handler came along on our patrol today. The dog is supposed to be trained to find snipers or anyone hiding in the jungles around us. He did just that this afternoon, charging out ahead of us into some heavy vegetation. Ernie Jefferson was on point. He carefully followed the path of the dog, followed by the anxious handler and Mike Danko. A burst of AK fire brought them all running back toward the rest of us as fast they could go, Ernie in the lead, followed by the dog, his handler and Danko. I guess the sniper must have done the same thing in the opposite direction. There was no sign of him as we swept back through the area where the shots came from.

✗ ✗ ✗ ✗

"Man, I can't stand this," I lament to Ed and Doc as we wile away the morning hours trapped within the confines of the bunker. "I'm bored to death."

"It's better than being out on patrol…isn't it?" Doc responds while

Tim Haslam

taking inventory of the contents of his medical bag for the tenth time in two days.

"I don't know that it is anymore. At least the day goes by a little faster when you're on patrol."

The concept of a day passing reminds me that I haven't checked off the days from my helmet calendar in a while. I'd drawn a band around by helmet when we were back at Firebase 30 last April and added 365 tick marks along it. I have to work backwards from March 15th of 1969 to figure out how many days I have left to go. My counting and arithmetic gets me to a discouraging result, *two hundred and ten days...not yet half way.* I study the camouflage cover of my helmet for a while longer for want of anything else to do. My "*I Like Asphalt*" button is starting to fade under the scratches and mud residue. My own hand-rendered artwork needs refreshing too. With my pen I trace over the *Porsche* logo and the *Rosemary* and the "*Thank You Local Board 83.*" I add a new section, listing the places I've been; Dak To, FB30, Misery Hump, Route 14 Bridge, FB25, Dak Pek, Ten-Seventy-Nine, Crows Nest, Ranger's Roost, Cambodia, Dak To, Firebase 18, Firebase 31.

"You're right, man. I'd rather be out on patrol then stuck here in this pig pen," Ed declares, "especially now that were taking prisoners and with the possibility of a little vacation down on the beach at Vung Tau."

"The way our patrols move, we're not likely to find any gooks that don't want to be found. We make too much noise and go too slow," I tell him. "Plus, you and I have the radios. Even if we do surprise Charlie, we're probably not the one's who are going to be doing the shooting."

"You're right about the patrols making too much noise but don't forget about the guy I shot last month. I should'a got an R&R for that."

"Sorry Ed...no body. Blood trails don't get you shit."

"There's a body somewhere out there. I know I got that guy."

I think for a minute about the implications of our conversation and an idea starts to take shape.

"Wait a second," I say, as I pull out my Dak Sut map, "I've got an idea. Suppose you and I went out, just the two of us. We take one radio and our weapons...that's it. The gook trail watchers have all been down around this area here where these three trails are all pretty close

Stars and Stripes and Shadows

together. Doesn't it make sense that they're probably coming up this way, along this one trail that goes all the way down to the valley on the northwest? So, you and I'll be trail watchers. If we go down this way, down this finger here we can move pretty fast, zigzagging down this steep part. It'll put us right above the trail about here. We can go early in the morning or late in the afternoon and catch them coming or going. If there turns out to be a lot of 'em, we just sit tight and use the radio. If it's just one or two, we take 'em. What do you think?"

"You think the lieutenant will go for it? Nobody's ever sent out a two man patrol before." Ed's question suggests that he's still thinking over the possibilities. "I guess we could. Yea, if Grossman goes for it, let's do it."

We run the idea by the newest-Six-Two when he and Sergeant Bollman return to the bunker a few minutes later. Bruce is excited with the idea and wants to go himself, but won't pull rank and bump either Ed or I out of our own plan.

"I don't know, it's not a bad idea, but just two guys going out is pretty risky," says Grossman, mulling over the unorthodox proposal. "How long would you be out?"

"A couple of hours, I guess," I answer. "If we go out just before the rest of our patrols come back in, we can plant ourselves along the trail and hopefully catch the gooks on day shift heading back home. It would take us thirty or forty minutes to get back here. So, if nothing happens we'd head back in just before dark."

"Were you thinking of doing this today?"

"Why not?"

"OK, I'll run it by the Captain at our noon briefing."

"The Captain will go along with it on one condition," Grossman tells us upon his return from the daily noon officer's meeting. "I have to go with you."

Oh, man… that's gonna fuck up everything. Three's too many. With just Ed and me this was going to be an adventure, it was going to be fun. Maybe if it was Lieutenant Falck or Lieutenant Riley, but Grossman…

"Sure, sir…that'll be fine," I say, knowing that there's no backing out of it now that new conditions have been imposed. "When do you wanna head out?"

435

Tim Haslam

"We'll go out at four. The other patrols will all be to the east of us. The mortar crews here know what we're going to do and have two reference targets already dialed in close to where we're going. You guys need to go up and get the exact coordinates for those targets before we go."

For the next few hours, Ed and I scurry around, more excited than we've been about anything in months, readying ourselves for our little adventure. We get the mortar targets marked on our maps. Ed agrees to hump the radio and loads in a fresh battery. We clean our weapons again, lightly lubricating the bolt and bolt-carrier. Bruce has loaned me his commando style CAR15, a cut down version of the M16. I strip out all the rounds from eight magazines and carefully reload them back in, ensuring the rounds and the magazines are clean, that the spring tension within each magazine is OK and that each magazine seats properly when inserted up into the receiver of the stubby rifle. We agree to take along two frags each and one canteen of water.

What about smokes? Should we take cigarettes? It would be better to be sitting out there reducing our anxiety by sucking in smoke. Will Marlboro smoke give us away? *No cigarettes.*

We're on our way a few minutes before four o'clock. I take the lead, moving as quickly as I can, trying to avoid any terrain that is heavy with vegetation. I don't have my machete, as we can't afford to alert anyone of our coming by hacking at the plants around us. Ed and the Lieutenant stay close behind me, concentrating on their efforts to keep quiet. We work our way down through the denser forest that surrounds the firebase until we come to a steeper slope populated only with tall slender trees. We stop to survey the ground ahead and the thicker jungle up behind us and off to the east. *Will we be exposed to snipers if we venture out into this clearing? We should be OK. Any snipers that could shoot us down there would have done so as we came down to where we are now.*

Grossman gets a read on our position. We should be about three hundred meters up from the trail. The slope down through the clearing is pretty steep and covered in a thick layer of slippery leaves. We'll have to traverse back and forth to make our way down.

Toward the bottom of the clearing we spot the trail slanting diagonally down to the east in front of us. The trail here has the clearing on the upslope side and heavier vegetation falling away on the down-slope side. It's not the best place for an ambush. If we missed on our first

436

Stars and Stripes and Shadows

shots, Charlie could dive off the trail into the jungle and have cover that would allow him to move in three directions. Charlie would quickly gain the advantage of maneuverability. We would have only the protection of a few scrawny trees.

"Let's work our way up to the west a little and see if things look better up there," the newest-Six-Two directs.

I have to work back up through the leafy hillside and away from the trail to make progress in that direction. We get lucky, after another hundred meters the trail turns sharply back towards us and rises up through the clearing with a series of short switchbacks. There's a brush-covered knoll up about twenty meters that looks down on the trail. When we get up there we realize that it's perfect. The trail comes up through the clearing about fifty meters toward the knoll, wide open on both sides—no place to hide. From the other direction the trail turns back to the west following a nearly level finger ridge, also through open terrain. We have clear fields of fire at people moving on the trail in either direction. We're well hidden and we can beat-it down the east side of the knoll if we have to, protected from return fire by the rising contour of the ground.

The Lieutenant determines our position and Ed calls it in. Then we work out our strategy. If one or two guys come up the trail, we wait until they reach the top of the switchbacks, about twenty meters down from where we are.

"Should we try to take them prisoner?" I ask Grossman, thinking for the first time that these are human beings we're setting a trap for.

"We probably should," says Grossman, unconvincing in his stance. "If they get up to that little jog in the trail I can fire over their heads from behind these bushes and tell them to chieu-hoi. If they don't, Ed will have the scatter gun fixed on them from where he is now and you'll have your fifteen covering them from down there to the left. We'll give 'em about two seconds to make up their minds...then everybody opens up.

If they're coming down the trail, we'll wait until they get to the same place. Tim, you'll have to fire the warning shots, Ed and I will cover...OK?"

"What if there's more than two of them?" Ed asks.

"If there's just three or four and they're in a pretty tight bunch we'll

Tim Haslam

take 'em the same way. Just make sure the first guy doesn't get passed that bend in the trail. If they're more spread out, we'll let them go by and call in mortar fire. Watch me…I'll give you a hand signal on what to do. A closed fist, we take 'em, an open hand, we let 'em go…OK?"

The adventure has now taken on a new dimension of reality. We have a choreographed plan for how we're going to kill people.

Each of us has settled into a nest within the brush, spread out about ten meters apart from one another, the Lieutenant furthest up the slope, Ed in the middle and me down and off to the east a little. I make sure that I have a round in the chamber of my little rifle and that the magazine is solidly seated. I run the thumb of my right hand up and down a few times, adjacent to the selector lever that switches the weapon from it's SAFE position to it's FULL AUTOMATIC position, simulating what I will have to do reflexively at the first sight of a gook, my right index finger on the trigger. I have to remember that the little sawed-off CAR15 bucks and jerks more than the M16. I'll have to keep a tight grip up on the plastic grip over the barrel with my left hand to keep it from jumping around too much in reaction to the rapid series of little explosions pressing back into the metal tubular stock.

There must be a thousand years of accumulated leaves compressed into the decaying carpet that I'm sitting in. There must be a thousand species of insects, spiders and reptiles crawling around within this biomass—searching, sampling, and ambushing each other without conscience or moral reservation. I don't have to search much to find representatives; the big-headed black ants, centipedes, a bright red spider the size of a quarter. *What about the dry land leeches? I know the little fuckers are down here somewhere. I know they're pinching and pulling their way toward the warmth of my blood right now. Shit! I don't have any cigarettes…how will I get one of them off?*

An hour passes before Ed whispers to us that all the other patrols have returned to FB31. The three of us are the only ones left outside the wire. If Charlie's going to come along into our trap, it'll be soon. The forest is darkening quickly as the sun must have dipped down beyond the higher western peaks. The clouds are thickening up too and a gentle drizzle is starting to work its way down through the foliage of the high trees. Our ability to see up and down the trail is starting to diminish

Stars and Stripes and Shadows

as the light fades. Charlie will be close before we can see him. The adventure is becoming less and less exciting. The original perception of the possible ends has been superseded by the real misery of the means. Our bravado is loosing its intensity in direct proportion to the fading light around us.

I need to re-adjust my legs. My left foot's starting to go to sleep, crimped up under my right knee. As I carefully straighten it out, I kick away enough leaves to uncover a fat millipede about six inches long slithering its way up toward my crotch, riding on the alternating waves of leg units rolling along each side of its shiny segmented body.

Let's get the fuck out of here!

I look up toward Grossman, waiting for him to shift his gaze down this way. At the first turn of his head, I wave my hand to get his attention. He takes notice of my hand movement. I point to the watch on my wrist. He nods in agreement. It's time to give up on our plan. We won't get to kill anybody this way today. We don't have a lot of time to get back before total darkness sets in.

Ed calls back up to the firebase and tells Wee John that we're on our way back in. He emphasizes that the Yards on our side of the perimeter need to be reminded that the three of us will be coming up through the wire in front of their position. They need to be reminded not to shoot us.

In an hour and half we're back within the dank, sludgy interior of our bunker, struggling through cans of Pork Slices, telling Doc all about our bold mission.

"Is that red patch still bothering you?" is all Doc has to say, noticing that I'm once again scratching intently down under the top of my left boot. "Let me take a look at that."

"Yea…I'd say that's ringworm for sure. I'll have to find out what we're supposed to do about that. Meanwhile, don't scratch it so much."

"But it feels so good, Doc. I'm not sure I want it to go away."

ӿ ӿ ӿ ӿ

"Hey Ed, Houston wants all the RTOs up at the headquarters' bunker," I yell over to Arter who's talking with a group of Five-Nine guys outside the next bunker up the line, "he's got some new codes to give us."

Tim Haslam

Roy Houston goes over all the new word-of-the-day codes for the next week with the band of RTOs collected outside the big bunker on this sunny morning. We've almost finished our note taking when Captain Hilton and another officer get our attention as they exit the command bunker, pulling on their helmets.

"You guys better straighten up and look smart," the Captain says to us, elevating his voice to be heard over the increasing drone of an approaching Huey. "The new Battalion Commander is coming in on that chopper to get a look around."

Even though Houston's done with our briefing, we all hang around to get a look at the new honcho who's going to be deploying us from now on, here and there within the shit. The outgoing commander—Ranger — Lieutenant Colonel Malone had earned everyone's respect. He seemed to have real respect for us too, preferring to use the mechanical weapons at his disposal rather than the flesh and blood type. Even with the little exposure any of us actually had with him, we could recognize the man under the Ranger code name and the silver oak leaf...he was a good guy.

Our first image of the new colonel stepping off the skid of the UH1 suggests that this guy's going to be different. His uniform is spotless, pressed and heavily starched. Even the camouflage cover on his helmet looks to be showroom fresh. The brass and silver adornments on his uniform reflect back glints of sunlight. There's no mistaking this guy is a big deal. There's also no mistaking that this guy is a big ego. Around his waist is a black leather pistol belt with a black leather holster on the right side. Within the holster is an ivory handled .45 pistol as clean and pristine as the rest of his superficial panoply. *This guy thinks he's General Patton!*

Captain Hilton and the other officer, who must be the Battery Commander from the 6th of the 29th, crouch out under the rotor wash to greet the new leader. After brief handshakes the Colonel and his entourage of polished-boots tiptoe along behind the two filthy line officers heading back toward the command bunker, all looking out of place out here in this wilderness.

The new, starchy Colonel pulls up short of the headquarters' bunker entrance and scans around the landscape, taking particular notice of the closer in bunkers, trenches and pits. He takes a long look at the

Stars and Stripes and Shadows

group of us loitering over at the edge of the sandbag wall encircling one of the 105s. He studies us with the eyes of a gentrified aristocrat passing by a leper colony. He sees filthy grunts staring back at him; some clad in faded tee shirts, others in unbuttoned fatigue shirts with the sleeves hanging down over their hands. Shredded pant legs hang over our mud-incrusted boots. Whiskers grown nearly to beard status and heavy, long moustaches covering most of the tired faces confirm our sloth and lack of military discipline along with the long bushy hair that presses out from under our helmets.

He has to do something about this. He has to exert his influence. He has to establish his leadership and reputation with the men.

"You people live like pigs," he blurts out, as a general proclamation for all who are able to hear.

"Captain, I suggest you get this pigsty policed up right now and get your men squared away. Why aren't these men wearing their tunics?"

Tunics? What the fuck does he think we are...the Roman fucking legion?

"I want to see the men here in proper uniforms and this mess cleaned up before I leave," Colonel Julius Caesar admonishes Hilton and the artillery officer waiting outside the bunker entrance.

"Yes sir...I'll see to it," the Captain responds without comment or objection. The West Point graduate and veteran combat commander has been in the army long enough to recognize this kind of officer. *Just take your lumps, grovel and kowtow at the appropriate queues and hope to hell that this asshole gets out of here quickly. There's nothing to be gained by opening up another front in the war against vanity and arrogance.*

The Captain relegates the assignment to Sergeant Madison, who immediately calls for all the Platoon Sergeants, who carry the message back to the rest of the grunts, who acknowledge the new Colonel's observations and directive with the same respectful commentary.

"You've gotta be shit'n me! We live like pigs? Who-the-fuck put us out here in this shit anyway?"

Sergeant Bollman pulls everyone in the Platoon out of their bunkers, reminds us all how to dress appropriately for the monsoon season in the Central Highlands jungles and then has us all sweep through our area picking up any of the cigarette butts that haven't yet sunk down below the surface of the sodden ground that we're wallowing through.

Tim Haslam

"What's this guy's code name?" Doc asks Bollman as he picks up a little can that formerly contained WHITE BREAD.

"I don't know," Bruce answers. "Any ideas on something appropriate?"

"How about anal-retentive…A-R, or Alpha-Romeo," I offer. "I think Alpha-Romeo would be really good. The guy thinks he's the alpha-dog and he's really in love with himself."

"What does anal-retentive mean?" Mike Beasley asks, wanting to ensure that he has the correct image.

"It's someone who tries to retain their feces. Taking a shit is a dirty proposition for them. You know; people who are generally obsessed with being orderly and tidy."

"This isn't a very good place for people like that," Beasley observes honestly.

"No shit!"

Chapter 14

Scarred

Dak To again. This time our visit is anything but relaxed. There's been lots of activity in the mountains to the west of here lately. Aerial reconnaissance and statements from the increasing number of Chieu Hois confirms that they're building up again to hit this place. We were hurried off the choppers that brought us back down here from Firebase 31 and sent immediately to our positions along the perimeter bunker line. We're a little further up the east side this time, closer to the north end of the base, closer to where Charlie can hide up on the lower slopes of Rocket Ridge and launch his missiles at us. Alpha Company has been here for several days now and occupies the bunkers on the west side of the perimeter.

As soon as we reach our assigned bunkers, we're sent off to retrieve more ammo, flares and grenades. We are also given, for the first time, flak vests to wear while we're here. The thick, hot vests stimulate another round of discussion as to their effectiveness at stopping various projectiles. The general consensus is that they'll work pretty well at stopping shrapnel, but not so well at stopping bullets. What ever they stop, it will have to be heading for our torso. Our faces, throats, limbs and genitals are all still unprotected against the hot shards that the North Vietnamese are planning to explode among us. Stay close to the bunker is the popular sentiment for the grunts of Bravo and Alpha Company during this stay at Dak To.

We seem to be getting a break from the rain here. The familiar gray clouds have been pushed around Rocket Ridge to the north, leaving the sky over the Dak To base clear and blue; hot and humid. Whoever's

Tim Haslam

in charge of the base defenses has determined that the amount of concertina wire springing around the camp is inadequate. We need to lay more. The army has plenty of wire and, during the day, the grunts have nothing else to do. This isn't one of the typical make-work assignments though. There's a true sense of nervousness pervasive throughout Dak To. The belief is that Charlie is coming. The belief is that this place will be the next Khe Sahn. *If more wire will slow down the people with the AK47s and the explosive satchel charges, let's string out lots of it...all we have...all we can get.*

The work, un-springing the coils of wire, stretching it out, stacking and securing it, is hard under the direct rays of the tropical sun. It's too hot to do this wearing these vests. It's too hot for shirts. The air is crisp and clear and quiet. We'll hear the thwumping of an enemy mortar or the ripping blast of a rocket launcher in time to retrieve the vests. This is a good time to catch some rays as we work.

A dirt trail skirts the perimeter just outside the wire along the section we're working. The trail disappears into a grove of banana trees heading eastward toward the village of Dak To. During our lunch break, the first contingent of local merchants arrives on the scene in hopes of conducting commerce with the wealthy Americans toiling out at the edge of the big encampment. Two Honda motor scooters, followed by a rising trail of dust, pull up near us, thirty meters across an open section that we have yet to secure with the new wire. The Hondas, the riders and their merchandise look familiar.

"Gee Eye wan boom boom?" the skinny man on the lead Honda yells over to us, shoving the two females riding behind him out into clearer view. Both girls seem to be as mal-nourished as their escort, their tight jeans and tee shirts pressing around just enough contours to suggest that there really are female forms underneath the stretched packaging. The two girls on the back of the trailing motorbike are dressed in silk ao-dais with their conical hats hanging over their backs.

"Numba one boom boom girls," escort number two declares enthusiastically.

I have to appreciate their thoughtful merchandizing approach. They've brought something for every taste, tight jeans or silk ao-dais, contemporary or traditional, passive or aggressive. The contemporary girls start posing and gyrating around as further evidence of their wherewithal...their chaperone

Stars and Stripes and Shadows

beaming with pride. The traditional pair is more stoic, more mysterious about their approach, hoping, apparently, to attract the more conservative sexual shopper. The display strikes me as both sad and comical. I can't tell how old any of this cast of characters is. The girls could be fourteen to twenty, the men probably around twenty. Is this a family business, I wonder...are there brothers and sisters within this troupe?

"How much?" a voice from our side inquires.

I already appreciate the presence of the slender whores and confident pimps. They have broken the monotony for a few minutes. They have given all of us something different to look at and something to think about...maybe even something to consider. I think about my own level of hormonally driven anxiety and curiosity. I consider the possibilities. I wonder at the logistics. I wonder if such an opportunity, back within the sheltered privacy of a dusty banana grove would be satisfying. I think about the images each guy returning from R&R has shared about his experiences with such high levels of appreciation. I think about the whole list of diseases that we learned about back at Fort Polk, that Doc Charlebois has validated...the symptoms, the consequences...the awkward explanations one would have to come up with. I think about the stories of VC whores imbedding razor blades within their vaginas.

You gotta be shit'n me? I think to myself as I watch two of the bare-chested grunts head over for a closer look at the offerings.

You gotta be shit'n me? I think to myself with even greater confusion as the two are led off into the trees by their chosen dates...the contemporary models apparently being the best match for their appetites. The two men have separated themselves from their weapons, their helmets, their flak vests and their buddies and are blithely skipping off into a banana grove, where who-knows-what waits for them. All for the opportunity to have a ten minute sexual interlude with a dusty teenage prostitute at a special reduced price of only five bucks.

Ten minutes away from this shit would be worth five bucks!

I sometimes wish I were a little more assertive, a little more adventurous, a little more curious.

�✕ ✕ ✕ ✕

Just before dark, the first mortar rounds drop down into the center of the complex, damaging only sandbags with their flying shards of

Tim Haslam

hot metal. The duster at the north end of the complex answers almost immediately, its forty-millimeter tracers arcing up into the jungled slopes overlooking the camp on the northwest side. From our position on the bunker line we can follow the line of the outbound rounds and see the puffs of smoke filtering up out of the trees. We can see where Charlie's hiding. We can see how close he is. The volume of fire put out by the duster is either on target or sufficiently close to give Charlie second thoughts about lobbing anymore rounds at us from anywhere near there.

The game of explosive tag continues well into the night. One or two mortar rounds drop down into Dak To from various spots within the surrounding jungle. Forty-millimeter rounds or our own mortars return the fire. One of the supply huts right in the center of the camp is hit. A round penetrates down through the corrugated steel sheet roof and explodes amidst some crates full of helicopter spare parts. Another one damages a deuce-and-half truck parked between two other huts. It'll need new tires in the morning and the passenger side door will let more air in from now on. None of us are hurt. There's no way to know what's happened to the resources of the other side. We put out about ten rounds to every one they shoot at us. We must be doing some damage.

It's another long night with the camp at two-thirds alert. There's little sleep to be had with the intermittent explosions and almost constant bursts of star shells that keep the place bathed in the unsteady shifting light from the slowly falling flares.

Charlie doesn't come. A few of his mortarmen, working the night shift, are enough to harass us, to keep us from getting much rest. The other North Vietnamese regulars are sleeping soundly out there somewhere in their tunnels, saving their energy for a better opportunity. Dawn finds us wearier than we were at the end of our workday yesterday; hoping that today will include some slack time, some time to get some sleep, to get rejuvenated a little bit, to build up some strength for tonight.

"We're moving out in two hours." Lieutenant Grossman tells us upon his return from the early morning pow-wow he was summoned to. "Make sure everybody has five days worth of C's, plenty of water and ammo…then have the squad leaders come see me," he tells Bollman,

Stars and Stripes and Shadows

signaling to the rest of us that we're about to go humpin' again.

"What now, sir?" I ask, "I thought we'd be here for a while. I thought this place was supposed to be in danger of attack."

"It's still true. This place is in danger of attack but, we think we know where the bulk of Charlie's troops are building up. A Lurp team out to the west of Rocket Ridge has been watching a steady stream of small NVA units heading into one of the valleys out there. We're going out into the mountains beyond those valleys and will work our way back this way. We'll try to catch them before they can dig in up on Rocket Ridge again."

"Is this just us...just Bravo? There could be a whole lot of them out there," I ask, concerned that we're about to head into the land beyond the big ridge where Charlie has ambushed so many Americans. This is the land of the A-Shau Valley, of Hill 875 and 1338. This is the area that every veteran of the Central Highlands has heard about. Lot's of people die out there.

"Alpha Company's coming too," says Grossman, already stuffing provisions into his ruck. "They'll go out first, landing on some hilltop about two klicks to the south of where we're going. Then we'll both start sweeping back this way. Delta and Charlie Company will be relieving us here."

"How about we just stay here and let Delta and Charlie do the humpin'. It seems like it would be a lot more economical," I say, rhetorically as I too start stuffing little cans into my ruck.

"I already made that request," the Lieutenant says. "I think the new Battalion Commander is punishing us for our sloppy appearance up on Firebase 31. I guess Delta Company was guarding a bridge somewhere when the new Colonel first visited them. They were all nice and clean and well behaved when he dropped by. I think he really likes Delta Company and doesn't want any of them getting bruised or dirty." The Lieutenant's sarcastic observation feels too much like the truth. We all feel like we're being sacrificed.

"Oh, and one more thing," adds the newest-Six-Two, saving the best for last. "We'll be the first platoon in."

Every helicopter in the Central Highlands must be assigned to this operation. By the time we get out onto the airstrip, there must be twen-

Tim Haslam

ty Hueys on the ground and at least that many honeybeeing around the skies nearby. Loaches and Cobras are also hovering around or making low passes over the landing strip, getting themselves pumped up for a fight. The clean well-disciplined lads from Delta Company have off-loaded from the Hueys on the ground and are on their way back to the dry comfortable bunkers. Charlie Company will arrive later.

The unmistakable rumble of an arc-light somewhere off to the southwest reverberates over the top of Rocket Ridge, suggesting that the area is being prepped for our coming.

"It's just a reuse," Grossman tells us. "The B52s are hitting a bunker complex about two klicks south of where we're going. They want Charlie to think that's our destination."

I don't know if I'm glad that the thousand pound bombs aren't obliterating everything around the area that we're headed for or not. I know that Charlie has figured out that such strikes are usually followed by American grunts riding in on their helicopters. Maybe all of the gooks are actually in the bunker complex being pulverized by the B52s. I wonder what our hilltop will look like. Will it be clear enough for a Huey to get down on? How will the area we're heading for be prepped? I quickly readjust the straps on my gas mask remembering the beginning of misery-hump.

"OK, here's how we're going in," Grossman starts out, explaining to the gathered around squad leaders, "I'll be on the first bird in. Haslam and Arter will both be with me; one radio on the Battalion push, the other on Company. Mike Ferlik and two of his men will go with us, one machinegunner and one rifleman. Grady, your squad's on the second chopper."

Grossman, who seems nervous now, finishes describing the order of our assault into the shit. Sergeant Littlejohn, who was transferred over to our Platoon to take over Bob Taylor's squad will be on the third helicopter followed by Tom Malone, a new guy, a graduate of the Army's NCO school—an instant NCO —a "shake-and-bake," who has been assigned to lead Steve Steven's old squad.

I don't like this! We'll be the first six on the ground; a new Lieutenant, two RTO's who will be busy with radio communication and three other men. This isn't much firepower. If Charlie's around and can

Stars and Stripes and Shadows

prevent any other choppers from getting in, the six of us are screwed big time. *I don't like this!*

Ed and I agreed that he'd keep his radio on the Company push and I would monitor the Battalion frequency. This means that Ed will be in constant contact with Captain Hilton's RTOs, Wee John and Roy Houston, until the whole Company is on the ground. Should something happen on the ground and we need help in the form of artillery, air support or medevacs, it'll be my job to contact the providers and make sure that they deliver.

"Ed, Bruce, listen to this," I say, gesturing with my arm for them to get closer to me and my radio. The first squad from Alpha Company just landed and started taking fire as soon as they got on the ground. No one's been hit, but there's enough small arms fire coming at them to keep them pinned down and to keep the next Huey from getting in to them. The RTO keeps asking for some kind of air support. "We need a gunship. We need a Cobra or something to help us up here. We're taking heavy fire from our north and west flanks. We're pinned where we are. We need help. Over."

"Roger that Seven-One-Charlie. There's a loach and two Cobras on their way. They should be there any second. Go to five-eight-nine-five to get into contact with them. Over."

"This is Seven-One-Charlie. Roger. I'm switching over to five-eight-nine-five. Out."

"Switch your radio over too," Bollman instructs me, anxious to hear the rest of the play by play for the isolated Alpha men.

"OK," I answer, twisting the two knobs on the top of the Prick25 to that frequency.

The helicopters are asking for smoke on the north and west sides of the men on the ground to mark the territory they can't fire into. They want coordinates or directions for where the enemy fire is coming from.

In another minute, one of the Cobras can see some of the gooks up on the adjacent ridge. They're starting to run...they'll be easy targets for his gatling-gun. There's more somewhere to the west. The men on the ground are still taking fire. The other enemy soldiers surrounding the grunts either don't yet see the Cobras or don't care. They don't want

449

Tim Haslam

to miss their opportunity to finish off the Americans who have flown into their yard. Maybe they think they can bring down our helicopters too.

"Medevac! We need a dust-off bird up here. One of our men's hit," the Alpha Company RTO shouts into the radio, his voice stressed and urgent.

I know what he's thinking now. I know of his confusion. He's on a frequency that connects him with the choppers. They're telling him things, they're asking him questions; they demand his full attention. He needs to get his request for a medevac out on the Battalion frequency or his own company push. He's apparently got the only radio on the ground down there and he needs to be in contact with people on three different frequencies. He can only hope that one of the chopper pilots will relay his plea for the dust-off bird. He can only hope that the right people are listening to him.

"Shit, man...they walked right into it," Ed says, thinking as much about what's about to happen to us as to what's going on with the Alpha guys.

"Saddle up," Lieutenant Grossman says, hurrying back over to us from a last minute meeting with the Captain. "We're going, now," he says to us, looking around for Mike Ferlik.

"Ferlik, Ferlik, let's go. We've gotta go now!"

"Do you know what's happening to the guys in Alpha up there?" I ask as Ed pulls me up to my feet. "It sounds like they landed right in the middle of a lot of shit."

"Yea...I know," is all the new Lieutenant says as Sergeant Ferlik and two of his grim faced men join us. Grossman leads us off at a quick pace toward the line of vibrating slicks spread out along the landing strip, their churning rotors pushing and pulling up the surface layers of red dust.

Even through the darkened goggles of their aviator's helmets I can see that the crew of our bird is anxious about this one. They too must know what's happening to Alpha Company. They know that Charlie knows we're coming. They know that they'll be driving the first chopper into unfriendly territory and that they have to get the six of us onto the ground out there. Only the door gunners study us though, as we approach the skids on either side of their machine. The pilot and crew

450

Stars and Stripes and Shadows

chief up in the cockpit are busy with the knobs and switches that control the UH1D. The door gunners evaluate their approaching cargo thoughtfully. The door gunners are thinking how glad they are that they won't have to be left out there. The door gunners are thinking about what a big target their flying machine is going to be as it hovers down toward the ground to let us off. We're all hoping that somebody will change their mind real soon about going through with this.

Mike Ferlik, the Lieutenant and I climb into the left side of the Huey, sitting with our legs dangling out the side. We want to be able to get out of this thing as quickly as possible when it gets near the ground. Ed and the other two men are sitting the same way on the other side.

The rotors start to grind at the air a little harder and the chopper starts to separate from the ground. A few feet up into the dusty air the pilot pulls us forward until we're out of the line of the other Hueys. He eases the tail around so that we're on a northward heading and throttles up. The tarmac races passed us to the south dropping further and further down below us until it abruptly transitions into the first forested ridge to the north of Dak To.

The chopper's climbing more acutely now and banking westward, causing the three of us on the left side to grab onto any part of the helicopter's structure within reach. We're looking down into the jungle sweeping by below us. In another few seconds the chopper levels out a little, still nosed downward and accelerating. I let go of the door track piece I've been clinging too long enough to notice that my hand is shaking. Not from the vibrating of the machine I'm riding in. It's shaking as a reaction to what I'm feeling. For the first time since I've been in this country—in this war—maybe for the first time in my life, I'm really scarred. I've worked myself into this…psyched myself out. I've chosen to react to everything this morning as though it were ominous. I can't say that I'm really afraid of getting hurt or even killed. It's an adrenaline driven anxiety that keeps building. I guess I'm like every other element of this force, man, machine and weapon; pumped up, fully loaded and cocked, racing at full throttle toward a place where death is the objective. *Something has to happen. Something will happen.* Up to now I've clung to the belief that nothing really bad would ever happen to me. Today is different. Today is a different feeling…a different belief.

The door gunner on our side stiffens up, leaning out to get a better

Tim Haslam

look at the landscape up ahead, keeping the barrel of his M60 aligned with the direction of his searching eyes. We're tracking above a heavily forested finger ridge. The UH1 is slowing. We're getting close. The pilot's looking for a place to put down. Then, with a sudden jerk of acceleration he banks hard to the left, again causing us to grasp at some part of the structure of the helicopter to keep us in. He continues the left-hand turn until we're coming up the finger again. The crew chief leans back and says something to Lieutenant Grossman. I can't hear what he says through the noises generated by the turbine and rotors. *Maybe there's been a change in plans. Maybe somebody's calling it off.*

The Huey slows again. This time I can see why. I can see just enough of the ground out the other side to see what's going on. There's a little clearing with a small bomb crater in the middle of it. There's just about enough room for the Huey to get over the crater. We'll get out there. I remember my first steps into misery-hump and what happened when I jumped down into the bomb crater out there. I remember the firing and the gas. I don't want a repeat of that.

The Huey pilot brings the chopper into a full hover off to the left of the crater. He moves the big machine backwards several meters somehow as both the door gunners nervously scan the surrounding ground for any signs of Charlie. Then the helicopter shifts its orientation a little to the left and the pilot slides the machine diagonally over the crater. He wants to keep the nose pointed out toward the clear air on this side. He doesn't want to have to nose through nor over the bigger trees at the eastern edge of the clearing should somebody start shooting at him. He's working hard to contain the motions of the hovering machine. He's trying hard to bring it down closer to the edge of the crater. He knows that with each second we're here the chances of Charlie getting close increases...we all know...we all want to get out.

He does it. He gets us close enough to step off onto the skid and then down into the soft soil dredged out by the exploding bomb. We're all out. We've all taken up a prone position, lying around the western edge of the crater looking out into the jungle, waiting for our ride to get away, waiting for Charlie to determine what happens next.

The chopper's just started pulling itself away from the clearing when the first jarring blast explodes from somewhere in the trees further down the finger to the west. An instant later one of the big trees in front of the

Stars and Stripes and Shadows

crater is split and splintered by another blast, sending the six of us burrowing into the soft red soil. They've fired a rocket-propelled-grenade at the chopper. Charlie's in a hurry, rushing to get a shot at the American helicopter before it can escape, taking a wild chance the missile will find its way through the forest obstacles. Another blast from the same area precedes the whoosh of the next RPG arcing out just to the rear of the fleeing Huey's tail rotor.

"Grenadier-One this is Eight-Two-Six-Two-Charlie. We're taking fire. RPGs coming from down on the finger to our west," I say into the radio as soon as I've regained enough control to remember my job.

"Tell them that we're about three hundred meters further down the ridge to the west than the designated LZ," Grossman yells over to me from his position five feet away.

I add the Lieutenant's information to the next call and listen to Ed echo the same thing into his handset, filling in Captain Hilton and the rest of the Company as to our situation.

"Mike, you need to get down into those trees down there," the Lieutenant says to Ferlik, knowing that we've got to establish a more aggressive response to whoever is out there launching the RPGs at us. If they can get one of their shrapnel laden rounds close to this crater, they can take us all out.

"We'll lay down covering fire. Get down into those trees and bring all the fire you can onto everything from that bamboo clump on down."

The newest-Six-Two starts firing down through a narrow open alley between the trees as Ferlik and his two men start running down toward a clump of brush off to the left. I have another little open swath out in front of me and start firing down that way too. I work through one magazine, firing short bursts, watching the bullets slam into the ground down the hill and into the vegetation thirty meters down. I force a second magazine up into the 16 as squelch breaks on my radio.

"Eight-Two-Six-Two-Charlie, there's a gunship in your area. He'll be over your position any second. Pop smoke and give him the position of the RPGs. He's on this push...he's Popeye-Five. Over."

Somebody must have learned something from Alpha Company's experience earlier and added some protective firepower to the team bringing Bravo Company in. A Huey gunship pounces over the ridge

Tim Haslam

to our north, a moment after the radio notification, asking for a target. I set off a blue smoke grenade down in the bottom of the crater and let the pilot know that three of us are here and three others are twenty meters off to the southwest. The gooks *are*, or at least *were*, thirty to forty meters straight down the ridgeback. The gunship dives down toward the target area in a slight right-hand bank unleashing rockets from the skid-mounted pods. It takes only a fraction of a second for the stream of rockets to start exploding through the vegetation. Anything still there has reached the endpoint of its life.

With the gunship now zigzagging back and forth down over the ridge-top, strafing through the plants and animals with its mini-guns, we can get back to the work of ensuring that the LZ is safe for the next chopper and Grady's squad. My hand isn't shaking so much now as I unscrew the cap of one of my canteens and wash away the dusty dryness of my mouth. I think we may have seen all there is of Charlie for a little while. It must have been a small unit that fired on us, perhaps just passing through this area on their way to join others attacking Alpha Company. The helicopters have driven them off and will keep them from building up in force around us. With the help of Grady's guys we go to work enlarging the LZ, quickly slashing away another ten meters of bamboo, vines and trees. The rest of the Company flies in and joins us without incident and the Captain hurries us all away from the LZ, cattle-driving us hard another klick and half up the ridge.

Business as usual!

✗ ✗ ✗ ✗

Another klick and a half up the ridge we enter into an old arc light zone, heavily cratered with some of the heartier plant life just beginning to sprout back out of the loosened soil.

"Stay back a second," one of the new instant-NCO Sergeants advises Bruce Bollman and me as we work our way up toward the front of the file where the Sergeant and two other men are gathered. The rest of the men are spread out behind us searching around the ruins for anything that may validate Charlie's presence here, before or after the bombing. I see the object in the new Sergeant's hand before Bruce does and can now see that he and the two other men at his side are looking down at the ground just in front of them.

Stars and Stripes and Shadows

"I think we've got a spider hole here. I'm gonna drop a frag down, just to make sure that nobody's down there," the man says, starting to reach for the pull ring on the hand grenade.

I don't know if it's my voice or Bruce's that screams out the loudest.

"No…no…don't drop that frag down there!"

The volume of our response and the urgent determination clearly underlying our plea freezes the grenade wielding Sergeant, erasing the confidant expression on his face and replacing it with a more confused look.

"That's no spider hole," Bruce declares more calmly as we approach to within a few feet of the group of concerned new guys now studying the hole in the ground in front of them more closely.

"There's a dud thousand pound bomb down there," I tell them, rounding at Sergeant Bollman's explanation. "Dropping that grenade down there would be a really bad idea."

"No shit man," one of the other stunned new guys says, taking a few steps back away from the round opening in the ground.

I look over and catch Bruce's eyes returning my expression. All either of us can do is shake our heads just as the true realization sets in of what might have happened had we been one or two steps further back from the three men anxious to explode their first hand grenade in the Nam.

ⁿ ⁿ ⁿ ⁿ

The second day out we come across what seems to be a sizable bunker complex well hidden under the heavy triple canopy. Charlie's spent a lot of time constructing and crafting this compound. It's a place they intended to use for a long while. Heavy logs have been cut, trimmed and entwined with one another to form the foundations of the protective structures on the surface. Below ground, the tunnels are honed out with professional artisan-like care. Within the tunnels are a wealth of supplies; ammo, rice-bags and medical supplies. They've worked hard to build this place, to bring in supplies for storage here, to conceal and protect their property here. Our job is to destroy it all.

Sergeant Rimmer and a couple of other volunteer tunnel-rats set to work crawling down into the inner reaches of the underground den,

Tim Haslam

placing blocks of C4 at various points and running the detonator wires back up through the surface entrances. The sound of the detonated plastic explosive barely reaches the surface. A silent little train of smoky dust crawls timidly out of the entrance holes several seconds after the blasts, confirming that the C4 has done its job.

As a final precaution against re-habitation, Rimmer and his crew have set one more set of charges, attaching each one to a large canister of CS gas powder. This time, once they've pulled themselves and the detonator wires up out of the holes, we all pitch in, shoveling up the entrances, plugging them with sandbags, loose dirt and mud. With the next blasts, the oxygen remaining within the arteries of the anthill is co-mingled with the released gas powder, completing the work of the exterminators. Charlie's not likely to want to come back here. If our work isn't sufficient deterrence, he knows that this place is now marked on every American map. He knows that the B52 crews can finish the job some evening without warning.

It's taken the better part of the day to neutralize Charlie's little base. Captain Hilton has found a place a few hundred meters up one of the adjacent fingers that's suitable for our night-defensive-position. So, we hump up there and set to work constructing our own camp. Six-Two Platoon has been assigned a section adjacent to the LZ that's been hacked out of a large stand of bamboo, leaving a bed of spikes, broken shafts and leaves and it's hard for us to find a patch of ground clear enough of the broken bamboo to lay out our hooch. Ed, Doc and I have to dig out a few little stumps and roots to smooth out the ground and then we decide to take a smoke break before we actually start lacing the ponchos together.

We're all relaxed on the ground, leaning back against our ruck frames, enjoying a quiet smoke. It feels good to be sitting here, bathed in the shafts of sunlight filtering down through the trees on this pleasant, dry afternoon. We're in no hurry to finish our work and no one of higher rank is pressing us to be more productive. We don't get too comfortable though before an inbound Huey, bringing fresh water and more C-rations disturbs our break, blowing a torrent of leaves and bamboo pieces over us. We're still too comfortable and too tired though to make any attempt to move out from under the rain of detached foliage

456

Stars and Stripes and Shadows

that's falling over us.

The smoldering Marlboro in my right hand limits my preening work to my left hand. I'm too tired to even hurry through the effort of sweeping off the leaves and things dumped on me as a consequence of the Huey's rude invasion. I reach across casually to brush some of the debris off my right shoulder when, for some reason, something within my peripheral vision catches my attention. I glance down onto my upper right arm in response to the subtle stimulus.

"Shit! Goddamn-it," I blurt out, jumping up to my feet, throttled by a full blast of adrenaline. "What the fuck is that?" I yell out, sweeping furiously away at my sleeve.

"What the hell is wrong with you?" Doc asks with moderate concern.

"Did you see that? Where the fuck did it go? Did you see that thing?" I ask of my two partners who must think I'm in the throes of some kind of hallucination.

"See what? What the fuck are you talking about?" Ed asks, still too unconcerned to pull himself up out of his reclined posture.

"That thing that was on my arm...there was some kind of a goddamned bug. It must have been a foot long!" I tell them as the image of the monster starts to consolidate within my consciousness and perhaps my imagination. "I was brushing off some bamboo, when one of the pieces started walking up toward my neck. The fucking piece had legs and a face and was poking at my neck. Goddamn-it...where the hell is that thing?"

I start kicking around at all the debris that's collected down at my feet, searching frantically for the latest forest demon that's attacked me, probing at each splintered piece of bamboo, looking desperately for the one that walks and eats grunts.

"I'm tell'n you guys, there's some kind of a giant bug down here. No shit, the thing is this long," I tell them, holding up my two hands, spread a foot apart, as though I were describing my first trout catch.

"No shit, shall we get our guns?" Ed asks, pulling in another drag of smoke.

The revenge-seeking piece of bamboo is nowhere to be found. It's flown off along with the other things blown about by the departing Huey or disappeared back amongst the other remains of it's brethren,

Tim Haslam

playing bamboo-possum, waiting for a better opportunity to exact it's retribution against the machete-men.

I continue scanning around the area as we assemble our hooch, kicking my way through every patch of leaves accumulated around. I check out the inside of the hooch thoroughly before putting myself or any of my gear in there. Doc and Ed have little concern over this latest threat. Their fears have to do with Charlie and what he can do to us. I'm the only one who knows what else lurks along this ridge top. I'm the only who can imagine what this thing, perhaps these things, are planning to do to us. I'm the only one who will have trouble falling asleep this night worrying about the walking bamboo that was probing around at the flesh of my neck.

Goddamn, I hate this place!

◢ ◢ ◢ ◢

Three more days pass by slowly under the ruck; off and on rain, up and down, hack and slip, trip, fall, sweat, itch…bleed.

On the fourth day we're moved to another location, helicoptered a few klicks further south. Again we're put down on a hilltop, once thick with bamboo and other vegetation that has recently been bombed into a heap of sticks and shards. Half of the Company is on the ground, the rest are still in transit on the shuttling Hueys. Another UH1 coming out from Dak To, loaded with more C-rations butts into the queue and lands atop the rubble. I join a group volunteering to off load the C's and crouch up under the spinning rotor to retrieve one of the cases. As I reach the skid I see a smiling Doc Davis climbing out of the Huey, dressed in clean fatigues. He's been on R&R and hitched a ride back out to us on the re-supply chopper.

"Hey Doc…what's happening?" I yell out to him, trying to be heard under the pressing air of the rotors. "How was R&R?"

"Man, man, man…I could really get used to that," he says, smiling more broadly, placing his hand on my shoulder. "That was *the* best, man…*the* fuckin' best!"

"Let's get out from under this thing and you can tell me about it."

"Right on," the still smiling Doc says as I pull back away from the chopper, cradling the cardboard case of rations. I hurry as quickly as I can to get out from under the pounding air and away from the rising

Stars and Stripes and Shadows

dust, picking my way through the remnant bamboo spikes.

"Damn," I hear Davis say, from a little behind me.

I turn and see that Doc is down on the ground, not smiling anymore, apparently having just tripped over something. He had his ruck and medical bag slung over one shoulder and was probably not very well balanced has he tried to follow me out away from the LZ. He was probably also still thinking about R&R; thinking about life away from the shit. I watch him rise back up slowly studying his right forearm. It's so common to see grunts tripping and falling out here that I don't pay much attention until I see the bright crimson stream dripping down from the dark brown flesh of his clean arm.

"Shit, Doc...are you OK?" I ask, putting down the crate and heading back toward him.

"I think I got sliced pretty good on one of those shafts," he says to me, squeezing at the underside of his arm.

As I reach his side, I can see that the blood is really flowing out of the long, deep slice through the soft flesh on the inside of his arm.

"C'mon, let's get off the LZ and over there by the trees so we can do something about that," I tell him and offer a hand to lead him over toward the shaded line of trees.

"I can't do much about this with my left hand. You're going to have to do the work. I'll tell you what to do," Doc says to me calmly, not registering any pain or concern.

Damn...there's a lot of blood! I think to myself as my head starts to throb a little, the heat and humidity seeming to have increased significantly in intensity. *OK, OK...shake it off!* This isn't the time to get squeamish about the sight of another man's blood flowing out of his body.

"What do you want me to do?"

Doc directs me into his medical bag and through the inner pouches. He wants this can of powder and that bottle of something and that stick of ointment and this butterfly bandage and a couple of field dressings. He keeps me busy. He keeps me from paying too much attention to the thick red fluid that continues to drip off his arm, over my hands and onto my mud-caked boots. He helps me pinch the separated flesh back together, holding it tightly as I apply the butterflies. The powders and fluids and ointments seem to be working. The blood flow has nearly

Tim Haslam

stopped. A few more swabs with one of the field dressings and then I wrap another clean dressing tightly around his arm, tie it off and look up for a confirmation that the job is done.

"OK…nice job…thanks," Doc says to me.

"Yea, man…that Kuala Lumpur place was really out of sight, man."

The smile returns to his face as he resumes his R&R narrative without any further comment about his arm or his wound or his blood or my lightheadedness.

"Doesn't that hurt, Doc?" is all I can think of to say, not quite ready to move passed my first surrogate medic assignment. His adventures in Kuala Lumpur can wait a minute or two until my own anxious state can settle back down a bit.

"Yea, a little. Man, you should see the women there…"

OK…OK…I guess some things out here are worth talking about and others are just too common to warrant much conversation.

N N N N

This hump is different from the others. The jungle and mountains look and feel the same. The heat, humidity, rain and mud are the same. The mosquitoes and leeches, the cuts and scrapes are all the same. The long nights of guard duty, fighting every second to keep my eyes open, to stay awake, are the same. The C-rations, the Marlboros, the warm water, the gravelly squelch and the radio chatter are all the same. But, everyone senses that Charlie is around here…that lots of them are around here. This is an area that is of value to him…that he'll fight for. So, every step up and down the fingers of these mountains is accompanied by careful probing scans with our eyes, and our ears are keenly attuned to separate out the normal sounds of grunts and jungle from the possible vibrations of other men with guns. We move through all this with greater alertness than ever before. No one gives in to the usual mental fatigue or fades off into the walking, daydreaming state that gets us through most days humping. Nervous energy and adrenaline renew the vibrancy of the forest colors. The size and shape and texture of leaves register's now within our consciousness. Every flutter and flinch of branch or vine or shadow elicits a reaction from us, draws our attention…our scrutiny. The men on point hack away the thick vegetation,

Stars and Stripes and Shadows

keeping their weapons ready to react to anyone disclosed on the other side of the tangled curtains opening at the strokes of their blades.

Things we find along the way confirm our senses and our fears; a few recently occupied bunkers here, an abandoned machinegun position there...fresh trails...trampled plants. They know we're here, combing the mountains for them. They don't seem to want to confront us...yet. We know they're watching us. Perhaps someone is watching down along the barrel of an AK47. *Perhaps he's seeking a prime target—an officer, an RTO.*

The usual physical exertion commensurate with humping these mountains under the weight of the ruck is exaggerated by the demands for sensory acuteness and for the constant mental evaluation of everything around us. When we stop for a break, the whole system shuts down. There's just enough motivational energy left to open and lift a canteen up to our dry lips. A cigarette's too much. Sleep for a minute or two before the bell sounds for the next round.

We just had a break? It couldn't have been fifteen minutes ago. It's just a little after eleven...too early for lunch. Why are we stopping again? What's happened?

"What's going on?" Grossman asks, verbalizing my same thoughts. "Why have we stopped?"

"I don't know. Houston just said to take ten. That's all he...wait a second." Houston's voice comes back over the radio interrupting my explanation to the Lieutenant.

"Roger. Out," I reply into my handset. "The Captain wants you and Bruce up there. I don't know why...maybe the war's over."

"More likely they've moved our destination out a few klicks," responds the newest-Six-Two, the beginnings of his own layer of cynicism starting to show through.

Doc, Ed and Mike Ferlik find their way up to where I've flopped down onto the ground to wait for the army's next decision. As this seems to be a bonus break, we all find the energy to light cigarettes and enough energy to discuss the possible implications of our surprise hiatus. None of our gloomy speculations however come close to what Lieutenant Grossman and Sergeant Bollman are about to tell us.

"We're going in. We're going back to Pleiku for a stand-down."

Tim Haslam

"Are you serious, sir? We're really getting out of here? We're really going all the way back to base camp...when?" The same series of questions comes simultaneously from all of us gathered around.

"Today," Bollman declares, before Grossman has a chance to round out the miraculous vision.

"We're gonna cut an LZ right here. Choppers will be here within an hour to take us down to Dak To where we'll get on trucks. We'll be at Camp Enari tonight."

The paralyzing fatigue and emotional emptiness that characterized our being just a moment ago have been somehow completely erased. There's a shared rebirth spreading among the grunts of Bravo Company. Fuck Charlie! Fuck the boonies! Fuck the shit! We're getting out of here. We're really getting out of here for a while and not just to the dry, dusty camp at Dak To. We're going all the way back to Pleiku, the closest thing to civilization that exists in the Central Highlands.

The happy guys from Six-One have mowed out a landing zone even before the volunteers from the other Platoons can get over there to help. Lighten our load; that's the only thing to do to kill the time waiting for the helicopters to come. Hundreds of little cans of various C-rations are punctured and left to rot out here. Only the most favored ones; peaches, pound cake and beans and weenies are kept. I can pour the water out of four of my six canteens. I put another fresh battery into my radio and discard the old one, adding to the building collection of suddenly valueless stuff accumulating around us.

A string of six Hueys shuttles us out of the shit and has us back down on the airstrip at Dak To by mid-afternoon. There is a great deal of excitement among the Bravo grunts; positive excitement. Nothing like this has happened in the six months that I've been here. This is the first real relief, the first real opportunity to believe that things can get better. Stand-down means a break. The Army, the Division, the Brigade and the Battalion have all agreed to give Bravo Company a rest. No patrols, no guard duty, no LPs, no radio watch and no bullshit details. Hot showers, clean clothes (there has to be clean underwear), hot meals, cold beer and soda, shopping at the camp PX, mail, movies and who-knows-what other pleasures await us at Pleiku. We're all anxious to climb onto the trucks lined up to convoy back down Route 14.

Six-Two Platoon is assigned to three trucks toward the tail end of

Stars and Stripes and Shadows

the column of vehicles. It's up to us to sort out who goes on what truck. I follow Mike Ferlik and most of his guys up onto the middle of our three trucks, arrange my ruck into a backrest and settle down onto the hard metal bed of the deuce-and-a-half. A couple of the newer squad leaders that have joined us recently, the ones right out of the Army's NCO school, climb up after me and settle in, happy to have the chance to go back to civilization so soon. Toby Lamberti hurries up toward the tailgate of the truck and pulls off his ruck, tossing it up into the cluttered bed.

"Here," he says to me, thrusting out his M16, "give me a hand with this."

I twist around just enough to reach over and grab the rifle butt that Toby's handing me. Just as I grasp the black plastic stock, something down in my lower back makes a subtle pop and sends a sharp jolt of pain up along my left side.

Damn! Ow…what the hell was that? I straighten up and try to twist myself back into a more upright posture hoping to correct whatever it is that's causing me this pain. It doesn't work. The sharp pain bites into my lower back and burns its way down the inside of my left leg. I try several other gyrations, trying to find some orientation that will end the pain. Nothing works. By now, Toby's settled in and can tell that something's going on with me.

"What's wrong?"

"I don't know, man. When I took your rifle, something sort of snapped down in my back. It hurts like hell. I don't know what I could have done."

"Where's Doc?" Toby asks, knowing that there's nothing he can do to help me out.

"I think he's on the next truck up. Don't worry about it. It'll be OK. I think it's probably like a cramp or something. If I can just get into a comfortable position here, I think it'll come around."

I don't know that I believe what I'm saying or not. I've never had an injury greater than a sprained ankle in my life and I can't recall ever feeling such sharp, lingering pain.

Just try to tough it out. There's nothing else to do anyway. I just have to sit here and enjoy the ride back down to Pleiku. It'll be fine by the time we get there. Then I can start partying along with everyone else. Whatever

Tim Haslam

I did to my back will be forgotten by then.

By sitting up straight and pulling my knees up slightly toward my chest I seem to be able to reduce the pain. *OK, OK, that's better,* I think to myself, greatly relieved, as the truck jerks forward and starts plowing into the heavy dust churned up by the line of military vehicles ahead of us. We're on our way. Things are about to get better.

Among some of the other cargo in our truck is a crate of fresh oranges. They get passed around quickly without any concern for authorization or ownership. Everything in this truck is now assumed to be for us. I haven't seen much fresh fruit in my time out here. The sweet juice and chewy fiber of the orange adds to the feeling of Christmas on this hot September afternoon. I remember how there was always a fresh orange in my stocking on Christmas morning. I think for a minute about home, the images starting to become a little clearer again. I remember our mantle and fireplace and the warmth of our living room as my sister and I plowed through the bounty of gifts always bestowed upon us. I remember when I was home on leave last Christmas. I remember being with Rosemary Christmas night, after the usual family gatherings. I wonder what Rosemary's doing right now. *What time is it back home?* I wonder if she's thinking about me. I wonder if she remembers me. I wonder if she's asleep. *I wonder if she smells like Shalimar.* I wonder why.

By the time our truck passes out of the opened gates at the southern end of the Dak To base I need to shift around again. I need to find another position that will be comfortable. I try a couple of things. There's still a lot of pain. Something's definitely wrong. The pits and bumps in the old road, slamming back up through the rigid frame of the truck don't help any. *This is going to be a long trip! I'm not having as much fun as everyone else.*

Route 14, running from Dak To back to Pleiku seems to be much longer than it was coming the other way so many months ago. There are the same intermittent attacks of rain though and the late afternoon sky is gray and dark, reminding me of the ominous feeling as we pass through the outskirts of the dirty old city of Kontum and through the other little mountain villages along the way. This time however, I know more about the dangers that I could only imagine when I last passed through here. The remote ARVN complexes, isolated out here in the

464

Stars and Stripes and Shadows

wilderness are cause for even more contemplation and trepidation than they were on my first trip. I now know about snipers and mortars and rockets. I know about the long dangerous nights out in these jungles. I know about Charlie and I know about luck. I know that in another couple of hours it will be night out here. I'm glad that I won't be spending the night at any of these bamboo fortresses. Even with the lingering pain in my back I'd rather ride this vibrating, bouncing truck out of the shit…even if takes days or weeks.

The sky is darkening further, fading from afternoon to evening as the convoy passes through the little valley to the north east of Pleiku. The valley that was the rallying point for the convoy that brought me out to the shit last March. From here on in, the road is shared with more and more Vietnamese, some on little motor scooters, most on old bicycles. They all seem to be in a hurry to get someplace. They want to get there before dark.

The truck behind us must have had a crate of oranges as well. I see one flung out of the back, aimed at a young man peddling along the side of the road. It misses him, but he nearly loses control dodging the fruit and almost turns into the ditch adjacent to the road. A moment later I see a hand reach out of the same truck and snatch a raggedy hat off of an old man peddling an even older bicycle slowly along. The truck obscures my view of the man before I can discern his reaction. The road bends around to the left a little and I can see that Lieutenant Reese in the truck behind us is the man representing my country to the people of Vietnam, the officer winning the hearts and minds of the people we're liberating from communist oppression. My back really hurts now. I'd like to shoot the asshole Reese.

Our truck pulls through the gate at Camp Enari just as the last fading remnants of dusk blush out of the western sky. The vehicles in the convoy separate at various intersections within the camp, heading for their respective unit headquarters and motor pools. The camp is alive with activity. Little bands of uniformed men stroll leisurely about the dusty streets, bathed in the stark brightness of electric light bulbs. I haven't seen such light in six months. The other men in my truck are showing signs of their own building excitement. They want to be off this truck and out walking around. They want to be heading for the NCO Club or the Enlisted Men's Club. They want to avail themselves

Tim Haslam

of whatever the camp has to offer, whatever is here that they've been denied for so long. I have the same deep wants, but can't overcome the pain that's compounded by every move and twist of my body. I'm starting to feel as though I'm going to be denied my stand down.

We pull up alongside the S1 office hut with the 3rd of the 8th sign outside. Before we can climb off, Bob Price and a Sergeant that I don't recognize come trotting out to greet us. Sergeant Bollman, who's been riding in the cab of our truck has exited the vehicle and walks over to meet the two men. I can see Price and Bollman standing side by side, fully illuminated by a large, bare light bulb attached to a telephone pole next to them. I'm struck by the dramatic difference in the appearance of these two men. Price is dressed in clean fatigues and wears an army-issue baseball cap. It's the contrast in the two faces though that's captured my attention. I can see the clean, shaven flesh of Bob Price's face. He looks much younger than I remember him when he was out with us in the field. Bollman's face, in contrast, is painted with the mottled, aging varnish of the grunt world. I hadn't noticed his face either until just now. I hadn't noticed any of our faces until just now. Now, here, under the artificial electric light, within the company of clean, civilized people, I can see what's happened to us. I can see on all of our faces the build up of months of living out in the shit; living out in an uncivilized world where you don't want to be seen. We look too much like creatures of the forest.

"Stay on the truck," Bollman advises us after a brief conversation with Price and the unidentified Sergeant. "There isn't enough hot water here for the whole Company to shower. We're going over to the 4th of the 42nd Artillery and use their showers."

Bollman helps the other two men throw two bundles of clean fatigues up onto the back of the truck and returns to the cab. It's almost completely dark now and the nighttime rules preclude the driver from using his headlights. Most of the roads through Camp Enari are straight, level and run at right angles to one another. The driver seems to know the way, proceeding slowly through the darkened streets.

It's been over five hours since I climbed up into the back of this truck; five dreadful hours and five thousand jarring, punishing bumps. I can barely get to my feet. There's no way I can lift my ruck. Lamberti helps me. Somehow I make it down onto the ground, hoping that

Stars and Stripes and Shadows

things will come around if I can stretch out into an upright posture. They don't. The pain finds new territory to penetrate; further down my left leg, down toward my groin and all the way up my back. I work my way over into the hut with the showers, taking six-inch steps. I don't know that I can get out of my fatigues and I sure don't want to ask anybody to help. I can see that there is clean underwear along with pants and shirts. I don't know how I'm going to get out of the disgusting, shredded rag that's been graphed to my body for the last six months. I'm not sure I can make it to the shower or that I can stand under the warm water.

The others have charged out of their filthy uniforms and headed into the showers, excitedly discussing all the possibilities of things to come. The Ivory Soap takes on new meaning here. There's even a bottle of shampoo being passed around. The faces of the young men are starting to emerge as the detergent solvents etch away the jungle residue.

Most of them are done and dressing before my slow painful struggle releases me from my own filthy clothes. My companion underwear deserves a more thoughtful separation. I'm in too much pain though and trying to hurry to catch up with the others and so, my constant companion boxers, nearly shredded away, get thrown into the trashcan without any farewells. Their tour of duty is complete. For them, the war is over, their duty fulfilled yet unappreciated, perhaps even resented; their retirement unceremonious; *they don't mean nothin'.*

The hot water has run out by the time I've inched my way under one of the showerheads. I don't know if the cold water feels good or bad. I know only that something is seriously wrong with my back and that the pain is severe. I stay just long enough to soap down quickly and rinse off. There's no time to shampoo my hair. Raising my arms is too painful anyway.

The new, clean underwear are somehow enough to give me a brief moment of pleasure and appreciation for something. Everyone else is waiting for me back on the truck. I'm keeping them from their celebration. I hurry into my new fatigues as much as I can and back into my grungy boots. I've never been in this much pain.

"There's nothing that I can do tonight," Doc Charlbois tells me back at the big tent that's been set up to temporarily house us.

Tim Haslam

"Come to sick-call in the morning. If it's still bothering you, I'll send you over to the 71ˢᵗ and they can check out what's going on."

"OK...thanks Doc."

I know that he's in a big hurry to join the others heading off to the appropriate clubs and the cold beers before the ten o'clock curfew drives them back here to the dark tent. For me the only celebrating will be from finding some body position on this hard cot that limits the amount of pain I'm in. For me, this will be one more long sleepless night. Tomorrow morning, I'll likely still be in the throes of misery from my back injury instead of the misery of a hangover earned along with my grunt friends. There seems to be an irony to this. This is the lowest point in my life. This is the loneliest I've ever been.

N   N   N   N

"It looks to me like you've got some pinched nerves down here," the fatigue-clad doctor says to me, pointing at the X-ray clipped up onto the lighted box on the wall. "It also looks like this disk down here is somewhat compressed. The nerves that come into the spinal cord through this disk space are probably being pinched. Have you done anything that might have put a lot of strain on it recently, or done something that might have compressed your lower back?"

Are you shit'n me? I've been hump'n around an 80 pound ruck...jump'n out of helicopters and tripping over everything in the Central Highlands.

"No, sir...I can't think of anything. I was just reaching for a rifle that this guy was handing to me when it went out. Everything was perfectly fine up until then."

"I'm putting you on a no-duty profile for a week. I want you to come back here everyday for ice-messages and physical therapy. It'll be uncomfortable for awhile."

With the doctor's paperwork in hand, I climb back onto the military ambulance truck that shuttles back and forth between the 71ˢᵗ Evac Hospital and Camp Enari over on the other side of Pleiku. Riding back over the rutted roads on the hard bench seats of the ambulance quickly offsets any of the beneficial affects of the therapy. The doctor has prescribed some pain pills and muscle relaxers that haven't yet taken effect.

Its late afternoon by the time I get back to the Bravo Company tents

Stars and Stripes and Shadows

and hobble my way over to my cot. Most of the others in the Platoon are milling around within the hot tent, sharing the merchandize they've purchase at the camp PX. There are lots of new cameras and radios to be tried out. Others are lounging on their cots, lost in a new magazine or paperback book or writing letters home on new, clean stationary. I continue to feel as though I've been cheated by fate out of this small reward. I'm sure my back will be fine again, just when this stand down is over and it's time to head back out to the boonies. A smoke helps a little. Sergeant Bollman's promise that we'll be getting mail later this afternoon helps more.

The mail arrives an hour before dinnertime. There's a letter from Mom and a formally typed one from Dad and two from Rosemary. It's been a long time since I got two letters from her at the same time. Her letters have been coming with less regularity, spaced further and further apart, each comprised of a nearly carbon copy narrative describing her job, her dad and how bored she is. Careful examination of the postmarks indicates that one of the two letters was sent nearly a month ago. It's been lost in the postal system somewhere and just coincidently arrived at the same time that her next letter reached me. The older letter is the same dispassionate diary of mundane things. There are no longer any feelings about us expressed; no concerns about me put forth; no mention of the long months remaining before we can be together again.

The latest letter is different, suddenly, there's a lot going on for her. There's a lot for her to tell me about. She's been hanging around with one of my fraternity brothers, Rick Wright and his latest girlfriend, Lisa. They've included Rosemary in just about everything they've been doing apparently. She's become a part of their circle of friends. She mentions lots of new names, people I don't know, girls and guys.

This letter does bring back the images of home. Parties on balmy summer Friday nights at Zuma Beach; going to the movies down in Hollywood or Westwood, going to the Old World on Sunset Boulevard afterwards for big syrup-laden Belgian waffles late at night; lingering over a cup of coffee at Denny's in the morning, wondering what to do the rest of the day. Her letter only describes the scenes. My imagination colors in the rest; the dialogue, the activities and the cast of characters; girls and guys. *Who's there with her? When will she tell me the rest of the story?*

Tim Haslam

N N N N

The Bravo Company stand down is in its third full day. I'm spending most of my days in transit to and from the 71st. Maybe I'm making a little progress or maybe I've just become so used to the pain that I've learned to deal with it a little better. I still can't find a comfortable position to sit or lay in and I'm still limited to tiny steps whenever I attempt to walk anywhere. The other guys are sympathetic and want to assist, but don't want to be held up as time is running out on their break. The pain pills that the doctor prescribed make me feel a little dopey anyway. I'm not very good company right now. I just want to sleep. I just want someone to shoot me. I just want to have a stand down for one day.

The word spreads quickly on the morning of the forth day that we'll be going back out tomorrow. I'm still on a medical profile and restricted from duty. *What's going to happen to me?* I'd gladly face Mr. Ruck and another six months out in the shit if my back would just feel normal again.

Around mid-morning, Captain Hilton comes through our tent with another new man. The solidly built black man with the Captain is First Sergeant Jerome Goodrum, Bravo Company's new first sergeant replacing Master Sergeant Madison who departed this morning for home. The Captain is introducing Goodrum to each of the few men still remaining within the tent.

"How you doin' Haslam? I heard you've been having some trouble with your back," the Captain says, sitting down on the adjacent cot.

"Yes, sir…I still don't know what I did, but it's pretty stiff and sore. The doctor over at the 71st says its pinched nerves."

"This is First Sergeant Goodrum," the Captain says, introducing the veteran NCO with the straight line little moustache and friendly smile.

"Sorry to hear about your back, son," Goodrum says, extending his hand. "I've had some back problems before myself. I know what kind of misery that can be."

"Thanks Top. Maybe you can tell me how long this will last."

"My guess is that it's probably going to be a while."

"That's one of the reasons we came by," the Captain says, transitioning the conversation from superficial to substantive. "We're pulling out tomorrow and we can't take you with us and I don't know when you'll

Stars and Stripes and Shadows

be able to rejoin us again. You'll have to stay here at base camp until the doctor's release you"

"Yes, sir," I answer, understanding the situation but still feeling like there's more to their visit than this explanation.

"Can you type?" the Captain asks, starting to get to the point.

"Yes, sir...I took typing in school and have had to type a lot of school stuff since then," I reply, wondering what my answer is about to get me into.

"Look, I hate to loose you out in the field. I need capable RTOs and squad leaders and I think you've got potential out there but, here's the situation. Bob Price, the Company Clerk is scheduled to DEROS next month. This is going to put Sergeant Goodrum and me in a bind. We don't have a replacement. Since you have to be here and you can type, I'd like you to start working with Price to learn his job. Then, when he leaves we'll at least have someone temporarily who knows the job. If your back has fully recovered by then we'll decide about finding another clerk and bringing you back out."

"So this is really just a temporary assignment?" I ask making sure I understand my options.

"Like I said, we need you to learn the job and fill in until we can work through what happens next," the Captain dodges my question, reminding me that I do what I'm told, that I don't have options.

Later that afternoon, Price comes by to congratulate me on my new assignment.

"Man, its way better here than out in the boonies. You sleep in a dry place. You eat hot meals in the mess hall. You can shower almost every day. We hardly ever get mortared here," Price tells me with true conviction.

In his ball cap, clean fatigues and glasses he looks like the Company Clerk. He wants to be the Company Clerk. He's happy. He's also going home in less than thirty days. Whatever else the job entails, that he's not telling me about, is insignificant to him relative to the risk of dieing out in the shit in his last month of service in Vietnam. I guess I should be happy too. There are a million compelling reasons why I don't ever want to go back to the shit. Every second I was out there, I wanted to be someplace else. I wanted to have all the things that Price

Tim Haslam

just described. I wanted to be dry and clean, free from the constant itch and sting. I wanted to be a little safer.

I watch the deuce-and-a-half full of unhappy grunts pull away down the dusty road towards the eastern gate, heading back towards the mountains and all that's contained there. I study the bandoliers, the belts of machinegun bullets, the frags, flares and mines hanging from the refreshed rucksacks accompanying Bravo Company back out. I've exchanged goodbyes with all my friends. I wonder who will be the new-Six-Two-Charlie. I wonder who won't come back. I wonder why I'm feeling so alone and depressed standing here in my clean fatigues and my ball cap. I wonder why I'm not feeling better about my future here within the heavily defended Fourth Infantry Division Basecamp.

"Get your hands out of your pockets, soldier," an unknown Lieutenant passing by suggests to me, breaking my moment of reflection. "Don't you have something you should be doing?"

An LZ fashioned by thousand pound bombs from a B52. (From the collection of Robert Stevson on the IvyDragoons website.)

The beginnings of a fire support base; this one may be FB30. (From the collection of Robert Stevson on the IvyDragoons website.)

Tim Haslam

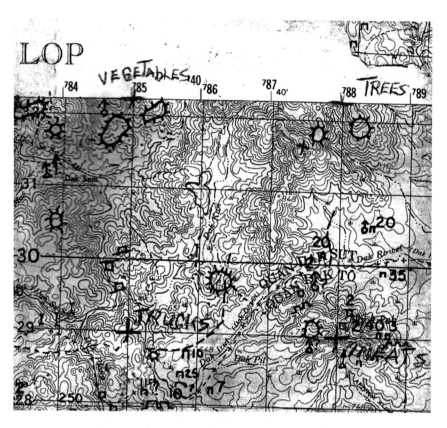

A section of my Dak Mot Lop map with reference categories marked; vegetables, trees, trucks and meats.

Stars and Stripes and Shadows

Fri. May 17,

Dear Mom & Dad,

We've moved again, and are now at another fire base on another hilltop. There a little more activity, however, we've been mortared everyday for the last three days. But it really isn't to dangerous. They only get off a couple of rounds and our own mortars and artillery and gunships are on them. We've only had one minor injury, and we tend to stay closer to the bunkers.

We've had a lot of air strikes in the area, which is also comforting, and last night we had three B-52 strikes in the area that really shook up the place.

I'm really getting sick of c-rats. and am still looking forward to your package.

Next episode on next page.

Tim Haslam

(Continued)

Mon. May 20
9:30 a.m.

As I was writing this letter last Friday we were mortared again, and I was persuaded to put off completing my letter. It was also the worst attack yet, as we had one man killed and 10 wounded. But they haven't come to close to our bunker. However we had two short rounds from our own mortars land a few feet away yesterday; but neither of them went off.

Joe has promoted to assistant squad leader, and that along with being RTO keeps me pretty busy.

We haven't had any rain for the last three or four days, but it's pretty cloudy, and tonight I am on OP outside the perimeter, so it will probably rain.

We also haven't had any mail sent out to me for about a week, and I hope they will get out here today.

One of my letters home. This one was sent from FB25. The "one man killed" was Sergeant Sterling Johnson.

Stars and Stripes and Shadows

The 155s at the bridge; I think this is the one that had us trying to plug our ears with cigarette butts – June 1968. (From the collection of Robert Stevson on the IvyDragoons website.)

The bridge along Route 512 over the Dak Poko – June 1968. (From the collection of Robert Stevson on the IvyDragoons website.)

Tim Haslam

A C7 Caribou that crash landed at Dak Pek, brought down by ground fire a few days before Bravo Company arrived there on other C7s.

```
'6   LINE UP  BACK
     427096   1358
     GRFMJH   DSQO
17th
     First  Woman
     41872   39506
     LJPBQ   YFZKD
18th
     Coke  Partly
     0374   928516
     ZMBN   QSVDFU
19th
     Zebra  Funds
     63109   52847
     MWHJL   CKIPG
20th
     Chart  Mobile
     92705   31846
     EGXPF   QJKDZ
```

Words-of-the-day codes for the 16th to 20th of August 1968.

Stars and Stripes and Shadows

Me, at Ranger's Roost – July 1968.

With Jack Wong and our bag of fresh fish. Note the front of my pants. I wasn't really that afraid of getting kidnapped; just got too close to the tank full of thrashing around fish. October 1968.

Tim Haslam

200 Pee; a 200 Piastre note, the currency of South Vietnam in 1968 and a Ten Cent Military Payment Certificate.

First Sergeant "Top" Goodrum.

Bob Price (with his finger in his M16) and I returning from a sweep for VC out to the west of Camp Enari – October 1968.

Tim Haslam

Stoney; outside the barracks. Note the symbolic commitment to the war on the door.

Marion Valentine (Val), right, and I outside the S1 office. Note that I'm still wearing elastic bands just below my knees to keep the leeches from getting any further up my anatomy.

Stars and Stripes and Shadows

Getting near the end...tired of it all.

Jim Welsh heading out for guard duty with his bandolier and cans of Black Label.

Tim Haslam

The last B52; on the ground at Cam Rahn Bay; taken just before I boarded the plane for home – March 1969.

Chapter 15

DA Form 1

"You have to be really careful with the carbons," Price advises as he diligently adjusts the clean sheets of paper and thin pieces of used carbon tissue behind the document form. "We have plenty of paper and DA-1s, but not much carbon paper. You have to make four copies of this, and that makes a bundle of paper that just barely fits into the typewriter." He's referring to the Army's Morning Report. Each and every Company level unit in the United States Army must fill out and turn in a Morning Report, every day, seven days a week, 52 weeks a year. The Morning Report is the main job of the Company Clerk, it's his primary responsibility and it must be done right.

"You're allowed to have three strikeover errors down here in the bottom part of the form, but no mistakes are allowed up here in the top part," he tells me pointing to the various sections of the form. It's mostly fill-in sections; DATE, UNIT ID, etc., etc.

"Down here, you can make a few mistakes. This is where you have to describe what's behind the changes to the information that's up here in these boxes."

Price is into this. This is just the kind of thing that gives him a real sense of importance and control. He's mastered the Morning Report. He's ritualized everything about it from carefully stacking and stapling the package together, to inserting it up under the roller of the big Remington typewriter, to the vertical alignment and tab settings. He takes great pride in the finished product. It's not going to be easy for him to hand it off to someone who may not be as passionate about it as he is.

"So, who's gonna care if you do make one too many mistakes?" I

Tim Haslam

ask, as he starts to peck in a series of mysterious acronyms into the blank squares across the top.

"Captain Walterhouse...he's the Battalion Adjutant," Price tells me, lifting his fingers up and away from the keys. He doesn't want his answering to be a distraction from his concentration.

"When we're done with it, it goes to the Captain over in that office." Price points to a closed door at the east end of the flimsy wood framed building that serves as the S1 office for the Battalion. Within the office are all the other Company Clerks for the Battalion plus a clerk whose primary responsibility is security clearances and background checking. At the west end of the office is another closed door with a sign that reads; MAIL ROOM. Everything in the office; the desks and chairs, the files and tables, all seem to be old Army Surplus. The individual clerks have personalized their space as much as they can. Several of them have big reel-to-reel tape recorders on tables behind their desks and an array of music is country-twanging or rock-and-rolling around the room. It's OK to smoke and nearly everyone does. There are three big fans, mounted on floor stands, attempting to generate some draft of cooler air through the hot stuffy confines of the little office. Everything and everyone is dusty.

Mud to dust! Still hot, still humid! This isn't much better than the shit.

"Walterhouse will look over everything on the report and—trust me—he will look at every letter and number that you type in. If he doesn't find too many mistakes, he'll sign it down here and you can pick it up in that tray over there. From there, you have to distribute and file the various copies. That's it...that's all there is to the Morning Report."

"How much time do I have to do it? Does it have to be turned in by a certain time?" I ask, nervously considering how long it's been since I typed up my term paper for Miss Gonziorosky's senior comp class, the last typewritten work I can remember doing that had a deadline and quality consequences.

"It has to be on the Captain's desk by ten. You'll have until eleven to fix any mistakes that he finds. Don't worry...on most days there's not that much going on that changes things on the report. If something happens though, and a lot of guys get wounded or killed, this thing can

486

Stars and Stripes and Shadows

really take a long time."

I've survived the last six months out in the jungles; being mortared, rocketed, sniped at, set upon by leeches, mosquitoes, fire ants and giant man-eating pieces of bamboo and now I'm facing the likelihood of court-martial and firing squad for failure to turn in the Morning Report—with no more than three errors—in time.

"So what happens if you don't get it done in time?"

"Captain Walterhouse is pretty good. When you're new, he'll cut you some slack. If he knows that you're working on it, he won't really start to get pissed until about eleven-thirty. The Captain's not the main reason you need to get done with this anyway. You need to get this out of the way so that you can get all the other things that need to done each day in time."

"I guess you're going to show me what 'all the other things' are?"

"Yea...in a minute," he says, twisting away at the carriage knob, releasing today's version of DA-1 for B-3-8. "First, I'll introduce you to the other guys here."

Still seated behind his desk, with me at his side, Price starts with the guy across the room, Jim Welsh the Delta Company clerk and works his way around counterclockwise; Bill Taylor Alpha's clerk, Dennis Maxey, Charlie Company, Rick Stone, the clerk of all secret things and Steve Loza the clerk for the headquarters staff, recon and weapons platoons. Welsh, Taylor and Maxey each wear the Combat Infantrymen's Badge (CIB) over the left-hand pocket of their shirts, as does Bob Price, indicating that they have all served time out in the shit, that they are all infantrymen by training and experience. Stone and Loza are the only people here actually trained by the Army to be clerks. This provides an endless source of ribbing and good-natured dissonance based on the class distinction between "real clerks" and "real grunts." Stone and Loza are up to it and can easily hold their own with the "dumbshit grunts" that've been fortunate enough to find their way into the exclusive S1 clerk's club. Stone and Loza are told frequently that they don't know shit about shit, or about the shit and never will, by the CIB'ers— "anybody who can type can be a clerk. It takes a special breed to be a grunt in the shit."

"Yea, right...anybody who can't type, or spell, or read, qualifies for that special breed!"

Tim Haslam

All of the guys are friendly and happy to have a new face joining them. The introductions have provided everyone an opportunity to take a break from their morning routine for a few minutes and to start a dialogue between them. I'm perfectly happy to keep on with the banter and discussion, but, Price, the short-timer, wants to get back to work. He starts showing me other forms that have to be filled in and routed here and there. He opens up several large routing envelopes and goes through the contents of each, explaining what they are and what I will have to do with them, clarifying how many mistakes are allowed with each process step, what the deadlines are and who has to approve them.

Basically, the job of the Company Clerk is to keep track of everyone officially assigned to the Company. It's no easy task. People in an infantry company in Vietnam are constantly moving around. People DEROS out and new replacements come in. Sick and wounded men go to various hospitals. More fortunate men go on R&R, which is a different status than men who are actually on formal leave. Men transfer to and from other units. Men turn up missing. Men die.

The clerk also has to keep track of what each man is. How many First Lieutenants, Staff Sergeants, Specialists Four and Privates First Class are there in the Company today and the clerk has to cite the official orders that authorize any change of status. There's a lot of paper to process and understand, all written in the language of Defense Department and Department of the Army abbreviations and acronyms. I hope I can learn this language and what to do with all this paper in the next few weeks.

Click...2, click...2, space, shift...click...S, click...e, click...p, space, click...6, click...8. There, good. I've got the first box filled in without a mistake. Price has given me a copy of today's DA-1 with an assignment to copy it as a means of getting familiar with the document and the old Remington. He won't risk any of the carbons in a practice session, so I just get one of the blank forms to play with.

"Be careful with the J, it sticks some times, so does the V but not as much, and the 7 and 8 keys tend to get locked together a lot, I think one of them is a little bit bent," Price tells me as I click and knob-twist and carriage return my way through the document. I get all the way

Stars and Stripes and Shadows

down to the section where I have to type in the number 1 in a block along the line that reads "COMMISIONED" under the heading "IN TRANSIT" and the sub-heading, "OUTBOUND."

"Damn it! I put in an upper case L by mistake. Can't I strike over that? There's still room in the block for me to correct it," I suggest to Price.

"No…not up in this section. No mistakes up here," he says forcefully, as though he understands the dire implications of submitting today's DA-1 for B 3/8 with such a blemish.

He gives me another DA-1 form. I remember all the right knobs and levers to release and twist and adjust to get the paper aligned just right.

Click……click……click……damn…retract…crumple…waste basket.

Insert…align…click……click……click……click……damn!

Finally, after only four discarded forms I make it all the way through the upper section and stay within the allowable three errors in the lower section. I did it. Each morning for the next ten days this will be the routine. Price will do *his* Morning Report, explaining what the changes are from the various orders and notification documents that show up each day. Then it will be my turn to slowly click out a duplicate. Once Captain Walterhouse has signed the Morning Report, the clerks are freer to manage their work without much external interruption.

Walterhouse often disappears for hours at a time and the other officers and senior NCOs assigned to the Battalion's base camp headquarters usually have duties elsewhere and rarely come in to S1 to bother us. The stereos get turned up and long periods of casual discussion take place. For the other clerks, who've mastered the routine here, this is pretty easy duty. For me, I'm still not comfortable around this place. My back still hurts, but that's not the main source of my discontent. For reasons I can't understand, I miss the shit.

Price introduces me to Marion B. Valentine, the Bravo Company mail clerk and asks him to show me around the rest of the camp. Valentine (Val) gladly accepts the assignment, starting with a thirty second tour of the mail room, explaining the complexities of his job. I remember Valentine from out in the field. I didn't know him though. He was in Six-One Platoon for awhile until he got sick with something.

489

Tim Haslam

The timing of his illness, similar to that of my back injury, put him back here at Camp Enari when he got out of the hospital just as a vacancy for mail clerk surfaced. Bob Price sent word out to Captain Hilton about the need for a new clerk and mentioned that Valentine was coincidentally passing through and met the qualifications. At the same time a whole pack of fresh replacements were heading out to the Company and the Captain agreed to solve the problem as Price suggested. With the Company Commander out in the field, the Company Clerk has a lot of power. A Company Clerk that understands how to use this power can find himself with a lot of friends—at all ranks.

Val walks me down the wooden walkway that runs between the tin-roofed billets and Quonset huts that make up the 3rd of the 8th Battalion area. By now I know where the mess hall and the showers are. Each of the buildings is surrounded with a sandbag wall, about four feet high. Most of the buildings also have a layer of sandbags on the roof. The sandbags serve as a constant reminder that the whole camp is in range of enemy rockets and mortars.

Val shows me where the aid-station is and fills me in on the sick-call routine each morning if I'm in need of medical attention. He points out some of the other structures and large metal containers that occupy space here and there between the permanent structures. There are several large cargo containers (CONEXs) that are used to secure more valuable supplies and ammunition, each locked and under the control of the various Supply Sergeants. At the end of the wooden walkway is the shitter, a small wooden structure that, like all other structures is surrounded on three sides by stacked sandbags. Along one of the inside walls is a wooden bench seat with six holes. A few roles of toilet paper are set here and there between the open holes. Under each of the holes is an old fifty-five gallon barrel, cut in half. Maintenance of the shitter and the six half-barrels is the sole responsibility of Tran, an elderly Vietnamese civilian who is allowed into Camp Enari each day along with hundreds of other Vietnamese who perform cleaning, laundering and kitchen duties for us. To most of the men here, Tran is referred to simply as the "shit-burner."

As we return along the wooden walkway, a very large black man exits one of the billets and heads towards us. Valentine immediately ceases his narrative descriptions of life hear and straightens himself up.

Stars and Stripes and Shadows

"Good morning, Sergeant Major," Val says to the big man as he closes to within a few feet of us.

"Morning Valentine...and who's this?" the Sergeant Major responds in a friendly voice.

"This is Haslam. He's going to be working with Bob Price as the Bravo Company Clerk. Price's going home in a few weeks."

"OK...I guess Valentine's showing you around and going over the rules with you."

"Right, Sergeant Major," I reply.

With the introductions only half completed, I'm not sure of the Sergeant Major's name. It doesn't really matter though. All I really need to know about this man is that he's the Sergeant Major. There's only one enlisted rank higher in the Army—a Command Sergeant Major. Sergeant Major's generally have more power and influence than anybody. Most officers below the rank of Lieutenant Colonel treat Sergeant Majors as their superiors. Even Generals treat Command Sergeant Majors with care and respect. It takes a long time to work one's way up through the enlisted ranks to reach E-10. They're the venerable plenipotentiaries of the Army. In every infantry battalion the arrangement is the same. The Lieutenant Colonel in command makes the strategic and tactical decisions and orchestrates the units in combat. The Sergeant Major runs everything else.

"I'm Sergeant Major Reynolds," he declares in the manner of a benevolent dictator, holding out a bear paw sized hand.

"Nice to meet you Sergeant Major," I say while attempting to stretch my own hand over the great catcher's mitt of a hand extended out at me.

"You might want to get that moustache trimmed up a little bit and it looks like you could use new, clean boots," SM-Reynolds suggests, still in a friendly, fatherly tone, as he pulls away from us, apparently on his way down to the shitter.

"I don't think I ever talked to a Sergeant Major before," I tell Val, as we return to our tour.

"Reynolds is really a pretty good guy," he tells me. "Just don't get on his bad side. When he tells you to do something, do it."

"What's he likely to tell me to do?"

"We have to stand formation every morning, right out here in front

Tim Haslam

of S1 at seven. Reynolds will take role and read off the duty assignments. Generally, because we have full time jobs here, we don't get any of the daytime assignments. It's the guys that are just passing through that get all the make-work, piddly-assed jobs. You know how the Army is; they don't like anybody sitting around."

"So, we just have to do our clerk job and that's it?"

"That's pretty much it during the day. We'll probably end up with some kind of guard duty assignment four nights out of the week though; either perimeter guard, perimeter back up, or reaction squad. Back-up and reaction squad aren't too bad. You just have to spend the night with all your gear over in that billet across the street. If anything happens you'll get deployed out to the perimeter or wherever the shit's hit'n the fan. If you draw perimeter guard though, you have to go out when it gets dark and spend the night out in one of the perimeter bunkers. It's better than guard duty out in the shit, but it still makes for a long night."

"What if we don't have any duty? What do we do at night?"

"We're pretty much on our own. We can go over to the EM Club until curfew. They also have movies almost every night over at the transportation battalion. The Dayroom here is open until curfew and we've got a little Canteen in a room attached to the main supply shed out in back that's sometimes open if the Supply Sergeant's can score any beer."

Clubs, movies, beer and sleeping on a dry cot, this is all starting to sound better. I think about the nightly struggles to stay awake through the long hours of black silence on LP and radio watch out in the shit. This has to be better.

Valentine leads me back to the S1 offices and has Bob Price make out passes for both of us so that we can expand our tour out beyond the Battalion area. The only place he really wants to take me to and really wants to go to himself is the PX.

The Post Exchange turns out to be a complex of commercial enterprises. There's a barbershop just inside the entrance as well as a massage parlor. Vietnamese civilians operate both. Val tells me that, although he's never been there, he's heard that the girls giving the messages will provide certain additional services for a price. There's a considerable line of men queued up outside the entrance to the parlor, confirming the

Stars and Stripes and Shadows

level of interest in messages among the young men of the 4th. The two Vietnamese barbers are sitting in their barber chairs reading Vietnamese newspapers. There's no waiting for a haircut.

The store part of the PX is pretty well stocked with goodies and they have a surprising selection of Japanese made electronics; Nikon and Pentax cameras, Seiko wristwatches, Sony radios and even some big Akai reel-to-reel tape recorders, all at reasonable prices. They also have all the necessary military paraphernalia that the Army doesn't supply. I buy one of the silver and blue Combat Infantrymen's Badges and immediately pin it on my shirt. It's my declaration to the non-combatant's here in base camp that I've been in the shit, that I'm really a grunt. I'll have my own uniforms if I stay here in base camp and I can have any of the appropriate patches sewn on by Vietnamese who work here. I decide to wait before investing in any such adornments. *Let's see how well base camp and I get along.*

Val and I loiter around the PX complex until just before chow time and then head back to the 3rd of the 8th for lunch. Along the way he points out where the main Division Administration group is, the Division Aid Station, and the central post office. The rest of the neighborhood segments we pass are the various headquarters for all the other infantry, artillery and armored units that make up the 4th Infantry Division.

We pass officers several times as we stroll along. Fortunately Val has re-learned the proper etiquette and snaps out salutes and, "good morning sirs" with the necessary flourishes and conviction. I follow his lead, echoing each sincere greeting.

"A lot of the officers walking around out here are on what's called courtesy patrol," Val explains. "They're between assignments and have nothing better to do and so the Division has them walk around looking for soldiers who are out of uniform or who fail to salute or some other major violation of protocol."

"What do they do if they find something wrong with somebody?" I ask.

"They write up something like a traffic ticket. They get your name, rank and service number and your unit. The citation gets sent to your company and it's supposed to go to the company CO for review and possible disciplinary action and a copy is supposed to go into your

Tim Haslam

personnel file. Believe me, the whole thing's a fuck'n game. It don't mean nothin'…still, it's a hassle. It's always better to look like your going someplace on business. Try to have something in your hand, some papers or something and take some of the side streets to get to the PX. You're less likely to run into one of the courtesy patrol officers that way."

"We receive and return salutes proudly in the Fourth Division!" the banner tacked up above the door going into S1 reads as another reminder to anyone who's pride may be in need of bolstering.

"I guess they take all the formal Army stuff pretty seriously around here," I observe out loud to Price as I return to our desk after lunch.

"Oh, yea, life out in the shit was a lot better in that way. There was always too much to do to get your job done and stay alive then to worry about bullshit like that. We were always lucky too. All the officers we had out there had their heads on right and didn't really give a shit about crap like that. A lot of the officers here at Camp Enari have spent their time out in the shit and don't like this stuff any better than we do. Anyway, you'll get used to it; you'll learn how to play the game here. We don't get fucked with that much.

"Here," he says, handing me a piece of paper, "this is a bulletin from some officer over at the 374th. The Division has sent it around to all the units to follow. It itemizes all the important rules for us to follow."

1. MEMBERS OF THIS COMMAND CONTINUE TO BE CITED BY MILITARY POLICE FOR UNIFORM AND APPEARANCE VIOLATION. THE FOLLOWING LIST OF POSSIBLE VIOLATIONS-
   A. MIXED UNIFORMS, I.E. JUNGLE AND STATESIDE FATIGUES
   B. NO SHIRT
   C. FATIGUE TROUSERS NOT BLOUSED
   D. NO HEADGEAR
   E. IMPROPER HEADGEAR
   F. INDIVIDUAL NEED-HAIRCUT
   G. INDIVIDUAL NEED-SHAVE
   H. NO INSIGNIA OF RANK
   I. NO SHOULDER (4TH INF DIV)
   J. NO US ARMY INSIGNIA
   K. SLEEVES ROLLED UP AFTER 1800 HOURS
   L. NO NAME TAG

Stars and Stripes and Shadows

M. NO INDENTIFICATION TAGS (DOG TAGS)

N. BUTTONS MISSING

O. SHIRT UNBUTTONED

P. NO BELT

Q. IMPROPER BELT (NOT QUARTER MASTER ISSUED)

R. DIRTY UNIFORM

S. UNIFORM WITH HOLES OR RIPS

T. DIRTY BOOTS (UNPOLISHED)

U. ZIPPERED BOOTS

V. SLEEVES CUT OFF

W. FAILURE TO RENDER PROPER MILITARY COURTESY TO AN OFFICER

2. THE MOST LIKELY AREA OF RECEIPT OF SUCH CITATIONS IS AROUND THE PX. PRIOR TO LEAVING THE COMPANY AREA, CHECK ABOVE LIST TO INSURE YOU ARE NOT VULNERABLE TO UNIFORM AND APPEARANCE VIOLATIONS.

//SIGNED//
TRUMAN F. MARTIN
1LT, SIG CORPS
EXECUTIVE
OFFICER

"I want you to start practicing something. You'll have to get this down," Price says, shifting the conversation back to the afternoon's lessons in clerking. He pushes a piece of paper over in front of me with the Captain's signature on it. *Roger T. Hilton* it says, easily readable in a simple unimaginative cursive style. Then he shoves over another with the same signature on it, *Roger T. Hilton*; same signature, same style, same everything.

"OK, this one's the Captain's signature," Price says, referring to exhibit number one, "and this one's my forgery of his signature," he declares, pointing proudly to the scrawl on paper number two.

"Wow, nice job. What do you use that particular skill for?"

"With the Captain out in the field, he can't possibly review and sign all the orders and other documents that require the Commanding Officer' signature. So, the Company Clerk has power of attorney. It's all cool. It's all legal. I sign everything for the Captain. Most of it has to go through Captain Walterhouse for review before it becomes official anyway. Walterhouse doesn't really have the time to study all of these

Tim Haslam

things and so getting his OK is usually just a formality."

"So you're really the guy that authorizes everything?" I ask, now in awe of this potential power.

"Yea, pretty much. For important stuff, like promotions and extended leaves and transfers I always send out a message to the Captain and get his approval before I make it official and put his name on it, but for the little shit that doesn't mean anything I just approve it."

I start in right away with my assignment, determined and motivated to master this aspect of my responsibilities quickly.

Roger T. Hilton. Roger T. Hilton. Roger T. Hilton.

N N N N

Two weeks have passed since Bravo Company returned to the boonies without me. Price, who now has less than a week to go until his DROS date, has taught me everything he can think of about the job and now let's me do it all, watching over my typewriter plucking and verifying everything before it gets submitted to Captain Walterhouse. I'm still *oopsing* my way through a lot of paper and am wearing out the precious carbons at a rate that has Bob concerned.

There's a lot of work here and not much time for goofing off. I'm at the desk by seven in the morning and finishing up at about seven at night unless there's some hard deadline for something, in which case I'm here further into the night. The other clerks put in the same kind of hours and effort and by the end of the day we're all pretty beat. The nights that I don't have any of the guard duty assignments it's nice to spend an hour or so with various small groups of the other guys who reside here. The Enlisted Men's Club is generally too crowded and too far away to go to except on the nights when we get done early and have more time to kill. The little canteen out in the back of the supply shack is a good place to get together and relax over smokes and cold beers when they're available. It's not uncommon for someone to have acquired a bottle of Jack Daniels somehow and shots of that help to make a party out of the little group discussions. More and more of my days are coming to and end this way, stumbling onto my bunk with the rest of the barracks spinning around me. The sleep isn't very restful and the commensurate headache stays with me through the morning formation, breakfast and most of the Morning Report. A little alcohol

Stars and Stripes and Shadows

and a little partying help to pass the time here. Why shouldn't a lot help more?

"What if they come today?" Price laments as he follows me up onto the back of the deuce-and-a-half.

"I'll bet they come today for sure," he adds, setting his bandoliers down on the bench next to him, referring to the long overdue official DROS orders that will be his ticket home. His DROS date is only four days away and he hasn't yet seen his official orders. He doesn't trust that the Army or the Defense Department will remember. He's worried that they've forgotten about Bob Price.

"So, what if they do? They'll be there when we get back," I tell him, adding my own bandoliers to the pile on the bench seat. My back seems to have now fully recovered and the doctor has released me to fulfill any and all work deemed necessary by my superiors to hasten our victory and the end of the war.

The Division's been getting concerned that Charlie may be building up close in to Camp Enari and that the VC are getting too bold in their activities in and around many of the neighboring villages. So, today, virtually everyone at base camp is being sent out on a search and destroy mission. A series of little convoys are spoking out from the base, following the various roads that lead to and away from camp in all directions. The trucks are to go out about seven klicks, let us all off and we're to sweep our way back to Enari on foot, killing all the NVA and VC we see along the way. Tanks, APCs and heavily armed jeeps are stationed all along the roads and out in the neighboring fields. Helicopters of all varieties dart around over the convoys as well as teams of O2's and Hobos providing air cover. I don't remember the grunts out in the field ever getting this kind of support. I guess the grunts are too far out in the shit. At the end of this day—this six hour operation—everyone involved will go home to the comforts of Camp Enari and reflect on the mission over hot food and cool drinks.

The land surrounding Camp Enari is different from anything I've been in so far. It's farmland; mostly rice paddies, with occasional patches of other crops working their way up through the sodden ground toward the hot sun. We can help ourselves to the little bananas pick-

497

Tim Haslam

able from the trees in the groves we pass through, cautiously searching out VC hiding places. The rice paddies present another set of obstacles, slowing our inbound progress. The flooded fields can't be waded through easily and the bordering dikes require a series of right angle detours to get across.

For me, I'm not too worried about Charlie out here. There's so many of us milling around with so much ready firepower along with us that Charlie would have to be crazy to start something. Charlie probably has the same view of this operation as the rest of us. It's just some bullshit effort suggested by a General somewhere who's been falling behind in his body count contributions. Along the way several farmers and villagers will be rounded up and brought in for interrogation. The reports will describe how numerous suspected VC were apprehended. A few shots may even be fired. A few people may suffer the consequences. It will serve to remind Charlie that the American's will spare no expense to keep him off guard.

Bob Price on the other hand is worried about everything out here today. He's too short to be out here with a rifle in his hand he thinks, and keeps saying to the rest of us. He's afraid of the potential irony. He survived eight months of his tour out in combat without a significant wound and now he's afraid that, as a clerk on his last bullshit patrol, he's going to get killed a mile outside of base camp. I guess I wish I shared his fears today—for the same reason.

The trek back in affords me an opportunity to get a closer look at real Vietnamese villages and people. Their reaction to our intrusion runs from obvious fear to barely disguised annoyance. Many of the people I see have to be VC. I can't tell which ones really are or which ones are sympathetic to which cause. I don't see anyone who seems too happy that we're here. The kids in these villages are unlike the happier ones in the Yard villages up in the mountains. They've learned that any outsiders are likely to bring trouble. The men, young and old, the women and the children in and around the villages just stop and watch us pass through, hoping that there will be nothing about themselves that attracts more specific attention from any of us. It's hard for me to remember that I'm here to help them. It's hard for me to believe that they appreciate the help. I guess that none of us can see the bigger picture. We're all way too far down into the shit to recognize the significance of this struggle for the greater good.

Stars and Stripes and Shadows

The day turns out to be nothing more than a long hike on a hot day; a tour through the surrounding neighborhood; a superficial check on the wellbeing of our hosts.

My first turn at perimeter guard follows the day's fruitless sweep outside camp. The bunkers out here are the biggest I've yet seen, obviously constructed by experts—not grunts. I can stand up comfortably inside and there are actually cots for sleeping. There are five of us assigned to this bunker and the adjacent elevated guard tower. One person is awake up in the tower manning the M60, another within the bunker and the other three asleep. It's not so bad. It's dry and comfortable. It's just one more long night.

In front of the bunker is a section of chain-link fencing. I guess it's there to intercept any rockets heading toward the bunker, preventing them from reaching a surface solid enough to depress the triggering mechanism. I don't know if this is proven theory or just a way to utilize some excess fencing material. I wonder what happens to sprays of M16 rounds being fired out through it.

As I stare out through the bunker port and the fencing into the quiet darkness it occurs to me that it's now October and that I've been in the Army almost a year now. I think about home and realize that a whole spring and summer have come and gone back home, come and gone without me. It all went on without me. My friends went to the beaches, they had backyard barbecues and they found some reason to celebrate every warm weekend evening. They partied, they played and they never appreciated for a second how valuable those moments were, how rich they were, how alive they were.

I never got to see the smooth flesh on Rosemary's slender legs take on the honeyed, bronze cast imparted by the Southern California sun. I didn't get to kid her about the few little freckles that sometimes show themselves across the bridge of her upturned nose when she's spent too much time exposed to the solar rays. I never had a chance to race my old 1957 Porsche over Coldwater Canyon, with her laughing at my side, on our way to the movies in Beverly Hills or Westwood. I never held her warm hand or embraced her body…touched her…kissed her. She was there in another world. I was here. For us here in the shit, there was no summer of '68.

Chapter 16

The Wraith

With Price gone, the days for me in the S1 office are long and busy. I've yet to develop effective countermeasures for all the various quirks of the old Remington and my own typing skills are still far below those of the other clerks. Each morning is a panicked struggle to meet Captain Walterhouse's deadline for the Morning Report. A few times I've knowingly submitted the Bravo Company DA-1 with one or two errors beyond the legal limit. I figured that it was better to take my lumps for the errors, feigning surprise at the discovered typos, than to get hammered for being late. In reality, the consequence was nothing; no lumps, no hammering, just the same signature on the bottom of the dissonant forms. I guess that the Captain has other things to do too and doesn't really tally his way through each of the reports submitted to him. I hope that the undetected violation won't have a detrimental effect on the war effort.

I've become friends with all the guys here in the office and the others who are considered permanent party here in base camp. They're all good guys and fun to be with when we're not working. I see Lieutenant Falck every once in a while as he passes in and out of here performing his new duties within the Battalion Headquarters structure. Like the rest of us who've come out of the jungle, he looks much different clean and barbered; he's the same officer though and the same person. All officers should be like him or Riley or Captain Hilton. I was lucky in that way when I was out in the shit. It could have been much worse with different kinds of people leading us.

Doc Charlebois surprised me last week, showing up at my desk

Stars and Stripes and Shadows

one evening. He'd just arrived on the afternoon convoy from Dak To. He tells me he's been given a new role as the assistant to the Battalion Medical Officer. He's out of the shit; he's earned a change of scenery and responsibility back here. He'll be missed out there but it's great for me to have him around here. He fills me in on what's been happening out with Company. It's the same old shit.

I can't say that I'm getting to know them but I'm getting familiar with the regular crew of Vietnamese that show up here each morning to perform their duties in service to us. They all have regular assignments, mostly within the kitchen and mess hall. Tran, the shit-burner, is the only male that I've seen among the local helpers. All the rest, about a half a dozen, are women ranging in age from about seventeen to maybe fifty. One of the older women, Thuy, seems to be the matriarch of the whole bunch and serves as the gang-boss, spokesperson and lead nego-tiator for any of the many side businesses that have developed or might have potential. She approached me early on, realizing that I was now assigned here and forcefully explained to me through her betel-stained teeth how things worked around here and about the services provided. They've developed a thriving independent laundry and seamstress ser-vice. For a monthly fee of about five dollars they'll take care of all of my laundry needs, fatigues and bedding and sew on any patches or badges that I desire to display on my uniforms. Everyone in camp seems to utilize this service. It's very clear to her that I will too and she'd like the first month's payment in advance.

The Vietnamese civilians that work here give me my first real chance to study some of the people who live in this country, the people we're fighting for, the people threatened by their potential role as a falling communist domino. None is more interesting than Tran. I see him only when I need to visit the foul smelling little shack out in the back of the Battalion area. I try to say hello to him as I come or go from his facility. He doesn't seem comfortable with this. I don't think it's the language. It's something deeper and more personal. He won't main-tain any eye contact and merely offers a barely detectable head nod in response to the greeting. He's always busy. Wearing high rubber boots and gloves he swaps out the half barrels used to collect the bodily wastes from the Americans. They never get anything close to being full before

Tim Haslam

Tran pulls them out and replaces them with ones that he's emptied and hosed out. He pulls the ones in need of attention out from under the little hinged door flaps at the back of the shitter and drags them several meters out into an open patch of ground where he pours gasoline over the contents and then drops in a match. There's always shit burning out here. There's always the smell of burning shit wafting over the whole Battalion area. The residual ashes get dumped out and buried. The barrel gets hosed out and lined up behind the shitter. There's always a row of cleaned out barrels ready to go. Tran has a routine and order about things that cannot be broken or modified.

I fantasize that Tran is a tragic character. Perhaps he was a mandarin back when Bao Dai was emperor of Vietnam; rich and influential, discharged when the countries first attempts at democracy set in. Perhaps he was a general in the army; powerful and corrupt, before the coup that overthrew President Ngo Dinh Diem back in 1963 sent him into exile by the next regime that questioned his loyalties. Perhaps he's really a VC officer, here to spy on us, preparing for the right moment to add grenades to his barrels before he slides them back under the asses of the imperialist Americans. Perhaps he's just an old man doing what he must do to survive. Whatever his motivations are, he's a proud man and he'll fulfill his responsibilities as though his life here and in the hereafter depended on it. His wrinkled, sinewy body reminds me of my grandfather and makes me realize how lucky I am that my grandfather's home now with a can of Schlitz beer in his hand watching the Dodgers or Lawrence Welk on the television.

N N N N

"Hey, you wanna get out of here for a while today?" Doc asks me, peering in through the office door behind my desk.

"Sure...do you have a way to make that happen?" I respond, eager to break out of the monotony of the routine.

"I have to take some mail over to some of the guys at the 71st and need somebody to ride shotgun. How about it, you wanna go? We can have lunch over at the Pleiku Air Force Base. I already checked with First Sergeant Goodrum. He says it's OK with him if you can get your clerk stuff taken care of."

"OK...I'm almost done with the Morning Report and everything

Stars and Stripes and Shadows

else I have to do can wait. What do I need to bring?"

"Bring your M16 and a couple of bandoliers...and your helmet. We'll leave in about an hour."

Doc, wearing his helmet pulls up outside the S1 shack in a jeep just as I come up the wooden walk with my weapon and ammo.

"It'll be good to get out of this place for a little while," he says, adjusting the bundles he has in the back seat. "The Air Force Base chow is almost like stateside food. We can go to the NCO Open Mess."

Doc's suggestion reminds me he's a Spec-5, an E-5, an NCO. I'm just a Spec-4, just an enlisted man, not an NCO.

"I'm not an NCO. How am I going to get in there?"

"Don't worry about that. They never really check anybody going in. You can put these on," he adds, pointing to the Spec-5 pins attached to his shirt collar. "I've got my Open Mess ID card that I can show them. You can show them your regular ID and tell them you just got promoted if anybody hassles us going in. It won't be a problem."

"OK," I respond, as Doc hands his pass to one of the MPs at the camp gate. A moment later we're out on the road heading east toward Pleiku, just the two of us in the little jeep. There are a few Vietnamese out on the road and others in the adjacent fields; some are VC, some aren't. I hope the one's who are VC realize that medics and clerks don't pose much of a threat, that we're not worth wasting bullets or explosives on.

"I have to make a short stop in town," Charlebois advises me as we bounce along the dusty road nearing the old city. "There's a little clinic that does a lot of stuff for the Vietnamese up here. They don't have much to work with and so we bring them some of our excess medicine and equipment. It'll only take a minute."

Doc turns the jeep onto one of the roads that heads into the outskirts of the squalid town. I feel more uncomfortable now, driving into this place, exposed in the little open jeep with nothing but my M16 and a few magazines of ammo. There aren't many people out on the streets and only a few visible around the dirty shacks and houses we're passing. Occasionally there are larger houses set back further from the road, built in the French Colonial style, perhaps once grand estates. They're no longer grand though. They haven't seen paint or fresh plaster since their French owners departed in 1954. The deteriorating facades now are

Tim Haslam

covered with dust, streaked by the tracks of dripping rainwater. Drying laundry hangs out of open windows along with dirtier items of clothing, blankets and towels. The yards, once lavishly landscaped, are now littered with the debris of castoff household items and the deteriorating remnants of once fashionable architectural adornments.

The town smells of decay, rot, sewage and smoke. There's no evidence of anything being built; of anything new. It seems to be a place where nothing grows or flourishes; where nothing improves. It's a place between life and death, a netherworld that people don't want to be in but have to be; a purgatory for the people trapped by the surrounding mountains and the ravages of war. I don't want to be here a moment longer than I have to either.

We pull onto a larger boulevard that starts to look more like a commercial section. Still, there are few people around. Pleiku is essentially a market town but the market place must be in some other section. I can imagine that at one time this street was a thriving thoroughfare with busy shops, restaurants and bars down at street level and professional offices and apartments on the second floors. Now most of the buildings are boarded up or simply open but vacant. A few people pass along the wide sidewalks on foot toting various bundles, probably returning from the market place, and bicycles are the only other vehicle traffic to be seen. Doc and I and our green U.S. Army jeep stand out like beings from another planet. I'd feel better if there were more olive drab around, more beings from my planet.

Doc pulls our jeep over to the side of the street and parks at the edge of the wide sidewalk in front of a row of decaying two story buildings. I can't see that there's any activity around anything here. There's no one on this section of sidewalk, no one visible around any of the doors or windows.

"Alright, this is it…the clinic's up those stairs," he says pointing to a stairway alcove unidentified with signage or addressing of any kind.

"You'll have to stay here and guard the jeep. I won't be long."

"OK, just make sure you're not too long. I don't like this much out here."

I light a cigarette as Doc disappears into the alcove. I check the readiness of my M16 and scan around the neighborhood. There's nobody on this side of the street that I can see. There's nobody around

504

Stars and Stripes and Shadows

at all. I start to find all the places that a sniper could be; windows, doorways and rooftops. Anybody peddling by could toss over a grenade without breaking stride. *C'mon Doc...hurry up!*

Several more uncomfortable minutes have passed when I spot someone coming along the sidewalk toward me. I'm not sure whom this is coming at me. I'm not sure *what* this is coming at me. Everything else around fades into insignificance as my full attention is drawn toward the creature working its way along the sidewalk toward me.

*Damn...*I think to myself. *What happened to him... or, is it even a him?*

Ten meters up the sidewalk from me now is, I think, a man, pulling himself along, a few inches at a time. Under his right arm is a straight wooden crutch, padded under his armpit with filthy cloth. There is no right leg. I can't tell how much of a stub is left, hidden within the baggy, urine-stained pajama pants he wears. His left arm hangs limply down to his side, the hand a mangled lump of scar tissue. The face though is the most severally damaged feature of this poor being. The whole right side of his face is gone. There is no eye, or even an eye socket. There is only a little vent-like opening where a nose should be and another slightly larger opening a little below that. There doesn't seem to be any jawbone under any of the waxy, scarred flesh. His left eye is the only facial feature to have survived the trauma that ripped away so much of his body and there is only the faintest glint of that visible within the scar tissues stretching across his face. *How can he be alive? How can he sustain what's left of his body?*

I can see that every move for this poor wretch is a struggle, a test of will power and determination. Every inch of flat sidewalk is a thousand feet up Mount Everest for the being resident within this dissembled remnant of a body. The subtle redirection of his vector and his focus becomes apparent to me however and I can tell that he's heading intentionally right for me. He continues the process of leveraging out his crutch, followed by a short sweep of his left leg, drawing him a few inches closer to the jeep. He repeats the agonized cycle over and over in macabre slow motion until he's pulled himself up immediately adjacent to where I sit alone in the passenger seat of the U.S. Army jeep. Here he stops, orienting himself toward me. His eye, only a few feet from mine seems to be studying me, evaluating me, or trying to com-

Tim Haslam

municate with me.

Goddamn it! I think to myself. *Who is this? Who was this? What does he want with me? What does he want from me?* No Hollywood scriptwriter or make-up artist could have imagined up such a hideous looking creature. I try not to look at him, but find that I cannot separate my own gaze from his. He is the stuff of nightmares. He is the personification of all that surrounds me; of the hopelessness of Pleiku under this gray sky, of the lonely isolation of these haunted mountains, of the frail nature of our beings and of the ultimate price of our stupidity. He is a poster-child from hell. He's somehow refused death or perhaps been denied its peace and dignity. He *is* the Nam and the shit. *What does he want from me?*

Because of his short slumped stature, the specter that is his face is nearly aligned with mine as he braces himself into place, standing motionless, gesture-less, expressionless, leaning on his crutch, staring at me. I don't know that he has any capacity remaining for hearing. I don't know what I could say to him anyway. *Does he want something...Piastres...MPC...food? Is he looking at my M16, pleading for me to end his suffering? Does he hold me accountable for all that's happened to him? Does he just want me to share in his plight and his pain for a moment, or, is he somehow trying to tell me that deep inside this mutilated form is someone just like me; that he too thinks and feels and yearns; that once, he too sat uniformed, in a military vehicle, performing his duties; honorable, noble, in service to his country and his beliefs. Does he just want me to know?*

I can't find any foundation for determining the right thing to do. I can only sit there, poking the index finger of my right hand nervously in and out of the trigger guard on my weapon, continuing to stare back at this silent soul that casts his blighted shadow over me. *Why did this person come to this place at this time?*

"Hey...Di-di...Di-di-mou! Get the fuck outta here!" Doc's voice shouts at us from somewhere behind me.

"Damn, man...get the fuck outta here," he adds as he climbs into the driver's seat, starts up the engine and jerks the jeep away from the curb.

"What the fuck was that?" he asks of me, flushed and out of breath.

Doc Charlebois is a kind, charitable and tolerant young man who

Stars and Stripes and Shadows

resorts to vulgarisms only as an extreme accompaniment to some emotional surprise. He's a medic because he prefers to participate in healing rather than harming. Doc's reaction was way out of character.

"I don't know what he was," I respond. "I've never seen anybody that was that messed up. He just came over and stood there. I don't know what he wanted. He just stood there."

"Man, when I came out on to the sidewalk and saw him, I thought maybe he was up to something. Just the sight of him startled the shit out me. I guess I shouldn't have been so pissed that way. Damn…that guy was really fucked up."

Neither of us looks back. Neither of us wants to know any more about the living corpse that's left back there on the wide sidewalk of this ghost city.

N N N N

I can't get the man's face out of my mind as I follow Doc around the halls of the 71st Evacuation Hospital. Within the wards, the sick and injured men rest on comfortable beds attended by caring doctors and nurses. They get their mail from home. For many of them, they will be going home soon and many of the ones going home will take with them the scars of war and many of them will leave portions of their youthful bodies here. I can't imagine that any of these men though, returning to the United States of America, will ever have to languish along the sidewalks of a lonely, dieing town in urine-stained pajamas. I'm sure we take better care of those who sacrifice.

Doc's cheerful conversation pushes the encounter with the wraith a little bit further down in my consciousness. We enter into the NCO Open Mess at the Air Force Base without any challenge to our credentials and gorge ourselves on the best food I've had since leaving home. *How does the Air Force warrant such good chow?*

By mid-afternoon, I'm back at my typewriter, thinking about where I've been and what I've seen this day; hell, the inside of a hospital and an American style cafeteria. *How can they all be so close together out there?*

Chapter 17

Jack and Judy

"I think I'm ready for R&R," I tell Bill Taylor, Jim Welsh and Stoney as we chase our beers down with swallows of Jack Daniels back in the smoky confines of the little canteen one evening, "I've been here seven months now and need a break."

"Singapore, man, that's the place. The babes there were unreal," Stone advises, beginning to relive his experiences in the bustling city-state. He walks us through every detail of his five days there, focusing more on the activities of the nights. His endorsement leads us into a more objective evaluation of all the other R&R sites; Penang, Kuala Lumpur, Taipei, Tokyo, Hong Kong, and Sydney. Hawaii is reserved for the married guys who can generally meet their wives there. Neither Welsh nor Taylor have had R&R yet and, like me, can only contribute what they've heard.

Valentine and Del Pinkerman, the guy in charge of maintaining all of Bravo Company's weapons, join us around the little table and pick right up on the evaluations of where I should go. Pinkerman's been to Hong Kong and launches into his moment-by-moment remembrances, impassioned even beyond Stone's narratives. He describes, not only the girls, but details all the places, the rituals, and the various pricing structures. He tells of the people who will come to your hotel room door within minutes of your arrival, trying to connect your needs and desires with the offerings at their various establishments. He offers guidance on how to dismiss such representatives and how to shop the city; how to get by the aggressive touts that shepherd the weak off the sidewalks and into their neon emblazoned thresholds; how to negotiate

508

Stars and Stripes and Shadows

with the mama-sans in the bars and what to say to the girl ultimately chosen to be your date. English is the official language of Hong Kong. *I'll go to Hong Kong!*

As Company Clerk, I get the monthly listing of seats available to the various R&R sites. I forward this out to the Captain who will provide the names and ensure that the men awarded the seats get back to Camp Enari in time. There are four seats to Hong Kong available this month to Bravo Company. I send the message out to the Captain; there are three seats to Hong Kong available to Bravo Company this month. Within a few days, Captain Hilton has provided the other names and all of us are scheduled for R&R, all at different times. I'll go by myself.

Valentine has volunteered to fill in for me with the Morning Report and the other clerks will help him determine what else is vital and must get done in my absence. The rest can wait until I return. Each remaining day before my scheduled departure I spend time with Del, getting educated about all things Hong Kong. He has advice for every person and place I'm likely to encounter, for every indulgence I'm likely to surrender to. He seems to have learned, in his five days there, how to manage the taxi drivers, the shop keepers, the tailors, the touts, the doormen, the bar tenders, the mama-sans and the bar girls. If I do as instructed, I will come back fulfilled in every way. I will have a new Seiko watch, a new Nikon or Pentax camera, a new custom-made suit and, if I've saved enough money up to now, a new Sony or Akai reel-to-reel tape recorder. If I do as instructed, I will come back with an empty wallet.

Up to this point in my life, any traveling I've done, beyond Yosemite Valley, has been planned and orchestrated either by my parents or by the military. Now, I must get myself from the 3rd of the 8th Battalion area at Camp Enari in the Central Highlands of Vietnam to the British Crown Colony of Hong Kong. I have to do all this by myself and I will have to make this journey accompanied only by strangers. If I can manage to get myself all the way there, I will have to explore this city and all that's contained within it on my own. I'm terrified. I'm excited.

N N N N

509

Tim Haslam

As the Pan Am 707 lifts off from the tarmac at the Cam Rahn Bay Air Force Base I feel like I can finally relax. I've managed to get myself this far via trucks and busses and a C-130 transport plane. I've got all of Pinkerman's guidance firmly implanted in my memory and money in the pockets of my summer khaki uniform. The others on the plane seem to be more vocal about their excitement. There's little doubt that this is an airplane full of American G.I.s on their way to a break from the Vietnam War. I can tell by the dialogues going around me that many of the men are pairing up together or forming larger groups for their assault on the city. I'm torn between the possibilities of going along with a crowd or taking advantage of the first opportunity I've had in seven months to be by myself for a little while, to have the freedom to go and do what I want or not go and not do what I don't want to. I decide to go it alone, even though the thought of heading out into a big foreign city in search of things and activities that I've had little or no experience with is pretty intimidating.

The stewardesses have handed out little brochures that clarify the rules of conduct for American Servicemen visiting Hong Kong. Foremost among the things to be mindful of is that Hong Kong is surrounded by Communist China and that the Red Chinese have a strong presence here in the city and a lot of influence. American Military Personnel are not to wear their uniforms while in Hong Kong, as this tends to irritate the communists. Also, within the brochure is a list of hotels that have rooms available for soldiers on R&R as well as a listing of recommended tailor shops that can provide us with civilian clothes. The rest of the brochure clarifies the do's and don't—mostly don'ts.

It's early on a Sunday evening, just before dusk, when the 707 slides down between the white, high-rise buildings, over the bay and settles down onto the runway at Kai Tak International Airport. Once we've retrieved the little luggage that we've been allowed to bring we're briefed one more time in an assembly room that also serves as the Customs station for us. We're told to pick one of the hotels from the list and find the bus outside that's designated to go there. From then on we're on our own.

The Park Hotel that I picked, for no particular reason, turns out to be a first-class place that fronts on Nathan Road, a busy thoroughfare through the Tsim Sha Suy section of the Kowloon district. The multi-

Stars and Stripes and Shadows

storied hotel sits on the corner of a busy intersection and overlooks the bay. The sidewalks and streets outside the hotel are busy with people and impatient little vehicles, as have been all the roads that have led us from the airport to here. There seems to be about a dozen of us that have chosen the Park as our home base and the other eleven, apparently more anxious to get going queue up at the check-in desk in front of me. The friendly staff at the desk gets through all the men in front of me quickly and just as quickly gets me signed in. I remember Pinkerman's first instruction and ask that most of my money be put in the hotel safe. I put my name on the envelope they give me, put two-hundred and eighty dollars in it and give it back to them for safe keeping. I watch the young, smiling Chinese woman add my room number, 512, to the envelope and continue watching until it's been placed in the safe and the safe closed.

My room turns out to be on the wrong side of the hotel to have a bay view. Actually it has only a view of the adjacent building and the intervening alleyway down below. The room's pleasant enough though and has a comfortable looking bed and my own shower. It has everything I need.

I haven't been in the room for three minutes when there's a knock at the door. *Pinkerman was right.* Upon opening the door I'm practically shoved back into the room by a thin Chinese man dressed in a wrinkled yellow shirt and narrow tie with a tape measure around his neck.

"Hi, Mr. American, I Mr. Cheng from the tailor shop right across the street. I can have everything you need to wear in just a few minutes. I make a nice suit for you too. I just get some measurements and then you come over in about a twenty minutes. You pay me then."

"Um, well," is my temporary response as I try to remember how I'm supposed to deal with this guy. "OK…actually I've already got a tailor shop that I deal with when I'm here in Hong Kong. Thanks anyway. Maybe I'll come over tomorrow and see what you've got." I extend my arms out to full length and sweep the disappointed man out the door. "Thanks…thanks for coming up…thanks…bye."

I grab my garrison cap and room key and head out the door before anyone else can get to me up here. I have my list of recommended tailors and stop at the front desk to ask for directions to the nearest one. I'm advised that the closest shop is on Austin Road, just a short

Tim Haslam

taxi ride away.

It's dark now outside and there seems to be no reduction in the traffic level either on the street or the sidewalk. As soon as I reach the curb, a taxi pulls around the corner and stops in front of me, apparently recognizing that a uniformed American must be on his way to a tailor shop. The street in front of the hotel is a one-way street in this drive-on-the-left-side city, and so the impatient driver, behind his right side steering wheel stares me into the back seat of whatever kind of little Japanese car this is. Once I'm in he turns to his left and awaits my instructions.

"I need to get to the Weng-Pei Tailor Shop in the Yu-Hing Mansion on Austin Road…OK?"

He stares back at me with blank irritation.

"You don't speak English, do you?"

"OK, can you just take me here?" I say, holding out the brochure and pointing to the address on the listing.

I get a terse head nod in response and the driver lurches us out into traffic. He has his right elbow resting comfortably out the open window with his right thumb secured to the horn button in the middle of the steering wheel. His left hand does the steering, the gear shifting and occasionally removes the cigarette from his teeth to flick the ashes out the window.

The streets are a showcase of lights and colorful signs arrayed around the open front shops. I'm going to be out in this world in a little while and I want to get the lay of the land. I try to spot the bars and night-clubs among the shops and restaurants. It's not hard. Pinkerman said that they're all about the same, offering the same kinds of refreshment, entertainment and companionship. American G.I.'s make up a good portion of their business and so we're treated well.

Three right turns, two left turns, two u-turns and twelve blasts of the horn is all that it takes to get the taxi in front of a four story building on a street that seems darker and much less busy than the other thoroughfares we've traveled along. The street-level storefronts seem to be closed, but I can see that there are lights on in what appears to be more shops upstairs. I pay the driver in Hong Kong dollars what I think amounts to about seventy-five cents. He seems satisfied and hurries off, leaving me alone on the street in front of, I hope, the Yu-Hing Mansion.

Oh shit…now what am I going to do? is my thought as I discover that the Weng-Pei Tailor Shop is one of the establishments on the first floor, one of the establishments that's closed. No other taxicabs are immediately visible on the street and from here and I can't see any more lighted or busier sections of the neighborhood. The only source of commercial activity seems to be on the second floor and so I head up the stairs in hopes of finding some friendly guidance.

Just to the left of the second-floor landing is a glass door that reads, Hung-Cheng Company, Tailors and Fine Men's Suiting. I check my recommended list of tailors but don't see that this name is on it. The light's are on though and I can see a Chinese man sitting on a stool behind a little counter, chop-sticking noodles up into his mouth. He's my only hope.

"Excuse me…are you open?" I ask nervously as I enter the little shop.

"Yes, yes…come in, sir…come in. How are you?" He says cheerfully, jumping off his stool, circling around the counter to further the greeting. "I am Jack Wong," he adds reaching out to shake my hand after a quick cleanup with the handkerchief in his left hand.

I tell him of my immediate need for some casual civilian clothes.

"Yes, yes, of course…I have everything you need. I have everything; slacks, shirt, shoes, belt…very nice…everything very nice."

He wastes no time in further negotiations and starts taking measurements.

"This your first time to Hong Kong?" he asks, as his tape measure stretches down from the crotch of my khaki pants to the top of my shined black Class-A shoes.

I remember one of Pinkerman's admonishments about never letting on that you're new in town. However, as I'm still in uniform, I'm sure Jack Wong has figured out that I've just arrived and that this is most likely my first trip here.

"Yes," is all I can think of as a response.

"Can I get you something to drink…something to eat maybe?" he inquires with what seems to be honest concern for my comfort and well-being. I'm not sure how to answer at first. I certainly didn't anticipate being provided with anything but clothes to wear on this stop in my adventure. I am hungry though, as I haven't had anything to eat today

Tim Haslam

except the little dry sandwich provided by Pan Am.

"What you like to drink?" Jack prompts, before I've had time to formulate by own response. "You like Vodka, Gin...Scotch...maybe beer?"

"Uhm, well, maybe some Scotch would be nice. Thank you," I reply, thinking he'll pull out a bottle and glass from behind his counter. Instead, he shouts out something in Cantonese that brings another man out from a back room. He introduces the man as his associate, Mr.Yang. I can immediately tell that Mr. Yang doesn't consider himself to be Jack Wong's equal in this association as his short responses and subtle head nods kowtow to the more assertive proclamations coming his way from the small, wiry man in the white shirt and narrow black tie. Mr. Yang makes a quick exit as Jack starts to show me a variety of shirts he has on one of the shelves. I pick out a long sleeve, ivy-league, light blue, oxford cloth shirt and we move on to a shelf full of casual pants. Before I've made up my mind about the right color of pants, Mr. Yang returns with an unopened quart bottle of Johnnie Walker, Black Label Scotch.

"Maybe a little soda, if you have it," I respond to Jack's inquiry as to how I want the Scotch, after Mr. Yang has delivered two glasses full of ice from the back room.

"You must be hungry," he declares, again in an honest, hospitable way.

I've been a little anxious about heading into some unknown restaurant by myself in this foreign city and so I answer in the affirmative.

"You like Chinese food?" he asks.

"Yes, very much," I answer, hoping that his idea of Chinese food is consistent with the kind of stuff that my dad used to go and get from the Hei-wei House over on Sepulveda Boulevard.

He shouts again for Mr. Yang who immediately transits from the back room, through the shop and out the front door. Jack continues to escort me through his inventory until I've picked out all the clothing I'll need to legally venture out into the nighttime realm of this city. He then points me to a little fitting room, where I become a civilian again for the first time in seven months.

Who is that? I think to myself as I study the civilian clad image reflected in the full-length mirror. There's some familiarity to the slender

Stars and Stripes and Shadows

body, but the mustached face is aged and worn beyond the remembered one that used to look back at me from my bathroom mirror at home.

"Very nice...all very nice," Jack says, breaking my reflection on my reflection. "Very handsome...everything seem OK to you?"

"Yea, everything seems fine...thank you."

Jack's carefully packaging my uniform up in a bag when Mr. Yang returns with dinner. He helps Jack lay out a feast of mostly familiar looking Chinese faire. Our glasses get refreshed with generous pourings of Johnnie Walker and then, Jack the Hong Kong Tailor and Tim the visiting American soldier sit down, chopsticks in hand, ready to dine and discuss our perspectives on the world.

None of Mr. Wong's offerings in excess of the clothes I've purchased seem to come with any hint of additional obligation on my part. The dinner and Scotch are offered strictly out of his personal sense of hospitality and he seems to be enjoying the chance to have a meal and discussion with someone other than the subservient Mr. Yang. For me, I feel like I've made a friend that can give me some guidance on how to proceed in my explorations of his city.

Jack understands clearly that this is my first night on R&R and that my plans most likely don't end at his shop. At the conclusion of our meal he tells me of the streets where I should go in search of entertainment suitable for honest American soldiers. He tells me too of streets and neighborhoods and certain establishments that I should stay away from.

"You meet nice girls, in good clubs, if you stay around this area... OK."

"Thank you very much Mr. Wong for all you're kindness," I tell him as I start to gather up my belongings.

"I think I would also be interested in purchasing a suit while I'm in Hong Kong if you can give me the approximate price," I tell him as an honest afterthought. I've been told by Pinkerman and others that suits and sport coats are really a bargain here. There's also something about buying a suit, without my father's assistance that adds another little credit to this right-of-passage.

"Oh, yes...I can make you a very nice suit, two-piece or three-piece suit. Which you like?" he says, pleased that I'm not one to simply eat and run.

515

Tim Haslam

"Well, I guess I'd like a three piece suit."

"OK, I can make you very nice suit for forty-dollars U.S."

"That would be very good," I tell him, thinking to myself that I could probably buy two at that price.

"You come back tomorrow and I get you measured and you pick out very nice fabric. OK?"

"Sure...OK...how about tomorrow afternoon?"

"Yes...come any time. Thank you, Mr. Has-ram."

Jack walks me out of the shop, down the stairs and out to the curb and waits with me the five seconds it takes for a taxi to jog out of the traffic flow in front of us. Once I'm in the back seat Jack tells the cabbie something in Cantonese and we immediately make our move back into the parade of oncoming cars and trucks, exercising some faith-based right-of-way protocol. This time, the several left, right and u-turns seem to take me back into a livelier part of town that doesn't seem to be too distant from my hotel. I feel like I could almost find my way back to the Park Hotel on foot from here if I had to, or wanted to.

The smells of the city are the first sensations to register with me as I transit from the cab onto the sidewalk. The nearly forgotten odors of motor vehicle emissions, oil and rubber ground into asphalt are conjoined with less familiar scents. Various aromas of mysterious cooking foods waft out from many of the street level storefronts where merchants and customers busily probe around hanging naked poultry carcasses and bins full of fish and flesh. Spicy incense and flowery perfume fragrances coming from other shops offset some of the stronger, more pungent vapors helping to make the overall sensation pleasant and suitable as a background for my adventure.

It's nearly ten o'clock now and everything seems to be open. Nearly all of the shops have customers and the sidewalks are crowded with a blend of Chinese people hurrying purposefully to some destination, young American and Australian soldiers hurrying purposefully in and out of the clubs and bars with touts of both Chinese and Indian descent trying to entice someone away from their purposeful hurrying and into their shops.

A wave of apprehension sweeps over me as I wander along the sidewalk, explaining to all the touts who beckon me that I don't have time right now to take advantage of their offers to come in and see something

Stars and Stripes and Shadows

I've "never seen before." Thanks. I start to wonder how I'm going to rally the courage to actually enter one of the bars or clubs, find my way through the scrutinizing stares of the inhabitants and settle in to the routines and rewards promised by Del Pinkerman, Bob Price and the other's who've gone before me. I don't know that I can do this.

No, damn-it! I'm twenty-one years old. I'm a combat veteran. I've managed to get myself from one foreign country to another, get to my hotel, get to Jack Wong's tailor shop, get through dinner—prepared who-knows-where, with someone I've never seen before, sharing Johnny Walker Black Label Scotch, and into the center of this city's entertainment district. I can't chicken out now!

On one of the corners, I find a nightclub. Larger and louder than anything I've passed by so far. I can see through the open front doors into the neon and strobe illuminated throng of people milling about or dancing. Everyone inside seems to be too animated to take notice of me if I go in and there's no doorman to have to work through. It seems safe, I'll start here, I think to myself, determined to follow through with the whole anticipated routine.

I was wrong. Nearly all of the young Chinese faces turn away from their groups or partners and scrutinize the tall American who's entered their place.

OK, there's no turning back now. I smile and excuse my way through several little huddles of fashionably dressed, beer drinking, cigarette smoking locals until I reach the bar on the opposite side of the room. I'm at first glad to see that there are two other "round eyes" at the end of the long bar, quickly working their way through glasses of pale colored beer. The two young men must also be G.I.s. I can at least get a reading from them on what this place is all about and what their recommendations are regarding other spots in the neighborhood.

"I'll have a San Miguel, please," I tell the unfriendly Chinese bartender in response to his silent presentation of himself behind the bar across from where I stand. I can see my two potential friends are refilling their glasses from San Miguel bottles, so that seems to be a good enough endorsement for me.

"Looks like ya just got in town, right, yank," the closer of the two men says to me as I hand the bartender a fist full of Hong Kong coinage. I wasn't expecting the Australian accent.

Tim Haslam

"Is it that obvious?" I ask rhetorically, glad to be able to communicate with someone who, at least on the surface, I can relate to. "Are you guys on R&R?" I ask, assuming that they're in the army too.

"Right you are...last night in town. Last chance to get all we can of the cold beer and warm ladies before we must return to our little gook friends back in the republic."

This time, I can tell that the Australian accent is being softened a bit by a heavy accumulation of alcohol.

"And what about you mate? What's your job in the Army of the United States of America... or, are you a Marine?"

"No, I'm just an Army grunt," I tell him, not ready to publicly reclassify myself as a clerk.

"Right. Right then, a real fightin' man. I believe that calls for a drink on me," the cheerful Aussie declares, gulping down the last of the San Miguel in his glass. "Actually, it'll be on him," he adds, thumbing over toward his partner. "He's the only one with any money left."

The second Australian has said nothing up to now and appears to be unlikely or unable to say anything intelligible as he slumps closer and closer toward the surface of the bar.

"Maybe I should buy the drinks," I tell him. "As you've already noted, I just arrived here."

"Right good man, Yank...another round for the grunts," my friend shouts over to the unappreciative bartender.

Over the next beer, he extracts from me my affiliation with the Fourth Infantry Division in the Central Highlands, my home near Los Angeles and my DROS date. In return I get; First Royal Australian Regiment—usually out in rice paddies somewhere and a hometown called Peebinga..."not Pee-bringer."

I soon realize that my inebriated, impoverished friends from the land-down-under aren't going to be very good company for the rest of my first night, and so I conclude our association with a fist tap and head back out toward the street in search of the kind of establishment my schooling has prepared me for. The traffic on the streets and sidewalks is starting to thin out and I'm feeling internal pressure to find the right kind of bar pretty soon. Mid-block I pass what seems to be a small cocktail lounge, identified by a string of neon martini glasses flashing on and off above the closed door. In front of the door is an old Chinese

Stars and Stripes and Shadows

man sitting on a stool. He smiles pleasantly as I pass by and responds with a simple "Hi" in response to my similar greeting. He makes no further attempts to entice me inside. A few steps past I conclude that the place of the flashing martini glasses fits the description of what I seek as well as anyplace else I've seen and as the greeter out front seems pleasant enough I decide to make my move.

"Hi," the man on the stool repeats as I approach again. Still on the stool, he reaches out and pulls the door open slightly for me. I'm not sure if I'm supposed to tip him or not. *I'll get him on the way out.*

It takes me a second to adjust to the subtle glow of the interior of the little club before things take shape. The bar runs the full length of the room to my right, fully stocked and equipped with all the appropriate saloon paraphernalia, set against a mirrored backdrop. Against the opposite wall is a row of a half-a-dozen little round tables set in front of one long bench, upholstered in red vinyl. Six sets of eyes follow my first few steps into the interior. On the right, behind the bar, the tender readies himself for my next move. On the left, at the far end of the bench, crowded around the last table, are four young Chinese women, studying me with polite interest while whirling straws around tall glasses on the table in front of them. Half way back toward me, seated on the bench is an older Chinese woman, dressed in an elegant traditional silk dress, peering over the top of her reading glasses at me. On the table in front of her is an open newspaper. My presence brings the occupancy of the room up to seven.

"Good evening, sir," the sleepy looking bartender says as I climb onto the third barstool down the line.

"Scotch and soda, please...Johnnie Walker."

"Yes, OK...on the rocks?"

"Yes...on the rocks, please."

Coinciding with the delivery a moment later of my Johnnie Walker on-the-rocks is the arrival of the silk-dressed lady.

"Good evening, sir. May I sit here with you a moment?" she asks in a clear, pleasant voice, any accent refined almost completely away. She's quite an attractive woman, somewhere in her late thirties, bathed in a little too much flowery cologne. She's exactly what Pinkerman and Price and the others described. She's the mama-san of this establishment.

Tim Haslam

"Yes, please, may I buy you a drink?" I offer, consistent with the protocol I've been coached about.

She gracefully maneuvers herself up onto the barstool to my left and says something in Chinese to the tender. *"Another glass of tea, but charge the American as though it was an expensive highball,"* is my take on the translation. It's OK though. It's all part of the process.

The mama-san has heavy responsibilities. It's her job to size up the clientele that come into the bar. She has responsibilities to the girls, the bar and to the clients. She's the screener charged with protecting the girls from psychopaths and scofflaws. It's also within her charter to make the best match ups between the personalities of the customers and the girls as well as to make attempts at equally distributing the customers among the stable of girls who work out of this bar. For all of these contributions, she receives compensation from the bar based on the number of glasses of tea are provided to her at the customers expense and a fee to, "buy a girl out of the bar" should she succeed in her matchmaking efforts.

"Have you just arrived in Hong Kong?" she asks, following a well-established checklist protocol. If I'm new in town, I'll have lots of money. If this is my last night on R&R I'll probably have very little money, but will likely want to spend all that I have. Anywhere in between and I'm probably still watching my budget.

"No, I've been here a few days," I offer back as a vague lie, figuring that puts me in the best negotiating position, hungry but not starved, solvent but not wealthy.

"Have you been to any of the other bars? Have you been with many of the girls?" This line of questioning is to determine whether I'm a shopper or a buyer.

Now she's got me. I'm not sure of the best response here. What if I have been to lots of bars and been with lots of "the girls?" How will an affirmative answer to either or both of the questions affect the negotiations? What if I say no? Then, what have I been doing, she'll be wondering. Am I abnormal in some way?

"Well, I've been to a few of the bars, but I haven't been with that many of the girls," I answer confidently, happy with myself for coming up with something that could almost be construed as the truth.

"May I introduce one of the girls to you?" she asks politely, pivoting

Stars and Stripes and Shadows

around slightly on her stool, gesturing in the general direction of the whirling straws at the back table.

Finally, we can cut through the preliminaries.

"Yes…I guess that would be all right."

The dim light and the distance to the back table make it difficult for me to get a good look at any of the girls and I remember that I'm expected to evaluate all the available girls before selecting my "date." *I don't think I'm going to be able to single out one young woman from this group and reject the others so publicly.*

"Perhaps I can recommend someone whose company I think you will enjoy?" she offers, relieving me of this uncomfortable responsibility.

"OK."

She presses the frames of her eye glasses back up a little tighter against her face and carefully slides off the stool. With tea glass in hand she heads to the back table and facilitates a muffled group discussion among the four girls. I guess it would be rude of me to spectate through this part of the process and so I keep my own eyes on the remaining Johnny Walker in front of me, pretending to be unconcerned about anything else. *I don't know about this?* I start thinking again. *I don't know if I can really do this? What am I going to say? How am I going to orchestrate all the remaining steps between this barstool and my hotel room? Don't wimp out now, asshole! Just go with the flow.*

After two more sips of the smoky scotch and three or four stabs at the floating ice cubes, while my courage ebbs and flows, I detect a presence closing in to my left. Before I have a chance to turn and identify the person approaching, a soft bubbly voice overrides the singing of the Moody Blues coming out of the jukebox back in the corner.

"Hi, my name is Debbie… and you ah?"

"Tim…" I respond nervously, wondering too late if it's OK to use my real name, "Hi."

Wow! I think to myself as a first reaction to the face behind the greeting. *She's a doll! She's really very attractive!*

"May I join you, please Tim?" she asks, something in her manner suggesting that it's OK for me to say, *"No…bring up the next offering for my scrutiny."*

"Yes, of course…please," I reply, stumbling over the foot rail as I

Tim Haslam

rise up to my feet.

I think the shopping part is over!

I want her to get seated quickly, so that I can sit back down and get myself at a better angle to take in her warm brown eyes and her subtle, Mona Lisa half-smile. Her silky, shoulder length black hair, cut in a perky contemporary style, frames her perfectly sculpted face, flawless in its complexion, genuine and inviting in its expression.

I want to stop here for a long moment. I want to rest right here after a year in the Army and seven months in the shit and just stare into this face. What ever's happened to me, wherever I've been and whatever I've done can be put aside for just a minute. I don't have to think about how far away home is, how far away Rosemary is, how I got here or how long I get to stay. I don't have to think about going back. For just a minute I've been beguiled into a perfect place. Debbie has given me this.

She eases me into conversation. Somehow I've bought a drink for her, another for me; another for the mama-san, I think. Maybe I bought one for the bartender and the other three girls. I don't know. I don't care. Everything and everyone in this dimly lit little bar has blended together into a carefree Renoir background. Debbie's face, her voice, her smell and her closeness have, in these brief moments emptied me out and filled me up. I just follow her lead in the conversation. She makes it easy. I can't take my eyes off her.

"Do you want to go somewhere else?" she asks, as the last drops of my latest Black Label are sipped out of the glass. As the glass comes down onto the bar, her small soft hand presses gently over the back of mine, eliciting a nearly forgotten feeling within me. *No, I don't want anything to move, to change. Yes, I'll go anywhere with you.*

"OK, sure."

My training takes hold again, coaxing me back in line with the routine.

"You must give me fifteen dollars, American, to give to mama-san and then we can go wherever we want."

With mama-san compensated, Debbie and I make for the front exit. I hold open the door for her and she tells me I should give the doorman a dollar. I straighten out one of the crumpled up dollar bills pulled from my pocket and hand it to the smiling man on the stool.

"No, no, one Hong Kong dollar!" she scolds me. For the rest of

Stars and Stripes and Shadows

the time that Debbie is with me, it will be her job to minimize the amount of money I give to anyone else. The fee I've paid to the mama-san entitles me to take Debbie out of the bar and for her to be my date. Anything expected on my part, beyond sharing her company in public places will require an additional negotiation between she and I and so, she therefore wants to make sure that I don't waste too much of my money on cameras or stereos or clothes or food or doormen.

She says she knows a fun place to go and pulls me by the hand back up the street. The fun place turns out to be the same club I was in earlier, where I shared a few moments with the two drunken Aussies and where the bartender and other patrons all seemed to think of me as an uninvited guest. She's dragged me inside before I have a chance to render my opinion about the establishment. This time my entrance brings a number of enthusiastic responses from various young Chinese men and women, dancing and smoking within the twisting reflections of colored neon. The enthusiasm is actually for Debbie, who seems to know everyone in the place. She keeps a grip on my hand as she makes her rounds from group to group, individual to individual, dragging me behind like a puppy on a leash. All of the dialogue exchanged is in Cantonese and there are no attempts at introductions or translations of anything said. Occasionally one of her friends will glance over at me, apparently in an attempt to properly place me into one of the subcategories of American assholes who buy friendship with Chinese girls.

What happened to the Debbie I was enchanted with back at the little bar up the street? I want to go back there. I want to be alone with her. I want to be with her on my terms.

"Sorry," she says, finally acknowledging that I'm still here. "I had some things I needed to tell my friends. Do you want to dance?" she asks, pointing to the adjacent dance floor where four energetic, animated Chinese couples are gyrating away to the Rolling Stones.

I'd rather go back to Firebase 25 in a typhoon.

"No, I don't think so. I'm not much of a dancer," I tell her, thinking this may come as somewhat of a disappointment to her and firmly establish my image as another dull guy to be endured for a few hours.

"That's good," she says with surprising energy. "Let's go sit down. Maybe you would like another drink?" With this, she pulls me through more of the crowd over to a small table covered in empty and partially

Tim Haslam

empty glasses. We sit down and for a moment I get a chance to get re-acquainted with the beauty of her face. Perhaps it's the brighter glow of the neon and strobe lights but she looks different now. She's still incredibly pretty; beautiful and desirable but she's only partially attending to me. I get everything on the surface but don't feel like I'm allowed below that anymore. I have to struggle to find the same promising character in her voice within the audible tangle of pounding music, clanging glasses and Cantonese expressions of youthful exuberance echoing around me.

Debbie orders the drinks this time, taking for granted that she understands my preferences. The drinks are delivered a few minutes later and added to the collection of glasses on the table. There's no effort made to remove any of the empties.

I think she actually gets something stronger than tea for herself. She makes her best effort to re-start the dialogue, to re-engage me in my own fantasy. It's nearly midnight now and I think I need to take the next step. I'm too tired and have probably had too much to drink to formulate any kind of convoluted strategy for getting her back to room 512 at the Park Hotel.

"Let's go to my hotel."

"I can't go with you to your hotel tonight," she responds immediately, followed by an apologetic smile.

What? That's not supposed to happen. That's not what she's supposed to say. Pinkerman...Price...what the hell is this about?

"Um, you can't go with me to my hotel?"

"No, no...I'm sorry...I can't tonight, I'm sick."

You're what? You're sick?

"You're sick?" I ask, leaning closer to her to ensure that I'm getting all this right.

"I girl sick," she says with a little touch of embarrassment in her tone and expression.

Girl sick...what the hell does that mean...girl sick? Oh...Oh...I get it. I understand what "girl sick" means. Shit! Damn!

After twenty-one and a half years of life, a year in the Army, seven months in the shit, an odyssey from Vietnam to Hong Kong, dinner with an unknown Chinese tailor, five glasses of Johnnie Walker and out-of-pocket expenditures of nearly thirty-five-dollars, my date is at that time of the month! This cannot be happening.

Debbie must have detected the pathetic deterioration of my expression and posture. She seems to understand that my expectations have been brutally dashed by the timing of her biological cycle. She wants to help.

"I have a friend I can call for you," she says with great enthusiasm.

"I don't think so," is my first reaction to her tended countermeasure.

"I don't know if that's a very good idea."

"No, it's a good idea, you will like her. She is very fun girl. I call her right now."

Before I can raise any more of an objection she's hurried off toward the alcove where the bathrooms and telephone are. She's back in five minutes with the news that her friend will meet us at the hotel. I'm thinking that this night is about to take a big turn for the worse. I'm heading for something that I'll have no control over. *What kind of a girl needs her friends to get dates for her at midnight in this town? This can't be good.*

Debbie and I enter the lobby of the Park under the disapproving eyes of the two night attendants behind the desk and sit down on one of the bench seats near the elevators. Here, in the steady subdued light and quiet of the hotel lobby, Debbie's soft warmth shines through again. I don't want to be with her friend. Sick or not, I just want to stay right here with this girl.

We're only here a minute or two when the revolving glass door entrance over to our left spins to life, catching the attention of the two attendants, Debbie and myself. The girl who shoots out into the lobby is nothing like Debbie in appearance. If Debbie has the appearance of a pretty, soft, warm, demure doll, this girl, obviously Debbie's friend has walked right off the cover of Teen Magazine. Dressed in a short red mini-skirt, white leather boots and tight white sweater—this girl is drop-dead-gorgeous. *Things are looking up.*

The friend moves quickly across the lobby toward us, her smile and buoyancy building with each step. Debbie springs up and gives her friend a quick hug, cackling something in Cantonese.

"This is Judy," Debbie advises me.

Before the other half of the introduction is presented, Judy jumps

Tim Haslam

up and wraps her arms around my neck and from a distance of about a half an inch says, "Hi, Teem."

I can see her sparkling eyes and smooth almond skin and, what's captured most of my attention, is that I can feel her. I can feel the contours and warmth of her body. I can feel the energy within this miniskirted package. I can smell the clean fresh essence of her pony-tailed hair and her skin and her breath. She's so close I can taste the sweetness of her warm breath. She has, in an instant, laid siege to all my senses, overcoming everything else. She's become part of me. She's very good. She's wonderful. She's found every one of my brain cells, that a moment ago were fascinated with Debbie, erased them, and injected the fullness of Judy back within them. She's taken over. She's in charge. I'll do whatever Judy wants, from this moment forward.

Debbie graciously excuses herself before Judy has released her grip around my neck and fades off into the Hong Kong night. I'll never see her again. I'll never get a chance to thank her for sharing her beauty with me when nothing else was more valuable. I'll never get a chance to thank her for Judy.

The two disapproving night attendants behind the desk have no clue of the complex human interactions that have just transpired in front of them. All they've seen is two bar girls and a horny American G.I. They've seen it all before.

Judy leads the way through the rest of the night with freight-train subtlety. She wants to fill in a few of the relevant voids about me and my status, left out of Debbie's earlier debriefing. She conducts the interrogation like a skilled barrister leading a witness through the essential facts necessary to finalize her strategy. Unlike a selfish prosecutor however, she offers a personal reward for every disclosure; a hug, a kiss, a touch, a laugh. The more I try to give her vague, evasive answers to her inquiries the more confused we both get about how long I've been her and how much time and money I have left. At various points within our interaction, both verbal and physical, she stops in an attempt to clarify some of the contradictions implicit in my terse answers.

"I don't understand you," she says several times. "It's OK though. You're not like the other Americans I've met. I like you."

I'll bet you say that to all the Americans.

The rest of my first night in Hong Kong, my first night away from

Stars and Stripes and Shadows

Vietnam, is a journey through an ethereal realm of sensations; soft, smooth and warm to the touch, sweet and sumptuous to taste and smell, every step accompanied by Judy's playful narration and ongoing questioning.

✷ ✷ ✷ ✷

It's seven-ish in the morning when Judy comes out of the little bathroom, fully revved-up for the rest of her day out in the city.

"What about tonight?" I ask, considerably more subdued about my readiness for the activities of the day. "Can I see you again tonight?"

"I thought maybe you were leaving today. Maybe I didn't understand you," she explains, making a final re-alignment of her ponytail.

"So, you will be here one more night?"

"Yes, maybe even longer than that."

"You're not sure how much longer you're going to be here? Americans always know when they have to leave."

"Well, I'm on a special kind of R&R and if I want to stay another day or two it's OK, I can."

Now she's really not sure of what to make of me, but seems willing to go along if I'm serious about wanting to see her again.

"OK, come to the Moongate Club on Kimberly Road at ten o'clock."

"That late, not until ten o'clock, I thought maybe we could have dinner?"

"No dinner, sorry, see you at ten," she offers as an explanation as she opens the door and enters the hallway. She blows me a kiss and pulls the door closed behind her, leaving me to float through another two hours of semi-sleep interspersed with re-plays of everything that happened last night. *Four more nights of R&R...little rest but lots of recuperation. Life is good! I wonder where Kimberly Road is.*

✷ ✷ ✷ ✷

Since my objective for the day is to explore as much of the Kowloon district as I can on foot and then cross over the harbor to Hong Kong Island, I leave the hotel right after breakfast and follow what I recall being the route to Jack Wong's. The morning desk attendant at the Park, apparently unfamiliar with my nighttime dalliances, happily provided

Tim Haslam

me with a street map of the district, confirming that it really was an easy walk up to Austin Road.

"Do you know where Kimberly Road is?" I ask as well, hoping that I'll be able to scout ahead for the Moongate. It turns out that Kimberly angles away from Nathan Road and intersects with Austin right near Jack's. *Perfect.*

The Moongate turns out to be in the middle of the block, easy to find, similar in appearance to the little bar where I met Debbie. I can't wait for ten o'clock, although I'm still excited about my opportunities to explore the city until then.

I find Jack once again alone in his shop. He's glad to see me and starts immediately inquiring as to the status of my appetites. I decline all his offers and he and I get to work looking through the bolts of suiting materials he has available. I narrow down my choices to a deep red-brown fabric and another lighter-beige with a hint of green to it.

"You know, Jack…why don't you make one of each color for me." *At this price it's not worth carrying on an internal debate over which color I prefer.*

Jack Wong is thrilled that his investment in Johnny Walker and dinner is paying off with unexpected dividends. As he proceeds with the measuring it occurs to me that Jack may know how I can go about finding a tour that will go out to the "New Territories" and the Chinese border. That's the only really tourist-like thing that I'm determined to do.

"OK, OK, yes…when you come back tomorrow afternoon for first fitting I can help you," he tells me as he chalks the lines for my pant cuffs.

With our business concluded he tells me the way to the harbor and the Star Ferry building where I can book passage on the ferry boat that crosses over to Hong Kong Island and the other half of the city. The energy of the city has overcome my lack of sleep and so the trek over to the harbor is a bright-eyed excursion through the scents and odors and sounds of the busy residents going about their lives on this bright sunny Monday. I get sucked in to a few of the clothing shops along the way by the assertive Indian touts outside, insisting that they have the one thing I need most in the world. The thing-I-need-most usually turns out to be a variation of the same black, yellow and green argyle sweater or a

Stars and Stripes and Shadows

more traditional silk Chinese tunic with something about Hong Kong embroidered on it. I'm able to maintain a strong defense against these temptations knowing full well how disappointed the proprietors must be in my lack of good taste. I'm not yet ready to enter any of the many shops whose windows are crammed full of Japanese manufactured cameras, watches and radios. There, I know the temptations would be too great to resist.

A small tobacco shop catches my eye with its display of various cigarette brands in the window. There are several packages, names and logos that I've never seen before set amongst the familiar Marlboro, Winston and Lucky Strike packs. I decide to augment my adventure further and buy a pack of foreign made cigarettes.

"A pack of...um...ah...Rothman's I guess" gets me an elegantly printed flip-top pack of cigarettes, made, who-knows-where in the world and some amount of Hong Kong coinage in exchange for the American dollar I tended.

The ride across the harbor on the Star Ferry caps the adventure. Boats are always fun for me. A big ferryboat, full of Chinese people, slowly plowing through a postcard image of sampans, row boats and ancient freighters, all set against a back drop of the city structures climbing up into the mountains on all sides puts me once again on sensation overload. This is fun. I could just ride back and forth like this for most of the rest of the day and at twenty-five cents Hong Kong, I could do it forever.

The ferry terminal on the Island side is set immediately adjacent to the city center and so I instantly find myself back among the schools of taxis and mini-trucks scurrying along the one-way streets. The high-rise buildings here seem to be more compacted than they were over in Kowloon. There is a greater sense of business being conducted over here too. More men in suits, more serious looking Anglos with brief cases and newspapers, more young Chinese women in dresses streaming in and out of the big buildings, plying their trades within the offices as energetically as the girls on the night shift over in the bars on the other side. Everyone in Hong Kong seems to have a purpose and role that they understand, accept and fulfill with enthusiasm. The pace and rhythm of the city around me continues to ward off my own fatigue. I can rest when I get back to Vietnam...back from R&R.

Tim Haslam

I go into the Hong Kong Hilton hotel, for no particular reason, except that it looks elegant and that a lot of American or European looking people seem to be going in and out. It is elegant, probably too much so for a grunt on R&R. The shops spread around the lobby level of the hotel carry lines of merchandize for people of other tastes and budgets than mine. I do get a cup of coffee and sit for a few minutes to observe the parade of well-dressed westerners scuttling about the lobby as I try to think through what I should do next.

Bob Price had told me of a place called the China Fleet Club, that's run by and for U.S. Navy personnel. He said it was a good place to buy most anything that I want, that I might find anywhere else in the city; cameras, stereos, watches, etc. They'll also ship anything I buy home at special military rates. *I guess I'll go there next.*

A short taxi ride gets me to the Club and a flash of my military ID gets me inside. The China Fleet Club is just as described. It's like a shopping mall and appears to offer everything I'd be interested in. The prices seem to be nearly as low as some I'd seen posted on like merchandize in the shop windows over in Kowloon and the fact that haggling is not part of the expected routine here makes it that much more attractive. I make the first big investment of my life in something electronic and buy a Sony reel-to-reel tape recorder. I add a tape recording of Simon and Garfinkel's <u>Bridge Over Troubled Waters</u> album and fill out the paperwork necessary to have it all shipped home.

The Club also saves me from the anxiety of finding a place for lunch. The spacious dining room is nearly empty at two-thirty as a cheerful young Chinese man guides me in to one of the white linen covered tables. He recommends the seasoned, sautéed prawns with wild rice and hovers over my right shoulder as I open the menu.

He's making me nervous. He expects me to decide right now. He's going to stay right here until I give him his orders. I don't see anything like a cheeseburger on here.

"OK, I guess I'll have the sautéed prawns," I tell him with as much confidence as I can muster, wondering what prawns are.

Across the room, sitting at a larger table, working quickly through large glasses of beer are two U.S. Naval officers, dressed in crisp white uniforms and another man, who must be either a British or Australian officer, similarly attired in a bright white uniform. I don't know how to

530

Stars and Stripes and Shadows

determine naval ranks, but the number of stripes on each man's epaulets suggests that they must be pretty high up the ladder. The starchy spotlessness of their outfits and their shiny white shoes makes me appreciate my soft cotton pants and oxford cloth shirt.

For all they know I'm an Army Major taking a break from my important military duties, or maybe I'm an official from the State Department, or the CIA. For all they know, I'm just as important as they are. My mission is actually classified and so I must sit here alone with my awesome responsibilities. *I think I'll order a beer too.*

These are shrimp! I think to myself as the waiter carefully twists the plate full of seasoned, sautéed prawns down in front of me.

"I believe I'd like a glass of beer," I tell the waiter when he asks if there will be anything else.

"Very good, sir. What kind would you like?"

What's the right answer? What kind of beer do important dignitaries usually drink?

"Whatever those officers are having," I tell him, as though I couldn't be bothered making such a trivial decision.

"Very good, sir."

The prawns or shrimp or whatever they are, along with the wild rice and the cold beer make up the best meal I've had since I left home. The starchy-whites must be on their third round of beers when I finally finish eating. I still have a third of my own beer left and am in no hurry to finish up and move on from this satisfying segment of the fantasy. The starchy's are now smoking along with their beer drinking...Tareyton's, a mundane brand of American cigarettes; a favorite among my fraternity brothers; the brand with the Micronite Filter, the brand that the black-eyed devotees on TV would rather fight than switch over. *Here's my chance to firmly establish my place in the hierarchy within the dining room.*

I slowly withdraw the blue lettered pack of Rothman's from my shirt pocket, lightly tap the top of the box against the palm of my hand to compress the tobacco just right, casually remove the cellophane wrapper and pull out one of the twenty filtered cigarettes. With the cigarette placed appropriately, thirty degrees off center, in my mouth, my Zippo ignites the extended end as I simultaneously contort my face

Tim Haslam

into just the right level of wince. Humphrey Bogart taught me this in Casablanca. I don't think any of the starchy's took notice. *Just as well. I'm trying not to attract too much attention to myself.*

N N N N

The taxi driver seems to be in a hurry to get me back to the Star Ferry terminal, jockeying his little car through the clogs and flows of traffic. At one point along the waterfront, the thoroughfare opens up and the driver throttles his cab up to a speed rarely attainable on the streets of this city. He jogs to the right at one point to get around a mini-truck plodding slowly along in the center lane. Just as he pulls around the truck, a mangy looking dog sprints over the median to our right, directly into the path of our taxi. I can hear the impact and swing my head around to see if I can determine what's happened to the dog. Happily I see the dog roll back up onto his feet and scurry the rest of the way across the street. The driver has made no attempt to stop or even slow down. I catch his eyes in the rearview mirror. He glances back at me and then briefly back out into the road passing away behind us and then back at me again. He gives me an expressionless half a second before returning his eyes to the road and traffic in front of him.

I wonder if the dog really has survived or if it had just enough of an adrenaline boost to run a few more yards. *Maybe what I heard was just the sound of the dog's tail being hit by the bumper. Maybe it really is OK. Maybe it's lying over on the other side of the road now...dieing...no one caring that his life is coming to end.*

The sound of the car and dog impact has snapped me out of my fantasy adventure. I think about Barney and home again. I think about how the once strong and vigorous German Shepard was struggling so much with his arthritis the last time I saw him when I was home on Christmas leave. He could barely get up on his own. He was not the same dog that accompanied me around our backyard realm, always willing to play whatever I wanted. I mentally scan around our whole backyard, remembering everything there, taking in every one of the walnut trees that I used to climb, the sections of lawn that I used to cut and the pool that my friends and I spent so much of our summer days and evenings in. I'll never see that place again. I'll never see Barney again. I wonder whose dog it was that we just hit.

532

Stars and Stripes and Shadows

✄ ✄ ✄ ✄

I can't wait until ten o'clock and so, at eight-thirty, after dinner at the hotel, I head for the Moongate in hopes of finding Judy earlier. The Moongate turns out to be much the same as the bar that Debbie worked out of, except that there's no doorman outside.

I've barely had time to adjust to the subtle glow within when Judy pounces out of the neon illuminated background, throwing her arms around me in a repeat of our initial contact in the lobby of the Park Hotel last night.

"Give me fifteen dollars for the mama-san and we can go," she tells me, apparently confidant enough in her personal level of authority within the Moongate hierarchy to orchestrate the process.

"Aren't I supposed to buy a drink?" I ask, remembering how pleasant my time with Debbie was last night at her bar and how unpleasant things turned out later once we'd left.

"No, c'mon…we go," she answers, looking up into my eyes with a sparkling sincerity and measure of connection that I've not seen since the night I left Rosemary for the last time. Perhaps it's just my imagination, or a subconscious desire to be appreciated simply for some personal uniqueness, but her look suggests that her motives go beyond the level of expected professional conduct. She really wants to be with *me*.

"OK," I tell her, as I hand her the buy-out fee. "Where do you want to go?"

She hurries to the back of the bar without answering me, spends thirty seconds with the lady sitting on the last barstool and then heads for the front door, grabbing my hand along the way. Once outside she stops and looks around.

"Give me a dollar for the doorman," she says matter-of-factly, without any acknowledgement that we just managed our way through the door without assistance from anyone.

"What doorman?" I ask foolishly. "We just opened the door ourselves."

She focuses her attention on the pedestrian traffic a few doors down and across the street, saying something, apparently to herself, in Cantonese and then, skillfully employing thumb and forefinger lets out a high pitched whistle, followed by another proclamation in Cantonese loud enough for everyone on the street to hear.

533

Tim Haslam

A middle-aged Chinese man, dressed in an ill-fitting suit, reacts to the summons, separates from a small clutch of bodies and jogs across the street towards us trailing smoke from the cigarette in his mouth. He hops up onto the sidewalk on our side of the street, slides around the two of us standing at the Moongate threshold and courteously opens the door.

That was actually worth a Hong Kong dollar, I think to myself as I hand off the payment to the smiling helper at the now-open door. The obvious fact that we're going the other way doesn't seem at all relevant to anyone involved in this transaction.

"I'm hungry," Judy declares, tugging me down the sidewalk. "Let's go have dinner...OK?"

It's been nearly half and hour since I finished the salad, steak, baked potato and ice cream sundae at the hotel and an opportunity to have a casual dinner with this girl would be better than anything else I could think of for the first part of our *date* tonight. My appetite for such a dinner is high, even if it involves eating more.

She leads me down the street, into the lobby of one of the tall buildings, up the stairs and into a first-rate looking Chinese restaurant. The hostess greets us as we enter, directing most of her greeting to me, trying to ignore Judy. Before I have a chance to acknowledge the greeting however, Judy injects herself back into the dominant role, parries and thrusts out a few short directives in Cantonese and leads the hostess and I over toward one of the better tables by the window. Once seated, with menus in hand she informs me of her own preferences, suggests what she thinks I would like and relays the plans to the now obedient hostess.

"You have girlfriend at home?" she asks, opening the conversation without bothering through anymore organized sort of segue.

She seems genuinely interested in my response, her eyes scanning intently back and forth across my face. I'm a little uneasy at first telling her about Rosemary. It was easier bragging to my grunt friends about my girlfriend, how pretty she was, how much fun she was and about all the things we did together. Those were generally just tag conversations anyway. None of us really cared that much about what the other guy had to say about his girl, we just each wanted to have the opportunity to bring up and share the images of our own girlfriends. Judy, it seems, wants to know everything. She pulls it all out—gently, patiently. She

534

Stars and Stripes and Shadows

prompts and probes, coaxing the remembrances into our conversation and I tell her everything. I tell her what Rosemary looked like, what we did, where we went. I tell her even that she's not been writing to me much anymore, that she hasn't had much to tell me for the last few months. I tell her that I'm not sure if Rosemary still feels the same way about me. I'm not sure if she misses me anymore, if she thinks about me anymore.

With each of my disclosures Judy's facial expressions conjoin with the feelings underlying my narrative. She smiles and laughs as though we were recounting our own past relationship. There's even a detectable sadness muting the sparkling luster of her eyes when I tell her of my concerns, accompanied by subtle twists of her mouth, expressing care and warmth. I'm too engrossed in my own stories and too beguiled by my companion here to wonder if this kind of directed catharsis is part of the package of services she offers or is a real expression of who she is and what she feels inside. It doesn't matter...I'm having a relaxed dinner with a beautiful girl. I'm having dinner with Judy and Rosemary. I'm relaxing, recuperating. I want to linger over this for as long as I can.

"You didn't eat much. Don't you like this?" Judy asks, bringing me back into the here and now.

"No, no, it's fine. I guess I was just too busy talking. How was your dinner?" I reply, taking note for the first time that she's finished every morsel on her plate and is now gently poking a toothpick around the spaces between her white teeth.

"C'mon, let's go," she asserts, dropping the toothpick down onto the carpeted floor. "What do you want to do now?"

"Let's just walk around for awhile...OK? I need to move a little."

The atmosphere of the city is more vibrant and alive now. With Judy's hand in mine, and no planned destination, the lights and sounds and smells wash over me, each step enhancing the intoxication of the evening. The stroll along the still-busy streets is a fantasy journey through a fantasy world and I know that there is more to come. Judy and all of this right now...Judy alone later.

"Let's go in here for just a minute," I suggest to Judy, in front of one of the few men's shops that doesn't have someone outside telling me about the wonders within. There's a pullover sweater displayed in the window that I want to get a closer look at. She doesn't seem too

Tim Haslam

enthusiastic about this, but follows along, her right hand tucked in around my left elbow. The Chinese shop keeper leads us to a stack of sweaters on a table toward the back of the shop and tells me that they're the finest in the city and that he'll make me a special deal and let me have it for only eleven dollars, U.S.

Judy immediately rips into the shopkeeper in high-decibel Cantonese, eliciting a submissive shrug from the surprised man.

"C'mon," she orders me, yanking me back toward the door, "I know a better place that has the same sweaters."

In the three seconds that it takes us to reach the door, the price has stepped down from eleven to ten to nine dollars, U.S.

The "better-place" doesn't have the same sweater, but does have one that's close enough and the shop keeper here, who Judy seems to know, is willing to sacrifice it at only nine dollars U.S. This seems a bargain to me and I agree to the terms. Judy carries on a quiet Chinese conversation with the shopkeeper all the way up to the register at the front of the shop where I hand him a ten-dollar bill. I think there must be some mistake when he hands me back three dollars change.

"No, it's right," Judy clarifies, having apparently added some final measure of influence to the negotiation without my knowledge.

Her final, "C'mon...let's go," gets us back to the privacy of room 512 at the Park Hotel.

I won't let her be in total command this time. I want to know some things about her. I want her to share more than just the warmth of her soft, supple skin, the essence of her hair and the electricity of her lips. No other of her *dates* ever wanted to know such things. None ever seemed to care. We spend the next several hours, learning, sharing and perhaps pretending that these moments are more than just an interlude, more than just an R&R; more than just a date.

✗ ✗ ✗ ✗

"Ah! Mr. Tim...you are right on time. How are you today? Have you found everything you want in Hong Kong so far?" Jack Wong says as I enter the door of the Heung Cheng Company.

"I have your suits ready for the next fitting. They will be very nice, very handsome. Come, try them on."

He leads me to the fitting room, where the two suits are hanging,

Stars and Stripes and Shadows

each on a separate wall hook. I try on the brown one first and wear it out for Jack's scrutiny. He tugs the sleeves into place, straightens the collar and balances the lapels. He makes a little mark here and a little mark there.

"Good, good. It will be finished tomorrow. It will be very nice."

We repeat the process with the green suit and the same results.

"You were going to tell me the best way to find a tour that would get me out to the New Territories and the Chinese border," I remind him as he places a couple of pins into the fabric of the brown suit.

"Yes, I have not forgotten. What are your plans for this evening?"

"Well, I don't really have any plans until about ten o'clock," I answer, thinking about the promise I made to Judy to meet again later.

With that, Jack picks up his telephone, dials a number and makes a very short declaration in Chinese to whoever is on the other end. Then, as he hangs up the phone, he yells out something, again in Chinese, that brings Mr. Yang and another, larger Chinese man from out of the back room. The other man, with a camera hanging from a strap around his neck, is introduced to me as Mr. Lim. I can tell that he speaks as much English as Mr. Yang...none.

With the smiling Mr. Yang and Mr. Lim staring at me, Jack puts on his own suit coat and then shepherds all of us out the door and down the stairs. Still, without clarifying our destination, he leads us out to the edge of the curb and looks down to his right, in the direction of the oncoming traffic.

"I have it all arranged," he finally discloses. "We will take you out to the New Territories and show you everything. It will be much better than a tour."

As I'm trying to sort through the implications of the situation, a shiny, black Mercedes Benz pulls up to the curb. Mr. Yang opens the rear door and beckons me to enter as Mr. Lim hurries around to the other side and Jack enters the front passenger seat.

"Hi, hi...Mr. Tim," the driver, Mr. Weng says as I'm introduced to the fourth member of my escort team.

Mr. Weng quickly inserts the Mercedes back into the flow of traffic with the same blind-faith determination as the taxi drivers, as Jack clarifies the details of our mission to everyone in the car who speaks Cantonese.

537

Tim Haslam

What have I got myself into? I'm thinking as I sit here, surrounded by four Chinese men, heading towards the outskirts of Kowloon in a black Mercedes Benz. I remember that Jack's shop wasn't on the list of recommended tailor shops handed out when I arrived. *Why has he been so hospitable? What's he up to? What are they all up to? Where are they really taking me?*

"Do you like fish?" Jack asks, twisting around fully in the front seat so that he's oriented toward me.

"Um, yea, I like fish," I respond a little nervously, still too distracted by the possibility of my kidnapping to remember that frozen fish-sticks are the only form of seafood that I really do like.

Fish...is that what I'm going to be eating for the rest of my life while in captivity somewhere deep in Communist China?

As our journey progresses out of the busy center of the city, Jack begins his pretended tour guide duties and starts telling me all about Hong Kong and Red China, pointing at sites of interest along the way. At one point we pass what looks like a military installation with two serious looking guards standing at attention on either side of the gated entrance. The guards, each with a shouldered automatic rifle, appear to be Asian, dapper looking in their light green uniforms and digger hats with the brims buttoned up on one side.

"Ghurkas," Jack tells me. "The Ghurkas have served as the guards for Hong Kong for a long time. They're part of the British Army but come from Nepal. They are very fierce men. Everyone is afraid of the Ghurkas."

We seem to be heading north along a road that follows the edge of the harbor. I can see the white buildings of Kowloon and across the bay in Hong Kong itself fading away behind us as the landscape shifts from urban to rural. There's still a lot of boat traffic visible out on the bay; large junks and smaller sampans, sail, motor and row about in all directions. It's another postcard scene that adds to the adventure of being kidnapped by four *commie* agents in their black Mercedes Benz.

As Jack continues his non-stop narrative descriptions of things along the way, Mr. Lim keeps taking the same profile picture of me from his position six inches to my left. *Maybe these will serve as mug shots for when I get booked into the detention and torture center for imperialist dogs.*

Mr. Yang says nothing, but smiles each time my head twists his way

Stars and Stripes and Shadows

and Mr. Weng, at the wheel, frequently validates the interesting attributes of whatever it is that Jack is describing. All in all, my abduction is a pleasant and informative experience so far and my captors are cordial and hospitable. I'm even encouraged to smoke, adding my cloud to that of Jack's and Mr. Weng's steady puffing into the polluted interior of the car. I can see a pack of Pall Malls in Mr. Yang's pocket, but he's so far refrained from lighting up. Perhaps his stature within the organization limits his privileges.

Weng begins to slow the black Benz as we approach what seems to be a village set close to the bay on our right. He swings onto a dirt apron at the edge of the village and parks among an armada of like-looking small vehicles. The others climb out with the smiling Yang holding the door open for me.

"Very good food here," Jack advises, as he leads the way off into the interior of the village. "Very good fish...very fresh fish here."

A long pier, jutting out into the bay forms the main street of the village. The pier, large enough to include a line of shops and restaurants along each edge, is busy with Chinese people, some shopping, some, apparently shuttling fish and other goods between the many boats tied up along the connected wharfs and piers. The air is a strong mix of fish, spice, seawater, cooking oil and motor oil. I can't see that there aren't any other American or European representatives within the throng.

I walk along, side by side with Jack, down a ramp that leads out onto the pier as he points out his favorite restaurant and describes the history of the village, Yang and Weng trailing along behind us. Mr. Lim tries to keep ten or fifteen feet ahead of us, turning every few steps to take our picture. Many of the locals stop to study us, wondering perhaps if the tall American being continually photographed is a celebrity. Sensing this, I ensure that my posture and demeanor are consistent with such expectations.

Jack turns out onto one of the connecting piers and directs me toward a ramp that leads onto the second boat in the line of sampans moored there. *Now they've got me. They're shepherding me onto this boat, where, I'm sure the pirate captain will sail me up the Yangtse River and deliver me to Mao Tse Tung for a sizeable ransom. They've got me surrounded, Lim in front, Jack at my side, Yang and Weng behind me. There's no chance to escape.*

Tim Haslam

The pirate captain seems to be a small, amiable man, anxious to show us the contents of a large open-topped tank in the middle of his boat. Within the tank there is a great variety of fish types swimming about within the clear water.

"What kind of fish do you like?" Jack asks seeming to be as proud of the array as the pirate captain is.

"Oh...uhm...I'm not sure," I respond, stalling to figure out a better answer, not recognizing any of the big mottled fish looking up at me.

"Actually, I really like prawns," I tell him, still carefully studying the swimming menu.

"Oh yes...you mean shrimp," he says enthusiastically and then relays my expressed preference to the captain in Chinese. The captain grabs a net and starts scooping large shrimp out of a second tank, further up toward the bow of the big boat.

"OK, OK...what else you like?"

"Well, I guess I'll trust your judgment. What do you like?"

Once again, Jack instructs the captain, who, along with one of his crewmembers starts pulling the identified fish out of the tank, placing them into a burlap sack.

Maybe this really is on the level and they really are just taking me for dinner, I begin to think as we depart the boat; Mr. Yang and Mr. Weng in possession of our dinner bags, Mr. Lim still documenting nearly ever move for posterity.

The proprietor at Jack's favorite restaurant leads the five of us to a table, instructing one of his own minions to take the bags from Yang and Weng. We each order beer and, following Jack's lead, light up cigarettes. Even Mr. Lim puts aside his photojournalist duties to smoke one of the Pall Malls offered to him by Yang.

We're all pals now, drinking our beer, smoking our cigarettes, nibbling on deep-fried something-or-other brought out to whet our appetites for the fish being prepared back in the smoky kitchen. Jack alternates the conversation between English and Cantonese, proving to be a good host and interpreter. Mr. Weng's questioning uncovers my Hollywood background, perking up the rest of the party and elevating my stature significantly among the group. Lim and Yang pass on their questions through Jack. They want to know if I've seen John Wayne or Jerry Lewis or Hoss Cartwright. No, just Steve McQueen, Charlton

Stars and Stripes and Shadows

Heston and Bing Crosby.

Enthusiastic "ah" and "oh yes," responses follow each of my motion picture industry disclosures. They're too genuinely enamored with all of this to be committed proletariat communists. I'm convinced now that I'm no longer in danger of being kidnapped. If I can survive the fish dinner I'll be OK.

My friends appreciate that I've chosen to forego the use of a fork and have instead followed their lead and taken up chopsticks to deal with the rice and array of fish delivered to us. The rice and shrimp/prawns are plenty to fill me up along with a few tastes of each of the other varieties of fish. It's all pretty good and a second round of Chinese beer makes it all even better.

With a couple of hours of daylight left after dinner, we return to the Benz and our trek out to the New Territories and the border. Jack directs Weng to a place along a mountain road where we have a view out to the west across a large valley. Jack tells me that the river cutting through the valley is the Shum Shun and that Communist China is on the other side. He points out a little complex of buildings on this side of a bridge over the river off to our right and tells me that this is the Loc Ma Chow Station with Ghurkas and British soldiers on this side with their Red Chinese counterparts occupying a similar complex on the other side.

China…I'm seeing into the real China.

At this distance I can just make out the figures of some of the Chinese guards over on the other side. There's no visible traffic on the road that leads westward away from the river. There are no other communists to be seen. The country is green and rich looking. It's a peaceful, pleasant scene. My friends seem to enjoy it as much as I do.

"I feel like I owe you something for all of this, Jack. Are you sure I can't pay you something for the dinner or gas or something?" I ask Jack as the Benz pulls up in front of the Park Hotel.

"No, no, no…we are happy to be able to do this with you. We will see you tomorrow when all your new clothes will be finished."

I shake hands with each of my smiling friends.

"Thank you…thank you all.

N   N   N   N

Tim Haslam

"You really are leaving this morning?" Judy asks, an hour before dawn on my last morning in Hong Kong. "For sure this time...you really must go today?"

"Yes," I tell her sadly, straightening up my khaki uniform shirt. "I have to be at the airport in less than an hour."

"I will miss you," she tells me, throwing her arms around my neck one last time. "Maybe you will come back here some day. Maybe you will find Judy again some day."

"I hope so..." I tell her, "I'll try."

For most of the airplane ride back to Vietnam, I sleep. During the awake time I relive each moment of my five days in Hong Kong until the reality of my destination sets in. *Back to the Nam...* back to the bullshit and the burning shit and maybe even back into the real shit itself. There's still something that wants me to go back out with the Company, to get away from the pretenses and protocols of base camp; to get back out where each day is a simple proposition, where Mr. Ruck sits at the top of the hierarchy and everything else struggles on equal terms for survival. There's still something within me that wants me to have an M16 in my hand...still something that drives me to use it.

Chapter 18

Nurse Wallace, Miss Kritch and Bob Hope

"Val, any mail for me?" I ask into the mailroom, knowing that Valentine is back in there sorting through the bag he brought in a few minutes ago.

"Nothin' yet."

I've made it through one more boring day with just the hope of new mail to look forward to. I haven't heard from Rosemary in almost three weeks. I haven't heard anything meaningful from her in as many months, but I'm still willing to tell myself that she's just busy, that she's not really very good at writing. It'll all be OK though, once I'm home. All this will be behind both of us and we can pick right up where we left off.

Four more months. Four more long months.

Two Bravo Company men have come in from the boonies on the convoy this afternoon. I have to get them settled in here temporarily until the Army figures out what to do with them. I'll have to make adjustments to the Morning Report tomorrow to indicate that they're back here. The Division Chaplain called one of the men, Gabriel Luna back, there's something that's happened back home that the Chaplain needs to talk to him about. I know Luna from our time together out in the shit. He's a good guy. I'm happy to see him, but uneasy about how to approach him given the circumstances of his presence here. He doesn't say much to me about this summons as I meet him getting off the truck from Dak To, but I fear the worst for him. Somebody in his family must have died. The other guy, Michael Hughes is a different

Tim Haslam

story. Hughes has been out with the Company less than two months. He refused to go on any more patrols. He's back here while the Army decides whether or not to court-martial him. Meanwhile, he's bad for the morale of the men out on the line. Hughes, it will turn out, is bad for the morale of the men everywhere.

Dealing with the two men is my last required duty of the day. I have no guard assignment tonight and tomorrow's Thanksgiving. All I have to do tomorrow is the Morning Report. I get the rest of the day off. I feel like celebrating tonight and head for our little canteen to join Doc, Pinkerman and anyone else that feels like celebrating too. When I get there I find that there's enough beer available in the ice tub for each of us to have four or five cans and Pinkerman's new quart bottle of Crown Royal will ensure that we all will consume way too much alcohol. We also have two cans of shoestring potatoes that somebody brought back from the PX today and of course we have plenty of smokes. We have everything we need to enjoy this Thanksgiving eve.

I run into Gabe Luna when I'm outside on a pee break and invite him to come and join us. He knows Doc and Pinkerman from our days together up in the mountains and seems happy to have the invitation. He follows me back inside, grabbing a beer along the way.

We all want to know if he's learned anything more about what's going on back home.

"It's my wife, I'm sure," he starts telling us. "She's been writing me how depressed she's become the last few months since I've been gone. We we're really close and she really depended on me for everything. She didn't have too many other friends and her own family lives on the other side of Denver...we're up in Colorado Springs. So, she's pretty lonely too."

"So, you think something might have happened to her?" Doc asks, following along the logical implications of Luna's description.

"No, no...I don't think anything really bad has happened to her. I wrote a letter to the Chaplain last month and told him what was going on. I thought maybe the Chaplain might be able to have somebody go out and see her and maybe try to help her out someway. I think that's what this is about. I think the Chaplain just wants to fill me in on what's going on."

Gabe's answer satisfies all of us that his take on things must be right

Stars and Stripes and Shadows

and that the Chaplain, in fact, will have good news for him. We go back to reminiscing about the good old days up in Dak Pek and behind Rocket Ridge.

"What's up with this guy Hughes?" I ask Luna after a lull in the war story telling, thinking that Gabe must know more of this story too.

"The guys just scarred, man. He's scarred to death. All he can think about is getting killed. He was worse than useless out there, man. The Captain and Lieutenant Nelson had to get him out of there. He was driving everybody else crazy. He's an OK kid I guess. He's just scarred to death."

"What happens to him now?" Pinkerman asks of me, as though it were up to the Company Clerk to solve the problem.

"I have no idea. I just show him back at base camp on the Morning Report tomorrow. What happens next is up to Top and Captain Walterhouse I guess."

The whole Hughes business is a downer. We're supposed to be having a party here. We need to get our minds out of the shit and back to faraway worlds. The beer and whiskey soon take over and enable livelier discussions about home, R&R, peace talks and the anticipated turkey dinner tomorrow afternoon. Within two hours, the beer and burning whiskey disables our abilities to articulate almost anything in a comprehensible way and so we spend the rest of our party time communicating with short spontaneous blurbs of inane thought, usually met with a, "right on!" or "fuckin-A!" or "it-don't-mean-nothin.'" At eleven thirty, with the refreshments all gone, we stagger back to the barracks; smoking, laughing and cursing the Army for keeping us so far away from any real reason to give thanks.

I guess we're alive…others aren't. I guess there's reason to be thankful.

Yesterday when I was young
So many drinking songs were waiting to be sung,
So many wayward pleasures lay in store for me
And so much pain my dazzled eyes refused to see.
I ran so fast that time and youth at last ran out.
I never stopped to think what life was all about
And every conversation I can now recall
Concerned itself with me and nothing else at all.

Tim Haslam

The hangover of Thanksgiving morning is a personal best for me, surpassing my most extreme efforts back at the fraternity house. It's all I can do to get the DA-1 and the carbons aligned within the old Remington. It's more than I can do to remember what goes into each box on the form. It's impossible to peck along at anything more than a snails pace with my palsied hands and my throbbing temples. Click………. click……….click. *Never again.* Click……….click……….click.

Half way through the marathon of clicking, one of my blank staring sessions is interrupted by the presence of someone hovering over my right shoulder.

"Hey," the someone says softly, apparently to me.

A painful twist of my head, reveals PFC Hughes as the violator of my space this morning. I don't have the energy or wherewithal to formalize or verbalize a response. The approximate direction of my bloodshot eyes will have to suffice as an acknowledgement of his presence.

Oh shit! What does he want? Not now…whatever it is…not now.

"I think I'm a homosexual," Hughes declares without any introduction or lead in to his disclosure, his own gaze fixed onto the Remington keyboard.

"What?" is the only response my alcohol-compromised reflexes can come up with.

"I'm a homosexual," he repeats, this time allowing his own bloodshot eyes to drift into contact with my studying stare. It's not alcohol though that's disturbed the clarity of vision suggested in this young man's eyes. Coffee, aspirin and the passage of a few painful hours will flush out the source of my self-induced punishment. For Hughes, there's something much deeper that's taken hold of him; something much less acute and transient.

"Why are you telling me this, Hughes?"

"You have to do something. Isn't there some kind of report or something that you have to fill out if somebody's a homo? You're the Company Clerk, right? Aren't you supposed to report this somehow?"

"Look, man, I'm still kind of new as Company Clerk. I have no idea what to do about something like that," I tell him, trying to be and sound sympathetic, shifting out of my own hangover misery and into a new realm of confusion.

546

"Maybe you should talk to the Chaplain or something."

"I did talk to the Chaplain. He said I should get such ideas out of my mind. He didn't believe me."

I'm not sure I believe you either. Whatever you are, or whatever's happened to you is something I don't understand.

"Look, man...why don't you just take it easy today, it's Thanksgiving. Get some rest, have dinner. I'll talk to the Captain tomorrow and see what the right thing to do is."

"Yea...OK," he says, the disappointment clearly reflected in his face and tone. He turns and heads back out into the dusty air and the heat waves shimmering up off the Marston mat surface outside the S1 office. The bright sunlight outside jolts me back into the painful reality of my hangover.

What's with that guy? What's he trying to do? Why would he say that?

Goddamn, shitty, fucking mess!

Thanksgiving?

The turkey dinner is less than half an hour away. There's time to read through all my latest mail one more time before heading over to the mess hall. My desk here in the S1 office is as good a place as any to relax and connect to home. The two fans circulating the hot air make the interior of the office a little more bearable than the barracks and Stone, Welsh and Taylor, who are doing the same thing, make good company.

Rosemary tells me that she went to a Halloween party with Rick and Lisa at somebody's house up on Laurel Canyon. She says she went as a Raggedy-Ann doll. She doesn't say anymore about whom else she was with or what she did, just that it was fun and that somebody there was dressed like a soldier, reminding her of me. I guess that's something, some acknowledgement of where I am and what I'm doing. I think about her made up to be Raggedy-Ann. I think about her made up to be Twiggy, or Joey Hetherton. I think about her, not made up to be anybody else, outside her front door, the last moment I saw her face.

"Where's Charlebois?" Sergeant Sweeney asks loudly entering the office. "Any of you guys know where Doc is?"

Tim Haslam

"I haven't seen him since last night," I tell him, adding to similar responses from the other clerks. "Why, somebody sick?"

"Not sick, no...it's some guy named Hughes. One of the guys in Alpha Company just found him in back behind the supply shed. He slit his wrists with a knife and was just sitting back there, crying and bleeding all over the place. I don't think he's seriously hurt, but we need Doc to deal with this."

"I'll help you find him," I tell Sweeney, feeling for some reason like I need to participate in whatever happens next.

What's with that guy? I think to myself as I begin my part of the search for Doc Charlebois. *Did he really try to kill himself? Should I have done or said something differently when he came to see me a couple of hours ago?*

Thanksgiving dinner in the dusty mess hall, in the stifling heat of Camp Enari, following an aborted suicide attempt isn't much like Thanksgiving back home. There's plenty of turkey, dressing, potatoes and bread and butter to fill up on and my friends and I are probably more appreciative of the meal itself than we ever were back home, as it's such a contrast to the usual bland fare that we've learned to endure here. There's no celebrating though. We're still surrounded by the shit, the smell of burning shit and the confusing image of someone like us who's so afraid of dying that he just tried to kill himself.

Hughes is now over at the Division aid station. He's somebody else's problem. He's out of my jurisdiction. An adjustment to the Morning Report tomorrow and I can forget about him. I'll need Captain Walterhouse's opinion about showing him as sick or wounded in action, or...?

With no duty assignment again tonight, I spend the rest of the evening on my bunk, reading the latest letters from home over and over again, surrounded by the transients of Bravo Company, coming and going in and out of the real shit. A blend of country, rock and roll and soul music hisses out of several transistor radios around me, each enhancing the individual images we retain of the places we've come from. I think about the dining room table in the house I grew up in and the faces of everyone who's always there at Thanksgiving. I don't know what the dining room even looks like in my parent's new house though and my

Stars and Stripes and Shadows

grandmother's face would have been missing this year. Barney wasn't there either this year, waiting outside for the table scraps and a pat on the head. This is my second Thanksgiving in the Army. Things back in the world continue to change without me. Next Thanksgiving, I'll be out of the Army though. I'll be out of the shit. I will have forgotten how shitty this all really is.

◢ ◢ ◢ ◢

"All right man...I'll see you when you get back. I hope everything turns out OK," I yell up to Gabe Luna as the deuce-and-a-half pulls away, heading off for the Pleiku Air Force Base where a C-130 will take him on the next leg of his emergency leave home. The Chaplain believes that Gabe's wife may be depressed enough to do harm to herself. Gabe and the Chaplain believe that his presence with her, even if it's just for a few days will be sufficient to bring her around; to strengthen her resolve and to allay her fears that she will be alone forever. I wonder if Gabe's wife is that different from Hughes. They're both so afraid of something that might occur that they're compelled to do something that ensures the occurrence. I don't yet understand that level of fear. For me, I'm more a victim of loathing for the circumstance I find myself in; separated from home and family and separated from my friends out in the shit performing the more relevant duties that we were all trained for; trapped in a bureaucratic netherworld of superficiality.

I've got to get over to the 6th of the 29th this morning as they have the only mimeograph machine on this side of Camp Enari. The S1 guys there will let me use their machine as long as I have my own paper. I had to cut a bunch of promotion orders this morning, carefully driving the typewriter keys through the thick surface of the ditto master that will be used for making the sixty copies that I'm obliged to send to various entities up and down the chain of command. Bob Price took me over there once on a similar mission. All I remember about the process is that it seemed pretty complicated and that if I mess up getting the ditto into the machine properly I'll ruin it and have to start over back at my typewriter.

The now common wind of the dry season is starting to kick up the fine red dust as I plod along the road eastward toward my appointment with the messy printing machine. My thoughts are still with Hughes

Tim Haslam

and Gabe Luna's wife and Gabe Luna and Barney. I'm not paying much attention to anything else around me. I do take notice of a man walking in the opposite direction though, on the other side of the street. At about thirty meters, I can see the two silver bars on the right side of his collar...he's an officer. I'm sure that he'll see that I have both my hands full, carrying the ream of paper in my right hand and the stack of fragile dittos in my left hand. I'm sure that he'll realize that it's impossible for me to render the required salute. I'm sure that he has more important things to do anyway than worry about whether or not some lowly enlisted man pays proper homage to his rank and stature.

"Good morning, sir," I say, along with a slight nod of my head as we pass one another. I don't hear any responding greeting and without any further thought on the encounter I return to my daydreams and my mission.

"Hey...hey soldier!" the voice behind me shouts out, a few seconds later.

I turn around and find the Captain jogging across the street diagonally toward me.

"Couldn't you see that I was an officer, soldier?" the Captain begins, as he closes the last few feet remaining between us.

Oh fuck...this is all I need.

"Yes sir...I could." *That's why I said 'good morning,* **sir***'... you dumb shit!*

WOOLEY, the embroidered patch over his shirt pocket says. There's another mysterious branch designation insignia patch on the left side of his collar that I don't recognize. It's not the crossed rifles of an infantry officer or the crossed cannons of an artillery officer. *This Captain Wooley's never been outside of base camp I'll bet.*

"We receive and return salutes proudly in the Fourth Division," Wooley reminds me, reciting verbatim the proclamation that's posted everywhere around Camp Enari.

"Don't you know that you're supposed to salute officers?"

"Yes sir, but I've got my hands full, sir. I couldn't, sir."

"Oh come on, soldier. You could have shifted those things around long enough to render a proper salute. It's just a bunch of papers."

"Sir, these mimeograph masters are pretty fragile and ..."

"Don't give me any lame excuses soldier. You men need to show

Stars and Stripes and Shadows

proper respect for superior officers. Do you understand?"

"Yes, sir." *You bet I understand, you moron! I understand that the Fourth Division can't find anything useful for you to do. I understand that whatever your military specialty is, there's not much of a requirement for it out here. I understand that your idea of respect is a lot different from mine. I understand that you're not in the same Army as Captain Collins or Captain Hilton.*

"I'm going to have to write you up for this," Captain Wooley declares, doing his best imitation of a motorcycle cop who's just pulled over one more motorist for failing to precisely obey the law, bringing him one step closer to meeting his daily quota of apprehended felons.

He takes down my name, rank, service number and pry's out of me, through determined interrogation, that I belong to Bravo Company, Third-of-the-Eighth Infantry.

"This will go to your Company Commander. He'll decide what disciplinary action to take. I hope you'll keep this in mind from now on. Carry on."

"Yes, sir," I respond with appropriate contrition, as I place my burdens down on the ground to allow an acknowledging salute. Wooley snaps back the gesture of mutual respect completely unaware that I have all the real power here. Wooley isn't smart enough to figure out that all these little "write ups" are sent to the appropriate Company Commanders via their respective Company Clerks. He's too engaged in the importance of his mission to recognize that the criminal he's just apprehended; the one with the paper and mimeograph masters, *is* the Company Clerk. The indictment of Specialist Haslam will be routed along with all similar indictments of Bravo Company soldiers directly into Specialist Haslam's waste basket. Captain Hilton has a real war to fight and doesn't have time for such bullshit. Specialist Haslam too has a real war to fight and doesn't have time for such bullshit.

Captain Wooley's diligence to duty has, however, for both of us, consumed five more minutes of our time here in this shit-hole.

ⁿ ⁿ ⁿ ⁿ

Damn-it! Only one more… if I make one more mistake I have to start all over. The Morning Report's taking forever this morning. I have to force myself to concentrate fully on my typing. I have to block out all

Tim Haslam

the other things going on around me; all the familiar songs vibrating out of the various stereos and radios arrayed around the office; all of the ongoing conversations taking place between my fellow clerks, the ones already done with their DA form 1's. *I really don't want to have to start all over again with this.*

The first salvo enters into my space, striking me in the left shoulder, breaking my concentration, forcing me to look up from the Remington. The source of the projectile apparently does not want to be identified. I scan around all the office space off to my left. It could have been Stoney, or Welsh or Taylor. It could have even been Valentine, who's now ducked back into the mail room. They're all looking busy however, concentrating hard on something or other on their desks. No one's going to fess up to being the person who threw the waded up paper at me. They're all part of the conspiracy though; but I'm not going to give them the satisfaction of being bothered by their adolescent attempt to distract me from my duties.

Welsh! This time I saw it out of my peripheral vision…it was Welsh.

I pick up the crumpled up paper ball that just bounced off my typewriter and fling it back at Welsh who ducks out of the way, allowing the return volley to carom off the Teac tape recorder on the table behind him. Bill Taylor allies with Welsh and fires two paper balls in my direction. Stoney balances the playing field, coming to my aid and throws one at Taylor. In another minute paper balls are flying all over the S1 office, each of us crumpling our rejected typing efforts as quickly as we can and hurling them back across the room at one another.

Bill Taylor expands his defenses through the use of a ruler and starts swatting back all the inbound rounds. This shifts the thrust of the game. Now it becomes a variation of baseball. Everyone pitches to Taylor. Strikes and balls are called. Singles doubles and homeruns are determined based on how far Taylor can hit the balls. Anything caught by any of us is an out.

Soon Taylor finds that there are too many obstacles between him and the various pitchers and so he clears a few things off his desk and actually climbs up onto it, crouching back down into a batter's stance. Now he can really blast back the inbound balls with great force. We each take turns, working clockwise around the room as pitchers. With

Stars and Stripes and Shadows

the release of my best pitch, coming in the third or forth round of the rotation, I see Taylor hesitate, frozen momentarily as a reaction to something behind me. The others seem to have frozen too and a silence has swept into the room. *Oh shit... I can only imagine what they're all now staring at behind me. Oh shit...it's gotta be Sergeant Major Reynolds at least, standing there about to send us all out to help Tran burn shit before he has us all shot.* I turn slowly around in my chair and scan up the body of the person standing in the doorway, somewhat obscured in detail by the contrasting brightness of the outside glare. It takes a second for me to take inventory of all the symbols that completely identify our visitor...actually only one really tells the story; the single black star on his right hand shirt collar.

Oh shit!

"Ten-hut!" Stone and Welsh blurt out simultaneously.

We all jump to attention. Taylor's unsure at first if should do so standing on his desk or retreat back down to floor level. He's on his way down when the General takes another step forward into the S1 office.

"Your Adjutant...I need to see Captain Walterhouse, your Adjutant," the Brigadier General says. We're all happy to see that he's not reaching for the .45 pistol holstered to his right side.

"In there sir...right in there...right through that door, sir," I sheepishly convey to the first real General I think I've ever seen.

"Carry on," is all he says as he passes through the litter of paper balls on his way to the Captain's office.

"We're dead, man. We're fucking dead," Welsh declares quietly as the rest of us hurry to clean up the ball park.

"Who is he anyway?" Stoney asks.

None of us have any idea who he is except that he's a fucking General and he just walked into our office and found the four of us behaving like a Junior High School English class with a blind substitute teacher. He's got to be in there right now discussing with Captain Walterhouse how many years we should each serve in Fort Leavenworth.

A few minutes pass with no sign of the General or Walterhouse. Our Remington's are all now fully loaded and our fingers are flying around the keyboards. Important military documents are being generated at a furious pace.

A half an hour has passed...an hour; nothing has happened; no one

Tim Haslam

has said anything…no Walterhouse…no General…no MPs.

Sergeant Major Reynolds shows up at the door to the office one-hour-and fifteen minutes after the great crime and passes right through the busy room as he does several times each day without taking note of any of us. He moves quickly over to the Captain's door; knocks and sticks his head in.

"Where's Walterhouse?" he asks back toward us as he retracts his head from the Captain's threshold.

"Don't know, Top…thought he was in there," I tell him, as I'm the closest one to him.

"Alright, I'll find him."

We never hear a word from Walterhouse or anyone else about the General's visit. We can only conclude that it must have been a military emergency of great importance and that the General just didn't really have time to arrange for the firing squad we all expected. Walterhouse and the Brigadier General must have exited out of the outside door to the Captain's office and just went about their business. Our business, at least for the rest of this day follows the straight and narrow.

� ✰ ✰ ✰

The two girls in the sequined mini-dresses are almost too skinny to be considered sexy and yet there's something captivating and sort of arousing about the way they sway and skip around to the drum beat and the awful rendition of the Beatles', I Wanna Hold Your Hand. The little, energetic band of Vietnamese has been invited into Camp Enari to entertain anyone without a guard duty assignment this night who's willing to sit through the ragged interpretations of early sixties rock and roll. Jim Welsh, Val and I all are free from night duties and so we've come for the show, bringing along a can of warm beer each. The volume and energy of the group and the prancing, shimmering vision of the two girls, each completely self-absorbed in their own seductive powers, makes the show pretty entertaining and a great alternative to any thing else that any of us might do this evening.

I'm starting to feel hot as I sit here watching the energetic interpretation…really hot. It's not a response to the gyrating females however, or the hot, humid air surrounding me. It's something else. This heat is internally generated. I don't feel so well in general all of a sudden. My

Stars and Stripes and Shadows

head aches a little and there's a subtle lightheadedness that has nothing to do with the half can of beer I've sipped my way through sitting here watching the slender female legs and the flop-haired guitarists. Something's wrong.

I tell Jim and Val that I'm heading back to the barracks. They're too entranced by the flash and flesh to care why. By the time I reach my bunk and crawl through the mosquito netting, all I want to do is sleep and my want is almost immediately realized…sleep comes quickly. For a couple of hours I sweat through a fitful sleep, similar in character to the night I spent up on Ten-seventy-nine with the punji-stake poison in my ankle. I wake up somewhere after midnight, soaked in sweat, my head still aching, my mouth dry, a little confused by the small, out of focus, points of light I can detect off in the distance. My left shoulder and arm hurt…they ache…I can't get comfortable. I don't have enough strength to get up and find water. I toss and turn and hope this goes away soon. I remember that Doc's on perimeter guard. I can't get to him to get any of his medicine to help until tomorrow. I wonder what time it is. I wonder how I'm going to get through the Morning Report tomorrow.

Somehow sleep returns, fitful again at first but then, at some point it shifts into the deeper state of nothingness where every mind and body component has completely shut down to rest; to recuperate.

The stirring of men around me in the filtered early morning light of the barracks brings me back into consciousness. The sweating's stopped. My flesh feels dry and cool and the headaches gone. My mouth is still cottony dry and I'm a little weak and shaky but all in all, I don't feel too bad. Whatever happened last night seems to have passed. A lot of water and some coffee and I should be OK again. I'm not very hungry though and there's nothing offered in the chow line in the mess hall to tempt me. Coffee will have to do for breakfast…coffee and a cigarette.

By the time I see Doc Charlebois at mid-morning, on my way back to the shitter, everything seems to have returned to normal and I don't bother to mention anything about how I spent the night. We both have other work to do. We both have another long day here in the Nam to get through.

I'm really tired at nine o'clock as I gather up my rifle, bandoliers

Tim Haslam

and ruck sack and head over to the tent across the street where the men assigned to reaction-squad must spend the night. Our job is just to be ready should something happen during the night. We can be deployed quickly to any point along the perimeter or sent outside the camp to counter any attacks. If nothing happens, we can just sleep through the night and then drag our gear back in the morning. For a night duty assignment, it's pretty easy.

As tired as I am, I can't seem to fall asleep. Then, I start to feel it again. At first, I think it must be my imagination. It's just the fatigue or the residual effects of last nights struggle with whatever had invaded my body.

I'm getting hotter again...no, I'm getting colder. I'm shivering a little. I'm hot too, though and my shoulder hurts again. There's no headache this time. *Goddamn-it! Why didn't I say something to Doc? Why didn't I get some medicine from him?*

I have a canteen of water on my ruck. I can get a drink. It helps a little. Whatever's happening is not as bad as it was last night. I just need to get some sleep and it'll be OK again. I worry and rationalize through a few more cycles of chills and fever before sleep takes over. It's deep sleep though. It's the kind of sleep demanded by a body focused on something unusual happening within its structures. There's no corresponding dreams or mental correlate to anything that's happening physiologically. My mind can't help in the needed response. My mind can only add a dimension of anxiety and confusion. My mind's been shut off for the remainder of this night.

I was right, all I needed was sleep. With the morning light, I pull myself up and find that everything's OK again except for a really dry mouth and a swig from the canteen overcomes that. I drag my gear back to the barracks and straighten myself up enough to stand formation in front of Sergeant Major Reynolds. I listen dispassionately as the big Sergeant Major declares that the upcoming day will be just like every other day here...long and boring and that I will have to end it out on perimeter guard tonight.

OK, OK...can I go to breakfast now?

A half a bowl of rubbery oatmeal, a cup of coffee and a cigarette constitute breakfast and then it's off to face one more DA form 1.

Click...click...click.

Stars and Stripes and Shadows

The day starts slowly and lingers along at that same pace over the next several hours as the heat builds up and the dust rises slowly back up into the air, onto my desk and into my lungs and the inner-workings of my typewriter. I'm working more slowly this morning…still a little shaky from last night I guess. I'm thirsty. My second and third cups of coffee don't taste very good. Noon finally arrives but all I want from the mess hall is a cup of Kool-Aid.

It's starting again. Goddamn-it! Why didn't I go on sick call this morning? Because I wasn't sick this morning! But I am now! I can feel it spreading all over me.

I go back to my bunk in the barracks and lay down. I don't get permission. I don't care. Maybe just a few minutes of rest will bring me back again. I'm really hot now…really, really hot. My eyes are sort of glazing over. My head's aching again and I'm feeling weak and kind of shaky all over.

It must be time for evening chow. I can tell that the other men in the barracks are heading off to the mess hall. I have to do something. I think I'm dieing. I have to find Doc. I pull myself up and work my way against the flow of traffic along the wooden walkway back toward the aid-station.

"Doc…I'm really not feeling so good!" I tell Charlebois the second I enter the door, seeing him sitting behind his desk.

"Sit down," he tells me, rising up from his chair, directing me to another chair just inside the doorway. I've barely made contact with the seat when Doc shoves a thermometer into my mouth, simultaneously placing his hand on my forehead.

"Shit, man, your temperature is a hundred and five. I've gotta get you over to the doctors at the Division Aid Station…c'mon."

He helps me up and leads me around to the back of the hut where a jeep is parked partially in the ditch adjacent to the dirt road, listing heavily toward the passenger side.

It takes every ounce of strength I have to keep from falling out as Doc lurches the jeep forward, jerking leftward onto the road.

"Why didn't you come to sick call this morning?"

"I didn't feel sick then. It's been kind of coming and going for the last couple of days but, in the morning I always feel OK."

Tim Haslam

"Just go in there and tell whoever's on duty what's going on," Doc tells me, pulling up in front of the hut with the big red-cross painted on the door. "I can't park here. I'll find a place to put the jeep and then I'll come back."

Inside, there's a counter running vertically through the front section of the hut. There's a Spec-5 sitting on a stool behind the counter reading through a stack of letters. He watches me meander from the door up to the counter across from him without saying anything until I come to a stop.

"What's your problem?" he finally says, as I reach a point just opposite him, leaning up against the counter for support.

"I have a temperature of a hundred and five. I guess I need to see a doctor."

"Why didn't you come to sick call this morning?" comes the anticipated response.

"I wasn't sick this morning!" I reply, trying to reflect as much attitude as I can about the irrelevance of the question.

"Well, I can't do anything now. You'll have to come back in the morning."

"Look, man, my medic just drove me over here from the third-of-the-eighth. He said I needed to see a doctor."

"There's nothing we can do now. You should have reported in to sick call this morning and you'll have to report to sick call tomorrow."

Maybe if I just let go of the edge of this counter, I'll collapse onto the floor and then this asshole will have to deal with me, I'm thinking as Dick Charlebois comes to the rescue.

"So, what's going on?" Doc asks as he enters the room, generally at me, but willing to receive a response from either of us.

"He says he can't do anything for me tonight. I have to come back in the morning."

"Bullshit!" Doc declares emphatically, "this guy's running a temperature of a hundred and six. We're not waiting 'til tomorrow. There has to be a doctor on duty here. Where is he?" Doc's determined tone has put the man behind the counter on the defensive.

"He's taking a shower."

"What?" Doc again reacts with astonishment. "This is an aid station for an infantry division in the middle of a fucking war and the

Stars and Stripes and Shadows

doctor on duty is taking a fucking shower? Bullshit...go get him!" Doc's elevating strength of purpose and determination is in direct proportion to my own fading strength and lagging sense of commitment to any outcome.

The man behind the counter relents to Doc's impassioned badgering and heads off in search of the doctor. Five minutes later a short man with a Lieutenant's bar on his partially damp collar leads the Specialist back into the office.

"What's going on here? What's going on with this man?"

For some reason, the Lieutenant Doctor skips the question about sick call, works his way quickly around the counter and looks me square in the eye.

"How long have you felt this way?" he asks, as his probing eyes scan quickly back and forth between my own malaised orbs.

"It's been off and on for a couple days, sir."

"Give me that thermometer, Drake," the doctor orders the Specialist who's remained on the other side of the counter.

Sixty seconds later, Lieutenant Doctor has all the evidence he needs.

"Admit this man now and get him into the IC unit."

⚡ ⚡ ⚡ ⚡

I see a red door and I want it painted black
No colors anymore, I want them to turn back
I see the girls walk by dressed in their summer clothes
I have to turn my head until my darkness goes

I see a line of cars and they're all painted black
With flowers and my love, both never to come back
I see people turn their heads and quickly look away
Like a newborn baby it just happens ev'ryday

I look inside myself and see my heart is black
I see my red door and I must have it painted black
Maybe then I'll fade away and not have to face the facts
It's not easy facing up when your whole world is black

Tim Haslam

How did I get in these pajamas? I wonder at one point after waking up out of a long fitful sleep. *I think I'm at the aid station.* However I got in the pajamas, they're now soaked in sweat and everything around me has a hazy, ethereal look to it. I have no idea how long I've been here; what day it is; or where my own uniform is. I don't really care about any of that though. I don't really care about any of the diffuse thoughts swimming around within my head...thoughts, dreams, sensations; all climbing over one another in this fever stirred soup of semi-conscious-ness. I can't care. I'm just an observer of the bizarre animation churn-ing out disjointed visions and sounds as the rest of my defenses rally to fend off whatever has invaded me.

"Too bad...too bad...too bad," I hear again and again. It's the same voice, repeating the same mantra from behind the same ominous dark cloud that I heard when I was up on Ten-seventy-nine, trying to sleep my way through the punji stake infection.

"Too bad...too bad..."

"I'm still not sure," I think I hear a different voice say; a voice less clear, barely understandable, coming from somewhere off to my left. "It could be malaria or mono or even hepatitis I guess. He doesn't seem to be getting much better, the fever's still high. As soon as the fever breaks, get him over to the 71st."

"Hey...hey, Hasland," a female voice seems to be saying. "How are you feeling this morning?"

There's a hand on my forehead.

"Your fevers dropped. How do you feel?

"Better...I guess...I'm thirsty. How long have I been here?"

"You've been here three days," the female in the green tee shirt and fatigue pants tells me. She has a stethoscope around here neck.

"We're sending you over to the 71st in about an hour. You'll need to get back into your uniform for the ride over there," she says, point-ing down to the foot of the bed, where the same dusty fatigues I had on when I came in here lie in a heap. They seem like they're a long way away. It seems like it will be impossible to get into them.

The military ambulance has no windows in the back part where I sit, leaning into the corner formed by the metal frame side and a wooden bulkhead behind the passenger seat.

It's stifling in here.

The only air flow drifts in through the open windows in the cab, carrying clouds of dust past the driver and the medic in the passenger seat. Across from me is another man apparently being transferred to the 71st as well. The right pant leg of his fatigues has been cut off above the knee, revealing a heavily bandaged lower leg, expanded in its girth, either by swelling or under-layer bandaging. He doesn't seem to be in too much distress though, as he smokes his way through the journey. Occasionally, he'll react with a wince or groan to one of the many sharp jolts relayed back up through the heavy metal frame of the ambulance from the road ruts. I don't have the strength to react to the same shocks. I try to keep my eyes closed in hopes of sleeping my way through the trip. I don't have the energy or the inclination to engage in conversation with anyone. I have a little bit of curiosity about the man's leg. I wonder if it's from a wound or from infected jungle rot or, maybe from ringworm that's been left untreated too long. My foggy attention shifts for a second down to the slowly expanding little ring of itchy redness that's been growing on my left ankle for the last few months. I guess I'll show it to somebody at the 71st.

"OK, everybody out," the way-too-cheerful medic says as he pulls open the rear doors of the ambulance.

My legs are barely up to the task of climbing down the step ladder to the ground and represent a rather shaky foundation once I'm there. The brightness of the mid-morning sun out here stuns my senses, nearly blinding me with the intense light coming at me from all directions. The light, the heat, the effort and my own diminished physiology combine to squeeze my head into a slight dizziness.

"Go on inside there," the medic seems to be saying, while the fuzzy outline of his arm points toward a double door at the end of the closest building, a thousand miles away. The bandaged-leg guy starts off, limping along at a fast clip. I follow slowly, cupping my hands around my squinting eyes, trying to limit the blast of glaring light that's slamming into me.

We're almost there when the right hand door is shoved open from the inside by someone dressed in fatigue pants and a green medical smock.

Tim Haslam

"Hold on a second," the female voice says to us in an abrupt and almost panicked tone. "You two'll have to stay out here for a few minutes...stay here," she says, pointing to a bench that sits under a little awning just outside the doors.

Bandaged-leg guy and I each reach the bench at about the same time. It's just in time for both of us. He seems to be in a lot of pain now and for me, the whole world is starting to spin faster and faster.

Twenty seconds on the bench and things start to settle down. The awning above us creates enough shade for me to visually focus on the things around me now. The medic from the ambulance is coming toward us. The woman in the smock has moved past us out toward what seems to be a helipad. Another, smock dressed woman bursts out the door followed by a similarly dressed man with what seems to be a radio. They too head quickly toward the open ground out beyond the parked ambulance.

"Get that thing out of the way!" I hear the man say; obviously referring to the ambulance that has just deposited us here.

The medic approaching us stops long enough to confirm that the driver of the ambulance has understood his instructions and is in fact getting 'that thing out of the way.'

"I guess they've got some wounded coming in on a dust-off," he tells us. "You'll have to stay here until they can get those guys triaged and inside. Just sit tight for a few minutes."

I think I can hear the popping, whirring sounds of a Huey somewhere off in the distance but, as my position here on the little bench only affords me a limited view of the sky I can't see it, or tell which way it's coming from.

Another few seconds pass. The chopper sounds are getting closer. The doors to my left burst open and a whole stream of people press outside, most carrying something, many have stethoscopes around their necks. The last several men in the accelerating pack are divided into teams carrying litters. They're all in a hurry to get out to the helipad. None of them pay the slightest attention to the two of us sitting here. I want to be inside, to be in bed but I'm just lucid enough to understand what this is about. I can wait.

There are actually two medevac birds slowing out of the sky toward the ground. The pad's large enough for both of them to land simultane-

Stars and Stripes and Shadows

ously, kicking up a spray of dust that slows the approaching detachment of medical personnel. The scene and its accompanying sounds have initiated an adrenaline burst within me. It's the first time since I've been sick that my heart rate's gone up, I can feel it pounding within my chest. It clears away some of the fog that's dulled all my senses but, at the same time, the things around me seem to be transpiring in slow motion. I can see everything with crystal clarity. The voices however, all competing for attention and priority are just a jumble of desperate sounds being sucked up out of the air by the spinning rotor blades.

Damn…there must be a lot of them.

Four…no five, men come off the Huey on the left. Three of them are passed down on the litters provided by the hospital staff. The other two, each holding bandaged arms, climb off on their on, assisted by the doctors and nurses. There seems to be more of the medical staff gathered around the other chopper. They're taking more time getting the litters off. I can see the attached blood-plasma bags being handed down from the helmeted dust off crew members to the nurses. Three litters start moving quickly toward us, each surrounded by people attending to the plasma tethered men. These three are badly hurt and there's a pervasive desperateness about this parade. Each of the attending faces is locked into focused determination. Each moving hand seems to know where to go to keep the damaged life systems functioning. Each step brings them closer to the ready surgeons waiting within the operating rooms inside.

For a brief second, as the first wounded men pass by, I have a sensation that I recognize them; that I know them. In another second I realize that what I recognize is the build up of sweat and filth that covers their pale, pained faces. They're grunts from the shit.

One of the Hueys lifts up and noses off, out of sight to the north. The other one's rotors and jet turbines are slowing, coming to a stop. It's staying here for awhile. I can see a helmeted man standing next to the open side of the helicopter with a radio handset pressed up against his ear. He's not part of the helicopter crew though. He has the look of a grunt. I see him exchange the handset with somebody still on board the Huey for a small bag. I recognize the bag as a combat medic's pouch as he starts walking this way. Now I know him…it's Doc. I don't know this particular medic; this particular man. But I know who he is…he's

Tim Haslam

their Doc.

Doc turns out to be a black man of average stature. His fatigues are covered in the usual layers of ground-in mud and dust. His shirt front and even his pant legs have something else added to the built up layers. They're spattered with blood spots, some already dried, some of the larger ones still damp. His face too shows the influences of something other than the usual dirt and sweat. Swaths of cleaner, light brown flesh are exposed down along each side of his nose. Tears did this. I can see, as he reaches us, that tears are still doing this.

"You got a cigarette?" Doc asks in our direction, stopping short of the doors.

"Here," Bandaged-leg guy hands him his Marlboro pack.

"What happened?" I ask, as Doc crumbles down onto the bench between the two of us.

"They're APC hit a mine," he tells us before lighting his Marlboro.

"Just above Kontum, up on route fourteen. We were on our way back up to Dak To. It must have been one big motherfuckin anti-tank mine," he adds emphatically, which at first seems to get Doc away from his built up tearful reaction.

"I was in a deuce-and-a-half, two trucks back from them in the convoy and it just about blew me out of the truck. It flipped the APC up on its side and blew pieces of track all over the place. Two of the guys in the truck behind them were hit with some of that. One's dead, the other one's pretty fucked up. All six men on the APC are pretty messed up. I guess you just saw them."

"The last three guys that went in looked like they were in pretty bad shape," I tell him, hoping that he'll have something optimistic to tell us about their prognosis. He doesn't say anything. I can see the tears building up within his eyes again.

"Are they all going to make it?" Bandaged-leg asks just as Doc gets up and heads for the doors.

"No."

и и и и

"Here, get into these," I hear as the blue pajamas are thrust at me. I'm sitting on a bed. A coarse, green blanket is stretched tightly be-

Stars and Stripes and Shadows

neath me. The bed is made up so as to conform to the highest military standards. There are other beds around me. There seem to be other people around me too. I can't really focus enough or care enough to notice the condition of the men in the other bunks that are nearby. The person who gave me the pajamas is asking questions. I'm trying to answer as I transition into the pajamas.

"When was the last time you ate?" the person asks at about the mid-point of the interview. I know now that it's a she and that she's jotting things on a piece of paper on a clipboard.

When was the last time I ate?

"I don't remember," I answer, realizing that I am sort of hungry.

"Can you make it to the mess hall?"

"I guess so," I tell her while trying to gage how hungry I really am.

"Ambulatory," I think I hear her say.

"You can lie on the bed," is the last thing I remember hearing. There was a strong emphasis on the word "on."

"Hey…hey buddy," a clear, male voice brings me out of my sleep. "Are you supposed to go to the mess hall for chow? If so, you better get going. They're closing down in a few minutes I think."

"Oh…OK, thanks," I respond to my *buddy* in the next bed down the line. As I pull myself upright I can see that there's a tray on a cart next to his bed. It's a dinner tray that he's apparently just finished with.

"They brought you your dinner?"

"Yea…they bring me all my meals. You told them you could make it to the mess hall and so they categorized you as ambulatory. That means you have to eat in the mess hall and that you can get to the shitter on your own."

"I didn't know I had a choice."

"Yea, well, it's too late now. If you want to eat you better make it over there. Its pork chops tonight…not bad."

"Where is it? How far is it?"

"Go out those doors," he tells me, pointing toward the end of the ward, down about thirty feet from the foot of my bed. "Then go left and follow the walkway. It's the first building on your right. It's not

Tim Haslam

too far. I went there yesterday so I could eat twice."

I have to stop just outside the doors and wait for a second while things stop spinning.

Left...he said go left.

The walkway is covered, like the ones that connected the buildings back at Valley College and there are supporting posts about every twenty feet. I can make it to the next post, then the next. At each post I have to stop and wait for a few seconds, holding on while I assess the likelihood of making it all the way. I reach the point of no return. Four more posts, followed by twenty more feet of walkway that runs off to the right and into the mess hall...I can make it.

Thankfully there's no line.

I get one of the metal trays, a knife and a fork. A short guy in a white cook's hat and apron scoops up something that must be the last pork chop-like thing that's left within the coagulated grease residue of the serving pan and shakes it off onto my tray. The only other remaining food available to me is sliced bread and one dish of chocolate pudding. I manage to get my tray and my first meal in several days over to the closest table. The chocolate is the only thing I can taste. It's also the only part of my meal that's supposed to be cold and that seems to help.

I'm not really motivated to get through it all. It's too much work for too little reward. I start thinking about the journey back to my bed.

All I had to do was say no! Shit!

N N N N

"All right, all right gentlemen, everybody up. Let's get those beds made up."

It's the same voice that made the 'ambulatory' determination for me yesterday.

First Lieutenant Wallace is the head nurse here in the Intensive Care Unit of the 71st Evac.

Nurse Wallace has all the power here. Everyone entering into the ICU including patients (ambulatory or not) and doctors do so under the oversight of Wallace. She has such self-assuredness and command presence that no one is ever sure if her pronouncements and rules represent Army Medical Regulation or First Lieutenant Nurse Wallace ego. She

Stars and Stripes and Shadows

runs a tight ship and everyone respects her authority. If one were to look more closely however they might find an attractive woman in her late twenties doing everything she can to do her job, perhaps sacrificing in the process what she might be down deeper. If one were to look more closely they might notice the depth of fatigue that's begun to age this girl's once pretty face. She's been here a long time. She's seen too much of the shit. She has control only of the eighteen beds in the ICU and perhaps, a strict set of rules will make up for some of her own fading ability to care.

"You can lie on your bed but not in it during the day," she says to me specifically as she passes down the line toward a couple of men still tethered to some form of fluid bags.

You've gotta be shit'n me! I'm in the intensive care ward and I can only lie "on" the bed!

The tethered guys seem to be given special dispensation from the rule; apparently if you're only semi-conscious and still in guarded condition the Army can overlook your sloth and lack of commitment to the war effort. Everyone else must make up their beds and make them up tight.

Wallace has disappeared from my wing when I finish my work. Good. I doubt if my effort would pass muster with her. I doubt if it would pass muster with my mom, who taught me about making hospital corners with sheets and blankets when I was about seven. I'm climbing right back up anyway! *What are they going to do if it doesn't measure up...send me to Nam?*

There's nothing about the idea of breakfast in the mess hall that's enticing enough or necessary enough to motivate me for such an odyssey. Coffee doesn't even sound good. A cigarette doesn't sound good. This scratchy blanket doesn't feel good. It's hot in here. *Or is it just me?*

Around mid-morning two men show up at my bedside and begin staring at me as though I might hold some interest for them. One is wearing a white smock with the ends of a stethoscope sticking out of the right hand pocket. The other man is in fatigues, Captain's bars on one side of his collar and the snake-wriggling-around-a-caduceus medical corps insignia on the other. A moment later Nurse Wallace shows up and hands them one of several clipboards she has in her possession.

None of them say anything to me. None of them checks my fore-

Tim Haslam

head for signs of eminent death.

"It looks like it's been several days," the smocked visitor says.

"The counts still pretty low," the fatigue-dressed guy adds.

"Still pretty high," Wallace replies to a muffled question. "One-oh-two, this morning."

"How's the appetite?" One of the men asks Wallace. The whole conversation has yet to utilize a personal pronoun that might connect me as the object of their analysis.

"Seems to be fine."

Fine...how the hell would she know that?

"OK, start him on some..." the Captain says as he starts heading over to the next patient in line. I didn't understand what he said to start me on but apparently Nurse Wallace had anticipated the diagnosis. She pulls out two plastic bottles from her smock pocket, shakes out two large pills from one and one smaller one from the other and hands them to me.

"Here...take these," she says to me, clarifying my role in the recovery plans.

N N N N

I make it to the mess hall at mid-day. I stuff myself on four forks full of spaghetti, a half a meatball and three spoonfuls of orange flavored Jell-O with bits of carrots trapped within it. I make it all the way back to the ICU with only one post stop. I'm feeling better.

"Excuse me...hi...excuse me," I hear from a soft, rather high-pitched voice.

I'm trying to hurry through cutting the grass and the lawn mower wheels keep falling off. *I have to get all of this grass mowed before I can go and join Rosemary who's waiting for me over in my Volkswagen in the driveway. Maybe I can just push it along without the wheels. Barney keeps dropping rocks in front of the mower. The Volkswagen's gone. There's an APC in the driveway. Barney goes over and drops a rock in front of the big armored vehicle.*

"*Stop, stop! Don't run over that!*"

"Excuse me...hi...excuse me."

I hear it again and, this time, open my eyes.

Stars and Stripes and Shadows

MISS KRITCH, it says on the nameplate pinned to her blue dress.

"Hi…how are you feeling?"

"Um, OK," I reply, pulling myself up into a seated position. Actually I am feeling better, a lot better. My head feels cool. I feel like things have finally changed.

"Is there anything I can get for you?" Miss Kritch asks through a gentle half-smile.

I study her for a moment before answering. She has the looks of a girl that wouldn't attract much attention. She's short and a little overweight and her bobbed, nondescript brown hair frames a pleasant but rather plain face. Still, there's something from within Miss Kritch that shines through the average-ness of her exterior that's most attractive. She's the opposite of Nurse Wallace. Where the shit of this war has worn away and worn down some of the external beauty of Wallace it has drawn to the surface the beauty of Miss Kritch.

"A toothbrush, I'd kill for a toothbrush," I reply immediately, running my tongue along the fur coated inner surfaces of my incisors. I can't remember when I last brushed my teeth and I can only imagine what my breath must be like. Almost instantly my passion about the toothbrush turns into a sense of regret at the phrase I've just used to describe what I'd do to get one. I need to back out of that impression somehow.

"Yea, if you could get me a toothbrush I'd really appreciate it. That'd be great."

"OK, sure…I can do that and toothpaste and everything else you might need to clean up…anything else; paper, pen, envelopes?"

"Yea, yea, all of that, if you can get it, thanks…thanks a lot."

"Where are you from?" she asks with genuine interest, suggesting that she doesn't have an allotted amount of time to process this stop on her rounds.

I tell her about Van Nuys and Hollywood and the movies and 20th Century Fox. She tells me about Missouri, her brothers and sisters and her favorite movie, *The Great Race*. Then she starts getting a little fidgety and says she'd better go and get my toothbrush. I wonder if it's her sense of duty or my breath that may have drawn her away from our pleasant conversation.

569

Tim Haslam

She's back within ten minutes with all that she promised and more. She's provided me with everything I need if I can manage to get myself to the adjacent building where the showers are. I thank Miss Kritch sincerely as she's the first person since Doc Charlebois to treat me as though I were something other than an unpleasant reminder of the things that dwell out in the shit. If I would have been wounded in action it would be different. These people are trauma specialists. They like to rebuild damaged humans in a hurry. They like to save lives and they will go to incredible lengths to do so. They must draw on every aspect of their training, experience, resourcefulness and luck to be successful here. They're not too concerned about the size of the scars that may result from their heroics. Most of the wounded men lucky enough to have been brought here don't care too much about such things either, at least not yet.

I find my way to the showers in the building behind the ICU. The shower room is just an open concrete floor bay with five shower heads protruding out of the wall on the west side. Like everywhere else in the military, there's no consideration given to privacy or modesty. I've grown used to this by now. However, the old Vietnamese woman mopping the floors within the shower area is a bit disconcerting. It's just me and the mop wielding mama-san in the shower room. She gives no indication that she's likely to leave now that I'm here. She gives no indication that my presence, dressed or otherwise, will deter her slow progress around the room, pushing and pulling the mop over the concrete. I have a more difficult time staying focused on my mission as I undress a few feet away from this female. *Oh well...it don't mean nothin' I guess.*

И И И И

"I think he's stable enough to move out of the ICU," the doctor tells Nurse Wallace during the usual mid-morning visit at the foot of my bed. Neither of them ever says anything to me; asks me any questions, solicits any input from me as to my opinion of how I'm doing. Nurse Wallace, in fact, seems to take more notice of how tightly tucked my blanket is.

"OK, we can send him out this afternoon," Wallace replies to the doctor.

Where will I be sent to this afternoon?

"All right, Specialist, you're to be moved out today," an unfamiliar nurse advises me as she wakes me up from my late morning nap.

"Where am I going?'

"Well, you're well enough now to go somewhere else for the rest of your recovery. You don't need any real treatment anymore. You just need to rest and get your strength back."

All right...I think to myself, *Japan, here I come.* I know from my clerk job tracking the movements of the sick and wounded that most of our men go a place called Camp Zama in Japan to do there recuperating. The one's who have returned from there have all said that it was a pretty good place.

"It looks like your going to the 6th CC," the nurse says, shattering the images of my R&R in Japan.

"6th CC...what's that?"

"The 6th Convalescent Center...it's a convalescent hospital back at Cam Rahn Bay."

Cam Rahn Bay! I came into this country through Cam Rahn Bay. I went through Cam Rahn Bay on my way to Hong Kong. Cam Rahn Bay is just one giant ugly military complex. Cam Rahn Bay is still in Vietnam! There must be some mistake!

⚡ ⚡ ⚡ ⚡

What is this, a DC-6 or a DC-7? I wonder as I look out over the two pajama clad men in the seats to my left, taking notice that the churning propellers are finally revving up. I've been sitting here, in my blue pajamas along with this planeload of recovering men for over an hour. At least a dozen tactical military aircraft have passed by the window as we've sat here waiting on the tarmac at the Pleiku Air Force Base. I'm guessing that the bomb laden planes are on their way up towards the mountains to the north to help out the grunts of Bravo Company. For some reason, I want to be up there with them now. I don't want to be here in my pajamas going to the 6th CC and I don't want to be the company clerk any more. I think that something will happen up there and that I will miss it. I also keep thinking that something more should have happened when I was out there before. I'm starting to forget about

Tim Haslam

all the little shitty things that happened every minute of every day out there that I hated so much and I still have this strange and uncomfortable desire to want to pull the trigger on my M16.

"You want a smoke, man?" the guy next to me asks, pushing his Marlboro box over in front of me.

"No, thanks," I tell him, hesitating for a second to think about whether or not I really might want a cigarette. I haven't had a cigarette since I got sick and the urge for one is just now starting to return. I look around and see that about half of the recovering men inside this hospital aircraft are smoking and the accumulating secondhand smoke within the cabin does little to whet my appetite.

Following my refusal, he pulls out one of the cigarettes from the pack and then pulls out a well-worn corncob pipe from his pajama shirt pocket. He twists apart the two sections of the pipe, separating the mouthpiece part from the corncob bowl. At the connecting end of the mouthpiece part is an irregularly shaped metal fitting that's covered with a thick residue of what must be built up tar. My curiosity builds as I watch him wipe this dark brown residue along the sides of his yet to be lit Marlboro.

What the hell is he doing?

He works diligently to get as much of the gummy gunk as possible from off of the fitting and onto the cigarette shaft. With the fitting almost clean, he re-assembles the pipe, places it back in his pocket and, using his finger, he smoothes out the transferred tar along the Marlboro and then lights up.

It takes about another ten seconds for me to figure out what this business was all about. The smell at first is pretty subtle but keeps building with each exaggerated puff from my seatmate. *Pot!* That's his marijuana pipe and the thick residue isn't the normal tobacco tar, it's built up cannabis sludge that, at least in his opinion, still has some medicinal or recreational attributes associated with it.

"You wanna hit, man? It's not much, but it's something.'"

"I guess not…thanks," I tell him as I study the three nurses standing together in the aisle up behind the cockpit hatchway. None of them seem to care about the fact that so many of their patients are smoking. I guess none of them even care about what's being smoked. Maybe that's why all of this goes on. Nobody seems to care.

Stars and Stripes and Shadows

⚡ ⚡ ⚡ ⚡

The 6th Convalescent Center seems to be a pretty big complex, residing on a low bluff just above the beach, looking out at the South China Sea and is comprised of an array of the usual Vietnam military-barracks style buildings. It's brutally hot here and the half dozen swamp cooler fans inside the ward I've been assigned to do little to make this place comfortable during the day. They have the same rule about lying on your bed here but they don't want you ever getting too comfortable even on top. None of us here are exempt from the daily "details" that require us to perform menial tasks around the grounds of the hospital. Our chores take up a few hours of the day. Meals take up about another hour followed up by the pill dispensing routines. The rest of the time we're on our own. There's a small library in the building next to the mess hall and I usually spend a few hours there each day. They have a few recent copies of stateside newspapers as well as the latest Stars and Stripes and enough books of interest to keep my mind occupied as I regain my strength. The library is also a pretty good place to hide to avoid volunteering for additional jobs.

They show movies nearly every night outside at a little makeshift theater that's been set up between two of the wards. This is the only pleasant aspect of life at the 6th CC as the balmy evenings are usually accompanied by soft ocean breezes and the movies seem to bring us a little closer to home for a couple of hours. There is also popcorn. Popped fresh in a little shack set back just beyond the rows of benches that comprise the theater seating. A bag of popcorn costs a nickel and is sold through a little open window by an attractive, but rather sullen-natured Vietnamese girl who sits up on a high stool exposing a fair amount of young female thigh flesh out beyond the hem of her mini skirt. Nearly everyone who attends the movies wants to buy popcorn. Lot's of us like popcorn. Everyone looks forward to his ten second glimpse of thigh.

Each long boring day at the 6th CC I regain a little strength but I'm not in any hurry to get back to my duties as Bravo Company clerk. I think more and more about the guys out in the boonies with the Company and want to be back with them. Another part of me thinks that's crazy, the part that remembers how each little scratch and bite and itch ally with one another into one big miserable syndrome of discomfort;

Tim Haslam

the part that remembers Mr. Ruck and Charlie and the pearl-handled-pistol Lieutenant Colonels who think we live like pigs. The stories on the front pages of <u>Stars and Stripes</u> remind me of what happens to grunts who stay too long out in the shit. The number of dead Americans continues to rise each day. *Maybe our new President, Richard Nixon will do something when he takes office next month. Maybe he can end the war next month. Maybe I should just try to wait it out here at the 6th CC.*

ⱻ ⱻ ⱻ ⱻ

One of the hospital staff members interrupts our dinner in the mess hall to tell us that the Bob Hope show will be coming to the Cam Rahn Bay Air Force Base tomorrow and that if any of us want to go, we can. We need to be back here at the mess hall at eleven hundred hours tomorrow morning, ready to go. The announcement is followed by a short question and answer period.

"Are we going to be provided with fatigues to go there?"

"No."

"What time does the show actually start?"

"Seventeen hundred hours."

"What are we supposed to do there between eleven hundred hours and seventeen hundred hours?"

"Wait!"

"Outside?"

"Yes!"

Six hours, sitting out in the torrid sun on the tarmac in my pajamas…I don't think so. It would take a lot more than a distant glimpse of Ann Margaret or Joey Heatherton or Raquel Welsh or anyone else to get me to endure that. I haven't been able to get through any four-hour stretch without the need to sleep since I got sick. I desperately need a diversion from the mundane tedium of this place but the thought of sitting out there for six hours is incomprehensible. I'll stay here.

Apparently, most of the pajama-clad population of the 6th CC was willing to endure the wait for Bob Hope and Company and so those of us choosing to stay behind are afforded a day without any work assignments, a day to do nothing all day long. After lunch I work my way down the sandy bluff that drops off behind our ward, bringing me close to the beach. I spend most of the afternoon there, sitting in the

Stars and Stripes and Shadows

sand with no one else anywhere in sight, throwing rocks and pebbles out into the waters that ultimately connect with Playa Del Rey. I think about going home. It's mid-December now, getting close to Christmas. A year ago I was just finishing up my basic training up at Fort Ord and about to head home on Christmas leave. It would be a grand homecoming. Everyone was glad to see me after my initial transition phase from civilian to soldier. None of us yet knew for sure that I was bound for Vietnam. Barney had a lot of trouble just getting himself up out of his bed to come and greet me because of his worsening arthritis, but he made the effort and, still able to wag his tail, he came over to me to sniff at both the familiar and unfamiliar scents of the close-cropped soldier that had been his friend his whole life.

Rosemary thought I looked so cute in my uniform and my buzz haircut. I couldn't wait to get out of the Army uniform and back into the more comfortable uniforms that young men in the San Fernando Valley were compelled to wear. I had two weeks over Christmas and New Years to be Tim Haslam again. Everything was the same at home. Everyone was the same. I was the same, for two more weeks I could go back to my world.

I wonder if my mail will catch up to me here. It's been more than three weeks since I've seen any message from home. Nobody back there even knows yet that I've been sick. I haven't been able to rally the energy to compose the set of letters that I must send to Mom and Dad, my sister and Rosemary, telling them of this latest phase of my adventure in Southeast Asia. Maybe I should wait awhile longer so that this news gets to them after Christmas. Maybe it would put a damper on their holiday knowing that I'm in the hospital with malaria. But, it's been so long since I've written maybe they think I'm dead.

I'm almost through with the last of the three letters, the one to Rosemary, when one of the medical staff comes through the ward, obviously looking for volunteers. There are only four of us in here now and it looks like he can use all of us.

"At nineteen hundred hours I'll be back for you all," the Staff-sergeant tells the little group of us that he's pulled together at the nurse's station in the middle of the ward. "You all have guard duty tonight. I'll have everything you need."

Guard duty! The patients have to pull guard duty at a hospital? What

575

Tim Haslam

kind of off-the-wall bullshit is this? I add that thought, almost verbatim into my letter to Rosemary.

I should have gone to see Bob and Ann and Joey. I leave off the part about Ann and Joey in what I'm telling Rosemary as I fill her in on the rest of the malaria story.

N N N N

"OK, someone will be around to check up on things about every two hours," the Sergeant of the Guard tells us after driving the four of us out to a bunker that sits up on a bluff above the beach, at the north end of the hospital complex.

"This is all we get?" one of my fellow volunteers asks with obvious reservations abut the readiness of this unit. I will learn in a little while that the spokesman is in fact a Marine.

"Three blankets, a fatigue jacket and one fucking M14 with one fucking magazine of ammo…what the fuck are we supposed to do with this?"

"Look man, don't worry about it. Nothing ever happens out here. One of you will be up and on guard while the other three of you can sleep. The guy on guard gets the jacket, the others get the blankets. The guy on guard gets the gun. Just kind of keep an eye on those boats out there," instructs the Sergeant, at the same time drawing our attention to a collection of raggedy looking sampans and junks that seem to be riding at anchor out about a quarter of a mile off shore.

"What the fuck do you mean keep an eye on them?" the Marine inquires with building impatience. "What if they start to come this way? What are we supposed to do?"

"Don't worry about it, they won't. They're out there every night," the Sergeant advises us impatiently as he clearly wants to exit this conversation and get back to the comforts of the hospital.

"Hold on a second," the Marine presses back. "If those boats move this way or if some dinghy or something comes this way, what do we do? Do we shoot them?" The Marine has apparently had better training than the rest of us. He wants clarity on his orders, he wants to know exactly what his mission is, and he wants to know what, if any, constraints he's under. The man in charge is not a Marine. He's not had any combat experience. He's part of a medical staff. He just wants

576

Stars and Stripes and Shadows

to get back to the movies and popcorn and his ten-second glimpse of smooth female thigh flesh.

"Look man, just use your own judgment but don't worry, nothing will happen."

"Yea, OK, I'll tell you what, if one of those boats even turns this way we're gonna fire."

"OK, whatever," the Sergeant, stepping up into the jeep offers as a final validation of command expectations.

Within a half an hour of our deployment out here, the glow of dusk over the mountains to the west has given way to total darkness. There are just a few pinpoints of electric lights visible down within the hospital complex to break the blackness as we work out our guard rotation and nobody objects to me taking the first two and a half hour shift, which doesn't officially start for another half an hour. Two of the men grab blankets and head into the bunker ready to start sleeping away another few hours of their tours in the Nam. The Marine's not yet ready to sleep and joins me sitting up on top of the bunker looking out toward the dark void where the cyclic sounds of the surf seem to have increased in volume.

He offers me one of his Winstons, which I take and he Zippos both of our cigarettes into life. It's the first smoke I've had in weeks. It's the first time I've even been tempted to smoke. Maybe I just wanted to be more like the Marine. Whatever the motivation is, the Winston adds a great deal of satisfaction to these first moments of duty out here tonight.

We fill each other in on our roles and experience here in this country. His story is a lot like mine. He got here just after the Tet Offensive back in March and was sent up to join the 3d Battalion, 26th Marine Regiment at Khe Sahn after most of the siege there was over. He joined a brotherhood of men who had endured some of the worst fighting so far in the war. He came to them as one of the replacements for their buddies who had died there. He would never be able to measure up to the men around him because of the timing of his service in the United States Marine Corps. He would have his opportunities to fight, to shoot and to seek shelter from the enemy's bullets and explosive projectiles but he would never have the right to say he was there like the men at Khe Sahn who had joined the Marines a few months earlier than he had.

577

Tim Haslam

"So what happened to you? How come you're here at the 6th CC?" I ask him after telling him of my own experiences and of the malaria that struck me down one night while watching mini-skirted Vietnamese girls dancing to the arrhythmic beat of a local band.

He holds up his left hand and I can see that the second finger, the ring finger, is missing. I can just make out that the stub of root has not yet healed completely, that it is still scabbed over.

"It was just un-fuck'n-believable," he begins. "We were on a convoy heading back to Da Nang from Phu Bai when we started to take incoming mortar and rocket fire. We had to get out of the trucks fast and when I jumped out the back I got my wedding ring caught on some part of the tailgate. It just snapped my finger right off. Incoming fire was pretty intense and I had to get down into a ditch on the side of the road next to the truck. It hurt like a motherfucker by then and was bleeding like hell. By the time the shooting stopped and the corpsman had me bandaged up, they were in such a hurry to get the hell out of there that there wasn't time to look for my finger or my ring. That's probably the worst part, man. My wife's gonna kill me when she finds out about the ring."

"So, she doesn't know about your finger, or that you've been in the hospital?" I ask, wondering if his plight too is thus far unknown to anyone back home.

"No, I wrote to her a couple of days later from the aid station but I only told here that I lost a finger. I didn't say anything about how it happened or about the ring. At first, the wound wasn't that big of a deal and I was supposed to go back out within a few days but then it got infected pretty bad and my whole hand started to swell up and then my whole left arm. So, they sent me to the surgical hospital to deal with all of that and then here to this place. Some fuck'n wound huh! No Purple Heart for this one."

"Yea, well this place is like that, lots of ways to get messed up that don't count."

The Marine with the missing finger and the lost wedding ring, whose going to be killed by his wife if he lives long enough to get home turns out to be from San Diego. We talk about life in Southern California all the way through the two-and-a-half-hours of my shift and a good part of his shift. The boats offshore seem to be staying put and we

Stars and Stripes and Shadows

advise the unconcerned person in the jeep who comes around at 12:30 a.m. that we have everything on this front under control. We reminisce on for a few more minutes after the sentry check and I'm really enjoying the company of someone who can share familiar images of Southern California as well as a few more of his cigarettes. As extreme fatigue is still an after effect of my malady, I finally have to head down into the bunker for some sleep. I'm in good hands, at least until the Marine's shift ends and as long as the ammo holds out.

ᚾ ᚾ ᚾ ᚾ

"All right gentlemen, everybody up. Everybody up... Merry Christmas," the first shift nurse keeps shouting as she paces briskly along the center aisle of the ward, shaking or kicking the foot of each bed.

What is this, some kind of Christmas ceremony? Some kind of special breakfast deal the hospital has in store for us on this Christmas morning? Shit...it's six o'clock. We usually get to sleep in later than this on regular days.

"Everybody outside," she adds as she reaches the east end of the cellblock.

I pull myself up reluctantly out of bed and join into the line of blue pajamas following Nurse Herald out through the west door into the staggeringly bright light of this special day. Once adjusted to the bright glare, I can see that there are three men waiting for us, a Captain, a Staff-sergeant and a Spec-5. The Captain has the caduceus insignia on his left side collar suggesting that he's a doctor.

"Sorry about this, men," the doctor Captain begins, "I know its Christmas but I need to have you help us out a little here this morning. We just found out that were expecting someone from the Inspector General's office here tomorrow to inspect the hospital. We want to make sure that everything's ship-shape. We don't need any hassles from the IG to distract us from our work of getting you guys well and back to your duties. Sergeant Calionzes here will fill you in on what needs to be done. Keep in mind that dinner will be served early this afternoon, around fifteen-hundred and that the cooks are busy working on a real feast. OK, sorry about this, Merry Christmas."

The Captain turns his attention away from our expressions of disbelief and down toward the face of his wristwatch as he turns away to

Tim Haslam

make his escape to the day-room where the rest of the staff is watching the football games played earlier back in the states.

Nobody in the blue pajama contingent has to verbalize the response. The unexpressed reaction to the Captain's Christmas morning message is precisely the same for every one of us; Army, Marine, Air Force, sick, wounded, black or white, generally genteel or generally crude...*you've gotta be fuck'n kid'n me!*

Before the sub-audible chorus can complete the expression, Sergeant Calionzes gently fills us in on the details.

"All right, listen-the-fuck-up. You'll find stacks of new sandbags at various points around the outside of this ward along with shovels and four piles of fresh sand. I need you to pull off any of these raggedy looking sandbags from the blast barrier and replace them with new ones. Any questions?"

Everybody has the same rhetorical questions. *Are you out of your fucking mind? What kind of off-the-wall bullshit is this? Why the fuck isn't the hospital staff out here filling goddamn sandbags on Christmas morning? Who the fuck's going to get their ass in a sling if the IG doesn't like the looks of the blast barrier around our ward? Not us! Will the IG care if a bunch of patients at this place die from heat stroke on Christmas morning?*

"All right, divide up into three man teams and spread yourselves out around the building. With this many of you, each team should have about fifty feet of the sandbag wall to re-build. It should only take a couple of hours and then you can have breakfast."

As I hold open the sandbags and watch my teammate shovel some of the sand into the bags and some of the sand into the sleeves of my pajamas I try to think back on what had been the worst Christmas of my life up to this point. Was it when I was eight years old and not allowed to wear my new football uniform to the dinner table or was it when I was twelve and got the slot-car racing set that quit working after the first twenty minutes or was it last year knowing that in another ten days I was going to have to go Fort Polk Louisiana for advanced infantry training? Whatever the prior Christmas disappointments or limitations were, those Christmas's were grand and wondrous compared to what's happening here. I'll bet the guys in Bravo Company out in the shit are having a better Christmas than this.

Stars and Stripes and Shadows

Our work restoring the ward to its peak combat readiness takes two and half hours, then we have breakfast. Then I get to lounge away an hour and half in the library, then an hour trying to throw pebbles across the ocean and finally its time for a nap.

I must have been sleeping for quite awhile and have gone into the realm of deep sleep that nothing in the world around me can penetrate.

Someone apparently can't stand that I've found such a place. Someone is trying to pry me back out of here.

"Soldier...American soldier...please, for one minute, please," a voice next to me seems to be saying. I must be dreaming that someone in Vietnam needs my help.

"American soldier...please...happy Christmas."

I awake and roll over to find an ARVN officer standing next to my bed along with two young Vietnamese women, elegantly dressed in full length ao-dais, each holding a basket full of wrapped gifts. The closer of the two women, the one in the dark blue, silk ao-dai is holding out one of the packages for me.

"Thank you, American GI, American soldier...happy Christmas," the nervous officer says to me.

"Happy Christmas," the girl handing me the package says in a soft, barely audible voice as I take the gift from her.

"Thank you," is all I can think of to say in response, wondering if my benefactors here are Christians or Buddhists or neutrals. Whatever their affiliations are I guess they want me to open their offering now. A quick glance into their baskets and I can see that most of the wrapped presents have to be pairs of thong sandals. The one they hand me however is a little bit larger and more irregular in shape. It's soft to the touch. It's some kind of cloth garment. I open up the package quickly, finding a really nice blue silk robe, embroidered with birds and dragons. I like it. I like it a lot. More than I would have liked a pair of thong sandals. I think the three Vietnamese here, my hosts in this land, are truly happy to see my reaction to their gift. We exchange one more round of thank-yous and then they move to the bed across the aisle. The ratio of thong sandals to silk robes turns out to be about ten to one within the ward. The few people getting the robes think that they're pretty cool. The reaction to the thong sandals is less enthusiastic but

581

Tim Haslam

it's something. I wear my robe for the next few minutes until its time to head off to the mess hall for our Christmas feast.

When I return to the ward after dinner, my Christmas present is nowhere to be found...*stolen*. *Goddamn-it!* Somebody else in this ward, somebody who got thong sandals as their Christmas present from the grateful people of the Republic of Vietnam, has my robe hidden under their pillow or their mattress. They didn't even leave their sandals in exchange.

Because it's Christmas there won't be any movie tonight.

Merry Christmas!

COMMANDER'S MESSAGE

Christmas has a special meaning for American soldiers in Vietnam. Amid the tragedy and ugliness of war, the Holy Season reminds us of the joy and beauty of peace. In a land whose people struggle for a better life, the Christmas message brings cheer and hope for the future.

We who serve in this distant land may be justly proud. On this Christmas Day, no finer gift may one provide than to give of his own that his brother might share what he himself enjoys. This is what we are doing as we assist in supporting the Vietnamese in their struggle to maintain independence.

My best wishes to each of you and to your families on this Christmas Day. As we face a coming new year, may we each pray for success in our mission, peace on earth, and good will for all mankind.

CREIGHTON W. ABRAMS
General, United States Army
Commanding

Stars and Stripes and Shadows

"That pile's for us," the truck driver tells the two of us, pointing to a pallet load of boxes just inside the warehouse door. My unknown friend and I have volunteered for another duty assignment that's brought us, still in our pajamas, on a re-supply mission that's taken us to various depots scattered around the vast Cam Rahn Bay complex. This one must be more commissary goods. I recognize a lot of the names on the boxes; Del Monte, Campbell's, Hunts, etc. We load it all onto the truck, climb on ourselves and settle in among the various boxes and crates for the hot, dusty trip back to the 6th CC and some rest. Actually, I'm feeling like I'm pretty much back to normal. The only lingering effects of the malaria now are a steady but subtle pain in my left side and off and on spells of shaking in my hands. I'm ready to get out of this place.

"How much longer do you think I'm going to be here?" I ask the duty nurse when we return from our supply mission.

"Well, let's see," she responds, thumbing through the clipboard full of papers that contain our latest status updates. "It looks like your count's still a little low but it's been coming back up pretty well. I'd guess you'll be released early next week."

It's been nearly a month since I got sick. Valentine sent me a letter that I received two days ago along with a pile of mail from home. He's been filling in for me as Company Clerk and seems to like the job, although he says he's got a growing pile of things that he doesn't really know how to deal with and so he's anxious for me to get back. I'm less anxious to get back to clerking and all that it entails at Camp Enari. I'm anxious to get out of the 6th CC though. I make up my mind to put in for some kind of transfer as soon as I get back to Pleiku. I've thought about this a lot lately. I want to be back with the guys in the Company but I really don't want to have to endure life out in the shit anymore. I decide I'll try to get a transfer to the aviation battalion and see if I can get a job as a door gunner on a Huey. I know how to use an M60 machinegun and I have combat experience. Flying around all day, returning to the comforts of Camp Enari or neighboring Camp Holloway or Pleiku Air Force Base wouldn't be a bad deal. People might still be shooting at me though. My next choice would be to apply to the Brigade's Long Range Reconnaissance Team. I think I could stand going out on the six and seven day patrols with the four man teams that

Tim Haslam

travel light, move fast and are supposed to avoid contact with Charlie. Between patrols, the Lurps get to spend a lot of time hanging around the clubs here at base camp looking cool in their tiger suits and digger hats. *Yea, I could do that.*

ℵ ℵ ℵ ℵ

It's been thirty-three days since Doc Charlebois dropped me off at the Division Aid station. I'm finally on my way back, finally dressed in fatigues again, sitting here in the cargo hold of this noisy C-130 along with three pallets of supplies and a family of Montagnards. One of the Yard kids, who's maybe two or three, has one of his legs heavily bandaged. I'm guessing that he's had to have some sort of special medical treatment, beyond the abilities of the Green Beret medics or even the Evac Hospital staff. I'm guessing that his father is probably someone of influence within the tribe, someone the Army needs cooperation from. I don't have to guess what being inside this giant flying machine is like for this primitive family…their terrified. Each shudder, twist, turn and shift in prop pitch of the flying whale brings the same concerned response from all of them. They're hoping the good spirits of their ancestors have the strength to keep this big machine up in the air all the way back to the Central Highlands. They look at me and my reaction for reassurance. I'm wishing the good spirits of my ancestors had the strength to turn this thing back to the east and carry it all the way across the Pacific Ocean. We both want the same thing. We both want to have our feet firmly planted on the ground of home.

Chapter 19

Tanks, Tigers and Chicken Little

"I got the morning report thing down pretty well," Val tells me on the first morning after my return. "Stoney and Welsh and Taylor have all helped me a lot but there's still a big pile of orders and transfers and shit here that I'm not sure how to handle. Taylor said they're not that urgent and that they could wait until you got back."

I look with dread at the deep pile of "orders and transfers and shit," thinking of the hours and days of loading and reloading the carbon papered sets into the unforgiving Remington and pecking my way through the various boxes on the various forms. I try to envision how many trips over to the 6th of the 29th I'll have to make to use their ditto machine and how many times I'll run into Captain Nothingbettertodo along the way. I'm glad to see Val and the others in the office though and Val reminds me that I'm actually getting 'short', just over two months to go to DROS.

"Are you thinking about extended at all?" Val asks, "Cause I'm hoping to take over as clerk if you're really going to be leaving in March."

I've had to start thinking hard about whether or not to extend my tour over here, not because I want to be here a minute longer than I have to, but the popular belief is that if you have less than six months left in your enlistment when you go home, they let you out of the Army altogether. If you have more than that, you'll have to take a stateside assignment for the rest of your time. For me, that would be staying here in the Nam for another fifty-three days. Right now I'm thinking that I could still endure fifty-three more days and that getting out of the Army in the spring would give me the summer at home.

Tim Haslam

"I'm pretty sure I'm going to extend," I tell a disappointed Valentine, "but I'm not absolutely positive yet. What's been happening with the Company out in the field?"

"It's been getting pretty bad up around Dak To again, a few more men wounded and one KIA."

"Who was killed?"

"One of the new guys, I guess a Huey gunship was trying to root out some gooks out in front of Six-Zero platoon and one of his rockets went short, right into the point squad.

Oh, and a whole lot of guys have DROS'd out and a lot more new guys have come in."

I had forgotten about how many of the guys out there were supposed to be going home in November and December and so that becomes my first order of business, to find out the names of the people who've made it home. I pull out the filed sheets of DROS orders and scan them for familiar names. They're all there; Ed, Bruce Bollman, Danko, Beasley, Elmer Charette, Mike Ferlik, Ernie Jefferson, Grady, Wee John, Roy Houston, they've all gone home. They all passed through here when I was in the hospital. I didn't get to see them, to say anything to them. They all made it though. They've all gone their separate ways back into the world.

Two and half more months seems like forever. Two and half more months plus fifty three days starts to look impossible.

"And Captain Hilton's got a new job to," Val adds to his report of changes. "He's now a Major and the Battalion Executive Officer. The new Bravo Company Commander's around her somewhere. He just got here yesterday and will be going forward in the next couple of days."

"What's his name? What kind of a guy is he?"

"Griffith, Captain Griffith, he's pretty straight-laced, pretty regular army. He's no Captain Hilton, but he seems to be an OK guy, I guess."

The information about the changes to Bravo Company has eroded away any possible interest I may still have had in wanting to rejoin them. The only familiar things out there would be the leeches, mosquitoes, Charlie and Mr. Ruck and I've had enough of them to last a lifetime.

Returning from my first trip down to the old familiar shitter, I

Stars and Stripes and Shadows

encounter Sergeant Major Johnson standing with another man. The Sergeant Major introduces me to my new commanding officer, Captain Edward W. Griffith who seems glad to see me and wants to get a complete status from me on the Company's strength and status. He wants to do that right now and we start walking together up the wood planked walkway toward the S1 office. When I first came up to Griffith and Johnson they were standing off to the left of the walkway just outside one of the Company billets and so when Griffith and I headed out I was on the right, starting a get acquainted dialogue with my new boss.

"I'm the superior officer, Haslam. The superior officer should always be on the right," he matter-of-factly scolds me as he maneuvers around to take up his earned position on my right.

"Sorry sir."

Shit...another one!

Griffith pretty quickly shows that there's more to him them just his rigid adherence to military protocol. He wants to know everything about the Company and about the men. He wants to know what I know about the shit. He's really a friendly, although sort of stiff, kind of guy. He'll be OK out there. I tell him that I need him to write his signature for me, that I will have power of attorney for him back here and will be signing things on his behalf. I want to tell him that Captain Hilton had promised to promote me to Sergeant last November if I stayed with the Company. I want to tell him that I've kept my end of the bargain although neither Hilton nor I were thinking in terms of Company Clerk or patient at the 6th CC when the deal was struck. Maybe I'll wait and mention it to Captain Hilton the next time I see him.

$$\mathcal{N} \quad \mathcal{N} \quad \mathcal{N} \quad \mathcal{N}$$

Jim Welsh left for R&R yesterday and the rest of us here in S1 have divided up his Delta Company work. I just heard this morning that Delta has been moved down south to a place called Mang Yang Pass and that the rest of the 3rd of the 8th will be going down that way soon. It turns out that our Brigade has been designated as the quick reaction force for all of Vietnam. If something happens anywhere in the country we get sent there. Right now, Charlie's building up at a place referred to as VC Valley that runs down to the southwest of Mang Yang pass.

Tim Haslam

The mountains down there aren't as high or as thick as those that surround Dak To and Dak Pek and so the grunts are probably thankful that they'll be getting away from the miseries of humping around the high mountains. There's plenty of NVA down there though and it's an area that's always been a Viet Cong stronghold. It has other dangers for the grunts too.

I've just started on the Bravo Company morning report when I get the call over the landline. Delta Company lost a man last night, not to a sniper's bullet or a mortar or rocket fragment, Charlie had nothing to do with his death. Friendly fire had nothing to do with it either. A new terror has entered the world of the Delta Company grunts. Actually the Delta Company grunts have entered into the world of the new terror.

One of the tired Delta men on guard duty last night could hardly make out what happened through the blackness surrounding him. There was barely enough of any kind of sound to suggest that something was really wrong over at the next foxhole. None of his experiences or reflexes or instincts developed through his months out here could help clarify what he thought he was seeing. Something large seemed to have sprung up from nowhere toward the foxhole thirty feet off to his right and seemed to pull away just as quickly dragging something nearly its size down through the cleared field of fire, down into the thicker jungle beyond. It took a few seconds for this man to accept that the shadowy specter was real and not just another fatigue derived half-dream image. Once convinced of his own state of consciousness the startled man on guard crawled back to the line of hooches behind him and roused everybody he could find. Nearly the whole platoon worked their way cautiously over to investigate the foxhole where the sentry thought he'd seen something. There was no one there, only a rifle and, a few feet out in front, a helmet. Delta Company headquarters was advised and the rest of the Company was put on full alert.

For everyone else in Delta Company the remaining hours of darkness were spent nervously scanning through the blackness, weapons held close and ready, including knives and bayonets. A few flares were sent up to aid in the search for whatever might be out there and to help find their missing man. The Delta Company commander decided to wait for first light to mount a search further out into the jungle. There

Stars and Stripes and Shadows

seemed to be little point, and a great deal of risk, sending more men out into the black jungle to search for a man who had been spirited away by some new form of creature, hostile to their presence.

The tiger must have somehow overcome Specialist Martin quickly and silently. Perhaps Martin had fallen asleep. The determined tiger had little trouble pulling Martin down across the cleared field of fire. Somehow he avoided the trip wires that should have popped the flares that should have alerted the company as to the presence of an intruder. The stealthy tiger pulled or carried Martin down another thirty meters into a swale separating the Delta Company hill from the adjacent one to the west. There, the tiger felt safe enough to start transforming Martin into sustenance for his or her great body.

The frightened men of Delta Company surmised all of this as the first filtered streaks of dawn penetrated through the trees, revealing the evidence. They found the unmistakable footprints of a large animal, a very large cat. The tracks were easy to follow down to the swale. There, a shredded fatigue shirt, a paste of blood and dirt and what seemed to be a human jaw bone was all that could be found. All that could be identified as Martin.

For the rest of the day Delta Company patrols searched every inch of ground within three hundred meters to the south, west and north. No other signs of Martin or the great carnivore that had so easily plucked him away from within the perimeter of heavily armed grunts were to be found.

The officers of Delta Company had to explore new territory that day. They had to answer questions and make decisions far outside the boundaries of their training and experience. Should the jawbone be tendered over to Graves Registration? Should it be sent home in a casket to his family? They don't even have Martin's dog tags. Maybe he should just be listed as missing in action? What action? What was wrong with our defenses? What must we do differently tonight? How the hell do we deal with tigers?

N N N N

Bill Taylor and Stoney are just returning from the mess hall, coffee cups in hand as I hang the phone receiver back up onto the box on the wall behind my desk.

Tim Haslam

"You're not going to believe this," I relay to them what I've just been told about what happened to Delta Company last night. At this point I only know that a man was dragged off and that all they found was a jawbone. I don't even know his name. I don't even know enough to properly update the Delta Company morning report.

"Yea, well you're not going to believe this either," Taylor tells me after listening to my news. "We're going out there."

"What…who's going out there?"

"You, me and about half the guys here at the battalion, day after tomorrow, Captain Walterhouse just told us. Johnson's been told to pull together a reaction platoon to go up there and relieve Delta Company. They want to build a fire base there but Delta Company's needed somewhere further down in VC Valley. The whole battalion's being brought down there as quickly as possible."

"Just us, one platoon of base camp commandos is supposed to relieve a whole line company and build a firebase?"

"No, not just us, I guess there'll be a lot of engineers to do most of the work and there's actually a road that goes all the way up to where they are. There'll be a platoon from the 1st of the 69th Armor there too with tanks and APCs.

"How long are we supposed to be out there?"

"Don't know. Johnson wants you and me and Pinkerman and Sergeant Littlejohn to meet with him after lunch to work out the details."

"You four are going to be squad leaders," Johnson begins. "You've all had experience out with your company's and you've been around long enough to know what to do. I'll give you the names of the men who are going with you at formation tomorrow morning. You'll have the rest of the day tomorrow to get gear together."

"How long are we going to be out there?" Pinkerman asks.

"A few days, maybe a week, things are going to be moving fast out there, they want a battery of 105s operational up there by the end of the day Thursday. The convoy leaves at oh-seven-hundred on Wednesday morning. Welsh, Stone, and Valentine will have to fill in for you back here while you're gone."

"Welsh is on R&R, Top," I remind Johnson.

Stars and Stripes and Shadows

"Oh, right…OK, Stone and Valentine will have to do it all I guess. I'll see if the Captain can find anybody else that might be able to help them out."

Bill Taylor and I make it back to the office and inform Stoney and Valentine about all of our roles in the new plan. Nobody's too happy. The lamenting has barely reached full steam when the ringing phone gets everyone's attention. As the only phone in the S1 offices is on the wall behind my desk I've become the operator and answering service for all the other clerks. Most of the calls we get are from the guys permanently stationed at the forward support bases telling us about people in transit back towards us or wounded people in transit to the 71st Evac or about dead people.

"No way," the others hear me say as a first reaction to the report coming in over the land line. They can tell by my look of disbelief that whatever is being communicated is not the usual report of guys coming back on the afternoon convoy, destined for R&R.

"Yea…yea…no shit?…no way…OK, OK, yea…shit man…OK, right."

"It's happened again," I tell the now gathered around clerks after I've taken in all the available details. "Another tiger attack…same place…last night and almost the same circumstances, only this time the guy survived.

"Who was it…how?"

"Beaulieu…Bernard Beaulieu, remember him? He hung around here for a few days a couple of weeks ago coming back from R&R. He was from Puerto Rico or some Caribbean Island, remember, he had sort of an accent and was just a really easy going guy who seemed way too happy for somebody going back out to the shit?"

"Yea, yea, I remember that guy," Taylor says. "The Sergeant Major kept having fun with him at morning formation on the days he was here just because he could make him laugh so easily. What happened to him? How'd he get away from a fuck'n tiger?"

"I guess he never saw it coming, he said it was like somebody just punched him hard on the side of his head, knocking him down into his foxhole. Next thing he knows, something really big's clamped its mouth over his face and is trying to pull him up out of the hole. Luckily, he held onto his M16 through the whole thing and somehow was able to

Tim Haslam

get a shot off. He doesn't know if he actually shot it or just scarred it away. He's only got a few cuts and scrapes on his head and face. He's one lucky son-of-a-bitch! They're sending him in to the 71st for a couple of days. There's no way he was going to spend another night out there after that."

"So they didn't find the tiger?"

"I guess not, no blood trails or anything. I guess it's still out there."

"I'll bet those guys in Delta Company string about a million trip flares tonight and will be on two-thirds alert for the rest of the time they're out there."

"Yea, well don't forget that we'll be out there tomorrow night."

✦ ✦ ✦ ✦

I'm working to get my knife blade as sharp as possible, sliding it carefully up and down the surface of the whetstone, trying to avoid stabbing or slicing myself whenever the deuce-and-a-half slams through a rut or pothole in the road. I'm glad to have a chance to escape all the bullshit of base camp for a few days but, being unsure of what kind of shit lays ahead I'm not wholly excited about this alternative either. The tiger adds a new dimension of concern too. There are likely to be fewer mosquitoes and leeches out here now that it's the dry season, but I know how to deal with them. I know how to endure their attacks and the after affects of their bites. Things would be different with a tiger. I don't expect to get much sleep out here.

The dusty road weaves its way through landscape that's been molded by humankind to a much greater extent than the environment surrounding Route 14 up in the higher mountains to the north. There are lots of small farms, generally surrounded by rice paddies, banana orchards and corn fields. A few times we pass what must have been sizable plantations, now unkempt, too costly and vulnerable to keep operational, the bed rows of the once productive trees have long been overgrown with invading strains of squatter plants, thriving on the amended soil. There are lots of small, dirty villages along the way too, adding smoky odors of cooking as well as the stench of human waste to the surrounding air. I keep a hold of my M16 as we pass near the villages. These are not Yard villages, the villagers here are Vietnamese,

Stars and Stripes and Shadows

some are VC, some don't have a preference for politics; none seem to appreciate our presence.

We've been outside Camp Enari for maybe two hours when the road enters a more densely forested section of ground, still generally flat. We've traveled long enough to have grown bored with all that's around us and those of us in the backs of the trucks have all retreated to our own individual daydreams of different worlds. Three short bursts of AK fire coming from off to our right re-awaken everyone associated with the convoy. The shots, coming from a cluster of small trees about sixty meters out, are directed at the vehicles in front of us. Our driver reflexively jerks our truck hard to the right and off the road onto an apron of knee high grasses. None of us in the back need any prompting or further encouragement to get out of the truck or to seek shelter behind it. There's little more than the taller grass blades between our truck and the lead spewing AK47s.

I remember that I'm officially the squad leader. I'm officially in charge of the other five men huddled tightly back here behind the exposed truck. We're not in any position to mount a counterattack. I just hope that Charlie doesn't have anything more than his AKs; an RPG could be the end of our truck and us.

Before I can formulate a next step, one of the APCs from the rear of the convoy comes charging up the shoulder of the road until it nearly slams into our truck. Just in time, the right side tread locks up and the still churning left side tread redirects the orientation of the armored machine out toward the trees and the gooks and the AKs. After another ten meters the driver locks up both treads and the instant the big machine ends its lurching skid, the .50 caliber machinegun up on top opens up. It would be suicidal for Charlie to fire again now. The machine-gunner up on top of the APC isn't waiting for targets, he has plenty of ammo and he keeps both his thumbs tightly pressed down on the trigger plate at the rear of his weapon. His fingers are clutched tightly on each of the two vertical handles mounted just in front of the trigger mechanism. His arms are directing the barrel of the big gun into various sections of ground out in the general vicinity of the enemy at the same time trying to compensate for the bucking recoil.

For what seems like several minutes the .50 caliber rounds continue to shred through everything out there. If the men with the AKs are still

Tim Haslam

alive they must now realize they've made a mistake. If they still cling to any thoughts of survival, those are about to be dashed. Grinding its way quickly up along the same shoulder is an M60 tank, anxious to have a crack at whatever it is that's exposed itself.

The tank commander directs his giant machine up along side of the APC and a second .50 caliber is added to the counterattack. Tactically the two heavy machineguns are more than enough to neutralize the meagerly armed adversary. For the young men operating these machines, it's not nearly enough. The one-hundred-and-five millimeter rifle jutting out from the tank's turret blasts out its first round. It explodes a fraction of a second later out beyond where the machineguns are firing; throwing up an aggregation of dislodged earth, plant mass and grey-brown smoke. If Charley's still alive, it's logical to assume he'd be trying to crawl away from the direction of the incoming machinegun rounds. If Charley's alive and behaving logically he's crawling right into the territory where the high explosive tank rounds are being directed. The young men operating the big armored vehicles have a chance to apply their training, to test their skills, to neutralize an enemy and to use up a lot of the ammunition they've been riding around with over these hot dusty roads. They're doing their job, they're relieving some of their pent up anxiety and boredom...they're having fun. With this shift in momentum, it's safe enough for us to work our way around to the front of our truck, taking up better spectating positions, watching the show of force and the pyrotechnic display. There's still a big adrenaline rush associated with the engagement, but little real drama anymore. The outcome is certain.

"Mount up! Mount up!" a Lieutenant standing in the middle of the road a few vehicles ahead of us is yelling. We need to get the convoy moving again. We've lost time. There isn't time to send anyone out into the battle ground to determine the effectiveness of our counterattack.

Once again I see this war as a series of insane skirmishes where we shoot at each other for a few minutes and then go on our way. There's been nothing gained for either of us in this encounter. The ground doesn't matter. The territory is of little importance. The Vietnamese attackers are probably dead. The American tax payers are out a few thousand dollars worth of ammunition and the main residual effect on the young men in this convoy is an elevated appreciation that we're still

Stars and Stripes and Shadows

alive, commingled with a private acknowledgment that there are lots more people with AK47s out in these forests and within these villages willing to perform such stupid acts.

❧ ❧ ❧ ❧

The place chosen for the next firebase is hard to recognize at first as a hilltop. The heavily rutted road coming up seemed to rise gently as it hair-pinned through the heavy vegetation up and away from the main road. Even at the top it's so overgrown and the surrounding trees are so large that it's impossible to see anything of the surrounding countryside that would confirm the height differential that would justify placing the howitzers up here.

This place is not virgin jungle though. It's been visited my mankind before; visited by men who also couldn't coexist with one another very well. A narrow finger radiates off toward the west, covered in high grass but only sparsely populated with trees. At various spots around the finger, I can see shapes of things manmade protruding up out of the grass. The shapes are wooden markers, carved into silhouettes of men; carved to look like soldiers…carved to look like Legionnaires wearing the distinctive kepi caps with the cloth shade hanging down over the backs of their necks. These are grave markers for dead soldiers from another attempt to civilize these mountains; dead French soldiers who died right here, killed by the Viet Minh fourteen years ago. Perhaps their spirits have joined the ancestors of the Yards and are happily smoking cigarettes and drinking thick beer as eternity ticks by. Perhaps they've just been transformed into the different life forms that have learned to survive out here, fighting each other only for nourishment and access to the suns rays. I wonder if just before they died they thought of this place the same way that I do…*the shit. On est dans la merde; ca ne veut rien dire!*

Delta Company pulled out from here earlier this morning, probably glad to be away from this place, glad to be on their way to some other sector of the shit where there are only humans and insects motivated to kill and consume them. There are only a few engineers up here when we arrive, protected primarily by three APCs and two tanks that have tracked themselves as far as they can up into positions around the perceived crest. There is also a Huey gunship prowling around the sur-

Tim Haslam

rounding airspace, perhaps searching for tigers.

We have our work cut out for us molding this place into a firebase. Our assignment is to set up housekeeping near two of the foxholes dug out by the previous residence, expand the field of fire out another thirty meters, build bunkers and help dig out the emplacements for the 105s due in tomorrow. There's barely any hope of getting enough of the jungle hacked away to clear the field of fire out that far by nightfall. It's my own personal plan to string as many trip flares as possible out in front of our foxholes. That's my priority before the night sets in and the nocturnal feeders come out. The bunker building and emplacement digging will have to wait until first light tomorrow.

After a short briefing by the Engineer Lieutenant in charge, I fill in my guys about the night plans. We're to divide up into three man teams; two thirds alert; two men awake, one sleeps. The two men on guard are to stay close to one another the Lieutenant advises and unnecessarily admonishes us to keep our weapons close at hand. There are only three radios to spread around the whole perimeter. If anything happens, if anyone hears or sees anything we're to send up a star shell flare. We're also free to fire at anything. The good news is that there is a battery of self propelled 155s somewhere down along Route 9 to the east that will be firing DTs around us all night. Every ten minutes they'll put rounds at various points outside our perimeter that should deter the larger animal species that might be attracted to us. This will be comforting for the two men on each team that are awake and on guard duty. For the third man, it will mean that any sleep to be had will come in short increments.

It's a long, long night back out in this new part of the shit and the whole experience out here has convinced me that I really don't want to go back out with the Company nor do I really want to go out with any long range patrol teams. I also realize now that I have too little time left in country to be granted a transfer unless I extend my tour by several months. I have only about fifty three days left now and that seems like forever. Even adding just another fifty three days that would get me an "early out" seems like a poor choice. I could actually be on my way home in fifty three days. Wherever I was assigned to back in the states for the remainder of by service would have to better than this. The whole "early out" thing may just be grunt rumor anyway. I don't know

Stars and Stripes and Shadows

of anybody that's actually done it. For all I know, I could extend that long and still have to go back and serve more time. An additional fifty three days of this kind of crap; of tigers and Charlie and tropical diseases and officers with nothing better to do than hassle me; of long nights on guard and dust and heat. I don't think so. I should go home at the first chance. I know I get thirty days leave when I go home. That's all I can think about now.

This is gonna take forever. Now that it's the dry season the surface layers of ground have hardened and the intertwined root systems of bamboo and other plants are making it impossible to dig out the first gun emplacement. After struggling for two hours in the hot sun, alternating shifts with the two D-handle shovels available to us, we've barely scratched the surface. We've been told that the guns are to be helicoptered in early this afternoon. *There's no way we're going to make it.*

"There's no way you're gonna make it like that," the Engineering Lieutenant says to us on his second trip by to inspect progress.

"Sir, this ground is really hard and full of roots. With just these tools, this will take forever," I explain.

"All right, there's a better way. You men take a break for a few minutes," the Lieutenant tells us before hurrying back up toward the top of the hill.

A short while later he's back with two other members of his engineer team, pointing out to them the ground that we've been trying to break through. Their discussion seems to be generating a level of excitement within the little group that is completely disproportionate to anything I can think of. Apparently it only takes a minute for the team to work out a better strategy for solving the problem and the Lieutenant and one of his men again head back up the hill. The other man, a Sergeant, comes over to fill us in.

"OK, here's what's gonna happen. Any of you guys know anything about explosives?"

Although all of us have experience out in the shit and have been around plenty of exploding things, we're hesitant to answer in the affirmative, we want a lot more information before we inadvertently volunteer for any work that involves explosives.

"OK, it doesn't matter, here's what we're gonna do. We've got lots

Tim Haslam

of things up in our truck to deal with problems like this. First, we're gonna set a shape-charge right in the middle of this area that you've started digging in. The shape-charge'll blow a hole straight down into the ground about ten feet that's maybe three feet in diameter. Then, what we'll do is put a fifty-pound cratering-charge down in there and set it off. That'll blow out everything in about a ten meter radius. After that, you'll just have to shovel out some of the loose stuff and clean it all up a little."

The plan sounds good to us, a whole lot better than inching our way through the rooted crust with our little shovels. There has to be more to our part of the plan though.

"So what do you need us to do?" I ask suspiciously.

"You guys can take a break for a little while. When we're ready to set off the shape charge you probably want to get down behind that tank," he tells us, pointing to one of the M60's stationed about fifty meters down the road. "When the charge goes off it's going to kick up a lot of shit. We'll give you plenty of warning though."

We find a shady spot a little ways down the hill toward the sheltering tank and settle in to watch the engineers ply their trade. We watch them carry down an odd shaped canister like device with a conical protrusion pointing down at the bottom. The device, about three feet high and eight inches in diameter is welded into a metal framework of supporting legs, all of it painted olive-drab. They set it in the middle of our diggings and start wiring it up. As they prepare the device, a helicopter climbs up diagonally toward the hilltop from down near the main road to the east. It's one of those flimsy looking, plastic bubble front little helicopters that seem too fragile for military use. It hovers for a brief minute over the top of the hill, seeming to observe all of our morning's activities and then it twists back over the trees to the south and disappears.

"All right, all right," the Sergeant yells down to us. "Get your men behind some shelter. We're about to set this off."

We waste no time getting ourselves down the hill and behind the big tank as the Sergeant and the other Engineers repeat the warning to all parties working around the hilltop. The Lieutenant stays up on the crest of the hill until he can see that everyone around is aware of the pending blast and has taken shelter. Satisfied that everyone is safe

Stars and Stripes and Shadows

from the likely effects of the blast he disappears back over the top of the hill.

"Fire in the hole...fire in the hole!" an unseen voice yells out. "Fire in the..."

Just as the final warning is issued, the bubble helicopter reappears over the treetops to the south, heading right towards the danger zone, about two hundred feet in elevation. The man with the detonator must have been facing north, toward the area of the explosion, perhaps trying to shelter his ears somehow, probably fully focused on what was about to happen, unaware that the helicopter was even there.

The explosion is a great, quick blast that cracks loudly through the humid air, sending an eruption of rocky debris straight up into the clear sky. A second after the shock wave passes the five of us, crouched down behind the tank, we peer up over the rear deck of the M60 to see what's happened. The eruption of material is raining down all around the hilltop. A few rocks of various sizes are falling out about fifteen to twenty meters up from the tank. We're in no danger. The bubble helicopter however seems to be in trouble. The front of the bubble is shattered and it's following an erratic flight path back down toward the main road, wobbling left and right along its center axis, fishtailing badly. The controls have to be damaged or perhaps it's the pilot that's damaged. We can see the whole uncontrolled descent of the broken helicopter. We can all tell that it's going to make contact with the ground, directed more by gravity than by the pilot's intent. Somehow the pilot manages to keep enough trim on the machine so that the skids on the undercarriage take the brunt of the hard impact. The skids weren't designed to absorb that much shock however and collapse upon impact. The cockpit containing the two men collides in turn with the ground a fraction of a second later, the tail of the machine bucks forward to an angle of about forty-five degrees, snapping the stabilizer drive shaft and then is jerked back to horizontal by the shuddering recoil from the impact. An instant later there is silence.

Everyone up here watches and waits for something that would clarify the status of the two men inside. There's nothing, just the dust settling. Within a minute a jeep appears from somewhere along the road coming from the north, hurrying over toward the crippled chopper. Men get out of the jeep, run over to the inanimate hulk and begin

Tim Haslam

probing and maneuvering around. A moment later they pull someone out, someone alive, and gently assist that person over to the jeep. One of the three men from the jeep stays with the extricated man, the other two men return to the broken machine. They appear from up here to be working steadily, diligently but at a pace inconsistent with a life-saving effort. They must know what we can only surmise.

In another few minutes a dust-off Huey settles down on the road out in front of the jeep. The injured man is taken on board and then two of the Huey's medics jump out, follow the jeep guys over to the downed chopper and together they pull a still helmeted body, limp and obviously lifeless out. The medevac bird lifts off, vectors back toward Pleiku. The jeep pulls back onto the road and continues on its way southward. It's time for everyone to get back to work.

The rumor spreads around the hilltop that the dead man was a Colonel from Brigade staff performing a general surveillance of this area. The follow-on discussions examine the possible sources of blame for this one. The engineers must have fucked up big time, not clearing the air space before detonating their explosives or maybe the little helicopter, flying low down below the tree line was out of radio contact, maybe somebody didn't understand what the message was. Maybe it was just an accident, nobody's fault, just another guy who was alive a few minutes ago and now, due to too much living out in the shit is dead...bullets, shrapnel, tigers, flying rocks...what's the difference?

Close to half an hour passes before the Sergeant comes back down and tells us that they're going to go ahead and finish blasting out the emplacement positions with their cratering charges. He warns us that these are considerably more powerful than the shape charge and that we should get well down the road when they're set off.

With the first warning, we head down the road another thirty or forty meters, down passed the tank. We have to be well out of the danger zone down here. There's nothing but a few trees to the side of the road to use for any kind of shelter, but at this distance we should be OK, we can just stand out here in the road and watch the show from a safe distance.

The third "fire-in-the-hole" alert doesn't even register in my mind. The shock wave nearly knocks me over and temporarily deafens me. It seems as though the whole hilltop has been exploded into a million

Stars and Stripes and Shadows

pieces all hurled violently up and out in all directions.

Oh fuck…we're not far enough away! We're not nearly far enough away!

The rocks and particles following the lower trajectories are bouncing down the road towards us, skipping rapidly, seeming to accelerate as they escape the explosive force that's propelled them. Some of them are large, bowling ball sized. I've never seen solid objects moving so quickly in my direction. I'm panicked, but can't work out an escape plan. Just as the first pieces skip by me, I realize that there's another problem to work out, a bigger problem. Forcing myself to take a quick glance up, I can see the sky above me has been shattered into a mosaic of shards that are just reaching their apogee.

Oh shit, shit, shit! A thousand meteors are now beginning to fall from their positions in the sky right above me. There's nowhere to go, there's no shelter anywhere around from this. By now my senses can only register panic, trusting my reflexes to find safe passage out from under the vertical barrage and away from the horizontal assault. I try to detect which falling pieces are most likely to hit me and I make feeble moves accordingly. It's impossible, there are too many of them, it's like dodging rain. Finally, I just surrender, grabbing onto my helmet, hoping that it will provide some form of shock protection for my whole body if I can narrow myself down under it somehow. I reflexively crouch down trying to limit the exposed parts of my anatomy to my back and my steel-bucketed head.

A few long seconds pass, accompanied by dull hard thuds and little explosions of bursting rocks and bouncing pebbles all around me. I try to straighten up a little, thinking that maybe I should just run. I get only a few inches up from my full crouch when something slams into my still partially bent left leg, just above the knee. The force bursts apart whatever the falling mass was, rock or compacted dirt clod, and knocks me completely down to the ground where I retract myself into a tight fetal position, grasping on to the assaulted knee, all the while being peppered and dusted with the smaller bits of debris still falling. My leg has to be broken. My knee must be shattered and there are still more bombs falling all around me. The lower part of my left leg seems to be going numb and the surface flesh all around the knee cap is stinging and burning.

Tim Haslam

Oh shit, is my first thought. *My leg must be broken,* enters my thoughts a second later before the fear of further battering takes hold of my senses again. In another few second's things seem to be settling down…fewer thuds…just the rushing sounds of small particles raining down, maybe it's safe enough to sit up and take a look around. I take a quick check upwards and am happy to find that the red-brown dust is the only remnant of the explosion still remaining in the sky, some of it falling, some rising up as a result of the cratering impacts of the bigger rocks. A glance up towards the hilltop finds the road littered with rocks of all sizes and a new crater up at the crest, just the right size for a one-hundred-and-five millimeter howitzer…mission accomplished.

Steve Sams and "Charlie Bear" Brown, two of the guys in my squad, two guys I've known ever since I started clerking can tell that I'm having trouble getting up and hurry over to see what's wrong and to offer help.

"I got hit in the knee. I think it might be broken."

"We'll get you up to the top and get the medic for you," Brown tells me.

He and Sams help support me as we make our way up through the lava field.

"Man, a broken knee like that would be the million dollar wound," Sams observes as we approach the crater.

He's right, I think to myself. *They'd have to send me to the hospital. It would have to take six or eight weeks to heal. He's right! I'm outta here! A broken knee can't be permanent. I'll recover fully just in time to go home.*

My feeling toward the overzealous engineers has just changed from anger and contempt to gratitude and admiration. When they set off the detonator for the cratering-charge they may also have set things in motion that will get me away from all the tedious labors of clerking, all the bullshit of base camp life, all that life here in the shit might have in store for me for the next two months of my tour here. They may have issued the ticket home. They may have saved my life.

"Fuckin-A, man…that's right, this could be it!" I tell my two, now envious crutches, forgetting about any of the ache and burning surrounding the area of my million dollar wound.

At the top of the hill we find that I'm not the only victim of the

Stars and Stripes and Shadows

expedited excavation. Two other men are being attended to by a medic and one of the engineers. One has his shirt off revealing an area of puffed up, blue-ish flesh along the right side of his back, pock-marked with several blood leaking contusions. He's hurt much worse than I am. There are likely broken ribs beneath the surface injuries. His million dollar wound will come at a higher premium of pain and suffering and medical intervention than mine. The other man is holding his left hand limply within his right hand and appears to be in the most pain of the three of us. Already his fingers and knuckles have swollen. I can guess what happened to him. Like all of us he must have reflexively tried to duck down under his helmet. He must have reached up and tried to hold onto the only little bit of shelter available to him. Something hard, accelerating down from the sky, must have impacted first with the fragile bones and tendons and nerves of his left hand before hitting the more resistant surface of his steel pot and insulating helmet liner. His head is undamaged, his helmet performed as designed. His hand was not so designed. He too will pay a higher price over a longer period of time for his good fortune.

"What's the matter with him?" the medic inquires of our trio, trying to mentally triage the wounded without being diverted from the immediate needs of the bleeding man.

"He's got a broken knee," Brownie replies, confident in our hopeful diagnosis.

"OK, sit him down over there. I'll get to him in a minute. Be careful not to bend his leg."

Brownie and Sams help me gently to the ground and we all light up cigarettes and wait for my turn with the Doc.

"I'm not sure that it's broken," Doc tells us after a few seconds of pressing and squeezing. It might just be badly bruised. We'll have to get you down to the 71st and have it X-rayed to make sure. The dust off bird will be here in about a half an hour. Do you want anything for the pain?"

"No, I'm OK," I tell him as he starts writing up the dust off tag that will travel with me, identifying me as an officially authorized injured person. The pain in and around my knee is already starting to fade. The other two damaged men aren't so lucky. They both appear to be

Tim Haslam

in a lot of discomfort and each moment waiting keeps them focused on the pain. Neither of them seems to feel lucky about what's happened to them.

Goddamn it, I begin to reflect after about fifteen minutes of waiting. *There's nothing seriously wrong with my knee.* The only pain left is a minor stinging around the little surface scrapes and the swelling is already going down. I stand up to validate my worst fear…that I'm fine. Sure enough, my leg is fully functional. It moves as intended, without pain. *Goddamn it.*

"I guess I won't need this," I tell the Doc, handing him back his ticket. "My knee seems to be OK…its fine."

I head back down toward the crater where the rest of my squad is cleaning out the skree from within the pit, looking back to see the dust-off bird take the other two men off to the 71st…off to the clean sheets and Nurse Wallace and Miss Kritch and the Vietnamese woman with the mop in the showers.

I remember how important it is to lay on your bed but not in it.

Chapter 20

Every Man for Himself

With all the men DROSing while I was in the hospital one of the little rooms at the end of the Bravo Company barracks became available and Sergeant Sweeney said I could have it. As the little room contained a bunk bed and two footlockers, I would have to share it with someone though. Fine…this would still be way better than life in the open bay part of the barracks where everything everyone does and says impinges on everyone else, where every individual odor blends together into a larger cloud of dust clinging stench. My own room, particularly on the nights when my roommate is on guard duty would mean privacy, a prized commodity, unavailable to me for the last fifteen months.

Staff Sergeant James Littlejohn Jr. is my roommate. I first met Littlejohn during our lazy days guarding the bridge over the Dak Poko a hundred years ago. Everybody likes Littlejohn. His black brothers respect him because he's older than most of the men out here, he's been in the army longer and mostly because he's got more for-real, no-bullshit street smarts than anybody else. Littlejohn has a million stories, all highly improbable but probably all true. He's too low key and too self effacing to make this stuff up. More than any of his other attributes though, Littlejohn is respectful of others and seems to appreciate the things he can learn from any other human being. I can always make him laugh. I can always teach him things he wants to know. He does the same for me. The Army is his home but he doesn't care that much about ever being the head of the household. Being a Staff Sergeant is OK…maybe Sergeant First Class again some day. Anything above that would probably involve too much work and too much responsibility.

Tim Haslam

Anything above that would be too much of a diversion from being Littlejohn and put too much stress on his easy going spirit.

"Man did you see how big the moon is tonight," Littlejohn asks me as he comes into our little room after completing the last of his duties for the night. Littlejohn's on light duty, he was pulled out of the field as a result of severely infected patches of jungle rot on both his arms. The scratching was too irresistible. The crud under his finger nails was too ripe with unfriendly micro-organisms and the healing wounds were too fertile an environment. For Littlejohn though, it's as good as the million dollar wound. The doctors say he can't go back out into the shit until it's all fully healed. Littlejohn thinks he'll never have to go back out again. First Sergeant Goodrum is somewhere in the middle. He likes Littlejohn, but hates any malingerers and so he keeps him busy with jobs and tasks that won't interfere with the healing process, truck driving being foremost among the duties and an assignment that Littlejohn relishes. He can drive trucks back and forth to Dak To or wherever for the rest of his tour. He's happy about his plight.

"Yea, it looked huge coming up over the mountains," I reply, lounging up on the top bunk, re-reading my latest letters from home. Neither of us have any guard assignments tonight. We're free to do nothing.

"Yea, that's right man, it was bigger when it first came up. You know about shit like that. How come it gets smaller as it comes up further? Is it closer when it first comes up?"

I explain to my receptive student what I remember about dust particles in the atmosphere and light refraction.

"So, which is bigger anyway, the moon or the sun?"

"The sun is thousands of times bigger."

"So, which is closer, the moon or the sun?"

"The moon, I think it's like two hundred thousand miles away and the sun is like ninety-eight million miles."

"No shit, ninety-eight million miles. Man, it's good that you know all this stuff. I wish I knew more about shit like that, man."

"Well, I don't know how much good knowing shit like that is doing me. We're both pretty much in the same place, doing the same thing. It don't mean nothin.'"

"No man, no...you been to college...when you get home you get

Stars and Stripes and Shadows

back there. A smart kid like you can do all right for yourself. This shit'll all be over some day and you can put all that stuff you know to good use…it do mean something.'"

Before Littlejohn can parent me more with his philosophy the door to our room opens revealing Joe Costas, one of the guys in transit back from the hospital. Costas is one of Littlejohn's best friends and is in fact referred to as "Little Joe" mainly because the two of them were always together during the quiet moments out in the shit, Littlejohn and Little Joe.

Costas and Littlejohn exchange fist taps along with a short exchange of street banter acknowledging how glad they are to see one another. Their open smiles and laughs confirming the underlying feeling.

"Hey man, how ya doin' Haslam?" Little Joe says to me as we tap fists, his broad smile still stretched across his face.

Costas has brought an unopened bottle of Jack Daniels that he insists upon sharing…without any objection or hesitation from us. In another minute we're settled in, canteen cups, containing way too much sour mash whiskey, in hand, Little Joe and Littlejohn sitting cross legged on the floor, me still up on my top bunk perch, a can of shoestring potatoes being passed around to help absorb the burning alcohol. Life is good.

Costas too is from Georgia and has been in the Army nearly as long as Littlejohn, with a similar track record. Somehow they've figured out that Littlejohn's ex-wife's cousin is married to Little Joe's sister and this brings on a detailed exploration and evaluation of people in the family that they both know. Each exaggerated remembrance, anecdote and description is punctuated with a great shared laugh, fist tap and "fuckin-A" or "damn-right" or "no shit, man." For me, this is like listening in to some radio soap opera and before too long they start to realize how entertaining I'm finding all of this. With an appreciative audience and continued encouragement from JD the stories get livelier and livelier.

"Here, man, here's what we're talkin' about," Littlejohn says at one point, extracting an envelope from his foot locker. He pulls out a bunch of photo strips, the kind taken for a quarter within the confines of one of those little curtained-off booths at the mall.

"Here, this is my now wife," he says, handing the first strip to Joe who renders his silent evaluation with another fist tap and then hands

607

Tim Haslam

the strip up to me. The images are of an attractive light skinned black woman, seeming to be much younger than Littlejohn, her expression suggesting some discomfort with the portrait process.

"... and this is my used-to-be wife," he declares with a laugh, handing Costas the next strip.

"Yea, that's her, that's her for sure, man...damn. When did you get this?" Little Joe takes considerably more time studying the used-to-be wife before relinquishing it to my custody.

"Man, I just got that last week," Littlejohn says, as I study the quite different images. This woman is closer in age to Littlejohn, attractive in a different kind of way than "now-wife," her long black hair falling off to one side of her head in a single tight braid. She's not shy or uncomfortable in the slightest in front of the impersonal camera lens. She wants the full essence of her internal being captured. She wants her personality to shine through. This isn't just a picture, it's a message. She's also topless.

Together, we sip and laugh and fist tap our way through the next two hours. Littlejohn explains further how his used-to-be wife hopes he gets assigned to Fort Sill, Oklahoma when he comes back to the states, as she's now living in Oklahoma City. Costas warns of trouble with the now-wife if he does. Littlejohn agrees with some reluctance deciding he may just try to find his way back home via OKC so that he might have one last chance to put closure between used-to-be and now.

I don't remember Little Joe leaving. It's just somehow become dark and quiet and the room has begun to spin. I'm trying to think through my own relationship. I'm wondering about whether Rosemary is my used-to-be girlfriend or my now-girlfriend. I haven't had a letter from her in nearly a month.

※ ※ ※ ※

"I guess Welsh isn't back yet," Captain Walterhouse says to me just as I'm finishing up the morning reports for both Bravo and Delta Company. "I guess you're filling in?"

"Yes, sir," I respond, suspecting that his question is about to be followed up with a new assignment.

"I need you to write a letter to Martin's parents. He's the guy who was killed by the tiger."

Stars and Stripes and Shadows

"Doesn't the Army or the Defense Department send them some kind of letter like that?" I ask, thinking that it's kind of late for this kind of thing.

"Yea, of course but they just send them a notification. This is supposed to be a more personal letter from his commanding officer and since Captain Brandt is out with the Company he can't very well do it and as Welsh is gone, I need you to do it."

What the hell am I going to say to this guy's parents…I hardly new the guy?

"Look, here's a couple of sample letters. Pick one that you think is appropriate, change it a little to fit the circumstances and sign it for Captain Brandt. Make sure that there are no errors on this. It has to look like it was done right. When you've got it finished bring it in to me."

I look over the three sample templates of personalized letters of regret coming from commanding officers. Each of them pertains to someone who has died in combat and how the brave sacrifice was typical of their unselfish service and dedication to duty. I find one that I think I can work with; change the wording that says *killed by hostile fire* to read *killed by hostile animal* and add a few comments about the general upright character of Specialist Martin.

…With my deepest regrets,

Sincerely,

Raymond L. Brandt, Captain, United States Army,

Commanding Officer, D Company, 3d Battalion, 8th Infantry.

Walterhouse reads over my rendition, this time seeming to be concerned more with the substance of the message than with typos and spelling. He does however discover the use of the word "to" instead of the appropriate "too" in one of the sentences and sends me back to try again.

"OK, good," is all he says after proof reading the next revision. "Oh…and here's a promotion allocation list that just came down…send it out to Captain Griffith," he adds, handing me a mimeographed copy of the orders.

"Yes sir."

Tim Haslam

January promotion slots available: B Company, 3d/8th
Staff Sergeant – E6: 1 available slot
Sergeant –E5: 3 available slots
Specialist Four – E4: 5 available slots
Commanding Officer to submit names NLT 1600 hours, 15 Feb.

I think back to last September when Captain Hilton and Lieutenant Riley both promised me a promotion to Sergeant in November if I worked for them. It's now late January and they have each been promoted out of that environment, rendering such promises null and void. I think I've done my part. I think I've done everything that was asked of me.

I type up a quick note to Captain Griffith, passing on the promotion allocations, asking him to send back to me the names of the people he wants to promote into the available slots: 1 Staff Sergeant – E6, 2 Sergeant – E5, 5 Specialist Four – E4. Please have the names back to me by 10 Feb, I'll take care of the rest of the paperwork and submit it all back up to Division.

It's been a long and busy day, keeping up with the Bravo and Delta Company clerking chores and fulfilling my duties as surrogate commanding officers. I've just lighted my end-of-the-day, kick-back cigarette when Pat Sanderson comes into the office and pulls Welsh's empty chair over in front of my desk with a big grin on his face. Sanderson too is in transit back from the hospital and of course, in no hurry to rejoin the Company out in the shit. Sanderson is another Southern Californian, actually from Beverly Hills and the one person in all of Bravo Company who has a background similar to mine. We've become friends.

"Look at this, man. Did you see this?" He asks, in almost a whisper, leaning forward over the desk, shoving a piece of paper toward me.

The paper is one of the periodic Division bulletins with various announcements. The last paragraph of this particular edition, dated yesterday, announces that there are three available R&R seats for Hong Kong, departing Cam Rahn Bay the day after tomorrow.

"Let's go," Pat says with great enthusiasm.

"I've already been on R&R," I tell him with great regret.

Stars and Stripes and Shadows

"So what, who's gonna care?"

"Well, Top Goodrum for one, Captain Walterhouse probably, and who's gonna do the work here?"

"Look, Welsh is due back tomorrow right? He owes you and Val likes doing all the clerk stuff anyway. He knows that you're short and he wants the job when you go. It gives him more practice.

"What about Top? He's not gonna let me go."

"What does he care as long as the work gets done. We're not taking the seats away from anyone else in the Battalion, plus I think I've got something else to offer him."

"What do you mean something else?"

"Last night at dinner I was sitting next to Top and Reynolds and they were talking about stereo stuff. Top was going on and on about this great Teac tape recorder that they had on sale for fifty bucks at the PX but when he got over there, they were sold out. So, we tell Top that if he let's us go we'll get him the Teac in Hong Kong, guaranteeing that he won't have to pay more than fifty bucks."

"OK, suppose he likes the idea but says it doesn't take two of us to go and get it."

"Well, we hold our ground. It's both of us or no tape recorder."

"Great, we're going to blackmail the First Sergeant. I'm get'n too short to start pushing my luck with him like that. I don't want to spend the rest of my days here as assistant shit-burner."

"Come on, man…Top's a good guy, he has a sense of humor. If he doesn't go for it he doesn't go for it but I know that he really wants this thing."

"So, you'll have the bases covered?" the half smiling First Sergeant asks me after a moment's contemplation of our offer. "It's no loss being without Sanderson, he's just another mouth to feed around here."

"Val and Welsh will take care of everything. I just need to be taken out of the guard rotation while I'm gone and there's a whole bunch of new replacements coming in over the next week that can fill in there."

"All I've got now is forty bucks. I spent the other ten I had for the tape recorder on a few other essentials," adds Top realizing that he's in the driver's seat in this negotiation.

Sanderson looks at me. I return a raised eyebrow sort of questioning

Tim Haslam

look along with a subtle nod.

"Not a problem Top, anything more than forty dollars is on us," Pat offers as a way to close the deal.

"If you don't come back with the Teac…don't come back!" First Sergeant Goodrum recommends as an alternate plan, affirming his permission. "I'll give you the forty the day you leave."

И И И И

I'm looking in the mess hall for Sanderson on the day before our planned departure. There are still some details to be worked out about our transportation to Cam Rahn and I haven't seen my travel companion all morning. The lunch time crowd is thinning out but there's no Sanderson. I spot Littlejohn at one of the tables, taking his time puffing through a cigarette, picking over the food remnants on his tray. I decide to get my lunch and join him. I'll find Pat later.

"What's the haps man?" Littlejohn greets me as I sit down across the table from him.

"You haven't seen Pat Sanderson, have you?"

"I saw him with Captain Nelson early this morning. It looked like they were heading off to the PX together."

"No shit, with Captain Nelson?"

Before our dialogue gets any further, a large black man places a tray full of food down on the table next to Sergeant Littlejohn and sits down, all the while glaring at me. The man is PFC Lewis Barnes. He's been sent back to base camp by Captain Hilton to face court-martial charges of insubordination, dereliction of duty and other charges. Barnes has a reputation as a trouble maker, as a black-power brother who has no use for any part of the white man's Army or war. He was drafted into the service of his country out of the Detroit projects, accepting the offer only because of a less attractive alternative offer presented to him by a municipal court judge. Everything he's done since has been with reluctance and resistance, taking advantage of every opportunity to encourage his black brothers to feel as he does about white people.

"What you doin' with this dude, man?" Barnes asks of Littlejohn, ensuring that his contempt for me and my kind is fully expressed.

"Man, lighten up," the thoughtful Sergeant replies. "Ain't you got yourself into enough trouble?"

Stars and Stripes and Shadows

"All the trouble I got is because of the whole world of honky bullshit that surrounds us. You got the same trouble," he indoctrinates Littlejohn. "You just don't want to stand up to it, man."

"What you doin' here anyway, man?" Barnes says, shifting the focus of his attitude over to me. "You gotta be one dumb motherfuck'n white guy to end up over here in this shit. Any honky with any brains at all can get out of this. There are plenty of brothers to send over here to fight this bullshit war. Why ain't you back at college or back working at some motherfuck'n vital job like cleaning swimmin' pools or some shit like that?

"There's no difference between him and you and me right now," says Littlejohn in his usual friendly, heard-it-all-before, style. "There's plenty of white guys live'n and die'n out in the shit."

"Yea, plenty of dumb-ass white guys. I'll wait for you outside."

With that proclamation, Barnes withdraws from the table and exits the mess hall.

It's Littlejohn's job to stay with Barnes wherever he goes throughout the court-martial process. It's also Littlejohn's job to see that Barnes fills out any and all paperwork associated with his plight. Barnes cannot read or write.

"Man, how much longer have you got to deal with that guy?" I ask.

"His trial actually ended this morning. They found him guilty on all charges. This afternoon I've got to get him over to the Fourth MPs and then go with him and them down to Long Binh where he's going to start his jail time."

"No shit…he's going to jail and he's just casually walking around like this with you?

"Well actually, he doesn't really know that he's going to jail. When they read the sentence, it was pretty hard to follow all the things that the judge was saying. They said he had to go down to Long Binh and then would be sent stateside. I don't think that Barnes really understood the part about being assigned to Fort Leavenworth or maybe he doesn't know that that's really a prison. He just heard the part about Long Binh and stateside."

"So, you're taking this guy to prison and he doesn't even know it?"

Tim Haslam

"Man, think about it. If he knew that he was on his way to four years in prison how much cooperation do you think he'd be give'n me. He'd be making my life fuck'n miserable. You know what he's all about and there are lots of guns around here, man. He'd shoot my ass first chance he got. He'd shoot my ass, your white ass and every other white ass he could see."

"So, what does he think is really going to happen?"

"Look man, I gotta job to do, I gotta get him down there to Long Binh and then my job is done, he's somebody else's problem. So, I read him the part of the orders that says we all go down there to Long Binh and then he's on his way back home."

"What? He thinks he's going home?"

"Yea."

"Man, are you crazy? What do you think he's gonna do when he gets down there and finds out that he's on his way to jail for four years?"

"By then he'll be in handcuffs with a million MPs around…he can't do nothin' and I'll di di the hell out of there."

"Damn, man…you better hope that he doesn't figure this out."

"No shit, man! No shit!"

I cross paths with Pat just as I'm leaving the mess hall. He's coming up the road out in front with a little bag in his hands.

"We need to be ready to go at nine tomorrow morning," I tell him. "We need to get over to the Air Base as early as possible to get on the wait list for flights to Cam Rahn."

"Why nine? Let's go earlier then that and make sure we're out on the first flight." "The first scheduled flight isn't until noon and they won't even let us sign in until eleven."

"OK, nine it is. Captain Nelson's going too. Maybe he can pull some weight for us over there."

Nelson's a good guy, just recently promoted to Captain after serving his time as a First Lieutenant Platoon leader out in the shit with Bravo Company. His men liked and respected him. He's of similar character to Collins, Falck and Hilton. I'm guessing that he can transition into civilian clothes and transition out of the role of a military officer. He'll be a good companion. Having two friends to make this trip with makes

Stars and Stripes and Shadows

it seem like a lot more fun.

Pat and I head back toward S1 to work out the rest of our plans for tomorrow and beyond. Along the way we pass Littlejohn and his still in-the-dark charge Lewis Barnes. The two of them are talking to James Ardis Jr., another of the Bravo Company brothers and one who can be easily swayed by Barnes racist views. Ardis too has a reputation, not so much as a rebel rouser type of trouble maker, but more of an attitude case about everything, always looking for the minimalist effort required to get by. When it serves his purposes he can also fit in with any of the other grunts from the shit, black or white. I see Ardis and Barnes fist tapping and laughing several times as we pass by. Barnes must be sharing his good fortune, describing how he's on his way home. Littlejohn glances over at me, laughing along with the two men, nervously masking his deception.

◢ ◢ ◢ ◢

"Screw it," I tell Val when he points out his fourth typo down in the narrative text part of the Morning Report. "I don't think Walterhouse is going to notice that."

It's only 7:00, I've got two hours to kill and could have done the Morning Report myself but I thought I'd let Val do it while I looked on just to give him a chance to remember how to do it while I'm still here.

"You still here, Haslam?" First Sergeant Goodrum says to me as he comes through the door.

"Not for long, Top. We're gone at nine."

"Well, in the meantime make yourself useful. Here's the roster for the convoy going out this morning. Go round up these four guys and get 'em up here, bag and baggage, ready to go."

"OK, who's going?"

"Wells, Ardis, Llamas and Costa," Top answers, tapping impatiently on his clipboard.

I head back toward the Bravo Company billet expecting to find all four men there. As I enter, Wells and Llamas pass by heading out, already aware of the convoy, already aware of their invitation; rucks on their backs, weapons in hand, the same dejected look on their faces. On the second bunk to my right I also find Ardis, reclining comfortably on

615

Tim Haslam

his back, a cigarette in his mouth, his hands locked together behind his head. He doesn't seem to be ready for anything.

"Ardis, you've got to be on the convoy this morning. You gotta get ready and up there right now."

"I ain't goin.'"

"What?" I ask him in reply to his short proclamation even though I heard him perfectly.

"I ain't goin'," he repeats without shifting out of his relaxed posture.

"Ardis, you don't have a choice. Your name's on the list. Top just sent me down here to get you Wells, Llamas and Costa…you gotta go."

"Look man, I said I ain't goin'. Fuck the convoy! Fuck Wells and Llamas and Costa…fuck Top and fuck you."

Ardis' response catches me completely off guard. I would have expected grumbling and profanity. I wouldn't have been surprised to encounter curses directed at the messenger, I would have expected a slow response to the call but I could never have imagined an outright refusal.

"Ardis, whadda ya think you're gonna do? What do you think Top's gonna do? You have to get your ass up off that bunk and get on the convoy. You don't have any choice."

Lewis Ardis Jr. pulls the cigarette out of his mouth as the beginning of his response to my latest challenge. He throws the cigarette down at my feet and brings his arms back out from behind his head. In his right hand he has a .45 pistol that he points right at my face, his own face now locked into a mask of determination, his eyes fixed upon mine, aligned behind the sights of the pistol.

"I…ain't…goin'," he repeats with slow, forceful deliberation.

"OK Ardis, OK," are the only words I can get out, looking over the barrel of the .45.

He's not really going to shoot me…is he?

I take a couple of backward steps as I try to think of something else to say or do in response to Ardis' .45-caliber-reinforced refusal. A short, flashbulb like image of Hong Kong passes through my consciousness, followed by an image of the First Sergeant's face when he finds out about Ardis and me and the .45. *Shit…I may not make it to Hong*

616

Stars and Stripes and Shadows

Kong. Shit...Top's going to be really pissed. Shit...Ardis, you had to pull this shit today!

"OK man, you ain't goin'. It don't mean nothin' to me," I tell the .45, continuing my backwards retreat toward the door. "Just put the gun away, man."

I make it out the door and find that there are two other men there. They must have made it out of the barracks behind me when Ardis first showed the weapon.

"What are you gonna do?" One of them asks me.

"Shit man, I don't know...tell Top I guess. It'll be up to him and the MPs to deal with this guy."

With that decided, the three of us hurry up the wooden walkway toward the road where the First Sergeant waits impatiently for his last convoy passenger.

"Where the hell's Ardis?" First Sergeant Goodrum asks as the three of us approach.

"He say's he isn't going, Top and he's got a .45. He told me he ain't goin', and he pointed the .45 at me and just kept saying that he ain't goin.'"

"Goddamn-it," Goodrum declares, pushing the three of us out of his way as he charges down the walkway back toward the Bravo barracks. The three of us, plus Pinkerman and Valentine who have overheard my explanation, all follow the First Sergeant, intentionally keeping a few yards distance between us and our lead element.

"Ardis, get your ass up off that bunk, get your gear and get up there on that truck," we can all hear the fearless Topkick exclaim the instant he enters the barracks, "and give me that goddamn .45."

We all wait for a response from Ardis or from his gun. A silent minute or two pass and then Ardis comes out of the door, ruck sack slung over one shoulder, his M16 in his hand, wearing his helmet backwards on his head, followed by Goodrum, pointing the barrel of the .45 down, inertly at the ground. Neither of them says a thing to any of us and the whole parade returns back up the walkway. Ardis climbs up on the deuce-and-a-half, joining Joe Costa, Wells and Llamas. Ardis looks pissed, but resigned to his fate. Actually, all the men on the truck have that same look.

I need coffee and a cigarette before I can return with Val to do battle

Tim Haslam

with the DA Form 1. I'm not sure if my hands are shaking now because of the residual effects of the malaria or because of the variation in this morning's work routine.

Doc Charlebois comes into the office a little before nine o'clock looking for me.

"Ardis shot himself in the foot," Doc tells Val and me.

"For real, he shot himself?" I ask.

"The truck wasn't even to the rallying point. He's already at the 71st. I guess you can take him off the morning report."

"How do I show that?" Val asks, seemingly more concerned with the administrative implications of Charlebois' news than with the substance of the message.

"Temporary Duty – Hospital," I tell him without hesitation, pointing over to the appropriate block on the form. "Right there, TDY-Hospital. Then we've got to adjust the strength numbers and deployment."

"I can't have any more strike-overs up in that section. That means we'll have to start all over again."

"Tomorrow...wait and show the change tomorrow...it don't mean nothin' today."

♂ ♂ ♂ ♂

It's almost ten-thirty when the bus finally pulls out of the main gate at Camp Enari heading for the Pleiku Air Force Base. Pat Sanderson, Captain Nelson and I, accompanied by a busload of other Fourth Infantry Division men, are all happily on our way now; out of the shit for a few days, on our way to various exotic Asian cities. Finally, I have a few minutes to relax after a busy morning coaching Val, helping out First Sergeant Goodrum and testing the mental discipline of Lewis Ardis Jr. and the sensitivity of one .45 caliber pistol trigger. Also now, I have something to do while the bus bounces along the dusty road skirting the edge of Pleiku. Val caught up with me just as the three of us were walking away from the 3rd of the 8th area and handed me a letter that had just come in with the day's mail. It was addressed to me and I could see by the hand written Colorado return address that it was from Gabe Luna. I tucked it into my pocket, as I didn't want anything to

Stars and Stripes and Shadows

slow down our progress toward Hong Kong.

No way, I think to myself as I make my way through Luna's narrative description. *No way,* I keep thinking as I follow along with the sequence of events that's brought Luna to the writing of this letter. *No way,* can I, at first, believe any of this.

Gabe Luna will not be coming back to Camp Enari, or the Fourth Infantry Division or Vietnam or the Army anytime soon. Gabe Luna's wife is fine. She always has been fine. The two of them are both fine and on their way to some undisclosed place somewhere in the U.S. or in a nearby land where they can wait out the rest of the Vietnam War together. Gabe Luna and his wife concocted the whole scheme. She was never the frail paranoid young wife portrayed in her letters or in her tearful interviews with Army Chaplains. He was never the protective, concerned, distant husband, desperately afraid of what his emotionally immature bride might do in his absence or in the event of his death. Together, they designed and carried out the whole scenario. The first week he arrived out in the boonies with the Company he knew that he had to get out. He knew that any price to be paid later was better than the price he was already paying out there; paying in the currency of fear, discomfort, isolation and longing. He told her so in his first letter home. She went immediately to work formulating a rescue plan. Once conceived, and shared, the script took on a life of its own and all they had to do was read their lines with sincere conviction. All they had to do was convince those whose jurisdiction is with the spiritual concerns of the grunts that their particular spirits were in jeopardy in ways unlike the spiritual concerns of every other grunt. The Chaplains could actually do something for these two members of the flock. They could do more than minister with words and phrases and rituals. They could actually influence events that would mend these threatened souls.

Damn! I'm thinking as the bus approaches the gates to the Air Base. *Hughes pretends a change to his sexual orientation and slices his wrists, Porter and Artis shoot themselves. Artis maybe thinks about shooting me. Littlejohn delivers a man to a jail term under the pretense of going home and Gabe and Mrs. Luna go AWOL by taking advantage of the better nature of the officers with the crosses on their collars.*

Is communism behind all of this? Ho Chi Minh?

Can I make it to the 15th of March?

Chapter 21

Farewells

"Haslam, hey man, what's happening?" one of the other khaki uniformed men already seated in the Customs Clearing room at Kai Tak Airport says to me as I follow the similarly attired line inside. We're all about to get our instructions regarding the rules of engagement while in Hong Kong.

"Lee, hey man," I say back to the soldier I recognize as Alan Lee, one of the guys I went through infantry training with back at Fort Polk. I haven't seen him since we graduated from there nearly a year ago. He's wearing a 25th Division patch on his shoulder and has also earned his Combat Infantryman's Badge. He's changed though. He doesn't look quite like the quiet, well mannered young Chinese-American I hung around with back there in the cold, wet Louisiana forests as we learned our trade. He wears the same unmistakable veneer common to all grunts-from-the-shit. Soap and water can't wash away the experiences etched into his young face. He knows the shit.

"You're on R&R too," I confirm with him and then introduce him to Pat Sanderson and Captain Nelson. The Captain amends my introduction, replacing his rank with *John*. I invite Lee to join us, at least for this evening and he seems happy to accept the offer.

I already know all the rules of conduct for American military personnel in Hong Kong and am probably more restless and anxious to get out of there than the others. On the plane I relived some of my experiences in Hong Kong; about the tenth time that Pat has heard all of this, but all new information to Nelson. We haven't yet worked out a game-plan for our assault on the city, agreeing that we would first get

Stars and Stripes and Shadows

checked into hotels, change into civilian clothes, which we all have and then, over drinks in the closest bar, we'll develop our strategy.

The Park Hotel turns out to be booked up, but they recommend the Meridian right next door. Fine…that only slows our progress down by a few minutes and the Meridian, although not quite as elegant as the Park has all the amenities necessary for our pursuits. One of the nearby tailor shop representatives follows the four of us as we make our way from the front desk to the elevators, extolling the value, quality and service available only at his shop. We respond in unison that we already have civilian clothes. Undeterred, he draws our attention to the many varieties of fine cameras and watches to be found at another of the nearby establishments he represents. He's still educating us as to the special offers available to us only this evening as the elevator doors slide together, curtaining off the remainder of his pitch.

"I told you," I remind my friends.

"So, are you sure that you want to go right off and find Judy?" Pat asks me as the four of us get comfortable behind the first round of San Miguel's delivered to us at the bar right next door to the hotel.

"Well, I plan on making it over to the Moongate before too long," I respond, "but I'm willing to tag along with you guys for awhile if you want to prowl around first. I'm sure that the mama-san at the Moongate can find dates for you all as well. Maybe I'll get a discount if I bring in all this business."

"Why wouldn't you want to shop around a little? There are a lot of women in this town. Why not sample more?"

I think for a minute about Sanderson's suggestion. I remember how anxious I was with the whole process the last time; of how nervous I was during my first contact with the bartenders and mama-sans and doormen, with Debbie and with Judy. I remember too, every minute with her. I'm not sure I want to go through the rigors and protocols of shopping around again. I'm not sure that such effort would yield experiences that would surpass those remembered.

"I don't think I'm likely to find anyone I'd like better than her," I tell them, leaving the impression that I'm open to the idea of further exploration. I'm also finding it most pleasurable, being right here, in this company, savoring the images of what's likely to happen over the

Tim Haslam

next few days and nights. I'm in no hurry to do anything or to make any decisions. I'm just enjoying the ride, comfortably whiling away a few more of the hours remaining between now and my DROS. I'm so content in the moment that I have almost forgotten that today is February 2nd...my 22nd birthday. Disclosing the occasion to my three friends gets me several more drinks through the course of the evening. At the same time there is a subtle limitation to our reaction to this milestone. Real birthday celebrations are, for all of us, associated with images of home.

Alan reveals to us that he speaks some Chinese although he describes his family's dialect as Guoyu and thinks that everybody around here speaks Cantonese. It's close enough though he thinks and we all believe that Alan's presence and ethnic background will be of value to us all. Our foursome is the perfect blend. Alan speaks the language. I've surveyed the ground before. Nelson has an officer's maturity and leverage and Pat has the percolating physiological longings necessary to set a rapid pace for our team.

"C'mon...let's go," Pat urges the rest of us as the second round of beer bottles approaches empty. "Let's see what else is around."

I suggest that we work our way up Nathan Road, remembering that there are numerous establishments consistent with our aspirations; thinking too that such a journey would not take me too far from Kimberly Road and the Moongate. And so off we go, happily onto the Kowloon streets just as the atmosphere is transitioning away from fading daylight and into the buzzing neon world where all things needed by American G.I.s are described and promised all along the busy sidewalks. The difficulty now is where to start the sampling.

The streets seem to be unusually crowded this evening, which makes it somewhat easier to shuttle past the touts outside the shops that hold no interest for us but also makes it harder for us to slow down to evaluate the similar facades of the bars and clubs. We have to adjust to the tide of people flowing along the streets.

"Let's just go in here," suggests Pat, steering us out of the throng and into a little alcove entranceway to a club labeled "Dragon's Song."

Alan and I, trailing Sanderson and Nelson by a few paces, catch up just as Pat opens the door, just as a familiar voice breaks out of the general cacophony of city noises surrounding us.

Stars and Stripes and Shadows

"Tim, Tim," I think I hear. I turn out toward the school of pedestrians swimming down this way along the sidewalk just in time to absorb one of the bodies flinging itself out of the crowd. The arms are around my neck an instant before my senses can identify the sound and feel and smell of my assailant.

"Judy!"

"You are here again! How long have you been here?"

"I just got here," I respond, still adjusting to her closeness. "I was going to come over to the Moongate in a little while."

"No, no... I no longer work there," she says, relaxing her grasp somewhat as she takes notice of the three other men with me. "These are your friends?"

"Yes, we all just got into town."

As I tell her this, I notice that she too is not alone. There are two other very attractive and similarly dressed young Chinese women with her. We work through all the introductions still tangled within the outer threshold of the Dragon's Song. The other girls are much like Judy, neither is shy or reserved. The taller of the two, Sandy, latches on to Alan Lee and immediately begins to explore his Chinese roots. Alan seems to have no objection to the inquiries or to the soft fingers that have interlaced with his own. In similar fashion and with even greater enthusiasm Pat has accepted the direct overtures of the third girl, April. Captain Nelson doesn't seem to register any disappointment about the shortfall of females associated with this accidental encounter. In fact, he seems to be a bit relieved. Judy, of course, has a friend she can call for the Captain. Nelson graciously refuses the offer, declaring a desire for independence in this evening's pursuits. We all enter the Dragon's Song, find a large table in the nearly empty club, order drinks and start the party.

The girls make it easy. They're very good at what they do. Whether it's natural ability or not, sincere interest or not, they ask the right kind of questions, they laugh and smile at the right times, they flirt and flatter and squeeze and beguile. They have us right where they want us. They have us right where we want them to have us. We have them right where we want them...for now.

After the arrival of our second round of drinks Judy insists that I dance with here and pulls me out onto the empty dance floor, telling

Tim Haslam

me how much she likes the song that's playing. I haven't heard it for a long time. I haven't reacted to the familiar melody for a long time. I haven't relived those moments for a long time.

> *Are you going to Scarborough Fair?*
> *Parsley, sage, rosemary and thyme*
> *Remember me to the one who lives there*
> *For she once was a true love of mine.*

On one of the last night's home on my last leave, Rosemary and I saw the Graduate. It was one of those wonderful nights where nothing that might happen tomorrow or the next day mattered. It was a night like so many others that she and I had shared over the two years of our relationship; a drive over one of the canyons that leads to Beverly Hills or Westwood while I listened to her updates on the days events; a movie, followed by a late dinner or just lingering over coffee somewhere while we compared notes about people like Ben and Mrs. Robinson, about Dustin Hoffman and Katherine Ross, about Tim and Rosemary. It was so easy and comfortable, so free and new, so clear and so simple and best of all, there were still moments of quieter closeness to come, outside her apartment door.

For a brief moment in time I'm blended within the now of Judy and the then of Rosemary. It's different though than Littlejohn's now and used to be. Both Judy and Rosemary are now, but only one of them is here.

Judy feels and smells and looks even better than I remembered. Everything about her combines into a rich elixir of soft fresh relief. She is a cool breeze on a balmy evening, a golden sun rise after a dark night. She is the catalyst that reactivates feelings I've nearly forgotten, feelings I've feared subconsciously were lost, feelings I've only had with and for Rosemary. There is something different about her though; there is something about this girl, this night in this place that I didn't detect the last time we spent time together three months ago. There is something more genuine in her comments, more sincere in her eyes and her touch. I think she is truly happy that I have come back and that we are together. There is something more than commerce suggested in the nuances of her reactions to me.

Stars and Stripes and Shadows

И И И И

The first few days of this R&R fly by much too quickly. We're trying to pack in too many things. Pat and I have successfully found the Teac tape recorder we owe Top, although it cost us an extra ten dollars each by the time we got it into the hands of the parcel post office at the China Fleet Club. We each have new cameras for ourselves and the two of us have become daily visitors at Jack Wong's tailor shop, becoming the mainstay of his clientele this week. Once again, he escorts us, including Alan, out to the New Territories, packed into the black Mercedes, treating us to dinner. We do more sightseeing on our own, Pat and Alan and I. Captain Nelson has decided to rest and recuperate at his own pace and our paths only occasionally cross in the lobby of the hotel. Judy, Sandy and April accompany us on several of our shopping excursions, driving the shop keepers crazy with their stubborn negotiating stances and their spirited rejections of the values portrayed by the touts and shop employees. By late afternoon each day the larger group dissipates into independent couples, each more free to follow their own desires at their own pace.

On the third night, Judy wants to go to the movies. She wants to see John Wayne in the Green Berets. The idea of going to the movies sounds great, but I'm not sure that I want to see a movie about the Vietnam War. She's insistent enough and I'm curious enough and so we go. John Wayne's version is nothing like the version I've been living through. His is World War Two with the Japanese replaced by the Viet Cong and, just like all the earlier war movies, the actors playing the bad guys are all Chinese. Judy thinks that I look like John Wayne. *I'll bet she says that to all the Americans.*

Pat and I visit Jack's shop for the final time on the morning of our last full day in town. We try on our latest purchases of suits and sports coats and write out our home addresses for Jack who's promised to package everything up and send it all back home for us. He continues to express his appreciation to us as we try to leave his shop, following us down the stairs and out into the streets, thanking us all the way. I know that I will never see this honest, friendly man again but I will never forget his natural kindness and his gracious assistance when I was alone in his world.

Tim Haslam

↯ ↯ ↯ ↯

I spend all of my last afternoon and evening with Judy. Mostly we just drift along the streets together, stopping into shops now and then, stopping for coffee or iced tea. We linger over dinner and are in no hurry to get back to the hotel. We're trying to slow the city down. We want everything going on around us to progress in slow motion. We both want this day to linger, to last, to freeze in time.

We're unsuccessful at stopping the world around us and in an instant we find ourselves sitting in the lobby of the hotel. We are the only ones there at 6:00 a.m. The bus to the airport will be along soon. I don't know where Pat or Alan or Captain Nelson might be right now or how they plan on getting back to Vietnam. Maybe Sandy and April and some other resident girl have captivated each of them and enticed them into staying in this pleasant and exciting place. Judy's perhaps trying to do this with me. She's trying to tell me things that I don't think she's ever said to anyone. She doesn't seem to know quite how to do this, what the right words are. It's the first time I've seen her struggle to communicate her feelings or to get her message across. It's the first time I've seen her unable to control the world around her.

"I never know anyone like you before, Tim," she tells me, clutching tightly to my hand, pressing her head into my shoulder, "I never feel this way about any American…about anyone."

She pulls herself upright and away from me for a moment and looks me in the eye. She punches me gently in the chest as a subtle smile brightens her face. "I don't want you to go. Can't you stay another day like you did the last time? Why can't you stay again?"

"I have no choice this time. I have to go. I wish I could stay. I wish I could be with you for a lot longer. I have no choice this time."

She hugs me tightly until the unwanted bus arrives out front. She too hears the squeak of hydraulic brakes on the damp street outside and tightens her grip even further.

"I have to go."

She pulls back just enough to bring her face in front of mine. Tears are in her eyes and more warm salty tears track down her soft almond cheeks. I kiss them away. I move reluctantly through the hotel door, leaving her inside and I head off, once again to Vietnam.

Chapter 22

DROS

"AIT Committee Group, 2nd BDE. Ft. Ord, California," the preliminary assignment orders read.

Fort Ord, California…I could do that. That'd be close to home. I could endure six months there. I could endure six months there easier than I could endure an extra fifty three days here.

My mind's now made up. There's no way I'm going to extend my service here in this place. I'm going home. I'm going back to everything and everyone that I left. I'm going back to the way it all was. I'm going back into the images I've clung to and revisited over and over, that have sustained me through eternal nights out in the rain, through torturous days under the ruck and through the fevered, foggy influences of Vivax Malaria. I'll get thirty days leave and then I'll go up to Fort Ord and play soldier for five more months. I'll probably be able to come home on weekend passes once in while and Rosemary may even be able to come up there and see me. My minds made up. I'm now a committed short-timer.

N N N N

It's the 5th of March when the actual DROS orders finally reach my desk.

Tim Haslam

DEPARTMENT OF THE ARMY
HEADQUARTERS 4TH INFANTRY DIVISION
APO San Francisco 96262

SPECIAL ORDERS   24 February 1969
NUMBER 55   EXTRACT

117   TC 246   Fol rsg dir.   MP.   TDN.   PCS.   TPA in CONUS   CIC 291A03

Rept to: Central Clearance bldg 4635 NLT 1000 hrs 2 days prior to PC for Out-processing
Rept date (Trans): To be ann in indiv PC. Indiv WP IAW PC instr rept to 22d Repl Bn, Cam
Ranh Bay Vietnam NET 24 hrs & NLT 12 hrs prior to PC and must have MTA (DD Form
1482) compl IAW AR 59-21 and USARV Reg 55-11.
Mo OS (curr tour): 12 UNOIDIC (NT 12 Mo)
Maj comd/agcy: Hq USARV Long Binh Vietnam
Lv data: 30 DDALVAHP   PCS (MDC): 5CE9
Tvl data: TDMAA. Max auth hand bag 66 lbs. 134 lbs excess bag auth. AMD: VCR-TCM-
3. U-(Local Ctl No)-AZ-03.

HASHAM TIMOTHY L US56713762 (559-91-6632) SP4 11B20 Co B 3d Bn 8th Inf APO
96262
Asg to: USARV Ret Det APO 96375 FFAT 1st Bn 2d Bde (WOMO) Ft Ord CA

DEROS: 13 Mar 69

Hasham? Goddamn-it…they mis-spelled my name! It's me though… my serial number, my social security number. Goddamn-it…this better not mess things up. If I have to become Timothy L. Hasham to get out of this place, so be it.

"Eight days," I shout out, throwing both my hands up into the air. "Actually seven days and a wake up and I'm outa' here."

"Right on," my fellow clerks chorus back in reaction to the news I've been awaiting for the last three-hundred and fifty seven days.

All right, the thirteenth… two days ahead of my expected DROS date. All right…it's real, it's really going to happen!

There are a lot of things I have to do to get ready to leave this place. There are a lot of out-processing steps associated with one's extrication from the shit. I have to check in with various sub-sections of the Fourth Infantry Division to sign out and get official permission to go home. Top and Captain Walterhouse still expect me to fulfill all my duties right up until the moment I leave. There's no slack cut to anyone just because they're short. Valentine still needs a lot of coaching on all the

628

Stars and Stripes and Shadows

tasks that I've learned to deal with and the war too is still going on. The war too must be dealt with.

The Battalion has been sent up into the mountains west of Kontum again to block infiltration routes. The 66th and 24th NVA Regiments seem to be gaining strength and are known to be moving towards Kontum and Polei Kleng, reinforced by engineering and artillery units. They want to regain the offensive and they want to strengthen their footholds in the highlands. The Fourth Division must stop them. Each day now, reports are coming to us about ambushes and firefights, about casualties and about deaths. Alpha Company encountered a Battalion sized force and had 19 men killed, the worst losses for the 3rd of the 8th since the battles of November, 1967. Two days later, Delta Company had seven men killed. Men in my Company, in Bravo Company, some that I knew well out in the shit, some nearly as short as I am and some new guys who I processed into the Company when they first arrived are being reported as wounded, some are reported as KIA. I see a familiar name on one of the reports, Alfred Lallave, a guy I went through AIT with back at Fort Polk. He had to be days away from leaving the boonies. He had to be days away from being extricated from the shit that he's been in for nearly a year. He was a short-timer too and now he's dead. He'll never see home again.

The reports aren't always accurate or have been inadvertently modified as they get passed on from the Company to the forward support base to Brigade and down to us. I get a report that one of our officers, Lieutenant Demarco has been shot in the eye. I remember Demarco coming through here just before I went into the hospital. He was a short, stocky good natured guy. I can see his face. It's terrible to imagine what a bullet through his eye would do. Happily, the official after-action report comes through a few days later and correctly describes his wound as, "shot in the thigh," probably the million dollar wound.

The Bravo Company grunts out in the shit, in fact all the 3rd of the 8th grunts out in the shit are in contact with Charlie almost every day now. I can't help but feel like I belong out there too. I feel like I'm missing out on something that I'm supposed to be part of and, at the same time, something that I don't want any part of. I feel like maybe I shouldn't be leaving this place yet. I feel like I can't wait to get out of this place. I don't know yet that I will forever struggle with these feelings.

Tim Haslam

ɴ ɴ ɴ ɴ

March 12th is almost over. My last DA Form 1 has been typed, submitted and signed off by Captain Walterhouse. All my own out-processing paperwork is done and I have only one more official duty to perform for the 3rd of the 8th. I have to take one last turn on reaction-squad tonight. It's no big deal. It still gives me time to say my goodbyes over a few beers before I have to check in at 10:00. I can sleep away my last night in the Nam in the tent just as well as in my little room. I can get to my DROS...get to my wake-up performing this one last duty. Nothing has ever happened during all the times I've had reaction squad duty. Nothing will happen tonight.

My friends have treated me to just the right number of beers to send me off to bed relaxed and ready for sleep; no spinning, no headaches, no vomiting. Just enough to ease me right into sleep without getting too caught up mentally in thoughts of tomorrow and the days to come.

I don't know what time it is or how long I've been asleep when the siren sounds. For the first seconds I forget that it's DROS day. We have to get on the truck and get out to the perimeter line...something's happening...*thwumping* and *kachunking* are happening. It becomes obvious as we approach the perimeter near the west gate that the in-bound mortars are falling closer to the bunker line than to the interior of the base. Sporadic flashes of gunfire coming in cracks and bursts spit intermittently out from the bunkers as star shell flares float down over the cleared ground out beyond the tangles of barbed wire.

The six of us in the back of the truck need no instructions on what to do or where to go when the truck slides to a stop at the edge of the frontage road, twenty meters back from the bunker line. The bunkers seem to be dangerously far off but there are two small foxholes about ten meters off to our left over toward the gate and we all scramble for them. Two men ahead of me jump down into the first hole when a third man, running next to be reminds me of what day it is.

"Hey, man, let me down there, I'm short...two weeks to DROS. I'm too short for this shit."

"Sorry buddy," I tell him as I jump down. "I'm going home tomor-row. You can be on top."

"No shit man," he says, more appreciative of my situation than the

Stars and Stripes and Shadows

other two men. "Leave it to Charles to fuck with you on your last night in the shit."

The incoming rounds stop as the outbound fire closes in on the sources of the thwumps. The Air Force will finish off the encounter. It turns out that a C-47 airborne gun platform, known to the grunts as Puff the Magic Dragon was on its way back to Pleiku from another night job up north when Camp Enari came under attack. A slight heading adjustment to the right brought Puff right over the western approaches to Camp Enari. The gattling guns mounted within the slow flying machine rain down thousands of rounds of 7.62 mm lead, a hail storm of red tracers that dices up wide swaths of vegetation out beyond the clearing. Charlie's done for tonight.

The Camp remains on full alert for the rest of the night and so we sit nervously out here waiting, smoking, cursing Charlie and laughing about the irony of an attack so close to our DROS dates. *Let's hope we've really escaped the more serious outcome of such irony.*

"There it is man," my not-quite-as-short partner says, pointing off toward the eastern edges of the night sky where the first blush of dawn is beginning to appear, "DROS, dude."

"Right on...finally!"

I made the wake up.

✈ ✈ ✈ ✈

"Just form a line along this walkway," the Sergeant barks out at us. "We'll get everybody taken care of. Just relax, nobody's going anywhere today. The DROS dates on your orders don't mean shit. Everybody'll get out in the next few days."

The next few days? Goddamn-it! I'm now going to have to spend the next few days stuck here at the Reception Center in Cam Rahn Bay.

The Sergeant's declaration strikes into me like hot shrapnel from another mortar round. *Goddamn-it! My orders say today! Why do I always have to follow orders? Why aren't these orders to be followed too...goddamn-it...a few days? Shit!*

When I reach the front of the line, I check in with the Specialist at the desk who's taking the brunt of each DROSing man's dissatisfaction with the situation. He tells me the same thing he's told everyone in line ahead of me.

Tim Haslam

"Stay within the Reception Center area and listen to the PA, we'll call your name when you're manifested on a flight out. Find a bunk in one the billets and get comfortable and be ready to go when you hear your name."

"How long do you think it's really going to be," I plead with him before relinquishing my place up here. "Is it really going to be a few days?"

"I don't know man. Things have been stacking up for about a week now, lot's of guys are rotating back home. I've heard that they're trying to bring in more planes to keep up but I don't know for sure when that'll happen."

The rest of March 13th, my promised DROS date, crawls by. I confine my movements to the latrine and the mess hall. The rest of the time I stay on my bunk in the sweltering barracks. I read Stars and Stripes. I re-read Stars and Stripes. I stop reading and re-reading whenever the PA system crackles to life. A few names are called, every few hours a few names are called. At this rate I'll be here forever. I'll be here for the extra fifty-three days I would have needed for an "early-out" and it won't count because I was officially DROS'd on the 13th. I'll get cheated out of my thirty days leave. I'll miss the date I'm supposed to report up to Fort Ord and I'll be reassigned to Fort Rucker, Alabama or Fort Sill, Oklahoma or some place far away like that. *Goddamn-it…the Army had no trouble getting me into this country right on time! Why the hell can't they get me out?*

Early on the morning of the 14th, two Sergeants come through the barracks assigning volunteers to various duty assignments around the Center. I escape conscription this round but realize that they'll be back. It'll be just my luck that I'll be snagged later in the day and will be mopping floors in the latrine when my name is called. I'll miss my turn, go to the bottom of the list and be here forever. I can't stay here in the barracks.

I wander away from the barracks, testing the range of the PA system by moving along the various paths that spoke out and away from my packed up gear. The mess hall and the PX are both in range, the PA announcements coming in loud and clear, instantly quieting the general din of noise that fills these crowded places.

I look through every item in inventory within the PX. I go back

Stars and Stripes and Shadows

and look at most of them a second time…maybe there's a label to read. I endure until lunch time. Twenty-seven names have been called since breakfast. Twenty-seven men have been paroled. After lunch I go back to the PX and scour back through all the merchandize. Perhaps something new has been added to the selection in the last hour. At 2:30 I buy a book of crossword puzzles and head off in search of some place where I can go to work on the crosswords, somewhere the two Sergeants can't find me. I spend the rest of March 14th, official DROS-plus-one, sitting on the ground outside the latrine, my back pressed up against the wall, penciling and erasing my way slowly through the first intermediate level puzzle.

At 10:31 a.m. on March 15th 1969, ten-hundred-thirty-one-hours military time, 1:31 p.m. California time, I hear it; "Hasham, Timothy L." right between Grassley, Jeffrey R. and… somebody. I hear it just as I'm sneaking back into the barracks after a trip to the latrine. It takes me twelve seconds to gather up my duffle bag, my little overnight case, my cap and my crossword puzzles and begin the delirious hump over to where the freedom busses come. I'm in an accelerating state of ecstasy and anticipation. It's really happening now. Nothing's going to stand in the way. The Army has stepped up to their responsibilities toward me. *I'm outta here!*

I can see that the engine is running on the olive-drab colored bus twenty meters away from the line of anxious men that I'm a part of. When I get to the front of the line I give a team of two unhappy men my name, I show them my ID card and I tell them "no" when they ask if I have any weapons. They wave me forth onto the bus.

The trip from the Reception Center to the Airbase is an ancient memory in reverse. The same scurry of military activity that I passed by going the other way a year ago, the same heavily armed vehicles on the road churning up the same clouds of red dust that choke up the hot air; the same ominous silhouettes of mountain ranges off to the west; the same sounds and the same smells. Everything is the same except the feeling. Leaving the shit feels much different than entering it. Knowing the shit however, makes the feeling even more fear laden than it was a year ago, when only my naïve imagination could paint pictures of the three-hundred-and sixty-five days between then and now, between in

Tim Haslam

and out. There's something about the feeling that dilutes the happiness of my eminent escape.

✄ ✄ ✄ ✄

The Boeing 707 is just sitting there waiting for us. The doors on this side of the cabin are open. The stair ramps are in place. *Why aren't we getting on board?* The Pan Am plane looks out of place against the backdrop of military aircraft and ground vehicles as it sits there, its nose pointing obliquely out toward the southwest as we all impatiently stare at it. The planes nose is pointing coincidently right at a B52 sitting quietly on the apron a hundred meters away. The giant Stratofortress seems so calm and benign relaxing over there, the tips of its great wings nearly touching the ground. In its repose it's difficult to connect the inert machine with the abundant broad scars left throughout the valleys and ridges of the Central Highlands by its vandalizing sorties. This is what brings the Arc Lights. This is what brings the whispering death from the sky.

"OK sergeant…what are we waiting for?" A full-bird Army Colonel up at the front of the line asks the Air Force Sergeant blocking our access through the wooden barriers that separate the line of homeward bound Army personnel from the 707.

"Sir, there's a contingent of Air Force personnel that are supposed to board first. They're inside that hangar but should be coming out any minute now."

"Air Force personnel…we're standing out here, all ready, waiting to board a commercial jetliner, waiting for Air Force personnel?"

"Yes sir," the Air Police Sergeant responds nervously, detecting a big jump up in the Colonel's irritation. I can see that the Colonel's wearing a Combat Infantryman's Badge just like mine. He has a 101st Airborne Division patch on his shoulder. He knows the shit and he knows bullshit when he hears it.

"Bullshit…we're getting on the plane," he tells the outranked and out-motivated Air Force Sergeant. "C'mon," he barks back to his enthusiastic United States Army supporters queued up behind him. "Let's go, there'll be room for the Air Force personnel."

Right on, Colonel!

Stars and Stripes and Shadows

A cheer goes up and spreads throughout the entire cabin of the 707 as it lurches into motion. The aggregated emotional energy of the passengers is probably greater than that of the four jet turbines gradually accelerating their pull through the hot dusty air. The plane ambles tooslowly along the apron all the way out to the western end of the runway and stops there for another agonizing few minutes. I have a window seat on the left side of the plane and so I can see out toward the north, out to where some of the great mass of the Cam Rahn Bay complex sprawls out; out to where the 22nd Reception Center and the 6th Convalescent Center reside, each too distant to actually be seen. I watch it all slowly pass back behind me as the plane taxis forward building up speed.

An even more passionate cheer goes up as the plane separates from the tarmac and the angle of ascent steepens. I watch the parked B52 shrink away until it disappears out of my limited line of site and then I return my attention to the things within range of my seat. I don't watch any more of Vietnam fade away.

The longest journey of my life is the last thing to be endured before I make it home to the United States of America.

✈ ✈ ✈ ✈

It seemed to take much longer to reach Yokota Air Force Base in Japan than it did covering the same route going the other way last year. What's even worse is that we have a two hour layover here. My Timex says that it's 2:25 p.m. suggesting that the flight up here took a little over three hours. The clock on the terminal wall says that its 12:25 p.m. here at the base just outside of Tokyo. The whole time thing provides an opportunity to fill in some of the layover delay. If my watch says that it's 2:25 p.m. and it's actually 12:25 p.m. here, what time is it in California? If I know that and I knew how long the flight from here to Seattle takes I could figure out exactly what time I'd set foot back on American soil. I check around with some of my fellow restless passengers and the consensus seems to be that the flight takes about ten hours. I start doing the math but can't really figure out what math to do, so I try to sketch out the problem. Before long, my scribbling attracts the attention of the two men sitting closest to me and they add their brain power to the effort.

"OK, OK...we're gonna leave at about 4:30 right. So just add

Tim Haslam

ten hours to 4:30 right. So...what's that...four-thirty, five-thirty, six-thirty...OK, two-thirty...we'll be there at two-thirty!"

"No, no...what about the time difference? Vietnam was like fifteen hours earlier, or was it later, than it is in California and it looks like its two hours earlier here than it is in Vietnam. So, we have to like add the ten hours to 4:30 and subtract thirteen hours from that, or do we add thirteen hours?"

"We're not going to California. We're going to Seattle. Does that make a difference?"

"Fuck no!"

We finally work out a solution that we can all agree on that has us arriving at McChord Air Force Base at 11:00 a.m.

"OK, eleven o'clock in the morning. On what day?"

"Oh shit."

"OK...it was Tuesday when we left Nam..."

After a much less concerted attempt to figure this out, we all agree that we don't really give a shit what day it will be. The important thing is that we have killed nearly thirty minutes of our layover time. For me, it's time to start working through the day ahead, whatever day that is. If we get to McChord at eleven, they've got to get us over to Fort Lewis. *How far is that? How long will it take to out-process there? Will they be able to release us the same day? If they do, how long will it take to get from there to the Seattle-Tacoma Airport? How long will I have to wait for a flight to L.A.? I think it's about a two hour flight.*

It's possible! I could be home before nightfall on whatever day it is that the plane lands in Washington. I'll have to see the sun go down and come back up one more time and that next sundown is just a few hours off. Why can't we just get back on the plane and meet the sun head on?

The crowded plane pulls along high above the Pacific Ocean waters that are more slowly flowing eastward along with us. Some of those same water molecules, originally came from up in this sky as monsoon rain. They've worked there way down from the mountains of the Central Highlands, down the Dak Poko and the San, down the Mekong and out into the South China Sea, across the Philippine Sea and thousands of miles of the Pacific Ocean. *I'll beat them to Playa Del Rey.*

Stars and Stripes and Shadows

Only the individual overhead lights are on in the cabin as we press on through the night sky. A few of the passengers seem able to sleep through these hours. Not me. Each time I close my eyes the world ahead starts to take shape and then the shapes decompose into details of who, where, when and how. The images answering each question collide into a nonsensical patchwork of thoughts. There's too much going on mentally to provide sleep any chance of breaking through. The adrenaline rush of anticipation is too great and easily trumps the regular cyclic releases of serotonin and the chemistry of sleep that my body really needs. My last real sleep was interrupted by the rockets and mortars that Charlie hurled at Camp Enari as their farewell message for me. *How long ago was that? What day was that?*

Only a few of the men who are awake are engaged in any kind of social behavior. A few muted conversations carry over the steady rush of outside airflow and engine hum. A few gin rummy games keep others from watching the second hands of their watches plodding around and around. Others drag their eyes across the lines and down the pages of paperback books, not really attending to anything the author is telling them. Several minutes can go by, several pages, before one realizes his own story is more compelling and has diverted all his attention. For some, all of the attention resides in the past; where they've been, what they've done, what was done to them. They have to relive all of it. They're not ready to let it fall away along with the increasing distance separating us from the Nam. For some of us, there can only be thoughts of what's to come.

"Blank...E...blank...ON?" I should be able to get this. I know this, "Wading bird." *C'mon, c'mon...I know this.*

I finally have to look away from the page in front of me, away from all the frustrating, erasure smeared blank squares surrounded by penciled in letters. Before I look at my watch for the ten-thousandth time I pull up the plastic shade covering the window. I can make out the shape of the wing...the sky's getting lighter.

In another few minutes others in the cabin make the same discovery. All the shades are pushed up into the slots above the windows. Everyone's eyes validate the same observation...the sun...dawn. We'll be able to see our way home from here.

Tim Haslam

"Just under two hours now," the pilot announces, further energizing his rapidly awakening passengers. "We should be on the ground at McChord a little after eleven a.m. Pacific Standard Time."

The worn out stewardesses bring breakfast to us within a half an hour of the Captain's announcement. The little cups of coffee jack up our metabolisms a little more but everyone seems to want to work slowly through the stiff scrambled eggs and sausage. Perhaps we can make breakfast take up another half an hour.

"Yes, please," to more coffee each time one of the stews passes by with a stainless steel pot in hand, "Yes, please"... "Yes, please."

I've only got three cigarettes left after this one.

We've gotta be getting close...it's ten-forty.

All I can see outside is the grayness of the clouded air we're streaming through. It feels like we're angling downward though. I wish we'd break through this. I want to see the United States of America the instant we pass over the coast line. For just a second I see a little patch of blue ocean down below. *Shit...we're still over water.* Then another patch; then a bigger one and then the gray disappears altogether revealing an expanse of white-capped water. I scan around my whole field of view looking for a boat or ship that would verify closeness to the mainland...only water, dull blue under the clouds, salted with white.

"The Olympic Peninsula is just ahead gentlemen," the pilot advises. "We'll be over American soil in one minute."

The announcement brings up another cheer and draws everyone in the cabin over to the nearest window.

There it is. Gray-brown land covered in gray-green trees up ahead of us, just above the wing, the image of land still somewhat obscured by the hazy atmosphere. The strip of visible land disappears for a long minute and then crawls out from under the wing right below me, greener now, clearer and sharper. I look for signs of life, of civilization, of American people. All I see is forest. The right kind of forest though, not jungle, the kind of forest you hike and fish and play in. The dense trees soon give way to more open land and manmade structures start to appear. The rural areas transition into suburban neighborhoods until finally the Tacoma skyline passes by as we draw closer and closer to the ground.

Stars and Stripes and Shadows

The pilot nearly cheats us out of our next and most compelling opportunity to raise a cheer as his landing is so gentle it takes us all a second to realize that we are, in fact, on the ground in the U.S. of A. The delayed cheering continues all the way down the runway, accompanied by fist tapping all through the cabin and various predictable personal comments. "Right on!" "Far out...we made it!" "Fuckin-A!"

A few of the first men down the stair ramps drop to their knees and kiss the ground; others coming along behind see this and join in the ritual. It's not the tarmac at McChord Air Force Base that I want to be kissing. I'm just as glad to be here and just as relieved and just as appreciative of all that this land means as the next guy, but this is slowing our progress toward the busses that will take us to Fort Lewis.

The bus exits the main gate and blends into civilian traffic. For the first time in a year I see American people going about their business; driving their pick-up trucks, their station wagons full of kids and their hand decorated Volkswagen vans. I can see their faces as they proceed through another day of their lives, safe and secure, protected from the rain, unconcerned about anything else arcing down from the sky. The faces are the confirmation. *I'm back... it's over......... it's over.*

✱ ✱ ✱ ✱

"Welcome home. We'll have you all out of here today," the female Lieutenant tells us as we enter into the first out-processing station at Fort Lewis, greatly relieving the pent up tension among us.

"We need your cooperation. So please pay attention at each station, follow the instructions and, I guess I don't have to tell you this, move quickly."

Paperwork...showers...new patches sewn on our Class A uniforms...more paperwork...pay vouchers and pay, in real greenbacks. We trade copies of the orders we've been carrying for copies of other orders that we're to carry on to our next assignment. A one-minute haircut, a medical check and one more bus trip; it all takes less than three hours. The Army can be efficient.

✱ ✱ ✱ ✱

"I really don't want to take any chance of missing the flight," I tell

Tim Haslam

the pretty blond woman behind the Western Airlines counter after she suggests that I buy a standby ticket that will save me a lot of money.

"I don't mind paying the full price if there's any doubt about getting on as a standby."

"You just got back, didn't you?" She asks, taking notice of the medals and badges on my uniform.

"Yea…that's why I don't want to take any chances."

"Don't worry," she tells me with a little wink. "You'll get on. Gate 8."

"Oh honey, I'm so glad you're back and safe," my mom tells me over the pay phone.

"What time does your flight get in?"

"Seven-twenty. Can you call Rosemary and let her know and maybe she can come with you to the airport?"

"Of course. She's been calling to find out if we've heard anything. She's going to be so excited."

"OK, great, thanks. Look, I've only got a few minutes before I have to get to the gate. I'll be on Western flight 318 from Seattle and it gets into LAX at seven-twenty, OK…I'll see you soon. Bye."

I have just enough time to stop into the little news stand shop within the terminal. I get a pack of cigarettes, three Clark Bars and a copy of the Los Angeles Times. I go up to the check-in counter at the gate hoping to get confirmation that I really don't need to be worrying about making this flight.

"The flight's not full. Don't worry…you'll be on it," another pretty Western Airlines girl tells me over a reassuring smile.

OK, I won't worry…too much.

"I'm still willing to pay the full fare if there's any doubt at all," I tell her, wanting to keep both of our options open."

"Don't worry, you'll make it."

"Can you tell when there's, like only one seat left?"

"Don't worry, I promise you…you'll make it."

I make it…Seat F, Row 4.

Cool…a window seat, right up near the front.

There's a businessman dressed in a suit and tie sitting in Seat D and

Stars and Stripes and Shadows

nobody in E. He asks if I've been to Vietnam a moment after I climb over him and click myself into place.

"Yea, I just got back."

"Well, welcome home," he lavishes upon me before returning to his Time Magazine.

I'm a little disappointed with his lack of interest. I'm back up on one of the adrenaline rush cycles and want to talk to someone. I want to share something. I want to get a response. Oh well, I guess I'll use the time to study the L.A. Times and see what's going on at home.

*Oh man, no...*I think to myself as I read the front page stories about all the rain that's been falling in Southern California and the mudslides and damaged property within the various canyons that surround the San Fernando Valley and out near the beach above Malibu. *Not rain, not here, not now.*

There are a few stories about the war, buried back within the front section and another story about the Paris Peace Talks. It seems that the negotiators are still arguing about vital issues such as the shape of the table that they are all to sit at. I wonder how many people will die back in Vietnam, on both sides, while such trivial matters are being re-solved. None of the news about the whether, the war or the priorities of the diplomats dampens my excitement for the moment however. Each second I'm getting closer and closer to home. That's all that matters in the world right now.

My watch says that it's six o'clock...less than an hour and a half to go. The time and distance remaining in my separation have finally shrunk down into a nearly bearable measure. The Western Airlines 727 and the planets are nearly aligned. I've just watched the sun drop over the partially cloud-obscured horizon, leaving a spectacular panorama of orange and red spiking out from the gold rimmed clouds.

Now that I've seen the sunset, I wish I were sitting on the other side of the cabin. Our approach to LAX is going to be from out over the ocean and I will be unable to see anything but the darkening surface of the water as we start to enter familiar territory. I won't be able to see the lights of the L.A. basin come into view. I won't be able to translate the patterns of varying light density that would represent familiar sections of town... most of the sections illuminating memories as well as landmarks.

Tim Haslam

"…patchy clouds and sixty-three degrees in the Los Angeles area," the pilot tells us at 6:58 p.m.

"…please bring your tray tables and seat backs into their full upright and locked positions," the head stewardess tells us at 7:09 p.m.

Nobody raises a cheer at 7:17 p.m. when the wheels of the Boeing 727 make contact with the ground of LAX, the ground of Los Angeles County, California, the ground of home. Hardly anyone even puts down their newspapers or their magazines or their paperback books to celebrate this milestone. No one but me, it seems, is consumed with anticipation about what will happen in just a few moments, about who will be throwing their arms around their necks as they file out of the ramp into the crowded terminal or about the resurrection that is about to occur. Life in the shit is about to come to an end and life as I remember it is about to begin again. I can't help but smile thinking that none of these people get it.

I'm surprised for the first instant I set foot out into the terminal that there aren't more people waiting for passengers. I think I detect my brother in law, Frank, before I actually see him. His six-foot-six-inch height registers in my peripheral vision, drawing my attention around slightly to my left. There they are; Frank, Nancy, Mom, Dad. Rosemary?

"Hi honey, I'm so glad you're here," Mom says along with her hug.

"Welcome home, son," Dad adds, smiling, shaking my hand. "I like that moustache."

"Welcome home, welcome home," Nancy adds in turn.

"Hi Tim…welcome home," I can hear Frank offer quietly as I complete a short hug of my sister.

"Thanks, thanks. You can't believe how great it is to be here," I tell them all as I shake Frank's hand. They all look the same. They all act the same, a little nervous perhaps but still able to resist any greater emotional displays. We're not a family of overt displays. We're not huggers. We're a family of depression era survivors. Nothing is ever too bad or

642

Stars and Stripes and Shadows

too good to move us out of our fairly narrow range of stoicism. Still, down below the surface, we're all glad in this moment.

"I know you're looking for Rosemary," Mom tells me, aware that some of my attention is diverted off into the crowds searching for someone else.

"She had a horseback riding lesson this evening. She'll join us at home later."

"Oh, OK," is all I can say in response, unsure of what that means but still willing to push the long anticipated reunion out a little longer.

The walk from the baggage claim area out to the parking lot seems awkward...short periods of uncomfortable silence lingering between short questions and answers about the salient details of the last few days. How was the flight? When did I eat last? When did I sleep last? Am I hungry? Am I tired? How was the whether in Seattle?

Fine. Yesterday sometime...I think. Two nights ago...I think. No. No. A little cloudy...I think. It feels like a conversation between strangers.

As we reach Dad's car Nancy and Frank break off for their own car. They'll meet us at Mom and Dad's.

At night, artificially illuminated, everything along the route back to the Valley seems to be the same. Traffic is light and we're making good time along the San Diego Freeway. Mom and Dad are quickly running out of superficial questions though. It doesn't seem like there ought to be lulls in the conversation however and, as I can tell I'm running on adrenaline fumes now, I try to fill the voids. If there's too much quiet time for thinking I'm afraid I'll finally shut down mentally or maybe I'll dwell too much on the relative importance of a horseback riding lesson on this particular evening.

"We got a mortar and rocket attack at the Division Base Camp the night before I left there. I think Charlie did it just for my benefit...just as a send off," I tell them, without giving any thought as to where that might lead the conversation.

"Oh, was anyone hurt?" Dad asks after a short pause, probably unsure of whether or not this is a subject to be pursued too deeply.

"No, nobody on our side anyway. We called in Puff and watched as the area where the rockets and mortars were coming from got blown

Tim Haslam

away," I respond quickly, glad that I got all the way through the explanation without saying shit or fuck or anything like that.

"What's Puff?" my dad asks as he steers his Lincoln Continental along the freeway, passed the rows of white head stones at the Veteran's Cemetery in Westwood.

"You know...it's one of those old CH-47s from World War Two that's been converted into a flying gun platform. They can really rain down a lot of bullets."

Again, I'm glad that I was able to resist using a term like pee-bringing or fucking shit or any of the other forms of verbal coloration that have become so firmly engrained in my lexicon. I'm not sure I'll be able to maintain this kind of discipline much longer given my current state of mental exhaustion and so I decide not to offer up any more war stories. I shift instead to a safer topic.

"The paper said you've had a lot of rain."

"Oh my, yes," Mom starts in. "It's been nonstop and really making a mess of things all around."

Right now, the rain is serving a purpose. It keeps both of them engaged in telling me things about the storms and the damage and the lack of good sense shown by the people who live in the houses built up on stilts along the canyon slopes. The rain narrative gets us over the Sepulveda Pass and several miles westward along the Ventura Freeway. It seems odd to me that we're going home this way. We should have stayed northbound on the Golden State to get to the home I remember. This route all looks just the same as it used to, all of it familiar territory. It's the destination that remains a mystery. All the familiar things however, including Mom and Dad, Nancy and Frank, seem to be just a little out of alignment with my memories. It's too subtle an error to really register within my consciousness. I'm probably just so tired that everything seems a little ethereal; a little dream like. When we get home, when Rosemary gets there, everything will fall into place. The foggy haze of the last year will give way to the clear reality I've been yearning for...all perfectly aligned with the images I've stored away in my mind.

After a short tour of the new house we all settle into the comfortable chairs in the living room, exchanging nervous glances at one another,

Stars and Stripes and Shadows

wondering what the appropriate topics for discussion might be. Mom asks once again if I want anything to eat. Once again I decline, but accept when Dad surprises me with the offer of a beer. I don't think my parents have ever seen me consume alcohol before. I think they were too busy at Nancy's wedding to notice how much Champagne I put away. My dad seems somewhat pleased as he hands me the opened can of Olympia Beer.

"Thirty days," I tell Nancy, answering her question about how long I have on leave. "I have to report back up to Fort Ord on the 15th of April."

"Oh, that's great. That's a long time," she says as she extricates a package of Benson and Hedges cigarettes from her purse.

*No shit…*I think to myself. *My sister smokes cigarettes. Right here in front of Mom and Dad, she's going to smoke a cigarette.*

"Want one Mom," she asks as though this were a common occurrence.

"Sure," Mom answers, reaching over to accept the offer. My mom has always smoked; one cigarette a night, sometimes two, never more than that unless it's a social occasion and she's among other smokers.

"Tim, you want one?"

"Uh, no thanks, I have my own," I declare with some caution, wondering if my nicotine use will require some further explanation or justification. I quickly pull out one of my Marlboro's and my Zippo. I walk over and light Mom's cigarette. Nancy beats me to the end of hers with her own small lighter. Dad's been fiddling with his unlit pipe ever since we sat down and follows our lead bringing the well worn pipe to life with a match. Frank apparently has been able to make it all the way through this last year without taking on any new vices.

I'm sitting here in the living room of my parent's new house, drinking a beer and smoking a cigarette. I guess my status as a veteran has earned me some privileges that college age sons were denied.

The beer and the cigarette relax me a little and give all of us, except Frank, something to do during the uncomfortable pauses. My enthusiasm for the moment jumps back up a few notches, but I'm still not sure that I have the confidence to begin any other Vietnam stories.

Mom comes to the rescue.

"So, honey, have you fully recovered from your bout with ma-

Tim Haslam

laria?"

"Yea, pretty, much," I tell them, thinking that was a hundred years ago. "My side still aches a little sometimes and once in a while my hands still shake a little, but it's no big deal."

"Your letters didn't make the hospital seem like a very nice place," says Mom as she gently presses out the stub of her Benson and Hedges in the ash tray on the coffee table in front of her. "It doesn't sound like you had much of a Christmas."

"Oh man...I couldn't believe some of the stuff they had us do there. Every day, they came up with some new kind of off-the-wall-shit for us..."

Oh shit...I just said shit! Right here in front of Mom and Dad and my sister and her husband, smoking a cigarette and drinking a beer. I just said shit right here in this living room...shit!

"Sorry, I mean...it was like...they could never really...like... leave us alone there. It was more like a prison than a hospital."

"Are you sure you're not hungry," Mom asks as a way of disintegrating the expletive still reverberating around the room.

"How about another beer," Dad adds, joining Mom in the diplomatic, hear-no-evil camp.

Before I can tender my latest refusal of their offers the doorbell rings.

Rosemary!

"Why don't you go," Mom says to me, "I'm sure that's Rosemary."

The journey from my chair to the front door rejuvenates and consolidates every thought I've had about Rosemary in the last year, how much I've missed her, how much I've longed for this moment with her, how much I've imagined, fantasized and feared. I can't wait to open the door but I'm also really nervous.

"Hi," she says softly.

"Hi," I tell her back, unable to contain a smile as I study everything about her revealed under the porch light. It's her round, wire rimmed glasses that catch my attention more than anything. I didn't envision them. What I did envision was an uncontrollable assault of arms locking around my neck, of soft lips pressing firm and warm against mine, of warm, salty tears to be kissed away from her smiling cheeks. I didn't envision the shy, coy, nervous posture standing still in front of me,

646

Stars and Stripes and Shadows

hesitating, waiting nervously for some additional clue or invitation or movement on my part.

I move forward and put my arms around her. She responds in kind as I draw her tightly to me. She accepts my kiss, joins me in it, uses it to remember, uses it in an effort to re-align and re-acquaint. We say nothing else. She clasps my hand and follows me back into the living room. Finally it's complete. Finally I'm back. I'm home. It's over...it's finally over.

N N N N

Over the next few days I get caught up on sleeping and eating and showering, relishing each of these basic activities as a hard earned privilege. Rosemary has to work each day and so I take Dad's other car, his 1958 Ford hard top convertible, the one I learned to drive in, and cruise around looking for my old friends or just driving by old places that might rekindle fond memories. The car is the most familiar artifact of my pre-war life and the trips through the old neighborhoods reconnect me to many of the images I've drawn upon over the last year.

Rosemary seems to have several compelling obligations that prevent her from spending time with me on most of the weekday evenings. On the weekends she wants us to be with our old friends, mainly with Rick Wright and his girlfriend Lisa and their school of friends, most unfamiliar to me. I don't get it yet that she doesn't want to be alone with me. I don't get it yet that her tempered reaction to me and her modest acceptance of my affections are symptoms of something more than the nervousness of getting reacquainted. I don't get it yet that life for her in the last year evolved at a different pace than mine, driven by different forces, accompanied by different people and different experiences. I don't get it yet that, for her, I was lost to the Vietnam War, that we were lost to the Vietnam War. I don't get it yet that it's over.

On the second Saturday of my leave it becomes apparent to me that the things going on between us are not just temporary adjustments but are truly indicative of different feelings and a different relationship. I find the courage, driven out of two weeks of subconscious disappointments and their corresponding feeble rationalizations, to confront her. She makes no attempt to refute my observations or to deny that things have, in fact, changed. She seems relieved that it's out in the open now

Tim Haslam

and that I understand where she is. She seems relieved also that she will no longer have to pretend anything for my benefit. She says she's sorry and then adds the explanation that penetrates through me with the impact of an AK47 round. It's my fault. I've changed.

Everything here in the world that I've recently returned to has changed…everything and everyone. I'm not the one who's changed. I'm the one who wants everything to be just as it was. I'm the one who wants to pretend that this last year was just a bad dream and that it's finally over. *What's happened to everyone else?* My friends and Rosemary's new friends all look different in their longer hair and different styles of clothes and wire rimmed, round glasses. They talk differently, adamant in their political opinions, righteous in their grasp of truth, arrogant in their simplistic interpretations of why things are the way they are and who's to blame and equally narrow in their views of what needs to happen to correct them. Most of these learned diatribes and railings against the old, establishment ways are proffered about under the haze of stale marijuana smoke in somebody's psychedelically adorned apartment. My presence at such social events seems to make it awkward for everyone. I've tried to understand the perspectives, even agreeing with many of the views, often sympathetic to much of the underlying philosophy. Still, sitting comfortably within these bastions of free expression, I can't help but think how odd it is that these people can so easily drift between their knowing views and their giggling appetites; their cannabis driven need for "munchies." It's hard for me to have as much fun as they are, being right and free and comfortable all at the same time, all with so little effort. I guess in this way, I have changed. I don't fit in anymore. I haven't learned how to do this yet.

The next weekend I go along with my parents to a party at the Palmer's, family friends that we've known since I was seven. All of their closest friends are there. All of the grown-ups that have been part of my developing life are there. It's great to see them all, to feel the warmth and sincerity of their greetings and their honest expressions of relief that I'm home, that I'm whole…that I'm alive. They want to know more about what happened for me and to me than most of my personal friends seemed to care about. They remember me at eight and twelve and sixteen. They know everywhere I've been and nearly

Stars and Stripes and Shadows

everything I've done up until this last year. They want to fill in the gap. Our conversations inevitably lead into politics and philosophy and I find myself, once again, pushed away from the clarity of their views and their easy consensus. They're just as right and adamant and righteous in their views as Rosemary's friends, proffered here under the haze of stale Viceroy and Benson and Hedges smoke and ice clinking scotch and soda. The views expressed here however see it all just the opposite from the perspectives of the longer haired members of the next generation. I guess I have changed. I can't accept their views either. For the first time in my life, I realize that the adults who have helped to raise me and groom me for adulthood might be wrong. I'm not sure I fit in here either.

I don't do much for the rest of my leave. I take the car and drive around, searching and thinking, unable yet to fully understand or accept that Rosemary is really gone. A few nights, I hook up with some of my longtime friends, a few I've known since high school, a few have been in the service, a few to Nam. We don't talk about that though. We drink beer and talk about the things that really matter; the Dodgers and the Lakers, our cars, our fantasy cars and girls. We make each other laugh. It seems just the same with them as it always was. We spend a lot of time remembering all the things that we used to do together, usually reflecting on how lucky we were to have gotten away with much of it. The alcohol, nicotine and apolitical camaraderie reconnect me somewhat for the few hours we're together. But, even here, within the familiar faces and stories and attitudes, it still doesn't feel quite right. It doesn't feel that we're right anymore in our superficial views of things. It doesn't really feel like I fit in here either.

The orders promoting me to Sergeant, the one's approved by Captain Griffith's power of attorney, are there at Fort Ord when I report for duty. I'm assigned to the Automatic Rifle Committee at the Advanced Infantry Training School. I become an instructor, teaching those bound for Nam how to maintain and fire their M16s. The trainees can see my Combat Infantryman's Badge. They can tell I've been there. I can get them to pay attention to what I have to say because I know the shit. There are a few things I really want them to know, a few things I know

Tim Haslam

that could save their lives out there in the shit. I wonder how many of the sleep deprived faces sitting there in front of me on the bleachers at Range 12 on those cold foggy mornings will not come home. I wonder if anything that I can tell them will make a difference.

The rest of that spring and the summer of 1969 pass by for me under the gray, overcast Monterey skies. There's not much to do there when I'm not giving classes to the bored trainees or sitting up in the range tower controlling their live fire exercises. The guys I work with there, all returning veterans, and I go into town once in awhile and drink beer in depressing bars. War protesters march outside the gates of the Fort several times. Some of us are sympathetic to their cause. Some of us hurl back epithets from inside the battlements. Some of us just aren't sure enough to react one way or the other.

On the 16th of October I'm released from active duty. A friend, released the same day, has a car and drives me all the way back to L.A. I move back in to Mom and Dad's house, take off my uniform for the last time and begin my new life. Everything around is still a glaring reminder that the world has changed, that lines have been drawn; lines between right and left, between right and wrong, between patriot and traitor, between one generation and another, between old and new, beer and marijuana, us and them. I don't like this world as well as the old one…the one I longed for every second I was in the Nam…the one I was going to return to. Maybe, once my hair grows out longer and I update my civilian wardrobe, I'll fit in better, I'll adapt to it all, I'll find my side of the lines.

I think about the war sometimes as I try to adapt to this world. I think about the men I knew in the Nam and what we had to do. I think about how lucky I was and how unlucky some others were. I think about how we lived and what we thought and what we said. Maybe we had it right then. Maybe we had it right when we kept saying…*it-don't-mean-nothin.'*

Epilogue

More than fifty-eight-thousand Americans died in Vietnam during the war. Twenty five hundred of those were from the 4th Infantry Division. 83 men from the 3rd of the 8th Infantry, were killed during the year I was there. Eight of those were from Bravo Company. Of those killed when I was there, I only knew a few. Death wasn't a daily occurrence for me over there. Violent struggles for survival with armed adversaries were rare and usually of short duration. The days out in the mountains and the jungles were mostly just long and tedious, repetitive in character, each marked by some new little wound or injury, inflicted by the permanent residents of that hostile place. Each moment out there however carried with it the expectation of inevitable combat and its possible consequences. Each day held a measure of pain, a measure of fear and a measure of dread. Each long day finally counted off added a measure of hope. Every one of us who endured those long days out there learned things about ourselves. We learned from our own reactions and from the reactions of those around us. It was all demonstrated; strength and weakness, determination and futility, courage and collapse. I can't remember all of the men who endured this with me. I can't sort out accurately who demonstrated what. I think we all probably demonstrated a little of each at some time or another. Collectively though, I will remember the men I served with as strong, determined and courageous. I'm proud to have been in that place at that time with those Americans.

It's now November 2005. After nearly three years I've finally finished the story. I've brought back everything I could remember, knowing that it was incomplete and fragmented, understanding that it has been incorrectly reconstructed. Back in February of 2003, at a little coffee shop in Alamo, California, I began writing this story. The first unsure keystrokes that day were accompanied by tears welling up in my eyes, coming from somewhere deep inside me for some reason I couldn't fully understand. As I add these last few words, the tears are back. This time I think I know why. This time they're telling me something. I've read the story over and over, re-written most of it several times to try to get it as right as possible. It's now as complete as I can make it and one thing is left perfectly clear to me...*I can't remember how shitty it all was!*

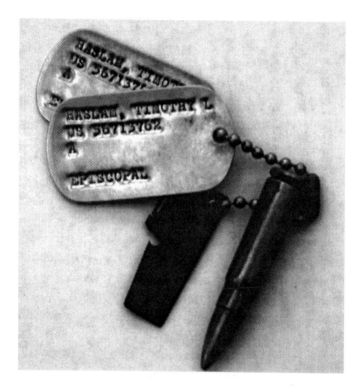

Author's Notes

General   Through the entire course of telling this story I've struggled over the use of names. After thirty-five years I've unfortunately forgotten many of the names of the men whose words and deeds remain more indelibly etched in my memory. I know too that I have inaccurately attributed things to people. I have considered making all the names fictitious as a more equitable means of allocating out my memories. However, as some of the names and faces and roles do remain strongly imbedded within my mind I have chosen to use them. Thus, this story is peopled with names, both real and surrogate. Some of the "real" people are also assigned to roles within this story that they may not have actually performed back in 1968. Should any of these men read this account, I hope that they will recognize the story as a synthetic consolidation of people and things. This is the story of a group of grunts and men struggling through the day-to-day rigors of life in the shit. I would guess that most grunts would recognize it.

Page x   Estimates of the total number of civilians killed that day at My Lai seem to vary greatly across the different sources I found, some as high as 500. The 347 figure is one of the lowest estimates. Even at that it was truly a massacre of devastating proportion…a *liberty of bloody hand* to a scale unlikely to have been envisioned by Henry V outside the gates of Harfleur. I've used information here gleaned from www.dreamscape.com/morgana/mylai.htm.

Page 5   Since I started writing this book and digging into the mass of information available about Army life in Vietnam during the war, I've been unable to find any other reference to the Douglas A1E Skyraider as a "hobo." However, that's my clear remembrance, bolstered by an old photo of one that I took on the runway at the Pleiku Air Force Base. On the back of the photo I had scrawled, "Hobo." Localized terms and tribal language are commonplace within units in the military. Perhaps it was just some Bravo Company grunt that started the term within our tribe.

Page 11   Advanced Infantry Training was conducted at various Army posts within the United States during the war. I went through mine at Fort Polk, Louisiana, where the school was known as "Tiger Land." For me, my advanced training was conducted in January and February of 1968, in very cold weather, including snow. Tiger Land was nothing like Vietnam. Much of the gear and equipment we were trained on was out dated and inappropriate for use in the jungles. I never saw tropical fatigues, tropical boots, rucksacks or machetes until I was required to use them in the Nam.

Page 13   Early versions of the M-16 rifle were known to jam easily. Improvements were introduced into these weapons later on that reduced the likelihood of jamming, but the reputation lingered and there was a great deal of superstition resident within grunt lore about what things would cause these guns to jam. I know from my own experience that an M-16 that's not been thoroughly and regularly lubricated will jam. I couldn't ever verify that a full, twenty-round magazine would cause a problem

Page 148   According to the American War Library, there were 123 B-52 missions conducted in May of 1968 in the II Corps Tactical Zone. Each dropped an average of 27 tons of bombs at an average per mission cost of $41,000.

Page 161   California Dreamin,' The Mamas and the Papas, 1966.

Page 166   One of the great sources for regaining clarity on long forgotten images is the website for the 3rd of the 8th Infantry Regiment (www.ivydragoons.org). I found this site sometime in the Fall of 2004 when I was well into this story. Many photos have been posted there. The photos brought back many memories, both of people and places. There are several photos posted there of the bridge over the Dak Poko as well as photos of the 155mm guns that were emplaced there, the ones that caused me to sleep with cigarette butts in my ears; the ones that probably account for my poor hearing today. There are also photos of the real Captain Collins, Lieutenant Falck and others.

Page 230   Both Sides Now, Judy Collins, 1968.   No other song stayed with me as much as this one while I was in Vietnam, I repeated the lyrics of this song to myself over and over again to escape the tortures of Mr. Ruck and to help pass the long nights on guard duty out in the silent blackness of the jungles.

Page 238   The Sounds of Silence, Simon and Garfunkel, 1965

Page 272   The Byrd's came out with a popular version of Mr. Tambourine Man in 1968, limited to just one verse of Bob Dylan's song. Actually I had heard Dylan sing the whole thing in person at the Santa Monica Civic Auditorium back in 1964 and had it on one of the Dylan albums I had. When I was a senior in high school I would listen to Dylan nearly every night, sitting in the darkness of our dining room where the hi-fi was, my mother unable to understand my attraction to such a voice or to such messages, chagrined that I could even consider such noise as music. The lyrics to the other versus of this song, written long before our involvement in Vietnam, seem to fit exactly with my remembered feelings and thoughts as I traipsed around those jungles.

Page 276   Homeward Bound, Simon and Garfunkel, 1966

Page 298   At some point, in one of my letters home to my parents I told them that we were near Dak Pek. My dad found a long article in the April, 1968 issue of the National Geographic about Vietnam's Montagnards. The article has numerous pictures of the Yards, their villages and the mountains around Dak Pek. I've kept that issue and it too has served to round out many of my memories.

Page 313   The background voice accompanying my two bouts with fevered responses to infection was a mystery to me for many years. Then, several years after returning home from Vietnam, I was at a friend's home and his four-year-old child was watching cartoons on television. He was watching a vaguely familiar old cartoon about Little Toot, a childish tugboat character. The cartoon caught my attention as I seemed to remember it from my own childhood. Somewhere in the story, Little Toot had been banished out to sea by the older tug-boats and was floundering around out in treacherous, stormy weather, under heavy dark clouds with an unseen voice repeating the "Too bad" declaration. I immediately made the connection. Perhaps I had first related to Little Toot while under the influence of the Chicken Pox, or Mumps?

Page 341 Another song that played over and over in my mind as I trudged around the mountains was Tom Jones' song <u>Green Green Grass of Home</u>, it seemed appropriate to replace Mary in the Tom Jones version with Rosemary.

Page 388 It took thirty-six years to solve the mystery of the dead man's name. The Ivy Dragoons website, which I discovered in 2004, has a "Tribute" section which lists all of the 3rd of the 8th men killed during the war. Knowing the man's Company, rank and the approximate date of his death, I was able to determine that it had to be Billy Monroe Gross from Columbus, Georgia, killed on July 23, 1968. After 36 years I was both glad and once again saddened to have a name to go along with the face and body of the dead man I helped carry out there on that gray rainy day.

Page 432 One of the best discoveries I made while searching bookstore shelves for backup information about the war was Michael P. Kelley's, <u>Where We Were in Vietnam</u>, Hellgate Press, 2002. This extensive research work provides a wealth of facts and knowledge about things, places and lore, from the famous to the obscure. It also is a rich source of links to associated websites. The reference to Dak Seang in this book refers to a heavy attack on August 18th 1968 by the 40th NVA Artillery and 101D NVA Regiment.

Page 473, 477 Studying the pictures posted on the Ivydragoon's website I found many familiar faces and places. One collection, that posted by Bob Stevson, brought back particular memories. The pictures of Bob himself were familiar. Bob in fact was one of the head-quarters RTO's, one of the Six-Charlies. I must have exchanged sitreps and other communications via the ANPRC-25s many times with Bob.

As his email address accompanied his photos on the website, I contacted him and asked his permission to use some of the familiar images. He graciously acceded to this request. It was also of value to me to have this contact with a fellow grunt from those days, the first I'd had in thirty seven years. Thanks Bob.

Page 545   Yesterday When I Was Young, Roy Clark, 1968

Page 559   Paint It Black, The Rolling Stones, 1966

Special thanks to Terry Degraff for the perfect cover design.

CPSIA information can be obtained at www.ICGtesting.com
Printed in the USA
LVOW06*0315021015

456648LV00002B/6/P